GENUINE REALITY

ALSO BY LINDA SIMON

William James Remembered (editor) (1996)

Gertrude Stein Remembered (editor) (1994)

Of Virtue Rare (1982)

Thornton Wilder, His World (1979)

The Biography of Alice B. Toklas (1977)

Linda Simon

GENUINE REALITY

A LIFE OF WILLIAM JAMES

HARCOURT BRACE & COMPANY

New York   San Diego   London

Library of Congress Cataloging-in-Publication Data
Simon, Linda, 1946–
Genuine reality: a life of William James/Linda Simon.—1st ed.
p.   cm.
Includes bibliographical references and index.
ISBN 0-15-193098-8
1. James, William, 1842–1910. 2. Philosophers—United States—Biography.
I. Title.
B945.J24S485   1998
191—dc21   97-29877
[B]

Text set in Garamond 3

Designed by Linda Lockowitz
Printed in the United States of America
First edition
F E D C B A

For Thilo and Aaron

"... the word 'or' names a genuine reality."

— WILLIAM JAMES
A Pluralistic Universe

"Life is in the transitions as much as in the terms connected; often, indeed, it seems to be there more emphatically, as if our spurts and sallies forward were the real firing-line of the battle, were like the thin line of flame advancing across the dry autumnal field which the farmer proceeds to burn."

— WILLIAM JAMES
"A World of Pure Experience"

CONTENTS

INTRODUCTION

The phantom of an attitude, the echo of a certain mode of thought, a few pages of print, some invention, or some victory we gained in a brief critical hour, are all that can survive the best of us.
                              — WILLIAM JAMES,
                    from his memorial to Ralph Waldo Emerson[1]

I

ON MAY 31, 1897, the holiday known since the end of the Civil War as Decoration Day, William James stood among the citizens of Boston, awaiting the unveiling of Augustus Saint-Gaudens's memorial to the slain Union hero Robert Gould Shaw. If others felt a flush of patriotism and pride, James, no ordinary spectator at this occasion, felt his throat tighten and his chest muscles constrict. In a few hours he would stand before the assembled crowd as the main orator. In a few hours, all would look to him to define the meaning of the moment.

Not for the first time in his life, nature seemed to sense his apprehension. It was raw, drizzly, the kind of day that reminds New Englanders of the inconstancy of spring, of the enduring metaphorical power of winter. Many thought it fitting that the event should occur under somber skies. Beneath the jubilation that stirred Bostonians that morning, there lay a chill of anxiety about the future: about the wars they would be asked to fight; about the sons, like the fair-haired young Shaw, whom they would be asked to sacrifice.

From a reviewing stand on the steps of the State House, Massachusetts Governor Roger Wolcott opened the commemoration; after his brief address, an American flag draping the sculpture was pulled away, revealing a striking bronze monument. In bas-relief and high relief, Saint-Gaudens had rendered the passion of Shaw's troops as they thrust themselves forward to battle, their faces reflecting the solemnity of their duty and the tragedy of their destiny. Shaw, mounted on a sturdy horse, rides beside them; above, an angel portends their future. The sculpture is as romantic, as poetic, as splendid, as anything that Saint-Gaudens ever created, but it is not a glorious paean to battle.

As thousands strained to catch their first glimpse of the monument, a cannon boomed from Boston Common, followed by a twenty-one-gun salute from warships in Boston Harbor. Then a parade began, led by veterans of Shaw's fatal assault. The Fifty-fourth Massachusetts was notable as the first black regiment to fight in the war, and now, more than three decades later, the survivors marched together for the last time. Soldiers, civilians, and seven burnished carriages carrying speakers and honored guests wound through Boston for two hours. The streets were thronged with people, some of whom were not yet born when Shaw was killed in an ill-conceived assault on Fort Wagner in South Carolina; many of whom had only heard stories of the famous Fifty-fourth Regiment. But for many more, the dedication brought back vivid memories of fear and loss.

The parade stopped at the Boston Music Hall, draped in bunting for the occasion, where three thousand were packed inside, grateful that this Decoration Day was mercifully cool. After a few remarks by Governor Wolcott, Boston's Mayor Josiah Quincy, and Reverend Edward Hall, the governor introduced the orator for whom the crowd had been eagerly, impatiently waiting.

As James stepped forward to deliver his address, the restless silence broke, and the audience burst into cheers, "*tremendous* and long continued," his wife, Alice, recalled, louder and more sustained than he ever had heard before. He did not expect such a reception—but then, he was not sure what to expect from a public appearance far different from the talks he usually gave. He had been so worried about his delivery that he took two elocution lessons from a noted instructor recommended by Harvard's president, Charles Eliot. As he rehearsed, he nearly lost his voice; indeed, the night before he was so sure he would not be able to speak that he and Alice rushed out into a driving rain to look for a physician who could help him. Finally, at nine o'clock, they found a sympathetic laryngologist, who sprayed his throat, gave him some lozenges, and sent him home.

Public speaking was nothing new for James, but neither were stage fright or psychosomatic symptoms. If he felt nervous before class lectures and talks to his academic peers, that feeling was nothing compared to this occasion, when he would be speaking before his immediate world. It challenged him "unlike anything I have done before," he said; "it has to be executed like a musical composition." The speech took months to write. He threw out his first few drafts after reading them to his family and to a friend who told him it was "no oration at all but an essay." He needed to rework it, James decided, "to get a little more color and rankness of flavor into it"; finally, to his great relief, he was able "to break away from the vulgar claptrap of war sentimentalism."[2] Once he was satisfied with his efforts, he decided that this time, unlike every other speech he ever delivered, he would not read from notes; although he claimed to have difficulty memorizing anything, he was determined to learn his forty-five-minute-long speech by heart. By early May, he knew nearly the whole of it.

For James, the oration at the Robert Gould Shaw ceremony marked a personal victory: his chance to demonstrate the "civic courage" he urged upon all Americans, and, even more, evidence of his stature as a leader among his contemporaries. Twenty-one years before, he had been so deeply certain of his own weakness and worthlessness that he doubted that he ever would take a place as a productive member of his community, ever achieve the status of *manhood* in a society that valued forthright independence, ever find a woman who could love so feeble a specimen of humanity as he. Although he was then teaching anatomy and physiology at Harvard, he did not see much future in it for someone so enervated: "My health is not strong," he wrote to a French colleague; "I find that laboratory work and study, too, are more than I can attend to."[3] He was a thirty-four-year-old man still living under his parents' roof, trying to exist on "a little spoonful" of energy that gave out, generally, by ten o'clock in the morning.[4]

"It's a strange freak of the whirligig of fortune that finds me haranguing the multitude on Boston Common," he wrote to his brother Henry after he accepted the invitation to speak, "and I hesitated a good deal what to do. But one ought not to be too ready to funk an honour."[5] That honor was only one of many that had come to James within a few months: he was nominated to deliver the prestigious Gifford Lectures on religion at the University of Edinburgh in Scotland; and he had been invited to lecture at the University of California. But the lectureships were not surprising for a man who had made a considerable mark in his profession since the publication of his *Principles of Psychology* in 1890. The Shaw speech was unexpected. After all, he himself had not fought in the Civil War, although his brother Garth Wilkinson James, who died in 1883, had been wounded seriously in the battle that killed Shaw; it was Wilky's service as an officer of the Fifty-fourth that served as rationale for choosing James as the main speaker for the day. But others, many others, would have been more appropriate if a Civil War association were required. Boston, and James's own circle of friends, abounded in eminent Civil War veterans. Booker T. Washington, relegated to a short concluding address, would have served well as the principal orator.

James had been chosen not because he was a professor of psychology at Harvard; not because he had written an acclaimed textbook and many philosophical articles; not even because his brother had been a member of the Fifty-fourth. He was chosen because he had the rare talent to inspire, even to mesmerize, his audiences.

At just over five feet eight inches tall, James was trim, robust, with luminous and engaging blue eyes. To his classes at Harvard, he customarily wore a sporty tweed Norfolk jacket with checkered or striped trousers, tan shoes, and one of the colorful, flowing neckties he collected in England or Italy. For more elegant occasions, such as a dinner with friends on Commonwealth Avenue, he would arrive in formal evening clothes, including silk hat and patent leather shoes, even if he were walking the three miles through Cambridge to Boston. "We so appropriate our clothes and identify ourselves with them," he wrote, "that there are few of us who, if asked to choose between having a beautiful body clad in raiment perpetually shabby and unclean, and having an ugly and blemished form always spotlessly attired, would not hesitate a moment before making a decisive reply."[6]

His distinctive dress underscored his unconventional personality, his love of spontaneity, his intellectual irreverence. James's public image, like his finely crafted writing style, struck some fastidious observers as "graphic and racy." Although he was the same age as many of his Harvard colleagues, he appeared younger, fresher, and more vibrant. He cultivated that distinction: the "material self," as he put it, was just as significant a part of a person's identity as the social self and the spiritual self.

Listeners called his talks "vitalizing." Often, when he gave a series of lectures, word spread so quickly between the first and the second that a larger lecture hall had to be secured for the increased audience; he was an energized and energizing speaker. "[I]t was impossible," a friend of his wrote, "not to be morally elevated by the smallest contact with William James."[7] He persuaded his listeners that he understood them, that he shared their concerns. As his student Walter Lippmann wrote, James "felt with all sorts of men. He understood their demand for immediate answers to the great speculative questions of life. God, freedom, immortality, nature as moral or nonmoral—these were for him not matters of idle scientific wonder, but of urgent need." Always impatient with philosophers who created systems of abstractions, James rooted his philosophy in palpable experience. "Sunlight and stormcloud, the subdued busyness of outdoors, the rumble of cities, the mud of life's beginning and the heaven of its hopes," said Lippmann, "stain his pages with the glad, sweaty sense of life itself."[8]

This glad and sweaty sense of life, this conviction that philosophy could not be divorced from political and social realities, informed his famous speeches—"Is Life Worth Living?," "The Will to Believe," his memorial to the noted Swiss naturalist Louis Agassiz, and his many talks on psychology to Cambridge teachers—all delivered a short time before he was asked to give the Shaw oration. He was the only man for the moment; his audience knew that. "I jubilate...that you have accepted," Henry wrote to him on hearing the news, "and I jubilate, above all with the conviction that you will be triumphantly uplifted."[9]

James was triumphant on Decoration Day, 1897. After the speech, he was overwhelmed with praise from those who were there and, in the weeks that followed, from many who were not. James deflected the praise onto the occasion, "an extraordinary occasion," he said, "for sentiment.... It was very peculiar, and people have been speaking about it ever since—the last wave of the war breaking over Boston, everything softened and made poetic and unreal by distance, poor little

Robert Shaw erected into a great symbol of deeper things than he ever realized himself.... We shall never have anything like it again." But he knew very well that he himself had emerged victorious: "Did you notice that applause," he remarked to Alice later, "it looks as if I were popular."[10]

II

THE SHAW ADDRESS, more than merely an affirmation of his popularity, marked James's debut into the political arena, where, he believed, he could help to shape the moral life of the nation. It is a moving speech, precisely honed, and transparent in revealing the anxieties and contradictions that pervade all of James's work and continue to challenge our understanding of him.

Once, writing to a graduate student whose doctoral dissertation he just had read, James chided her for accusing him of inconsistency. "You take utterances of mine written at different dates, for different audiences, belonging to different universes of discourse," he said, "and string them together as the abstract elements of a total philosophy which you then show to be inwardly incoherent."[11] Mere scholarly exegesis, he said, was not adequate to assess his work. Yet he was well aware that inconsistency was a complaint others voiced about him throughout his career.

James could not be anything other than contradictory. He lived, alternately, in two different universes—one, unified and monistic, inherited from his father; the other, pluralistic and changeable, imagined by Darwin: James wanted the best of both. He admitted to being, at once, a "tender-minded" and "tough-minded" thinker. When he titled an article "The Sentiment of Rationality," the play on words reflected the dynamic movement between emotion and reason that characterized his own thinking. He was a scientist with the disposition of a philosopher and a philosopher with the perspective of an artist. He was convinced of his own essential complexity: certain that his public personality contradicted a hidden, more authentic, self.

Inconsistencies in his political writings can support a view of James as apolitical, politically naive, or so violently disillusioned with political process that at least one scholar has called him an anarchist.[12] He urged each citizen to take a moral stand, but cautioned that political reform was best left in the hands of "true men," educated and informed, who could be trusted, for one thing, to divert their innate "battle-instinct" from involvement in yet another war. In some writings, he speaks with the passion of Whitman, embracing multitudes; in others, he speaks as a patrician Boston Brahmin. And he presents us with contradictions in more areas than just his political essays.

Although he complained about Americans' thoughtless worship of "the bitch-goddess SUCCESS,"[13] from the time of his first vocational crisis James recognized the need to create himself as a marketable commodity, and he never relinquished that task. While his brother Henry perpetuated the myth that none of the Jameses knew or cared anything about business, William James cared passionately: he wanted to make money, as much as possible. When he published each of his works, he defined his self-worth as much by the number of printings he sold as by his colleagues' critical acclaim. James devoted more than a decade of his life to producing books for a popular audience and to taking his philosophical ideas on the road for well-paid lectures. Convinced that he was underpaid at Harvard, he tried several times to find more remuneration elsewhere. His works are peppered with allusions to the marketplace because he was embedded, as were his readers, in a culture that put a "squalid cash interpretation . . . on the word success."[14]

He campaigned to affirm the validity and worth of other people's experiences, but he could be intolerant of his friends and family. Although he persuaded nearly everyone he knew of his deep interest in them, he admitted that his show of compassion was not always sincere. Empathy posed a problem for him, a problem that troubled and isolated him. He wrote that we can connect with others' experiences only by supposing them to be like our own, but that sense of connection often eluded him, and he yearned for communion. "[W]e with our lives are like islands in the sea," he wrote,

> or like trees in the forest. The maple and the pine may whisper to each other with their leaves, and Conanicut and Newport hear each other's fog-horns. But the trees also commingle their roots in the darkness underground, and the islands also hang together through the ocean's bottom. Just so there is a continuum of cosmic consciousness, against which our individuality builds but accidental fences, and into which our several minds plunge as into a mother-sea or reservoir.[15]

Many of his friends and colleagues found this "cosmic conscious-ness" in the embrace of religion. James could not. Religion tormented him throughout his life. Although he could not pray, he desperately wanted to believe in God. He attended Harvard's morning chapel each day at a quarter before nine, and he made sure his sons did, too. He begged his wife, whose religious convictions were deep and unques-tioned, to help him in his spiritual quest. She did, in part by sharing his unflagging devotion to psychical research. Certain that investiga-tions into hallucinations, mediums, hypnotism, and automatic writing might reveal a verifiable realm of spirits and transempirical conscious-ness, James helped to found the American Society for Psychical Re-search and served as one of its most dynamic officers. But to correspondents who were skeptical about the supernatural, he mini-mized his interest, claiming that psychical research was a matter that diverted his attention from more conventional intellectual pursuits.

His sister, Alice, said that he was as hard to pin down as quicksilver: he was, and he is. Perhaps that is the reason he remains so endearing and so refreshingly contemporary. Unlike many other nineteenth-century in-tellectuals, buttoned into their stiff white collars, calcified in our col-lective memory, James strides easily, inquisitively, into our own time, urging us to notice him.

Portraits of James on the jackets of his books show him at his most professorial: contemplative, serious, iconic. If he is not reading, he stares at us with the abstracted gaze of someone consumed by tran-scendent thoughts. Perhaps the best known of these photographs is a series taken late in his life. At sixty-seven, James had the appearance of an old man, aged by a long battle with heart disease. His beard was grizzled, his eyes tired. Even when he is posed facing the viewer, he looks inward, thinking so intensely that a vein on his forehead bulges. That forehead is enormous; he is, in that portrait, the most cerebral of beings.

But his diaries, manuscripts, many thousands of letters, and seven-teen volumes of published works reveal an image of James more like a snapshot taken at Putnam Camp, his beloved retreat in the Adiron-dack Mountains. He stands with a group of friends, leaning against the rustic Shanty, the gathering spot for the camp's residents. He appears to be in his early fifties, his beard is graying, his hairline has receded. He is dressed in a plaid sport shirt, his thumb hooked in the waistband of his rumpled hiking pants. Between two fingers, he holds a slip of paper, perhaps a note he made that morning when he was reading on a special, secluded ledge where he knew he would not be disturbed. But reading was not his main occupation at Putnam Camp.

In the Adirondacks, he felt an authenticity of being that eluded him elsewhere; here, he could celebrate himself as a rugged participant in the strenuous life. The smell of balsam, the golden afternoon light, the crisp air generated, he said, "a state of spiritual alertness" that is reflected, in this photograph, in his eyes. He may have hiked up Mount Marcy that day; perhaps he would scramble up the Gothics tomorrow. The climbs were exhilarating, not only because they were so physically demanding: James was afraid of heights.

III

JAMES'S "HIDDEN SELF" emerges from his writings, works of unexpected intimacy and uncommon spirit. In those writings, as we see his continuing struggle with identity, with problems of morality and authority, and with his enduring spiritual quest, we discover the significance of his life—to himself and to us—as much in what he called "transitions"—"spurts and sallies," brave starts, willful gestures—as in his achievements. If we are to understand him, we need to look at those moments of decision and indecision; at places where he imagined alternatives to paths prescribed by his culture, his class, his father; at times when the word "or" named a desired reality.

That word gives us, in effect, a distillation of his philosophy. Pragmatism, pluralism, radical empiricism—these name James's legacy to us. The terms are broad, amorphous. Even in James's time, to his enormous frustration, the "brief nicknames," as he put it, were easily and persistently misunderstood. Rejecting philosophical systems of transcendent abstractions, James meant his philosophy to offer a process of thinking, of making sense of experience, and of justifying decisions. Pragmatism, pluralism, and radical empiricism, then, describe attitudes, dispositions, perspectives.

Pragmatism is a method of problem solving that looks to the consequences of ideas to define the truth of those ideas. Pluralism urges our openness to multiple perspectives because, James wrote, "there is no possible point of view from which the world can appear an absolutely single fact."[16] As an empiricist, he asks us to consider so-called "facts" as hypotheses to be tested against our experiences in a changing environment; what makes him *radical,* he explained, is his conviction that unity, oneness, and order in the universe is itself a hypothesis.

This summary of James's central arguments only hints at their liberating power for his contemporaries and for his heirs. James himself brought to philosophy a rare combination of personal experiences and perspectives. He never studied philosophy in any academic setting, but instead learned metaphysics from his father, whose ideas, generously thought of as eccentric, celebrated a monistic universe presided over by a benign spiritual force, a Creator, whose goodness might emanate into receptive individual consciousness. Free will, choice, agency, and authority were antithetical to Henry James Sr. who cautioned his children against any "narrowing" profession and urged them simply to "be." His eldest son, brilliant, competitive, ambitious, found that goal stifling.

As a compromise between "being" and engaging in a profession, James chose art. It seemed to him that becoming an artist would help him to achieve the spiritual transcendence that his father expected from him and also allow him the possibility of contributing, in some productive way, to the community at large. Some philosophical colleagues believed that James's experience drawing and painting shaped his perspective for the rest of his life. James was an artist, his friend Théodore Flournoy wrote, "in his extraordinarily vivid and delicate feeling for concrete realities, his penetrating vision in the realm of the particular, and his aptitude for seizing on that which was characteristic and unique in everything that he met."[17] Although James's career as an artist was short-lived, he never relinquished his attention to concrete realities and brought to his philosophy an abiding conviction that only the realm of the particular could yield the truths he sought.

James's most extensive formal training was in science. With the youthful goal of becoming a Thoreauvian naturalist, he eventually enrolled for more rigorous study at the Lawrence Scientific School. Not interested in pursuing laboratory research, he chose instead, though with little enthusiasm, to study at the Harvard Medical School. Deciding against practicing as a physician, he applied his background in medicine to the teaching of anatomy and physiology at Harvard.

The trajectory of James's early career, however, does not represent the whole of his experience. At the same time that he was testing his interest in science, he was fashioning his own curriculum as a psychologist. He was motivated both by a desire to resolve urgent questions about his own mind and by a conviction that the science of psychology, just emerging from its philosophical roots, would suggest a new architecture for the structure of personality and a new understanding of human potential. This training as a psychologist, combined with his background as an artist, enriched and complicated James's philosophy.

In the 1870s, when James began to shape his identity as an intellectual, the clash between science (notably, Darwin's theory of natural selection) and philosophy—in the form of German idealism and British empiricism—was at its most clamorous. Darwin taught his contemporaries that the natural world was characterized by spontaneous change, interaction between the individual and its environment, and, most significantly, by choice. For philosophers who would function only in an ordered and unified universe, these ideas were threatening. For James, eagerly attentive to particulars, practiced in scientific method, and searching for an affirmation of his own authority, these ideas seemed copiously fertile. They defended the single most important discovery of his life: the will to choose. To his intellectual heirs, James's perspective made him a visionary—of literary modernism, quantum physics, and cubism—of a world, his student Gertrude Stein wrote, where "everything cracks, where everything is destroyed, everything isolates itself."[18]

Underlying the methods of inquiry and problem solving that James called pragmatism, pluralism, and radical empiricism is his exhortation to imagine possibility, to define chance as a gift, to be bold enough to act on one's desires. In a world of renewal, flux, and novelty, the ends were not as important as the process of change. Whatever exists, in any case, is continually being revised by what will follow; whoever we are, at any moment, is who we will become.

IV

"[H]E HAD A PROFOUND admiration for other types of mind," one of James's students recalled, "just because they seemed like other universes."[19] He admired, especially, men who had vanquished inner demons and overcome social constraints. "I have just been reading Darwin's life," he reported once to a friend, "and, whilst his nervous system makes bad nerves respectable, the tale of it shuts the mouth of all lesser men against complaining.... It makes anything seem easy."[20] When he met someone new, he probed persistently to discover all he could about them, to understand how their experiences made them who they were, to see where those experiences intersected with his own: all this, to learn more about himself.

Eager to plumb the depths of his identity, he believed that one essential route was through a multiplicity of experiences. From his responses to those experiences, from the patterns of those responses, he would learn something new about himself. More experiences—varied, novel, risky—had the potential to yield a portrait of himself as knower, perceiver, interpreter, actor. He championed the new, he hungered for astonishment. The next book, the next encounter, the next mountaintop, would reveal, surely, an unexpected vista. A vista that, in barely perceptible or in profound ways, could change one's sense of self. Experience was his salvation, his religion.

Some subjects seem hostile to the enterprise of biography. But James welcomes inquiry. "Philosophic study," he once wrote, "means the habit of always seeking an alternative, of not taking the usual for granted, of making conventionalities fluid again, of imagining foreign states of mind." He might have been defining the biographer's task and the reader's as well: to discover the possibilities of two lives, our subject's and our own, to imagine foreign states of mind within our subject and ourselves.

By 1903, when James spoke in Concord, Massachusetts, at the celebration of Emerson's centennial, he felt himself racing against time to write his philosophical "message to the world," to produce the books by which he wanted to be remembered: *Pragmatism, A Pluralistic Universe,* and *The Meaning of Truth.* He worried about what "few pages of print" would survive him, what significance future generations would see in his work, how he would be remembered by those who never had known him. Memories, he told his Concord audience, captured "so slight a thing" compared with the fullness and richness of a life; memory reduced the cacophony of experience to "a mere musical note or phrase" that could do no more than suggest an individual's complexities. Still, he added, "happy are those, whose singularity gives a note so clear as to be victorious over the inevitable pity of such a diminution and abridgement." He was not happy at that moment, not certain that he could emanate that clear, enduring musical note, not convinced that he would wage a victorious battle over oblivion.

Something of James will never be known by those of us in search of him. We will never know fully what it was like to have a conversation with him, to climb with him to a peak in the Adirondacks, to walk with him around the deck of a steamship bound for England, to sit in his class as he invented his philosophy. All we have, really, are a few pages of print, and a need to make sense of a life: his and, no less, our own.

GENUINE REALITY

JAMES FAMILY GENEALOGY

William (1771–1832)
m. (1) Elizabeth Tillman
    (1747–97)

         Robert (1797–1821)

         William (1797–1868)

m. (2) Mary Ann Connolly
    (1779–1800)

         Ellen (1800–23)

      m. (3) Catherine Barber
        (1782–1859)

Augustus (1807–66)	Jennet (1814–42)	Catharine (1820–54)
Henry (1811–82) m. Mary Robertson Walsh (1810–82)	John Barber (1816–56)	Ellen King (1823–49)
	Edward (1818–56)	Howard (1828–87)

William (1842–1910)
m. Alice Gibbens
    (1849–1922)

        Henry (1879–1947)

        William (1882–1961)

        Herman (1884–85)

        Margaret Mary (1887–1950)

Henry (1843–1916)

        Alexander (1890–1946)

Garth Wilkinson (1845–83)
m. Caroline Eames Cary
    (1851–1931)

        Joseph Cary (1874–1925)

        Alice (1875–1923)

Robertson (1846–1910)
m. Mary Holton
    (1847–1922)

        Edward Holton (1873–1954)

        Mary Walsh (1875–1956)

Alice (1848–92)

Chapter 1

MORTIFICATION

IN THE LATE 1800S, the trip from Cambridge, Massachusetts, to Syracuse, New York, was long, convoluted, and uncomfortable. But it was a trip that William James undertook regularly in his role as overseer of the James family property. He traveled to Syracuse at least once a year, often more; and whenever he went, he had money on his mind. For himself and his siblings, a few stores on Salina Street, owned by the family since the eighteenth century, meant mortgages and repairs, bankers and agents, and most of all, rent. The Syracuse property supplemented James's income, subsidized his travels, had helped pay for the publication of his first book, and always served as a reminder of his origins.

He was descended from one of America's richest men, a captain of industry so wealthy that, rumor had it, only John Jacob Astor exceeded his fortune. Then as now, wealth meant power, and the first William James, grandfather of our philosopher, was a powerful man: restless, decisive, fiercely willful. He believed, with unwavering certainty, that money and power reflected a man's ultimate achievement.

When our William James stepped off the train in Syracuse each year, he was convinced that he had rejected his grandfather's mercenary values; he believed that he would be judged by his teachings, his writings, what he called his "message to the world." He identified himself with an intellectual elite that pretended to have finer preoccupations than cash. James never knew his grandfather, but he knew that his own father had repudiated the business tycoon who raised him, and he and his siblings professed that they, too, had no respect for "the counting-house."

Yet James's private and public writings are peppered with meta-phors drawn from the world of business, and he strived, with no apol-ogy, to shape his publications for the marketplace. His philosophical works, focused as they are on questions of free will and human poten-tial; his personal struggles with power and authority; and his anxiety about his self-worth suggest his affinity, by more than blood, with his grand and looming patriarch. The first William James, of course, did not consider philosophy a suitable occupation for any of his descen-dants. Family legend has it that he was known as "the Patroon."

WILLIAM WAS EIGHTEEN when he emigrated from Ireland to America in 1789, twenty-two when he arrived in Albany, where he would make his fortune, take three wives, and sire thirteen children. His career as a businessman began when, with a partner, he opened a small store that sold tobacco and cigars. The shop soon expanded to include dry goods and groceries, but James was not satisfied with being a modest mer-chant. Shrewd, sharp, ambitious, he built a tobacco factory, leased and operated the saltworks of Syracuse, and, among many civic roles, served as first vice president of the Albany Savings Bank, director of the New York State Bank of Albany, and trustee of Union College. He was a significant force in the decision to build the Erie Canal, which es-tablished Albany as a major center of trade.

Billy James, as his friends called him, first married when he was twenty-five. Just starting out as a merchant, he chose a wife suitable to his station: Elizabeth Tillman, twenty-two, the daughter of a mariner. Nine months and three weeks after the marriage, Elizabeth died, a few days after giving birth to twins.

Two years later, James married again. Mary Ann Connolly was twenty, the daughter of a New York merchant and substantial landowner. Like James, she came from Irish ancestry, but unlike her husband, she was a practicing Catholic. James, during his two years as a widower, rapidly increased his business holdings. He now had two stores, and he had just built a tobacco factory. He was thriving as a businessman and in love with his wife. Within the year, Mary Ann was pregnant, and in April 1800, the Jameses became parents of a daugh-ter, Ellen. In June, James took a partner to acquire yet another store, larger and grander than the others. The summer of 1800 was an ebul-lient time in James's life. With three children, a young and lovely wife, and four flourishing businesses, James was by all accounts a success. But the summer ended, and his family again was struck by tragedy. In October, when she was just twenty-two, Mary Ann died.

Twice a widower, with three small children, William James needed a wife. Three years after Mary Ann's death, he found one. Catharine Barber, the twenty-one-year-old daughter of Judge John Barber, a New York State assemblyman, seemed a likely choice for the thirty-two-year-old James, whose businesses and landholdings afforded him a prominent place in Albany life. Catharine was rather timid, it seems, not given to displays of emotion, but no doubt she and her family thought that William James would be a good match. William and Catharine were married on December 16, 1803, a few months after James became a naturalized citizen. During the next twenty-five years, they would have ten children, eight of whom survived to adulthood. In 1809, their third son, Henry, died when he was two months old. Two years later, on June 3, 1811, they bestowed the same name on their fourth son.

Henry James grew to be an active and independent child who exhausted himself running and playing and who was glad that his parents were too busy—his mother with many children and a house to run, his father with business, banking, and political concerns—to bother him.

Catharine Barber James, often pregnant, usually sequestered herself at home. Although both her father and husband were eminent figures in upstate New York social and political life, Catharine seems to have been uneasy in society, frequently retiring to a corner with a book when her husband had visitors. Henry remembered that his mother was much more comfortable with social inferiors than with those of her own class. It surprised him, he said, that she could get so much pleasure from having a conversation with a seamstress. While Henry enjoyed chatting with the family's coachman, gardener, maid, or cook, he was aware that his relationship with the servants "could not be one of true fellowship, because the inequality of our positions prevented its ever being perfectly spontaneous."[1] As an adult, Henry generously explained his mother's preference in friends as a reflection of her "democratic" spirit, but more likely it reflected her shyness, lack of confidence, and the intimidating presence of her overpowering husband.

Although Catharine kept an orderly household, requiring the children to maintain regular hours for study, meals, and play, Henry recalled later that he "felt no absolute respect for [this order], and even violated it egregiously whenever my occasions demanded."[2] Those occasions included visits to the local confectioner's, where he ran up debts far greater than his small weekly allowance and which he paid by pilfering change from his father's drawer. Or he would take his rod and run off to go fishing or pick up his gun and go hunting.

His father, less concerned with the daily control of his children, seemed "easy" if not "indifferent." William James rarely asked his children how they were doing at school or what interested them or who their friends were. Looking back on his childhood, Henry came to regret this lack of closeness with his father, but when he was young, the indifference allowed him considerable freedom. Beginning at the age of eight, for example, the precocious Henry frequented the local cobbler's shop, where a few young men worked in the back room making shoes. Henry often stopped in at the cobbler's for a drink of whiskey or wine before going to school; sometimes he did not arrive at school at all.

The cobbler's shop gave Henry an experience of a world far different from the conventional, pious atmosphere of his overstuffed and overpopulated home. The young cobblers were bawdy and irreverent, and Henry coveted their approval. He and his friends—who included the sons of the governor of New York—smuggled from their homes fruit, cakes, eggs, and even aged Madeira to share with the cobblers. And Henry brought novels, which, he remembered, "they were fond of reading, and their judgements of which seemed to me very intelligent. The truth is, that we chits were rather proud to crony with these young men, who were so much older than ourselves, and had so much more knowledge of the world."[3] If his parents disapproved of his companions, so much the better. If his mother imposed rules and curfews, he simply ignored her.

Living with such a crowd, not including servants, it is no wonder that the young Henry noticed "a certain lack of oxygen" at home. Although there were many children, only one, Augustus, four years older, was a boy near his own age. Otherwise, he had two half brothers fourteen years older, and two others five and seven years younger. With few comrades within the family, Henry looked for friends away from home. He led an unfettered life, except for "paralytic" Sundays, when his parents' rules were unalterably enforced:

> we were taught not to play, not to dance nor to sing, not to read story-books, not to con over our school-lessons for Monday even; not to whistle, not to ride the pony, nor to take a walk in the country, nor a swim in the river; nor, in short, to do anything which nature specially craved. How my particular heels ached for exercise, and all my senses pined to be free, it is not worth while to recount. . . . Nothing is so hard for a child as *not-to-do*.[4]

His family, he said, like most American families, lived in "contented isolation," thoughtlessly accepting religious dogma because it was prudent to do so, following social conventions and expectations without reflection. But even if Henry rejected religious ritual, he inhaled the basic tenets of his parents' Protestantism and constructed his own theory of sin and redemption. It was a sin, Henry believed, to behave rudely to other people. Hurting another's feelings made Henry fear "the terrors of hell" and "a dread of being estranged from God and all good men." And he felt the blessings of God whenever he "had a marked escape from fatal calamity." These escapes were not infrequent, he claimed, considering his taste for hunting, sports, and generally running amok. "I distinctly remember," he wrote later, "how frequently on these occasions, feeling what a narrow escape I had had from rock or river, I was wont to be visited by the most remorseful sense of my own headlong folly, and the most adoring grateful sentiment of the Divine long-suffering."[5]

His parents were equally grateful, fearing as they did that his imprudent escapades would lead to injury or even death. One can imagine that they implored their impetuous son to slow down, be careful, be good. Henry was not malicious, but he was not obedient.

If we know few details of specific escapades, one is imprinted in James family lore. Sometime during his years at the Albany Academy—the exact date is unclear—Henry participated in an experiment with a group of boys and their tutor in a field in front of the school.[6] To learn some principles of flight, the boys made balloons that were heated by igniting flax balls dipped in turpentine. When the balloons rose, the fiery balls fell to earth, where the boys stamped them out. One day, however, in the fury of kicking and stamping, the boys sent a burning ball sailing up into a nearby stable, where the hay instantly caught fire. Henry, arriving first on the scene, thought that he could stamp out this fire just as he and his friends had done in the field. But the blaze was too strong, turpentine spills on his trousers ignited, and Henry's right leg went up in flames.

The burns were severe and the pain agonizing. If Henry had felt remorse after his narrow escapes, how much more he suffered now, when his own misjudgment, his own wildness, left him bloody and charred. If he felt ashamed whenever he disappointed his parents, how much more wounded he felt now, seeing their worry and grief. Henry, who had exulted in the role of family rebel, now became the focus of the family's constant attention and pity.

That pity was more evident from his father than his mother, and made Henry aware, as he never had been before, that his father cared about him. Henry's only memory of his mother at that time was of her coming into his room at night to pull the covers over his shoulders: she did not speak to him; she did not offer comfort to her son, wakeful from throbbing pain. She only tugged at the covers, turned, and left. Henry decided that she must have been sleepwalking. When William showed unrestrained anguish over his son's suffering, Catharine, uncomfortable with open displays of emotion, felt that she had to impose "due prudence" on his behavior.

William's extreme despair may have been compounded by other recent losses. A few years before, his eldest son, Robert, had died. Robert, his father's favorite, had been groomed to succeed William in business and already had taken charge of some of his holdings. His sudden death, while he was on a family visit in Geneva, New York, was a stunning blow to William. Two years later, in the spring of 1823, his beloved daughter Ellen, the only child of his marriage to Mary Ann Connolly, died, leaving behind a year-old child, Mary Ann. Threatened with the loss of another child, William wanted desperately to save him. Henry, in spite of his earlier bravado, wanted to be saved, and he wanted to be loved. His father's anguish convinced him, finally, that his father did love him; it was the first time that his father seemed to see him as an individual, not merely one among many of his offspring.

For a few months after the accident, with Henry prostrate from pain, liquor, and tincture of opium—laudanum—the family mustered hope that the wounded leg would heal. In the spring of 1827, the burns seemed to be healing rapidly; but during the summer and in the fall, progress reversed. "Henry's leg is not as well at present as it was in the Spring," his sister Jannet wrote to Marcia James, wife of her half brother William, in November 1827. The following April, Augustus James reported again to William "that several black spots had appeared on his leg which it was feared were the forerunners of *mortification*." The family's doctors advised amputation, and "after mature deliberation on their part, and indeed of us all, it was concluded to perform the operation."[7] A month before his seventeenth birthday, on May 6, 1828, Henry was prepared for surgery.

Amputations were common in the early nineteenth century. If a wounded limb did not heal, there were no antibiotics to arrest the spread of infection. The only recourse was to cut off the offending limb, hoping that the surgical wound might heal more successfully. Although the operation was performed often, it was, as the *Boston Medical and Surgical Journal* reported, "difficult to do well."[8]

The operation, without anesthesia, took about half an hour from the first cut to the final tying of the blood vessels. First, a tourniquet was applied to cut off the blood supply to the lower leg. Henry lay on an operating table, fully conscious, held down by a surgeon's assistant, with his knee extending beyond the table edge. With an amputating knife, the operator, as the surgeon was called, cut into the skin below the knee all around the leg. Drawing back the skin about two inches, he sliced into the muscles with a scalpel, and into the bone with a saw. When the bone was sawed through far enough, he was able to snap it off, making as clean a break as he could. While the actual cutting took only a few minutes (six, in Henry's case), finishing the procedure, which meant tying off the veins, arteries, and tendons with silk ligature, was excruciatingly slow. Finally, with the wound wrapped in a cloth, Henry was carried to a bed, dosed with laudanum. After an hour or so, the wound was dressed with an adhesive plaster.

For several days after the operation, Henry was watched for fever, nausea, diarrhea, pallor, high pulse, or other signs of infection. Dressings were changed daily, and the wound was inspected. Physicians and surgeons were powerless to do anything but wait, watch, and pray. Healing depended more on the strength of the patient than on the skill of the surgeon.

Henry was strong and healthy, but as he recovered from surgery, he did not feel as hopeful as his physicians. Confined to his bed, Henry realized that he was lame; he would be lame forever. He was no longer an ebullient, energetic adolescent. His childhood, innocent, careless, and benign, had ended violently. And it was his own fault. His punishment was pain, physical affliction, and relentless boredom. One day after another was like those paralytic Sundays that he chafed against and despised.

Henry had few personal resources to sustain him as he lay bedridden. He was not the kind of boy who lost himself in the imaginary worlds of books. He did not sketch or paint. He had always been impatient during periods of enforced reflection. Besides, he was groggy from pain-killing narcotics and liquor. For the two years surrounding his surgery, Henry James was an invalid, dependent on his family, cut off from his friends. In those two years, he changed irrevocably.

In his later writings, James argued that children should be unfettered, allowed to indulge their natural impulses. Childhood, for him, was a time of "divine rapture" and "magical light." The dictates of religion, which he saw as an "outrage to nature," would repress children and "draw a pall over the lovely outlying world of sense." More important, religion asked children to defer to an inviolable authority, a cruel and hateful God, who wanted to deny the child expression of his individuality. This God that James created in his private universe acted upon the child in the same way that James's injury affected him: "as an outside and contrarious force. . . . The conviction of his supernatural being and attributes," James said, "was burnt into me as with a red-hot iron, and I am sure no childish sinews were ever more strained than mine were in wrestling with the subtle terror of his name."[9] In perpetual battle with this hostile force, James said that, as a child, he could never feel pleasure or happiness without an underlying sense of fear that God would strike in retribution.

The Character of a Swindler

THE YOUNG MAN, leaning on his crutches, who finally walked unsteadily out of his home at the age of seventeen wrestled not only with a hostile God, but also his own confused feelings about his self-worth, manliness, and ability to love and be loved. Disillusioned and depressed, he squirmed irritably in his family's embrace: he wanted to be loved, but he felt pitied. When Henry lost his leg, he believed he lost control over his life: physically, because he was dependent on his parents and could no longer escape from home; emotionally, because his "animal spirits" had been smothered, and he could no longer identify himself with his sensuous, seductive friends at the cobbler's shop.

William and Catharine James had made decisions for Henry during his years of invalidism; in the fall of 1828, they made another: Henry would go to college, Union College in Schenectady, to be sure, where his father was the mortgage holder and major trustee. And he would board at the home of Dr. Eliphalet Nott, the college's president. Although Dr. Nott appears to have been a congenial man with ideas on religion more liberal than those of William and Catharine James, Henry still felt a lack of oxygen in his new home. He still was watched, reined in, circumscribed.

Moreover, he had little interest in Union's prescribed studies of classics and mathematics; he rebelled against his father's inflexible decision that he study law. Because he had been tutored at home, Henry was able to enter the junior class, but he was less concerned with academic standing than he was with reviving his social life. As quickly as he could, he joined the newly formed Sigma Phi Fraternity and plunged feverishly into its activities. His passion for the sensuous life proved expensive. With a love of oysters and good cigars, he managed to run up huge bills on his father's account. Within a year, Henry James had achieved a widespread reputation as an irresponsible spendthrift and drunk.

"I have heard, and your friends generally have heard enough of your conduct to cause us much pain and solicitude for your safety and future usefulness," Archibald McIntyre, a friend of the family, wrote to Henry in the fall of 1829. "I consider you on the very verge of ruin." McIntyre urged Henry to obey his father and study law, or at least "one of the learned professions." He could not believe that Henry would be so foolish as to disgrace his family and throw away his opportunities, and he urged Henry to promise his father to obey him. "If you do not," McIntyre warned, "you will lose all respectability, all support, independence, every thing valuable in life. You will be shunned by the good—you will be miserable."[10]

But Henry could not help himself. He simply could not bow to his father's authority and demands; he had to prove that he could live an independent life. A few days after receiving McIntyre's letter, Henry fled from Union College and, as he wrote to his friend Isaac Jackson, took "the great step" on his personal "pilgrimage" to freedom, away from his father's sphere of influence in upstate New York.[11]

Now ambling on a wooden leg, Henry made his way to Boston where he quickly found a job as proofreader for the *Christian Examiner,* a Unitarian newspaper, and lodgings in the home of its editor, Francis Jenks. His bedroom on the first floor contained four large bookcases, a small sofa, a bed nestled between two armoires, and a painting of Lorenzo de' Medici by Mrs. Jenks. "This room is sacred to me," he wrote to Jackson.

If his work—checking quotations and writing short notices— sometimes proved tedious, Henry found satisfaction enough in pleasing Jenks, who was "very liberal in his encouragement." He continued with his study of languages, this time blissfully on his own, and read impulsively from the odd collection of books in his room. "My ambition is awakened," he said, although at the moment that ambition had no specific focus.

His social life improved from what it had been at college, with a new circle of acquaintances who spurred more mature interests than he had shown in Schenectady. He was drawn to hear the noted Unitarian minister William Ellery Channing and came away feeling that there could be no "higher treat than one of Channing's practical sermons." No one seemed to care that he was the son of the wealthy magnate William James. Through the Jenkses, he was "launched," he said, into a brilliant circle of Boston society who, Henry reported, "afford me every requisite attention." He even met a woman who seemed to him the model of a perfect wife—unfortunately she already was married. For the first time since his terrible accident, Henry was happy.

William, of course, was not. On first hearing that Henry had fled from Union College, William vented his rage to McIntyre, in whom he confided his family troubles. He was incensed, he said, that "A son who was reared not only by anxiety and prayer but with liberality to profusion—Has so debased himself as to leave his parents [*sic*] house in the character of a Swindler."[12] Later, trying to provoke McIntyre's sympathy, he added that he was not so much angry as sorrowful: "It is difficult to conceive of the wound'd spirit of a man in my situation," he wrote; "[M]y heart pities a poor unfortunate son—who has so perverted the mercies of a kind providence" that could make him "one of the most respectable members of his family and of the community."[13] He asked McIntyre to serve as intermediary, conveying a message to Henry that was meant to inspire both fear and contrition: tell him, said James, "that when he finds how base he has acted,—and when deceived and despised by himself and all others;—to come to me and I shall endeavor to screen him from infamy and as far as possible from reproach."[14]

There is no evidence that Henry was deceived by his colleagues in Boston, but if McIntyre's message reached him, Henry may well have felt a renewal of the guilt and self-hatred that beset him after his injury. Certainly, he craved his father's love, even if that love was mixed with pity. Instead of insisting that Henry come home to study law, James now offered to protect his prodigal son, to forgive him, and to shelter him. Henry could not resist his father's will, nor his own craving for his father's love. By spring, he was back at Union College. In July 1830, he graduated with his class.

While his classmates went on to continue their professional studies or enter the business world, Henry refused to pursue fame or fortune. Instead, he decided to persist in the kind of work he had done in Boston, this time on the *Albany Daily Craftsman,* a four-page newspaper consisting mostly of advertisements and some combative political editorials. In the conflict with his father over his future, this choice was Henry's small victory.

He was soon to discover, however, that his father ultimately triumphed. In December 1832, William James died of a stroke, leaving an estate of more than a million dollars. But James had left an intricate trust that singled out Henry and his eldest brother, William, from receiving the same benefits as their siblings. Unlike his twin brother, Robert, William had rejected participation in the family business. His father saw this rejection in much larger terms: William did not share his values, recognize his power, or bow to his authority. Instead, William chose an intellectual life: he went to Princeton and then, apparently to his father's dismay, entered the Princeton Theological Seminary. When praise for William's sermons reached the James family in Albany, the elder James became irate that William had succeeded despite his opposition. Henry mentioned his father's reaction in a letter to his brother. "Papa desires me to be particular in telling you that this ought to show you the necessity of increasing ardour in your studies," he wrote, "and of gaining the acquaintance of his most respected friends."[15] The Reverend William James had a distinguished career, preaching at the Murray Street Church in Manhattan, and later in Rochester, Schenectady, and Albany. But his father never approved, just as he did not approve of Henry's flagrant disregard of his wishes. Both sons were left with only a small annuity.

Henry respected William as "a capital person in mind."[16] When his brother was about to visit in 1827, while Henry was still recovering from his accident, Henry wrote that he looked forward to the visit "with a view to the ultimate improvement of my mind, or to an immediate assistance to my spirits and resolution."[17] When William and Henry essentially were cut out of their father's will, they decided to act together to sue the estate. More important, William convinced Henry to make a move that, given the context of Henry's life up to that point, seems astounding: in 1835, Henry entered Princeton Theological Seminary.

We do not know why he made this decision. Although his association with Dr. Nott and Mr. Jenks spurred his interest in religious matters, he seemed not to aspire to the ministry. But with no guarantee of an income, with no professional training and a deep disdain for business, he had few choices. Perhaps he saw that William had acquired the respect and authority that he himself desired, that William was engaged in authentic philosophical inquiry, and that William was not, so far as he could see, demonstrating the religious hypocrisy that he had seen in his parents and their friends. Certainly William agreed that Henry had been "impoverished intellectually" by the religious upbringing of their home and might enlarge his views if he devoted himself to serious study.

A Diviner Self

HENRY MAY HAVE BEEN eager to begin this study, but he soon felt disappointed. His classmates, he discovered, were interested not so much in ideas as in vocational training. "The ordinary theological student," Henry wrote, "has a fatal professional conscience from the start, which vitiates his intellectual integrity. He is personally mortgaged to an *institution*—that of the pulpit—which is reputed sacred, and is all the

more potent in its influence upon his natural freedom on that account."[18] The other students were committed to the rituals of the
church, while Henry yearned to understand how God was manifested
in human nature. He began to feel that familiar sense of asphyxiation.
"My recollection of Princeton people," he wrote to his friend Joseph
Henry, who taught natural philosophy at Princeton, "is that they are
virtuous, agreeable people up to a certain pitch," but then insufferable
in their commitment to religious dogma.[19]

Despite his growing discontent at the seminary, James continued
his studies with unusual persistence. Even after he and his brother received word that they had been successful in breaking their father's
will, the newly wealthy James (he was guaranteed an annual income of
more than ten thousand dollars) did not give up his place at the seminary. But the money gave him freedom to travel, and in the summer of
1837, he made the bold decision to go to Great Britain. During the
four-month trip, James explored his family's roots in Ireland, was fitted for a cork leg to replace his heavy wooden one, and discovered the
teachings of the theologian Robert Sandeman.

In Sandeman, James discovered a kindred spirit. Sandemanianism
had survived the death of its founder more than sixty years before to become a popular sect among rebellious Protestants. Its tenets excited
Henry: Sandemanians threw off the pretense of church rites and hierarchy in favor of simple and more primitive religious rituals that emphasized brotherhood among worshipers. They scorned self-righteousness
and believed that God's grace was bestowed on those of pure faith,
rather than those who aspired to good works. In Sandeman's universe,
James's accident was not a punishment for inherent evil; nor did James's
penchant for sensuous pleasures deny his participation in the religious
community.

James returned to Princeton feeling more restless than when he had
left. He confided these feelings to a friend, Hugh Walsh, a New Yorker
who harbored similar doubts about his vocation for the ministry. They
decided, once and for all, to leave the seminary. Walsh could return to
his family in New York City, but James knew that he had no place in
Albany. At Walsh's invitation, he, too, went to New York.

At twenty-six, Henry James cut an attractive figure. Of medium
height and sturdy build, with a ruddy complexion and intense eyes, he
could afford the well-tailored suits that he so well liked, and his stylish

cane seemed more a dapper accessory than a physical necessity. Independently wealthy, he no longer had to concern himself with earning a
living or following a career. He was as free as he had been as a child,
with all his wants and needs paid for by his father's legacy. If he could
no longer roam the fields and hills of the countryside, he did manage to
navigate city streets. He realized that he would not find answers to his
questions about religion, human nature, and society from the Princeton
Theological Seminary or any other institution. Yet he was persuaded
that he could find those answers on his own; and he believed that the
search was sufficiently important to occupy his time and efforts. If
James would not become a cleric, he would become a pundit.

This was the Henry James who, when he visited the Walsh family
in 1838, met Hugh's sisters, Mary and Catharine. Both in their
midtwenties, the Walsh sisters, by the standards of the time, were
spinsters. Neither was a beauty, but they had a warmth and serenity
that attracted Henry, and their interest in his ideas buoyed his ego.
Henry began to think about marriage.

As far as Mary and Catharine were concerned, Henry seemed a
good prospect as a husband. Their brother respected him and enjoyed
his companionship; he came from a good New York family; and his income was more than adequate. We do not know how Henry decided
between Mary and Catharine, who both were eager to marry, nor what
about Mary generated his strong feelings of attraction. Family portraits
of her, taken much later, show a woman more stolid than sweet, her
face set in a tight-lipped expression that cannot be called a smile. But
the youthful Mary stirred Henry's sexual desire; he wanted her, and she
consented.

Marriage offered Henry affirmation of his manliness and his ability
to fulfill a prescribed role in society: husband. For Henry, the family
was society in microcosm, and success in the sphere of the family was
no less significant than success in the world of business or politics. As
much as he professed to rebel against conventions, he saw advantages
to sharing his life with a sympathetic listener and nurturer. And, of
course, he would have sex. Although in future essays, Henry idealized
marriage, at twenty-six, the carnal possibilities were central. "Marriage
is a sacrament which women interpret in so much more celestial a
sense than men," he commented many years later to Ralph Waldo
Emerson.[20]

Henry was interested, too, in the spiritual deliverance that he believed would result if he joined his life with a woman's. Convinced of the essential bestiality of his own character, he hoped that Mary could save him. Woman, he wrote, offered a man "a diviner self than his own; a more private, a more sacred and intimate self than that wherewith nature endows him." In allying himself with the purity of a woman, he could enact a "passionate divorce . . . between himself and his baser nature." Sex, then, becomes a positive force for society, rather than the merely "sensual or selfish sentiment" that it might be without the sanctity of marriage.[21] Henry believed, also, that women should be submissive to their husbands, who naturally must dominate their wives, children, and servants.

Henry remained in New York for the next two years, spending much of his free time visiting with the Walshes, courting Mary, and persuading her, her mother, and her sister that the marriage should be solemnized outside of the church that he despised. Finally, he succeeded; and on July 28, 1840, Mary and Henry were married in the parlor of the Walsh home in Washington Square—not by a mere justice of the peace, but by Isaac Leggett Varian, the newly elected mayor of New York. The bride wore a light muslin dress—it was, after all, midsummer—and, in an uncharacteristic gesture of elegance and celebration, a glimmering gold headband. A week shy of her thirtieth birthday, Mary Walsh became Mrs. Henry James.

Chapter 2

GESTATION

HENRY ADMITTED that his marriage to Mary was no intellectual match, but he felt genuine affection for her, and she was able to give him the moral support that he craved, serving as an eager listener to his often eccentric ideas. Her letters to her mother-in-law in Albany report on her "dear Henry's" philosophical inquiries, writings, and lectures with sympathy and respect, evidence that she knew enough about religious, social, and political issues to comment helpfully, but not enough to challenge Henry's assertions.

Judging by Mary's later penchant for tethering her children, she probably preferred having Henry at home with her most days and every evening, constantly in sight. He quickly grew dependent on her company and looked to her for affirmation. For the rest of his life, Mary's affirmation often was all that sustained him.

Although in his essays Henry argued for the subservience of women (and children and servants) to a dominant patriarch, Mary wielded considerable power within the family. Later, her sons described Mary James as a pillar of strength and devotion: self-sacrificing, loving, giving, and caring. She was nurturing, and Henry wanted to be mothered. She was also anxious and controlling. Early in the marriage, for example, she was afraid of Henry's "keeping company" with his friend Parke Godwin, a writer and a bristly, outspoken social critic, because of habits that she considered dissolute. Gradually, as she saw that Henry was not being led astray, she relented and allowed the friendship to continue. But she was always vigilant.

Some of her anxiety was fueled by her husband's disability. Because Henry sometimes fell when he walked, especially when he refused to use a cane, Mary needed to be watchful whenever they made excursions into the city. She also needed to be alert to the emotional needs of a husband who was subject to spells of depression from a variety of causes: his own inner demons, overwork, lack of recognition by his peers, and a general sense of the vulgarity of American culture. "Life is not by any means a victory, but simply a battle," he once wrote to his brother William.[1]

Henry spent most of his time at home, studying, writing, and preparing lectures. In the late 1830s, he devoted much of his intellectual effort to publicizing and expounding upon Robert Sandeman. In 1838, Henry published—at his own expense—an edition of Sandeman's *Letters on Theron and Aspasio,* with his own unsigned two-page introduction. Two years later he summed up his thinking about Sandeman in a pamphlet, *Remarks on the Apostolic Gospel.* Ultimately, however, Sandeman failed to help Henry resolve the thorny questions about religious and personal authority that so painfully disturbed him.

Even as a rebellious child, Henry struggled with the idea of authority, both in his family and in the Calvinism in which he was raised. Certain that he was not valued by his father or his father's God, James, throughout his life, protested against the idea of hierarchy in the church, society, and even the family; he railed against the conventional standards by which men were judged superior or inferior, respectable or unworthy, and tried to generate his own criteria, based on an individual's capacity for loving God. Yet at the same time, James himself strived for recognition by his peers. He wanted to speak before admiring crowds; he wanted his books to sell in large numbers; he wanted his name to be known among his contemporaries; he wanted to be remembered by history.

As he worked, alone and unrecognized, on subjects that did not capture the public imagination, he felt increasingly isolated. After first hearing Ralph Waldo Emerson lecture in the spring of 1842, he wrote to him of his earnest search for God's love, a lonely quest that "severed [him] from friends and kindred" except, he noted, from his loyal wife.[2] He could not abide conversations with "church people" because of their "disgusting narrowness," and so he cut off relations with the most likely audience for his ideas.[3] Mary, therefore, became vitally important in his life; yet she alone was insufficient.

By April 1841, Mary James was pregnant. When they first were married, the Jameses had taken rooms at the Astor House, and soon after moved to a rented house on Washington Square; but for Mary's confinement, they decided to return to the hotel. In the 1840s, the Astor House, on Broadway between Vesey and Barclay Streets, was called "the wonder of the time," an oasis in New York's crowded business and residential district. With its lush interior garden, well-tended flower beds, and an expanse of lawn beside it, the Astor House was both a sumptuous refuge and one of New York's most prestigious addresses. There, on Tuesday, January 11, 1842, William James was born.

Now they were three—and more. With a baby came the need for a nurse and for the increasing presence of Mary's sister, Catharine. Aunt Kate, as she was called even by Henry and Mary, still was unmarried, and like many such female relatives, moved from her mother's home to that of her married sibling. The family needed room, and Henry took the first suitable opportunity: he bought a house in Washington Square from his brother John.

Washington Square, a nine-and-a-half-acre tract of land that once had been the city's principal military parade ground, by 1842 was one of its finest neighborhoods. Bordered by Waverly Place and Fourth and MacDougal Streets, it was convenient to the elegant shops on Broadway, the omnibuses that traveled to the sparsely populated northern regions of Manhattan (that is, above what is now midtown), and the local markets. Living on Washington Square allowed Mary close proximity to her mother; and Henry was only a few blocks from the New York Society Library, where, for a membership fee of twenty-five dollars, he could borrow books and attend lectures.

Shortly after the Jameses settled into their new house, Mary discovered that she was again pregnant. The period of her pregnancy was one of gestation for Henry, as well. His new friendship with Emerson was flourishing, and with it, James's hopes for recognition and accolades. By 1842, when the two men first met, the thirty-nine-year-old Emerson already had published *Nature,* his eloquent exposition of the tenets of transcendentalism; had delivered "The American Scholar," his acclaimed Phi Beta Kappa address at Harvard in which he defined, as much as Emerson ever defined anything, the role of the American intellectual. Emerson stood at the center of a thriving intellectual community in Concord, Massachusetts, where his friends included the writers William Ellery Channing, Bronson Alcott, and Margaret Fuller. Unlike James, he did not labor alone, unrecognized. Instead, he was a popular speaker who also published in many respected journals. He was a good man to know.

Emerson found James "wise, gentle, polished, with heroic manners, and a serenity like the sun."[4] James called Emerson "a fellow pilgrim" and saw in him a kindred spirit whose public demeanor masked inner sadness and vulnerability. At the time that James met him, Emerson was desolate, grieving over the death of his five-year-old son, Waldo, from a sudden attack of scarlatina. But Emerson could not afford to indulge in his grief for long: he needed his lecture fees to support his wife and two young daughters. Within weeks of Waldo's death in mid-January, he forced himself to fulfill his speaking obligations. "In New York lately," he wrote when he returned, "as in cities generally, one seems to lose all substance, & become surface in a world of surfaces. . . . This beloved and now departed Boy, this Image in every part beautiful, how he expands in his dimensions in this fond Memory to the dimensions of Nature!"[5]

James, no stranger to depression, sensed Emerson's need for sympathetic companionship and for a respite from the forced conviviality of hotels, restaurants, and meeting halls; he invited Emerson to his home. If the visit afforded some solace to Emerson, it proved a boon to James as well: according to family legend, Emerson was moved "to admire and give his blessing to the lately-born babe who was to become the second American William James."[6]

In 1842, however, it was not William who coveted Emerson's blessing, but Henry himself. He wanted Emerson to guide his intellectual and professional life, to advise him on lecturing so that he did not return from his talks brooding over his ability to interest his listeners; he wanted Emerson to help him decide if he should study science or persist in religious inquiry. He wanted more than the genial kindness that Emerson offered to everyone else. "He wants an expression of your faith, or to be sure that it is faith," Henry David Thoreau wrote to Emerson after he had talked with James for a few hours.[7]

James's repeated requests for help intensified after his second son, his namesake, was born on April 15, 1843. In May, James admitted to

Emerson that he was suffering from a "spell of blues" that he thought was caused by "two days prevalence of east winds and dyspepsia." His depression, though, more likely is linked to the birth of the "fine little boy . . . [who] preaches to me that I must become settled somewhere at home."[8] The infant underscored his feeling of worthlessness. As usual when he was depressed, he withdrew from social relationships; succumbed to old, familiar feelings of self-hatred; questioned his capacity for love and friendship and his ability to contribute to society.

Though this depression was generated by the birth of Harry, it also reflected his growing disappointment with Emerson. Early letters to Emerson suggest that James looked upon him both as spiritual brother and father. But whenever James ascribed those roles to a friend, the relationship—sooner rather than later—deteriorated. He tended to see intellectual brothers as rivals and spiritual fathers as oppressors. As much as he wished to draw close to Emerson, therefore, he contrived to distance himself by finding exasperating, unsupportable faults. James discovered, for example, that he felt increasingly irritated by Emerson's "provokingly perverse way of speech." He hated himself for feeling such irritation and wished he could love fully and uncritically. "It all comes of some lurking narrowness in me," he wrote disingenuously to Emerson, "which shall be discovered if so it be—but which nevertheless shall be legitimately discovered, that is, through the experience of growing life."[9]

Certain that he needed his own experience of growth, James, nevertheless, found that his attention and energies focused on the growing life of his infant sons. While William and Harry had all possibilities open to them, Henry became increasingly aware that many possibilities already were closed to him. He could not, he feared, reinvent his identity. Instead, he realized that his roles within the family demanded conformities and compromises that threatened to stifle his sense of individuality. His children expected him to take a position of authority. More than any of his friends, these children required James to open his heart. But James was afraid he could not. "Every narrowness I have ever grown out of," he wrote to Emerson, "I have first hugged and hugged as if it were a blanket for eternity." His narrowness, his determination to be independent and solitary, had given him security—had, in fact, given him an identity that he was not sure he could relinquish. It had protected him against his father and the disdain of his peers.

But now his children threatened to pull this blanket from him and leave him, emotionally, naked.

With Henry suffering such conflicted feelings toward his two young sons, the children depended critically on Mary's attentions. We have only hints of Mary as a young mother, but those hints portray a woman who believed that babies were demanding "tyrants" who needed to learn that they could not "rule" their mother. When they cried at night, she was apt to let them "bawl a good bit" as long as she knew they were not hungry or stuck by a diaper pin. If their physical needs were met, her duty was done. When Harry was born, she felt no regret in seeing Willy "shoved off" to her sister's care, a pattern that would repeat itself with the birth of each James child. She claimed to admire their growing independence, pity them when their "strength of arm or of will" failed them in asserting their rights among their siblings; but she also was irritated when they resisted her control. "I never see infants now," her third son wrote when he was long past childhood, "without discerning in their usually solemn countenance a conviction that they are on their guard and in more or less hostile surroundings."[10]

Mary looked for quick remedies for distress in her children and in her husband, as well. To alleviate Henry's depression, she suggested that he get out of the house; a visit to Emerson in Concord might be just the thing to lift her husband's spirits. But the solution would not be so easy: Henry needed more than a transitory distraction. Besides his doubts about his ability to love, he felt growing uncertainty about his vocation.

Whenever James became deeply troubled, his immediate environment became intolerable, and his first move was flight. He not only needed to get out of the house, he needed to get out of New York City. In May 1843, a month after Harry was born, James put his house up for sale. The profit on the transaction, he decided, would finance a radical change for the Jameses. At first, he thought he might move to the country, separating himself physically from the intellectual centers that he found so hostile, and "communicate with my *living* kind, not my talking kind—by life only."[11] But he realized that living an exemplary life, unheralded, would not satisfy him.

There was, of course, another route, one sanctioned by many Americans of his class: settling in Europe. By the summer of 1843, he decided to leave America. "Mr. James talks of going to Germany soon with his wife—to learn the language," Thoreau told Emerson. "He says he must know it—can never learn it here—there he may absorb it and is very anxious to learn beforehand where he had best locate himself, to enjoy the advantage of the highest culture, learn the language in its purity, and not exceed his limited means."[12] But by the end of the summer, James had changed his mind about the destination. It would not be Germany, where, without the language, he would be at a serious disadvantage in participating in "the highest culture"; instead, he would take his family to England.

A Nest of Hell

ON OCTOBER 19, the Jameses, including Aunt Kate, sailed east on the *Great Western.* "How long I shall stay, and whether I shall gain what I go for specially, or something instead which I have not thought of, and all questions of that class—I am of course in the dark about," he wrote to Emerson before leaving.[13] He was going, he said, to study the book of Genesis in order to support his idea that the text "was not intended to throw a direct light upon our natural or race history, but was an altogether mystical or symbolic record of the laws of God's *spiritual* creation and providence." His exposition on this theory would, he thought, "contribute a not insignificant mite to the sum of man's highest knowledge."[14] He was going, also, to pursue his readings in science, about which Emerson did not share his enthusiasm. And he hoped to find friends who might help him gain the recognition that he failed to achieve in New York. One of those friends, he decided, would be Thomas Carlyle, "the very best interpreter of spiritual philosophy which could be devised *for this age,* the age of transition and conflict."[15] James brought with him to England a letter of introduction to Carlyle from, appropriately enough, Emerson himself.

As soon as he settled his family in London, James presented himself to Carlyle, who, James hoped, might offer him the affirmation that he simply could not elicit from Emerson. The meeting was a disaster. Carlyle was wary of most Americans, and although he was willing to make an exception for a friend of Emerson, he still treated James with the same condescension that offended other visitors. "The worst of hearing Carlyle," reported Margaret Fuller after she visited him a few years later, "is that you cannot interrupt him. I understand the habit and power of haranguing have increased very much upon him, so that

you are a perfect prisoner when he has once got hold of you. To interrupt him is a physical impossibility."[16]

Apparently, Carlyle intimidated James so severely that the latter
took to stuttering in his presence, behavior not recorded by anyone
else who knew James. "James is a very good fellow," Carlyle wrote to
Emerson, "better and better as we see him more. Something shy and
skittish in the man; but a brave heart intrinsically, with sound, earnest
sense, with plenty of insight and even humor. He confirms an observation of mine . . . that a stammering man is never a worthless one."[17]

James, for his part, as soon as he realized that Carlyle would never
respect him in the way he needed to be respected, deemed Carlyle intellectually limited. While Carlyle was "wont to question established
institutions and dogmas with the utmost license of scepticism, he obviously meant nothing beyond the production of a certain literary surprise, or the enjoyment of his own aesthetic power." Carlyle bristled at
the idea that he would be considered a reformer and also that he would
be considered a lover of humankind. He was neither, he declared; and
James regretfully agreed. Moreover, James was disheartened to find
that Carlyle's overriding emotion toward his colleagues was that of
pity: "'Poor John Sterling,' he used always to say; 'poor John Mill, poor
Frederic Maurice, poor Neuberg, poor Arthur Helps, poor little
Browning, poor little Lewes,' and so on; as if the temple of his friendship were a hospital, and all its inmates scrofulous or paralytic."[18]
James had not moved, at great effort and expense, to a place where he
would be trivialized and ignored. Although he enjoyed the company of
Mill, Lewes, and especially John Sterling, another friend of Emerson,
he realized within a short time that England would not give him what
he sought. In January 1844, he packed up his household once more
and crossed the channel.

When James fled from England after less than three months, he
still was in search of the "higher culture" that he had come to Europe
to find. That search was more difficult than he had anticipated, and it
unsettled his entire family. All the Jameses were seasick on the way to
France. "Willy didn't know what to make of it at all," Henry wrote to
his mother, "and screamed incessantly to have 'the hair taken out of his
mouth.'"[19]

In Paris, they could not find adequate lodgings; the city was damp
and chilly; and James, without fluent French, felt alienated from the

culture. Little Harry, barely a year old, was the only family member who seemed undisturbed by being uprooted from England. Henry was tense and depressed, Mary and Kate bore the burden of calming him and overseeing the children. Two-year-old William was agitated: "Our wretched Paris excursion broke him up a little," Henry reported.[20]

There was nothing to do, Henry thought, but return to "tidy old England"—not to London, this time, but to the countryside, which he remembered fondly from his previous visit. The crossing in late April was calm, and although Harry was distressed because of teething, William seemed more serene. Of his two sons, William was the most volatile. He was cheerful when the family was settled but easily upset by change. He was a restless, active child, just as his father had been, and certainly he was bright, eager to chatter with adults. Henry, reflecting his desire to do away with family hierarchy, taught his son to call him and Mary by their Christian names—William called them "Henwy" and "Mawy," because he had trouble pronouncing the r—as if they were friends or comrades.

Dispensing with parental titles was unusual at the time, but fostering a sense of equality within the family was not. In advice books to parents, experts suggested that strict discipline and harsh punishments were detrimental to the spirit and personality of the child. This point of view marked a change from the parental role of the late eighteenth and early nineteenth centuries, when parents, especially fathers, used fear to foster obedience and punishment to underscore fear. Mid-nineteenth-century fathers, redefining their role as nurturers, needed to create roles for themselves different from those of their own parents. Henry, who desperately wanted to reject his father as a model, nevertheless had difficulty conceiving this new role. He was in charge, the protector of his wife and children, but felt inadequate, burdened by his new responsibilities and by responses toward his sons that he did not understand.

As he watched Willy and Harry playing, he often was overwhelmed by a surge of odd memories and disturbing feelings. "I confess to some potent pullings now and then, dear Ma, in your direction—'nursery' remembrances and 'little-back-room' remembrances come over me not infrequently," he wrote to his mother when the family was settled in England once again. They had found a house, Frogmore Cottage, in Windsor, where the children had fields in which to play, and their nearest neighbor was the Duchess of Kent. With "trees and flowers and shady walks, and a fine fruit garden running round the sides of the house," Henry thought they would have a wonderful summer. Yet as he watched his children play, as he looked out upon Great and Little Parks, his own childhood memories darkened his spirits, making "Windsor Castle seem a great ghastly lie, and its parks an endless sickness not to be endured a moment longer."[21] Henry had no way to analyze these feelings of betrayal and affliction, no language to describe the connection between his sons' thriving and the flourishing landscape of the English countryside. He knew only that whatever was so pleasurable for others became, for him, ominous.

While he believed that his children should evoke feelings of love, protectiveness, and joy, Henry experienced a range of negative emotions: troubling memories of his own youth; envy of the children's opportunities to experiment and grow without strictures and responsibility; regret over opportunities lost, regret over childhood lost. These emotions, so contradictory to his image of a good father, made him feel contemptible.

Writing offered no consolation: on the contrary, he suffered a chilling sense of self-doubt. He wondered if his ideas were truly original and significant. Would anyone care about them? Sometimes, he felt satisfied with his theories, but more often, the whole task seemed futile. Then, one chilly afternoon in late May, Henry found himself sitting alone at the dinner table after his family had finished and retired upstairs. Watching the dying embers in the fireplace, suddenly he was overcome with fear and trembling.

> To all appearance it was a perfectly insane and abject terror, without ostensible cause, and only to be accounted for, to my perplexed imagination, by some damnèd shape squatting invisible to me within the precincts of the room, and raying out from his fetid personality influences fatal to life. The thing had not lasted ten seconds before I felt myself a wreck; that is, reduced from a state of firm, vigorous, joyful manhood to one of almost helpless infancy. The only self-control I was capable of exerting was to keep my seat. I felt the greatest desire to run incontinently to the foot of the stairs and shout for help to my wife,—to run to the roadside even, and appeal to the public to protect me; but by an immense effort I controlled these frenzied impulses, and determined

not to budge from my chair till I had recovered my lost self-possession. This purpose I held for a good long hour, as I reckoned time, beat upon meanwhile by an ever-growing tempest of doubt, anxiety, and despair, with absolutely no relief from any truth I had ever encountered save a most pale and distant glimmer of the divine existence, when I resolved to abandon the vain struggle, and communicate without more ado what seemed my sudden burden of inmost, implacable unrest to my wife.[22]

The crisis, he said later, was a mystery to him. He could not guess at its cause, but he knew immediately the result. "One moment," he said, "I devoutly thanked God for the inappreciable boon of self-hood; the next, that inappreciable boon seemed to me the one thing damnable on earth, seemed a literal nest of hell within my own entrails."

Henry's breakdown caused an immediate shift in power within the family. Now Mary and her sister had three children to care for, but one was thirty-three. Henry needed to be shielded from disturbances, including the demands of his two young sons. Deeply depressed, in a "ghastly condition of mind," he no longer participated in the life of the family. Suddenly, for Willy and Harry, the father who continually hovered over their activities inexplicably withdrew. He competed with his sons for his wife's attentions; he needed to be soothed, loved, nurtured. He needed to be treated like a child.

The Strangest Lightness about the Heart

HENRY'S BREAKDOWN, beginning with what appears to have been a panic attack, generated ongoing anxiety and depression that allowed him to abdicate the roles he found threatening: parent and writer.[23] James set high standards for himself: he would not be satisfied simply with writing an interesting essay about his views on Genesis; he aspired to contribute "a not insignificant mite to the sum of man's highest knowledge." His calculated use of the double negative is a familiar strategy for James: while apparently sounding modest, in fact he boasts about his intellectual prowess. During his stay in England, he wanted to produce a book that would both justify his living abroad and earn him the recognition he coveted. He was pursuing this goal alone, far from the few friends he could count on in New York, far from his and Mary's family and from familiar surroundings.

His feelings of vulnerability were compounded by the demands of being a parent—and not just a good parent, but an excellent, inimitable parent. While Mary had the task of nurturing the children's "subjective identity," his role as father, he believed, carried with it the huge task of giving to his children "the objective individuality or character they claim in themselves."[24] Mary took charge of the children's private feelings; he, of shaping the personality and responses that they presented publicly. This distinction between private and public, subjective and objective, would haunt his children throughout their lives.

James was not the conventional Victorian father who saw his children at prayers and dinner. He was always at home, and when he lifted his gaze from the pages he was reading or writing, he focused on his young sons toddling in the garden. As his letters reveal, James planned many family activities to respond to his perception of his children's needs; these excursions and visits sometimes were curtailed by the children's health or fatigue, and, no doubt, Henry's hopes about his children's responses to his outings often were not realized. He quickly learned that developing theories about raising children was far easier than putting those theories into practice. Nevertheless, he persisted in trying to shape his children according to his own beliefs about human potential and intellectual development. After all, he believed, the world would judge him by the behavior and intellectual brilliance of his progeny.

Anxiety about his children's intellectual development, however, was not the only burden that James bore. In an essay that he published years later he gives us a hint of another source of oppression: his agonizing need to protect his children from sin. For some time, he wrote, he had been overcome with feelings of guilt about his own transgressions. Even so benign a memory as having thrown snowballs at a younger brother seemed to him an unpardonable sin; "every dubious transaction I had been engaged in from my youth up, no matter how insignificant soever," he wrote, "crept forth from its oblivious slime to paralyze my soul with threats of God's judgment."[25] Convinced of his own evil, he was overwhelmed with self-hatred.

His children, though, were pristine in their innocence. They had not yet confronted nor committed sin, and he desperately wished to protect them from the inevitable contamination that would make them "odious to any human heart." But there seemed only one way to keep them pure: through annihilation. "I *did* say in my inmost heart incessantly," he wrote to a friend later, "'take these children away before they know the soil of sin.' What dreadful mystery of sin haunted me night and day. I have been on my knees from morning till night (this strictly between ourselves) sometimes determined as it were not to let God go, till he gave me some relief in this direction."[26]

Henry found no relief through prayer. Instead, he became obsessed with the feelings of powerlessness generated in him by his children. "I am sure," he said, "that I am incessantly belittled by my parental anxieties, that my life is robbed of half its possible freedom and joy by my insane attempts to constitute myself into a Providence for my children and so supplant the Divine Providence."[27] If Henry later came to realize the insanity of his quest to usurp God and assume complete power over his children's lives, in the 1840s he was not yet enlightened.

In response to his feelings of inadequacy on every front, he simply wanted to give up. "With no attempt there can be no failure; with no failure no humiliation," his son William wrote many years later. "So our self-feeling in this world depends entirely on what we *back* ourselves to be and do. . . . To give up pretensions is as blessed a relief as to get them gratified; and where disappointment is incessant and the struggle unending, this is what men will always do. The history of evangelical theology, with its conviction of sin, its self-despair, and its abandonment of salvation by works, is the deepest of possible examples, but we meet others in every walk of life. There is the strangest lightness about the heart when one's nothingness in a particular line is accepted in good faith."[28]

Immediately after his crisis, James stopped working on his study of Genesis. He had no interest, he claimed, in pursuing any intellectual efforts. He visited some physicians who advised that he take a water-cure treatment—England had many spas for such a purpose—a popular remedy for nervous exhaustion. Baths, mineral water, and inactivity, however, did not help; James resented being thrown into the company of "a few morbid specimens of English insularity and prejudice" and grew tired of hearing an "endless 'strife of tongues' about diet, and regimen, and disease, and politics, and parties, and persons."[29] During those months of health seeking, he made a critical decision: he would stop writing. He never had had even a glimpse of the truth about the Scriptures or anything else, he decided. He was a fraud. "Indeed," he wrote, "an ugly suspicion had more than once forced itself upon me, that I had never really wished the truth, but only to ventilate my own ability in discovering it. I was getting sick to death in fact with a sense of my downright intellectual poverty and dishonesty."[30]

But if he would not be a seeker after truth, a philosopher and writer like Emerson, what would he do? Who would he be? He did not take long to find an answer. While taking the detested water cure, he struck up a friendship with one Mrs. Chichester, who suggested with some authority that James's crisis in May was what the Swedish mystic Emanuel Swedenborg called a vastation—a positive catharsis, as Swedenborg saw it—and although the experience caused him initial distress, it would lead, she assured him, to renewed health. Encouraged by the gentle Mrs. Chichester, a woman of "singular personal loveliness," James looked up Swedenborg's books in London, where he also encountered James John Garth Wilkinson, a genial London physician who devoted his energies to translating, editing, and popularizing Swedenborg.

James's discovery coincided with a surge of interest in Swedenborg among many of his friends. But while some were enthusiastic enough to base a theology and new church on Swedenborg's writings, more sophisticated thinkers approached Swedenborg with a bit of skepticism. "Very dangerous study will Swedenborg be to any but a mind of great elasticity," Emerson commented in his journals.[31] In 1844, James's was not a mind of great elasticity, and he lit upon one idea of Swedenborg's as a kind of mantra: the rejection of selfhood. To know truth, James learned from Swedenborg, one had to give up "natural prejudices and prejudices of education," the most perilous being "that which makes selfhood the greatest of realities, and consequently inflates the heart of man with all manner of spiritual pride, avarice, and cruelty."[32]

As James understood him, Swedenborg believed that self-hatred was as mistaken as self-love. In fact, Swedenborg argued, obsessive morbidity of conscience was caused not by actual reflections on misdeeds, but on the annoying interference of "certain ghostly busy-bodies intent upon reducing the human mind to subjection, and availing themselves for this purpose of every sensuous and fallacious idea we entertain of God, and of every disagreeable memory we retain of our own conduct."[33] Swedenborg, then, lifted from James the crushing burden of his guilt and convinced him that his psychological affliction was caused by "a brood of ghostly loafers who had at last very nearly turned me out of house and home. . . . The first step toward my acknowledging the evil of my doings," he concluded, "is my perception of its being a foreign influx or importation."[34]

By blaming mischievous spirits for his depression and guilt, James was free to believe that he himself was a good, indeed, a splendid, person. The true essence of selfhood, Swedenborg taught him, came from God and therefore could be nothing other than good.

Rejecting the self allowed James to give up striving for success as an intellectual. There was no need for competition in Swedenborg's universe, where all were equal, all capable of sharing in Divine love. Good works and acclaim did not make anyone more worthy than another. Here, at last, was a philosophy generous enough to obliterate James's self-hatred and deprecation and to mollify his anger and impatience toward others. Men who aspired to exert authority over him were deluded; they were actors in a universe in which he did not believe.

Reading Swedenborg and talking with Wilkinson helped to alleviate James's depression. But with renewed energy came familiar feelings of restlessness. In the fall of 1844, Mary became pregnant again; around the same time, Henry decided to take another trip to Paris, and then, more drastically, to leave Europe and return home. The Jameses stopped first in New York City, where Mary and Kate visited with their family, and where, on July 21, 1845, the Jameses' third son was born, named for Henry's new mentor Garth Wilkinson.

In the fall, the Jameses traveled to Albany for an extended stay with Henry's mother, and by November, Mary was again pregnant. Robertson James—this time, the Jameses chose a name from Mary's family—was born the following August. Without a permanent home of their own, for the next two years the Jameses traveled between Manhattan and Albany, descending upon their relatives—notably Catharine Barber James and Elizabeth Walsh—for months at a time. The indecision about where they settled reflected Henry's changing ideas about what would be best for his children: William, four, and his three younger brothers.

In fact, now that Henry had relinquished his own selfhood, he could dwell even more obsessively than before on his children, on rescuing them from illusions and saving their pure souls. Children, he believed, should be raised in protracted innocence, shielded from the materialism and vulgarity of society. His sons would grow up to believe in the innate goodness of their own impulses, to follow their inner lights—their spirits lit by Divine love. James's manipulation of his family was a social experiment that he believed could not fail. He raised his sons to despise conventional notions of success, to scorn society's images of manliness, to embrace democratic and egalitarian ideals, to look to no authority other than their benign father. His children became his world, and he theirs.

Besides Swedenborg, Henry discovered another thinker to help him conceive of the world he would create for his children. As Mary explained eagerly to Mrs. Garth Wilkinson:

> Speaking about the future & the children, my dear Henry & I have lately been receiving a whole flood of light & joy upon this subject, by an insight into the glorious plans & prospects which Fourier opens upon the world. Henry has been reading to me a most charming little book by our friend Madame Gati de Gammon, & translated by our old friend Mrs. Chichester. As fiction it is more beautiful than any romance I ever read, but if true, (& I *feel* that it must be so, or if not, as my hopeful loving Henry says, something better must be) it will not only banish from the world poverty with its long list of debasing evils but it will remove every motive to cruelty, injustice & oppression, which the present disordered state of society has given birth to, & nourished in the selfish heart of man.[35]

Fourier, whose thinking inspired the establishment of many utopian communities in the mid-nineteenth century, believed that people did not need laws or restrictions in order to live in harmony with one another; the community of humankind would thrive simply by nurturing an individual's inner goodness. Men and women would choose their vocations, their mates, their spiritual practices, according to their own particular nature. No vocation is better than another, no way of living is better than another, no personality is better than another. Diversity would lead to harmony as human beings accept and celebrate their differences.

By the very nature of their ideas, Swedenborg and Fourier affirmed for James his own role as a philosopher. If all men were equal, then James was as significant a thinker as Swedenborg or Fourier, Emerson or Alcott. If all men held equal authority within society, then James, at last, and with no chance of failure, could achieve his deepest desire.

Chapter 3

APPETITES AND AFFECTIONS

1847–1855

IN THE SUMMER OF 1847, with "four stout boys" all under six, Henry and Mary James rented a house at 11 Fifth Avenue in Manhattan. By late autumn, Mary was pregnant with her fifth child, and the Jameses finally decided to settle in New York City. Their long visits to Albany had been crucial for James: at last, he had proved to his many relatives that he was not the ne'er-do-well who had shamed his father, but the respectable head of a quickly growing family and an industrious writer and lecturer.

In the two years after his return from England, Henry had reestablished contact with Emerson, Alcott, and other friends who were eager to hear his ideas. They encouraged him to lecture—in fact, they helped him find receptive forums—and to write. In 1845, after he spoke before the Young Men's Association of the City of Albany on "What Constitutes the State," he was asked to submit the lecture for the *Harbinger,* the journal of the American Union of Associationists, social reformers inspired by Swedenborg and Fourier. As its prospectus proclaimed, the journal was "devoted to the cause of a radical, organic social reform as essential to the highest development of man's nature, to the production of those elevated and beautiful forms of character of which he is capable, and to the diffusion of happiness, excellence, and universal harmony upon the earth."[1] James could not have found a more appropriate home for his writing.

The men who wrote for and edited the *Harbinger* became James's intimate circle: newspaper editor Horace Greeley; George Ripley, a founder of the socialist community Brook Farm and former managing

editor of Emerson's *Dial;* Charles Dana, who had taught Greek and
German at Brook Farm and who later became editor of the New York
Sun; George William Curtis, also a former Brook Farmer; James's
longstanding friend Parke Godwin. If these men were not renowned
writers, at least they were better esteemed than the "vague and female"
authors who sometimes deposited themselves in James's parlor. As
much as he enjoyed an audience of women with literary pretensions, he
preferred to be surrounded by men who would publish his essays. The
success of the *Harbinger,* James hoped, would sweep him to promi-
nence. The journal clearly was so central to his life that when William
and his playmates decided to form a club, they called it the Harbinger
and even produced their own publication. Like their father's *Harbinger,*
the boys' journal included poems, one written by William.

In early November 1847, James learned that the *Harbinger* was
leaving Brook Farm, just outside of Boston, to set up its offices in
Manhattan; there was no question that James wanted to be nearby. Immediately, he put down a deposit on one of the many new three-story
brownstone houses built north of Washington Square, at 58 West
Fourteenth Street, between Fifth and Sixth Avenues. The city was
being aggressively developed with these town houses: in 1849 alone,
more than sixteen hundred were built in the Jameses' neighborhood.
Some New Yorkers resented the monotony of the structures, but James
was more interested in space than in architecture. A few months after
their arrival in the spring of 1848, their family again increased by one:
on August 7, when Henry was thirty-seven and Mary thirty-eight,
Alice, their first daughter and last child was born.

Although James boasted of having no profession save that of eternal student and seeker of truth, during this period he seemed determined to make writing his career. "How much more honorable this,"
he insisted, "than upon one derived from the merciless warfare of Cedar
& Wall Street?"[2] Each morning, he sat at his writing table for hours of
intense labor on his lectures and essays.

Whether his subject was Swedenborg or Fourier, socialism or social contracts, he always returned to his singular obsessions: spiritual
life and the problem of individual authority. He insisted on discussing
socialism from, as he put it, "the highest point of view"—abstractly
and philosophically—rather than in practical, concrete terms.

His public, however, hungered for solutions to pressing political and social problems: in 1848, violent revolutions erupted in major European capitals; in Ireland and western Europe, famine and poverty generated unprecedented immigration to America—in the 1850s more than a million newcomers from the British Isles alone swelled the population of America's cities; the slums of New York, Boston, and Chicago were beset by disease, violence, and political corruption. Many popular speakers were active in reform movements that focused on temperance, education, housing, health, and, not least, abolition of slavery.

James, however, was not among these ardent men and women calling for radical, tangible changes. Although he was well aware what topics interested audiences of the time, he would not, or could not, meet their needs.

James believed that social problems resulted from personal repression. Society itself shackled humans by limiting both their authority over their own lives and their opportunities to express their essential nature. According to James, society condemned each man to live "under law successively to his wife, his children, his relatives, his neighbors, his fellow countrymen. . . . [Society] has given the individual expansion, but only in a downward or subversive direction, such an expansion as you give the prisoner, not by breaking his chains and bidding him be free, but by enlarging and multiplying the wards of his prison."[3] In many essays and even in letters to friends, James repeatedly railed against the obligations thrust upon him by family life: "The sentiment of responsibility," he wrote, "grinds human life into the dust."[4] As much as he professed to love his family, he wished he could be free from thinking always about "the necessity of providing subsistence, education, and social respect for myself and my children. To these narrow limits society confines all my passion, all my intellect, all my activity; and so far denies me self-development."[5]

When individuals were enslaved by social constructions, James argued, it was no wonder that violence and crime resulted. Certainly he acknowledged that murder and robbery were evils, but he believed that people would not commit such acts unless forced by society to strive for wealth or fame. "We should give up the indolent and futile habit of blaming the thief, the liar, the adulterer, the drunkard for their abominations," he exhorted his listeners, "and place the blame where alone it truly belongs, upon our defective social organization."[6] When critics accused James of not acknowledging the difference between good and evil, he defended himself by assuring them that he knew the difference—but he ascribed the cause of good and evil acts to social constraints rather than personal weakness or defects. Human beings were essentially good, he claimed: how could they be otherwise, when they were invested with Divine spirit?

James appeared to some of his colleagues to be "of the class of purely ideal reformers, men who will lounge at their ease upon damask sofas and dream of a harmonic and beautiful world to be created hereafter, while they would probably be the very last to whom the earnest worker, in any branch of human concerns, could resort for aid with any prospect of success." While no one disputed James's intelligence, many regretted that his ideas had the frustrating propensity of "breaking into spray and impalpable mist, glittering in the sun, and descending to earth with no weight or mechanical force to effect any great end."[7]

James, ever sensitive to criticism, complained about his audiences as much as they complained about him. He told Garth Wilkinson that he had developed a "horror of pen and ink," and he confessed to Emerson that he did not much enjoy speaking to "literary men. . . . Catch them out of the range of mere personal gossip about authors and books," he remarked, "and ask them for honest sympathy with your sentiment or an honest repugnancy of it, and you will find the company of stage-drivers sweeter and more comforting to your soul."[8] James preferred stage drivers not because he was a champion of democracy nor of the intuitive good sense of uneducated people, but because he dreaded the censure of his peers. "The fact is," he wrote to Emerson, "I am in a very bad way I am afraid, for I cannot heartily engage in any topic in which I shall appear to advantage."[9]

Bronson Alcott concurred, agreeing that James's themes "are a little unpopular," but blaming his shortcomings as a speaker on his aggressive manner, "his bearing too consequential and knowing, as of a man with Kingdom-Come in his brain." James, thought Alcott, had a "voracious intellect, subtle, sinuous, clear, forcible, and swift, voracious of guile as a cormorant of its prey. A terrible logician and audacious even to the verge of duplicity."[10] Certainly he did not project the serene presence of his friend Emerson, who had speaking engagements from New York to Chicago, Boston to Philadelphia. Although James delivered many lectures in New York and Boston, he never attained his friend's popularity. Even when his work on the lecture circuit seemed to thrive, James felt that his position as an important intellectual was precarious.

Harry remembered that his father worked as if he were "under pressure for his bread and ours," but the nature of his work was as mysterious to them as it might have been if James left each morning to go to Wall Street. Yet if they did not fully understand what their father was writing or why, they recognized how central writing was in their father's life, how exalted an occupation.

At the same time, however, the children learned that, for their father, being a writer was onerous and dangerous. Henry Sr. seemed to derive little satisfaction from his work, but instead, as William recalled, "despised every formulation he made as soon as it was uttered."[11] He often was irritable, rudely interrupting Mary's activities with the children, impatient with their needs. Sometimes he became depressed, although not as dramatically as he had in England; nevertheless, his self-absorption during those dark periods caused him to withdraw from family life and demand Mary's constant attention.

The children learned that a writer worries about what readers will think of him, and they discovered, from Henry's reaction after he returned from some of his lectures, that their father often had a hostile, frustrating relationship with his audience. His essays usually found a home in small journals threatened with imminent demise. On February 10, 1849, the *Harbinger,* which had faced financial trouble since its inception, published its last issue, cutting off an important outlet for James's work. James had been a significant contributor, publishing nearly a dozen book reviews and nineteen essays, including "Human Freedom," "Is Human Nature Positively Evil?" and "Love and Marriage."

At first, it seemed that there might be another opportunity to find a readership: The American Union of Associationists was eager to continue a journal and authorized Parke Godwin, the *Harbinger*'s editor and James's friend, to solicit funds for a monthly magazine. Godwin asked James to serve as coeditor, a position he coveted. But Godwin's efforts failed to produce enough support. For James, the failure of the *Harbinger* was a personal failure, a rejection of his ideas, and, more important, the loss of sustaining fellowship. For his family, the loss of the *Harbinger* meant enormous changes.

Urchins

AT THE END OF AUGUST 1849, James's discouragement led to a feeling of restlessness; as he had six years before, he decided to leave the country and sail for Europe. In part, his decision reflected his search for a hospitable intellectual community, in part, his concern over money: James worried about finances all of his life; he knew nothing about managing money and was determined not to learn. "Our consensus . . . was amazing," Henry Jr. wrote about his family later; "—it brooked no exception; the word has been passed, all round, that we didn't, that we couldn't and shouldn't, understand these things, questions of arithmetic and of fond calculation, questions of the counting-house and the market."[12] If there was any single force that undermined freedom and spontaneity, Henry Sr. believed, it was an individual's need to earn a living. Yet as much as he boasted of his lack of connection to the business world, he knew that he was burdened with the task of providing for his family, and he knew that the financial climate of America affected their welfare. Still smarting from his father's derision over his profligate ways, James needed constantly to prove to himself, his family in Albany, and his cautious wife that he could live economically.

In 1849, with a household consisting of five children, numerous servants, Mary, and Aunt Kate, economy seemed a formidable challenge. He knew that his brownstone on Fourteenth Street needed to be enlarged, at least to accommodate a playroom for the children, who were now doubled up in the available bedrooms. Bob even had to sleep with Aunt Kate.

Moreover, a cholera epidemic that took more than seven hundred lives between May and July in 1849 convinced James that the city was an unhealthy place in summer. The stinking garbage that littered the streets and the packs of dogs, pigs, and goats that rummaged in the trash made even his neighborhood repulsive. The family needed a country home, and country homes were costly. Europe seemed a cheaper alternative.

Settling in Europe, he believed, also would allow him more control over his children. The boys, he wrote to Garth Wilkinson, because they had no playroom in the house, cavorted with friends outdoors, where they learned "shocking bad-manners." It seems unlikely that at the ages of three and four respectively Bob or Wilky could have shocked their father with their bad manners; nor does it seem likely that Harry, by all accounts a docile and obedient little boy, would have suddenly, at the age of six, become incorrigible. Which leaves William.

MUCH OF WHAT WE know of William's childhood comes from Harry's memoirs, written a few years after William's death, when Harry himself was ill, often depressed, and inclined to romanticize lost youth. Although the portrait that emerges is bathed in a golden glow of nostalgia, homage, and love, certain consistencies help us to understand William as a boy. He was quick, restless, egotistical, short-tempered, clamorous for attention and praise, and openly curious. Not only Harry, but the whole family, saw William as occupying a special place among the children. Although barely more than a year older than Harry, his position as firstborn, his precocious intelligence, and his willfulness defined him as a leader among his siblings and even among his friends. As Harry describes him, William seems hardly ever to have behaved like a child: even in nursery school, according to Harry, he was confident, brilliant, and independent.

He craved, he demanded, recognition of his obvious talents. One favorite pastime among the James children and their friends was mounting theater productions, which William conceived, directed, and in which he took the lead as "constant comic star. . . . I remember how far ahead of us my brother seemed to keep," Harry recalled, "announcing a 'motive,' producing a figure, throwing off into space conceptions that I could stare at across the interval but couldn't appropriate." William's interest in these productions, as in so many other of his childhood activities, was not in the camaraderie among his peers, not even simply in enjoying the spirit of creating and imagining, but in winning the acclaim of adults. His parents, assorted James and Walsh relatives, and their friends usually were eager to admire, but the admiration that William coveted most was his father's. The surest way to win that admiration, William realized early, was by homage and emulation. It is no wonder, then, that William chose the name Harbinger for his boys' club: he wanted to become part of, to identify with, his father's dearest project. If the world at large would not keep the *Harbinger* alive, then

William alone would revive its spirit. In addition, William took to emulating his father's public personality: fearless, voluble, even terrifying. "A Robespierre in argument," Bronson Alcott remarked. "No man wields a logic so swift and fatal."[13] That was the image that William aspired to; that, he believed, was the boy his father wanted.

William's aggressive behavior, however, met with censure—certainly from his mother, who preferred her children quiet, and even from his father, who saw in his son a potential competitor to his role as Robespierre. Despite James's optimistic prediction that raising children in an atmosphere of freedom would result in the expression of their divine goodness, William was not always good. He could be rebellious and demanding. Whenever their father told the children stories of his own youth, Harry remembered that "each hero of each thrilling adventure had, in spite of brilliant promise and romantic charm, ended badly, as badly as possible. This became our gaping generalisation."[14]

The cautionary tales, however, had no effect on William's behavior: when he turned his well-honed verbal ferocity on his father, James responded violently. Just as James himself had been repeatedly flogged with a black strap when he misbehaved in school, now he angrily lashed out at William—but with an even harsher instrument of punishment. More than fifteen years later, William recalled his father's method of discipline: "I never suffered more pain since Father used to spank me with a paper cutter in fourteenth street," he told his sister, "nor hardly ever more cold."[15]

No one reading Henry Sr.'s passionate paeans to essential human goodness could have suspected the level of violence in his household. The beatings openly contradicted his much-publicized ideas about children's ingenuousness and their need for nurturing environments. James denounced the churches and schools that had corrupted his own spirit when he was young. He wanted something different for his own children: an environment that would not wound them, crush them, inhibit them, and fill them with self-hatred. In the egalitarian, socialist society envisioned by Fourier, and promoted by James, their needs would be met, they would not have to struggle to earn a living, and they would be free, therefore, to focus their lives on spirituality and creativity.

From an early age, Harry remembered, the James children were taught that their task in life was to convert "simply everything that should happen to us, every contact, every impression and every experience we should know" into "Virtue, as a social grace and value." But the children did not understand how they were to express virtue; they did not know "what was suggested and expected." They understood only that their father had a horror of conceit, arrogance, smugness: "he only cared for virtue that was more or less ashamed of itself."[16] William, though, was not at all ashamed of his quick mind, his curiosity, and his talents. He wanted approval, but his father maintained that all he really valued was spiritual purity.

James believed that he alone could teach his children this "spiritual decency." He refused, of course, to allow them to join any established church, a decision with which Mary, who had left her own church at Henry's urging, concurred. Although he sent them to schools and found them tutors, he disparaged much of what they learned. According to Fourier, whose ideas on personality and education inspired much of James's thought, children should not be stuffed with information, but instead should move through a variety of activities throughout the day so that their many "passions" (love, personal ambition, sensuality) could be stimulated. As James saw it, they should be nurtured to become Artists.

By Artist, of course, James did not mean a painter who studied at an academy, rendered pleasant scenes on canvas, and sold his works at a gallery; he surely did not mean a poet who wrote uplifting lyrics for popular magazines, nor did he mean a musician who displayed his talent at concerts. These, according to James, were artisans, whose pretense to art he scorned. For James, Artist meant a free spirit who obeyed "his own inspiration or taste, uncontrolled either by his physical necessities or his social obligations. . . . The Artist . . . works only to show forth that immortal beauty whose presence constitutes his inmost soul."[17] The Artist was an individual with neither obligations nor connections to society, submitting to no one's demands or judgment. The Artist did not need to earn a living; in fact, if the Artist set himself to producing anything, he was bound to fail in fulfilling James's criteria for success. "To live or to act is more than to produce," he wrote. "The poet, painter or musician is not the perfect man, the man of destiny, the man of God, because the perfect man is so pronounced by his life or action rather than by his production."[18] James's distinction between the practicing artist and the exemplary Artist confused the children; in late adolescence, William would plead with his father to clarify his ideas about art and explain why he objected so passionately to William's studying painting and drawing. But as a child, William knew nothing more than that the Artist was, for his father, a glowing ideal.

THE JAMES FAMILY did not leave America in the summer of 1849. By fall, James's mood had brightened, buoyed by his reception at the Town and Country Club in Boston in November, where he had been invited to speak at Emerson's request. James felt guardedly optimistic about his status among his peers. There would be other talks, thanks to Emerson and Alcott; Emerson persuaded James that he was indispensable to help him arrange lectures in New York; and James decided to compile his lectures into a book. Published at his own expense, *Moralism and Christianity* collected an essay and two talks on James's favorite subjects: Divine Man; the relationship of socialism, civilization, and the individual; and morality.

Instead of building a playroom or buying a country house, the James family decided to leave Fourteenth Street in summer and vacation at one or another hotel not too far from home. New Brighton, a resort community on Staten Island, a twenty-minute ferry ride from Manhattan, became, for a few years, a favorite spot. The village of New Brighton attracted sophisticated Bostonians, New Yorkers who wanted easy access to their Manhattan businesses or homes, and wealthy southern families escaping sultry heat. The Jameses first stayed at the Pavilion Hotel, renowned in its time, a grand villa with a large saloon, two huge wings of guest suites, and a two-hundred-foot-long promenade across the front, where families could take an evening stroll.

The Jameses might have heard about the attractions of Staten Island from any number of their friends, including Emerson, whose brother, Judge William Emerson, lived there, or Henry David Thoreau, who tutored the judge's son for half of 1843. For Thoreau, Staten Island was an Edenic garden, shaded by cedar, gum, and tulip trees, fragrant with red honeysuckle. When he was not teaching his student Latin, he roamed in the woods and fields, looking for new flowers, listening to the crickets and the roar of the sea. Publicity for New Brighton boasted of its "solubility of climate," but in the summer of 1854, when the Jameses rented a small house instead of staying at the sumptuous Pavilion, the weather was memorably oppressive. "It has been abominable, terrific, atrocious, suffocating," Henry complained.[19] The family never vacationed there again.

Mrs. Walsh

THE FOURTEENTH STREET residence often was crowded when relatives visited, but in 1853, the household lost one member: Aunt Kate, at the age of forty, was getting married. The year before, Kate had moved out temporarily to nurse her brother John, who lived a few blocks downtown. Freed from the scrutiny of her sister, her brother-in-law, and the five "vociferous nurslings," as Henry called his children, she encouraged the attentions of a wealthy sixty-year-old widower who had been discreetly courting her. Captain Charles Marshall seemed, to the Jameses, a bit too rigid in his habits and rather humorless; but still, responding to Kate's apparent happiness, they were delighted when she agreed to marry him. "I hope she will make him spend all his income," Henry remarked.

Kate's marriage meant more room in the nursery, but less of an audience for Henry's diatribes and one less parent for the children. Kate, Henry commented with regret, "has always been a most loving and provident husband to Mary, a most considerate and devoted wife to me, and an incomparable father and mother to our children. She has paid all the servants' wages over again by her invariable goodhumour and kindness, and been both sun and stars to us whenever our skies have been overcast by dread, or the night of any great sorrow has shut us in."[20]

She served as accomplice to Henry and Mary in convincing the children that dread and sorrow never occurred. Harry remembered sitting at breakfast, for example, eliciting from his aunt details about their stay in England in 1843. As Harry evoked the scene decades later, Kate described the period as an idyll, omitting any hint of Henry's breakdown and ensuing depression. Aunt Kate was a dominant force in the children's lives. As a surrogate parent, she shared Mary's ideas of child rearing more than her eccentric brother-in-law's: children, the two sisters believed, should be docile, obedient, and cheerful. Harry best fulfilled their expectations; the others suffered their aunt's brisk orders and wide-ranging anxieties. Bob complained later that no mother should delegate her role to another woman, and even Alice, who as a child had a pleasant relationship with Aunt Kate, recalled her oppressive personality. Kate, said Alice, was "a person so apparently meant for independence & a 'position'" who instead was forced to invest her energies in other people's lives: "she had but one *motif,* the intense longing to absorb herself in a few individuals . . . & how much the individuals resisted her, was, thank Heaven! but faintly suspected by her."[21]

William resisted her mightily, especially her efforts to rein his activities. It seemed to him that Kate always imagined the worst that could occur in any situation, and he anticipated her disapproval whenever he went too far or too fast. Even as an adult, when once he nearly was pushed out the back of a crowded horsecar, he predicted to his sister, "Aunt Kate may, and probably *will* have shoot through her prolific mind the supposish: 'How wrong in him to do sich! for if, while in that posish, he should have a sudden stroke of paralysis, or faint, his nerveless fingers relaxing their grasp of the rail, he would fall prostrate to the ground and bust.' To which reply I reply that when I go so far as to have a stroke of paralysis, I shall not mind going a step farther and getting bruised."[22]

Unfortunately for William, Kate's absence was brief, lasting from just after he turned eleven until he was thirteen. Marshall, cold and demanding, made Kate's life impossible. He was "accustomed to command only to be obeyed,"[23] and so, of course, was Kate. Within two years, risking inevitable gossip, she returned to her sister's family, keeping as a souvenir of her marriage the honorific "Mrs." before her maiden name. Disappointed at her failure to command her own household, she apparently never gave up hope of remarrying. In 1869, when Kate was in her late fifties, Harry reported to William that she and two traveling companions were growing "a bit tired of each other & owing partly to the presence of an insane & partly to the absence of a sane, gentleman among them, have not introduced a 'foreign element' into their circumstances to the degree they would have liked."[24]

The Parental Optimism

JAMES, DETERMINED to raise his children unconventionally, occasionally acquiesced to providing some formal schooling for them. In New York, the children were taught French and German by a succession of tutors, each of whom, in turn, disappointed their exacting employer;

and the boys were sent to a succession of nearby day schools, whose pedagogy inevitably incited James's disapproval. The boys were embarrassed and confused about the reason for their tutors' dismissal. Some may have been incompetent, others intolerably eccentric, but a darker worry lurked in the children's minds: Were they dismissed because their young charges failed to learn what their father wanted them to learn? Were the pupils, and not their tutors, the ones at fault? Was their father unhappy with them? Since James never discussed his decisions with the children, they never knew.

Later, Harry guessed that one reason for the change of tutors was his father's characteristic idealization of new acquaintances, what Harry called "the parental optimism." Interviewing candidates for the job, he likely discussed his own ideas about what the children should learn and how they should be taught; only those tutors who agreed would be given a chance to prove their abilities. At first, then, James probably believed that the new tutor would be no less than brilliant; when he discovered that she was merely competent or that her teaching methods were not precisely what he wished for, he was disenchanted and disillusioned. Just as in his relationships with his friends, his disappointment made him impatient and scornful.

As a result of the succession of tutors—and of a similarly frequent change of schools—the boys came away with an amalgam of inconsistent knowledge. Their early education lacked rigor, continuity, and any underlying pedagogy. It reflected their father's erratic ideas about what children should know, how they should be taught, and how they were to understand autonomy and authority.

In 1852, James decided that the boys should learn languages more systematically than they did with one or another of their tutors, and to that end sent them, finally, to the Institution Vergnès, not far from the Jameses' home. The school was presided over by Vergnès himself, an elderly, irritable schoolmaster who set a rigid curriculum for his charges, mostly boys from well-to-do Mexican and Cuban families. Harry remembered a "complete failure of blondness" in the generally gloomy atmosphere. The boys learned some French, but James, dissatisfied as usual, allowed them to attend only for one year.

Richard Pulling Jenks ran a smaller school nearby, with only a few rooms—the Institution Vergnès took up two floors—staffed by only a few teachers. A Mr. Dolmidge, lean, beardless, and mild mannered,

taught writing; a Mr. Coe, drawing. Coe, a large man with a shock of
thick white hair and a commanding presence, was a talented teacher,
inspiring by encouragement and by involving the students in his own
work, which ranged from tiny "drawing cards" to larger oils on panel
boards.

For the James brothers, the Pulling Jenks school was a new kind of
educational experience. Short, paunchy, bald Jenks, William said later,
was the most congenial of their instructors; in fact, he added, "the only
one to whom the art of exciting an interest or inspiring a sympathy
could be in any degree imputed."[25] But William was excited more by
Mr. Coe than Mr. Jenks. At eleven, he discovered that he loved to
draw. Now, anyone looking for William at home could be sure to find
him in the back parlor, bent over his pad, drawing for hours on end,
absorbed and totally content.

William had a talent for art. His graceful sketches show a sure eye
for detail, texture, and light, and an easy line. But when he sat drawing for hours and hours, he was doing more than honing his skill. In
the bustling James household, drawing gave William a refuge from his
mother's scrutiny and his father's harangues. When he concentrated on
art, he could shut out intrusion; when he drew, he could render reality
the way he saw it and not as his father, for one, interpreted it. Mr. Coe
praised his young student unequivocally, invited William to see his
studio, and sent the boy home with samples of his own work. But the
person William wanted most to impress was unresponsive. At the age
of eleven, William did not understand why if his father so passionately
glorified the Artist, he was not interested in William's productions.

The boys had attended the Pulling Jenks school for a year when
James again decided to withdraw them and try another school. At the
ages of ten and eleven, Harry and William began to inquire about why
they were taken away from a school they so much enjoyed. Their parents gave them no reason, however, and the boys were left to draw
their own conclusions. But if we look at later patterns of Henry's separating William from schools and mentors, it is likely that William's
enthusiasm for art and for Mr. Coe frightened his father. If Coe gave
William the emotional support that he needed, if he affirmed the
child's talents, he threatened to supplant James's influence over his son.
James could not allow that to happen. The boys surmised only that

Pulling Jenks moved on to another position, perhaps uptown. They never knew for sure.

The new school did not clear up their confusion. Forrest and Quackenbos, another neighborhood institution—Harry likened it to a "shop" rather than a school—offered two tracks of instruction: Classical, in which William was enrolled, and Industry and Usefulness, where poor Harry landed. Since Henry Sr. thought little of Harry's intellectual abilities, he decided that the eleven-year-old should be exposed to accounting.

Certainly James's choice of schools for his children did not reflect in any way the educational philosophy that he published, nor did he respond to his children's personalities, needs, or interests. He was motivated only by his own need to protect his offspring from the corrupting influence of anyone else's ideas. In repeatedly changing their educational experience, he necessarily exposed them to a plethora of ideas and teaching methods, but this diverse exposure was not his goal. He was more urgently motivated to abort their relationship with anyone who might intellectually attract them or lead them too deeply into ideas that Henry Sr. deemed dangerous. The pattern of education that began in New York continued throughout Europe, as James moved his sons from school to school in city after city; and it did not end until William, far into adulthood, finally claimed a vocation.

Dangerous notions, however, did not reside in classrooms alone. Among his friends in New York, William counted foremost one Edgar Beach Van Winkle, a few months younger than William, who lived two doors away. The Van Winkle family was far different from the Jameses: Edgar Simeon Van Winkle was a well-established lawyer, a member of the Dutch Reformed Church, and a more typically Victorian patriarch than Henry Sr. Van Winkle; his wife, Hannah; and their four children (Edgar had three sisters) did not live the peripatetic life of the Jameses, but traveled only between Manhattan and Connecticut's Litchfield Hills, where the family had a summer estate.

The Van Winkle family provided a stunning contrast to the Jameses. Besides being anchored by a father who was both a professional and pillar of the community, the family seemed steeped in "a regular maze of culture."[26] The Jameses, on the other hand, wandered through a bewildering forest of cultural experiences. One evening the children might be taken to a performance of Shakespeare; more often they would see a contemporary farce with such characters as "Nan the Good-for-Nothing" played by actors of varying quality. "[S]tupefaction grew sharp in me and scepticism triumphed," Harry noted, looking back on the theatrical excursions, "so vulgar, so barbarous, seemed the array of types, so extraordinarily provincial the note of every figure, so less than scant the claim of such physiognomies and such reputations."[27] The children felt a similar reaction to the works of art they saw when they accompanied their parents to galleries, a frequent after-dinner activity. If some of those works were great, others, Harry suspected, were nothing more than fakes or forgeries. It would take years, and many visits to reputable European museums, before Harry and William could make sense of their early exposure to painting.

If Henry and Mary James did not have the ability to discern dross from gold, the Van Winkles apparently felt no such confusion. "I didn't then know about culture," Harry conceded, "but Edgar must promptly have known."[28] William felt a strong kinship with Edgar, who seemed to him "one of the only chaps I ever knew who had any ideas of their own."[29] Those ideas would not have pleased Henry Sr. Edgar, after all, was being raised conventionally to make his contribution, socially and professionally, to a society whose aesthetic, social, and moral values he upheld. Edgar attended the University Grammar School where he was preparing for college and a career.

Despite—or perhaps because of—the differences in their upbringing, William and Edgar became close friends as they grew up together on Fourteenth Street. Edgar was a member of William's Harbinger Club, and he served as William's confidant throughout his adolescence. Edgar and his family represented stability, conformity, and respectability—qualities that William yearned for in his own life.

Among other boys who inspired William's interest were the family's orphans. His cousins Albert Wyckoff (who, besides being an orphan, was also an only child), Augustus Barker, and the sons and daughters of Henry James's sister Catharine seemed curiously enviable, "somehow more thrilling," Harry remarked, "than parentally provided ones." Deprived of ever feeling homesickness, Harry thought it would be blissful "to be so little fathered and mothered." Overseen by three parental figures, included as companions in their parents' every outing, William first, Harry soon enough, and the other children after them wished for some freedom from the "intensely domesticated" James household. Their straining toward independence did not elude their father.

In 1855, William turned thirteen. The difficult child, James thought, would be uncontrollable as an adolescent. Drawing upon his own memories and his selective observations, James saw puberty as a dissonant and "extremely unhandsome" period of development:

> The urchin has outgrown the jacket and dickey of infancy, but is still a world too small for the standing collar and long-tailed coat of manhood. His actual powers are small, but his instincts are unlimited. He has the thoughts of boyhood, but he utters them with a voice more hoarse than the adult man's. He has the sentiment of freedom, but he knows no positive or manly methods of demonstrating it. He attempts it chiefly by rudeness towards his progenitors, calls his father the old man, and his mother the old woman, and gives out, on every occasion, a suspicion that they have been over-estimated. He renounces the customs and statutes of the paternal mansion, bullies the servants and his younger brothers, and hastens to involve himself in courses which afflict the older people with the saddest auguries of the future man.[30]

James dreaded the day when William would renounce his customs and statutes. And despite his public arrogance, he was never certain of his own strength as an intellectual: he feared that if William deemed him "over-estimated," his assessment might, indeed, be justified. If adolescence were difficult in general, James thought, it was worse in America, where dissent and rebellion were cherished cultural traits. William, he decided, needed a more structured society, where the transition from youth to adulthood was circumscribed, where personal rebellion was not so easily tolerated, where William would be a stranger to the culture as a whole and not so likely to be seduced by the examples of other adolescents. On June 27, 1855, the family left for Europe.

Chapter 4

OTHER PEOPLE'S RULES

1855–1860

WHEN WILLIAM DEPARTED on the *Atlantic* with his family in the summer of 1855, he left not only his friends and the home where he had spent most of his childhood, but a sense of independence that he would not recapture in Europe. Despite having three anxious caretakers, the James children were allowed considerable freedom to roam beyond their Washington Square neighborhood, even as far as Eighteenth Street, where, Harry later recalled, they discovered peacocks and fawns in the garden of a mansion. They inspected theater posters on Fifth Avenue billboards, whetting their appetite for the raunchy productions they later attended with their father. Often, they spent Saturdays at P. T. Barnum's American Museum, which offered displays of art and natural history, sometimes titillating, often bizarre. If New York was the country's largest, grandest, and most fascinating city, to William it seemed as comfortable and intimate as a village. The New York of his childhood, Harry said, had a "family-party smallness" and a palpable sense of community.[1]

The Jameses drove into London in a carriage overflowing with baggage, including a heavy load of books by Swedenborg that Henry Sr. transported to all his destinations and reverently laid out wherever the family settled. Harry sat next to the driver, William crushed inside with the rest of the family, which included Aunt Kate and Annette Godefroi, a French *au pair*. The children had been tantalized for months with alluring descriptions of European life and landscape, but William, by that time, knew better than to expect reality to match his parents' vision. He was not surprised to find London far different from the city they had portrayed: dirty, dull, and so huge that it was intimidating. Fortunately for William, the family planned to leave quickly; they were bound for Switzerland, where the schools had earned an international reputation for an enlightened pedagogy that Henry and Mary hoped would benefit their sons.

Their departure was delayed, however, when Harry fell ill with malaria, apparently contracted during the previous sweltering summer at New Brighton. On bad days, he suffered from fever and chills; on days when he was well, the family could travel. The sickroom dictated the family's progress. Haltingly, after stops in Paris and Lyons, the Jameses arrived in Geneva.

In early fall, with the air crisp and the sky cloudless, Geneva sparkled. The city was elegant, quieter than London and, to William, far more charming. The family installed themselves in part of a gracious villa, with a quiet, shady garden, not far from the school where William, Wilky, and Bob were enrolled as boarders.

The boys' new residence was no less accommodating. The Pensionnat Roediger, housed in an old villa, was surrounded by woods, rolling fields, and leafy arbors. The school prided itself on its excellence in teaching languages and on a warm, responsive atmosphere that would have pleased Johann Pestalozzi, the prominent educational reformer whose ideas about children's freedom of expression, much like Fourier's, had attracted the attention of American parents and teachers. The Pensionnat took some forty-five pupils, mostly from France and Germany. Each time the Jameses visited the school, they noted with satisfaction the multilingual bantering among the students and were pleased by what they called "the relation" between teachers and their joyful charges. Surely they could not have found a more "genialised, humanised, civilised, even romanticised" environment for the boys.[2] Harry remembered that the school "had the air of the happiest home."[3]

When we read Henry Sr.'s letters and essays written during the few months the children were enrolled, we discover, however, that he chose the school not because of its nurturing atmosphere but rather because its headmaster had a reputation for being able to discipline difficult children. Henry wrote to his mother that he was impressed by Achilles Roediger, "a man of great sense and I should judge of enormous practical power. . . . He is said to possess the power of ruling refractory boys in a very remarkable degree, and that without ever going to extremities in the way of compulsion, but by perfectly gaining their respect and confidence, and so binding them to his will. I certainly never met a man in my life of more powerful personal magnetism."[4] Far more significant to Henry than the extensive playground facilities (including gymnastic equipment and a nine-pin bowling alley), Sunday concerts, and bountiful dinners was the behavior of the students. "All the pupils are made gentlemen in deportment," he reported shortly after his sons were enrolled, in one of his frequent contributions to the *New York Tribune.*[5]

The Jameses had more opportunity than other parents to observe the daily life of the school. As much as they praised Roediger, they were uncomfortable about having their sons live at school for the first time, away from their discerning care. Most afternoons, Harry, who still was recuperating, accompanied his parents to the school, where they visited with William, Wilky, and Bob. These visits, which singled out the James boys from the other boarders, also kept them from entering fully into the activities of the school, from making close friends, and from developing a sense of loyalty to their new community. As it turned out, the distance that their parents created served the children well: after only a few months, Henry Sr. withdrew his sons from the Pensionnat Roediger, and the family left Geneva. Harry claimed that the reasons for leaving were "doubtless well known to ourselves at the time," even though forgotten later; but it is just as likely that the children, once again, did not know why they were being removed from school, why their father was dissatisfied, and how their own performance may have influenced his decision. At thirteen, William wanted the challenge of Roediger's curriculum and, even more important, the chance to test himself against other boys his age. But his needs were secondary to his father's.

Henry admitted only that he and Mary decided "that the schools are greatly over-rated." But he had no specific criticisms of the curriculum nor of the teachers' qualifications. Indeed, whenever he referred to the teachers he noted that they and the students behaved as if they were all one happy family. When he and Mary visited the school, however, they felt they were not part of that family, but merely invited guests.

Roediger, as head of the children's new family, became transformed in Henry's mind from a charismatic and powerful figure to a threaten-

ing rival; and Mary, too, felt that her role as a mother was being undermined by the attention that the children received from their teachers. Although Henry Sr. admitted that the children were thriving, he
was troubled. Just a month after he wrote to his mother praising the
school, he notified her that he had changed his mind: "home tuition
will be the best for all of them; . . . while it will be much the least expensive, it will also be greatly to the interest of the children both in
moral and intellectual regards." Certainly it was in Henry Sr.'s best interest that the children leave the Pensionnat Roediger: He would regain the central position in their lives, and he would be able to leave
Geneva, which had come to bore him. "The town is . . . very dull for
one who has no active pursuits," he told his mother, "and I think we
shall all feel better for a change."[6]

So the many valises and cases were packed, the Swedenborg library
set into boxes, and the entourage assembled. Across France, across the
channel they went. London, for the second time, was no brighter nor
more appealing for William. It was a gray, dreary city of no apparent
charm, shrouded in such dense fog that he could hardly see the buildings across Berkeley Square, where the Jameses had rented a small
house. This central location seemed promising to William, until he
was told that he and his brothers could not play in the streets as they
did at home. Nor would they be going to school, as they did in
Geneva. Instead, Henry Sr. placed an advertisement for a tutor who
could instruct his sons in Latin "and the ordinary branches of an English education."[7]

The response was overwhelming. Candidates crowded into the
Jameses' front hall, pushed up the stairs, and pressed against the door
as they awaited an interview. Whatever James was looking for this
time, he found it in one Robert Thomson, a shy, awkward young Scottish teacher, as different from Roediger as anyone could be.[8] The boys
spent each morning with Thomson, but the curriculum he invented for
them failed to make a lasting impression. Later, Harry could remember nothing of what he studied with Thomson, and William called the
year in London vacuous.

Their father, however, was delighted with the change. Each morning, when the boys were in Thomson's care, Henry Sr. sallied forth to
meet one friend or another. Now that he was a noted lecturer and published author whose *Lectures and Miscellanies,* in fact, had received two

complimentary notices in the *London Leader,* he dared to renew his acquaintance with Carlyle; he also saw Thackeray, whom he had met in
New York, and, of course, his friend Garth Wilkinson. When his Albany relatives, no doubt wondering about the cause of the family's
many sudden moves, guessed that they would soon return to America,
Henry retorted that they meant to stay. In fact, they were moving from
the center of London to the quiet suburb of St. John's Wood, where
their neighbors would include the Wilkinsons, and where they had
rented a furnished house on Marlborough Street, larger than their New
York town house, for a mere £250 per year.

William spent his fourteenth birthday in the house on Marlborough Street, with its garden and pleasant view, neither of which interested him. Although his father noted that his sons "were never so
sweet and good," William certainly was bored. He found St. John's
Wood monotonous and depressing. First he had been uprooted from
his friends at home, then from his classmates in Geneva; in London, he
knew no one. Because he was not attending school, he had no way of
meeting boys his age. He had no companions other than his younger
brothers and much younger sister. He missed the generous grounds of
the Pensionnat Roediger; in St. John's Wood, he had nowhere to play.
Instead, his outings consisted of sedate strolls with his brother Harry,
both boys dressed uncomfortably in high hat and gloves, or of forays to
one or another London landmark under the benign but uninspiring su-
pervision of Robert Thomson.

William knew very well that the life of a fourteen-year-old held
other possibilities. London, he later told Harry, had been "a poor and
arid and lamentable time, in which, missing such larger chances and
connections as we might have reached out to, we had done nothing,
he and I, but walk about together, in a state of the direst propriety."[9]
Henry Sr. did not notice his son's mood; he was, his children later admitted, curiously unable to empathize with other people's feelings. But
it also was in his interest to ignore any signs of William's discontent:
Henry wanted to stay in London; he did not want to consider any reason for another move. An unusually quiet son seemed nothing but
good and sweet, causing no trouble in the family, keeping his feelings
to himself.

William might have been a bit happier if he had known that his father's enthusiasm for England soon would wane. By the middle of

spring in 1856, Henry Sr. grew tired of British social life and culture. When he traveled on the omnibuses to the center of London each morning, no one responded to his eager efforts to strike up a conversation. He decided, once and for all, that Carlyle was impossible—"the same old sausage, frizzing and sputtering in his own grease"; Thackeray, honest enough, but limited in his views; and Garth Wilkinson tedious.[10] The intellectual community he hoped to join did not embrace him. The English, he decided, were vulgar, provincial, complacent. "Their love is clannish," he declared to Edmund Tweedy. "They love all that near their own living, but they don't even *see* any one outside of that boundary."[11] The final affront occurred when one of his editorial letters to the *London Leader* was published in so "shockingly mutilated" a form—two-thirds of the piece had been omitted—that he believed readers would think him simply ridiculous. London was no longer a viable city for the Jameses. This time, the family would go to Paris.

A Queer Way of Living

THEY ARRIVED IN EARLY June and settled into an apartment on the Champs-Elysées that Henry and Aunt Kate had found when they scouted the city a few weeks earlier. Opulently furnished in gilt and mahogany, this apartment, leased for only two months, served as a base from which Henry and Mary searched for a more appropriate residence for the family.

William's initial response to Paris was relief. The city, he wrote to his Fourteenth Street friend Edgar Van Winkle, was "a direct contrast to London. The sky is blue; the houses are white & everything else is red. . . . The sun and the white plaster and the bright colors are all very dazzling." Still, he added nostalgically, New York was prettier.[12]

Yet though Paris made a glittering first impression, in the course of a month, William painted a darker picture. "People talk about Paris being such a beautiful city!" he wrote to Edgar. "I never was more dissapointed [*sic*] in my life than I was in seeing Paris." The streets were dark, narrow, and reeking with stench; the Tuileries garden was "the ugliest place of the kind I ever saw," he wrote, but his specific complaint reflects more a feeling of physical than aesthetic discomfort: "At one end near the palace," he told Edgar, "there are some flowers, but no trees. So you can't go near the flowers in the day time for fear of being scorched by the sun. In the other part there are some trees the shade of which is perfectly black, they are so thick. A kind of damp chill goes through you as soon as you go under them." A kind of damp chill overtook him when he entered Parisian shops, too, because of the rudeness and dishonesty of the shopkeepers.[13] His response to French merchants was affirmed by his parents, especially by Mary, who undertook most of the shopping. Always suspicious in money matters— even when her own children were involved—she found the French manner of conducting business intolerable. France, William concluded, would not be pleasant. But his parents had just taken an apartment for fourteen months, and although William knew that plans could be changed according to his father's whims, he suspected that they would stay.

Paris was as lonely for him as London. Still, he knew no one his age; still, his parents would not allow him to explore on his own. Instead, he resumed his dull walks with his brothers. And the apartments into which the family squeezed, unlike the spacious houses they had rented in Geneva and London, were claustrophobic. "It's a queer way of living, this, all huddled up together on one floor," he observed.[14] Decades later, when he returned to Paris and managed to gain entry into the flat on the Champs-Elysées, William was surprised to find the rooms *"larger* than I had supposed them."[15] At the time, they had seemed stifling.

The apartment served as home and school for the five James children. Bob and Alice had a French governess for their instruction; William, Harry, and Wilky were taught languages and mathematics by the cool and demanding Monsieur Lerambert. Henry Sr. himself took over the instruction of history and geography. James apparently preferred to hire tutors for subjects that he believed had no connection to social or philosophical issues. When he looked for a school for his children, at home or abroad, he usually chose institutions that specialized in language instruction. If his children learned languages, he believed, they would have the impressive veneer of an upper-class education; but he himself would furnish his children with ideas about history, politics, and religion instead of allowing outsiders to discuss these sensitive areas with his impressionable offspring. The children would learn to see the world, past and present, from his own point of view.

Despite a division of labor that should have pleased him, James soon found Lerambert unacceptable. He was arrogant, first of all; and second, he would not take the children on excursions in the afternoons, so a Mademoiselle Danse had to be employed, as well, to chaperone Harry, Wilky, Bob, and Alice. William did not, or would not, join them. Perhaps it was the double expense that inspired James to reconsider the efficacy of home tutoring and to send the children, once again, to a school. This time, he found the Institution Fezandié, a newly opened language school. But it appears that James saw their attendance as a short-term experiment because he soon disclosed to them his new enthusiasm: they should be educated in Germany.

To that end he and Mary traveled twice to Frankfurt, Heidelberg, and Bonn to check on the availability of housing, the choice of schools, and the extent of the foreign community. As much as he wanted his children to learn French and German, James was fluent in neither. His contentment in any community, then, depended on whether there were sufficient American or English expatriates in residence. In Paris he had a few friends, including a couple who lived in the same building as the Jameses. He had heard that some of his New York neighbors were then in Germany, but when he and Mary visited the cities on their tours, they found no one who knew them and nothing that pleased them.

They still were undecided about their future when they left Paris to vacation in Boulogne for the summer of 1857. Although the vacation was marred by Harry's falling ill with typhus, they found the city pleasant and far less expensive than Paris. William, especially, loved it: he was enrolled immediately in the Collège Imperial, where he studied science, mathematics, literature, and French in classes that contained many English boys. At last, he had a chance to make friends his own age. When the school closed for vacation, he found that Boulogne offered a number of pleasant diversions, among them rowing and "equestrian, or rather asinine, exercise."[16]

Nevertheless, the family returned to Paris in the fall, intending to resume their stay. But shocking news from America interfered with their plans. "Hardly had we arrived," William reported to Edgar Van Winkle, "when we received a letter from my Father's agent telling us we must economize, for our income for the present year would be diminished."[17] Henry was stunned; the summer's financial panic had not seemed a reality until he was told that his own funds had been compromised severely. His first response was to book passage home—but where would they live? Their Fourteenth Street house was leased;

rentals were too expensive; their Albany relatives were unable to board seven Jameses. Boulogne seemed a frugal alternative.

William was delighted. "I was heartily glad to leave Paris," he wrote to Edgar, "which I detest as much, and more, than you do New York."[18] He took up his studies at the Collège, where he found the instruction in science excellent and his mathematics teacher "a real manly fellow." If the literature instructors were "inflated, pompous, pedantic," still they did not detract from William's overall enthusiasm for the school. That enthusiasm was inspired not only by his daily experiences, but more by the plans he was making for his future.

William had written repeatedly to Edgar Van Winkle, who already was enrolled at Union College, asking about entrance requirements and trying to assess his own preparation for the school. William believed that the haphazard preparation he had received from his father's tutors would be useless when he presented himself as a candidate for admission. But at the Collège, he was receiving, at last, *formal* instruction: classes, he hoped, that might be equivalent to the education he would be getting in an American school. In Boulogne, for the first time since the family had come to Europe, he felt that he was living in a world parallel to the one he had left behind—the world he was eager to rejoin.

In January 1858, just as he turned sixteen, William wrote a heartfelt letter to Edgar about "certain subjects" that tormented him. Worried about his future, he sought Edgar's advice, particularly about Edgar's own choice of study at Union College, civil engineering. William had only a vague idea about the profession of engineering—or, indeed, about any other profession—and could elicit few details from anyone he knew. Whatever information he did have seemed discouraging: "Everyone says that the business of a civil engineer is a very bad one," he told Edgar, "as the market is so overstocked that there is no opening for a new comer." At that moment, of course, William had little access to people with whom to discuss his career—except his father, who, of course, would discourage the choice of civil engineering. But William did not trust his father's opinion, and he wanted Edgar to explain his reasons for studying engineering so that he could decide for himself if it were a field that might interest him. "I don't care about making a fortune," William assured Edgar. "I only want to have a pleasant occupation and enough money to live upon."

Deciding on a pleasant occupation, however, was daunting for the sixteen-year-old. He urged Edgar to respond quickly. "Five minutes or so whenever you have the leisure will be a very small tax upon your time, & I am sure you would write willingly if you knew how much I wanted an answer."[19]

Edgar soon wrote to his tormented friend, but the information he provided did not assuage William's worries. In fact, when William next wrote to Edgar, he appeared more agitated than before, in part because he seems to have had a long talk with his father. Now he was concerned not merely about gleaning enough information about various professions, but about discovering his own true passions, the better to express them in his vocation; he worried not merely about finding a pleasant occupation that would allow him to support himself, but about making a lasting contribution to humanity.

Choosing a profession would not be so difficult, he confided to Edgar, "if society was decently ordered. Everyone, I think, should do in society what he would do if left to himself." But William had no idea what he would do if left to himself. As one of the top three students in his mathematics class, he believed he would do well to pursue a career in science. But he knew no scientists; he knew nothing about what they did as their daily work or how much they earned. When his father talked about scientists, he envisioned men engaged in a grand philosophical pursuit of Truth rather than in the mundane work of chemical, botanical, or biological study and experimentation. Henry Sr. saw William as a scientist much like the naturalist-philosopher Henry David Thoreau, who had visited the Jameses occasionally when he lived on Staten Island. Thoreau knew the species of fish in Walden Pond as well as he knew anything, could identify the flora and fauna of Concord, Massachusetts, and also, to James's great admiration, resolutely defied social conventions in his search for spiritual authenticity.

"If I followed my taste and did what was most agreeable to me," William told Edgar, ". . . I would get a microscope and go out into the country, into the dear old woods and fields and ponds—there I would try to make as many discoveries as possible,—and I'll be kicked if I would not be more useful than if I laid out railroads by rules which others had made and which I had learned from them. If in the former case I do not vindicate my existence better than in the latter, then I'm no man. I'll tell you what else I think I'll do. I'll be a farmer, and do as much good in the Natural History line as I can. How much that is, God only knows," he added. "I pray t[ha]t I may do something."[20] At the end of his long, tortured exposition about his vocation, he added a few lines puzzling in their apparent contradiction of all that he already had written. "I think you have made the best choice of a profession that was possible," he told Edgar. "An Engineer in the present state of society is far more glorious than a Naturalist, and as f[ar] as I remember you have a great vocation for the calling."[21] William may have felt that he had insulted Edgar's career choice and wanted to make amends, or reflecting on his passionate evocation of his future as a naturalist, he may have realized the absurdity of his proposal. Whether or not he then agreed with his father's rage against society's demands, he was aware that the world in which he lived offered ample opportunities for an individual to make a contribution through a conventional job. Edgar's father had a recognizable profession—lawyer—and neither he nor Edgar seemed any the worse for it. If Edgar had decided to live by others' rules, William respected that decision. But it made his own all the more confusing.

He did make one important resolution in France, however: he would go to college. "I think the best thing I can do will be to enter Union," William wrote to Edgar, "though I don't know whether Father will consent. I am not yet decided about being an engineer but at all events an engineer's education will do me no harm."[22] His goal seemed increasingly possible because, suddenly, the Jameses were headed home.

In Boulogne, Henry Sr. had created a situation similar to the one from which he fled three years before: his children were enrolled in school where they had many friends and some congenial, respected instructors; several of those instructors praised William for his talents in areas that Henry Sr. trivialized. Because the Collège attracted students from all levels of society, Henry was losing control over the friends with whom his children associated. And Henry himself was cut off from an intellectual community that made him feel important. Clearly, it was time to leave.

By late spring, the Jameses were in London, briefly, before returning to America. They rented Dudley House, one of eight cottages with two drawing rooms, four bedrooms, and a dining room that lined Dudley Place, near Harrow Road in the Paddington section of the city. The houses had identical light-brown stucco exteriors and green doors; they differed only in their pretentious names. "All this monotony is tiresome enough as you may suppose," William remarked to Edgar, "and I shall be glad to leave London." Now that the three-year trip was nearly ended, William offered his assessment of the experience: "I think that as a general thing," he said, "Americans had better keep their children at home." Although he profited by some of his educational experiences—he read and wrote French well, he said—still he regretted that he missed "the general routine which we would have done in America. I am less advanced in Mathematics, and have done a less *quantity* of study, have crammed less than I would have done at home." While he conceded that the family's travels had not been a loss for him, however, he was convinced that "the others might just as well have staid at home."[23]

With Edgar's help, he figured out that he could qualify to enter in the first- or second-year class at Union, depending on how the college considered his school record, and again he urged Edgar to respond to his questions about entrance requirements as quickly as possible "for every day is precious, believe me."[24] He was exuberant, then, when his father decided that instead of leaving London at the end of July, the family would depart six weeks earlier. On June 30, he was back in America, at last.

Castles

THE FAMILY SPENT July reunited with their many relatives in Albany. One day William and Harry went off by themselves, taking the train to Schenectady to visit Edgar Van Winkle at Union College. As they walked around the campus, they eagerly pictured themselves there as students—William soon, Harry a bit later. Although they knew their father felt no loyalty to the school, they themselves, encouraged by Edgar's anecdotes, felt a strong attachment. Edgar urged them to apply, but they needed little urging. They returned to Albany firm in their resolve to become college men.

They quickly discovered, however, that they had no power to decide their future. Henry Sr. angrily refused to consider the possibility

of college for any of his sons. "When I left you the other day at Schenectady," William wrote to Edgar,

> it was with the almost certainty of becoming within a few months
> a fellow "man" with you at Union College. But I was greatly mis-
> taken; for on coming to speak with my Father on the subject, I
> found much to my surprise that he would not hear of my going
> to any College whatsoever. He says that Colleges are hot beds of
> corruption where it [is] *impossible* to learn anything. I think this
> opinion very unjust but of course, much as I should like, myself,
> to go to Union, I must abide by his decision.[25]

Henry's reaction to William's plans hardly seems shocking in light
of his previous educational decisions for his children. But William's
surprise underscores the atmosphere of secrecy that characterized
James family life. William had never discussed his yearnings for college with either of his parents; Henry had never hinted at the educational future of his children. When the family returned to America,
the children believed—based on nothing in their own experience—
that they would resume a normal life for young people their age. Part
of that life included higher education—at Harvard or Yale, if not
Union College. Instead of going to Schenectady, though, William was
bound for Newport, Rhode Island, where his parents had decided to
spend the summer and, possibly, longer. "The castle we had built . . .
crumbled," Harry wrote. It would not be the last time the two brothers would engage in "crude castle building"; and surely not the last
that their father would demolish their dreams.[26]

Although at first William was disheartened by Henry Sr.'s unwavering hatred of colleges, he had learned from experience that any of
his father's decisions might be changed if only the right set of circumstances occurred. He hoped that his father might accede to his wishes
if only he pleaded his case more earnestly. This optimism buoyed his
spirits, and in his first months in Newport, William appeared enthusiastic about his new home. After so long in European cities, he was delighted with the country setting—the cottage was surrounded by four
acres of land. Furthermore, in Newport, they were among old friends;
his parents knew many families summering in the town, and William
found some companions in the neighborhood. Once again, the children could be independent: William and his brothers were able to

swim, fish, row, ride horseback, take long walks along the shore, and spend hours exploring the village and beyond.

But throughout August, William's encounters with his father were tense; they argued about the way William was spending the summer and continued to spar over the issue of college. Although Henry wrote enthusiastic descriptions of his children's summer activities, at home he unaccountably was annoyed, accusing them of useless idling and, according to William, asserting that "it would have been impossible for any of us to have been so idle had we been abroad." When Edgar sent a letter apparently arguing for the value of a college education, William showed it to his father "who admitted its truth, but said that 'the moral atmosphere of Colleges was very debasing.'"[27]

Besides drawing upon his own experiences at Union College, Henry no doubt heard similar stories about drunkenness and wild behavior at other schools. In Cambridge, for example, it was not surprising to see undergraduates staggering in the streets in broad daylight after imbibing spiked punch from buckets in Harvard Yard. Their drunken antics included breaking windows, setting bonfires, and hooting outside the residences of unpopular instructors.[28] As annoying as this behavior was to the college's administration and the disapproving populace, it was hardly as serious as the prevalence of "sexual vice" with the city's many local prostitutes. Though not all Harvard men were dissipated and unruly, Henry had no faith that his son would resist. He therefore could not relent: William belonged at home, under his own keen watch.

By early September, Henry Sr. was so irritated that he decided he had made a mistake to come back to America at all. "I have grown so discouraged about the education of my children here, and dread so those inevitable habits of extravagance and insubordination which appear to be the characteristics of American youth," he wrote to his friend Samuel Ward, "that I have come to the conclusion to retrace my steps to Europe, and keep them there a few years longer."[29] Keeping his children isolated from a world that offered them choices, temptations, and satisfactions had become a consuming struggle.

Henry's sense of crisis, however, diminished in the fall. By mid-November, William told Edgar that his father had put the trip off until spring, "but I doubt if we go then. We have taken a house here until May, and I should not at all wonder if we should give up our house in New York & settle down finally in Boston or Cambridge, as they seem to be the most respectable places in the United States."[30] William's prediction may have reflected his own desires rather than his parents': If the Jameses did settle in the vicinity of Cambridge, he might yet have a chance at higher education—at Harvard, perhaps, or at the Lawrence Scientific School, whose lofty reputation had reached the ears of the Jameses.

But in the fall of 1858, William could do no more than hope. After an idle summer, he looked forward to a winter only slightly more productive. His brothers were enrolled at the Berkeley Institute, run by the Reverend William C. Leverett, a recent graduate of the Harvard Divinity School, cheerful but, as one former student noted, "insignificant."[31] William, though, was too advanced for that school. He stayed at home, teaching himself math, practicing German with a local governess, and studying drawing with William Morris Hunt, the town's resident artist. Except for two neighbors his own age he had no companions and, after Boulogne, acutely felt the lack of friends, of admiring instructors, and, most important, of a sense of control over his future. "I think sometimes with regret of the imposing streets of Schenectady and the palatial walls of Union," he wrote to Edgar, "where I might now be distinguishing myself, but however—."[32] There was nothing he could do but bow to his father's will.

Submission, however, was not enough. Even though his children were following his pedagogic plans, Henry was edgy and critical, prone to unpredictable bursts of anger. When William took responsibility for training a puppy the family had adopted, Henry lashed out in derision at the way he exerted authority over the capricious animal. Although William did not shrink from beating the dog when necessary, his father furiously berated him: "Never, never before did I so clearly see the utter & lamentable inefficiency & worthlessness of your character; never before have I been so struck with your perfect inability to do anything manly."[33]

Certainly for Henry, controlling others was evidence of his own strength of character. William, however, wanted to prove his worth in other ways—by making decisions for himself, acting independently of his family, and moving into the future instead of stagnating at his father's feet—but the only way he could gain independence was to find the key to understanding his father's expectations. That key seemed buried in Henry Sr.'s obscure definition of manliness and his vague, complex notions about responsibility and self-fulfillment.

Henry taught William that to be a man, he must discover his "ideal selfhood" and act "not in obedience to either physical or social constraint, but in obedience to his own ideas of goodness, truth, and beauty." A man is never satisfied merely with honor and wealth; in fact, success generates "an aching void which all the wealth, of all the kingdoms of the world, would only make more insatiate." The highest activity of a man's life is the "inspiration of ideas," but this contemplative state is threatened always by the constraints of nature and society. To the extent that a man tries to fulfill his physical needs and adhere to social prescriptions, he is undermining his potential.[34]

For the next few years, as William tried valiantly to integrate these ideas into his own thinking about his future, he referred repeatedly to the "moral question," which at times exhausted and frustrated him. In the context of the James family, this moral question did not focus on ethical dilemmas, but rather on how an individual could live in a manner that was true to his nature. Even people acclaimed for their "enlarged sympathies" and "ardent humanitary zeal" were morally worthy, in Henry Sr.'s eyes, only if their motivation was generated not by the "beck of society" but "from a far deeper ground, namely, an intense perception of human unity, and an intense disgust therefore of every voluntary infraction of it."[35] William, though, at seventeen, had not generated an intense disgust for society. Instead, he hoped to become part of it—just as his friends were.

Edgar Van Winkle, following a socially prescribed path to a profession, soon would be independent, self-supporting, and respected. A Newport friend, fellow art student Jim MacKaye, was following a different, but equally attractive path—even against his own father's wishes. Although the elder MacKaye had urged his son to go to Yale, Jim had been so inspired by William Morris Hunt that he decided to go to Paris to study with Hunt's mentor, Thomas Couture. Yet Jim's decision did not meet with rage; his father seemed to understand his son's need to leave adolescence behind and make his own way in the world.

On the afternoon before Jim left Newport, he and William sat for hours on a stone wall overlooking the sea, sharing their dreams. They had been at that spot many times before, sketching. They had walked together at the water's edge to a lovely, quiet cove they called "Paradise"; they had swum, with Harry and their friend Tom Perry, at Easton's Pond. They had read Robert Browning and talked about poets, poetry, and the creative spirit. But now their companionship was ending; William was losing a trusted confidant, a friend who had shared the heady experience of Hunt's drawing class, and one of the few people in Newport who knew of William's growing attraction to art. As evening turned to night, Jim and William stood and shook hands for the last time. In the morning, Jim would embark on an adventurous future; William turned back toward home.

Light of Truth

THIRTY-FOUR-YEAR-OLD William Morris Hunt had traveled on a convoluted road to arrive at a career in art. At sixteen he entered Harvard, planning to become a surgeon. But undergraduate life proved too constricting for his tastes; he preferred sculpting and playing piano or violin to learning anatomy, and he preferred any activity to studying. Harvard suspended him on disciplinary grounds, a decision that proved no loss either to Harvard—which later awarded him an honorary degree—or to Hunt. In 1846, in Europe with his mother and siblings, he decided that he would continue studying sculpture, first in Düsseldorf and then in Paris; but shortly after he arrived in Paris, he saw a painting by Couture and, legend has it, declared, "If that is a painting, I am a painter."[36] Immediately, he enrolled in Couture's newly established art school. Six years later, when he discovered the work of Jean-François Millet, he was so enthralled that he sought out the little-known Millet in Barbizon, befriended him, and tirelessly promoted his work.

Hunt was free to follow his impulses, artistic or otherwise. Family wealth sustained his early career; marriage to an heiress kept him free from financial worries for most of his life. Because he did not need to earn a living, he saw no reason to pander to critics. "This doing things to suit people!" he exclaimed. "They'll hate you, and you won't suit them. Most of us live for the critic, and he *lives on us*. . . . If the birds should read the newspapers they would all take to changing their notes."[37]

Tall, thin, muscular, with gleaming, penetrating eyes and aristocratic elegance, Hunt was animated by a fount of nervous energy. Im-

petuous, flamboyant, irreverent: there was no one like him in Newport. "He was quick and alert," a friend noted, "most cheery and responsive; a wonderful *raconteur* and even mimic, everything became
dramatic in his handling."[38] He was also a born teacher, encouraging,
gentle in his criticism, and unstinting in his praise. He believed that
art came not from imitation of the masters, but from sources within
the artist. The important element of any work, he said, was "feeling."
"This *feeling* is what makes the difference between a wooden thing and
a beautiful fascinating picture," he said; "there must be *responsive feeling*
in a man, or he is not an artist."[39] The artist's task was not to paint
"cloth and cheeks," he said, but "the light of truth."[40]

Hunt treated his young students more like colleagues than disciples. He respected them, affirmed their talents, urged them to experiment. His excitement about art was infectious: "in the studio," wrote
Harry, who also took classes with Hunt, "I was at the threshold of a
world."[41] But more important than what he taught was how he lived:
Hunt was the model of a young, vibrant artist who created an aura of
glamour and excitement around him, who lived in a world of sensuality and beauty. William began to imagine himself in that world, and
when he listened to Hunt's ideas about his work, it seemed that he had
found the man his father had conjured up as the ideal Artist. Hunt insisted on personal authenticity; he did not covet popular approval. He
could be as innovative as he wanted to be. He lived according to his
own lights. "Art," Hunt told his students, "is about the only occupation in which people can do what they please without consulting their
neighbors."[42] Hunt, in many ways, seemed to echo what William long
had heard from his father. Surely, he thought, his father would be as
enthusiastic about Hunt as he was.

Again, he was mistaken.

Henry Sr., conflating William's interest in art with his admiration
of Hunt as mentor and model, could not abide a rivalry with a man
who was younger, more successful, more exciting to his son than he.
William, Henry decided, had developed "a little too much attraction
to painting—as I supposed from the contiguity to Mr. Hunt: let us
break that up[,] we said, at all events." Henry saw William's future not
in an artist's studio, where he might be surrounded by admirers and
acolytes, but alone in the woods. "I hoped," Henry said, "that his career would be a scientific one, as I thought and still think that the true

bent of his genius was towards the acquisition of knowledge: and to give up this hope without a struggle, and allow him to tumble down into a mere painter, was impossible."

In the struggle for William's future, of course, Henry had more power than Hunt. He could take William away from his art classes, from Newport, even from America. "Let us go abroad then," he announced, ". . . and bring him into contact with books and teachers."[43] William was shocked. Since the family's return in the spring of 1858, he had been trying to persuade his father to come to that precise decision; he desperately wanted to be brought into contact with books and teachers at Union or any other college. But to go abroad for such experiences was absurd. Henry Sr. claimed that he could not find a house for the family in Cambridge and therefore could not send William to the Lawrence Scientific School unless he lived separately from the family, a prospect that Henry found dismaying. But William, at sixteen, would have joined a large population of students living on their own. There were ample opportunities for boarding, and the trip from Cambridge to Newport was short enough to make frequent visits home an easy possibility.

Just as Henry had explained earlier trips abroad by asserting concern for his children's education and spiritual well-being, he again used them—the younger children's spiritual life also needed the European influence—as excuses for this new adventure. More likely, though, the decision was inspired by Henry's sense of his own failure. In the fall of 1858, more than sixteen years after he had first met Emerson, he finally visited his friend in Concord. At a gathering with Bronson Alcott, James insisted on dominating the evening with his criticisms of society and approval for those who disobey its rules. "He charges society with all the crime committed," noted Thoreau, also a guest, "and praises the criminal for committing it. But I think that all the remedies he suggests out of his head . . . would leave us about where we are now." Emerson's aunt, Mary Moody Emerson, who suffered no fools, became so irritated by James that she scolded him for his "lax notions": the visit was not a success.[44]

As personal relationships deteriorated, his professional life became even more dismal. At the *New York Tribune,* where James had published letters, editorials, and reviews since 1850, his supercilious tone and moral pretentiousness offended its editor, Horace Greeley, who summarily cut James off from further publication. James's last book, *Christianity the Logic of Creation*, published before the family returned in 1858, had received derisive notices. "There are two very bad things in this American land of ours," he had written to a niece years before, "the worship of money and the worship of intellect. Both money and intellect are regarded as good in themselves."[45] With its myopic view of human worth, America simply could not appreciate so complex and creative a thinker as Henry James. He would not give his countrymen a chance to reject him any longer. "I am a good patriot," he wrote in his letter announcing the family's departure, "but my patriotism is even livelier on the other side of the water."[46]

Good Bye to Everything

WHEN THE JAMES children were small, about a week before Christmas, Henry Sr., seizing a moment when Mary was out, gleefully brought his children to the closet where their gifts were hidden to let them peek at the bounty they were going to receive. And every Christmas morning, the children conspired to protect their father's indiscretion and their mother's feelings by exclaiming with delight and gratitude over their gifts. The performance became more polished each year.

Alice was not alone in resenting those spoiled Christmases: "What an ungrateful wretch I was, and how I used to wish he hadn't done it!" she later confessed.[47] But like her brothers, she never revealed that her surprise was feigned; the children learned early that artifice was a useful strategy in their household.

The Christmas ritual, one of many similar scenarios requiring dissimulation and pretense, helps us to understand William's letter to Edgar Van Winkle announcing that within days he would be leaving for another stay in Europe.

> I suppose your lively imagination could hardly have conceived such turpitude on the part of a being endowed with a human heart; but it is none the less true that we are to be torn from our friends and from our Fatherland once more.
>
> I for my part am very sorry to leave America, though the rest of the family, to all appearance are delighted.[48]

Although the rest of the family may have responded with convincing delight when Henry first made his proclamation, the children soon confided their sadness to one another. They expected, William reported, "to have a sufficiently dismal time at Geneva this winter,"[49] and they were palpably sad over leaving their friends and neighbors. On October 3, the night before they left Newport for New York, William and Harry bade a solemn farewell to Jim MacKaye, who had returned from Paris the previous spring, and Tom Perry, who remembered sinking to the "depths of boyish despair" at the prospect of losing his companions. Writing to Tom just hours before boarding the SS *Vanderbilt*, Harry admitted that he was thinking "much more of what I leave behind than what I expect to find. Newport and the Newporters are surrounded with a halo, in my mind which grows brighter and brighter as two o'clock draws near. . . . Good bye to you and every body and every thing!"[50]

The trip was rough: in eleven days on the ocean there were, Harry reported, not eleven hours of calm weather; the family arrived both dispirited and exhausted from their struggles with the "Demon of the Sea." Even so, there was no time for leisurely recovery. A day after landing at Le Havre, the family went to Paris and then on to Geneva, this time to try different schools from the one the children had attended during their last educational experiment. Wilky and Bob were put into a boarding school in the country; Alice attended a local school for girls; Harry enrolled at the Institution Rochette near the Jameses' hotel; William went to the Academy, precursor of the University of Geneva. Of the four, William had the best match: he studied science and mathematics with as much success as he had before and by spring had been invited to join the Société des Zoffingues, a social club for Swiss students. Although William later complained that during his entire stay in Switzerland, he had never seen the inside of a Swiss home ("the aristocratic and respectable Genevese are very exclusive and reserved in their demeanor towards strangers," he wrote to Edgar Van Winkle),[51] the club afforded him the experience of informal student life. When William found out that he could invite a friend to one of the society's festivals, he chose Harry, who remembered a rowdy gathering where "[d]rinking, smoking big German pipes and singing" were the main activities.[52]

Harry's schooling proved less congenial: the Institution Rochette taught engineering and architecture, neither of which interested Harry, who hoped to learn Greek and spent his few free hours reading books about Eastern travels. After a short time as a full-time student, he shifted to being an "externe," who was allowed to come only for certain classes and then leave. There was no student club for Harry, and no friend other than his older brother. Wilky, too, complained of life at the Pensionnat Maquelin, where he and Bob boarded. The quality of teaching was inferior, he said, and there were daily fights between students and instructors.

Although in Newport, Henry Sr. had protested that he wanted to keep his family together and not send any of his children away to school, he conveniently forgot this goal once the family arrived in Geneva. Wilky and Bob returned only on weekends, and for several months, Henry himself left the family to stay in London, presumably to write and try to make connections with colleagues. These connections, as before, proved tenuous. Early in July, the Jameses left Geneva. Only Bob stayed behind: he had begged to join his classmates on a hiking trip with an instructor. While Henry, Mary, Wilky, and Alice went to Interlaken, William and Harry were allowed to go hiking, too, through the Alps from Geneva to Chamonix, Martigny, and Loéche-les-Bains. After about a week, they met up with the rest of the family at Interlaken.

Although they were accompanied by a guide and covered part of the excursion by carriage, the trip was an exhilarating adventure for the two brothers. Harry described the hike as dangerous and thrilling. He and William crossed two glaciers and clambered up to "wild dreary and barren" peaks where "[t]he growth of everything but the enormous rocks is stunted." They trudged for hours through snow as deep as they were tall, but crusted with ice so thick that they did not sink. They were cold and tired by the time they reached the hospice at St. Bernard, where they were welcomed for the night. Although the monks gave them warm slippers and a hearty dinner, the hospice provided only limited comfort. The beds were damp and lumpy, Harry said, and in the morning, they discovered "grim and ghastly" corpses lining the walls of a storage house because the ground was too frozen for burial.[53] The physical trials—including, for Harry, an injured foot—only made the hike more splendid. For William, it proved to be more than a test of stamina and agility: in the dramatic setting, away from his family for the first time in years, he affirmed his decision that he would be—he was—an artist. He wanted to continue his studies with Hunt. He wanted to go home.

He did not reveal this decision to his family when he and Harry joined them at Interlaken, but instead spent three days visiting the required tourist attractions along with many other summer vacationers. But as soon as they all arrived in Bonn, where Henry Sr. intended to board his sons with families so that they could learn German and prepare for the next year's schooling in Germany, William told his father what he had decided. Henry was surprised, but this time willing to listen—and not only listen, but to act. On July 18, he wrote to Edmund Tweedy, reporting that William "felt the vocation of a painter so strongly that he did not think it worth my while to expend any more time or money on his scientific education! I confess," Henry said, "I was greatly startled by the annunciation, and not a little grieved, for I had always counted upon a scientific career for Willy, and I hope the day may even yet come when my calculations may be realized in this regard. But as it was I had nothing to do but to submit; and as our motive to stay in Europe was chiefly derived from the imagined needs of his education, so now we are glad enough to turn homewards, and let him begin at once with Mr. Hunt."[54]

On the same day that Henry wrote to Tweedy, Harry announced the startling news to Tom Perry: Henry Sr. had booked passage on the *Adriatic* for September 11, not two months away. "We are going immediately to Newport, which is the place in America we all most care to live in. . . . Willie has decided to try and study painting seriously, and wished [to] return home and do so, if possible with Mr. Hunt. That is the reason, at least in a great measure the reason (for his going home need not necessitate our all going) of this determination."[55]

Tom did not question the reason—he was glad enough that he soon would see his friend. But Tweedy immediately responded with a word of caution: Was James, as usual, making too hasty a decision in returning home? Had his reasons for being in Europe changed so drastically? Henry, though, insisted that he knew what he was doing. His children were homesick for friends, he explained; none of them, except for William, was thriving at school—none of them, he said, had intellectual capacities; and now James reversed his opinion that America was a den of sin. His children had a sentimental attachment to the idea of America that he could not counter. He was returning, he told Tweedy, "profoundly persuaded that no wilder hallucination exists, at least in reference to boys who are destined to grow up into American men. America is the 'lost Paradise restored' to boys and girls both, and it is only our own paltry cowardice and absurd ducking to old world conventionalities that hinder their realising it as such at once."[56]

Henry Sr.'s self-effacing response to William's decision might suggest that for the first time he felt sympathy for his children, for the first time understood their needs to establish roots in their own culture, for the first time realized the impact of their feelings of alienation in Europe. Henry's quick capitulation to William's request might suggest that he recognized that he no longer had the right to control his eighteen-year-old son's destiny. But his relationship with William before and after the family returned home belies those conclusions; James, as before, was acting in his own interests, responding to his own restlessness and discouragement, escaping from a claustrophobic atmosphere that he himself had created.

Chapter 5

SPIRITUAL DANGERS

1860–1865

WHEN HE WAS THIRTY, William James visited Newport for a few days and, he wrote to his sister, "went through our old stone cottage which was dismally mildewed and dirty inside." In the bedrooms, the wallpaper was peeling from the walls; the landscape he once had seen from his bedroom window was obscured by the new growth of trees. His memories, though, were painfully vivid. "The ghost of my dear self with his ignorance and weakness seemed to look out strangely at me from the whole place," he told Alice. "It was the same in Pelham Street & wherever I went, and made the total impression of the visit a very sad one. I don't care to go there again—except as to a new place forgetting the associations of the past."[1]

Harry described William as so spirited and optimistic, so determined and self-assured, that he could flower in any waste. But by the time he came home from Europe in September 1860, he was wilted from an intense struggle with his father, enacted in person during the weeks they were together in Bonn and by letter after his parents left for Paris, where they remained until the family sailed home. Despite agreeing to return—and despite his claims that he was returning for his children's benefit—Henry Sr. persisted in arguing against William's becoming an artist: he was repulsed by the idea that his son would engage in an occupation so spiritually and intellectually vacuous. William, trying to understand his father's concerns, bravely defended his own needs. Having brought his father to the point of returning, however, William did not want to risk another turnaround. Certainly he felt angry about Henry's continuing derision of his feelings, and he worried that when they talked, he would not be able to hide his hostility. Once, at a friend's house in Bonn, he came close to asking his father to clarify his thoughts about art and artists, but afraid of inciting his father's anger, he held himself back.

Ten days after his parents left for Paris, he received a letter from his father admonishing him that he and his brothers must behave with "self-respect and purity" now that they were on their own in Germany. Assuming that William would take on a paternal role in his absence, Henry gave him a chance to prove that he was mature and responsible. William rose to the occasion, reporting with a dash of condescension about the welfare, study habits, nutrition, and behavior of his three brothers. The boys seemed comfortable about using William as conduit for their own messages to Henry Sr. Bob, for one, a few days short of his fourteenth birthday, decided that when the family returned home, he would go to work in a dry-goods store—he had heard the salaries were good, even for an adolescent—and wanted William to break the news to Henry. "Poor little Bobby!" William wrote, echoing his father's view of his youngest son.

From his lofty perch as surrogate father, William finally dared to ask Henry to "set down as clearly as you can on paper what your idea of the nature of art is. Because I do not probably understand it fully, and should like to have it presented in a form that I might think over at my leisure." To persuade his father that he would consider his ideas sympathetically, William assured him that despite his impatience and insolence when they were together, he thought fondly of Henry when they were apart. "I never value my parents (Father especially) so much as when I am away from them. At home I only see his faults and here he seems all perfection, and every night I wonder why I did not value them more when they were beside me." He even asked his mother and Aunt Kate to forgive him for his "cruel and dastardly" behavior; but his father's forgiveness, he hoped, would take a more concrete form: a letter condoning William's choice of vocation.[2]

Within a week, William received a reply from Henry, but it did not satisfy him. William wanted to understand why Henry objected to his becoming an artist, "what were *exactly* the causes of your disappointment at my late resolve, what your view of the nature of art was, that the idea of my devoting myself to it should be so repugnant to you." Instead of responding to these concerns, Henry replied with characteristic vagueness about "the spiritual danger in wh[ich] a man is if he allows the bent of his esthetic nature (supposed strong) to direct his activity." A sensuous life, he implied, was not what he wanted for his son.

Fueling William's frustration, Henry merely repeated the points that he had made when they talked: he was afraid that William was not mature enough to distinguish between being an artist and a mere artisan. William might be talented, but talent was nothing that Henry admired; a true artist worked not to have his talents praised, not from a desire for critical approval, but from inner passion. Henry imagined most pseudoartists as egotists who deceived themselves about their own worth. He failed to be convinced by William's protestations of his spiritual integrity.

Yet William derived some small comfort by Henry's acceptance of "the *fact* of [his] being an 'artist.'" If he conceded that William had the right to shape his own identity, William had won a significant battle in his fight for autonomy. Power, after all, was William's goal: power to create, to give concrete expression to his experiences and sensibilities, to affirm his interpretation of reality. Art would give him this authority, and he saw no reason why these powers should lead to his moral debasement. "I do not see why a man's spiritual culture should not go on independently of his esthetic activity," William wrote to his father, "why the power which an artist feels in himself should tempt him to forget what he is, any more than the power felt by a Cuvier or Fourier would tempt them to do the same."[3] But according to Henry, Cuvier and Fourier, one a scientist, the other a philosopher, had found ways to meld their private desires with their public actions; they did not devote their lives merely to pleasure and self-fulfillment, but to social and philosophical reform. Certainly, he believed, these heroes did not care about public approbation.

Henry's persistent denial of William's authority over his own life, his repeated assertions that William did not know enough about art, or the world, or himself, to make a decision, undermined William's confidence. "My experience amounts to very little," William admitted, "but it is all I have to go upon." Responding to Henry's fear that art would cause William to be "degraded," he insisted that painting and drawing yielded for him "spiritual impressions the intensest and purest I know." He acknowledged that he understood his father's concern

about the moral dimension of the decision to pursue a career in art—
"duty to society &c &c."—but still, he told his father, "my life would
be embittered if I were kept from it. That is the way I feel *at present,*"
he added. "Of course I may change."[4] Henry was prepared to do everything he could to generate that change.

By the time the family left Europe, William's resolve had been
weakened by his father's assaults. Yet at least he, unlike his siblings,
had a definite plan for the near future; while he studied art, the other
children had no idea how they would occupy themselves. Harry, for
one, did not want to return to the Berkeley Institute. He harbored instead the "very silly wish" to go to college, knowing, of course, that his
father's opinions on that question had not altered. Nevertheless, despite some "prudential uneasiness" about his future, Harry, along with
the other James children, longed for America.[5]

The passage home was rough; the idea of home made it bearable.
At one o'clock on Monday morning, September 24, 1860, the *Adriatic*
docked in New York. At nine, the Jameses stood once more on their
native shores.

Paradox

AFTER A FLURRY of correspondence, Henry Sr. finally secured another
residence in Newport: Jim MacKaye's house on Kay Street, where
William had found a "second home" during the family's previous stay.
Newport, long popular with summer vacationers, had become a village
of emotional quarantine for Americans returning from expatriation.
Newport's air of impermanence—its population waxed and waned with
the seasons—appealed to those who felt alienated, or oppressed, by
more stable and entrenched communities. One could live in Newport
for months, or even years, without giving up the illusion that the stay
was, after all, no more than an attenuated hiatus in something else
called real life. Newport was a refuge, and in 1860, the James family
needed just that. Europe had "fatally disconnected" the Jameses from
their future, Harry wrote; Newport let them pretend that their detachment from any productive occupation was only another form of leisure.[6]

William, of course, had important goals: to resume his place at
Hunt's school, to prove to his father his passionate engagement with
art. It seemed a happy coincidence that the first friend William met
after landing in New York was John La Farge, the twenty-five-year-old

painter who had come to study with Hunt a few months before the
Jameses left. William had been enormously excited by La Farge's arrival. "There's a new fellow come to Hunt's class," he announced
breathlessly to Tom Perry. "He knows everything. He has read everything. He has seen everything—paints everything. He's a marvel!"[7]

La Farge had not been everywhere; he had neither read nor seen
everything, but to William and Harry he seemed mysteriously foreign,
"quite the most interesting person we knew," Harry said. Six feet tall,
with dark, silky hair and fierce, if myopic, gray-green eyes, La Farge
seemed far more sophisticated even than Hunt, to whom he could be
icily condescending. But his egotism and aloofness were reserved only
for those who claimed authority over him. Though Mary James, for
one, thought him self-centered and pretentious, with William and
Harry he was warm, engaging, seductive. La Farge "opened up to us . . .
prospects and possibilities that made the future flush and swarm."[8] Primary among those possibilities was becoming an artist.

Born in New York in 1835, La Farge was educated at a private
school in Manhattan, followed by a checkered college career. Always a
rebellious student, he was expelled in his junior year of college for
fighting with a classmate. An uncle intervened to get him readmitted,
and he graduated with his class in 1853.

At eighteen, La Farge underwent the same torment over his career
that William was experiencing. He had been drawn to art ever since he
was a child, encouraged by his grandfather, who was a miniaturist, but
discouraged by his father, who envisioned a more stable and respectable profession for his son. La Farge felt that he had no choice but
to acquiesce to his father's demand that he become a lawyer, and immediately after graduating from college, he apprenticed himself to a
law firm.

When he was twenty-one, however, La Farge embarked on an extended tour of Europe. In Paris, he took classes with Couture and, like
Hunt, the experience changed his life. Although he deferred to his father and resumed reading law after he came home in the fall of 1857,
he also established connections with the art community in New York,
meeting, among others, the architect Richard Hunt. La Farge's crisis of
vocation came to a sudden end in June 1858 when his father died,
leaving him a generous legacy. He put his law career behind him and
set out to train as an artist. When Hunt recommended that La Farge

study with his brother, who also had worked with Couture and had just set up a school in Newport, La Farge left New York and, in the spring of 1859, became William's classmate.

When William first met La Farge he did not know how old he was and guessed that he might be seventeen—just William's age at the time—suggesting his immediate feeling of identification with La Farge. Now, though, when they met again in New York, La Farge seemed older, changed. In fact, during their year apart, La Farge's life had changed considerably. He had fallen in love with Tom Perry's older sister Margaret, but the affair had not gone smoothly. La Farge was Catholic, Margaret not, and the Perrys tried to break up the relationship by moving the whole family to Louisiana during the winter of 1859–60. La Farge, though, would not be put off. In April, he followed Margaret south, proposed, and was accepted. In a few weeks, he told William, they would be married in Newport. With marriage imminent, La Farge once again confronted the question of his career. He had his inheritance, and Margaret was wealthy in her own right, but La Farge felt the burden of becoming a husband and, he anticipated, a father. He would buy a house, he would support a family: he needed to think of art not just as personal expression but as a means of earning a living.

Yet despite a gnawing concern about his future, he shared William's excitement about their life in Newport: the hours of discussions about Balzac and Browning, the long days of drawing and painting in the secluded studio. Set behind Hunt's gracious home, Hill Top, surrounded by trees, the school seemed a place apart and protected from the rest of the world. The artists of Newport managed to create a "wondrous esoteric quarter," Harry wrote, "peopled just by us and our friends and our common references" and isolated, imaginatively and aesthetically, from "the vast remainder of the public at large, the public of the innumerably uninitiated even when apparently of the most associated."[9]

This wondrous esoteric quarter, however, was being invaded by the marketplace. Although both Hunt and La Farge derided critics and the power of the public, neither could avoid concern with the economic implications of creativity. When William last studied with Hunt, the artist had recently returned from six months of travel in the Azores following the death of his infant son. Personally and professionally, he was in a period of transition: grief over the loss of his son gave way to

joy over the birth of a daughter; he had decided to apply his talents to
teaching as well as to painting; and he was experimenting artistically
with landscapes, figure studies, and genre paintings. Although his
work was not applauded by critics, especially those in New York, he
seemed more concerned with authenticity and self-fulfillment than
with popular appeal.

When William returned in 1860, however, Hunt's career had taken
an important turn. Through his wife's wealthy connections, he had become a sought-after portrait painter for New England's aristocracy.
Now, as Hunt's students worked in the cool, gray-walled classrooms of
his studio, their teacher was occupied in his own quarters painting like-
nesses of rich and famous men or, more often, their wives. During the
year that William was absent, Hunt's submissions to the National
Academy of Design in New York and the Boston Athenaeum had been
greeted with enthusiasm, and Hunt discovered that he coveted praise,
after all. He worked now with an eye toward Boston and toward fame.

As William—and Harry, too, who had nothing better to occupy
his time—sketched various subjects, including their cousins Gus
Barker, who modeled nude, and Kitty Temple, who sat for her portrait
as she sewed, Hunt plied his trade as a portrait painter. At around ten
each morning, he would greet his sitter, arrange the pose, and set to
work until lunch, when his wife arrived with a tray of wine and exotic
cakes made from a recipe they had brought home from the Azores.
While Louisa Hunt sat next to the sitter on a divan covered with an
oriental rug, Hunt summoned his students to range themselves around
the room and listen raptly as he talked of art. The respite did more
than relax the sitter—which Hunt claimed was its main purpose; it
provided an artistic outing for Mrs. Samuel Gray Ward, Mrs. Joseph
Randolph Coolidge, Mrs. Robert Shaw Sturgis, and their friends. As
Hunt played the part of the urbane cosmopolite and sensitive artist, he
honed his talents for flattery and supplication, neither of which came
naturally to him. He claimed that the afternoon's sitting was more productive than the first because his sitter always relaxed after the food
and wine; but for Hunt, the real triumph of the day was the sitter's
feeling of camaraderie with the painter and the recommendation of his
work to a friend or neighbor.

Through the winter of 1861, William devoted himself to working
with Hunt, earning praise from both his teacher and La Farge. William

drew beautifully, they agreed. He was a talented artist. But William was learning something more than drawing and painting. He learned that artists were subject to the whims, preferences, and dislikes of their audience. He discovered, as Harry put it, "the grim truth of the merciless manner in which a living and hurrying public educates itself, making and devouring in a day reputations and values. . . ." He heard about "victims who have been buried alive."[10] The emotional life of an American artist, as exemplified by Hunt and La Farge, was not characterized only by the spiritual intensity and passion that William was seeking, but by worry, resentment, and often indignation.

William realized that if he devoted his life to art, he would place himself in the same relationship to an audience as his father had had throughout his life: always he would be seeking ways to make himself known to the public, always he would be hoping desperately that the public would approve. As an artist, he would spend his life trying to reap adulation, fearful of failure every time he created a painting or drawing. If Hunt and La Farge, each far wealthier than William, were worried about finances, then how would he fulfill his modest dream of simply supporting himself?

Certainly his father continued to provide a chilling example of a man at the mercy of an unappreciative public. Now he had joined the battle between religion and science, taking much the same view of the working scientist (as opposed to his ideal Philosopher-Scientist) as he did of the artist: science, he proclaimed, was nothing more than a "subordinate power of the mind."[11] Just as the artist "is incapable of any properly spiritual joy in his work because he sees it to be an insubstantial thing at best, a mere shadow or image of his own shadowy power, or his own unreal self," so the scientist could only approach, but never succeed in, attaining real knowledge.[12]

Nevertheless, he asked Edmund Tweedy, who was in England when the Jameses returned to Newport, to buy a dissecting microscope for his son. "Willy needs it & will be much obliged," he added.[13] Whether William said that he wanted to continue studying science, or whether Henry decided that a microscope might serve to lure William away from art we cannot know. Certainly we know that Henry kept up his campaign against William's choice of career. "[W]e wholesomely breathed inconsistency and ate and drank contradictions," Harry remembered. "The presence of paradox was so bright among us . . . that we fairly grew used to allow, from an early time, for the so many and odd declarations we heard launched, to the extent of happily 'discounting' them; the moral of all of which was that we need never fear not to be good enough if we were only social enough: a splendid meaning indeed being attached to the latter term."[14]

The James Family Theater

IN THE JAMES FAMILY, the splendid meaning attached to the word "social" had more the flavor of theater than of communion. Henry wanted his children to appear happy, voluble, outgoing, and brilliant. Appearance was everything. When they were very young and he was obsessed with protecting their pure souls from sin, he worried more that they might appear hateful to others than that they would suffer themselves. When he criticized Emerson for his fatuous ideas about nature, he defended his position by observing that Emerson "breeds no love of nature in his intellectual offspring."[15] If a man is judged by his influence on others, then surely one's children were the most telling evidence.

From the time the children were young, he encouraged their home theatrical productions, plays that they wrote and performed for each other and for the family's visitors. William, especially, plunged into these productions with enthusiasm. If he could direct the plays, he was happy; if he could be the star performer, so much the better. Henry and Mary so admired the children's theatricals that performance began to permeate the family's daily life.

Several visitors to the James household echo the testimony of Edward Emerson who was so startled by the aggressive banter at dinner one evening that he thought the children would attack one another. Mary assured him, however, everyone was safe: this display of raucousness was normal for the Jameses at mealtime, she explained. Edward's sister Ellen also reported the rollicking family life: "the funniest thing in the world," she reported, "is to see this delectable family together all talking at once. Edith [her sister] and I spend all dinner-time in convulsions."[16] The James family at home, Ellen said, was a carnival every day.

But if Henry whipped up conviviality to impress the family of Ralph Waldo Emerson, when he did not take on the role of director, the comedy turned flat. "I go to the James's, the parents are away, and those unhappy children fight like cats & dogs," Tom Perry recorded in his diary. No one had any privacy, solitude was rudely interrupted, and, at the end of his visit, Perry was so sorry for Harry, in particular, that he invited him to stay with him.[17] Lilla Cabot, who later married Perry, described "the poky banality of the James house ruled by Mrs. James where HJ's father used to limp in and out and never seemed really to 'belong' to his wife or Miss Walsh, large florid stupid seeming ladies, or to his clever but coldly self-absorbed daughter who was his youngest child."[18]

In the James family theater, William took on the role of male lead, striving to be central to the family's attention and to garner unconditional admiration. With a nimble facility for quick, biting retort and a talent for sarcasm, he could be hugely entertaining; and the object of his efforts was praise and more praise. In Geneva, for example, he composed grandly extravagant poems for everyone in the family, except Henry Sr., who was traveling at the time. But approval from his mother, aunt, and siblings was not enough for him: he wanted Mary to show the poems to some friends "to be read, and admired by them," Alice reported. "We have all come to the conclusions that he is fit to go to the lunatic asylum," she advised her father.[19]

Many of William's youthful letters to his parents, and especially to Alice, reflect the arch, hyperbolic banter that substituted for conversations in the James family. If William was the brilliant hero, Alice was the only family member who could play the ingenue; that is the role he gave her, and the role, for too long, that she willingly played. She was "the cherry lipped, apricot nosed, double chinned little Bal" who "inflamed the hearts of her lonely brothers with an intense longing to kiss and slap her celestial cheeks,"[20] William wrote in a letter to his father when Alice was twelve. Of course, Alice would read this letter or hear it read aloud.

Although William's youthful letters to Alice seem to reflect an inappropriate "romantic feeling" of brother for sister, the letters were not intimate communications, but public documents, only nominally meant for Alice, read by the rest of the family and assorted friends, perpetuating the public roles played by each family member. Not until Alice was nineteen did William address letters specifically to her, a change that was so notable, she could not help but comment. "The admirable practice which you have begun of addressing your letters to me I hope you wont think of abandoning," Alice wrote. "The rest of the family were all torn with jealousy at my being treated with such distinction."[21]

Even letters from friends *to* the children were available for public scrutiny. Although Harry protested noisily after his father opened one of his letters from Tom Perry, his objection did not change the family's behavior. Years later, when Harry submitted his first signed story to the *Atlantic Monthly,* he gave the magazine Tom Perry's address for "their letter of reject, or accept. . . . [T]heir answer," he noted, "could not come here unobserved."[22] When William and Harry finally were living away from home, their correspondence, especially to each other, became more intimate and subdued; later, they advised one another which sections of letters must be removed before the document was put into circulation. But as the children were growing up, the world of the James family was a public stage.

The roles that earned accolades at home, however, seemed less satisfying when the children took their acts, so to speak, on the road. No one but William addressed Alice as "dearest darling," "beloved," "chérie de jeune bal," or "sweetlet." Although Alice was more than capable of responding to her brother's flippant hyperbole with wit and sarcasm, still, she became increasingly aware of the disparity between William's allusions to romance and her own lack of suitors. While friend after friend became engaged and married, Alice, by the time she was in her midtwenties, was convinced that she never would marry, that she was not the pretty, winsome, flirtatious young woman her brother had invented, but one among the "depressed & gloomy females" doomed to become old maids.[23]

Wilky, too, within the family, was thought to be gregarious and friendly, easy to talk with and to know. Shy Harry envied his garrulousness. After the Jameses returned to Newport, Henry sent Wilky and Bob to school in Concord, Massachusetts, where Wilky, from one classmate's account, was a popular and beloved student.

> Wilkie, was incomparable: besides being the best dressed boy in the school, and in manners and talk the most engaging, his good humor was inexhaustible. . . . He was sixteen years old when he came to us, but appeared older by two or three years, being self-possessed and having the bearing of a man of the world. In the company of the ladies he was entirely at ease, and devoted; they all loved him.[24]

But after a year, Wilky wanted to come home. Bob had refused to go back to the school, and without his brother there, Wilky felt disconnected and alone. Only with his brother could he reveal a part of his personality that he never showed to outsiders. The James children had yet to learn how to permit their private selves to emerge in public—even among friends.

Many years later, when William contributed an entry defining "person" and "personality" to *Johnson's Universal Cyclopaedia*, he noted that "person" derived from the Latin *persona*, meaning "theater-mask, part (in a play)" itself derived from the Greek term for "mask"; "the word person is still sometimes used to denote the corporeal appearance of a man rather than his inner attributes, as when we say that he possesses an agreeable person, or is personally repulsive."[25] As he was growing up, William was tormented by his conviction that the agreeable personality he assiduously created for presentation to the world hid a repulsive inner self.

Science

WHILE HE WAS STUDYING with Hunt, William continued the scientific investigation that had excited him all during his youth. Harry remembered watching William's chemistry experiments, which involved transferring liquids from one test tube to another and sometimes heating the test tubes over a flickering flame. William often emerged from his makeshift laboratory with stained fingers and, to Mary's dismay, spotted clothing. In Boulogne, he set up a darkroom where he developed photographs, often of Harry. But the subject did not matter to William as much as the process of development: of transforming subjective perception into a tangible, shared reality.

If chemistry proved the more adventuresome science, biology also attracted the young naturalist, and as he had predicted to Edgar Van Winkle when he wrote from Europe, William tramped into woods and fields to collect specimens and pond water to examine with his microscope. William had an abiding interest, Harry recalled, "in the 'queer' or the incalculable effects of things."[26] To Harry's consternation, he dared to test the effect of chemicals on humans by imbibing some himself; and he bought galvanic batteries with which he gave shocks to anyone brave enough to be a subject.

His artist friends encouraged William's interest in science. La Farge, especially, was interested in photography and optics, and wanted to understand more about sensation and perception. Science, La Farge believed, had great lessons to teach art. But William's interest in science was independent of its connection to art: science challenged him and art, increasingly, did not.

Harry said that he was not surprised that William gave up art: his brother rejoiced in making connections, establishing relationships among ideas, exploring, and working at something that was rigorous and strenuous. Certainly the pattern of great enthusiasm followed by great disillusionment was entrenched in the James household, enacted repeatedly by Henry Sr. And just as Henry's disenchantment often was caused by deteriorating personal relationships, William's rejection of art was provoked, in part, by his reassessment of the temperamental La Farge. When La Farge descended into dejection, he lashed out at anyone in his path, including William, who more than once was wounded by La Farge's sharp criticism. William reluctantly came to the same conclusion as Mary: La Farge was, indeed, arrogant, pretentious, and sometimes bitingly vicious.[27] Sometimes William adored him; but he no longer trusted him.

William's outstanding reason for rejecting art as a career, however, was fear of failure. Later, William admitted that he would have had an easier time choosing a career if he had not been so concerned with immediate "results," but in 1861, results were a persistent worry. In art, results were measured by sales, and William had no confidence that he could compete in the marketplace of aesthetics. He knew that he was talented, but he was convinced that he did not have the persistence, imagination, and flexibility to become a critically acclaimed and financially successful artist. He would be to Hunt and La Farge what his father was to Emerson and Carlyle.

Although William's decision to give up art does not seem surprising, Henry's abrupt agreement to allow William to enroll in the Lawrence Scientific School does. But in the spring of 1861, Henry found himself cornered. Just as William made his decision to leave Hunt's studio, Abraham Lincoln called for seventy-five thousand volunteers to fight for the Union. His request met with enthusiasm throughout New England where many men William's age acted on their abolitionist convictions and enlisted. William's favorite cousin, William James Temple, just three months younger than William, left Harvard to join, as did Gus Barker. William, at nineteen, was swept up in the patriotism that inspirited Newport: he would be a soldier, and on April 22, just days after Lincoln's call for volunteers, he signed up as a ninety-day volunteer in the Newport Artillery Company, making himself available for recruitment into a state militia unit.

His father responded with alarm: he unalterably refused to allow his two eldest sons to fight in the war—Bob and Wilky, at age fifteen and sixteen, were too young—and he believed that many other parents also were trying, some vainly, to keep their patriotic and, he thought, naive offspring from enlisting. He described himself holding on to the coat-tails of William and Harry, even though the "the scamps pull so hard." He told them that they were too young to die; and in any case, no government was worth dying for. Nor, it seems, did Henry believe that slavery was an issue that merited so dramatic a response as war.

Ever since Lincoln's election, Henry had been outspoken about the national crisis. In March 1861, he told a Newport audience that the Civil War, more than a conflict between North and South over the issue of slavery, was part of a longer and deeper struggle to realize a transcendent ideal of liberty. No political system, not even democracy, could foster the kind of spiritual enlightenment necessary to prevent the enslavement of any individual, black or white. Fighting for the Union, then, in James's estimation, was irrelevant.

William, though, did not see it that way, and his movement to enlist may have pressured Henry into proposing an alternative: if William agreed to stay out of the war, he finally could leave home and enroll in the Lawrence Scientific School.[28] Judging from the speed with which William's interest in art waned, Henry might have believed that William would last only a year at the Lawrence Scientific School before returning to the richer source of erudition that his father could offer. In fact, William's stay in Cambridge may well have been presented to him as a yearlong experiment, judging from a schedule that William sent to his family early the following November: he would complete a year in Cambridge, then come home for a term before returning to Cambridge for further study. This one-term respite seems an odd proposal, unless he agreed to the plan before he left. Henry may have believed that a half-year interruption would give William time to realize his mistake and change his mind once again.

Henry warned William, as usual, about maintaining his integrity in the face of pressures to conform, and he reminded William of his propensity to take up tasks with enthusiasm, only to drop them later. This time, however, William wanted to prove his father wrong. "I can be as independent as I please," he wrote to his family, "and want to live regardless of the good or bad opinion of everyone. I shall have a splendid chance to try, I know, and I know too that the 'native hue of resolution' has never been of very great shade in me hitherto. But I am sure that that feeling is a right one, and I mean [to] live according to it if I can. If I do I think I shall turn out all right."[29]

But if he did not—what then? William's repeated "if's" reflect his continuing doubts over his commitment and abilities. Could he make decisions to direct his own life, or would he forever be dominated by his father? Was he capable of knowing himself? Was he capable of acting on his own beliefs, even if he risked the bad opinion of everyone, including his parents? Could he manage to live independently?

The earliest letter we have from William's first year in Cambridge responded to Harry, who apparently informed William that Mary missed him. Framing a rather mundane letter enumerating the young men with whom he already had become acquainted, William assured his "poor desolate Niobe of a Mother" and the rest of his family that he did not feel at home in Cambridge and suffered "several pangs since being here at the thought of all I had left behind at Newport, especially gushes of feeling about the *place.*" The thought of his mother's grief made him "shed tears on the floor of the P. O.," he said. When he continued his letter the next morning, he had somewhat calmed his fevered response and asked Harry to remind their father to send money.[30]

His family, however, was determined to elicit continued affirmations of his devotion. The next day he received a letter from his mother describing the family's Sunday dinner; using a strategy that would become familiar to William, she informed him that his father had had a headache. Reporting illnesses and indispositions served Mary well in her effort to inspire guilt, if nothing more, among her children. William gushed back that her letter brought tears to his eyes. "I shall enjoy home as I never did before when I get back," he wrote.[31]

In subsequent letters, William referred to his homesickness always with the exaggerated theatricality that seemed expected of him. Thinking of home, he said, "makes my hair curl for joy"; often, he pictured "the lustre of far-off shining Newport all silver and blue" with the "heavenly group" of his family waiting for him. But soon after a visit from Harry in November, he sent his family a sketch of themselves that belied his effusiveness.

Henry Sr. stands at the center of the group, wearing his customary top hat and leaning on a cane. Bewhiskered and bespectacled, the patriarch of the family links arms with Harry, depicted as a dapper young man somewhat taller than his father. Aunt Kate, wearing a bonnet, shawl, and hoop skirt, holds Harry's hand; and beside her, his hands jauntily in his pockets, wearing a scrappy-looking cap, stands Bob. To the left of Henry Sr. stands Mary, portrayed as nearly indistinguishable from her sister. And at the far left, slightly apart from the group, the fingers of both hands splayed out on her skirt, is thirteen-year-old Alice. William, the artist, is missing; and so is Wilky, who at the time was visiting with him in Cambridge.

But there is something odd about the cartoonlike sketch: except for Henry Sr., whose mouth is hidden by his beard, and Harry, who appears slightly puzzled, all of the Jameses are frowning most emphatically. They look unhappy, even angry. And there is something odd, too, about a parenthetical phrase that William inserted to describe the "heavenly" group: "all being more or less failures, especially the two outside ones"—that is, Alice and Bob.

This was not a group to inspire homesickness, and yet in two weeks, William noted, he would be home for Thanksgiving, "home, home, home to the hearts of my infancy and budding youth," he sang; home to the place, he would later write, haunted by his own "dear self with his ignorance and weakness."

But despite his father's expectations of failure, William did not come home defeated. He had made acquaintances both at the Lawrence Scientific School and Harvard College, including the ebullient Francis J. Child, professor of English, who took his meals at the boardinghouse where William lived, and a brilliant young classmate, Charles Peirce, son of mathematics professor Benjamin Peirce. James went to lectures and art exhibits and was studying hard. He did not much like chemistry, partly because he was required to complete fifty dull experiments before the term's end, partly because he was not inspired by his teacher, Charles William Eliot, a stately, taciturn New Englander who, one of his students recalled, was "cold as an icicle."[32] Eliot, William thought, was not "a *very* accomplished chemist"; William, Eliot thought, was not an overly accomplished student. Although he acknowledged that

William was "interesting and agreeable" and possessed "unusual mental powers," he noticed that William seemed more interested in other branches of science than in chemistry, and that in the laboratory, he preferred "novel experimenting" to the requirements of the course. Eliot also concluded that William's work was undermined by his "ill-health, or rather by something which I imagined to be a delicacy of nervous constitution."[33]

This "delicacy" became evident during the spring semester of his first year, when he began to miss classes in quantitative analysis and did only moderately well on the examination for Eliot's course. By that time, however, James had decided that chemistry would not be his field, nor Eliot his mentor. Instead, he wanted to study with Louis Agassiz and become a naturalist.

Agassiz was fifty-four—four years older than Henry Sr.—when James first heard him lecture on natural history in Boston, but he seemed far younger than Henry Sr., and far more energetic. His international reputation and personal magnetism made him the star of the Lawrence Scientific School. For some in the Harvard community, his anti-Darwinism only added to his charm.

Darwin's *On the Origin of Species by Means of Natural Selection,* published in 1859, inflamed debate among naturalists and philosophers, who protested against both Darwin's method of research and his astonishing results. Agassiz, along with many of his colleagues, refused to take Darwin's theory of natural selection seriously: it contradicted nature, he asserted; it posited a godless universe. James was among many who flocked to Agassiz's lectures attacking Darwinism; but it was not Agassiz's theoretical position that drew him to those talks.

Instead, he was attracted by Agassiz's conviction that to become a scientist, one should not be stuffed with information, but learn to think independently and creatively. James talked with a classmate who had been studying with Agassiz for two years and came away seeing "how a naturalist could feel about his trade in the same way that an artist does about his."[34] Agassiz's naturalist did not learn about the world from reading books, but, as William had planned long before, from going out into the woods, observing acutely.

Competing with Agassiz for James's interest were such men as the biologist Asa Gray and the anatomist Jeffries Wyman. In his late forties when James began to study with him, Wyman was a cautious, moderate, shy man who had graduated from Harvard some thirty years before, took a degree in medicine, and, like most American scientists at the time, then studied abroad. Since 1847, he had taught at Harvard College, the School of Medicine, and the Lawrence Scientific School. Although Wyman was as reticent as Agassiz was dynamic, James soon discovered that he had a "filial" feeling for him and came to rely on Wyman for advice about his future.

After taking a semester off, James was back in Cambridge in the fall of 1863, trembling over his fate. By then, Harry had enrolled in the Harvard Law School, the first step, or so it seemed, to a recognized profession. His younger brothers, too, had taken decisive steps in their own lives: Wilky and Bob had enlisted in the Union army: Wilky, in the famous Massachusetts Fifty-fourth, the first black regiment, led by Robert Gould Shaw, the son of a family friend. At Harvard, scores of men also had joined in the war, and the ideals of manliness and valor infused the atmosphere of Cambridge.

In this charged context, William confronted his own unease and vacillation. By mid-January, he wrote to his cousin Kitty Prince, he had "to make finally and irrevocably 'the choice of a profession.'" The prospect was chilling. "I have four alternatives," he told her: "Natural History, Medicine, Printing, Beggary." Beggary, he suggested, would pay best. He tended toward natural history, but he was sure that he never could support a family on his salary as a naturalist. Medicine would be more lucrative, "but how much drudgery and of what an unpleasant kind is there!"[35] He felt paralyzed as he looked down a diverging road: "One branch," he wrote to his mother, "leads to material comfort, the flesh-pots; but it seems a kind of selling of one's soul. The other to mental dignity and independence; combined, however with physical penury."[36] He guessed that she would advise him to choose the fleshpots, but he attributed that choice to cowardice.

Although William was eager to declare himself emotionally liberated from his family, he was not quite ready to take on the burden of financial independence. His father had taught him that "mental dignity" was possible only if one need not worry about financial responsibilities; if that were true, then surely the family that so deeply valued mental dignity would continue to support him. William implied that his vocational decision would be easier if his parents could find a home in Cambridge, which the Jameses apparently had been putting off.

Without room and board, he would be free to work under Agassiz at the Museum of Comparative Zoology, earning $400 to $500, which amply would cover his personal expenses.

Instead of pursuing a career as a naturalist, though, James heeded Wyman's counsel and finally made the decision to enroll in Harvard's medical school. He began in February 1864, with little enthusiasm. Since his family relied only on homeopathic physicians, James did not feel any esteem for traditional medical training. He called the curriculum "humbug" and concluded that the efficacy of a physician came more from "the moral effect of his presence on the patient and family, than by anything else."[37] But at the age of twenty-two, he was not about to reverse another decision. His period of searching and experimentation was ended, and his relative independence ended, too. After paying for room and board for two children for nearly two years, the Jameses finally rented a town house in Boston's Beacon Hill, where William and Harry relocated in the spring of 1864.

Isolated Circumstances

AS JAMES BEGAN his second year in medical school, he was offered another chance to test his interest in becoming a naturalist: Agassiz was recruiting volunteers to join him on an expedition to Brazil to collect specimens. The trip, financed by Nathaniel Thayer, one of the wealthiest men in Boston, would cost James some six hundred dollars, but the expense, he decided, would be worth it.[38] "W.J.," he said to himself, "in this excursion you will learn to know yourself and your resources somewhat more intimately than you do now, and will come back with your character considerably evolved and established."[39] His family agreed—at the very least, James would be participating in research with one of the greatest living naturalists—and his father and Aunt Kate came up with the necessary funds to make the trip possible.

The Thayer Expedition would take James the farthest he ever had been from his family. At the Lawrence Scientific School, he was within a short trip to his brother Wilky in Concord, his father visited frequently, and letters flew back and forth between Cambridge and Newport. But as soon as the *Colorado* departed from New York on April 1, James found himself in "isolated circumstances" that sent him spiraling into depression. The passage was rough, he reported home, but he did not suffer nausea, only homesickness. "[F]or twelve mortal days," he wrote, "I was, body and soul, in a more indescribably hopeless, homeless and friendless state than I ever want to be in again."[40]

During the first weeks of the trip, he was irritated and uncomfortable. Fleas, mosquitoes, and ringworm produced violent itching; he had diarrhea, the hotels were bad, and his tasks seemed useless: "*nothing* has been done wh. cd. not have been done just as well by writing fm. Boston," he said. Moreover, he was not sure how he felt about Agassiz, who was egotistical and overbearing, yet inexplicably fascinating. "He is doubtless a man of some wonderful mental faculties," he confessed, "but such a politician & so self-seeking & illiberal to others that it sadly diminishes one's respect for him." Of one thing, however, he was certain: after a few weeks of collecting specimens and working in a makeshift laboratory, he knew he did not want to be a naturalist. "When I get home I'm going to study philosophy all my days," he wrote to Harry.[41] The message, of course, was meant for Henry Sr.

His distress was compounded when, early in May, he became seriously ill. At first, he thought he had smallpox; Agassiz later revised the diagnosis to the milder varioloid, which sometimes afflicted those who had been vaccinated against smallpox. He was quarantined in the *maison de santé*, fed chicken and rice, and felt generally miserable. He wanted to be home. "My coming was a mistake," he wrote to his family. "I am now certain that my forte is not to go on exploring expeditions. . . . I am convinced now, for good, that I am cut out for a speculative rather than an active life."

Although he had gone on the expedition to reach just such an epiphany, he felt disappointed by what he had learned about himself. In physical prowess, he was sadly deficient. "The grit and energy of some men are called forth by the resistance of the world. But as for myself, I seem to have no spirit whatever of that kind, no pride which makes me ashamed to say, 'I can't do that.'" What he did have, he said, was "mental pride and shame which, although they seem more egotistical than the other kind, are still the only things that can stir my blood." He would come home and devote himself to "striving to set things at one in [his] own topsy-turvy mind."[42]

This curious admission of "mental shame" made him reluctant to share his revelation with anyone outside of his immediate family. If his parents told anyone else that he was coming home, he warned them, "I absolutely forbid anything to be said about my motives. They are no one's business. If pushed you can say you don't know and that I had seen all I wanted and did not care about prolonging it."[43]

His father was predictably sympathetic to his son's anguish: William, it seemed, had made yet another mistake. Henry's letters were so tender that they evoked a sweet, if puerile, response: "My Dearest Daddy," William began, "Great was my joy the other evening . . . to get a batch of letters from you." But by the time he answered his father's solicitous letters, William no longer needed consolation. As he recovered physically, his spirits improved. He became caught up in Agassiz's enthusiasm for the expedition, which, Agassiz wrote to his benefactor, Thayer, was yielding specimens "about four or five times more extensive & important than I had expected."[44] Agassiz convinced James that he valued his contributions, and Elizabeth Agassiz, whom James described as "an angel," nurtured him.

In part, his new enthusiasm was generated, too, by a growing sensibility to the exotic—and erotic—environment. By July, although he still complained about trouble with his eyes, a consequence of his bout with varioloid, James waxed euphoric about the landscape and inhabitants; and by August, he felt that the "real enjoyment" of the trip at last had begun. His voluptuous letters suggest a sexual awakening, veiled, of course, as a naturalist's reverie. "I am tasting the sweets of these lovely forests here," he wrote exuberantly; those forests, he added, were "not as grand and tangled as those about Rio, but more soft and smiling and much more penetrable." Heady with thoughts of that softness and allure, he was "arouse[d] . . . and beg[a]n to feel as if there were a little of the human being left in me—Still in these ashes glow their wonted fires."[45] He decided to see out his full commitment to the expedition.

As he devoted himself to the project, he developed the kind of filial relationship with Agassiz that made both men comfortable: James needed a strong mentor to guide and praise him; Agassiz enjoyed paternalism. James saw that he could, indeed, learn much science, and Agassiz felt no inhibition about keeping his assistant focused on his tasks. "I am getting a pretty valuable training from the Professor, who pitches into me right and left and wakes me up to a great many of my imperfections," James wrote home. "This morning he said I was 'totally uneducated.' He has done me much good already, and will evidently do me more before I have got through with him."[46] Agassiz may have been bombastic, but he was a disciplined scientist who knew how to accomplish his goals. Clearly, he recognized James's brilliance, but he often felt exasperated by James's disorganized, unfocused, and often self-defeating behavior. "James," Agassiz warned him once, "some people perhaps consider you a bright young man; but when you are fifty years old, if they ever speak of you then, what they will say will be this: That James—oh, yes, I know him; he used to be a very bright young man!"[47]

Besides challenging him intellectually, the trip tested his physical resources. He discovered that faced with storms, capsizing canoes, and roaming tigers, he could act decisively and sensibly. But in one test of his manliness, he felt frustrated: he could not win the attentions of a native woman. At a dance given in honor of Agassiz's crew, he was attracted to the lovely young women with "splendid soft black hair," exuding "the most wildly melodious perfume." But he could not communicate his desire. "It is disgusting in the last degree to live in a country & feel yourself a foreigner, to be prevented by the trammels of a foreign tongue from giving vent to the thoughts that arise in your soul," he wrote to Alice.[48] The fair Jesuina was not the only object of his attention: there was also Alexandrina, Mrs. Agassiz's housemaid, whose portrait James sketched; women bathing, spied from afar; and one pretty girl in the village of Obidos with whom James claimed he was in love.[49]

His inability to communicate the "shades of emotion" that overcame him had more complex cause than merely lack of language. In a notebook in which he recorded his impressions of the trip, James described a spider monkey that became his "best friend." The monkey was so fond of him that whenever James came into sight he would jump on him, wrapping his arms, feet, and even tail around him. When James managed to tear himself away from the passionate embrace, the monkey would enact a tragic pantomime of utter rejection—until something came along to distract his attention. "This excessive mental mobility of monkeys, their utter inability to control their attention or their emotions, so that they are as completely possessed, by whatever feeling happens to be uppermost in them at the time" seemed to James pitiable. But as "creatures of impulse" they seemed "*interesting* in the young ladies [*sic*] sense of the word."[50] James, on the other hand, always on guard, always keeping his emotions under control, failed to attract the interest of young ladies.

In one ambiguous diary entry, however, he describes an encounter that may have yielded some measure of success: he came upon Agassiz entreating three handsome Brazilian women to allow themselves to be photographed. Agassiz believed they were "pure Indian" and wanted the photographs for scientific research. "Apparently refined and at all events not sluttish," James reported, "they consented to the utmost liberties being taken with them and two without much trouble were induced to strip and pose naked." How much James participated in taking "utmost liberties"—and even what those liberties were—we cannot know; yet when one of the group's Brazilian associates came in and observed the scene, he pointedly asked James if he had been sent from the Bureau of Anthropology.[51]

Cradled in his hammock each night under the stars, setting out before dawn in a canoe to collect fish, drinking Portuguese wine, dancing: for James, Brazil was a kind of paradise. In early December, anticipating his return home in just a few months, he was filled with conflicting emotions. As he sat writing by candlelight, wearing a shirt and linen trousers, breathing the perfumed air that wafted in through the open doors and windows, he hardly could imagine the New England winter—or his previous life. On the one hand, he claimed that he was tired of the monotony and isolation of the country and eager to return to his studies. But on the other hand, "the idea of the people swarming about as they do at home, killing themselves with thinking about things that have no connection with their merely external circumstances, studying themselves into fevers, going mad about religion, philosophy, love and sich, breathing perpetual heated gas and excitement, turning night into day, seems almost incredible and imaginary." He predicted that he would feel "many a pang of nostalgia for this placid Arcadia."[52]

Chapter 6

DESCENT

1866–1870

WHEN JAMES RETURNED to the cold, dark New England winter, he became once again, at the age of twenty-four, a student; once again, a son dependent on his parents. His Brazilian experience helped him arrive at two important conclusions about himself: first, although he was drawn to intellectual life, he believed that his lack of logic and his "mobile temperament" made it necessary for him to circumscribe his intellectual activities; second, he was convinced that there was something essentially troubling about his relationships with women.

Love seemed an unattainable goal. When Henry Sr. had tried to justify his decision to come back to America, he told Edmund Tweedy that his children wanted "friends among their own sex, and sweethearts in the other," and he added that he hoped they would all make early marriages.[1] William would be the first to test this possibility, but he hardly knew how to begin. His competitiveness and egotism had not impeded his friendships with men, but he had no experience in treating women in any way except with condescension.

William learned from his father—and found echoed in the culture at large—that women were at the same time intellectually inferior to men, but spiritually purer. "[I]n your intercourse with pure women study to do nothing and say nothing and feel nothing but what would elevate them in their own self respect and the respect of their kind," he once counseled Bob.[2] Marriage to a good woman allowed a man to reject his baser instincts and attach himself to "a more private, a more sacred and intimate self than that wherewith nature endows him."[3] Yet Henry's warning against lustful thoughts contradicted his own openly

flirtatious behavior and his lascivious interest in public scandals that
had any sexual component.

It seemed to William, moreover, that it was not Mary's purity and
sacred soul that Henry valued, but rather her limitless emotional support and unqualified praise. Writing from Bonn when his parents were
in Paris, William recalled a typical family scene: Alice would be reading a novel and nibbling fruit; his mother and Aunt Kate would be sitting in armchairs, "with their hands crossed in front of them, listening
to Father, who is walking up and down speaking of the superiority of
America to these countries, and how much better that we should go
home."[4] It did not matter, of course, what discourse engaged his father:
Mary and Kate would sit in silent approval. When Henry went to lecture, Mary always accompanied him, creating a flurry of excitement as
the two left the house, fluttering with praise when they returned.
Whenever Henry left the family on one or another rare excursion
alone, he was welcomed home with great sympathy for the trials he endured and the loneliness he felt. "[D]ear old good-for-nothing homesick papa," as Alice called him, needed his two wives and five children
to bolster his vulnerable ego.[5]

William understood from his parents' marriage that a wife necessarily gives up her independence and defers to her husband's needs.
Primary among those needs was a safe haven from the assaults of the
world. "In the outer world," William wrote,

> a man can only hold good his position by dint of reconquering it
> fresh every day: life is a struggle where success is only rela-
> tive ... ; where failure and humiliation, the exposure of weak-
> nesses, and the unmasking of pretence, are assured incidents; and
> he accordingly longs for one tranquil spot where he shall be valid
> absolutely and once for all; where, having been accepted, he is se-
> cure from further criticism, and where his good aspirations may
> be respected no less than if they were accomplished realities.[6]

William yearned for just such a refuge where he could strip off his mask
and be recognized "absolutely and once for all," where his weaknesses
would be tolerated, where a woman who cared for him would encourage his dreams, affirm his identity, and love him unconditionally.

During the first month that he was home, his cousins Kitty and
Minny Temple were staying with the Jameses, and William was pressed

into service as their escort to parties. "The consequences were a falling in love with every girl I met," he wrote to his friend Tom Ward.

Among the girls to whom he was attracted, none was so appealing, and so disturbing, as Minny Temple herself. Minny and her three sisters—Kitty, Ellen, and Henrietta—were wards of the Jameses' most loyal friends, Edmund and Mary (Temple) Tweedy, who took in the children when Mary's brother, Robert, and his wife, Catharine James (a sister of Henry Sr.) died within a few months of each other in 1854. In Newport, no family was as close to the Jameses as the Tweedys and the Temple children. The girls' older brother, William James Temple, who was killed in action in 1863, stood out as William's and Harry's favorite male cousin; Kitty was a comfortable companion, serious and sedate, who could sit at her sewing for hours while modeling for William and John La Farge. But Minny, by all accounts, was an extraordinary young woman with whom, Harry said, everyone was in love. Slender, dark-haired, graceful, and spirited she was refreshingly honest and unusually self-possessed. Other women in William's circle—the fastidious Theodora Sedgwick, for example, who also had taken art lessons with Hunt—seemed too exacting, earnest, or fussily sentimental: sentimentality, in William's estimation, was a quality not desirable in women, but irritatingly prevalent.

Minny had her own strong opinions and did not shrink from making them known. She had the courage to spar with Henry Sr., whose ideas she found depressing; had no patience with her younger cousin Alice, whom she found dreary; and did not deign to cultivate Mary's favor. Mary and Alice resented her, furthermore, for accepting their liberal hospitality when she so obviously disliked them.[7] Harry adored her. William was confused.

To Harry and Tom Perry, Minny was "a young and shining apparition," charming, vivacious, generous in spirit, and totally unconventional. She lived according to her own perceptions and sensations; William, on the other hand, had been taught to watch himself, to consider always what others—especially his father—would think, to deny his own feelings. In a gesture of solidarity with his family, he treated Minny with "unsympathetic hostility." But by the time he became reacquainted with her in Boston, he found that like his brother and many of his friends, he was enchanted by her.

Oliver Wendell Holmes Jr. and John Gray flirted with Minny, and it is likely that William did, too. But his flirtation consisted of light-hearted banter, the kind he had practiced for so long with his sister. Although Minny attracted him, he could no more communicate his feelings to her than he could to the Brazilian women who had aroused him. He felt buoyed by Minny's company, but frustrated by his own inhibitions.

There were other young women in Boston who interested him: Ellen Hooper, who later married Ephraim Whitman Gurney, a professor of history at Harvard; her sister Clover, who married Henry Adams; and especially Fanny Dixwell who, as James knew, was being courted by Holmes. Perhaps because he knew that Fanny was involved with another man, William was able to admit that he was attracted to her and to shower attention on her. Fanny "is about as fine as they make 'em," he told his brother Wilky. "She is A 1 if anyone ever was."[8]

Fanny, a cousin of William's medical school classmate Henry Pickering Bowditch, was a little more than a year older than William. The eldest daughter of one of Boston's most prominent families, she wore her pedigree with grace. Socially adept, Fanny knew when to sit demurely and when to discuss paintings and poetry. She herself aspired to be an artist, but since her eyes often troubled her, she doubted that she would realize her dream. Fanny had none of Minny's spontaneity, curiosity, or sharp intelligence—but she was winsome, and William felt unusually comfortable with her. With Holmes in Europe in the summer of 1866, he took to visiting, often. His pursuit was a source of amusement to Holmes's mother, who reported to her son that Fanny was getting "visits from Bill James, who appears to go there at any time from 9 o'clock in the morning—I told her to let me know how the flirtation got on—she says he is a person who likes to know his friends very well—I had a little fun with her, about him, & told her I should write to you about it."[9]

Fanny made a difficult summer bearable for James. Along with other medical students, he was working at the Massachusetts General Hospital; while his family vacationed in Swampscott, he lived in a rented room, visiting them on weekends. Still, he felt uncertain about his future in medicine and, just as important, about his own potential to do any significant work. He had come to the conclusion, he confessed to Tom Ward, "that each man's constitution limits him to a certain amount of emotion and action, and that, if he insists on going under a higher pressure than normal . . . he will pay for it."[10] James Jackson Putnam, a medical school classmate who frequently visited the James family, remembered James quieter and more withdrawn than he was in later years. Instead of coming to the medical school laboratory in Boston, James often would work alone in a laboratory he set up at home in Cambridge, where his family had moved. Self-regulation became James's personal prescription for health, but it proved a bitter draft. When Tom Ward, prey to debilitating mood swings, scoffed at James's apparent "animal contentment," James admitted that he was "less quiet than you suppose."[11]

In the fall, after Holmes returned and recaptured Fanny's attentions, William began to descend into an uncontrollable depression. His studies at medical school involved him in both dissections and dissimulation. Like his classmates, he was busy "toadying the physicians, asking them intelligent questions after lectures, offering to run errands for them &c," to court their favor for hospital appointments. Each student was supposed to call personally at the home of the professors and trustees. "So I have 16 visits to make," he reported to Alice. "I have little fears, with my talent for flattery & fawning, of a failure."[12]

But by spring, he knew he could not accept the appointment that he had managed to elicit by his charms. He was depressed, irritable, emotionally exhausted. He suffered from back pain and chronic gastric problems. He could not concentrate. He confided to his father that he had recurring thoughts of suicide. But outside of his parents and Harry, no one suspected his distress. When the Temple sisters visited in January and again in April, William apparently mustered his strength to persuade them that he was as vivacious as always.

To his other siblings, all of whom were facing difficulties in their own lives, he wrote letters of unwavering cheerfulness. Alice was in New York under the care of Dr. Charles Taylor, an orthopedic surgeon who treated women of delicate nervous dispositions with a combination of massage, exercise, and rest. Wilky and Bob were in Florida struggling— against their own inexperience, an unhappy financial partnership, and inhospitable Southern politics—to make a success of a cotton farm. They knew nothing about William's own struggles, but rather heard from him about friends, theater excursions, parties, and teas. He did not tell them—he would not tell anyone for months—that he was ill.

William feared that his breakdown bore out his father's conviction that studying medicine was a mistake. Philosophical science was the only choice Henry Sr. condoned; *applied* science was something to disdain. Yet when William considered withdrawing from medical school, giving up his training, and doing nothing but stay at home, the prospect was intolerable. Home, he said, "had become loathsome."

His description arose partly from his own dark vision of his life and prospects, partly from the depression and physical illness that pervaded the Quincy Street household from the fall of 1866 through the spring of the next year. Even Mary had been ill, though she shamed the malingering James men by continuing heavy housework "like a little buffalo." Harry suffered from the back pain and indigestion that would plague him throughout his life. William did not exaggerate when he explained to Alice that he refused an invitation to a party by pleading "domestic affliction."[13]

When William decided to quit Boston for Europe, the traditional Jamesian refuge in times of distress, Henry readily agreed. In Europe, William could study, read, perfect his knowledge of German, and, by the way, see that his father had been right all along. Mary, worried as usual about the expense of the trip, acquiesced only after William assured her that he would live "very quietly and economically."[14]

Philanthropy

ON TUESDAY, APRIL 16, James sailed, stealthily, for Europe. Because he swore his family to secrecy about this latest collapse, hardly anyone knew why he left. After his father blurted out the news of his imminent departure to Oliver Wendell Holmes Jr. one evening, William scribbled a hasty note cautioning Holmes "against telling any one I was going away yet. Father told you prematurely—I should prefer to have it 'come out,' like an engagement all of a sudden when everything is definitely settled."[15] William's curious comparison of leaving home and becoming engaged reveals an unspoken motivation for the trip: in Europe, away from the scrutiny of his family and overly curious friends, he might have the opportunity to pursue a woman who attracted him without fear of censure or failure. He might actually fall in love; a friendship might "ripen into familiarity," as he hopefully put it, and perhaps even lead to marriage.[16]

Sexual urges, he confessed to his friend Tom Ward, once compelled him "to escape from a mere physical nervousness" into an act that he later regretted—masturbation, perhaps, or possibly an experience with a prostitute. "The tho't of what *might* have been the result of it makes me shiver now," he added. "But I feel so to speak as if in that respect I had 'come of age' through the experience."[17] But mere satisfaction of sexual needs was not what James wanted during this trip.

Never as adventuresome a traveler as his brother Harry, William searched for safe places: he preferred small provincial cities to European capitals, and homey pensions run by grandmotherly women to any kind of hotel. If he had not intended to enroll in a German university, he might well have headed to Boulogne, of which he had fond memories. Instead, after a few days in Paris, he went to Dresden, "a decorous and dry little city," the Jameses' friend Charles Eliot Norton once commented, which had become "the 'residential abode' of a large colony of Americans, many of whom are of a sort whom one does not see at home, and does not wish to see abroad. . . . It has become little more than a not very brilliant satellite of Berlin."[18]

Life in Dresden did nothing to lift James's spirits. He spent the summer of 1867 in such "doleful dumps" that he tore up the few letters he managed to write to his friends, afraid of giving them "too unpleasant an impression" of his condition.[19] He was lonely and bored, trapped in a monotonous routine that he had no strength to alter: he took cocoa and an egg for breakfast, read until lunch, napped, and in the afternoons, he sat in his room and read. Through his window, he watched the sun set across the roofs and listened to the murmur of the city from the market nearby. Those hours, he said, recalled languid afternoons at his grandmother's house in Albany that made him feel that his life had stopped in eternal twilight: instead of solving his problems, he found himself obsessively returning to the same depressing thoughts. Each evening, after a light supper, he often took long, aimless walks, occasionally ending up at a terrace overlooking the Elbe, where, as respite from his trials, he drank enough beer to cause the "most delightful reveries."

Although he told his mother that he dreamed of home, it is more likely that these reveries featured the coquettish young women who attended a boarding school across the street from his pension. Sometimes, in the hours he spent in his room, he longingly peered at them through a telescope. Once, he caught sight of a particularly beautiful dark-haired woman, perhaps eighteen years old, sitting at a window. She stirred him so violently that, he confessed to his mother, "I begin to think my heart will not wither wholly away."[20] But the potential withering of his heart worried him. He dared not approach the object of his desire, and he wondered if he would ever meet a woman who would respond to him with the same intensity that he felt, time and again.

James's disclosure to his mother was not the intimate revelation it appears to be. With his arch tone and inflated description (the letter is peppered with exclamation points as James describes the "ravishing apparition" with her "mute-appealing, love-lorn look"), James transformed his experience into a farcical melodrama. At the same time, however, he knew that he would inspire his mother's consternation, irritating her at a safe distance. Mary was unduly worried about William's succumbing to a woman's temptation. She believed that he was inclined to become carried away with emotion and would fall in love too easily and not wisely. Without her intervention, he might make a dreadful mistake. William was not concerned with mistakes, but with an atrophied heart.

James's conviction of his own social awkwardness made him feel an affinity, he said, to the British, who "have the faculty of *blushing* which is denied to the French and comparatively to the Germans" and who seemed to him socially inhibited.[21] Nevertheless, he considered himself more urbane than most of the Americans he met, who, with their "hungry, restless look" behaved as if they were "unhooked somehow from the general framework."[22] Unfortunately, to many who knew him then, James could have been describing himself.

By midsummer, when his mental and physical health showed no improvement, James consulted a physician in Dresden who recommended the baths at Teplitz, some forty miles away, in what is now the Czech Republic. Early in August, James decided to try "the cure." Teplitz, the oldest spa in Bohemia, was more monotonous than Dresden, even though James arrived well into the "season," when the spa was at its most populated and its parks and promenades filled with a fashionably dressed, international clientele.

The water cure reflected the holistic medical theories in which most physicians believed: in a controlled, "hygienic" environment, the body's natural restorative powers would heal diseased organs. But a carefully regulated diet, fresh air, and mineral waters were not the only requirements for a cure. The patients themselves had considerable responsibility if they were to get well: they needed to commit themselves to a calm routine, free of distracting thoughts; they needed to focus their willpower entirely on good health.

The regimen's effect on James is uncertain, and, as his letters attest, probably irrelevant to his health. His willpower was focused on wrenching himself from his father's intellectual influence and on facing the consequences of that rupture; their relationship was a continuing distraction. At the same time that William wanted generous financial support from his father, he wanted independence. At the same time that he declared his opposition to his father's ideas, he longed for Henry's approval. "You live in such mental isolation," William wrote, "that I cannot help often feeling bitterly at the thought that you must see in even your own children strangers to what you consider the best part of yourself."[23] William's bitterness, however, was tempered with regret.

His contradictory motivations make William's Teplitz letters curious documents: he flatters Henry in one sentence and scores him in the next, blames himself for his lack of understanding and accuses Henry of obfuscation. But one thing is consistent throughout the Teplitz correspondence: William's anger toward Henry for denying the value of personal achievement and personal experience. His father's example and teachings undermined what he now saw as healthy, gregarious, productive life.

He rejected, viscerally and philosophically, his father's belief that true morality and spiritual integrity could be achieved only by self-abnegation and communion with God. Instead, he believed that "philanthropy"—human sympathy, companionship, and communion—offered a singular path toward personal salvation. "*Everything* we know and are is through men," William proclaimed to Tom Ward, in letters that elaborated on the themes he took up with his father. "We have no revelation but through man. Every sentiment that warms your gizzard, every brave act that ever made your pulse bound and your nostril open to a confident breath was a man's act. However mean a man may be, man is *the best we know*."[24]

Henry, of course, disagreed; and William decided to ignite, if not resolve, their conflict by attacking one of his father's articles, a recent essay on Swedenborg in the *North American Review*.[25] In choosing to take issue with a published work, William was aligning himself with his father's many other critics, men who did not hesitate to demolish the weaknesses in Henry's thinking. Attacking an essay, moreover, felt safer to William than jousting with his father in person. Where in conversation, Henry tended to recast and revise his assertions in an effort to deflect criticism, he could not so easily retract what he had polished for publication.

Henry argued, as he had so many times before, that selfhood was illusory and that spiritual fulfillment depended upon submerging one's consciousness in that of the Creator. But William, who saw himself as a pantheist at best and, at worst, an atheist attacked the idea of a unitary Creator. Unless he could acknowledge his own authority and identity, William believed he never would find a practical solution to the "moral business" that he had struggled with for so long.

Instead of clarifying his ideas, however, Henry responded by undermining William's authority: William could not understand him because he was still at a "puerile" intellectual stage. His "purely scientific cast" of thought made it impossible for him to think like a philosopher. "Ontological problems seem very idle to the ordinary scientific imagination," he wrote, "because it is stupefied by the giant superstition we call Nature." The scientist was trained to observe, the philosopher to reflect, he told William; if William would only take the time to reflect, he surely would come to the same conclusion as Henry: that Nature was a human construct, a hypothesis derived to give a sense of unity to disparate observations.[26] Reality lay only in God.

William refused to come to that conclusion. "[W]e ourselves must be our own providence," he wrote to his father.[27] Friendship first, work second, he decided, would yield "all the Good and True and High and Dear" that humankind could achieve. "[It] seems to me," he told Tom Ward, "that a sympathy with men as such, and a desire to contribute to the weal of a species, which, whatever may be said of it, contains All that we acknowledge as good, may very well form an external interest sufficient to keep one's moral pot boiling in a very lively manner to a good old age."[28]

If William seemed decisive and strong in letters to friends, however, he insisted on portraying himself to his father as troubled and dispirited—partly to justify the expenses of his trip, partly to elicit

Henry's sympathy. Although William's decision to go to Berlin rather than take an "after cure" at another spa suggests improvement in his health, soon after he arrived in Berlin, he sent a confidential letter to his father reporting that he was no better. His back still caused much pain, especially after any social interaction; his stomach still caused distress; and his spirits were as low as they ever had been. Just as in the spring, "the pistol the dagger and the bowl began to usurp an unduly large part of my attention."[29]

Letters to friends contradict his suicidal confession. In the first weeks after his arrival in Berlin, he claimed that the city was exciting, with an attractive, intelligent population. He planned to take courses at the university, had a comfortable room near the school, and was feeling "like a new man." By December, though, his tone changed; it was harder than he had expected to enact the "philanthropy" that he believed was so essential for his life. Despite the arrival of Tom Perry, who was rooming with him, he yearned for companions. His friendship with a young woman remained only that; and, to aggravate his loneliness, he received from his sister "the longest list of engagements and weddings" from among their Boston circle. "[A]ll the world seems to be getting married," Alice announced. All the world, that is, except for her twenty-five-year-old brother.

"Berlin is a bleak and unfriendly place," William wrote to Henry Bowditch. It was difficult to make connections with the "rude and graceless" Berliners because "you have to make all the advances yourself; and your antagonist shifts so between friendliness and a drill sergeant's formal politeness that you never know exactly on what footing you stand with him." His studies proved as unsatisfying as his social life because of his slow progress in reading German.

He envied Bowditch who, he imagined, was "rolling on like a great growing snowball through the vast fields of medical knowledge and are fairly out of the long tunnel of low spirits that leads there by this time." He knew that a medical career was over for him; he knew that he could not teach science because he felt physically unable to do laboratory work; the most exciting prospect he could imagine, he told Bowditch, was writing for a medical journal—of course, he admitted, "I hate writing as I do the foul fiend."

If only he could find a job, something that would give him enough money "to keep body and soul together for some years to come" and required him to do nothing but read, he imagined that he would be reasonably content. He wondered if Bowditch would be interested in a partnership: "you to run around and attend to the patients while I will stay at home and, read[ing] every thing imaginable in Eng[lish], Germ[an], & French, distil it in a concentrated form into your mind."[30]

While he waited for inspiration about a new career path, he turned to reviewing, a logical outgrowth of his voracious and wide-ranging reading. In 1865, he had published two unsigned reviews in Charles Eliot Norton's *North American Review:* one on Thomas Huxley's *Lectures on the Elements of Comparative Anatomy,* another on "The Origin of Human Races," an essay by Alfred Wallace. He told Norton that he would be pleased to review other books on biology. But when he again took up reviewing in Germany, he did not want to limit his scope to science. He knew that Harry was earning money by publishing stories regularly in the *Atlantic* and the *Nation,* and it seemed to William that writing might be a possible career for him, too. After laboring with great effort over a review of Herman Grimm's *Unüberwindliche Mächte,* William sent it to Harry for editing and, if he deemed it worthy, forwarding to the *Nation.*

"I liked your article very much & was delighted to find you attempting something of the kind," Harry replied. "It struck me as neither dull nor flat, but very readable." He sent it on to the *Nation,* where it was published at the end of November. Grimm's novel was a bildungsroman about an aristocrat who realizes that he cannot live on his family's past glory, but must shape and assert his own identity. Surely William found the theme appealing, and although he pronounced the book "somewhat slow and tame," he wrote a warm review. Despite his protestations that writing was so difficult for him, Harry's praise helped inspire William to continue with his new role as literary critic.

Always his closest companion within the family, Harry, in the months following William's return from Brazil, grew to become a trusted friend. William could count on his sincere compassion, not compromised by his own demands. He shared William's opinions of the family atmosphere and understood his need for privacy. William's suffering caused Harry to believe that the two were close in temperament, and his letters to William in Germany underscore that affinity. At the same time that Harry expressed his sympathy for his brother's feelings, he made clear that he, too, was not well. Like William, he was "not fit for anything—for either work or play." He believed that he could recover if he were able to "strike a happy medium between reading &c, & 'social relaxation,'" but there were few opportunities for such relaxation in dull, wintry New England. "I haven't a creature to talk to," he complained.

Harry, who loved Europe far more than William ever had, envied his brother's stay in Germany. When William tried to minimize the importance of being abroad, Harry protested: "Don't try to make out that America & Germany are identical & that it is as good to be here as there. It can't be done." First of all, the James family (who, Harry reported, were "as usual—whatever that may be called") were not in Germany. And their home was as loathsome as it had been when William left. "Life here in Cambridge—or in this house, at least," Harry confessed, "is about as lively as the inner sepulchre."[31]

William sensed as much from his mother. Wilky was back from Florida, where he and Bob had attempted to become cotton farmers. After their crops had failed from too much rain and an infestation of caterpillars, Bob simply gave up; now Wilky was afraid that he could not run the business without his brother. Ill with malarial fever, Wilky was weak, gaunt, and depressed. Bob had come back as well, but he caused such discord in the family that they could not wait to see him leave. "He is perfectly wretched at home," Mary told William, "and makes us all very uncomfortable."[32]

William had no intention of returning to Cambridge before he achieved some important changes in his life. But as autumn turned to winter, he felt that he was not making any progress. Christmas, celebrated among his acquaintances with a sentimentality that he could not share, depressed him. The darkening days depressed him. His solitude depressed him. "The ghosts of the past all start from their unquiet graves and keep dancing a senseless whirligig around me," he wrote to Oliver Wendell Holmes. He could not read, he could not study. He decided to try, again, a cure at Teplitz.

Emotions of a Loving Kind

BY THE TIME HE left Berlin, James had come to the unhappy conclusion that he would never share an intimate relationship with any human being. "I have grown into the belief," he wrote to Holmes, "that friendship (including the highest half of that which between the two sexes is united under the single name of Love) is about the highest joy of earth and that a man's rank in the general scale is well indicated by his capacity for it."[33] His own rank, he believed, was shamefully low.

If he were inherently cut off from romantic or sexual passion, still he might discover "a constructive passion of some kind," such as Holmes had found in the law. But not since the early days in Hunt's studio had James experienced the kind of "artistic satisfaction" that he now sought and that he imagined Holmes felt. "[T]he limits of my own mind," he confessed, "conspire to give my thoughts a vague emptiness wherever feeling is, and to drive feeling out wherever the thought becomes good for anything."[34] Depression had so dulled his emotions that James hardly could feel anything, much less intellectual excitement. Yet despite his apathy and enervation, he plodded forward in his plans for a career.

Those plans centered on the possibility of studying physiology with the intention of applying his discoveries, however insignificant he thought they would be, to the new science of psychology—not a surprising choice, given his continued brooding about his own personality. But since he believed that he could not work in a laboratory because of his "bad memory and slack interest in the details"—not to mention his weak back—he could not conceive of how he would translate his interest into a career.[35] He might become a professor of "moral philosophy," but, he wrote to Holmes, "I have no idea how such things are attainable, nor if they are attainable at all to men of a non-spiritualistic mould." How could a man who believed that God might well be dead or, James said, "at least irrelevant," claim any moral influence on American youth, even those in some unheralded, rural college?[36]

As he fought against recurring depression in the spring of 1868, he clung to the idea that work might redeem him. If he led an active life, distracted from the longing that so often beset him, he might make some lasting contribution to humanity and to defining his own sense of self. As he told Tom Ward, his only hope in dark times was that he would make a "*nick,* however small a one, in the raw stuff the race has got to shape, and so assert my reality."[37] His ambiguous final phrase implies that he hoped, simply, that other human beings would recognize his own existence; but a similar passage in a letter to his brother

Bob complicates James's meaning. Referring to their "in various ways dilapidated family," James insisted that he and Bob need not give up their hopes of sloughing off an unfortunate emotional legacy: "the world is as young now as it was when the gospel was first preached," he wrote. "And our lives, if we will make them so," he wrote to Bob, "are as real as the lives of anyone who ever lived." Existence and reality, for James, were not equivalent. His own existence, characterized by despondency and apathy, did not feel like real life. Only in struggling, striving, and willing would he feel truly alive.

Teplitz, he believed, was the first step on the road to productivity. If he wanted to enroll in physiology courses in the summer semester at Heidelberg, which was his immediate goal, he needed to become stronger.

In Heidelberg, he would study with Hermann von Helmholtz, the most important physiologist in Europe, and his former student Wilhelm Wundt, whose *Contribution to a Theory of Sensory Perception* and *Lectures on the Mind of Man and Animals* recently had been published. In Helmholtz and especially in Wundt, who was reputedly more accessible, James believed that he would find energizing mentors who would help him to transcend the antiquated training he had received at the Harvard Medical School where anecdotal experience had as much, or more, weight in the training of physicians as laboratory results. James recognized that new scientific discoveries would change the practice of medicine radically. He hoped to be part of that change: "it is a misfortune," he wrote, "for a medical man to be born at this period of chaos and transition, to live in an age half-way between the comparative clearness of ignorance and the transparency of true wisdom, in waters, as it were, which are just beginning to precipitate their contents."

In reviewing a report on the state of physiology in France, James argued that a physician, "if he have any ambition . . . must start with an education which (literary or not) must be as thoroughly physical as that of the engineer and miner"; physiology was destined to become "the light in which medicine is to work." More than chemistry, anatomy, or zoology, physiology aimed "to control and change the phenomena" of which living organisms were composed, not merely to identify and classify them. Understanding the physiology of the process of nutrition might lead to preventative or curative intervention; understanding the physiology of sensation might lead to intervention in diseases of the mind, or at least to furthering the understanding of the relationship between mind and body, which, during James's season of despair—and long after—was of central interest to him.[38]

Three weeks into his monthlong cure at Teplitz, James received a "beloved letter" from his mother, begging him to come home and allow her to nurse him back to health. If Teplitz did not work last summer, why did he think it would have any efficacy now? Perhaps it would not, but home, at that moment, was not an alternative. Although James admitted that he felt worse than before he arrived in Teplitz, he insisted that the regression was "a good sign and the normal result of the weakening effect of the baths."[39] He expected to feel appreciably better as soon as the cure was over.

But he continued to decline. There was nothing to do, he decided, but to take another cure—hoping fervently for success. This time, feeling a small improvement, James decided to go again to Dresden, rather than return to Berlin. He again stayed at the pension of the grandmotherly Frau Spangenberg, where, in May, he met Catherine Havens, a twenty-nine-year-old music teacher from New York, who, like James, was in Europe for physical and emotional resuscitation. The two were thrown into each other's company—they were the only boarders at the time—and James found that he enjoyed their afternoon rides, their long talks on the garden steps, and Catherine's evening piano recitals.

By the end of May, James was entirely miserable: Catherine's talent and pursuit of a career served as an affront to him. Complicating those feelings of self-deprecation was his dawning sense of Catherine's attraction to him. He was confused about his own feelings: Did he love her? Could he respond to her love? Was a self-proclaimed neurasthenic the only possible lover he could attract? One evening, while listening to Catherine play, he experienced "a sort of crisis. The intuition of something here in a measure absolute gave me such unspeakable disgust for the dead drifting of my own life for some time past," he wrote in his diary.[40]

A few days later—just about the time that Catherine left Dresden—the crisis became more acute. He felt powerless to control his life, and as Kate Havens drifted away, his frustration was palpable. What was the use of loving, he asked in his diary, if "one cannot expect to gain exclusive possession of the loved person." He might feel "mere delight as often as the lovable quality is displayed—but no pretention to earn a sort of right over it so that it may be produced for our benefit as often as we will it." If he did pretend that his presence might inspire the "lovable quality . . . and circumstances snub it, the reaction is painful." To protect himself from that pain, he needed to keep his feelings in check, to feel only what was "proportionate" to the reaction that he could expect from the woman.

His brief flirtation with Catherine sent him into a philosophical spin about emotional alliances. Love and friendship, it seemed to him, were "egotistical passions" that depended upon loyalty and a desire for continuity. But love was more dangerous because it involved something else besides: a desire on the part of the lover to possess the beloved—"without so much regard to those qualities that make it worth possessing"—and a desire on the part of the beloved to be possessed.[41] Unless both parties craved love equally, unless both parties invented enduring reasons for mutual esteem, someone would be hurt; James had no doubt that he would be the victim. To protect himself, he must limit his feelings "to the *particular* moment," rather than behave as if those feelings would continue into the future. With enough self-control, he would be safe.

After Kate left Dresden, William corresponded with her, anticipating another meeting. He had recovered somewhat from the overpowering feelings that she had aroused; now he was afraid of sinking "ever deeper into the drifting slough of indifference," a kind of emotional anesthesia that he saw as a symptom of his incapacity for love.[42] By the time they had been apart for several months, he convinced himself that he could not risk a romantic relationship; he warned Kate that the man she thought she knew was not the real William James. He had presented to Kate the "model of calm cheerfulness and heroism" that had become his public self, and he wanted to assure her that he was not that brave hero, but "a much meaner being": "feeble, egotistical, cowardly, hollow."[43] She could not count on him to be her lover.

Key-note

BY THE FALL, William had not improved sufficiently to warrant his continued stay in Europe. His plans to study in Heidelberg had come to nothing, and his flight from spa to spa—he tried a French cure at Divonne, to no avail—did not impress his benefactors. "I am sure I have something better to tell you than you will be able to learn from all Germany—at least all scientific Germany," his father had written the year before.[44] Now, he insisted that William come home for his health and edification. On November 7, William boarded the *Ville de Paris*. "This vagabond life," he finally admitted, "is not the thing for me."[45]

He quickly discovered that life at home was not the thing, either. The inner sepulchre, as Harry had characterized 20 Quincy Street, had turned into an infirmary, where William became the third patient. Harry was suffering from back pain, constipation, and low spirits; Alice only recently had begun to recover from a severe breakdown that had afflicted her throughout much of the previous year.

As Alice later described her collapse, she shared many symptoms with William: she was overcome with violent, tempestuous, uncontrollable feelings that included thoughts of self-destruction; she became so enraged at her father that she wanted not merely to reject his ideas, but to murder him; and she felt imprisoned by her "moral" temperament. For Alice, the "moral business" of her life was to be good, to exert unwavering self-control at every moment:

> Conceive of never being without the sense that if you let yourself go for a moment your mechanism will fall into pie and that at some given moment you must abandon it all, let the dykes break and the flood sweep in, acknowledging yourself abjectly impotent before the immutable laws. When all one's moral and natural stock in trade is a temperament forbidding the abandonment of an inch or the relaxation of a muscle, 'tis a never-ending fight.[46]

Her breakdown made Alice the center of watchful attention in the family. Unlike Mary and Aunt Kate, whose emotional stability was the envy of the James men, Alice had proven herself as delicate as her two eldest brothers and as deserving of special privileges. One of those privileges was the right to insult her parents. When Henry Sr. tried to dissuade Alice from going to Newport without him, for example, she told William and Mary "that her main wish in going was to get rid of him & Mother"; William was amused at her retort: "I was very glad to find her understanding so clearly her position," he told Harry. "She has seemed very well indeed since you left."[47]

Harry, aiming at his own round of cures at Malvern, England, and the art galleries of Italy, sailed for Europe within four months of

William's arrival home. He, like William, sent back detailed health bulletins—Harry's focused largely on his impacted bowels and weak back; unlike William, he used his year abroad to stake out his future.

William's back, the barometer of his emotional state, continued to be unpredictable, and he tried various treatments, including blistering and electrical shocks, to effect some positive change. Rest, of course, was a critical component in his regimen, and, at the same time, provided a welcome excuse to keep him from studying too hard for his medical exams. Now that he had rejected the possibility of ever practicing, however, he was free to claim that medicine seemed fascinating. "On the whole," he wrote to Tom Ward, "it seems to me there is no occupation on earth from which men of very different temperament and gifts can get more life & growth of character and wisdom than this."[48]

In June, when at last he earned his degree, James became a member of what he acknowledged was "an important profession." But the achievement had little impact on the volatility of his emotional life. He was left, he said, with "a good deal of intellectual hunger" that he did not know how to satisfy.[49] Still, he believed that he had not found a way to reconcile his essential nature with his contribution to humanity. First, of course, he needed to define that essential nature, a daunting task. In moments of relative strength, he saw himself as willful and powerful, someone who could stand up to intellectual challenges and plunge exuberantly into his experiences; but in darker times, he saw himself as a "morbid" personality who brooded over his weaknesses and could draw upon only limited stores of energy. Until he understood who he was and what he was capable of, he could not make sense of "the moral business" that his father had taught him was the crucial task of his life.

For the next few years James suffered cycles of buoyant hope and desolation. In the summer after graduating from medical school, he vacationed with his parents and Alice in Pomfret, Connecticut, where he seemed to his vigilant mother improved over his condition in the spring. Mary was not as sympathetic to her eldest son as she was to Harry. While she had scrutinized every dollar that William spent during his European trip, she urged her "dear reasonable over-conscientious" Harry to "[t]ake the fullest liberty and enjoyment your tastes and inclinations crave, and we will promise heartily to foot the bill."[50] What William needed, she believed, was just the opposite: not

self-indulgence, but regular habits of moderate exercise and benign diversion. Summer in Pomfret seemed to prove her correct.

The Bootts—Francis, a widower, and his daughter Lizzie—were
visiting the Jameses. Lizzie, who drew, painted, and sang, provided
just the distraction, Mary said ("the artistic atmosphere that . . . suits
Will exactly"), to inspire William to take up his old role as "the life of
the party." "Lizzy is such a simple unconscious creature, with such an
entire absence of coquetry about her," Mary reported to Harry, "that
there is no danger I think of her exciting any personal fascination over
him."[51]

Even if William had been attracted to Lizzie, he would have had
trouble courting her in the presence of his attentive family. When
Mary shifted her attention from Alice, who was discussing Harry's stories with William's friend John Gray, she watched William and Lizzie
lounging on the grass under the trees and listened as they talked about
"a wide range of subjects—art, languages and literature. What a striking instance she is," Mary reported to Harry, "of what a careful and
thorough education can accomplish."[52]

Mary was contrasting Lizzie to Minny Temple, whose restlessness,
impracticality, and flightiness inspired Mary's derision; but she could
just as well have been contrasting the thoroughly accomplished Lizzie
with her own daughter, who never had the privilege of a careful and
thorough education, who had no outlet for whatever talents she might
possess, and whose social life included a sewing bee, an occasional
evening at the theater, and the lifting cure, or therapeutic gymnastics.

If Alice James, at twenty-one, was on her way to becoming another
first-class spinster, Minny Temple, who found the very idea of marriage
depressing, never would live to achieve that status. "T'were well you
spake not of the 'deposit' in Mary Temple's lungs to anyone," William
wrote to Wendell Holmes. "Some people have a morbid modesty
about letting such things be known to any one."[53] Minny was not considered morbidly modest; but certainly James believed in the protective power of secrecy, and he tried to protect the dying Minny. As she
faced the annihilation that he had imagined for himself, she engaged
William in religious doubts and worries that centered on the validity
of her uncle Henry's ideas and her capacity for faith. William, who was
in the midst of reading his father's works, could have found no more
receptive audience for his own many concerns. But Minny proved to be

more than an intimate correspondent: she served as a living example of all that William was not and hoped to be: emotionally honest and fearlessly pagan.

William saw Minny during the summer of 1869, in the fall at her sister Ellen's wedding, and in mid-November when she visited the Jameses in Cambridge. Each time she was more ill than before, each time he felt more affection for her. Still believing himself incapable of becoming anyone's lover, he did not try to analyze his feelings for Minny; he would never have to act on them. Instead, he took on a more comfortable and practiced role: mentor, a role that, for James, contained a decidedly romantic, if not erotic, aura.

After Minny left the Jameses in November, William wrote to Tom Ward asking him to send an English translation of Wilhelm von Humboldt's *Letters to a Female Friend* to Minny, at his expense. The book he had promised to Minny was a collection of letters written by Humboldt, an eighteenth-century Prussian statesman, philosopher, and philologist, to Charlotte Diede, a woman he had met at a spa when they were both in their early twenties and never saw again. But the friendship that they began at the spa endured a long separation; thirty years later, at Charlotte's initiative, they became intimate correspondents.

Humboldt was one among many German authors—Kant, Schiller, Goethe, Herder—who captured James's imagination. "These men were all interesting as *men*," he wrote to Harry, "each standing as a type or representative of a certain way of taking life."[54] James identified with these writers who seemed, like him, to be struggling to overcome a tendency toward inhibiting intellectualization. Schiller once commented to his friend Humboldt "that the principal cause which prevents your success as an author is the predominance of the reasoning over the creative faculties of your mind, whence arises the preventive influence of criticism over invention, which is always destructive of mental production."[55] James assessed his own shortcomings in just the same way.

Besides teaching James "a certain way of taking life," Humboldt's letters to Charlotte suggested a manly role—teacher and guide—that James would assume in his relationship with many women throughout his life. He hoped that his talent for epistolary preaching would inspire Minny to echo Charlotte's feelings that his letters, like Humboldt's,

offered "an inexhaustible source [of] . . . strength and courage. . . . I
needed no other nourishment for my mind," she confessed to Humboldt, "no other book for my instruction, no clearer light for my soul."[56]

Humboldt was a widower with several grown children when he
began writing to Charlotte; he had had a successful career as a diplomat; his *Aesthetic Essays on Goethe's "Hermann and Dorothea"* had earned
him praise as a literary critic; his papers on the relationship of language
to thought and identity had given him an international reputation as a
philosopher of language; he was working on a massive study, *The Diversity of Human Language-Structure and Its Influence on the Mental Development of Mankind,* that would be published a year after his death. But
it was not his erudition that drew Charlotte to seek his guidance, but
his moral strength and his ability to shore up her spirits.

As much as William wished to be Minny's spiritual guide, he was
not so sure he merited her respect. Although he described her with a
tinge of condescension, William had no doubt of Minny's considerable
strengths. "She is after all a most honest little phenomenon," he wrote to
Harry, "and there is a true respectability in the courage with which she
keeps 'true to her own instincts'—I mean it has a certain religious side
with her. Moreover she is more devoid of 'meanness,' of anything petty
in her character than any one I know, perhaps either male or female."[57]
Minny's "moral spontaneity" was the very quality to which he aspired.

William, unfortunately, felt that he shared his sister's "moral temperament," a hidden repulsiveness that necessitated constant watchfulness.[58] This use of the term "moral" to describe personality was not
peculiar to the James family, but they did give it their own special emphasis. "Moral," as used by nineteenth-century physicians in diagnosis
of mental illness, referred to one's public conduct. Socially acceptable
behavior resulted from self-control or willpower; moral insanity occurred "as soon as the will has lost its influence on the actions of the
feelings."[59] If these feelings were pure and admirable, they required less
self-control, of course, than if they were bestial, shameful, and odious.

Insanity, in nineteenth-century medicine, meant unhealthiness of
any kind, not specifically mental illness or, in its most extreme form,
madness. William called his back pain "dorsal insanity." Moral insanity ranged from mildly antisocial behavior to criminality. Behavior
diagnosed as "moral alienation" included forgetting business appointments and using "lewd language before females, and oaths as exple-

tives in ordinary conversation."[60] Even minimal moral insanity could make one a difficult companion.

When Mary James evaluated William's improvement by his sociability, she applied criteria that were widely shared by physicians—and laymen—at the time. In mental hospitals, morally insane patients were said to be improving, for example, when they conducted themselves decorously in public spaces of the hospital and participated, with some measure of enthusiasm, in social activities.

Within the James family, though, moral health had more stringent requirements than public performance. Certainly willpower was an important component of the "moral business," but "will and moral and intellectual power" were distinct.[61] Willpower, as William explained it to Tom Ward, enabled him to take decisive action on his own behalf: if he found no spiritual sustenance in the idea of God, for example, he could will himself to "make the enjoyment of our brothers stand us in the stead of a final cause" and will himself to "lead a life so active, and so sustained by a clean conscience as not to need to fret much."[62]

Moral power, on the other hand, was a quality that, at the time, William believed to be inherent and unalterable. An individual's moral quality emerged from the deepest sources of personality, the hidden self. Minny's moral temperament—pure, honest, spontaneous—did not require concealment; she could allow her emotions to burst forth unchecked because they would not disgust or offend. But both her cousins Alice and William feared the quality of their moral temperaments. Only through a fierce exertion of willpower could they succeed in hiding what they could not bear to reveal.

Minny's moral spontaneity was an affront to William's own pretenses. Long after Minny had died, he said that he wished she could have known him as he was later, when he had found, after a painful search, qualities of his personality that he believed had been hidden during the time he knew her.

On her part, Minny felt that she knew James more deeply than he thought possible. William, she said, was "a rare creature, and one in whom my *intellect* . . . takes more solid satisfaction than in almost anybody—"[63] He was "one of the very few people in the world that I love—'& no mistake.' He has the largest heart as well as the largest head—and is thoroughly interesting to me—And he is generous & affectionate & full of sympathy & *humanity*."[64]

William's thoughts on religion became the central theme of their correspondence in the winter of 1869–70, when Minny found herself, during sleepless nights, questioning her faith in Christianity. Was Henry Sr. right, she wondered, in his notion that Christ should persuade us not of our innate goodness, but rather of our inherent impurity? When William asked her if she felt "separated from God," as he did, she replied that she did not; yet she knew that religious rituals did not interest her, and that she performed such acts "with weariness & grudgingly."

At one point during the months they corresponded, Minny had a "momentary vision of Redemption from thinking & striving, of a happy Rest this side of Eternity" by giving herself up to Henry Sr.'s idea of negation of selfhood in favor of communion with God. But she could not sustain that vision—"it does n't stay—and so back swings the universe to the old place—Paganism—natural Religion, or whatever you call the belief whose watch word is 'God and our own Soul'—And who shall say there is not comfort in it—One at least feels that here one breathes one's native air—welcome back the old *human* feeling, with its beautiful pride, and its striving—its despair, its mystery, and its faith."[65] What was a liberation for Minny was oppression for William. When the universe swung back to pantheism, paganism, atheism, he felt unmoored and terrified.

"If I had lived before Christ," she confessed to him, "Music would have come like a divine voice to tell me to be true to my whole nature—to stick to my key-note & have faith that my life would, in some way or other, if faithfully lived, swell the entire. . .harmony. This is a grander music than the music of the spheres—Of course the question will always remain, What is one's true life—& we must each try & solve it for ourselves."[66]

As William tried to solve just that question, to find his keynote, he again fell into a depression as black as any he had yet experienced. His back pain spread upward into his neck and arms; he tried galvanism, but the electric shocks did nothing to alleviate the intense pain. To help him sleep, he tried the hypnotic drug chloral, but took so much that his eyelids became inflamed. At the same time that he was collapsing, he never relinquished his role as Minny's adviser, urging her at one point "to behave like a man & a gentleman" if she wanted "to outwit fate."[67]

William could not act on his own advice. All he could count on in his joyless, lonely existence was his own will, which offered only limited consolation:

I may not study, make, or enjoy—but I can will. I can find some real life in the mere respect for other forms of life as they pass, even if I can never embrace them as a whole or incorporate them with myself. Nature & life have unfitted me for any affectionate relations with other individuals—it is well to know the limits of one's individual faculties, in order not to accept intellectually the verdict of one's personal feeling & experience as the measure of objective fact—but to brood over them with feeling is "morbid."[68]

Yet brood he did, matching Minny's physical decline with his emotional descent. In mid-January, he suffered a "great dorsal collapse"; on the first of February, he "about touched bottom." He had to make a choice, and make it at that very moment, he believed, about whether he would "throw the moral business overboard, as one unsuited to my innate aptitudes, or . . . follow it, and it alone, making everything else merely stuff for it."*

---

*There has been considerable interest about whether, at this time, James checked himself into the McLean Hospital, a mental asylum then located in Somerville, Massachusetts, close to James's home. Although later, after its move to a beautiful campus in Belmont, it became a refuge for the wealthy and celebrated (the poets Robert Lowell and Sylvia Plath were among its famous patients), McLean's in the 1870s treated men and women from all walks of life, including domestic servants, students, farmers, sailors, and clerks, as well as lawyers and businessmen. In a recent article, Alfred Kazin writes that the Harvard psychologist Henry A. Murray "revealed to me at one point in his life James had put himself into McLean's" ("William James: To Be Born Again," *Princeton University Library Chronicle* 54 [Winter–Spring 1993]: 248). Psychiatrist Ruth Tiffany Barnhouse, who did her residency at McLean's in the 1950s, told me that she, too, had seen records that James had been a patient at McLean's several times for treatment of depression. This observation was confirmed for her by William Herbert Sheldon, also on the staff of McLean's. Sheldon had personal interest in James because he was his godson; he later became the founder of the much-debated "Constitutional medicine," arguing that by examining a person's posture and physique one could assess temperament and intelligence. His theories led to the taking of nude "posture photographs" of undergraduates at prestigious New England colleges, a practice that continued from the 1940s through the 1960s. Sheldon suggested that he saw records of one hospitalization, did not cite the date, but said that James was a patient in midwinter. The question is: which midwinter, and, furthermore, was Sheldon confusing our James with his son, also William, who also suffered bouts of depression and could have been a patient at McLean's early in the century.

In *Manhood at Harvard* (New York: Norton, 1996), Kim Townsend quotes a letter from Henry Sr. to Harry, written after meeting Horatio Alger in the spring of 1870. "Alger talks freely about his own late insanity—which he in fact appears to enjoy as a subject of conversation and in which I believe he has somewhat interested William, who has talked with him a

Whatever inspired William's crisis—and his relationship with Minny is implicated—he responded immediately by committing himself to his father's mandate for successful living. Giving up the moral business would mean, after all, giving up the search for authenticity that had been crucial to his existence for more than a decade. He decided that he had never given the moral business a fair chance, only "as an aid in the accomplishing of certain utilitarian ends of attaining certain difficult but salutary habits. . . . But in all this I was cultivating the moral interest only as a means & more or less humbugging my self. Now I must regard these useful ends only as occasions for my moral life to become active."[69]

Hardly the epiphany that James wanted to experience, his commitment to the moral interest served, at least, as an antidote to his claim that willpower alone could sustain his life. But the path, he discovered, was pitted and strewn with emotional debris. And within a few weeks, he touched bottom once again.

Minny died on March 8. In his diary, William drew the outline of a headstone, on which he wrote her initials; March 9, the date he

---

good deal about his experience at the Somerville Asylum" (43n.). The ambiguous "his" makes it difficult to know if Alger talked about his own experience, or James of *his* experiences. "Experience," furthermore, for James, might have been visits to McLean's for the purpose of research, which would have been consistent with visits to mental asylums elsewhere, or visits to a friend who may have been a patient.

On the other hand, there are gaps in James's correspondence during two winters of his depression: from January 27, 1870, until March 4, 1870, and from December 29, 1870, until April 8, 1871, which could be explained by a stay at McLean's, or just as well by depression so profound that he could not write to his friends. McLean's allowed me to examine patient intake logs from 1866–72, the period when I thought it was most likely James would have sought help there. To protect the privacy of patients, names were deleted from the record log, but other information—date of admission, age, sex, occupation, diagnosis, and residence, were available to me. I found nothing that correlated with the facts of James's life during that period. I did discover, however, that in the 1870s there were a few prevalent diagnoses for mental illness among men of James's age: overwork and anxiety, heredity, and masturbation. Any or all of these complaints may have concerned James at the time.

I relegate this discussion to a footnote because I believe that whether or not James checked himself into McLean's is a minor point in his biography. Psychoanalysis and psychotherapy did not exist as we know them today. James would have been offered bromides to help relieve his anxiety and help him to sleep; he might have been offered electrical therapy to stimulate his nerves and allay depression. The primary service that McLean's would have provided was separation from his family and therefore from the context that exacerbated his symptoms. Even if we had his patient records, other records that I saw merely documented symptoms and noted prescribed medication. They offered no explanation about cause and only the most perfunctory notes of conversations between patient and physician. The best sources for understanding James still are his own writings about his mental state at the time.

learned of her death; and a cross. The stark drawing reflects his grief and loss far more than the effusive eulogy he wrote two weeks later, containing advice for Minny on how to behave in the afterlife. Only one line rings true: "Acts & examples stay," he wrote. Minny would haunt him forever.

Chapter 7

ABSOLUTE BEGINNINGS

1870–1874

IN 1901, WHEN HE was fifty-nine, James looked back at the two psychological perspectives available to him in the last decades of the nineteenth century as he searched resolutely for a way to understand his own personality. The first was what he called "classical" psychology, which, James said, considered "the human mind . . . largely an abstraction. Its normal adult traits were recognized. A sort of sunlit terrace was exhibited on which it took its exercise. But where that terrace stopped, the mind stopped; and there was nothing farther left to tell of in this kind of philosophy but the brain and the other physical facts of nature on the one hand, and the absolute metaphysical ground of the universe on the other."[1]

Classical psychology had been countered by "romantic improvers," whose inquiries resulted in a darker and thornier landscape. Instead of focusing on the normal adult mind, these psychologists were interested in pathology. They found their subjects in mental hospitals, prisons, even among children who did not, after all, behave in the reasoned and self-controlled manner of sane adults. These subjects promised to yield new secrets about the workings of the mind—even of a mind such as James's, which he suspected was not pathological, yet still contained elements that did not display themselves on any sunlit terrace.

Works by classical psychologists and romantic improvers, as well as by philosophers, self-proclaimed mystics, and popular self-help writers, dominated James's reading in the 1870s. These texts, he hoped, might offer consolation, guidance, and insights about his own feelings of fragility, about his fear of being overtaken by a madness that seemed, always, to lurk at the threshold of his consciousness. In a small back room in Quincy Street, with its two green chairs and, as Harry put it, "their old, not especially cheerful associations," James, unemployed and unattached, sat, day after day, and read.[2]

If sometimes he felt enlightened, more often he became dissatisfied and frustrated. John Stuart Mill and Alexander Bain, James's intellectual godfathers at the time, helped him to sustain a belief in the significance of willpower, but they also convinced him of the immutability of the moral temperament. James could will himself to control his feelings, his ideas, his actions—but he could not essentially change the person he was, a person subject to recurring, debilitating depressions. Although James occasionally could rouse himself to celebrations of the will, his sporadic proclamations did not lead to any decisive change in his daily life.

One evening—his depressions worsened with the waning light—James went into his dressing room to retrieve something when suddenly, "without any warning, just as if it came out of the darkness," he was overtaken, he said, with "a horrible fear of my own existence."

> Simultaneously there arose in my mind the image of an epileptic patient whom I had seen in the asylum, a black-haired youth with greenish skin, entirely idiotic, who used to sit all day on one of the benches, or rather shelves against the wall, with his knees drawn up against his chin, and the coarse gray undershirt, which was his only garment, drawn over them inclosing his entire figure. He sat there like a sort of sculptured Egyptian cat or Peruvian mummy, moving nothing but his black eyes and looking absolutely nonhuman. This image and my fear entered into a species of combination with each other. *That shape am I,* I felt, potentially.

He had no way to protect himself against transforming into the idiotic youth, he thought, and "became a mass of quivering fear."

"The lunatic's visions of horror are all drawn from the material of daily fact," he concluded.[3] But his own selection from "daily fact" reflected deep anxiety: The mental patient James recalled was notable because he suffered not from the common pathology of moral insanity (alcoholism and excessive masturbation, for example) but from epilepsy, which, although often misdiagnosed and misunderstood, could not be cured by strengthening a patient's will. An epileptic patient was at the mercy of his own biology.

The epileptic that James conjured, however, was an extreme case: "entirely idiotic," not someone who merely experienced seizures, but a young man who had withdrawn from the human community. William's fear was generated from his feeling of identification with this pathetic young man; he believed that he would become a monster, "absolutely non-human," bestial. But it was not simply the hallucination that generated such horror, but the *combination* of perceiving the hallucination and giving way to fear. There was a moment, he implied, when he could have made a choice not to feel fear but instead to believe that he possessed enough strength to defend himself against encroaching madness.

James resolved to tell no one, especially not his mother, about what had occurred. He claimed that he did not want to disturb her complacency; he also did not want her complacency to trivialize his momentous experience. If he would suffer, at least he would maintain his psychological and emotional independence from someone who could not understand what had happened to him.

The experience precipitated a period of dread: he hated being alone, especially going out alone at night, and he awoke each morning "with a sense of the insecurity of life that I never knew before, and that I have never felt since. It was like a revelation; and although the immediate feelings passed away, the experience has made me sympathetic with the morbid feelings of others ever since."

James's panic attack begs for comparison, of course, with the "vastation" that his father experienced in Windsor when William was a toddler. Because we do not know when James's attack occurred, we cannot know whether he already had read any version of his father's testimony—which was first published in 1879—or if he had heard Henry's story as he was growing up. Certainly there are inescapable parallels between the testimonies of James and his father: Both attacks occurred suddenly at a moment of apparent calm. Central to both experiences was a crouching, motionless, yet threatening figure. Both attacks rendered the victims immobile, generated long depression, and seemed to have some religious connection.

But William's version has a stronger psychological veracity: he presented himself as depressed to begin with, not hopeful, cheerful, and vigorous as Henry Sr. claimed to have been—a claim that his son later recognized was false. In Henry's version, some powerful "influences fatal to life" had "ray[ed] out from [the figure's] fetid personality," and threatened to annihilate him. William, reflecting changes in psychological theory since 1844, understood the figure to emanate from the workings of his own mind.

One crucial difference lies in the effects of the attack on each man: Henry's fear and trembling led him to discover Swedenborg, a discovery that changed his perspective forever. William, on the other hand, attests to a religious epiphany that seems gratuitous. Describing the fateful evening in *The Varieties of Religious Experience,* James claimed that the attack had "a religious bearing . . . I mean that the fear was so invasive and powerful that if I had not clung to scripture-texts like 'The eternal God is my refuge,' etc. 'Come unto me, all ye that labor and are heavy-laden,' etc., 'I am the resurrection and the life,' etc., I think I should have grown really insane." James footnoted this reflection on the "religious bearing" to refer readers to his father's confession of his "vastation" in *Society the Redeemed Form of Man.*[4]

The religious connection that William ascribed to the experience, however, seems only to justify including the anecdote in a volume about religious experiences. There is nothing in James's correspondence or journal entries for the period in which the attack occurred to reveal any religious conversion or epiphany; on the contrary, he insists on his inability to participate in religious ritual and doubts the existence of God. "It seems to me," he wrote to Harry, "that all a man has to depend on in this world, is in the last resort, mere brute power of resistance."[5]

Yet on April 30, 1870, he suddenly decided that resistance might not be all he could rely upon and entered in his diary a statement that appeared to signal an enormous change:

> I think that yesterday was a crisis in my life. I finished the first part of Renouvier's 2nd Essay, and saw no reason why his definition of free will—sustaining of a thought *because I choose to* when I might have other thoughts—need be the definition of an illusion. At any rate I will assume for the present—until next year—that it is no illusion. My first act of free will shall be to believe in free will.

Belief in free will was no less than an act of faith. After all, he had been persuaded by Bain that will can never be free, but rather constrained by an individual's personality and social context. James had defined will as energetic determination leading toward productive activity that would result in coming "into *real* relations" with people.[6]

Inspired by Charles Renouvier, however, his thoughts about willpower had a different focus:

> For the remainder of the year, I will abstain from the mere speculation & contemplative Grübelei in which my nature takes most delight, and voluntarily cultivate the feeling of moral freedom, by reading books favorable to it, as well as by acting. After the first of January, my callow skin being somewhat fledged, I may perhaps return to metaphysics study & skepticism without danger to my power of action.[7]

For the next eight months, he vowed to cultivate a new habit: a sense of moral freedom—like Minny Temple's "moral spontaneity"— an abdication of the watchfulness and self-criticism in which he formerly engaged. He would will himself to refrain from brooding upon the defects of his personality, even though he enjoyed it so thoroughly, and make sure that he read nothing that would compromise his new direction.

Renouvier offered James something more than the British positivists: "The knowable universe is for him, as for the school of Mill and Bain," James wrote, "a system of phenomena, and metaphysic is an analysis or inventory of the elements. But among these elements he finds the *possibility,* which British empiricism denies, of absolute beginnings, or, in other words, of free-will."[8] Absolute beginnings, for James, meant that he was not bound to a self inherited from his parents, determined by his physiology, or prescribed by society; he could create and define a new and potentially liberating self.

> For the present then, remember:
> Care little for speculation
> Much for the *form* of my action
> Recollect that only when habits of order are formed
> can we advance to really interesting fields of
> action. . . . Not in maxims, not in Anschauungen,
> but in accumulated *acts* of thought lies Salvation.

James decided that directing his will to the formation of new patterns of thinking was more important than merely willing himself to productivity. New intellectual habits necessarily would lead to new acts; but forming those habits—most significantly, self-reliance and self-confidence—was a crucial first step.

Hitherto, when I have felt like taking a free initiative, like daring
to act originally, without carefully waiting for the contemplation
of the external world to determine all for me, suicide seemed the
most manly form to put my daring into; Now, I will go a step
further with my will, not only act with it, but believe as well; believe in my individual reality and creative power. My belief to be
sure *can't* be optimistic—but I will posit life, (the real, the good)
in the self governing *resistance* of the ego to the world.[9]

James's cautionary chorus certainly included his parents; one wonders, in fact, who else had the ability to make him feel that suicide was
the only original act he could perform. But by "external world," James
also meant the larger template of social, intellectual, and religious beliefs that he felt he could not resist. Rebellion, however polite, required
a sense of daring that only practice, and the application of willpower,
might develop.

Although Renouvier caused no immediate revolution in James's life
and although James's belief in free will would be tested repeatedly for
many years to come, his "crisis" of 1870 marked a significant change in
the way he imagined his future. Not long before, he had earnestly
praised Robert Browning's elegy to an unheralded scholar, "A Grammarian's Funeral," because it seemed to capture the spirit of his own
life. The Grammarian, ignored by his own society, might be recognized
for his contributions only generations after his death. "It always
strengthens my backbone to read it," he admitted, "and I think the
feeling it expresses of throwing upon eternity the responsibility of making good your one-sidedness somehow or other . . . is a gallant one, and
fit to be trusted if one-sided activity is in itself at all respectable."[10] But
with the help of Renouvier, he saw that he might not be condemned to
live an obscure life circumscribed by self-inflicted limitations. He
might be able to rally his forces, assert his own reality, and thrust himself into a tumultuous, competitive arena of ideas. Now another sentiment from Browning seemed more apposite: "When the fight begins
within himself/" Browning declared, "A Man's worth something."[11]

A Solid Job

DESPITE HIS COMMITMENT to act and to assert his own individual reality,
James, in the early 1870s, was a person to whom things happened. Some
of those things were propitious. One of them was teaching at Harvard.

In the fall of 1868, Harvard's president Thomas Hill resigned and was replaced temporarily by Andrew Preston Peabody, a Unitarian minister and Harvard's Plummer Professor of Christian Morals. For eight months, the university's Board of Overseers searched for a new leader from among its ranks and without, finally settling on thirty-five-year-old Charles William Eliot, who had taught James chemistry at the Lawrence Scientific School and in 1869 was teaching at the Massachusetts Institute of Technology. Harvard's choice of Eliot, although unconventional, was at the same time cautious. As a scientist, Eliot was interested more in curriculum development than in groundbreaking research, an orientation that was important if Harvard were to offer a science program attractive to new generations of students. Although he was not a clergyman, which disappointed some on the Board of Overseers, who worried over students' morals, he was deeply entrenched in the values of Yankee Unitarianism. "Eliot was the non-pareil schoolmaster to his age,—an age that worshiped the schoolmaster and clung to him," one alumnus recalled. He was devoted less to science, art, and literature than to right living. He was genteel and articulate, but "regarded cultivation somewhat as Michael Angelo regarded the painting of the Venetian school,—as a thing fit for women. Life was greater than culture. No ideals except ideals of conduct had reality for him."[12]

James was among many who were surprised by the announcement of Eliot's appointment. "C. W. Eliot was confirmed President yesterday," he wrote to Henry Bowditch. "His great personal defects—tactlessness—meddlesomeness—and disposition to cherish petty grudges seem pretty universally acknowledged; but his ideas seem good and his economic powers first rate,—so in the absence of any other possible candidate, he went in. It seems queer that such a place should go begging for candidates."[13] But the appointment would prove to be fortuitous for James.

Eliot, intimately familiar with the science resources at Harvard, was determined to improve the quality of instruction and facilities. Among his former students, he had been impressed with the energetic Henry Pickering Bowditch who, at the time of Eliot's appointment, was studying physiology in Europe. As fellow medical students, Bowditch and James faced the same choice: whether to practice as physicians, ensuring their financial security, or to pursue further training to become research scientists without any certainty about opportunities for work in America, where physiological research was stalled by the efforts of zealous anti-vivisectionists.

Although James had assumed that Bowditch would become a physician, Bowditch was attracted to the opportunities for research that beckoned from Europe. After earning his medical degree in 1868, he went to Paris, hoping to study physiology and neurology. When James met him there during his own European sojourn, he found Bowditch discouraged about the poor laboratory facilities and desultory instruction. But unlike James, Bowditch did not allow initial discouragement to dash his hopes; he decided to go on to Germany, reputedly the best center for research in the world.

James witnessed Bowditch's progress with a mixture of pleasure and envy. "I was truly glad to hear of your determination to stick to physiology," he wrote to Bowditch. "However discouraging the work of each day may seem, stick at it long enough, and you'll wake up some morning—a physiologist—just as a man who takes a daily drink finds himself unexpectedly a drunkard."[14] Bowditch was fortunate enough to find a place in the Leipzig laboratory of the renowned researcher Carl Ludwig, where he became not just a physiologist, but an impressively trained and respected researcher.

Unlike James, Bowditch enjoyed the rigors of laboratory work. Among Bowditch's achievements in Leipzig was his invention of "a little apparatus . . . attached to a metronome for the purpose of marking time on a revolving cylinder covered with smoked paper." This device, significant for standardizing the results of physiological experiments, met with admiration from Bowditch's German colleagues; his reputation as an innovator soon made its way to Cambridge. If anyone could lead Harvard into a new era of scientific education, Eliot believed, his former student Henry Bowditch was the man.

In December, Eliot asked Bowditch to return to Cambridge to deliver a series of lectures on physiology. Bowditch, however, decided that his efforts would be more amply rewarded in Germany and turned down the offer. But the tenacious Eliot persisted: a year later, he offered Bowditch an assistant professorship of physiology at the Harvard Medical School and the opportunity to reform the medical curriculum. This time, Bowditch agreed to come home.

When Bowditch arrived in Cambridge in 1871, he seemed older, more confident, and more settled than James expected. Now thirty-one, he had recently married a young woman he met in Leipzig. Surely he still had the same "sagacious eyes" that James remembered, the same pointed beard that gave him a gnomelike appearance, the same sly sense of humor. But he no longer shared James's indecisiveness and doubts; he was ready to take a powerful position in a field that he found creative and satisfying.

Physiology, Bowditch argued, must be the central subject for medical students. While his predecessors—most notably Oliver Wendell Holmes Sr. and Henry Jacob Bigelow—believed that anatomy could be taught from lectures and texts, Bowditch agreed with Eliot that students needed to work in laboratories. "The University recognizes the natural and physical sciences as indispensable branches of education," Eliot proclaimed in his inaugural address, ". . . but it would have science taught in a rational way, objects and instruments at hand—not from books merely . . . but by the seeing eye and the informing fingers."[15] Unfortunately, the medical school lacked adequate space in which to set up such a laboratory. While Bowditch had brought the latest new equipment back from Germany, there was no place to house it except in two attic rooms of the dingy old brick medical school building on North Grove Street in Boston, near the morgue, the jail, and the Massachusetts General Hospital. Nevertheless, with a table, a sink, and a tub for frogs in one room, and instrument cases and books in the other, Bowditch and his students set to work.

Despite his professional responsibilities and his marriage, Bowditch renewed his warm friendship with James. During the 1871–72 academic year, Bowditch welcomed James into his laboratory and his home, sharing with James his responses to recent works on physiology. As much as he respected James's sharp intelligence, he, like other accomplished friends, no doubt was mystified by James's inability or unwillingness to pursue a career. It seems likely that Bowditch was trying to give James's life some positive direction when, in the summer of 1872, Bowditch asked James if he would take a vacant course on anatomy. All that was needed, he assured James, was Eliot's approval. Eliot, who remembered James as a student, voiced no objection, and in August, James was offered his first professional job.

The offer interrupted a bout of the "philosophical hypochondria" in which James so ardently indulged. He could read not more than four hours a day, he said, and "fits of languor" gave way to periods of "nervousness, wakefulness, uneasiness." He recognized immediately the salutary effect of having a paying job. "The appointment to teach physiology is a perfect godsend to me just now," he wrote to Harry, "[providing an] external motive to work, which yet does not strain me—a dealing with men instead of my own mind, & a diversion from . . . introspective studies."[16]

As much as he looked forward to teaching in the spring semester, however, he refused to consider the appointment as the first step in a teaching career; nor did he give up his commitment, announced during his Brazilian trip, to devote himself to philosophy. Instead, he was content to "keep up a small daily pegging at my Physiology" in preparation for the temporary course: he spent his time reading, sitting in on Bowditch's fall semester lectures, and working in Harvard's laboratory.

This activity caused a noticeable improvement in his spirits. Yet the prospect of teaching, within his grasp as a possible career, generated misgivings over the path he abandoned in 1861. "I have regretted extremely letting my drawing die out," he confessed to Harry. "I have been of late so sickened & skeptical of philosophic activity as to regret much that I did not stick to painting, and to envy those like you to whom the aesthetic relations of things were the real world."

In part, his skepticism about philosophy seems to have been inspired by pressure he felt to come forth with "fearfully knowing discriminations" when he talked with such men as Chauncey Wright, Charles Peirce, and, no doubt, his father.[17] This lack of confidence in his own authority generated anxiety about his ability to succeed as a teacher. He was, however, pleasantly surprised.

Even by his own high standards, he performed successfully in the classroom: performing, after all, was one of his most impressive skills. While he complained that he could not excite some of his dull students, he managed to engage the attention of many others. "So far," he reported to Harry, "I seem to have succeeded in interesting them . . . and I hear expressions of satisfaction on their part." Teaching was stimulating for James, as well: "I should think it not unpleasant as a permanent thing," he admitted. "The authority is at first rather flattering to one."[18]

Within the academic community he felt useful, competent, talented. He boasted to his mother that he believed "he had the power of interesting his class, and felt himself increasing pleasure in exercising

it." Cambridge gossip rang with praise for his "delightful" and "splendid" job.[19] Mary, relieved at William's productivity, although skeptical
about his endurance, conceded that "with his fresh and lively way of
looking at things," William seemed a natural teacher.[20]

Henry Sr., however, was not about to correlate the rise in his son's
spirits with his engagement in teaching or any other profession. He
held back from commenting on William's new buoyancy until, one afternoon, James burst out, "Bless my soul, what a difference between
me as I am now and as I was last spring at this time!" The outburst
gave Henry Sr. permission to ask what, according to William, had
caused the change; Henry admitted, however, that he posed the question with a good deal of trepidation because he was afraid of "interfering with" or "possibly checking" William's good spirits. This hesitancy
suggests that William responded uncomfortably during such conversations, interpreting his father's questions as threats to his authority and
as invitations to assert those "fearfully knowing discriminations" of
which he felt uncertain.

Surely the topic of a profession still generated tension in the James
household, and William was not about to concede that his new emotional health resulted from a job. Instead, he told his father that he ascribed the change to reading Renouvier and Wordsworth, and to
"having given up the notion that all mental disorder requires to have a
physical basis." Henry, delighted, interpreted the answer as evidence
that William was "shaking off his respect for men of mere science as
such."[21]

But William felt more ambivalence than he revealed to his father.
He noted in his diary his decision "to stick to biology for a profession
in case I am not called to a chair of philosophy, rather than to try to
make the same amount of money by literary work, while carrying on
more *general* or philosophic study. Philosophy I will nevertheless regard as my vocation and never let slip a chance to do a stroke at it," as
long as those strokes were made in the privacy of his Quincy Street
quarters.[22] Yet at the same time that he professed his unwavering commitment to philosophy, his reading of Bain, Herbert Spencer, Shadworth Hodgson, and Wilhelm Wundt reveals that he had decided also
"to fight it out on the line of mental science," which seemed to him a
fertile intellectual field that merged scientific research, anecdotal data,
analysis, and philosophical reflection.

He was increasingly impatient with physiologists, anatomists, or biologists who merely collected facts and presented them as significant contributions. "Our complaint," he wrote in a review of a textbook on mental physiology, "is, in one word, that a fact too often plays the part of a *sop* for the mind in studying these sciences. A man may take very short views, registering one fact after another, as one walks on stepping-stones, and never lose the conceit of his 'scientific' function, or reflect that he is only . . . a brick-maker, and not an architect." If one would understand the workings of the mind, as James hoped to do, the natural sciences seemed inferior to philosophy "in producing a certain quality of mental texture."[23] Yet philosophy that ignored science seemed equally deficient. And philosophy as a profession seemed as frightening a prospect as art.

When Eliot offered James the chance of teaching both physiology and anatomy for the next academic year, he accepted reluctantly, believing that he may have condemned himself to "clinging to those subjects for the next ten or twelve years, if I linger so long." Yet the decision seemed "the wiser, if the tamer" than "the other and nobler lot in life," which was to work at philosophy independently, as his father had done.[24] Philosophy, he thought, "as a *business* is not normal for most men, and not for me. To be responsible for a complete conception of things is beyond my strength." The natural sciences, on the other hand, offered a "stable reality" of facts that he would not have to criticize, question, or otherwise grapple with in his daily work.

James had seen, from his one semester of teaching, that daily responsibility positively affected his moods, his energy, his self-esteem. The natural sciences were real, tangible, respected, not a reality that he had to invent for himself and defend as a means of livelihood. He preferred to earn a salary—even so modest as six hundred dollars a year—and to enjoy the considerable psychological benefits of teaching. "It has turned out a solider job than I anticipated," he said. "I have done enough now to show me that the duty of teaching comes kindly to me, and that I probably should become a good instructor with practice."[25]

Dead Civilization

DESPITE HIS INITIAL enthusiasm for teaching, despite his commitment to Eliot to continue in the fall of 1873, James dipped into a familiar depression after his course ended. He decided that the improvement in his health was not so dramatic as he had claimed, and he wondered if he should continue at Harvard. While teaching was "of great moral service," it also proved exhausting. Tired, but unable to sleep, he feared that another year of teaching—with even more students, now that his course had gained popularity—would be intolerable. Perhaps the summer might revive his spirits; if not, he warned Eliot that he might have to back out of the job that awaited him. As usual, he planned to leave the country and join Harry in Italy.

James might have been as fatigued as any new instructor after the tension of a first semester of teaching, but his interpretation of this fatigue as his latest collapse reflects a recurring pattern of behavior: As long as an activity could be perceived as an experiment—such as studying art with William Hunt, assisting Louis Agassiz, or even beginning work at the Lawrence Scientific School—James entered into it with great enthusiasm. But as soon as persistence could be interpreted as commitment, he found an excuse to retreat. James could not reject what his father had taught him so long and so well: whatever work he chose would erode the core of his identity. Work would make him a new, a different, a compromised man. Work was a terrifying risk.

Naturally, his father was sympathetic to his retreats, but this time James was reluctant to ask his parents for money to finance his travel; he did not want to add to their financial worries, newly inspired by Wilky and Bob, neither of whom was on firm financial footing. After their Florida farming enterprise failed, the two brothers found jobs with the railroads in Milwaukee. But Mary and Henry, who saw their younger sons as unreliable and weak willed, were concerned that this new career path might not prove any more successful than the last. As William made his plans to travel to Europe, Bob, who had married in the fall of 1872, was expecting his first child; Wilky was engaged, hoping to marry as soon as he could earn enough to support a wife.

William was aware that his parents anticipated offering more financial help to their younger sons: "in Wilk's and Bob's present condition I have no right to ask father for a cent," he wrote to Harry. Instead, he proposed to find a student who wanted to travel to Europe with James as his tutor. "This," he wrote to Harry, ". . . wd. deprive me of the ever recurring strain and fever of lecturing and the great fret of pressing against and always overstepping my working powers which during the past 6 months has so unstrung me." He could also study, preparing himself for the vague future that he envisioned in the line of mental science.

His only worry, he confessed, was "excessive loneliness & ennui." In Cambridge, he had various social distractions to keep him from "being shut up face to face with ones [*sic*] impotence to do anything." But in Europe—even with Harry's company—if his reading and walking were constrained by ill health, what would he do?[26]

Harry reassured him and urged him to come. But as late as mid-July, William still wavered: "such a step wd. be about equivalent to desperation of any continuous professional development, and wd. leave my future quite adrift again." He regretted his "parasitic life" at home, but he was incapable of rallying his efforts to resume teaching.[27]

He spent July and August traveling, without his family, to several resort areas: Magnolia, on the north shore of Massachusetts; the Isle of Shoals, off the coast of Maine; the Catskill Mountains in New York. Resting, socializing with some attractive young women, and sailing had a tonic effect. But when he returned home at the end of August, any thoughts of resuming his position were undermined by his parents. His mother feared that teaching was simply too much of a strain for him: "He seemed to have gained a great deal by his summer relaxation," Mary told Harry, "but since coming home, after doing two or three hours study, he says his head gives out and all the strength goes out of his legs."[28] His father, predictably, came to the conclusion that William's newly chosen profession was at the root of his troubles and advised that he resign immediately. William was not sure. He felt "much tougher," he told Harry, but at home, where philosophical hypochondria was a way of life, he lost his resolve.

Aunt Kate, always an accomplice to the wishes of her sister and brother-in-law, came up with a thousand dollars to finance the trip. William booked passage on the *Spain*, bound for Liverpool. "[F]or a year I am adrift again & free," he announced anxiously to Harry. "I feel the solemnity of the moment, & that I *must* get well now or give up."[29]

In the context of yet another expedition in search of health, the idea of freedom lost the luster that it had when promoted by Renouvier. To be free, at the moment for James, meant to be bereft of a community that affirmed his identity as an intelligent, capable, responsible adult. No one flattered his ego, no one praised his competence, no one cared whether he existed or not. "I feel as if I might die to night and

London not feel it," he sighed in despair just days after he arrived.[30] In embracing freedom, James incurred a crucial loss.

By the time he joined Harry in Florence early in November, he regretted all that he had left behind. He had made a mistake in believing that Europe would restore him to health; Europe, he quickly realized, had nothing to offer him. Florence was "strangely small and dusky," he informed his mother. "The human race here has a debilitated look, undergrown and malformed esp[ecially] the women, so that it is hard to believe it to be the great italian people whom Taine and Stendhal &c bully us with."[31] He might also have added his brother Harry, although Harry was not given to exhibitions of bullying. Still, Harry's love for Italy was so well-known among the James circle that one friend predicted the two brothers might have a serious falling out over the relative merits of Florence and Rome.[32] If their companionship was strained, however, only part of the cause was William's vociferous scorn of Italy.

More troubling to William was his brother's literary productivity and financial success: Harry, by this time, was fully self-supporting as a writer, earning, he claimed, some three thousand dollars a year. "To write a series of good little tales I deem ample work for a lifetime," Harry wrote to a friend. "I dream that my lifetime shall have done it. It's at least a relief to have arranged one's lifetime."[33] Certainly arranging his own future would have been a relief to William, and his suppressed envy emerged in sly aspersions of Harry's character. When William divulged to his family that Harry had become "an utter slave" to "spirituous liquors," on which he squandered much of his earnings, William was diagnosing in Harry the family's most despised form of debauchery—alcoholism—and attacking the fiscal responsibility for which Harry always had been praised.

When the two arrived in Rome, they could not find adequate housing and decided to live separately—William at a hotel, Harry in lodgings he had occupied during his last visit. Their stay was cut short, however, when William suffered a feverish attack, which he diagnosed as a mild form of malaria; believing Florence to be a better climate for recovery, the brothers traveled north once again—much to the regret of Harry, who wished he could have stayed longer, and to the relief of William, who was oppressed by the preponderance of Roman churches. In Florence, Harry, in turn, became ill, succumbing to "a bilious attack complicated with a very severe rheumatic stiff neck" and a persistent and severe headache of apparently inexplicable cause.[34] Their consecutive collapses made William feel renewed affection for his brother, whose emotional responses so mirrored his own; he was glad that he was on the spot to nurse him. But as soon as Harry recovered, William made plans to leave. He first headed to Dresden, where he knew he would find the Tweedys. Then, he went home.

He explained his new resolution to his family, via a letter addressed to Alice:

> I begin to feel . . . strongly that at my time of life, with such a set of desultory years behind, what a man most wants is to be settled and concentrated, to cultivate a patch of ground which may be humble but still is his own. Here all this dead civilization crowding in upon one's consciousness forces the mind open again even as the knife the unwilling oyster—and what my mind wants most now is practical tasks, not the mere theoretical digestion of additional masses of what to me are raw and disconnected empirical materials.[35]

When James left Europe at the end of February, he had no practical tasks in mind. He would arrive home too late to teach in the spring and was not certain that he would have—or that he would accept—a job for the next academic year. But America—or, at least, the hallucination of America that had driven the family home from Europe in 1860—is where he wanted to be; only in America, he believed, would he find his future.

A Creative Dignity

AS HE ACCOMPANIED Harry through Florence and Rome, William burst out, more than once, "Oh, if this were only a real vacation after a long stretch of work—not a simple prolongation of the effort to get well—how much more I should enjoy it!"[36] His resolve to work, however, evaporated as soon as he entered the atmosphere of 20 Quincy Street. Once again, William began to complain, confiding in his parents every slight moderation of his physical and emotional state. His mother, decidedly, was no longer interested. "He keeps his good looks but whenever he speaks of himself says he is no better," she wrote to Harry. "This I cannot believe to be the true state of the case, but his temperament is a morbidly hopeless one, and with this he has to contend all the time, as well as with his physical disability."[37]

Insistently morbid within the confines of his home, nevertheless he was energetic and exuberant elsewhere. Anticipating a return to teaching in the fall, he began again to work in Henry Bowditch's laboratory, and he resumed reading and writing reviews for the *Nation* and the *Atlantic Monthly*. The books he read—manuals of mental hygiene and studies of mental physiology—confirm his renewed determination to become an authority in the field of mental science.

For James, this field had wide boundaries. If the dry accumulation of statistics held little interest for him, he was more than ready to follow less conventional paths to understanding the mind and discovering hidden layers of consciousness. One of those paths was spiritualism, which had titillated public interest for some twenty-five years, since a celebrated case of ghost rapping, involving the testimony of two young girls in upstate New York, began no less than a rage for psychic phenomena.

During the next decades, while a credulous public flocked eagerly to séances and other so-called manifestations of the occult, respected scientists in America and Europe—including the British physicist Michael Faraday, American chemist Robert Hare, and renowned naturalist Alfred Russel Wallace—conducted investigations to try to verify, disprove, or explain apparently supernatural phenomena. Their findings, however, were disappointingly inconclusive.

James was among many intellectuals who would not dismiss the possibility that experiences of the paranormal might yield psychological or philosophical insights. In 1869, he reviewed *Planchette: or the Despair of Science,* a compendium of anecdotal accounts of psychic experiences, for the *Boston Daily Advertiser.* At once captivated and irritated by the book, he complained that it included no reports of systematic, controlled experiments, but merely personal evidence. Yet he was fascinated by the possibility that he, too, might experience a realm in which "pianos float, 'soft warm hands' bud forth from vacant space, and lead pencils write alone."[38]

In search of such an experience, he decided to conduct his own investigations in spiritualism. There was no lack of opportunity: demonstrations of mesmerism, mediums, and the newly popular table turning abounded in the Boston area. James had heard about a table turner, a woman who was said to raise a piano by psychic force; James thought she would offer as suitable a beginning as anything else. He discovered, much to his disappointment, that she was a fraud: instead of having strong psychic powers, she had an unusually powerful knee. But he was hardly discouraged. "If I go on investigating," he wrote to Kate Havens, with whom he still corresponded, "I shall make *anyhow* an important discovery: either that there exists a force of some sort not dreamed of in our philosophy, (whether it be spirits or not)—*or,* that human testimony, voluminous in quantity, and from the most respectable sources, is but a revelation of universal human imbecility. I hate to settle down into this last conviction," he confessed, "and so would like to give the thing more of a trial than I have done yet."[39]

James saw no contradiction between his investigations into spiritualism and his work at the Museum of Comparative Zoology, of which he became the acting head in the fall of 1874 after the sudden death of Jeffries Wyman; or his membership in the Harvard Natural History Society, which he joined in December 1874. To scientific men such as James, psychic phenomena were no less "real" than invisible natural forces—gravity or electricity, for example—and no less worthy of intellectual inquiry.

Besides spiritualism, James was interested in the effects of mind-altering drugs and the possibilities of such chemicals to open new understanding of personality. He tried many such chemicals on himself, including chloral, amyl nitrite, and hashish, with varying success, if success be measured by insights gained. Sometimes his doses made him ill for days.

In 1874, he received from one Benjamin Paul Blood a pamphlet entitled *The Anaesthetic Revelation,* which seemed to James worthy enough to merit a review in the *Atlantic Monthly.* Blood was a forty-year-old self-proclaimed philosopher—"an idle, indifferent and amateur fraud," as he described himself—who lived in Amsterdam, New York, and had heard Henry Sr. lecture many years before.[40] With only a small readership for the essays and letters to editors that he published locally, he made a practice of widening his audience by sending his writings to "literary men." Since James had no literary reputation at the time, it seems likely that Blood sent the piece to Henry Sr. or even Harry, then the most notable literary man of the James family. In any case, as soon as William read it, he took it up with enthusiasm.

Blood claimed that after breathing nitrous oxide gas and other anesthetics, he experienced a kind of epiphany *"in which the genius of being is revealed."* He suggested that others must have experienced the same kind of revelation, but since the moment of transition from anesthesia to full consciousness was so transitory, the impact of the experience was lost. James conceded that Blood's idea would be considered "crack-brained" by many readers, but he urged an open mind. "Ontological emotion, however stumbled on, has something authoritative for the individual who feels it," he cautioned. "But the worst of all mystical or simple personal knowledge is its incommunicability." Intuition cannot be defended, he said; only the "intellect, with its classifications and roundabout substitutions, must after all be clung to as the only organ of agreement between men."

Yet clinging to the intellect often meant rejecting alternative views of reality. He preferred instead to try to interpret Blood's experience within a larger context of psychology and philosophy. As much as the idea of chemically induced revelation interested him, one element made him doubt Blood's apprehension of some hidden knowledge. "What blunts the mind and weakens the will is no full channel for truth," he concluded, "even if it assists us to a view of a certain aspect of it; and mysticism *versus* mysticism, the faith that comes of willing, the intoxication of moral volition, has a million times better credentials."[41]

James had discovered, in "the faith that comes of willing," a creative dignity that was no less than exhilarating. In the fall of 1874, he resumed teaching at Harvard. This time, instead of sharing a course with Thomas Dwight, he took over Natural History 3 (Comparative Anatomy and Physiology) by himself. His social life was filled with Sedgwicks, Gurneys, Emersons, Lowells, and Longfellows—all friends of the James family—supplemented with his own circle of friends: the acerbic Chauncey Wright, his medical school colleagues Henry Bowditch and James Jackson Putnam, his colleagues in the Natural History Society, and the participants of a men's dinner club, who seemed to him lacking in "the irresponsible confidingness of boyhood" that, at the age of thirty-two, he still enjoyed.[42]

As he reported about his social life to Harry, who returned from Europe in the fall of 1874, only to leave shortly afterward for New

York, he was apologetic about taking such pleasure in the "ultra quietness, prudence, slyness" of the provincial New Englanders. "You will be discouraged, I remain happy!" he exclaimed. If life in America was not as aesthetically rich as life in Europe, still he believed that only on his native soil could he nurture the intellectual seeds for his future.

Chapter 8

ENGAGED

1875–1878

FOR THE FIRST TIME in his life, James's decision to pursue a career seemed to him an optimistic choice rather than the "narrowing" compromise against which his father had so ominously cautioned. There was nothing narrow about choosing to study and teach physiological psychology, a field in which invigorating research was defining psychology as a new science. "I have never felt so well and have never on the whole been so busy," William wrote to Harry. Besides teaching, he was working at the Museum of Comparative Zoology, reading "absolutely nothing of a 'general' sort," and writing reviews and articles for the *Atlantic Monthly,* the *North American Review,* and most prolifically for the *Nation.*[1]

He met with success on all professional fronts. Charles Eliot was so pleased with James's work that after the fall semester of 1875, he raised his salary to $1,200 and promised a further raise, to $2,000, for the next year, "which," James told Harry, "will be a sweet boon if it occurs."[2] If teaching was not always intellectually stimulating, still it was a respectable profession that provided him with steady remuneration, an affirmation of his worth, and a chance to make some "deep impression" on young men.[3]

Besides the time and effort he devoted to teaching, James found new stores of energy to fuel his intellectual life. Emulating his productive younger brother, he took to staying up until midnight reading and discovered that "it enlarges very much the day. You can judge from it too how much more 'capable' I am than I have been," he told Harry.

"In fact I am enjoying my excellent condition enormously."[4] He also set aside time to write, an activity that he now found less difficult and more satisfying than before. From the spring of 1875 through the fall of 1876, James reviewed seventeen books, mostly for the *Nation,* on physiology, psychology, and philosophy.

In these early unsigned works, James heralds a new philosophy that responds to the scientific work of physicists, physiologists, and experimental psychologists. "[I]t is the men engaged in the physical sciences who are now pressing hard in the direction of metaphysical problems," he wrote in one review, "and . . . it would be sheer folly not to expect from their trained cunning in experiment, their habits of patience and fairness, and their willingness to advance by small steps at a time, new results of the highest importance." Calling psychology "the antechamber to metaphysics," James applauded the "detachment of mind" with which researchers, not burdened by "philosophical antipathies," could conduct their experiments.[5]

For James, Wilhelm Wundt was "the most praiseworthy and never-too-much-to-be respected" of the new psychologists because he formulated theories of the mind based on introspection and experimental investigation.[6] James cited, in particular, Wundt's notion that an individual's interests mediated experience by causing him to filter out certain sensations or impressions and to pay attention to others. "*My* experience," James announced, "is only what I agree to attend to."

Throughout his career, James focused attention on the differences between intellectualization and apparently spontaneous mental processes. To what extent, he asked, were feelings merely the sum of physiological processes, and to what extent were they the result of "synthetic judgments" shaped by one's personality? Did emotions exist at all beyond their physical manifestation as bodily changes? What "useful purpose," in terms of human evolution, was served by having consciousness "superadded to life"?

These questions located James on the new intellectual bridge between metaphysics and experimental psychology. Engaged in the philosophical issues generated by scientific inquiry, he insisted that his aim was not merely to contribute to "gratuitous" metaphysical discourse. If such philosophizing "simply ends by 'indorsing' common-sense, and reinstating us in the possession of our old feelings, motives, and duties, we may fairly ask if it was worth while to go so far round in order simply to return to our starting-point." Instead, philosophy should make some "practical difference" in real lives.

In his own life, he claimed that no thinker exerted a greater practical effect than Renouvier, who had helped James to lift himself from despondency by convincing him that "in every wide theoretical conclusion we must seem more or less arbitrarily to *choose* our side." For James, choosing between one course of action and another had never seemed arbitrary. Decisions were fraught with danger: he might reveal a part of his personality that would offend others; he might make a "wrong" choice and disappoint his parents. Too often, James retreated, making no decision rather than taking a risk, but Renouvier persuaded him that even "doubt itself is an active state" and "suspense itself would be a choice." In that case, he might as well act.[7]

Daring Thinkers

AS WORK AND ACTION liberated him from depression, James felt able to participate in the intellectual community that flourished in Boston and Cambridge. That community consisted of many informal associations of men—and, rarely, women—who met to discuss their common interests. In the 1860s, Harry mentioned that he and William had been invited to join a German Club, founded by a woman friend; they responded coolly to the invitation. Men's dinner clubs, on the other hand, received more enthusiastic attention. One group to which William belonged consisted of writers, editors, and lawyers, including such eminent Bostonians as Henry Adams, William Dean Howells, Tom Perry, and John Gray. Although James found the club "hopelessly swamped in its buttoned up Boston respectable character" and tediously "middle aged," he did not reject invitations to occasional dinners.[8]

James was more attracted to the company of men with whom he could share and test his ideas. In the early 1870s Harry told Charles Norton that William, Wendell Holmes, "& various other long-headed youths have combined to form a Metaphysical Club, where they wrangle grimly & stick to the question."[9] Mary apparently objected to the smell of cigar smoke when the wrangling took place at her home; and Henry Sr. was not above joining the men—all in their thirties, they hardly could be called youths—to interject his own views on religious matters.

The name of the club was ironic, seditious. None of the members was trained as a philosopher and none wanted to be identified as a metaphysician whose discourse seemed mere "gibberish." Three members—Oliver Wendell Holmes Jr., Nicholas St. John Greene, and Joseph Bangs Warner—were lawyers; John Fiske was a historian; Chauncey Wright and Charles Sanders Peirce were scientists. James's perspective, rooted in his scientific training, also had been shaped by his experiences as an artist, experiences that had honed his attention to concrete detail and urged him to question the relationship between perception and emotion. His readings in physiology and psychology provided a fertile bed for the ideas that he was just beginning to formulate; but philosophically, he still was his father's son. "'Boyish,'" one member remarked about James, "is a well-chosen word to express both our common judgment of his present, and mine in particular, of his future. . . . One remains a boy longer in philosophy than in any other direction."[10] Especially if one is the son of Henry James Sr.

Despite a lack of formal philosophical background, James and his fellow club members, no less than the philosophers who occasionally joined them, were agitated and intoxicated by Darwin's theory of natural selection. That theory generated huge, overarching questions about the relationship of science to philosophy and of philosophy to action. What philosophical perspective, they asked, could respond to a natural world characterized by random and spontaneous change, where the individual and the environment acted upon one another, and—most of all—where choice made a difference? If neither German idealism nor British rationalism sufficed, then what alternatives did they have? The responses ranged from Chauncey Wright's unyielding positivism to James's visceral inclination to pragmatism.

Wright, more than a decade older than James, was proof that genius alone could not produce greatness. Large, homely, unkempt, and socially inept, Wright lacked the drive and perseverance that might have made him an influential thinker. Except for a few reviews and articles, he published nothing. And even these pieces, James noted, were so poorly written that they did not serve his ideas to best advantage.

An agile and combative debater within the confines of the Metaphysical Club, outside of that group Wright enjoyed the company
of young children more than adults. When he was invited to lecture
on psychology and on mathematical physics at Harvard, his droning
monotone proved so unpopular with the students that the offer was
not renewed. Popularity, however, did not interest Wright. He was satisfied to support himself by working as a "computer" for the *Nautical
Almanac,* a job that gave him ample time for theoretical speculation. A
solitary bachelor, Wright found hospitality in the homes of many Cambridge families, the Nortons and the Jameses among them; but he returned each evening to his lonely rooms, where, at the age of forty-five,
he died of a stroke.

James was attracted to Wright's positivism: the tangible world of
daily experience was, for Wright, the only reality. James, however, was
more interested than Wright in the subjectivity of experience, in the
commonsensical perception of continuity among experiences, in a basic
human longing for transcendent meaning. Wright, he noticed, did not
seem to share this longing ("the *objectivity* of a phenomenon is its significance," Wright maintained),[11] and James, therefore, saw his philosophy as essentially nihilistic. "Chauncey is the damnedest rationalist
that I ever saw," James exclaimed once to George Palmer.

Wright's lack of emotional empathy, both in theory and practice,
was echoed by Charles Sanders Peirce, whom James met when they
were classmates at the Lawrence Scientific School. Peirce, three years
older than James and the precocious son of Harvard mathematics professor Benjamin Peirce, was no more socially skilled than Chauncey
Wright. James described him as "a very 'smart' fellow with a great deal
of character, pretty independent & violent though."[12] The independence and violence that James noticed informed Peirce's philosophical
writings and threatened his personal relationships. He refused, in lectures and articles, to accommodate himself to the needs of audiences
or readers. He offended acquaintances by his apparent hostility. He
complained, even as a young man, that the Cambridge community
felt "very antagonistic" to him, forcing him into a "position of oblo-
quy."[13] When confronted with evidence of his own antagonism, he explained that he had lost the ability to communicate because he was a
recluse, but more likely he was a recluse because of his brash tactless-

ness. James, after years of feeling intimidated by Peirce's "sententious manner and his paradoxical & obscure statements," found a strategy for taming the "thorny & spinous" personality: "grasp firmly, contradict, push hard, make fun of him," he advised, "and he is as pleasant as any one."[14]

In the 1870s, James recognized in Peirce a genius who was responding boldly to questions that nettled all of the club members. A semiotician and logician, Peirce focused on the ways signs convey meaning and reflect the consensus of a community about what reality is. As James listened to Peirce's talks at the club's gatherings, as he read Peirce's articles—especially "The Fixation of Belief" and "How to Make Our Ideas Clear"—in the *Popular Science Monthly,* he found affirmation for his own conviction that philosophy must move beyond abstract metaphysics and incorporate scientific methodology. But Peirce went further than James in hailing the process of observation and experimentation as necessary for ascertaining truth. An idea cannot be known, Peirce said, without considering the consequences of that idea: the effects of an idea are inseparable from the idea itself. Although Peirce and James someday would disagree about the implications of that assertion and although Peirce would strain to distinguish what he called "pragmaticism" from James's grand and amorphous "pragmatism," in the 1870s, the two men saw themselves as philosophical comrades, foot soldiers in an exhilarating battle against idealists, rationalists, Unitarians, and, for James at least, his own father.

In 1874, the Metaphysical Club welcomed to its fold the Scottish émigré Thomas Davidson. Gregarious and kind, with a rustic simplicity that set others at ease, Davidson quickly became a close friend of James, even though they did not always agree on philosophical issues. Often impatient with his fellow club members, Davidson, James remembered, would "crack the whip of Aristotle over us."

At the time when James first met Davidson, both men were thinking about the social effects of philosophy, both were reacting against the encroaching tide of Hegelianism that threatened to dominate philosophical thought, and both were concerned about their own sense of spirituality. Besides the philosophical group to which they belonged, they found these issues taken up by another earnest association of New Englanders who met in Boston's Beacon Hill.

In the fall of 1867, the Reverend John T. Sargent and his wife, Mary, began a club in their home at 77 Chestnut Street in Boston, devoted to exploring religious, philosophical, and social questions. The purpose of the Chestnut Street Club, as the group was first known, "was to bring together at intervals a few men and women of culture, most of whom were known to be daring thinkers on subjects of the highest import, and furnish them with an opportunity for uttering their thought to an audience capable of appreciating its scope, of criticising its worth, and of developing its relations."[15]

Daring as the thinkers were, they decided they needed a more evocative name for their association: they would be the Radical Club, and they attracted such eminent speakers as Emerson, Longfellow, and the aging Henry James Sr. Among the appreciative audience one could find Julia Ward Howe, the tireless reformer Elizabeth Peabody, John Greenleaf Whittier, and Lydia Maria Child. The setting belied the club's radical intent: The Sargents' home was tastefully affluent, and the room in which the club met suitably ornate. Hung with layers of curtains, draperies, and valances; furnished with intricately carved chairs and tables; decorated with imposing gilt-framed oil paintings and a pantheon of marble busts, the atmosphere of the Radical Club appeared entrenched in Victorian conventions.

The participants, however, strived to resist those conventions. Here, one could listen to Emerson redefine Christian tradition; Henry James Sr. rail against the "vicious principle of personality"; or Thomas Davidson incite a debate about the causes of individualism. On one afternoon the fertile subject of evolution was taken up by Mark Twain; on another, by geologist Nathaniel Shaler.

Conversations about religion generated the most controversy. Julia Ward Howe, who chronicled the club in her memoirs, confessed that some ideas "pained and even irritated me. The disposition to seek outside the limits of Christianity for all that is noble and inspiring in religious culture, and to recognize especially within these limits the superstition and intolerance which have been the bane of all religions . . . offended not only my affections, but also my sense of justice."[16]

Although the offerings of the Radical Club were uneven, and by the standards of the Metaphysical Club hardly radical, James attended occasionally, sometimes in the company of his father. Henry Sr., however, proved a more regular member. Early in 1876, on one of the occasions that Henry went alone, he returned, so family legend had it, with an uncharacteristic air of excitement. He had met the woman William would marry, he announced. Her name was Alice.

Alice

ALICE HOWE GIBBENS was born on February 5, 1849, in Weymouth, Massachusetts, where her grandfather, Christopher Webb, had been a prestigious lawyer. Her mother, Eliza Putnam Webb, was twenty when Alice was born; her father, Daniel Lewis Gibbens, at twenty-four, still had not found a steady career. The couple had married in 1847, the same year that Gibbens graduated from the Harvard Medical School; but he chose not to practice, instead embarking on a variety of short-lived business ventures. Some of these took him far from New England. Occasionally his family joined him: they all settled in California when Alice was seven, for example, and Gibbens became involved in ranching; but more often, Eliza Webb Gibbens returned to her mother's home in Weymouth with her three daughters—Mary was born in 1851 and Margaret in 1857—and waited for her husband to return.

The family's life may have been more stable when Gibbens was away than when he was in residence: he drank heavily, especially under stress, and his binges were followed by periods of such depression and self-recrimination that his wife feared that he would commit suicide. He urged better behavior from his daughters: "You must both try to be gentle and to make everybody as little trouble as you possibly can," he wrote to ten-year-old Alice and her younger sister Mary.[17]

Alice was brought up to be quiet, agreeable, and responsible. She learned to play piano, to sew, and to keep her feelings to herself. When, at the age of sixteen, she confessed to her father that sometimes she felt overcome by sadness, he told her she "must resist as there is nothing gained by being sad without a cause. . . . So whatever you do, be cheerful—I try very hard to look and talk cheeringly, even when my thoughts seem experiencing a cold, northeasterly storm."[18]

Alice soon came to have little faith that the professed values of the adults around her would be congruent with their actions. Even as a young child, adults often seemed to her misguided and hypocritical. Her family, for example, declared themselves sympathetic to the plight of slaves, but instead of adding their voices to those of abolitionists, her grandfather became president of the African Colonization Society, a group that advocated returning blacks to Africa. Alice considered her grandfather "more off the track than any pacificist." Unfortunately, her own mother did not see the error of his ways.

After she read *Uncle Tom's Cabin,* Alice, outraged at the cruelty and injustice perpetrated against slaves, became as ardent an abolitionist as any ten-year-old could be. When, a few months later, she learned of John Brown's raid on Harpers Ferry, she felt that "a great bell had tolled" in her moral life. The afternoon of his execution, she recalled, was particularly stunning. Incredulous because no one around her was mourning Brown's death, the grief-stricken Alice took her eight-year-old sister Mary by the hand "and with all the hopeless incommunicativeness of childhood we fared forth for a long walk without a word to our mother." As they were returning home, however, Alice caught sight of black festoons draping the front of the house of a prominent Weymouth citizen, "and," she remembered, "a great lifting of our hearts responded to that token that there were grown ups who cared."[19]

The Civil War and its aftermath came to have a devastating effect on the Gibbens family. In November 1862, Daniel Gibbens boarded a steamboat for New Orleans to take a position as clerk to one Thomas Dexter, a friend of Gibbens's who was serving as state treasurer to the city's military mayor, James F. Miller. At a salary of $166 per month, Gibbens was earning a decent wage for the time, a more steady income than he had counted on in the past. "[Y]ou must remember," he wrote to Alice, "it is for you all that I stay, to endeavor if possible to earn a home that we may enjoy together bye and bye."[20] If there were any money to spare, he also meant to buy a melodeon: "they are as good as a small organ," he said, "and I am very fond of the music."[21]

Even with these goals in mind, Gibbens found his experience in the South depressing: "there is a gloom about the streets that is very apparent," he wrote shortly after he arrived in New Orleans.[22] After the war ended, he followed Dexter to Mobile, Alabama, where the atmosphere was no brighter. Any display of triumph among the blacks was set against a backdrop of eerie silence in the white community. "The city is very quiet," Gibbens reported to Alice on the Fourth of July. "The military fired a salute of thirteen guns at sunrise, but there were no bells rung nor other indications of joy. The blacks are out in full dress and made quite an appearance in procession escorted by the black

troops."[23] The somber display contrasted with the exuberance he imagined at home. He urged Alice to go to Boston on the Fourth: "no such
celebration has ever been, or will be seen again," he wrote. "Every individual there will feel as if they were part and parcel of a grand
thanksgiving Jubilee."[24]

For Alice, the grand thanksgiving would come in August, when
her father was expected home. Her mother already had begun looking
for a house, where the family could settle at last. But his departure was
delayed by one month and then two, as he stayed on to continue his
service to Dexter. That service included companionship and, possibly,
embezzling. "The news was brought that my friend Dexter was here-
under arrest in close confinement," he wrote to his family in October.
Dexter was accused of stealing more than three thousand bales of cotton, and of selling a government position for the sum of twenty-five
thousand dollars.

Although some friends urged Gibbens to flee immediately, he decided that he "would not leave otherwise than openly"; soon he learned
that he could not leave: he was wanted as a witness.[25] As much as he
protested his innocence, many believed that Gibbens could not have
been a close associate of Dexter's without knowing of his shady financial dealings.

When Dexter fell, he pulled Gibbens with him. "With the retiracy
of Mr. Dexter," the *Mobile Daily Times* reported at the end of October,
"we are sorry to be obliged to chronicle that of Dr. Gibbens also."[26] But
the extent of Gibbens's illegal activities remains a mystery. In late
spring, he told Alice that he had been given "the handsomest set of di-
amond wrist buttons and shirt studs, that you ever saw," but did not di-
vulge the donor of the extravagant gift.[27] During the summer, he
confessed to Alice that he was involved in "a little speculation" for
which he had "furnished the capital for half the profits."[28] Besides divulging his financial schemes, Gibbens also reported home the occasional robberies of which he and Dexter had been victims. With
diamonds and embezzled cash as bait, the two may have been easy prey.

As he waited to be called as a witness in Dexter's trial, Gibbens became overwhelmed by the scandal. He began to drink and probably
to inhale sulfuric ether for more effective anesthesia. At about eight
o'clock on the morning of Sunday, December 3, he apparently committed suicide. He was found with his throat slit by a razor; he bled to

death, the *New Orleans Times* reported, in less than two hours. He was forty years old.

Instead of welcoming their father home with celebration, Alice, Mary, and Margaret stood with their mother to receive Gibbens's embalmed body. Eliza Gibbens was not prepared for widowhood. Although for many years she had been acting as head of the family during her husband's absences, she felt inadequate to the sudden burden of new responsibility. A quiet, diffident woman, she turned gratefully to her eldest daughter for support. She was not, and never would be, disappointed.

Gibbens's estate provided his family with a small, but decent, income. For a few years, they managed at home. But in 1868, when Alice was nineteen, they decided that they could live more comfortably abroad. They settled in cities that attracted other Americans: Heidelberg, Dresden, Florence. But by 1873, even Europe was not cheap enough for their declining fortunes. They decided to return to America, hoping that Alice and Mary would find work. Instead of returning to their hometown of Weymouth, they settled in Boston, where the Gibbens sisters soon found positions at Miss Sanger's School, where they were popular teachers. One student remembered Alice and Mary as "beautiful girls."[29]

Alice's occasional attendance at the Radical Club was not surprising for a young woman with a lively mind and an interest in religious questions. Certainly she stood out among the other female members of the club, most of whom were far older than she. There was something warmly appealing about her; besides Henry Sr., she attracted the attention of the eminent John Greenleaf Whittier, who became a special admirer. When Alice did not attend meetings, she could depend on Whittier to send her a report of whatever was discussed.

Despite his long and painful struggle for emotional independence, James decided to meet Alice Gibbens. Perhaps Henry's announcement regarding his future daughter-in-law piqued his curiosity; perhaps James was certain that he would prove his father wrong; perhaps he felt, at the age of thirty-four, that he needed to take any opportunity to meet a possible mate. Whatever his reason, James returned to the Sargents' home, alone, enlisting Thomas Davidson to introduce him to Alice.

The woman he encountered appeared far different from women who had attracted him in the past, and yet the attraction was undeniable. She had none of the spritely energy of Minny Temple nor the coy flirtatiousness of Fanny Dixwell. She had neither the delicate features nor narrow waist that convention dictated a young woman should have. In photographs, she appears only a few inches shorter than James, which would make her about five feet four. Her weight, however, far exceeded his: for most of her life, she was more than stout. But that stoutness gave her an air of solidity, even serenity, that made James feel comfortable in her presence. She had a soft, melodic voice, a generous sense of humor, and the most beautiful eyes that he had ever seen. Later, when a friend told William that Alice had "eyes *like a prayer,*" he responded, "That is just the expression I have been seeking all my life, but just escaped finding."[30] "Prayerful" was, indeed, an appropriate word to reflect the certainty that Alice felt about her own sense of spirituality. "[H]appy-go-lucky tumbling into things and tumbling out again," William later commented, was not part of Alice's personality; instead, she was intelligent, articulate, serene, steady.[31] His father was right.

Their shared interest in the intellectual discussions at the Radical Club was matched by their amusement at the pretensions of some of its members. In March, Alice sent William a copy of a satirical poem that she had cut out of the *Boston Sunday Times:* "The Radical Club" parodied the likes of Bronson Alcott, Elizabeth Peabody, and Julia Ward Howe, among other famous members—men and women whom James sometimes found insufferable.

The friendship between William and Alice flourished throughout the spring, sweeping William toward the crisis he had faced many times in the past: Could he love a woman? Could a woman love him? The first evening he called on Alice at home, he found her alone—her mother and sisters had gone to the theater—and noticed a certain enigmatic expression on her face that puzzled and captivated him. Alice seemed at once so girlish and so mature, so ready to depend upon him and yet so capable in her own right. He was falling in love with her, he thought, or at least, with the idea of her that he had created for himself. As he had done so many times before when he met a woman who attracted him, he began a debilitating process of self-analysis and recrimination.

James spent much of the summer away from Cambridge, where his father was slowly recovering from what appears to have been a stroke.

"His docile passivity is very pathetic & so is the devotion of Mother Alice & A.K. to him. I ran away 3 days ago, the recitations being over for the year in order to break from the studious associations of home," William told Harry.[32] Among his many destinations were Newport; New York, where his cousin Henrietta Temple was married; Philadelphia, for the Centenary of American Independence; and, at the end of the summer, Putnam Camp.

On the way home from Philadelphia, he stopped in Connecticut for a visit with Kate Havens, perhaps to test his feelings for her, or hers for him, perhaps merely to complicate his situation and thereby divert his energies from thinking about Alice. William and Kate took "a long and beautiful carriage ride" that James insisted would "gleam eternally like an oasis in the withered waste of my life's memory."[33] But he had been distracted during the whole of it: Alice was much on his mind throughout the summer, and never more than during the weeks he spent at Putnam Camp.

Retreat

IN ONE OF HIS earliest essays, James considered the weighty subject of summer vacations, on which he took a most definite stand. "The fact is," he wrote, "that every man who possibly can should force himself to a holiday of a full month in the year, whether he feels like taking it or not" both for the benefit of "irresponsible enjoyment" and "tone of mind and health of body."[34] James never had to force himself to take a vacation, even before he held any job.

During the summer of 1875, he, Henry Bowditch and his brother Charles, and James Jackson Putnam, all former medical school classmates of James's, headed for Keene Valley, a small town in the northern Adirondacks. While Lake Placid, Saranac Lake, and Saratoga Springs were popular vacation spots in the area, Keene Valley still was rustic and undeveloped in the 1870s, when James and his friends arrived. They found rooms at Beede's Boarding House, from which, accompanied by a local guide, they set out on strenuous hikes in the surrounding mountains—Noonmark, Sawtooth, Hedgehog, and Marcy—where no trails had yet been blazed. Keene Valley, with its balsam-scented woods, cold mountain streams, and wild fields, was, James thought, one of the most beautiful places on earth.

The following year, when Beede informed his four boarders that he was selling off some land and a spartan shack, they decided to chip in for a cooperative vacation spot. With the Shanty, as they called their living quarters, and a few rustic outbuildings, Putnam Camp was established.

Despite his dorsal problems and recurring malaise, James revived in the Adirondacks. Keene Valley was his private terrain, a world in which he moved unfettered. "As a walker," James Jackson Putnam recalled, "he used to be among the foremost, in the earlier years, and it was a pleasure to watch his lithe and graceful figure as he moved rapidly up the steep trails or stretched himself on the slope of a rock, his arms under his head, for resting." He had a strange way of climbing, lifting his weight with his lower leg instead of raising himself with the higher; but, Putnam said, this stance only added to his agility. When not mountain climbing, James spent hours reading, usually fifty pages a day. He had a special spot where he secluded himself with a book: a ledge overlooking the Ausable River, where he could lie, sheltered by trees, on a bed of pine needles.[35]

The Adirondack Doctors, as James called his hiking companions, were among his closest friends and colleagues, and served as continuing links to Harvard's medical school, where both Henry Bowditch and James Jackson Putnam taught. In Bowditch's Harvard laboratory, and in the laboratory that Putnam had set up in his own home, the three men conducted neurological experiments, sometimes using themselves as subjects. Of the three, Putnam was involved most directly with psychological pathology in his work at the Massachusetts General Hospital, where he served first as Electrician—mild electrical stimulation was a popular treatment of nervous diseases at the time—and later as Physician to Out-Patients with nervous diseases.

Putnam, four years younger than James, met James when both were studying at Harvard Medical School. One afternoon, in their anatomy class, James congratulated Putnam on his admirable recitation: "I was greatly impressed at once with the frankness of his expression, the generosity of his manner, and the peculiarly attractive quality of his voice," Putnam recalled.

As their friendship grew, Putnam visited James at home, where he was treated to a display of Jamesian banter that seemed to Putnam amusing, but sometimes intimidating. "I remember listening one day with trepidation," he wrote, "when Mr. James, Senior, gathered his face into a half-humorous, half-thunderous expression and then rolled out a series of denunciations on the people who insisted on misusing the word 'quite.'" As for his friend William, Putnam noticed that at home he seemed "somewhat quieter and gentler in manner than he afterward appeared to be."

At Putnam Camp, James was free from paternal domination. The strenuous life of hiking and mountain climbing affirmed a sense of manliness that eluded him elsewhere, especially in his parents' home. But complicating his visit from mid-August to September 1876 was Alice's residence nearby. She was staying with a friend at Beede's boardinghouse; she and William saw one another often; and soon he came to the exhilarating, incontrovertible conclusion that he was in love.

He realized, of course, that he must take some action—at the very least to declare his love to Alice. The prospect left him paralyzed, sleepless, feeling as if he were "split . . . into two beings": one, the public William James who could pursue a lighthearted friendship with an appealing woman; the other, the helpless private James whose needs never could be articulated, who had to repress and control his feelings.

He wished that in this affair of the heart he could "throw the responsibility of deciding on the other person," but he knew that the responsibility was his alone.[36] He hesitated, he worried, he thought and thought again. Finally, sometime in the fall, he bared his feelings to Alice: "To state abruptly the whole matter: I am in love, *und zwar* (—forgive me—) with Yourself."[37]

Just as he had done with Kate Havens, however, he tried to convince Alice that he was not the man he seemed to be. Among James's turbulent feelings in those days of indecison, longing and fear were the most prominent. Consumed with desire for Alice, he nevertheless feared that his habit of chastity and "instinct of personal isolation" would impede their sexual relationship. Although he believed that sexual impulses were "instinctive, in the sense of blind, automatic, and untaught," he also knew that even so powerful a force could be repressed by "slight differences in the individual stimulus, by the inward condition of the agent himself, by habits once acquired, and by the antagonism of contrary impulses operating on the mind." Among those contrary impulses was "ordinary shyness," caused, according to James, by a fear of failing to please, to fulfill another's expectation.[38] He wondered if he were man enough to marry.

A Feeling of But

IN HIS *Principles of Psychology,* James suggested that the language we use to describe feelings is inadequate to the depth and range of our emotions. "We ought to say a feeling of *and,* a feeling of *if,* a feeling of *but,* and a feeling of *by,*" he wrote, "quite as readily as we say a feeling of *blue* or a feeling of *cold.* Yet we do not: so inveterate has our habit become of recognizing the existence of the substantive parts alone, that language almost refuses to lend itself to any other use."[39] During his twenty months of courting Alice, James could well be described as suffering from a feeling of *but.* Whenever Alice told him she loved him, he countered with a host of reasons that she should not; if she intimated that she would break off their relationship, he lunged forward in passionate pursuit. The protracted wooing tried Alice's patience; caused William continual, gnawing anxiety; and more than once seemed doomed by James's insistent self-deprecation.

At the start, when he wrote to Alice protesting his love, he asked her to name "any absolute irrevocable obstacle" that should prevent his suit. He understood that she hardly knew him and certainly could find his avowal of love inappropriate. Of course, he informed her, there were innumerable reasons why she *should* not love him in return. "To a certain extent," he wrote, "I will suppose you feel a sympathy with me, but I can furnish you with undreamed of arguments *against* accepting any offer I may make."[40] But for now, he was making no offers. He simply wanted her encouragement. He got it, and it unnerved him.

The feelings that Alice provoked in James resulted in some of the most clotted writing he ever produced. His letters during the fall of 1876, by his own admission, were "shadowy & hard to interpret," but Alice certainly could understand that William saw her as more than an object of love; she was to be a source of deliverance. Unlike William, Alice was not beset with religious doubts; she believed in the supernatural, in a realm of guiding spirits, in God. He wanted her to enlighten him. "My attitude towards Religion is one of defence rather than of adoption," he explained. "I see its place; I feel that there are times when everything else must fail & that, or nothing, remain; and yet I behave as if I must leave it untouched until such times come, and

I am driven to it by sheer stress of weather." He looked to her to teach him "that certain goods are *real,* and compel me to live so as to merit them."[41]

The burden of his needs apparently proved too much for Alice, and she began to express doubts about their future together. Perhaps she was frightened by his claim of being "split as it were into two beings."[42] Or perhaps by evidence that the poor emotional and physical health he claimed he suffered was, in fact, true. James spent a wretched fall, and by Christmas, 1876, he convinced himself that the relationship was over. He told Tom Ward that Alice no longer cared for him; he was desolate.

But he did not give up, and by March 1877, he thanked her for "recognizing" him, a term that would recur throughout their courtship. James yearned for someone to perceive and love the authentic, the dark, self that lay somewhere in the deep recesses of his being. "Dearest friend," he wrote to Alice, "now that you *recognize* me, the horrible lonesome pang is removed from my existence, and I feel as if I could happily look upon you, whatever you decided to do."[43] She was his friend, his truest friend, and she gave him courage to keep pursuing her. "Some day, God willing," he told her, "you shall read the bottom of my heart."[44]

In the spring of 1877, a year after they met, Alice agreed that the courtship could resume, a decision that William received with both ecstatic and "vigilant" thoughts. His vigilance was directed partly toward making sure that the relationship kept him off balance. As he explained to Alice, he saw his defining trait as the need for "active tension" in any situation. He wanted to trust that his desires would be fulfilled, but he did not want to believe in a guaranteed outcome. "Make it a guarantee," he told her, "—and the attitude immediately becomes to my consciousness stagnant and stingless. Take away the guarantee, and I feel . . . a sort of deep enthusiastic bliss." It is no wonder, then, that the relationship did not proceed smoothly. Many times, to revive his masochistic exultation, William tormented himself with the thought that Alice would change her mind. "Last fall & last winter," he admitted to her, "what pangs of joy it sometimes gave me to let you go! to feel that in acquiescing in your unstained, unharnessed freedom I was also asserting my deepest self, and cooperating with the whole generous life of things!"[45]

In the summer of 1877, Alice made plans to travel to Canada with a friend, plans that James saw as a threat to their future. He tried to persuade her to come to Keene Valley instead or, at least, directly afterward. There, in an atmosphere in which he thrived, he could show himself to his best advantage. But Alice apparently thought that staying in Keene Valley, even in the company of her sister and friends, would be improper. She went to Canada, and in the fall of 1877, James again announced, this time to his brother Bob, that his relationship with Alice had ended.

Yet after she returned, he revived his pursuit, this time with more confidence that, although there were no guarantees, she continued to have strong feelings for him. Sometime during the winter of 1877–78, she wrote him a note that threw him into a state of "frenzy"—a state that persisted through the winter and well into the spring. By May, he gathered all his courage and, finally, during a walk on the Boston Common, he proposed that they announce their plans to marry.

On May 13, 1878, Oliver Wendell Holmes received a card signed by William James and Alice Gibbens. It contained a single word: *Engaged!*

Chapter 9

GIFTS

1878–1882

SINCE JAMES HAD kept his relationship with Alice a secret from all but
a few intimate friends, his engagement proved "a bombshell," as Mary
Tweedy put it, for the rest of his circle.[1] But if it was a shock, still it
was a cause of great rejoicing. "It filled my soul with joy unutterable at
the thought of what must be your contentment and happiness," Wilky
wrote. "It is certainly the greatest piece of news you have ever inflicted
upon the world, and I supposed the greatest event that has ever tran-
spired in the family."[2] It was, without doubt, the most crucial event in
William's life. Alice's acceptance of him seemed, to James, nothing
less than a miracle. "Nature is too strong for all of us so I succumbed
long ago," he wrote to a friend, "why *she* succumbed Heaven only
knows but she did."[3]

For William, marriage meant more than the uniting of two lovers;
it was, in the Jamesian sense, a moral issue: the declaration of a new
identity, affirmation that he could reject a life of chaos and despair and
instead could choose serenity and peace. "To me," he wrote to Alice,
"such decisions seem acts by which we are *voting* what sort of a universe
this shall intimately be. . . ."[4] In casting his vote, James reaffirmed the
decision he had made eight years earlier, after reading Renouvier, that
he would act "without carefully waiting for contemplation of the external world to determine all for me."[5] He acted, finally, alone, in his
own interest, to fulfill his own needs.

Marriage, he believed, necessarily would focus his responsibilities
on the needs of his family, preventing him from indulging his persistent emotional and physical hypochondria. The new regularity and

pattern of his daily life, he hoped, would produce the tranquillity for which he longed. But most important, he would be delivered from loneliness and solitude. Love, James wrote later, "transforms the value of the creature loved as utterly as the sunrise transforms Mount Blanc from a corpse-like gray to a rosy enchantment; and sets the whole world to a new tune for the lover and gives a new issue to his life."[6]

When William and Alice became engaged, they apparently planned a fall wedding. But at the end of June, Alice confided to her friend John Greenleaf Whittier that she was to be married "very quietly, as seems best" in mid-July. She anticipated his surprise and regretted that the change of plans meant that he would not be able to attend the ceremony. "I am surprised myself," Alice admitted, "but being very busy is a great blessing, for the leaving home and solemn change makes these last days very grave ones."[7]

Alice Howe Gibbens was twenty-nine and William James was thirty-six when they married on Wednesday, July 10, 1878. Unlike his father, James was married by a clergyman. The ceremony, conducted by Reverend Rufus Ellis, a longtime friend of the families, was held at the home of Alice's grandmother in Boston. The James family was underrepresented: although Henry and Mary witnessed the event, none of William's brothers attended; nor did his sister, Alice, who was suffering from a severe emotional breakdown.

While many of her women friends were engaged or newly married, Alice James had neither prospects nor hopes for her own future as a wife. Everything that marriage offered to a woman—public affirmation of her femininity and charm; sexual fulfillment; authority over home, servants, and children—was denied her. Instead, she was destined to be a spinster and a virgin, solitary and innocent of a woman's initiation into full adulthood; she would be, eternally, the James family's youngest child.

The marriages of her brothers Wilky and Bob also made Alice aware of her fate but did not generate the same kind of reaction. William's marriage was different: he was the last of the James children to leave home—in effect, abandoning Alice to her parents. His bride, more than the women Bob and Wilky had married, was welcomed warmly by the Jameses and their circle of friends: Charles Eliot and his wife were not alone in expressing their "ravishment" to Mary and Henry after first meeting Alice.[8] Both Henry and Mary James treated her as a new daughter, and their own daughter, frustrated and enraged, collapsed.

William reported to Henry the "sad summer" caused by Alice's breakdown as the family saw her symptoms worsen, improve, and worsen once again. Shortly after the wedding ceremony, Alice seemed to rally.[9] But in September, Henry Sr. reported to Bob that she had become hysterical and had threatened suicide. For Alice, the period that coincided with William's happiness was a spiritual death. "I have been dead so long," she wrote in her last diary entry in 1892, "since that hideous summer of '78, when I went down to the deep sea, its dark waters closed over me and I knew neither hope nor peace."[10]

No one in the James family connected Alice's breakdown to William's marriage. Henry Sr., in fact, refused to recognize any cause at all except "a diabolic influx into the human mind from the spiritual world, to which something in her temperament has rendered her peculiarly susceptible."[11] While the family waited for the diabolic spirits to depart, Aunt Kate came to help Mary, and all attention turned anxiously to the sickroom. It was a place from which William was glad to escape.

Early in July, he traveled to Putnam Camp to reserve a cottage for the honeymoon. "Hey diddle diddle!" James crowed, announcing to Alice that the camp could accommodate them for six to eight weeks. Directly after the wedding, the couple traveled first to New York City, from which they began a journey north. On the second night of their honeymoon, they stayed in the resort city of Saratoga Springs at the opulent Grand Union, purportedly the world's largest hotel, with its marble floors, garden courtyard, and broad piazza. From Saratoga Springs, they took trains, boats, and carriages to Putnam Camp.

Sentiment and Rationality

ALICE WAS SHY; William, as one might expect, was agitated during their first days of marriage. For the newlyweds, the camp offered "romantic and irresponsible isolation" and, at last, they began the sexual relationship for which William so ardently longed. Nevertheless, as much as William wanted to be alone with Alice, his desire to show her off and to create an audience before whom he could perform his new role as husband impelled him to invite Josiah Royce to join them on their holiday. Royce, apparently realizing that his presence might not be appropriate, declined.

William and Alice spent their days reading, bathing in the nearby stream, and walking in the woods. They also shared in another project: writing philosophical articles. William dictated; Alice, as she would continue to do throughout their marriage, served as amanuensis and respondent. During the previous winter, James had realized, with a sense of urgency, if not panic, that he needed to produce evidence of his intellectual abilities if he wanted to further his career. Within the Harvard academic community, his lack of formal training in philosophy was no liability. But he knew that if he wanted to apply for positions elsewhere, he needed to establish himself more firmly as a theoretician and scholar.

He proposed to write for several journals, foremost among them the *Journal of Speculative Philosophy,* the first American journal of philosophy, edited by William Torrey Harris, to whom James sent his "Remarks on Spencer's Definition of Mind as Correspondence."[12] This essay, which appeared in the January 1878 issue, was James's first signed publication, a fitting preface to his later work.

Although James had read Spencer's *Principles of Biology* when it was published in installments in 1868 and used Spencer's *Principles of Psychology* in his Natural History 2 course in 1876–77, he soon became "completely disgusted with the eminent philosopher."[13] Applying Darwin's theory of evolution to the human mind, Spencer posited a human being for whom survival was the only goal of life. The idea seemed to James reductionist and offensive, resulting in a superman who would be insufferably dull—but that was not James's only objection to Spencer's vision.

Survival, James believed, was only one of many competing interests that influenced thought and action—and, James wrote, "are all that makes survival worth securing." Love, play, art, philosophy, "the rest of religious emotion, the joy of moral self-approbation, the charm of fancy and of wit": these interests—idiosyncratic, sensuous, and ultimately inexplicable—were denied in Spencer's philosophical system.[14] But James would make them central to his own system of philosophy: "Interests, then, are an all-essential factor which no writer pretending to give an account of mental evolution has a right to neglect."[15]

If James's essay did not quite dispose of Spencer's theory, still, it established his position in a noisy debate about philosophy's changing boundaries, about the potential of science to transform the discipline,

and about the usefulness of philosophical abstractions. That debate engaged Harvard's philosophy department, where James proved himself
an energizing force by daring to champion both current German research in physiological psychology and the writings of Renouvier.

Within the department, however, James's enthusiasms were not always appreciated. In 1880, when James became an assistant professor
of philosophy, his colleagues included Francis Bowen, the sixty-nine-
year-old Alford Professor of Philosophy, who opposed Darwinism,
transcendentalism, and any pedagogical changes suggested by Charles
William Eliot; and George Herbert Palmer, teacher of ethics, trained
as a Congregational minister at Andover Seminary, who had become
chairman of the department in 1876. Palmer was popular more for his
generous manner than his sharp intellect. George Santayana likened
him to "a father confessor, never shocked at sin, never despairing at sin-
ners . . . Palmer was a fountain of sweet reasonableness. That his methods were sophistical and his conclusions lame didn't really matter."[16]
They mattered to James. Palmer, he wrote to G. S. Hall, "is an extraordinarily able man, but associating with him is like being in a dentist's chair, the whole while."[17] When Palmer joined the growing
number of philosophers who aligned themselves with Hegel, James
dismissed him as "a born prig."[18]

Courses in philosophy also were taught by members of the Divinity School, including its dean, Charles Carroll Everett (like Palmer, a
Hegelian); the Unitarian minister Andrew Preston Peabody, who
taught ethics; and the reform-minded Francis Peabody, who taught social ethics. As in many other colleges, the department, small and staid,
was still wresting itself from the influence of religion.

As James embarked on his career as a scholar, few publications
were devoted to philosophy. The *Journal of Speculative Philosophy* had
been begun by Harris, who, with his friend Henry Brokmeyer, were
the mainstays of the St. Louis Movement in Philosophy. Harris had
come to St. Louis in 1857 to teach shorthand, and by the time he
established his journal, was assistant superintendent of schools. He remained in St. Louis until 1880, when he moved to Concord, Massachusetts, where he lectured on Hegel at the Summer School of
Philosophy and joined informal gatherings of philosophers in James's
circle. Although James was an ardent anti-Hegelian, he overlooked his
antipathy to Harris's ideas as he courted Harris as a possible publisher.

James felt far more welcome as a contributor to George Croom Robertson's *Mind,* which had been inaugurated in January 1876, financed by Robertson's mentor Alexander Bain. *Mind,* the first British publication devoted to studies of psychology and philosophy, focused on exploring the place of the new science within the larger domain of philosophy. That place was not yet assured: psychology, at Harvard and elsewhere, was taught within departments of philosophy as a theoretical, rather than experimental, discipline. Robertson aimed to provide a forum where the latest work in psychology would be available to serious philosophers. Opening such work to debate would enable philosophers to evaluate the new discipline according to their own rigorous standards.[19]

James found in Robertson an attentive and sympathetic editor. While Harris frequently annoyed James because he preferred to publish translations and florid poetry rather than original (i.e., James's) philosophical essays, Robertson proved eager to substitute James's work for that of other writers. In 1879, "Are We Automata?" and "The Sentiment of Rationality" appeared in *Mind.* In these essays, James expanded upon the significance of interest and motivation both for everyday behavior and for the profession of philosophy.

Activity and Faith

BY THE TIME THEY returned to Cambridge at the end of the summer, Alice was pregnant. Married life, James wrote, was "an easy & natural state which I wish I had entered years ago."[20] But with a wife to support and a child expected, he became uneasy about his professional prospects. In 1878–79, he taught three courses: Natural History 3 (comparative vertebrate anatomy), Philosophy 4 (psychology), and Philosophy 20 (physiological psychology on both the undergraduate and graduate level). Drawn more to psychology and philosophy than to anatomy, James hoped to move into a philosophy department—at Harvard or, if necessary, elsewhere—and to make an impact in the field with his new psychology textbook, for which he had signed a contract with Henry Holt in June 1878. He had been recommended to Holt by his Metaphysical Club associate John Fiske as an astoundingly well-informed scholar in the field.

James had great professional and personal expectations for his new textbook. It would be evidence, he told Alice, that he was not a man who lived "*wholly* in projects, aspirations, & phrases, but now and then [has] some thing done to show for all the fuss." *The Principles of Psychology,* he assured her, would support them from the proceeds of its sales.[21]

In September, he corresponded with Daniel Coit Gilman, president of Johns Hopkins—where he had lectured the previous February on "The Brain and the Senses; and Their Relation to Intelligence"—about a possible appointment there. But by the end of the fall semester, after talking with Charles Eliot, he decided to stay at Harvard after all. Eliot assured him that if a professorship in the philosophy department became vacant, James would be the favored candidate to fill it.[22] While he waited, James took the opportunity to add to his salary by proposing to deliver twelve Lowell lectures and to teach women at the Harvard Annex "for not more than four hours a week and for not less than $4.00 an hour."[23]

Marriage did not cause a revolution in James's emotional state, but in small, incremental ways created a sense of independence and stability. Although he and Alice set up housekeeping only a few blocks from his parents' home, it appears that James tried to keep his distance from 20 Quincy Street. Once, when he needed a book from his family's library, he sent a student, George Gordon, to call on his father. "I thought it was strange," Gordon recalled, "to send me, an unknown student, to an unknown home, to unknown inhabitants, to find a book, but I went." When the aged Henry Sr. answered the door, glowering in his customary skullcap, the mission became even more puzzling. "What do you want? . . . What's your name, and who are you?" the old man demanded. When Gordon admitted that he was William's student, Henry glared at him with hostility—but he finally invited him in. "Are you a believer?" James asked.

Gordon not only was a believer, but a graduate of the Bangor Theological Seminary, and his disclosure sufficiently assured Henry Sr., who proceeded to relate an anecdote about his sons William and Harry. When the two were young, it seems, Harry declared that he believed in God, but not the church. "If you believe in God, you have got to believe in the church because God is the church," William retorted, rendering his brother speechless. Henry Sr., of course, took Harry's side in the debate—a debate that still smoldered, threatening to flare up at any time.[24]

Besides establishing some distance from the philosophical tyranny of his father, James's sense of independence and manliness were affirmed by the birth of his first child, Henry III, on May 18, 1879, which elicited this description to his brother Bob:

> My domestic catastrophe is now a week old. Babe and Mar [mother] both doing very well indeed. The former has a rich orange complexion, a black head of hair, weight 8½ lbs keeps his eyes tight shut on the wicked world and is of a musical, but not too musical disposition. . . . I find I have a strong affection for the little animal—and tho' I say it who should not, he has a very lovely and benignant little expression on his face.[25]

James, genuinely enchanted by his offspring, told Alice that he hoped "little Embry," as they called their infant son, soon might have a sibling. Still, James acknowledged that being a father brought new worries and anxieties. These preoccupations weighed heavily enough so that by the spring of 1880, his annual end-of-year collapse became exacerbated. His students noticed vast mood swings: from brilliance to lassitude, from energy to exhaustion.[26] He suffered, as before, from eye trouble, sometimes severe enough that students had to read their examination books to him. "I am so run down this year," he wrote to Bob, "that I have just decided to spend $500 . . . to spend the vacation in Europe."[27]

Recovery from his ailments, though, was not the primary purpose of the trip. This time, besides seeking a therapeutic benefit, James was going to Europe for intellectual sustenance; he hoped to meet some of the European philosophers with whom he had been corresponding and to expand the parameters of his small philosophical "club."

By the time James left in the summer of 1880, he had published, besides some half-dozen reviews and his remarks about Spencer, "Brute and Human Intellect" and "The Spatial Quale" in the *Journal of Speculative Philosophy*, "Quelques considérations sur la méthode subjective" in Renouvier's *Critique philosophique*, and "Are We Automata?" and "The Sentiment of Rationality" in *Mind*. These articles in major American, French, and British journals placed him in eminent company and attracted the attention of colleagues both at home and abroad. No longer an obscure instructor of anatomy, he had established himself, at the age of thirty-eight, as a respected philosopher who seemed, to his friend Josiah Royce, at least, to be founding a new school of philosophical inquiry.

The basis of this new school, as Royce understood it, lay not in its propositions, but in its broadening of philosophical questions by taking a psychological perspective and its concern with connecting philosophy to human action. Why, James asked, should anyone become a philosopher? What is the process by which we make decisions and achieve understanding? What are the consequences of our assumptions? In "The Sentiment of Rationality," and "Rationality, Activity and Faith," James explored the first question and decided that his own motive for philosophizing was to discover a "rational conception" to explain the "fragmentary and chaotic" experiences of everyday life, and so to feel "ease, peace, rest. . . . The transition from a state of puzzle and perplexity to rational comprehension," he said, "is full of lively relief and pleasure."[28] If rational conceptions posited a closed system, however, if they had no room for novelty, then they could obscure concrete experience, prevent the philosopher's active engagement in the real world, and fuel a sense of anxiety about change and spontaneity.

For James, the passion for simplification and explanation (the passion, that is, for a system of universal abstractions) needed to be balanced—even outweighed—by "the impulse to be *acquainted* with the parts rather than to comprehend the whole."[29] The mind that focuses on the concrete "loves to recognize particulars in their full completeness, and the more of these it can carry the happier it is. It is the mind of Cuvier *versus* St. Hilaire, of Hume *versus* Spinoza. It prefers any amount of incoherence, abruptness and fragmentariness . . . to a fallacious unity which swamps things rather than explains them."[30] The philosopher who rejects "fallacious unity" is free—in fact, is compelled—to make decisions and participate in daily life. "The impulse to take life strivingly," James wrote, "is indestructible in the race."[31] That sentence could serve as an epigraph for many of his future works.

Lustrous Figures

AS HE CONSIDERED motivations for philosophizing, James argued that a person's "emotional constitution" directed his affinity to one or another philosophy. His European trip gave him the opportunity to test that theory as he became acquainted with many of the men whose works he had been reading, responding to, and reacting against. After meeting the British philosophers Shadworth Hodgson, Alexander Bain, and even the redoubtable Herbert Spencer, James felt relief at their accessibility, even fallibility. Anxious about feeling intimidated, James found his new colleagues physically smaller and emotionally more vulnerable than he had imagined. Hodgson, for example, seemed to James "bashful & amiable . . . [and] very modest. . . . He laughs very easily and when doing so easily chokes."[32] Bain, one of James's early idols, was neither as erudite (he did not read German) nor as physically imposing (he resembled "a very respectable little old family servant") as James had anticipated. The "little hickory nut of a scotch man" had "no atmosphere to his mind . . . and altogether makes me glad to have seen him once but never more."[33] Spencer was amiable but self-satisfied, a man "who has the simple ends and feels that he has succeeded in them."[34] As these philosophers became transformed in James's mind from powerful, daunting intellects to gracious colleagues, as they listened to James and encouraged his ideas, he began to see the reality of his taking his place among them. When Hodgson agreed with him about the worth of Charles Renouvier, James felt validated. "You can't think how it pleaseth me," he wrote to Alice, "to have this evidence that I have not been a fool in sticking so to R."[35] Nor, he was convinced by his new colleagues, had he been a fool to disparage Spencer.

Buoyed by his European encounters, James returned to Cambridge more confident in his own philosophical perspectives. In an address to the Harvard Natural History Society, he once again argued against Spencer by championing the importance of singular individuals, rather than external forces, in shaping history. Social change, James argued, was due to "the Grants and the Bismarcks, the Joneses and the Smiths."[36] When the talk was published as "Great Men, Great Thoughts and the Environment" in the October 1880 issue of the *Atlantic Monthly,* James discovered that he had generated a heated debate. In January and March 1881, James was attacked in articles by John Fiske and Canadian naturalist Grant Allen, whose *Physiological Aesthetics* James had criticized in a *Nation* review four years before. Both defended Spencer against what they saw as James's irresponsible misreading.

In May, within his savage memoir of Thomas Carlyle, Henry James Sr. himself entered the debate by questioning the very notion of personal greatness. Just because a man is recognized by others as "a lustrous figure," Henry Sr. wrote, and "wins oftentimes so loud a renown" does not mean that he is truly worthy of such esteem. Such a man might be "domineering and irritable to the pitch of insanity . . . and his judgments are apt to be purely whimsical, or reflect his own imperious will." Henry was thinking of Carlyle as he wrote; the characterization, however, surely fit Henry James himself. If anyone could change the world, Henry concluded, it would be the man of excellent spiritual character, the humble man who defers to goodness and truth. "Character, or spiritual manhood," he insisted, "is not created, but only communicated." Such individuals are the true generators of reform.[37] While the essay can be read as a justification of his own modest career, it also served as a cautionary word to his son, ambitious for fame and, increasingly, for money.

In the spring of 1881 James again corresponded with President Gilman about a possible position at Johns Hopkins. The terms he suggested reflect a growing certainty of his worth to any philosophy department: he asked for a contract of four or five years, the first to be spent on sabbatical in Europe at a salary of $2,000; for the remainder of the contract, $5,000 per year, considerably more than Harvard was paying.[38] Gilman was willing to consider James's application seriously and invited James to come to Baltimore for a visit. James, who never warmed to Harvard's president, thought that Gilman "in philosophical intelligence is certainly worth a dozen Eliots."[39] But despite the camaraderie the two men established, within days of the visit, Gilman declined James's offer; like other American universities, the department preferred importing a scholar from Europe.

James did not betray his frustration to Gilman. "Altho' it does not just gratify my highest hopes," he wrote, the decision "enables me to subside upon my present circumstances with a tranquil mind and a feeling that there is nothing that *I* at any rate can do to better them."[40] His present circumstances at Harvard precluded a sabbatical for the 1881–82 academic year; he would have to wait another year, Eliot told him, since his service as instructor and tutor did not count to fulfill the teaching required before he could take a paid leave.

In the summer of 1881, the Jameses retreated to Keene Valley, in which romantic setting Alice again became pregnant. As he awaited the birth of his second child, James suffered, if that is not too strong a word, the death of his mother. Mary James died in January 1882, after a brief bout with bronchitis. During her illness, she was nursed by her daughter, her sister, and her husband. Bob was in Cambridge, too, but Harry arrived home from Washington, D.C., just after the funeral. "It has been a severe loss to all of us," William remarked, "but father and my sister, the two who presumably might suffer most from it, are bearing it very well."[41] If the two who grieved most deeply were very well, one can only surmise that William himself suffered little.

Mary's death elicited a response from her son that would be repeated after many future losses: a sudden sentimental epiphany about the value of the person lost, regret over the quality of their relationship, and a promise to treat others with more generosity. Years later, James admitted that after Mary's death "every thing about her seemed so different to me from what it ever had before, that I was indignant at my blindness, and resolved as far as possible to feel my human relations during life as I should after death, in order to feel them after death more as I did during life."[42]

This reproof suggests that James took responsibility for the lack of warmth between him and his mother; he was simply unable, he said, to recognize her strengths and attributes. But it is doubtful that he valued those strengths or could name those attributes. Throughout his youth, James found her controlling, demanding, annoying—traits that Mary, it appears, found equally unfortunate in her eldest son. The complacency and self-sufficiency that other family members admired in Mary caused William to doubt the complexity of her personality. He felt emotionally superior to her precisely because he could suffer— intensely, frequently, and, to her dismay, dramatically.

If her death caused only a ripple in his emotional life, he did consider a possible gain: buying his father's house. In the end, however, Henry Sr. and Alice, deciding that the Quincy Street home was too large, did sell—but not to William—and moved to Boston's Beacon Hill.

On June 17, 1882, James became the father of another son: this time, in the family tradition, named for him. In the months following Billy's birth, James was away from home frequently on one or another errand, including overseeing family business in Albany. James's repeated absences after the births of his children suggest that he was escaping from the responsibilities and disruptions caused by a newborn. But Alice, wanting to devote herself to her infant's care rather than to

William's, apparently welcomed her husband's absences during these periods. With her mother and sisters nearby (in fact, Alice and the children lived with her mother during some of William's absences), Alice enjoyed the strong support and close companionship of her family.

That support became vital for Alice when William again sailed to Europe in September 1882, leaving her at home with four-year-old Harry and three-month-old Billy. Finally taking the sabbatical that had been refused him the year before, James told his friends and family that he was going abroad to confer again with his European colleagues, learn more about their work and ideas, and especially to make progress on *The Principles of Psychology,* already years behind its due date. As in the past, however, the threat of a nervous collapse figured significantly in his decision to go to Europe.

Before he left, James succeeded in convincing President Eliot to hire Josiah Royce as his replacement. Royce was the first of several faculty members—George Santayana and Hugo Münsterberg among them—hired because of James's influence. Their presence dramatically changed the character of the philosophy department, but James never managed to create a cohesive "school" to promote his own ideas. Instead, under his guidance, Harvard's department became notable, perhaps appropriately in the context of James's philosophical views, for its intellectual diversity.

Royce, whose interest in the religious aspect of philosophy was shaped by Kant and Berkeley rather than Unitarianism, brought a fresh voice to Harvard; and he proved to be a stimulating colleague and loyal friend for James. He had met James seven years earlier when he stopped in Boston before departing for study in Germany. Immediately, James recognized something special in Royce, despite his social awkwardness and his odd appearance. Short and stocky, Royce had an unusually large head, bright red tousled hair, nearly transparent eyelashes, intense blue eyes, and full lips that seemed in a permanent pout.

Royce was bright, ambitious, and, at that moment, very much in need of a mentor—traits that appealed to James enormously. Born in the small California mining town of Grass Valley, Royce had grown up circumscribed by his parents' poverty and his spirit shaped by their strong religious faith. In the Royce home, the Bible served as the most significant work of literature, history, and moral teachings.

When Royce was eleven, his family moved to San Francisco, wrenching him from the quiet solitude that he had come to value. In the city, he was shunned by other young boys, who found him physically unattractive and personally unappealing. Yet if he failed in the parks and playgrounds, he succeeded admirably in the classroom where his teachers quickly affirmed his talents in mathematics and science. He advanced so quickly that he was able to enter the University of California College of Civil Engineering as a freshman at the age of sixteen. There, he excelled so markedly in both science and the humanities that, urged by the university's president Daniel Coit Gilman, the townspeople of Berkeley were moved to raise the money for his postgraduate studies abroad.

After a year at Leipzig and Göttingen, Royce was offered a fellowship at the new graduate school at Johns Hopkins, where Gilman had taken over the presidency. At the end of his first year, Royce visited James and poured out his self-doubts and worries. Those feelings were familiar to James: surely, at the age of twenty-one, he had been even more distressed than Royce about his future. As he would with so many young men later, James leaped eagerly into the role of counselor, encouraging Royce to continue his studies, assuring him that it was possible to succeed in a career in philosophy—especially for a man as talented as Josiah Royce.

Royce graduated from Johns Hopkins in 1878, receiving one of the first four doctorates awarded, but found to his disappointment that the only position offered was from the English department at the University of California at Berkeley. Longing to teach philosophy at an eastern college, he returned reluctantly to what he saw as the wasteland of the West.

James sympathized, but could not help him until his sabbatical created a vacancy. Royce embraced his Harvard position eagerly, determined to please both colleagues and students; as he confessed to a friend, "I do not want to go back to California, and took this place so as to get in the edge of a wedge somewhere on this side of the Continent."[43]

He drove in his wedge firmly during three years of temporary appointments; finally, in 1885, Eliot offered him an assistant professorship in the philosophy department, where Royce spent the rest of his career. He owed this success in no small way to James's support, and

James knew it. "Please give me *all* your impressions concerning him," William wrote to his wife during Royce's first semester at Harvard, "for I feel as if I had *made* him, after a fashion."[44] Royce's success was no less James's: proof of his power, his influence, and his stature among his peers.

Chapter 10

AN ENTIRELY NEW SEGMENT OF LIFE

1882–1884

AS JAMES TRAVELED through Germany and Austria in the first weeks of his trip, he found himself, much to his surprise, recalling the distress and loneliness of his 1867 stay in Dresden and Berlin. Again, he said, he had come to Europe to solve "much the same problems, to be met in much the same way, with patience." Now, though, he believed that the trip could revive the hopefulness, confidence, and happiness that Alice had inspired. "No symphony or opera or organ strain ever had more solemn tones than have made up our deep deep indefeasible relation to each other, my friend, my sister, my wife, my own," he wrote to Alice. "I feel your existence woven into mine with every breath I take, dear; and I am so full of pity for the poor creatures who have to live alone. . . . I never knew before what the sacred meaning of the word home meant."[1]

Home, of course, meant his two sons as well, and he missed tumbling on the floor playing "wild beast" with his three-year-old. "Your poor Dad has got no home now," he wrote to little Harry, "but just rolls around the world, sleeping in another bed almost every night. Sometimes he almost feels like crying to get home to Momsy & Culturmensch & Willyam & all."[2] Yet he believed that he needed to be in Europe, away from home and family, to achieve the goals he set out for himself: to improve in physical and mental health, and to work on his psychology textbook.

Just as he had sent health reports to his parents during his Dresden trip, he kept Alice apprised of changes in his eyes, improvements in his insomnia, his physical reactions to the weather, and his general sense of heartiness. These reports served partly to defend the expense of his trip; but Alice, although as frugal as his mother in many ways, encouraged James's stay in Europe.

Alice regained her strength fairly quickly after Billy's birth, and by late September had dismissed the baby nurse, managing by herself, with the help of her mother and sisters. When she and the children visited Henry Sr. in Boston, he found her thriving and thought his grandsons were "the most interesting children I ever beheld." Harry, especially, so "full of glee in inventing things that have never happened" was "too good to behold. He is manifestly too knowing for either his father or mother," Henry Sr. wrote to William, "and I alone have a doctrine—that of God's *natural* humanity—that can keep his intellect clear. But," he added, "I am going to die long before his intellectual needs will require me, and you must let him read my books."[3]

Death was much on Henry Sr.'s mind in the fall of 1882. He still grieved the loss of his wife; a history of heart disease and strokes had left him debilitated. Now, a combination of physical frailty and depression took its final toll: at the end of November, after a minor attack of nausea, he decided that he was dying. Although his physician diagnosed the illness as merely indigestion and predicted that Henry Sr. would make a full recovery, a visit with her father-in-law persuaded Alice that "[h]e has distinctly made up his mind not to live, and without disease, that, at 73, is a good reason for going."[4]

While Aunt Kate hoped that he would change his mind, his daughter felt "horrified . . . to the core of my being" when a friend suggested that she urge Henry to eat. Just as Henry had reacted with apparent equanimity to her own threats of suicide, she believed it was his right—indeed his privilege—to die whenever he wanted to. "Imagine my wanting to stay the will of God," she said, "and add a second to the old man's hours!"[5] He refused Aunt Kate's offerings of a bit of meat, a bit of bread, even some brandy. Sometimes he simply turned his head away, gazing, it seemed, into another world. Sometimes, he exploded in anger: "What vile-tasting stuff," he exclaimed after swallowing some water, "and what a vile world!"[6]

Yet as calm as she appeared, Alice confided to her sister-in-law that if Henry Sr.'s death seemed imminent, she would summon Harry "to share the responsibility" of burdensome decisions. Certainly she did not want William, who would offer none of the gentle consolation or serenity that Harry always had provided for his sister.

On Sunday, December 10, the summons became necessary. That night, a short time after William arrived in London to visit with Harry, they received an ominous telegram: "Brain softening possibly live months all insist Wm. shall not come." Although William admitted that he and Harry had long anticipated their father's final heart attack or stroke, they were not prepared for this sudden news with its frightening diagnosis. "Softening of the brain" implied a marked change in behavior, perhaps dementia—perhaps, they feared, violent rage. Worrying as much about Alice's reaction as about their father's deterioration, Harry quickly booked passage home. Despite the admonition that William stay in London, his first impulse was to return, as well. "I wanted to get to see him if possible before the end, & to let him see me and get a ray of pleasure from the thought that I had come," he said.[7] But on quick reflection, he changed his mind: his father, after all, might not even recognize him; and his father's recognition was essential for William. Harry, then, departed alone on December 12, leaving William in his Bolton Street flat.

His wife, who wrote almost daily, was torn between urging William to return and fulfill his filial duty and to stay away and acquiesce to his sister's wishes. Finally, she decided that her sister-in-law was right. "It is not *hard* to tell you that you could not be much comfort to that household now," Alice wrote to her husband. "Your father has grown indifferent to things and people. I am struck continually with the change in his relation to Alice. She seems off his mind."[8] William would not respond well to indifference. If he were disappointed and distressed by his father's reaction, he would require consoling, and no one would have time to devote to his needs. By his own admission, William was a demanding member of the family, depending on Alice to read to him, take dictation of his articles, find lost objects, and calm him when, as he put it, he fell into "a sort of a rage."[9] William was well aware that he could be a burden. "You must have full hands enough without me to nurse and smooth down," he wrote to Alice.[10]

Resigned never to see his father again, William awaited news from Boston with—as he put it—"intense eagerness," a word that describes accurately his feelings at that moment. For his father, death would bring release from unbearable loneliness and dejection. For himself, William said, it would mean the beginning of "an [e]ntirely new segment of life."[11]

As William waited, reflecting on his relationship with Henry Sr., he blamed himself for the tension between them; he had been, he said, emotionally "stingy and grudging."[12] In a much-reprinted farewell to his father—a letter he knew would be read by the whole family— William acknowledged indebtedness to the "central figure" of his life:

> All my intellectual life I derive from you; and though we have often seemed at odds in the expression thereof, I'm sure there's harmony somewhere, & that our strivings will combine. What my debt to you is goes beyond all my power of estimating, so early, so penetrating and so constant has been the influence.

He promised that he would edit and promote his father's works, and he apologized for the "trouble I've given you at various times through my peculiarities."

Despite William's effusions, the letter underscored his independence. He was, he told his father, a "creature different from yourself"; and those differences, one might conclude, were bound to inform his decisions as he went about promoting and publicizing Henry's works. William would assume a powerful role as editor, selecting *"extracts"* (here he underlined the term) according to his own evaluation of the importance of his father's ideas.[13]

Henry Sr. never saw his son's farewell. After several fainting spells, he refused to get out of bed, he refused food, he slept longer and longer; when he was awake, he preferred to turn his head toward the windows and gaze into the light. In his final days, when his physician administered opium to make him feel more comfortable, he babbled, often unintelligibly. Sometimes he cried out with longing for his dead wife. Sometimes, he told Aunt Kate, he had strange visions, once of some old men sitting along the wall doing nothing, he explained, but "taking a kindly interest in me."[14] And at the end, according to Aunt Kate, he murmured, "Oh, I have such good boys—*such* good boys!"[15] Those were his last recorded words. He died, more peacefully than his boys imagined he would, on December 18.

Henry Sr. was buried on the morning of December 21, in the family plot at the Cambridge Cemetery. The small group of mourners included the two Alices, Mrs. Gibbens, Mary Tweedy, Francis Child, and Fanny Morse. Bob was the only son in attendance. Harry disembarked in New York at noon, too late, where he was given a letter from his sister informing him that the funeral had already taken place. As he made his way to Boston, he shored up his courage to face a household overcome by grief and emotion. When he finally arrived at 11:00 P.M., however, he found an atmosphere of unexpected serenity. His sister Alice, who planned to leave the next morning for a few days' rest at Katharine Loring's home on Boston's north shore, was nearly ready for bed. She and Aunt Kate, who appeared "quite unexhausted," quietly and calmly supplied Harry with details of his father's last days. "The house is so *empty*," Harry wrote to William. But no one asked for William's presence: "All our wish here is that you should remain abroad the next six months," Harry assured him.[16]

William, who learned of his father's death before Harry did, from an announcement in the London *Standard*, felt momentary shock and an initial reaction of grief "more, much more than I expected."[17] But the grief was not enough to keep him from lunching and dining with friends. In the next days, sadness gave way to a new sense of power and freedom. His father, whose admonitions echoed in his mind each time he made a decision, whose censure he had feared and whose praise he so coveted, became transformed at once from a looming presence to an image "smaller, less potent, more pathetic."[18] William admitted feeling "[t]he sweetest sense of stability & balance . . . at the thought of him & Mother being in the same place, apart no longer."[19] He began to think of his own mortality and to reflect on the legacy that he would leave to his children and to the world. When he told his sister that their father's death would prove "the most important change in all your life," his words applied equally to himself. "In some ways, it will be a great nakedness, in others," he knew, "great freedom."[20]

THROWN INTO CLOSE proximity with her brother-in-law, William's Alice discovered that she often felt depressed after being in his presence, despite her warm feelings toward him. Harry seemed to her so stolidly "middle-aged."[21] "I think your brother Harry makes one miserable in a fine, inexplicable fashion," Alice wrote to William. "How wide these differences in nature are, and how I thank God for yours—your nature darling—which shelters mine so warmly."[22]

Alice observed with regret her sister-in-law's inexplicable rudeness and coldness to her aunt Kate. Nor did Alice understand the strained relationship between Bob and his sister although she knew very well that William's own relationship with Alice often appeared antagonistic. Despite appearances, however, he professed that he was her "loving brother . . . ready to help you and cooperate for your comfort in any way that lies in my power."[23] According to William's Alice, only Alice's friend and companion Katharine Loring and Henry were able "to smooth the troubled waters" resulting from Alice's displays of temper and suffering.[24] Part of Katharine's success with Alice was caused, it seems, by her administering larger doses of opium than the doctors recommended; part by her overbearing and officious manner.

Alice's relationship with Katharine worried the family, but no one felt able or willing to interfere. William's Alice reported that Henry once tried to talk with her about his sister and Katharine, only to stop short when Aunt Kate walked into the room. Alice suggested to William that his sister and Katharine might eventually tire of one another; it is likely that others in the family shared her hope.

Although there were only veiled hints that the Jameses considered Alice's relationship with Katharine as improper, they were frank about censuring the way Katharine controlled Alice and anyone else who came under her purview. Katharine, William said, was "a pure official, doing her duties as such splendidly; but to be met by an official when one turns to a human, is unpleasant."[25]

Nerve Healing

ALTHOUGH JAMES HAD told family and friends that he was going to Europe to seek a rich intellectual context to stimulate his work, as usual, his compelling reason was his recurring insomnia, restlessness, and depression—and the disruption these problems generated in his family life. With a new infant, Alice simply could not provide the emotional support and attention that William required during one of his "collapses." "You know, darling," William wrote, "how much of humbug there was in my coming abroad 'to see the other psychologists', & how it was really done for that other reason, & how I knew all along that my deeper intellectual ends would be much better served by staying at home with you."[26]

Certainly those deeper intellectual ends were not met in the first months of the trip. William was getting no work done and felt guilty about spending so much on travel with so little results. But after his father's death, with an inheritance assured—William and his siblings shared the income of an estate worth about $95,000 in cash and properties—his feeling of guilt diminished.

Still, despite moments of great satisfaction about his writing, James sometimes felt frustrated and impatient. He disliked London intensely: the weather was terrible, there was little natural light—a condition that always worsened his eye trouble—and he was tired from the endless round of social obligations every evening. When William hinted that he might want to come home, however, his family strongly discouraged him. An early return, his brother warned him, would seem "a melancholy profession of failure (as regards your projects of absence,) & sort of proclamation of want of continuity of purpose."[27] Henry knew that the threat of public humiliation had influenced many past decisions, but William had changed.

Outraged at Henry's interference in a matter that, William believed, should be his alone to decide—or at least his and Alice's, he told Henry that he now knew "just how one's half-crazy relations feel when they get letters of good counsel," referring, no doubt, to his own admonitions to his brother Bob. William insisted that his status at Harvard, and his colleagues' esteem, was unassailable; that Henry could not understand the reality of his life in Cambridge; and more important, that he did not appreciate that William was a married man who missed the companionship—and here we must understand physical companionship as well as emotional—of his wife: "any place near *her*," he declared, "is a good bit better than any place where she is not." No longer would he tolerate being treated "like a small child who didn't know what his own motives or interests were."[28]

Alice tried a gentler persuasion, asking simply if William would be giving up a chance at good health and good work if he came home too soon. Yet her motive may not have been entirely altruistic: For months she had helped to nurse her father-in-law while tending to her two young children. She was tired; and if she delayed a reunion with her husband, she would put off the likelihood of a third pregnancy.

Alice prevailed, at least for the moment, and James agreed to stay in Europe. Soon he announced that he was writing energetically about "the difference between feeling & thought," and formulating "some *really* big & simple views in psychology which will make the book . . . a new starting point in the Science."[29] Yet just days after that happy pronouncement, he succumbed to "the usual annual collapse" that he claimed to experience every February and changed his mind: he must come home. He was depressed, his eyes were bothering him, and he could not write.

During this desolate time he traveled to Paris, returned to the neighborhood where his family had lived when he was a child, and managed to visit their former apartment. The view and even the wallpaper were unchanged, yet what he saw contradicted the memory he had formed of that circumscribed period of his youth. "The rooms, strange to say, looked *larger* than I had supposed them," he reported to his wife. "It was rather touching & bro't up many reminiscences of Father & Mother in those days."[30]

James arrived home in mid-March, and by early May, Alice again was pregnant. James's eye trouble and depression persisted into the spring; he complained of poor progress in his writing and "muddled and clotted" thoughts. In an effort to sort out his ideas, he consented to give a few lectures at the annual Summer School of Philosophy in Concord, Massachusetts.

James did not hold the Summer School in high esteem, although occasionally he attended lectures that were delivered by one of his friends or colleagues. Begun in 1879 under the direction of Samuel Emery, Frank Sanborn, and William Torrey Harris, the school attracted some fifty participants, mostly women teachers, for the four-week sessions of ten lectures per week on philosophy or literature.[31] In 1883, topics included a discussion of the eighteenth-century Scottish empiricist David Hume, a reassessment of Hegel, and a look back at Puritan philosophy. James offered three lectures on psychology, which he soon shaped into an essay, "On Some Omissions of Introspective Psychology," for *Mind*.[32]

Now, four years after he agreed to write a psychology textbook incorporating the brave new work of experimental psychologists, James took a cautious look at their findings. Data about nerve responses and perception served to sustain a view of thought "broken into bits," and made to fit what James saw as false theories of mind. He feared that as psychologists examined anecdotal data to question mental activity, *states* of mind would receive attention, while "the stream of thought," or relational processes, would be ignored. Wary of nouns, he examined instead parts of speech that acknowledged nuance, relationships, or connotation: "there is not a conjunction or a preposition, and hardly an adverbial phrase, syntactic form, or inflection of voice, in human speech," he wrote, "that does not express some shading or other of relation which we at some moment actually feel to exist between the larger object of our thought."[33] As soon as psychologists imposed a rigid noun-based rhetoric on their observations, James warned, they were in danger of blinding themselves to a rich variety of data.

The relational term that most concerned James at the moment was "therefore." If we see a black bear approach from the woods, do we feel fear and *therefore* run? Or do we run, and therefore, by the act of running, generate in ourselves a feeling of fear? In "What Is an Emotion" James discussed for the first time his theory that our emotions are generated by action in response to stimuli: we are sad because we cry, we fear because we run. To one correspondent who was not convinced, James explained,

> Of course my "theory" about the emotions is quite independent of what species of mental operation the emotion is consequent upon,—whether a reflective judgment or a "perception." It confines itself to saying that, when once there, the emotion consists of a complex of feelings of bodily change. I used the word perception untechnically and for brevity's sake to cover all sorts of cognition. I don't wonder that the theory failed to convince you. I find that of my friends, the only ones to whom it seems plausible are the physiologists, and that is not *necessarily* a point in its favor.[34]

James seems more interested in considering the control of emotions rather than their generation.[35] While he admitted that emotions are difficult to feign, he knew from his own experience that they could be altered by one's will. Rather than responding with shame, regret, or dread, for example, one can learn other responses—responses more conducive to a feeling of well-being. "There is no more valuable precept in moral education than this," he wrote, "if we wish to conquer undesirable emotional tendencies in ourselves, we must assiduously, and in the first instance cold-bloodedly, go through the *outward motions* of those contrary dispositions we prefer to cultivate."[36]

James continued to argue for the centrality of the will in a talk he gave in the spring to Harvard divinity students, published later in the year as "The Dilemma of Determinism."[37] Determinism was not a dilemma for James; he rejected any philosophy that holds an "antipathy to the idea of chance,"[38] that negates the efficacy of free will and personal power. Where determinists use "chance" to imply chaos and degeneration, James saw the term as neutral at worst, and, at best, "eulogistic." "The idea of chance," he wrote, "is, at bottom, exactly the same thing as the idea of gift . . . [a] name for anything on which we have no effective *claim*."[39] The gift, for James, was the power to shape and interpret reality.

Local Dramas

IN HIS OWN FAMILY, William and his brother Henry—who, with relief, finally was able to drop the *junior* that for too long had tagged after his name—emerged as the two most powerful figures, the decision makers to whom others turned in distress. Unfortunately, there was ample distress among the Jameses in the years following their parents' deaths.

In May 1883, Alice entered the Adams Nervine Asylum, a small, private institution in the Boston suburb of Jamaica Plain, where, during a three-month stay, she followed a regimen of rest, food, and isolation that was supposed to alleviate her nervous symptoms. She was only slightly better when she left the institution, however, and spent the next year trying other treatments, including massage and a galvanic therapy—the application of low levels of electricity to various locations on the body—purported to be effective in stimulating the nerves. Finally, in the summer of 1884, Alice rallied: she socialized with friends, and her spirits seemed to improve. Later that year, she decided to travel to London with Katharine Loring, hoping that in a new environment she would continue to recover. Her brothers encouraged the decision; William, in fact, predicted that Alice might thrive so well in England that she would not think of returning home. Perhaps this prediction reflected his own wish to be relieved of his responsibilities for her now that he had a growing family of his own. As Alice improved, Wilky, suffering from heart disease, began to fail rapidly. Diagnosed with nephritis, in mid-November 1883, with his brother Bob at his bedside, he died.

At the time of Wilky's death, Bob was enjoying a rare, if temporary, period of health and stability. Depressed and alcoholic, he was a trial to everyone who cared about him: his wife, children, and siblings. In the fall of 1884, he turned up in Cambridge, dissipated and overweight. He confessed to William that he had been having an affair and felt confused and overwhelmed. For William, whose past advice to Bob often was unheeded and even resented, this episode confirmed the hopelessness of his brother's future. As much as William believed in the possibility of growth and change for himself and others, he was convinced that Bob was incapable of change. "Bob seems to me a mere hollow shell of a man, covering up mental disease," William wrote to Bob's wife. "I shall always be tender with him, because I seem now to be his only friend here, and it is good to have one refuge. He is his own worst enemy—Pity it is that you should be buffeted about at his chariot wheel."[40]

As his two younger brothers suffered, however, William and his family thrived. In January 1884, the Jameses became parents of a third son. The birth of another boy, however, caused a serious problem: now that the names Henry and William were assigned, what would they call their child? William's choice—Herman Hagen—puzzled Henry. What possible connection, he wondered, did a Herman Hagen have to the James family? As it turned out, very little. Hagen, William said, was "an inestimable old Colleague of mine . . . to whom I have no other way of testifying my affection, as he is the hardest man in the world to talk with."[41] Why James wanted to testify to his affection in so dramatic a way remains a mystery.

Hermann August Hagen, a noted entomologist, had come to Harvard in 1867, at Louis Agassiz's invitation, to head the entomological department at the Museum of Comparative Zoology. In 1870, at the age of fifty-three, he became professor of entomology. Although at the time, James seemed convinced of a sense of kinship with Hagen, a letter written to Alice nine months after their son's birth suggests that the friendship suffered a rift, perhaps caused by Hagen's reputedly short temper.[42] Henry objected strenuously to the name. He thought middle names superfluous, he explained, and he disliked "the idea of giving children the *whole* names of others."[43] Nevertheless, despite Henry's suggestions of several names he thought more appropriate, the Jameses insisted on Herman.

James stayed at home after Herman's birth; this time, Alice and the children left Cambridge to vacation in upstate New York. After the academic year ended, he set himself to the task of editing his father's works for publication, a project he approached with unusually high spirits. As his first book, it seemed less daunting than the still-unfinished textbook on psychology. Surely, he thought, it could be completed during the summer, published quickly, and—crucial to his plan—begin to earn royalties.

The book gave William a chance to wrestle with his father's ideas and emerge victorious: his father, at last, could not contest his interpretation. "I have been having a wonderful solemn kind of week with poor old Father's ghost, deep into whose intimacy I have wrought," he wrote to Alice. "I feel as if I had stated the gist of him in a way he would be glad of and glad that I should do."[44]

It is not likely, however, that Henry Sr. would have been pleased at his son's characterization of his thinking as narrow, "peculiar," and arcane. "With all the richness of style," William wrote in his introduction, "the ideas are singularly unvaried and few. Probably few authors have so devoted their entire lives to the monotonous elaboration of one single bundle of truths."[45] The single truths that his father expounded centered on the negation of the self and the exaltation of God. In essay after essay, book after book, he made the same point; yet after he had finished each work, William said, "disgusted with the insufficiency of the formulation (he always hated the sight of his old books), [he] set himself to work to say it again."[46]

In a tone at once unctuous and condescending, William portrayed his father as frustrated and unhappy. "Mr. James scorned to apply the word religion to any experience whose starting point was not pessimistic," William noted, and reasonably suggested that his father would have been better off living in a theological age.[47] When individualism, free will, and personal achievement were so roundly celebrated, Henry's denigration of selfhood attracted few sympathizers.

Although James often found his father's writing inaccessible, he filled the introduction with long, florid quotations and advised readers not to "*squeeze* the terms or the logic too hard."[48] For himself, he admitted "the deepest of all philosophic differences" with his father: that between philosophical pluralism and entrenched monism. He expected his readers to agree with him that pluralism "is a view to which we all practically incline when in the full and successful exercise of our moral energy" because pluralism holds that each individual is "a match for whatever evils actually confront us."[49] His father, in attacking pluralism, attacked his son's deepest convictions.[50]

James's shaping of his father's work was hardly a testimony of respect or a celebration of genius, yet he appeared to be shocked by negative reviews. Both William and Henry protested a particularly chilling assessment in the *Nation,* where, because of the family's friendship with the magazine's editor, they had hoped for a more sympathetic reading. James may well have felt that his own reputation as a philosopher would attract readers to the volume—and bring in royalties. To his disappointment, sales were few, and he did not even earn back his investment in the publishing costs. "Alas! poor Father!" he exclaimed to Henry. "It is sad."[51]

Beyond the Parapet

AS JAMES EVOLVED a philosophy rooted in experience, focused on the consequences of concrete behavior, and impatient with the metaphors and assumptions of established religion, he also maintained a fervent involvement in psychical research. Like many scientists of his time, James believed that scrupulous and rigorous investigation of psychic phenomena—mediums, thought transference, extrasensory perception, and even reported sightings of ghosts—might yield secrets that, for psychologists and philosophers alike, as yet remained impenetrable.

For James, psychical research offered a way to explore human consciousness outside of "classical" psychology. This school, he said, hoped to formulate clean, clear, simple laws to explain the workings of the mind. "The facts," he said, "must lie in a neat assemblage, and the psychologist must be able to cover them and 'tuck them in' as safely under his system as a mother tucks her babe in under the down coverlet on a winter night."

James and his fellow psychical researchers believed that the mind was vastly more complex, with dark and murky corners that might be illuminated by studying individuals who were under hypnosis and in trance states, or those who experienced amnesia and multiple personality. "A mass of mental phenomena are now seen in the shrubbery beyond the parapet," James wrote. "Fantastic, ignoble, hardly human, or frankly non-human are some of these new candidates for psychological description."[52] So, too, he hoped, explorations into psychical phenomena would result in useful material. "I believe," he said, "there is no source of deception in the investigation of nature which can compare with a fixed belief that certain kinds of phenomenon are *impossible.*"[53]

For philosophers, too, psychical research had the potential of yielding evidence of a transcendent consciousness, an Absolute: a realm beyond the natural and concrete world. Perhaps, James thought, psychical research could bring him to the spiritual epiphany that he longed to experience. "I confess," he wrote to Davidson,

> I rather despair of any popular religion of a philosophic character; & I sometimes find myself wondering whether th[e]re can be any popular religion raised on the ruins of the old Christianity without the presence of that element which in the past has presided over the origin of all religions namely a belief in new *physical* facts & possibilities. Abst[r]act considerations about the soul & the reality of a moral order will not do in a year, what the glimpse into a world of new phenomenal possibilities enveloping those of the present life afforded by an extension of our insight into the order of nature, would do in an instant. Are the much despised "spiritualism" & the "Society for Psychical Research" the[n] to be the chosen instruments for a new era of faith? It would surely be strange if they were, but if they are not, I see no other age[n]cy that can do the work.[54]

If some philosophers and scientists despised spiritualism, many ordinary men and women energetically explored the possibility that life "on the other side" existed. Séances were popular entertainment, and reports of hauntings and telepathy peppered popular magazines. James saw little value in amateur spiritualism, such as a camp meeting he attended in August 1884 and found "extremely depressing." "We spent the evening at a rather striking circle in which a man told lots of definite things to about 6 other sitters," he wrote to Alice. "This A.M. I saw 3 other performances, one of mesmerism, the others of so called spiritualism—nauseous!"[55]

These "depressing" demonstrations, however, took up much of his time, as James searched for evidence of authentic psychical phenomena. On many research expeditions, his wife eagerly accompanied him. Alice encouraged, and often directed, her husband's interest. After Henry Sr.'s death, she confided in William: "If one impression stronger than all others is left to me from those days, it is the unutterable reality, *realness, nearness* of the spiritual world."[56] William yearned to feel that unutterable reality.

His conviction that it would be useful to investigate "ghosts, second sight, spiritualism, & all sorts of hobgoblins," from a scientific perspective made him greatly sympathetic to the efforts of a group of prominent British intellectuals who, in 1882, established the London Society for Psychical Research.[57] Founders of the SPR included Henry Sidgwick, a lecturer in moral science at Cambridge University; Frederic W. H. Myers, who had been one of his students; Arthur Balfour, who later would become England's prime minister; and William Fletcher Barrett, a physicist and member of the Royal College of Science in Dublin, who labored defiantly to establish the SPR because of his frustration in publishing the results of his own investigations of telepathy. The London SPR attracted significant interest from major literary figures, including Tennyson, Lewis Carroll, and the redoubtable John Ruskin.

The society owed its early success to Edmund Gurney, also a former student of Sidgwick, who, at the age of thirty-five, gave up his practice of law to devote himself to psychical research. Although some of his colleagues scoffed at this decision, Gurney believed that James understood. "Absence of income, & loss of reputation, or rather (since I have not much to lose) a gradual positive reputation for being weak in the head, are of course disadvantages," he wrote to James, "but I should be a hypocrite if I pretended that in my own hedonistic calculus, such things weigh against the interest of the subject, as compared e.g. with the well-ploughed fields of law. . . . You, at any rate, are not among the friends who will be quite confident that I am or rather that we are making an egregious blunder."[58]

Certainly James was not among those critics, and he had ample company. When William Barrett led a contingent of psychical researchers to America in late August, he was met by an erudite group of men in Philadelphia and Boston who were eager to hear about the work of the London Society for Psychical Research. Among his welcomers were Simon Newcomb, the head of the astronomy department at Johns Hopkins and arguably the nation's most famous scientist; Edward Pickering, head of the Harvard Astronomical Observatory; Charles Sedgwick Minot, professor of anthropology at Harvard;

George Stuart Fullerton, who taught philosophy at the University of Pennsylvania; Alexander Graham Bell; Henry Bowditch, dean of Harvard's medical school; G. Stanley Hall, who taught psychology at Johns Hopkins; and, of course, James himself.

The forty-year-old Barrett, a rousing speaker, earned credibility from his impeccable scientific credentials. He persuaded his listeners that psychical phenomena deserved as much attention as such scientific phenomena as electricity, magnetism, light, gravitation—none of which was visible or tangible except through its effects. If electricity could travel unseen, why not thoughts? If gravitation pulled objects toward earth, why not a psychic force that would cause objects to rise?

Nor was he above demonstrating his own psychical expertise for the entertainment of his audiences. At a Philadelphia gathering, he hypnotized a woman volunteer, evoking "perversions," as he put it, in her sense of taste and physical perception. Under his spell, she confused the taste of sugar and salt, much to the amusement of the spectators. In addition, he easily convinced her that she could see him floating gracefully near the ceiling of the auditorium. Although the performance offered nothing new for men and women who frequently attended demonstrations of mesmerism, thought transference, and rappings, still Barrett's audience was delighted. Here, they decided, was no crank. Their enthusiastic response, Barrett confessed, was "a novel and gratifying experience."[59]

With Barrett's encouragement, James and his colleagues held meetings in September and October to discuss the feasibility of establishing a formal organization of psychical researchers in America. Barrett assured them that they would be deluged with testimony and evidence once they made their work public. Their ability to test and verify psychical phenomena, therefore, would be hugely enhanced. Of course, he warned them, once they declared their interest in psychical matters to the world at large, they might be subject to ridicule. "But out of alchemy came chemistry," he told them; "and out of astrology, astronomy. There may be much in these extraordinary accounts of second-sight, thought-reading, apparitions, and so forth, fit only to ridicule; but if there are any facts at the bottom, we want to find them."[60]

After several more planning sessions, the American Society for Psychical Research held its first meeting on December 18, 1884, with members and associates totaling about 250. Astronomer Simon Newcomb, whose caution regarding spiritualism and whose criticism of the methodology of the British SPR was well-known among his colleagues, agreed to take on the presidency. "I think Newcomb . . . was an uncommon hit," James commented; "—if he believes, he will probably carry others."

Immediately, James and Henry Bowditch, both officers, sent a questionnaire and solicitation for volunteers to all members and associates. The society set up a roster of subgroups to conduct research on thought transference, mesmerism, apparitions, and even such special phenomena as divining rods. As a member of the Committee on Mediumistic Phenomena, James was interested especially in the names and addresses of private mediums who would consent to be examined. "I take it the urgent thing," James wrote to Thomas Davidson, "to rescue us from the present disgraceful condition, is to ascertain in a manner so thorough as to constitute *evidence* that will be accepted by outsiders, just what the *phenomenal conditions of certain* concrete phenomenal occurrences are. Not till that is done, can spiritualistic or antispiritualistic theories be even mooted. . . . And what we want is not only truth, but evidence." Although he knew the members would be "lucky if our scientific names don't grow discredited the instant they subscribe to any 'spiritual' manifestations," he also realized that scientists alone—rather than "literary men, philosophers, or clergymen"—could advance the cause of psychical research as a means to explore a new, and undiscovered, reality.[61]

Chapter 11

THE LOST CHILD

1885–1887

JAMES SET UP A laboratory where he worked each day, following his own experimental inclinations. He discovered that he could put some individuals under hypnosis "even without waving my hands," but he attributed his success more to his subjects' willingness to relax than to his own "peculiar power."[1] He easily found cooperative subjects among students and colleagues who believed, as he did, that hypnosis might yield important insights about subliminal mental states and the possibility of thought transference.

As he investigated all manner of psychical phenomena, he was most engaged by sessions with mediums. Frequently attending séances in the company of family and friends, he hoped to find a single "white crow," as he put it, to prove to himself that not all crows were black: a single authentic medium to prove that not all were frauds. Psychical research was hardly at the fringe of intellectual activity among educated men and women, as a brief survey of the SPR roster confirms. Active members included Phillips Brooks, one of Boston's most influential religious leaders; the biologist Asa Gray; editor William Torrey Harris and publisher Henry Holt; James and Charles Putnam; Josiah Royce; Moorfield Storey; Edmund Tweedy; Andrew D. White, the president of Cornell; the lawyer John Ropes; and psychologist and physician Morton Prince. SPR Associates were equally notable: Felix Adler, the founder of the Society for Ethical Culture; Julius Seelye, president of Smith College; James's former student Theodore Roosevelt; and, from the Harvard faculty, George Palmer, Francis Peabody, and Nathaniel Shaler.

The interest among faculty members proved infectious for students already skeptical of the assumptions of established religion. One such student was Glendower Evans, who had met James after entering Harvard in 1875 and began a friendship that continued even after he graduated, took a degree from Harvard Law School, and joined the prestigious Boston firm of Shattuck, Holmes & Monroe. Although Oliver Wendell Holmes was fifteen years older than his new colleague, he recognized an intelligence in Evans that energized his own thinking. "Mr. Evans," Holmes would announce, beginning their daily discussions, "I am ready to contradict any statement you will make."[2]

James felt the same kind of esteem for Evans and welcomed his interest in serving as an assistant in psychical research by taking notes at séances. As usual for James, when he liked a student, especially a student who saw him as a spiritual guide, he brought him into the family's life. As soon as he learned that Evans had become engaged, he encouraged Alice to call on Elizabeth Gardiner, the bride-to-be, and arrange to see the couple socially.

Gardiner needed to spend only a few minutes talking with Alice to recognize her sharp intelligence, kindness, and emotional generosity. At the time, Gardiner needed an understanding friend as much as her husband did. Not so certain as he that religion should—or could—be sloughed off, she was beset by spiritual conflicts. While William was sympathizing with Glendower's doubts, Alice sustained Elizabeth's need to believe. Her serene faith comforted Elizabeth; Alice's words, she said, "seemed to carry a message from Heaven."[3]

Alice's equanimity, however, was sorely tested in the spring of 1885. In March, she fell ill with scarlet fever, requiring her to be quarantined in the bedroom and causing a significant disruption in the Jameses' family life. Alice could communicate with William only through the closed bedroom door; the children had to be removed to their grandmother's; and James was worried that he, too, was incubating the illness. At the time, scarlet fever required a drastic response even after the illness ran its course. When Alice recovered, James wrote to his sister, the bedroom "will be disinfected with sulphur fumes, everything in it will be washed, the walls painted & papered, and left open to the winds of heaven for many weeks."[4] Still, the Jameses were reluctant to move the children back; they first thought of renting another house for the spring, but eventually they decided to leave the children at the Gibbenses', where their grandmother and aunt Margaret could care for them.

By June, Alice was well, but the respite was short-lived: she and Herman both caught whooping cough. It seemed prudent, therefore, to remove the entire family from Cambridge to more healthful country air, and James and Margaret Gibbens took the two older boys to Pottersville, New Hampshire, to look for a suitable residence for the rest of the summer. His month in the country was no vacation for James, who discovered that child care, even with Margaret's experienced help, was a trial. The boys, six and three, were so active and noisy that supervising them, James said, was "a labor fit to break the back of Hercules."[5]

He and Margaret decided to split their responsibility: James was in charge until just before lunch; Margaret then took over until late afternoon. Margaret also had the sole jurisdiction for the "peculiarities in William's bowels" which she alone, apparently, could manage.[6] "Both Margaret and I have successfuly done our duty towards these children," James wrote to his wife, "but I doubt whether other two human children ever had so much need of being 'taken care of' as these. Active entertainment all day long . . ."[7]

Soon, however, his troubles in caring for Harry and Billy became insignificant compared with the tragedy that had begun at home: Herman was not recovering. Leaving his children with his sister-in-law, James rushed back to Cambridge. The pudgy, placid child whom James called "the flower of our little flock" had developed complications of bronchial pneumonia. Wracked with high fever, by early July he quickly worsened, suffering four convulsions within a week. Alice took him to her bed and nursed him night and day, sleeping not more than three hours, if that. The child was so profoundly ill that the family's doctors were surprised each time he survived a fit of convulsions; but finally he had no strength to fight. On the night of July 9, gasping for breath on his mother's bed, he died.

Alice, after weeks of nursing that followed her own serious illness, was exhausted. In a photograph taken soon after Herman's death she appears gaunt, pale, her skin almost translucent, with an expression in her eyes at once wistful and stunned. James knew that Alice's grief would take a heavy toll. "Of course there will now be a collapse," he realized. But for the moment, at least, she was "mellow & free from morbidness."

The next day, in a haze of grief, William and Alice planned their son's funeral. They chose a small wicker basket as a coffin and lined it with soft flannel. They engaged the venerable Unitarian minister Andrew Preston Peabody to conduct the service. At six o'clock on Saturday morning, July 11, they took a buggy the few miles from Cambridge to Belmont where, in the woods, they gathered birch branches and pine boughs, ferns, grasses, and wild flowers to cover the wicker coffin. Laying their dead child gently in the basket, they arranged sprays of leaves at his head, grasses at his feet, flowers on his chest. "I have always looked down on these dressings," James wrote to Aunt Kate, "but there is usually a human need embodied in any old human custom, and we both felt this most gracefully."

Later, at the Cambridge Cemetery, where Mary and Henry also lay, Peabody recited "a gentle little prayer," and closed the tiny coffin's wicker lid. "[A]nd there he lies," James said, "one more experience to bind me and Alice together, one more taste of the intolerable mysteriousness of this thing called existence."[8]

Soon after the funeral, William informed Henry of his son's death, focusing more on Alice's feelings than on his own. He confessed that because he had left Herman so much in Alice's care, he felt "as if I had hardly known him or seen him at all." And as much as he grieved for the child, he also was moved deeply by "the spectacle of Alice through it all. The old word Motherhood, like so many other old words, suddenly gets an unsuspected meaning."[9]

The old word "motherhood" had long held ambivalent meanings for James: against the cultural image of virtue and self-sacrifice, he construed a far less flattering portrait, sent to Alice during his visit to Germany in 1882:

> Dear, perhaps the deepest impression I've got since Ive been in Germany is that made on me by the indefatigable beavers of old wrinkled peasant women, striding like men through the streets, dragging their carts or lugging their baskets. . . . All the mystery of womanhood seems incarnated in their ugly being—the Mothers! the Mothers! Ye are all one! Yes Alice dear, what I love in you is only what these blessed old creatures have; and I'm glad and proud, when I think of my own dear Mother with tears running down my face, to know that She is one with these.[10]

Now, however, with the illness and death of his son, he perceived
a new facet of the mysteries of womanhood—and one that yielded a
more generous characterization of his wife. Alice's devoted care of Herman was nothing but angelic; and nurturing afforded Alice a privileged and intimate connection to their child that he could not share. In
his *Principles,* James is curiously reticent about the topic of "parental
love." After asserting that it "is an instinct stronger in woman than in
man," he fills out his discussion with a long passage by the German ed-
ucator Georg Heinrich Schneider, who offered a condescending description of the love of a mother for her "ugly, piping cry-baby." The
"hideous little being," according to Schneider, could turn a vain, self-
centered, fastidious woman into a creature of devotion and altruism.
To the "worthy Schneider," whose patronizing tone apparently eluded
James, he added just one note: "the passionate devotion of a mother—
ill herself, perhaps—to a sick or dying child is perhaps the most
simply beautiful moral spectacle that human life affords. Contemning
every danger, triumphing over every difficulty, outlasting all fatigue,
woman's love is here invincibly superior to anything that man can
show."[11]

Alice's grief, he saw, was visceral and intense, while his, lament-
ably, seemed to him "general, abstract." Alice felt "the *reality* of the
moral life, which at other times we press so little against we may doubt
if it's there. This has brought me nearer to you than ever before,"
James wrote to Alice weeks later, "so near that it is almost absolutely
near."[12] Even so, he could not experience grief with the same ferocity.

Henry responded immediately with his sympathy for William and,
even more, for Alice. "[B]abies," he wrote, "are soft memories & Alice
will always throb to the vision of his little being."[13] That vision, she insisted, never left her. Always, she said, Herman was in her thoughts. "I
think of my little Herman—," she told Elizabeth Evans, "where is he
now? He does not tell me. But I might as well have asked him, before
he was born, what his life in this world would be. How could he have
conceived of sight and hearing and of moving about freely in this wonderful world? Had I tried to tell him, he would have shrunk back in
terror and begged to stay safely in his mother's womb."[14]

If Henry Sr.'s death had intimated for Alice the nearness of the
spiritual world, Herman's death made belief in that world an urgent
necessity for both William and Alice. "I believe [in], I almost feel im-

mortality, or peradventure something infinitely better," Alice said; "but life and immortality are surely calling to us all—and more than ever I want to listen."[15] They simply could not accept the notion of their son's total annihilation: human immortality must be possible. "It *must* be now," James wrote to his cousin Kitty, "that he is reserved for some still better chance than that, and that we shall in some way come into his presence again."[16]

It seems no coincidence that a few months after Herman's death the Jameses became vigorously involved with a medium who, Alice believed, could keep alive her connection with her lost child. The medium was Leonora Piper, and she would figure large in James's personal and professional life for decades to come.

Under Control

LEONORA EVELINA PIPER was twenty-six years old, living in Boston with her husband and year-old daughter, when the Jameses first visited her. Piper had come to their attention after Mrs. Gibbens, who had heard of her reputation from friends (who themselves had heard about her from their maid) paid her a visit and returned home so excited that one of her daughters scheduled a sitting for the next day.[17] Both women reported that Piper, in a trance state, had mentioned many names that could be familiar only to the Gibbenses. Their testimony sent the Jameses to Piper's Pinckney Street home within a few days.

For both William and Alice, a trance medium offered more potential for an authentic connection with the spiritual world than a materializing medium, such as the one they visited shortly before Herman fell ill. In early June, James reported to his cousin Kitty Prince that he and Alice were going to the Massachusetts Institute of Technology "to see a materializing medium tonight,—the most promising we've yet got hold of."[18] Materializing mediums boasted of the ability to create phantasms, visible and sometimes palpable manifestations of spirits. Sittings with such mediums usually were conducted in a closed compartment, or wooden cabinet, that shut out all sources of light. One winter, James and George Palmer, as part of their investigations for the Society for Psychical Research, attended such "cabinet seances" every Saturday. Although the performances were dramatic and, for some, even thrilling, the two men did not find one materializing medium that seemed to them to possess genuine psychic abilities.[19]

Leonora Piper was not a materializing medium: her talents did not lie in emanating phantasms, causing tables to rise or spirits to rap. She presented herself merely as a passive conduit, whose body and voice were available to spirits of the dead, enabling them to send messages to the living. She became, for the Jameses, an enduring link to the "white radiance," as James put it, behind the veil of natural reality.[20]

At their first visit, Piper not only mentioned the name of Alice's father (calling him at first Niblin and then Giblin) but, more significantly, the name of their lost child, which, although it emerged as Herrin, was close enough for the Jameses. She also provided unusually intimate revelations about many members of the Gibbens family. "My impression after this first visit," James wrote later, "was, that Mrs. P. was either possessed of supernormal powers, or knew the members of my wife's family by sight and had by some lucky coincidence become acquainted with such a multitude of their domestic circumstances as to produce the startling impression which she did."[21]

Alice was desperate for a sign that Herman's spirit existed and was accessible to her; and perhaps she believed that Piper, with a young child of her own, intuited her need. At one sitting, Alice recalled, Piper, who apparently knew nothing of the special burial that the Jameses had devised, described Herman "with his hands full of daisies, and [she also related] other sweet nothings (from the point of view of science) which meant everything to me."[22]

Although James believed that Piper may well have used expert sleuthing to discover facts about his own, more famous, family, he was certain that knowledge of the Gibbenses, past and present, could not be so easily obtained. Nor, he thought, could Piper know intimate details of his own household: she mentioned the recent loss of James's waistcoat, for example, and she described in detail the death throes of a cat that James had killed with ether. "She was strong on the events in our nursery," James said, "and gave striking advice during our first visit to her about the way to deal with certain 'tantrums' of our second child, 'little Billy-boy,' as she called him, reproducing his nursery name. She told how the crib creaked at night, how a certain rocking-chair creaked mysteriously, how my wife had heard footsteps on the stairs."[23]

The Jameses were impressed, also, with Piper's personality and demeanor. Unlike self-promoting mediums who advertised for clients in the *Banner of Light,* a popular spiritualist journal, Piper appeared almost reluctant to share her special talents. She was, by several accounts, a modest young woman whose shyness itself enhanced her credibility for the Jameses. She preferred to meet with only a small number of people, sometimes her husband and father among them, in a private alcove of her home. Her husband explained that she felt "bashful" about succumbing to a trance state in the view of large groups. She claimed not to understand the quality or cause of that trance state and admitted that ever since childhood she had experienced some incidents of extrasensory perception which seemed just as mysterious to her as to those who benefited by her.

Although Piper consented to give sittings, and be paid for them, she did not seek the notoriety that James eventually bestowed upon her. In fact, when James told her that he was reporting about her for the *Proceedings of the American Society for Psychical Research,* she asked for partial anonymity; he referred to her only as Mrs. P. Nevertheless, she apparently encouraged, or at least cooperated with, James's interest in her. He attended at least twelve sittings in the first nine months after he discovered her; and he sent scores of friends, who supplied James with additional testimony. Glendower Evans served as notetaker as James questioned her. Besides undergoing trances, Piper consented to be hypnotized by James not just once, but at least five times, until he was satisfied that her trance state was sufficiently distinct from her reactions under hypnosis.

In a trance state, a medium was dominated by one spirit, usually male, and as James noted, usually a "grotesque and somewhat saucy personage." This dominating spirit was known as a "control," who relayed messages and information to one or another of the sitters. When the Jameses first met Piper, her control called himself Dr. Phinuit, a French physician who had died some twenty-five years before.

Although James concluded that Phinuit most likely was not French (he hardly knew any French words), not a physician, and perhaps not even a former living being, still he ascribed to Phinuit a personality that was in every way distinct from Piper's. Unlike the timorous and gentle Mrs. Piper, Phinuit was opinionated and vociferous; while Mrs. Piper's memory seemed unremarkable, Phinuit could recall minute details of his encounters with sitters. Moreover, besides relaying trivial and mundane messages from the dead to their living relatives, Phinuit gave pointed moral lectures with an arrogance and psychological insight that, James said, Mrs. Piper could never match.

James's candid profile of Phinuit helps us to understand how deeply the sitters needed to feel intimidated by the external "control." Many sitters who had slipped away from the religious moorings of their youth looked for new sources of spiritual authority. The control presented himself as such a figure, a stern patriarch who, from his vantage beyond daily reality, told sitters how to conduct their lives. One of Piper's controls, after the raunchy Dr. Phinuit, called himself Imperator; another, more pointedly, Rector.

For James, Piper's apparent innocence and passivity underscored her authenticity. While he often was suspicious of professional mediums, he responded with enthusiasm to testimony of psychical experiences in ordinary people. For a time, James apparently hoped that Alice, with her unwavering belief in psychical phenomena, might be able to cultivate mediumistic powers.

Although James was a more sophisticated participant than most who gathered in the presence of mediums, he shared with them questions about the possibility of an Absolute, an Oversoul, a God; about the role of religion in a scientific age; about the notion that only through scientific investigation could reality be apprehended; about the visceral human need for faith. Herman's death, his encounter with Mrs. Piper, and his editing of his father's *Literary Remains* made those questions immediate and urgent. As he confronted the contradiction between his father's monism and his own professed pluralism, he could not deny feeling a certain longing for the kind of solace and moral righteousness that Henry Sr. derived from his religious beliefs. "There are moments of discouragement in us all," he wrote later, "when we are sick of self and vainly striving. Our own life breaks down, and we fall into the attitude of the prodigal son. We mistrust the chances of things. We want a universe where we can just give up, fall on our father's neck, and be absorbed into the absolute life as a drop of water melts into the river or the sea."[24]

Religious Longings

JUST AFTER HIS father died, James wrote to Alice, pleading with her "not [to] leave me till I understand a little more of the value and meaning of religion in Father's sense, in the mental life & destiny of man."[25] Alice shared that task with many others, most significantly Josiah

Royce. For George Santayana, who was an undergraduate at Harvard in the 1880s, James and Royce were "the 'young' professors of philosophy, they represented the dangers and scandals of free thought, all the more disquieting in that their free thought enveloped religion."[26] The two men agreed that since the Civil War, and the engulfing wave of Darwinism, religious life in America had eroded. Young men such as they felt little attachment to the beliefs of an earlier generation, and they tried, as Royce put it, "to come to some peaceful understanding . . . touching the ultimate meaning and value and foundation of this noteworthy custom, so widely prevalent among us, the custom of having a religion."[27]

From 1883, when James returned from his sabbatical and joined Royce in the philosophy department, the two young professors— James, the older by thirteen years—spent long hours in each other's company, grappling with such issues as the inexorable connection between religious faith and action, morality, and ethics. They discussed pessimism, altruism, skepticism, and the possibility of an Absolute that might, or might not, be reconciled with scientific inquiry. Early in 1885, Royce completed *The Religious Aspect of Philosophy,* a book that reflected many of those conversations, as he acknowledged by twice thanking James in his introduction.

"It seems to me a book of genius decidedly," James declared. Royce, he wrote to Carl Stumpf, was surely "[t]he most promising man we have in this country," both an able philosopher and, equally important, "a very complete human being, alive at every point." He recommended Royce's new book to Stumpf, especially the second half, which asserted "a new argument for monistic idealism, an argument based on the possibility of truth and error in knowledge . . . seeming to me to be one of the few big original suggestions of recent philosophical writing. I have vainly tried to escape from it. I still suspect it of inconclusiveness, but I frankly confess that I am *unable* to overthrow it."[28]

Although James's later writings on religion seem to contradict many of Royce's assertions, his excitement about the book helps us to understand his own doubts and needs at this particular moment in his life. A few years before, James had expressed his incredulity over "[t]he entire modern deification of survival *per se,* survival returning into itself, survival naked and abstract, with the denial of any substantive excellence in *what* survives, except the capacity for more survival still";

Darwinism, applied philosophically, seemed to him "surely the strangest intellectual stopping-place ever proposed by one man to another."[29] James proposed a wider and more complex intellectual realm, in which motivations other than mere survival compelled human behavior. "What I care for," he told Shadworth Hodgson, "is that my moral reactions should find a real outward application."[30]

Royce agreed. All men, he said, "want religion to define for them their duty, to give them the heart to do it, and to point out to them such things in the real world as shall help them to be steadfast in their devotion to duty."[31] Belief in the Absolute, then, did not interfere with one's ability to know the world through concrete experience, but rather afforded individuals a consensus of values on which they could base their actions.

Doubt, too, could be a positive force, inspiring a renewed commitment to religious beliefs by those who may have followed, through habit or fear, the beliefs in which they had been raised. "We are not content with what we learned from our fathers," Royce wrote; "we want to correct their dogmas, to prove what they held fast without proof, to work out our own salvation by our own efforts."[32] As James searched for a way to make sense of his father's monism in light of his own belief in free will, he found Royce's worldly perspective on the Absolute, at least as he thought he understood it, potentially liberating.

James might reject the idea of God as authority and religion as superstition, but still he yearned to believe that there existed some force, something that transcended his life, that both understood him sympathetically and, he said, "cared for" him and those ideas which he held important and vital. "I simply refuse to accept the notion of there being *no* purpose in the objective world," he told Thomas Davidson. "In saying 'God exists' all I imply is that my purposes are cared for by a mind so powerful as on the whole to control the drift of the Universe. This is as much polytheism as monotheism."[33]

This embracing, protective, and utterly sympathetic God would offer personal solace but not necessarily moral guidance. Even in a universe whose general drift was controlled, there still were singular instances of injustice that asked for a response from such sensible men as James and Royce. "In what ways," James asked, "does the oneness come home to your own personal life? By what difference does it express itself in your experience? How can you act differently towards a universe which is one?"[34]

In his *Religious Aspect of Philosophy*, Royce characterized and attacked two prevailing models of moral behavior that he and James found unsatisfactory: the romantic and the professional comforter. Romantics, more sensible than most to the "stir of modern life," felt stranded, their "theological ideals . . . shattered."[35] After an initial sensation of freedom, if not euphoria, the romantic found that without a creed to guide him, to help him distinguish good from evil, to teach him how to act morally, he was a dejected soul, "condemned to fleeting emotions," who could not help but develop a pessimistic view of life.[36]

In contrast to the erratic romantic, buffeted by waves of emotion, some individuals, motivated by their religious beliefs to do good, took on "the office of comforter," searching for problems that evoked their feelings of pity and sympathy. When they directed these feelings at the poor, destitute, and unhappy, they felt a new sense of importance, even of power. At a time when self-righteous social reformers had a growing presence in urban life—James himself knew many of them—the professional comforter was a familiar type, but it was not a type that James wanted to emulate. In fact, he found professional comforters irritating.

Permanent social change, James believed, would not result from the moral behavior of a few self-conscious individuals, but only from a consensus of shared values. For a community to share values, its members needed to feel a sense of common purpose and a common philosophical perspective. Despite the diversity of its population, America, it seemed to James, could foster this spirit of national unity. "In England america and germany," he commented in 1871, when an uprising in Paris during the Franco-Prussian War showed him the consequences of national divisiveness, "a regular advance is possible because each man confides in his brothers. However great the superficial differences of opinion there is at bottom a trust in the power of the deep forces of human nature to work out their salvation, and the minority is contented to bide its time." But in France, he saw no such trust, but rather a debilitating "love of external mechanical order" based in part on "old orthodox conceptions, religious & social."[37]

By the 1880s, James saw that in his own country the minority was not contented to bide its time, nor the majority to trust in the deep forces of human nature. Too practical a nation to succumb to the allure of idealism and determinism, America needed a philosophy that would nourish its citizens' individuality, foster their sense of community, and encourage their conviction that the world could be changed through their own energy and will.

This belief underlay his response to violent disputes between labor and capital that resulted in hundreds of strikes—more than five hundred in Boston alone—devastating destruction of property, and an alarming number of human casualties. To James, who occasionally suffered inconveniences because of rail or streetcar shutdowns, the upheaval seemed "a most healthy phase of evolution, a little costly, but normal and sure to do lots of good to all hands in the end."[38] The good, as he saw it, was the articulation of common values and goals among masses of workers. The Knights of Labor, for example, had grown, since its founding in 1869, from a tenuous band of nine tailors to a membership of 100,000 skilled and unskilled workers by 1885. "If it succeeds," James commented, "it will be one of the greatest events in history, for it *can* only succeed by the exercise of virtues that very large bodies of men have never been able to show."[39]

James's guarded optimism proved prescient. Neither the Knights of Labor, nor any other of the conglomerates of unions that arose in the 1880s, managed to create a cohesive body of workers with coherent goals. In 1884, though, one goal seemed widely shared: the working day should be no more than eight hours long. Employers, of course, were not sympathetic to shortening the workday, and in May 1886, 350,000 workers in more than ten thousand businesses decided to test their collective strength.

Among those workers were the employees of International Harvester in Chicago, who were picketing outside of their plant on May 3 when fighting broke out among strikers and strikebreakers. Police attempting to control the melee killed six strikers; many were injured. The next day, the Black International, a militant group of laborers consisting mostly of German and Polish immigrants, called a protest gathering in Chicago's Haymarket Square. The rally began peacefully—even Chicago's mayor attended in a show of support for the workers—but later, police attempts to disperse the crowd met with violence: a bomb exploded, killing a policeman; the riot squad retaliated, and more than a hundred people were left wounded.

James, and many others who read the news the next day, felt no sympathy for those they identified as the perpetrators of violence. The "senseless 'anarchist' riot in Chicago," James wrote to his brother, "is the work of a lot of pathological germans & poles. . . . All the irish names are among the killed and wounded policemen. Almost every anarchist name is continental." Not surprising to James, nor to many others, the eight men arrested as anarchists and accused of the bombing were "continental."[40]

These foreigners, according to James, were "pathological" because they had no vested interest in preserving American identity, no sense of national cohesiveness. Violent demonstrations did nothing but set one American against another, inciting suspicion, splitting the society into warring factions. Convinced that violence must be stopped, James refused to sign a petition against the imminent execution of the convicted anarchists, although he was urged to do so by his brother-in-law William Mackintyre Salter, who was the leader of the Society for Ethical Culture in Chicago; by his sister-in-law Mary; and by his wife.

"When you're not sure, don't act," James offered as his excuse to Salter. "It is very hard to forecast consequences, and all that is said about making martyrs and embittering the working classes fails to affect me, if the men be guilty." He thought it more important that workers learn that anarchism "is no playing matter, and to make them feel responsible, is to make a few of them suffer all the consequences. Hereafter, every one will be warned by the execution that if he joins such a society, he does it with knowledge of the risk." Since the case had been tried responsibly, James saw no need to retry it by public opinion. Insisting that he had "a perfectly good conscience in withholding my name," he added: "Nothing is expected of the likes of me so no construction can be put upon it if nothing comes from me."[41]

Although this controversy was not the last time James would disagree with his brother-in-law's political views, he soon realized that with growing fame and authority, much was expected of him in the manner of firm moral leadership and ethical philosophy.

Another Kind of Person

"THE MORE WE LIVE the more attached we grow to the country," James wrote to his brother. Like many Cambridge families, the Jameses looked forward to summers away from the city. Now, they were spending a second vacation in Jaffrey, New Hampshire, a village at the base of Mount Monadnock, just across the Massachusetts border, where they had retreated after Herman's death. But rentals required yearly house hunting and, in the long run, seemed financially imprudent. They decided, by the end of the summer, that they wanted a home of their own.

Although Keene Valley always would remain James's favorite retreat, its inaccessibility made it a poor choice for the whole family. Far better, James thought, would be a site in New Hampshire, more easily reached by train and carriage, where the landscape was beautiful and, he heard, the land cheap.

In September, James set out on a real estate search that ended at the base of Mount Chocorua, in a town called, infelicitously according to James, Tamworth Iron Works. The "small farm" that interested him consisted of seventy-five acres, most of it woods, the rest hayfields. The shingled, green-trimmed farmhouse, built in the year James was born, needed considerable work, but it was large enough—fourteen rooms, eleven with doors that opened to the outside—included a big barn, and looked out at Chocorua Lake and the mountain. "It is only 4 hours from Boston by rail and 1 hour's drive from the station," William told Henry. "Few neighbors, but good ones; hotel a mile off. If this is a dream let me, at least, indulge it for a week or so longer!"[42] The asking price was $900, but James purchased the property for $750, planning to spend another $2,500 in repairs and renovation.

In the next few years, the house became a consuming passion for the Jameses. Built by itinerant carpenters, the building itself had not held up well. Besides making necessary repairs, James changed the landscaping so that the house, which was fairly level with the nearby road when he bought it, would afford a wider view. "Most people buy a site and then put a house on it," he told Henry. "I have bought a house and am now creating a site round about it, lowering the level of the landscape, in order to make the house appear on a little higher ground."[43] The alterations required moving the barn and some stone walls, changing the grade, and cutting down whatever trees blocked the openness that James desired.

While Alice took charge of overseeing the workmen, James was involved in the decisions, even on so minute a matter as cutting out knots from the tables he ordered built and inserting smooth inlaid blocks to replace them. Sometimes this first experience with home renovation proved frustrating: "I have told you 1000000 times that I had no knowledge of floors," William wrote in exasperation to Alice, "and thought we have better leave all but kitchen, pantry etc till we learned something."[44] Sometimes, his grand plans were foiled by Alice's frugality, such as his desire to put a lift in the house to carry coal, ashes, laundry, and food from one floor to another. At first William insisted on installing it: "For once I'll assert my supremacy in this marriage!" he declared.[45] But he quickly backed down, agreeing that unless he could find people who "praise it highly, and say that their 'help' would much grieve over its annihilation, out of love for you and your horrid little midgy nature I will not put it in."[46]

At the end of the summer, James felt unusually refreshed, and "more in the mood for the college struggle" that he faced annually as the school year began. Still, he had made too little progress on his psychology book, and in the past year had spent too much time, he decided, on psychical research. With regret, he decided to cut back: "But I feel quite convinced at the end of my year's work," he wrote to George Croom Robertson, "that this sort of work is as worthy a specialty as a man could take up; only it *is* a specialty, demanding an enormous sacrifice of time, and in which amateurs will be as inferior to experts as they are in most other departments of experience."[47]

Another reason for withdrawing may have been the unexpected death of his assistant, Glendower Evans, the past March. Evans's death was shocking for the Jameses and devastating for Elizabeth Evans. As tribute and consolation, she incorporated his name into her own, becoming known from then on as Elizabeth Glendower Evans; she wore nothing but black; and, like Alice in search of her lost son, she became a devoted follower of Boston mediums. Her aim, though, was hardly the scientific verification that had interested her husband and James.

Without James, the SPR was in jeopardy of failing. Like him, other members were too busy to spend long hours collecting and examining testimony of psychic experiences, interviewing mediums, and conducting experiments. What the group needed was a new infusion of energy, someone who could oversee its work, manage its budget, and direct its focus. In the spring of 1887, help arrived from England in the person of thirty-two-year-old Richard Hodgson.

Hodgson, a native Australian, had earned an undergraduate and a law degree at the University of Melbourne. In 1878 he entered the

University of Cambridge, where he became a student of Henry Sidg-wick and, through him, was drawn into the core of friendships that sustained the London Society for Psychical Research. Hodgson com-pleted his degree in moral sciences at Cambridge in 1881, and then, subsidized by Sidgwick, went to Germany for six months to study phi-losophy, ethics, psychology, and zoology. When he returned to En-gland, he took a post lecturing on literature and philosophy for the University Extension program.

Hodgson was a large, hearty man, sharp and irreverent. At Cam-bridge, he refused to wear the obligatory black evening suit, preferring to attire himself in rumpled brown. Before his graduation, he so fiercely balked at having to kneel before the vice-chancellor at the cer-emony that his friends worried that he never would relent. Hodgson, like many other members of the SPR, hoped that his belief in the oc-cult would be supported by rigorous scientific investigation and was eager to expose frauds. To that end, he agreed, in 1884, to go to India to investigate the work of Countess Helena Petrovna Blavatsky.

Blavatsky's Theosophical Society claimed to possess documents proving the existence of mahatmas, mystics who were able to project their spirits out of their bodies. Some members of the SPR, however, believed that the documents—and the mahatmas—were fraudulent. Hodgson's task was to find out. Relying on the skills of British hand-writing experts and his own acute powers of observation, Hodgson concluded, after a few months of investigation, that Blavatsky not only was a fraud, but also a Russian spy, sent to India to inflame anti-British sentiment. Although his findings stirred up fervent defense of the Theosophists, he emerged from the investigation as a hero of the SPR, a trusted evaluator of the paranormal. In that capacity, he seemed just the man to revive the flagging spirit of the American Society for Psy-chical Research.

Although he was not so sure that the job could be done, Hodgson was persuaded to come for one year, for a salary of fifteen hundred dol-lars, raised partly from donations solicited by SPR members, including James. In April 1887, Hodgson arrived in the United States to serve as secretary of the ASPR, with duties that ranged from investigating re-ports and witnesses to overseeing every financial detail of the organiza-tion. "I practically 'boss' this Society of 400 members," he wrote to a friend.[48]

With Hodgson in charge of the daily work of the ASPR, James plunged into work on his *Principles*. As in the past, the work stimulated him so greatly that he could not sleep. Irritable and depressed from persistent insomnia, he turned first to his usual remedy of chloroform. When that did not help, he turned to another source: mind cure, a form of psychotherapy that combined hypnosis, relaxation, and what then was known as the talking cure. His friend George Dorr claimed to have had success with a certain mind-cure "doctress" that he visited in 1886. Now James, exhausted by sleeplessness, decided to seek her help.

James had no reluctance to try popular remedies for neurasthenic symptoms. In the past, he had experimented with diet, a regime of gymnastic exercise called the "lifting cure," galvanism, and a menu of mind-altering drugs. He was staunchly and noisily opposed to the efforts of some Boston physicians to license health practitioners, however unconventional their credentials or their treatment. "Words cannot express my contempt for much of the medical legislation that is current," he exclaimed, "based as it is on a theoretic surmise, grafted on an insufficiently observed fact, generalized by pedantry, promulgated by love of dominion, and adopted by credulity as the rule of life. Let every man be his own observer," he advised, "and believe in no results that are not obvious; and let him be ready for the angel with the scythe whenever it comes."[49] With little respect for the medical education that had given him license to practice, he believed that physicians had no corner on the treatment of human ills.

James's visits with his mind-cure practitioner took place in the afternoon, between four and five, and, as James described them, consisted mostly of a nap. "I sit down beside her," he wrote to his sister, "and presently drop asleep, whilst she disentangles the snarls out of my mind. She says she never saw a mind with so many, so agitated, so restless, etc. She said my *eyes* mentally speaking, kept revolving like wheels in front of each other and in front of my face, and it was four or five sittings ere she could get them *fixed*."[50] Although James seemed pleased at the evaluation of his mind as such a complicated piece of machinery, he did not find the treatment immediately beneficial. After ten visits, he told his cousin Kitty Prince, who herself had been the subject of many attempts at therapy, he saw little improvement. "I cannot see that the mind cure has done me any positive good," he wrote, "though I shall go twice more, having resolved to give the good woman at least a dozen sittings, for fair trials sake. She has done wonders for some of my friends."[51] Yet a month later, when finally he could sleep more soundly, he changed his assessment. He was much improved, he reported to Henry, experiencing nothing less than "a new lease of youth," which he attributed to "the Mind Cure in which I have been dabbling."[52]

Although James suffered from insomnia, trouble with his eyes (that often resulted in stronger, and eventually, bifocal, prescriptions for lenses), and intermittent depression, in the early years of his marriage, he never sank to the depths of blackness that he had experienced in his youth. Usually his depression was caused by fatigue, such as his annual end-of-the-semester exhaustion or his beginning-of-the-semester discouragement. "It is always a dead sort of thing," he reflected, "beginning the college year. The loutish faces, all so passive, and so stupid that they will not swallow even when you put the foot within their jaws."[53] As soon as he saw those faces as individuals, each with his unique experiences and perceptions, his enthusiasm grew. Sometimes he became depressed when his writing did not progress well; sometimes depression followed bouts of illness.

He no longer saw himself, however, as "a man morally utterly diseased," but decided instead that all human beings, not only his father's children, embraced a "sick soul" as part of their personality. This "sick soul" might have special needs—for the consolation of religion, for example—that the healthy-minded portion of the personality did not; but, as he understood it, those needs were neither pathological nor shameful.

James attributed the change in his personality to Alice: "I have got out of that whole frame of mind," he told her, "not by any acute change or act or discovery, but simply gradually and by living with you, and it now seems so far off as to belong not only to another person, but almost to another kind of person."[54] While his marriage was an enormous force in changing his self-perception, he also enlarged his experiences of other people, as well: students, colleagues, friends, and his own children, who provided living examples of the wide range of personalities functioning happily, healthily, and productively.

IN THE SPRING of 1887, after an easy and short labor, Alice gave birth to their fourth child and only daughter, Margaret Mary. Named for her two maternal aunts, Peggy, as she was called, seemed to James "a queer little thing with a long nose—quite unlike any of the boys except that her complexion resembles Harry's. You can't tell what they are going to look like at this age. The strange thing is you *can* tell so well what their character & moral disposition is. It is a perfectly distinct and positive thing in each, when two days old."[55] Her character, James decided immediately, was "modest, tactful, unselfish" and, he added, "quite different from a boy."[56] In fact, she exhibited the very qualities that made her mother so endearing.

The boys not only were different from Peggy, but from each other. Harry, whose imagination Henry Sr. so praised when the child was three, soon outgrew his penchant for lying. By the time he was ten, he had become a stolid little boy, intellectually advanced (he was ahead of his grade in school), with none of the volatility that characterized most males in the James family. He liked to recite stories that he read, and although James sometimes found them endless, he also admitted that Harry put them over very well. "He is a good boy who will never cause anxiety," William told Henry, "—not a James, so far as I can see, whilst Billy is eminently one."[57]

William's namesake was as unlike his brother as anyone could be, with an "excitable & nervous" disposition complicated with asthma, stomach problems, and a temper. To his father, though, "beloved Williamson" seemed "the most delightful little being you ever saw; never lacking in a retort, and I think Father must have been like him when young."[58] William had been like him when young, too, more than he wanted to admit.

The volatility that characterized James's personality in his youth, though, leveled off for the rest of his life. Certainly, as his wife testified, he could be more exuberant, more overtly excited by life than other adults. Friends, too, noted his spontaneous ebullience about new experiences and new ideas. "He looked freshly at life, and read books freshly. . . . The last book he had read was always 'a great book'; the last person he had talked with, a wonderful being," his friend John Chapman wrote.[59] And the next experience ripe with possibility.

Chapter 12

FAMILY ROMANCE

1888–1890

IN MID-JANUARY, Alice, the three children, and the family's German governess packed up their trunks and set out to spend the winter in Aiken, South Carolina, a fashionable resort town not far from Augusta, popular with northerners eager to escape the cold and a host of seasonal respiratory ailments—bronchitis, pneumonia, tuberculosis. Aiken's population of two thousand more than doubled in the winter months, as vacationers filled its luxurious hotels and, as the Jameses did, more modest guesthouses. Alice's mother had gone to Aiken the previous winter, taking Billy, who suffered from asthma. Impressed, no doubt, by the elegant ambience, flourishing gardens, and salubrious climate, Mrs. Gibbens recommended Aiken to the rest of her family. From mid-January until mid-May, James was home alone, with only a few servants and the family's pet dog, Jap, for company.

Alice had left under the customary cloud of tension and recrimination that preceded all departures: whether William was leaving Alice or Alice, William, there were bound to be arguments, tears, and letters of apology from William to Alice for weeks after the departure. It was a pattern that had begun for James long before, when he was a young man leaving his parents' home; and it was a habit that he found difficult to change. "I think of you all speeding away through the darkness in your narrow room and feel (as ever under the same conditions) the most [remorse] for all my shortcomings tow'ds you, when you were by my side," James wrote. "That is the way in which I always think of my dear dear mother now. Alas! Alas! It should not be the way."[1] Yet it was the way, repeatedly, caused partly by the rush of packing and preparation, partly from James's guilt at feeling so strong a need to separate himself from his family. Alice assumed that some of the blame was hers because she tended to smother William with attention and advice when he was so occupied with his own concerns.

After Henry Sr. died, when she herself felt the full burden of the stifling attentions that James women could foist upon another human being, Alice experienced a moment of regret for her behavior and wrote to William promising not to "*fuss* around you so much, nor will I be always referring to the plan just before you. I find that method when applied creates a sense of hurry which must have been hard to endure."[2] Her good intentions notwithstanding, leave-taking never became any easier.

As much as James loved his family, still he felt a strong "instinct of personal isolation" that made him strain against all bonds. When that instinct took hold of him, he became restless and irritable, treating Alice with the same impatient condescension that he once had shown his mother. His occasional conflation of Alice with his mother was, to some extent, well-founded. Like Mary, Alice was the organizer and arranger of family events; she was nurse and nurturer; she soothed, assuaged, mediated. She also was frugal, sometimes frustrated by her husband's extravagant spending for clothing, often, or for works of art. While James thought nothing about ordering new shirts and buying attractive foulards, Alice had to be persuaded to buy a new dress or a piece of jewelry; and when she agreed, she needed further encouragement to wear the item and not bury it in a drawer. Once, traveling in Europe with William, Alice used some money her mother had sent her to buy a ruby ring. But the ring, James reported to Mrs. Gibbens, "has not been on her finger *once,* but sleeps in the bottom of her trunk—she seems to think she is not good enough for anything good."[3] James called her self-denial "diseased humility."

But Alice carried self-effacement only so far; she was forthright about asserting her opinions and letting her husband know when he had exceeded the bounds of her patience and goodwill. One recurrent cause of her anger was James's tendency to flirt casually with acquaintances and even family servants. During her stay in Aiken, for example, she became upset and depressed when he thoughtlessly wrote that he had kissed one of their maids. James thought his affectionate nature should please, rather than anger, her. "I often have a desire to kiss people," he explained, "(which I regret to say I have never yielded to except in the one instance wh[ich] you know). . . . It has nothing to do with any deeper confidence, and doesn't seem to me to conflict with any pre existent relation of the *heart;* it is merely a natural expression of passing tenderness and cordiality."[4] Apparently Alice did not forgive his transgression quickly: a few days later he was still apologizing. "Jealousy," James noted succinctly in his *Principles,* "is unquestionably instinctive."[5]

Possibly to atone for his indiscretion, more likely because he missed her, James told her that he had been moved to take out a packet of his old love letters to her. Reading them inspired not only a protestation of love, but of lust; not only devotion, but homage. He discovered, he said, how much he had changed, how deeply she had changed him. During their courtship, he had seemed "a man morally utterly diseased," he said, and it was no wonder that he had felt "scruples" about marrying her. "No decently feeling man can be a sinner and look with equanimity towards playing the part in the world's life of a sound member," he told her. But he was a sinner no longer, thanks to her. Although Alice was no stranger to depression, migraine headaches, and various degrees of moodiness, still James saw her as essentially healthy-minded: strong, practical, and optimistic; and her spirit had infected his own with an abiding sense of happiness.

He longed to see her, and in the next weeks, the two planned a reunion in New York during William's spring recess. Clearly William looked forward to the resumption of their sexual lives: their separation, he told Alice, seemed "a sort of second second edition of that primal estrangement" of their courtship "where imaginations took the place of deed. But it *will* make us intimate when we come together again, won't it dear?" Apparently Alice expressed as much eagerness for their reunion as he did. "I rejoice so tremendously in this accession of freedom and moral lustihood on your part," he told her, "and hope it will never fade."[6]

Alice's "lustihood," however, was tempered by her fear of another pregnancy. The dates they were to meet, she cautioned William, seemed perilous. He disagreed: "The April recess will be just the time unless you have deceived me in the past!" he assured her.[7] In any case, William was not adverse to having more children. With Alice, her mother, and her sisters in charge of the nursery, infants did not burden his life or imperil his solitude.

If James was ardent and attentive as a husband, he delegated the children's care to Alice. Writing to his friend and fellow psychologist James Mark Baldwin, James admitted interest in an article Baldwin had published about babies. "My wife has often put her babies to sleep by flaring up the gas upon them, but equally well by suddenly turning it down," James wrote. "She thinks the hypnotic effect comes from any sudden *change*. I admire your energy over the creatures: I don't think anything could hire me to put my baby to sleep more than one day at a time."[8] Yet though he retreated from child care, still he imagined himself as the mainstay of family life.

In the summer of 1888, when the family was at last together in Chocorua, William described to Henry a scene that he thought would serve for one of his novels "as a picture of domestic happiness." It was a warm afternoon in mid-July, and on the lawn, a mattress was airing out in preparation for the arrival, the next day, of Richard Hodgson. On the mattress sat Alice and Peggy, "the madonna and child," Alice, in a blue print dress, sewing and smiling down at Peggy,

> immensely big and fat for her years, & who, with quite a vocabu-
> lary of adjectives and proper names, and a mouthfull of teeth,
> shows as yet, although in her sixteenth month, no disposition to
> walk. She is rolling and prattling to herself, now on mattress &
> now on grass, and is an exceedingly good natured, happy, and in-
> telligent child. It conduces to her happiness to have a hard
> cracker in her fist, at which she mumbles more or less all day, and
> of which she is never known to let go, even taking it into her bath
> with her and holding it immersed till that ceremony is o'er.[9]

William admitted having a "romantic feeling" about Peggy that he did not have for his sons; his tender description of her and Alice in the sun-bathed afternoon reflects a romantic feeling about family, as well.[10] With Peggy as the center and focus of the scene, James defines family as "madonna & child": the angelic mother engaged in a solitary domestic task; the child evidence of her ample nurturing. At the moment, William knew that Harry was off on his own, riding a pony; he had no idea where Billy and the governess had gone. But their presence only would have interrupted the idyllic scene that, for William, defined the quality of his family's life.

Chocorua provided the picturesque backdrop for his imaginative construction of *family*. He had created the setting, but still he felt uneasy about his identity as patriarch. He described to Alice once "a most vivid daydream" he had had "of myself as I *ought* to be, sitting on our upper piazza at Chocorua with your mother and Margaret sitting on either side of me, their hands clasped in mine, you nestling at my feet, and we talking over the old remembrances of your bygone life in Europe, I tranquil and murmuring and selfless, like Bob. I feel it potential in me, and 'twill come out yet."[11] Not surprisingly, James had this daydream on board the *Cephalonia,* bound for Europe, alone.

Crucial to his reverie are women, adoring women, who are confiding in him recollections of their life in Europe during the difficult period after Alice's father had died. Central to their lives in every way, James portrays himself as husband, father, supporter: pillar of the family and happy in his roles. Happy, he said, "like Bob." But his comparison with his brother is an odd brushstroke in this idealized portrait. Certainly Bob was on William's mind during this period, but not because he was tranquil or happy—quite the opposite, as William well knew. Invoking Bob contributed to William's feeling of comparative worth.

Although James admitted that he had not yet achieved the tranquillity of family life that he described in his daydream, still, the stability and warmth that he did enjoy contrasted palpably with the sad existence of his brother Bob. Living in Concord, Massachusetts, with Mary and their two teenage children, Bob once again had succumbed to alcoholism. Belligerent and self-absorbed, Bob was a trial to his family, including William, with whom he frequently quarreled. William did not understand why Mary did not return to her family in Milwaukee, and seemed to think it a failing of willpower that she stuck so faithfully to her husband.

William concluded that Bob was doomed by the "pathological mental condition which is part of his very nature. He has *no* affection. And yet in his crises he goes through the emotional expressions of an angel. Now that his property is in trust, one great danger is averted. But I wish the poor wretch could die in one of his bad sprees—it would be so much future misery averted for him as well as for his family."[12]

William's diagnosis of his brother reflected the prevalent medical belief that alcoholism was hereditary and incurable; as William well knew, others in the family had been subject to the same affliction. Although he never resisted giving Bob advice, William believed that nothing would save his brother. Early in 1888, Bob seemed particularly vulnerable, behaving with hostility toward Mary and William, and eventually suffering such a "bad spree" that William decided he needed to be hospitalized. Although a friend suggested that Bob be committed to a penal reformatory, William sought a more therapeutic environment. He found a hospital for alcoholics in Hartford, Connecticut, to which he escorted his unhappy brother. William, however, had no hope that Bob could be cured. "I think his brain is getting more set in these irascible grooves," he reported to Henry, "but there are no delusions properly so called, and he is n't technically insane. We must live on makeshifts from 6 months to six months. The only manly and moral thing for a man in his plight is to kill himself; but Bob will ne'er do that, Im sure. Meanwhile they have over $3000 a year income and Mary sticks to him like a burr, in spite of everything. I wish she would n't."[13]

If William seemed unfeeling toward the unfortunate Bob, his actions reflected a deep concern. He served, at Bob's request, as his financial and legal trustee; he rushed to Concord whenever Bob broke down; he consoled Mary; he searched for a place where Bob could be treated. His harsh diagnosis of Bob, however, is consistent with James's need to convince himself of his superiority over his siblings, despite his genuine and deep love for them. Because the others, Henry and Alice, gave him no cause to condemn them, he found reasons to pity them.

His relationships within his family were echoed in his professional relationships. James liked to surround himself with vulnerable young men who were trying, as he once did, to extricate themselves from emotional or metaphysical ties; he had endless patience to listen to the ideas of one or another "crank" who posited a new way of philosophizing. Less comfortable, although sometimes inspiring, were men of equal ability and brilliance. James carried with him from childhood a need to be perceived as the best, the most brilliant: a genius. We can see in many relationships that what began as a friendship based on shared interests—and unequal status—soon turned sour when the friend made a bold professional leap. This was the case with G. Stanley

Hall, who had been James's student at Harvard from 1876 to 1878, earning the first American doctorate in psychology.

Although there was a difference of only two years in their ages, James fell easily into the role of mentor and Hall of "disciple and at best amplifier."[14] James, flattered by his student's deference and admiration, kept Hall apprised of his progress on the *Principles* and confided some problems about "the ghostly tribe of unfelt feelings" that he was trying to work out. "I long to talk it over with you," he wrote to Hall, who was then studying in Leipzig. "How lonesome psychologists are in this world of matter!"[15]

When James traveled in Europe in the summer of 1880 he met up with Hall in Heidelberg, where they spent some twelve hours together, ranging over various philosophical topics. As much as he acknowledged Hall's brilliance, still James saw himself as more powerful and influential. Twice, he wrote to Daniel Coit Gilman recommending Hall for a position at Johns Hopkins.

Their friendship flourished after Hall returned and shared in James's enthusiasm for psychical research. But during that period James himself tried to solicit an offer from Gilman, and in 1883, when Hall finally won an appointment to the psychology department at Johns Hopkins, their friendship began to develop problems. Hall's experimental research laboratory and his publications on psychology threatened to eclipse James's work. He was growing in stature, and in 1886, when rumor reached James that Hall was going to start his own *American Journal of Psychology*, the friendship seriously foundered. When Hall finally mentioned his new publication to James, he did not ask for a contribution but asked James to review the journal for the *Nation*. The review never materialized: first James confessed that he felt "quite paralyzed" about writing "for fear of displeasing" Hall; finally, he summarily declined the invitation. "I started to write with the heartiest good will to the job," he told Hall, "but found myself so subtly inhibited that it would not go."[16]

Inhibitions about making public statements did not keep James from criticizing Hall in private correspondence. "Hall is a wonderful creature," he wrote to George Croom Robertson. "Never an articulate conception comes out of him, but instead of it a sort of palpitating influence making all men believe that the way to save their souls psychologically lies through the infinite assimilation of jaw-breaking german laboratory-articles. If you try to draw any expressible theoretic conclusions from any of them, he won't hear it."[17]

Yet as a rival, Hall managed to spur James to work—faster, harder, and with more determination—to finish his *Principles*. "The feeling of rivalry lies at the very basis of our being," James declared, "all social improvement being largely due to it."[18] A psychology text-book, James knew, would raise his stature in the field and make him a viable competitor against Hall and other colleagues. He must produce, or face the consequences of his failure.

When James found out that Hall was being lured from Johns Hopkins to take on the presidency of Clark University, he felt unusu-ally "stirred up" by the news. At a "grand newly endowed university," Hall would be in complete charge of a psychology department and its research facilities, with the opportunity to move forward uninhibited by conservative colleagues. Hall's good fortune, besides inciting James's jealousy, also renewed his desire to leave Harvard, where he often felt undervalued. Hall's move, he thought, might mean a chance for his own advancement. If he were invited to replace Hall at Johns Hopkins, it would be "a rather hard thing to decline"; certainly he would be re-luctant to uproot his family, but still, he reflected, "I do believe in keeping the ball rolling, and I know that every man who leaves a col-lege for the sake of higher pay elsewhere helps to reform our system of underpaying intellectual work."[19] He anticipated a salary of at least five thousand dollars and looked forward to leading the young faculty that President Gilman preferred to appoint: "crude youngsters with reputa-tions to make, who were full of zeal and from whom lots of work could be got."[20] If Gilman offered him the job, he told Alice, he would have to accept as the "manly thing to do."[21] In the end, the manly thing was not required of him. He was not offered the position, but stayed on at Harvard, took over the teaching of ethics when Palmer left for a year's sabbatical and, in 1890, was appointed professor of psychology.

International Relations

ON MARCH 6, 1889, at the age of seventy-seven, Aunt Kate died. Once a central figure in the family, by the time she died Kate was peripheral to the lives of all her sister's children. Henry, who responded most sen-sitively to her death, admitted feeling "an immense relief that the beloved old Aunt has been set free," although he could not help but "mourn a little & feel sad" at the loss of one connection to his past.[22] His sister Alice, who at first was upset at the news of Kate's final illness, became even more distraught when she learned about Kate's will. Although Kate bequeathed ten thousand dollars to William and his family, she left Alice merely a "life interest" in some pieces of silver and a shawl. "As if," Alice commented, "the silver shd. come to disaster thro' theft, fire or flood, I shd. be quite unable, out of my income, to make it good. . . . A life-interest in a *shawl,* with reversion to a *male* heir, is so extraordinary & ludicrous a bequest that I can hardly think it could have been seriously meant." Alice decided to renounce her interest in the silver, and asked if her brothers would be kind enough to renounce *their* interest in the shawl, making her "its absolute possessor. I may, or may not," she warned them, "leave it to you in my will, but if I should, it will be entirely a voluntary action on my part & in that way you must look upon it & accept it with any ravages wh. moth & rust may have brought about."[23] With this posthumous affront visited upon her, Alice did not mourn Aunt Kate.

Although William and his wife traveled to New York to represent the family at Kate's funeral, he did not seem grieved over her death, either. He decided to use a thousand dollars of the money she left him to finance a summer respite in Europe. The trip would enable him to attend the first International Congress of Physiological Psychologists in Paris, to reconnect with his psychical research friends in England, and to visit Harry and his sister, whom he had not seen for five years. It was a difficult summer for him to be away from home: he and Alice were building a house in Cambridge, just outside of Harvard Yard, at the same time that they were renovating their property at Chocorua; but his personal needs superseded practicalities. On June 22, he sailed on the *Cephalonia.*

After a brief excursion to Scotland and Ireland, James arrived in London in mid-July and remained there for ten days before leaving for Paris. He felt considerable anxiety about seeing his sister again and worried about even telling her that he was coming. "Alice used to be so perturbed at *expecting* things that in my ignorance of her present condition I don't venture to announce to her my arrival," he told Henry. "But do use your discretion as to when & how she shall be informed."[24]

Henry was as anxious as William about their sister's reaction to the impending visit. Although Henry assured William that Alice "*delights,* in general, in your letters," he knew that they had had an awkward interchange over the provisions of Aunt Kate's will. Alice thought William sounded angry; William thought Alice resented his inheritance. The truth, Henry said, was that she was "keenly & I think not unjustly wounded by the *exceptional* provision" of the silver and shawl. Henry assured William that once they saw one another, "all complications will *of themselves* drop out."

There was no harm, however, in being cautious. The day after William arrived in London, Harry went to have lunch, alone, with Alice. At the end of the meal, pale and trembling, he burst out: "I must tell you something! . . . William is here, he has been lunching upon Warwick Castle and is waiting now in the Holly Walk for the news to be broken to you and if you survive, I'm to tie my handkerch[ief] to the balcony." Alice, after taking two hundred grains of a bromide, reacted with what she called "extreme propriety." William was allowed to enter.

He found her lying in bed, "white as a sheet, with outstretched arms into which I threw myself and all was over," he reported to his wife. Visibly upset about her reaction to William's recent letter, Alice exclaimed repeatedly, "You understand, don't you, it's all my body, it's all physical, I can't help it." After the initial outburst, she calmed, and William sat with her for the rest of the afternoon. She said that she found him unchanged; he told her that she looked just as she had five years earlier, except that she was noticeably thinner. Her spirits, however, seemed undiminished. "She was witty and animated and curious about everything and the tone of invective and sarcasm which I have always read as shrill and hard in her letters, is *uttered* in the softest most laughing way in the world, and gives an entirely different impression." They had formed a new bond: as William described it, "the electric current is closed between myself & sister, and . . . the non conducting obstruction is wholly melted away. It is a great relief."[25]

Alice, too, described her feeling of renewed closeness to her brother, but not as the soldering of a broken wire. For Alice, the meeting had been a complicated, sensuous, "strange experience, to have what had seemed to be dead and gone all these years suddenly bloom before one, a flowing oasis in this alien desert, redolent with the exquisite *family* perfume of the days gone by, made of the allusions, the memories and the point of view in common, so that my floating-particle sense was lost for an hour or so in the illusion that what is forever shattered had sprung up anew, and existed outside of our memories—where it is forever green!"[26]

Allusion, memory, and her own "floating-particle sense" inspired Alice's latest occupation. At the end of May, just weeks before William arrived, she began a diary that she was determined to keep secret from her brothers. "I shall at least have it all my own way," she said, "and it may bring relief as an outlet to that geyser of emotions, sensations, speculations and reflections which ferments perpetually within my poor old carcass for its sins."[27] Even had he known about the diary, however, and the rich fount of experiences that she recorded, James still would have characterized Alice's life as "terribly deprived." Any life bereft of public performances and public recognition was, in his estimation, sadly circumscribed.

Even his brother Henry, whose prodigious literary output he so envied, inspired his pity. "Harry," he wrote to his wife, "has covered himself, like some marine crustacean, with all sorts of material growths, rich sea weeds and rigid barnacles and things, and lives hidden in the midst of his strange heavy alien manners and customs, but these are all but 'protective resemblances,' under which the same dear old good innocent and at bottom very powerless-feeling Harry remains, caring for little but his writing, and full of dutifulness and affection for all gentle things." James could not acknowledge that Harry's writing, which already had established him as one of the most acclaimed novelists of his time, was worth such devotion; instead, it served his own ego to characterize Harry as socially and emotionally deficient, weak and childlike. As if that characterization alone did not establish William's superiority, he added another fillip: "I am sorry to say that he is saving not a cent of money, so that my vision of him, paralyzed, in our spare room, is stronger than ever. He seems quite helpless in that regard."[28] Paralyzed, Harry could no longer write; paralyzed, he would depend, totally, on his brother's ministrations.

James escaped from the cheerless world of his siblings to visit with Frederic Myers and Henry Sidgwick and his wife in Cambridge, where they conducted thought-transference experiments, observed a hypnotist, and discussed the future of psychical research. The man James most wanted to see, Edmund Gurney, had committed suicide the year before, and James felt his loss profoundly. With Gurney, he said, he

had found "the most nourishing communion."[29] Myers and the Sidgwicks, on the other hand, made him uneasy. Myers, for one, had "a
very intense and energetic character, suggesting despotism, meanness
and all sorts of things lurking in the background, which I didn't all-
together like."[30] The Sidgwicks seemed to him, unappealingly, "the in-
carnation of pure intellect—a very odd appearing couple."[31]

Although he criticized the Sidgwicks for their overly intense engagement in psychical research, he himself became unusually excited
when his wife reported that she was having "spiritual experiences" of
her own. Hoping that she could develop the powers of a medium—a
medium-in-residence surely would be a boon to the household—
James told her that if she had more such experiences, she must call for
Richard Hodgson immediately, and even Mrs. Piper.

Psychical matters continued to be the focus of James's attention at
the International Congress of Physiological Psychology, where European researchers considered, among their main topics of concern, hypnotic phenomena and telepathic hallucination. For James, however, the
conference was more important for "the friendships made, the intimacies deepened." Here, he first met Swiss psychologist Théodore
Flournoy and the young German researcher Hugo Münsterberg.

Despite twelve years' difference in their ages, Flournoy and James
found common bonds both personally and professionally. Flournoy, a
vigorous man with a trim Vandyke beard and intense eyes, was less
voluble than James, but just as eager for new friendships. Both men
were interested far more in creating psychological theory than in
amassing experimental data, both took seriously the field of psychical
research, both were married with growing families and the burdens of
household concerns.

Flournoy, who taught psychology at the University of Geneva, preferred to consider the influence of subconscious forces on personality
and to investigate "supernormal or metaphysical phenomena" rather
than to direct the university's psychology laboratory.[32] Like James, he
refused to relegate psychical exploration only to "theosophists, mystics,
and occultists."[33]

After James returned home, he and Flournoy wrote often to
each other about their respective psychical investigations, especially
Flournoy's observation of mediums. In an effort to explain mediums'

talents, Flournoy formulated a theory that mediums regressed into a kind of mental infancy, where their imagination ranged unfettered and their subconscious was receptive to psychical influences.

If Flournoy was, for James, a kindred spirit, twenty-six-year-old Münsterberg was more like the brilliant, admiring young men who surrounded him at home. But it was his brilliance, and not his admiration, that first attracted James. By the time they met, James had read the younger man's *Die Willenshandlung* and called it "much the most original and vigorous thing on the will with which I am acquainted."[34] As he wrote to his brother Henry later, James believed that Münsterberg was "the ablest experimental psychologist in Germany . . . he is in fact the Rudyard Kipling of psychology."[35] Münsterberg had been a medical student at the University of Leipzig when he took a summer class with Wilhelm Wundt and decided, instead, to enter the new field of experimental psychology. In 1884 he completed his course work for a medical degree; and the following year he received a doctorate in philosophy. He began teaching at the University of Heidelberg, where he completed his medical dissertation, and then moved to lecture at the University of Freiburg, where he set up an experimental psychology laboratory at his own home, for want of university facilities.

James was impressed both by the quality of Münsterberg's work and the strength of his personality. He seemed older and more assured than his years. "He was a great, husky German," recalled one student, "with a confident yet friendly smile that was modified somewhat by a vigorous moustache curled slightly higher on one side so that it somehow suggested hardness. When he was piqued he had a look of ferocity that students said he had acquired by trying to look like the Kaiser."[36] James found him "extraordinarily engaging," and he did not notice at all the "hardness" that others sometimes commented upon. Münsterberg, he wrote a few years later to Josiah Royce, was "not of the heroic type, but of the sensitive and refined type, big, inclined to softness and fatness, poor voice, vain, loquacious, personally rather formal and fastidious I think, desiring to please and to shine . . . fond of traveling and of all kinds of experience, interested in many intellectual directions, and talking anything rather than 'shop' when he gets out of harness."[37]

He was an ambitious young man unsure of his future within the German university system. As a lecturer without a permanent position, he depended on students for his livelihood: the more he could attract to his lectures, the more he was paid. As a researcher, he knew he could not go far without more elaborate apparatus than he could afford personally. Although he may not have liked to "talk shop," it is likely that he alluded to his future plans in conversation with James, planting a seed that soon would flourish.

The Continuity of Associations

JAMES HAD GONE to Europe, he said, to "break up the continuity of associations" that had become routine and dull. Even before the Congress had opened, that aim had been accomplished. He returned home in good spirits, rested from his break, energized by his meetings at the Congress, affirmed that among his sad relations, he was the most blessed.

Unfortunately, Alice had not enjoyed a similar refreshment. Instead of being flattered and stimulated by new encounters, she had tended children and supervised carpenters. A badly sprained ankle only added to her distress. She was tired, and William was not overly sympathetic. "I wish we had come abroad together," he wrote to Henry, "—but it is too late for regrets, and her turn will come ere long. . . . my expedition was a perfect success as it stands."[38]

Alice became more exhausted and depressed as summer turned to fall. Returning from the upheaval in Chocorua to their still-unfinished house in Cambridge, she discovered that her husband's enthusiastic return had resulted in her fifth pregnancy. Whether the prospect of another child lifted her spirits, we do not know.[39] But a miscarriage in October sent her further into depression; and soon her sorrow was compounded by the death from diphtheria of her two-year-old niece, the daughter of her sister Mary. "The maternal instinct is something the intensity of which no man can understand," William commented.[40] That instinct fueled her anxiety about her own children: throughout the late fall and winter, with Billy and Peggy unable to shake off persistent colds, a spate of new diphtheria cases occurred. One distraction, a different kind of burden, was packing the family's belongings for the move to their new home.

It was a relief, finally, to be living in the gambrel-roofed, wood-shingled house at 95 Irving Street that would be their permanent home. But they would not feel completely settled for several months: each morning, painters, wallpapers, and carpet layers arrived to finish their work, creating dirt and disorder. When the last dustpan had been emptied, however, the Jameses looked around them with considerable pleasure. The house, designed by architect William Ralph Emerson with innumerable suggestions from the Jameses (so many, in fact, that Emerson thought James had saved at least two thousand dollars by spending the summer in Europe),[41] was a gracious residence with a large entrance hall, a welcoming parlor, and, its most prized feature, a grand library—more than twenty-two feet wide and twenty-seven feet long—with floor-to-ceiling bookcases, a wide fireplace, and a generous desk. Two sofas and several deep, overstuffed easy chairs invited visitors. Its southern exposure made the room unusually bright and cheerful; from its many windows, one could look out on the lawn, the garden, and the woods through which Irving Street had been cut. The library connected with the parlor, allowing James to jump from his desk and join visitors. "At home, *I* am in Elysium," he sighed. "I didn't know that material comfort could do a man such inward good."[42]

Here at last, in the library he had so carefully designed, he set himself to complete his textbook. By his own admission, he was not a facile writer. Although sometimes he produced a manuscript for an article in a fit of inspiration, most often he labored mightily, writing and revising, throwing out what he had done and beginning again. The *Principles* posed a particularly difficult challenge, he said, first because his assertions needed to be supported by scientific evidence; second, because he felt the keen and critical eyes of other philosophers and psychologists peering over his shoulder. "[A]lmost every page of this book of mine is against a resistance which you know nothing of in your resistless air of romance," he wrote to Henry, "the resistance of *facts,* to begin with, each one of which must be bribed to be on one's side, and the resistance of other philosophers to end with, each one of which must be slain. It is no joke slaying the Helmholtzes as well as the Spencers."[43]

Looking out on a bloodied plain of fallen aggressors, William envied the "resistless air of romance" that allowed Henry and their friend William Dean Howells—novelists whose works James followed devotedly—to create characters, plot, *life* within the safe circumference of their own imagination, observations, and intuition. Howells's recent *A Hazard of New Fortunes,* which focused on issues of moral behavior and social reform, was a great book, William thought, because of the richness of its characters, "flexible human beings . . . instead of puppets."[44] "Ah! my dear Howells," he sighed, "it's worth something to be able to write such a book, and it is so peculiarly *yours* too, flavored with your idiosyncrasy."[45] James hoped that his *Principles* would be just such a book: reflecting his own acute observations, flavored with his own personality, and, most important, truly a work of literature.

With such high aspirations, it is no wonder that he claimed to have rewritten each page of his new book four times or more. Throughout the winter and spring, he worked intensely, feverishly, to complete the manuscript that, he said, "has been sticking to me like an old man of the sea for the last 8 or 9 years." Finally, on May 17 at 9:00 P.M., he sent momentous news to Alice in New Hampshire: "The job is done!" On quick reflection, he deemed it not a bad job, at that: "as I see it as a unit, I feel as if it might be rather a vigorous and richly colored chunk."[46] "Congratulate me!" he declared to his friend, psychologist Christine Ladd-Franklin. "I have this day finished the manuscript of a 'Principles of Psychology' which ought to be out in September. . . . I feel like a barrel with its hoops gone! and shall grow young again."[47]

A few days later, he packed up his nearly three thousand pages of manuscript, mostly handwritten, insured it for one thousand dollars, and sent it to Holt in New York. He was overwhelmed with a feeling of freedom from "that interminable black cloud" and a sense of his own accomplishment. The book, he told Alice, "proclaims me really an efficient man—and last not least 'the 2nd Messiah' about to be!" On their honeymoon, he had promised her that he would support her by the royalties from the book; now, it could be a reality. "Even that may come to pass, my beauteous bride! At any rate, darling it does give me some comfort to think that I don't live *wholly* in projects, aspirations, & phrases, but now and then have some thing to show for all the fuss." No longer could he consider himself "a thing of glimpses, of discontinuity, of aperçus, with no power of doing a big job"; *The Principles of Psychology* proved that not only could he write a book, but, with only three exceptions, "the *biggest* book on Psychology in any language."[48] He was a man among men. With the publication of Howells's *Hazard of New Fortunes,* his brother's *The Tragic Muse,* "and last, *but by no means least,* my psychology," he wrote to Harry, "the year 1890 will be known as the great epochal year in American literature."[49]

Holt, who had been waiting twelve years for the manuscript, had proofs ready by mid-June. James stayed alone in Cambridge for six weeks correcting fourteen hundred pages, making so many last-minute changes that he ended up owing Holt some three hundred dollars. Early in August, Alice came back from Chocorua to help him, at the same time taking over her usual domestic chores. By the time she arrived, however, another reader also had joined in the huge task, James's dear friend Sarah Wyman Whitman.

Barely a year younger than James, Sarah Whitman was an artist by profession and disposition. A painter, book designer, and stained-glass maker, she exhibited frequently in Boston galleries and at the National Academy of Design and the Society of American Artists in New York. Elegant, affluent, and charming, she surrounded herself with beautiful objects and brilliant people, gathering at her homes in Boston and Beverly interesting and accomplished men and women upon whom she lavished effusive attention.

Born in Lowell, Massachusetts, Sarah Wyman spent her childhood in Baltimore and returned north after she married Henry Whitman, a wool merchant, when she was twenty-four. The marriage was not a success, although Whitman, apparently, was, providing his wife with two homes and himself with a yacht. By the time James met her, she rarely spent time in her husband's company. Sometimes he flitted in and out of the house, only glimpsing the rich world of friendships that she had created for herself.

By the 1880s, Sarah Whitman was beloved by scores of Boston intellectuals, including, to name just a few, Elizabeth Agassiz, Sarah Orne Jewett, Lizzie Boott, Charles Norton, John Jay Chapman, and Fanny Morse. At a philosophical club that she began in her studio, young intellectuals gathered to discuss philosophy, aesthetics, religion, social reform—or merely to gossip among themselves. James was a frequent guest, as were Royce and Oliver Wendell Holmes. Whitman had a notable talent for making each of her friends feel especially worthy of her admiration. "Clever men love to be appreciated," John Jay Chapman wrote of her, "and when, as rarely happens, a woman is found with so much enthusiasm for intelligence that she turns a special reflector on anyone possessing it and gives him the shock and glow of recognition, the clever men will flock about her, and a sort of salon will arise."[50] James was especially susceptible to such recognition; Whitman, he said, was "the most admirable woman," and she became his intimate and trusted confidante.[51]

Top left: William James, grandfather of the psychologist, emigrated from Ireland to the United States in 1789. After settling in Albany, New York, he became one of the richest men in the country. Portrait by Ezra Ames.
FRICK ART REFERENCE LIBRARY

Top right: After a riotous youth, Henry James, Sr. became a serious theologian. This daguerrotype dates from the 1860s.
BY PERMISSION OF HOUGHTON LIBRARY, HARVARD UNIVERSITY

Left: Mary James, William's mother, was a powerful force at the center of the family. At the time this portrait was taken, William would have been in his twenties.
BY PERMISSION OF HOUGHTON LIBRARY, HARVARD UNIVERSITY

Top left: For some years, William hoped to become an artist. Among his fellow students at art school was John La Farge, of whom William drew this sketch.
BY PERMISSION OF HOUGHTON LIBRARY, HARVARD UNIVERSITY

Top right: At age 18, right, with two unidentified companions.
BY PERMISSION OF HOUGHTON LIBRARY, HARVARD UNIVERSITY

Right: Another of William's portraits, of one of his cousins, Kitty Temple.
BY PERMISSION OF HOUGHTON LIBRARY, HARVARD UNIVERSITY

Right: William was attracted to Kitty's sister Minny, shown here about 1861.
BY PERMISSION OF HOUGHTON LIBRARY, HARVARD UNIVERSITY

Below left: The Jameses, as drawn by William in a letter to the family, November 1861.
BY PERMISSION OF HOUGHTON LIBRARY, HARVARD UNIVERSITY

Below right: William's sister, Alice, at age 21, in 1869.
BY PERMISSION OF HOUGHTON LIBRARY, HARVARD UNIVERSITY

Right: One of William's younger brothers, Garth Wilkinson James, at age 24, in 1869.
BY PERMISSION OF HOUGHTON LIBRARY, HARVARD UNIVERSITY

Below left: Alice Howe Gibbens spent several years in Europe before she met her future husband. This photograph was taken in Dresden in 1873.
BY PERMISSION OF HOUGHTON LIBRARY, HARVARD UNIVERSITY

Below right: At age 27, in 1869, a time of great emotional and physical stress.
BY PERMISSION OF HOUGHTON LIBRARY, HARVARD UNIVERSITY

Left: The parlor at 13 Chestnut Street, Boston, home of the Radical Club, where William met Alice Gibbens.

Middle: James spent many vacations at Putnam Camp, in Keene Valley in the Adirondacks.
BY PERMISSION OF THE ADIRONDACK MUSEUM

Bottom: Standing, left, with unidentified companions at Putnam Camp.
BY PERMISSION OF THE ADIRONDACK MUSEUM

Top left: Alice with the Jameses' first child, Henry, born in 1879.
BY PERMISSION OF HOUGHTON LIBRARY, HARVARD UNIVERSITY

Bottom left: The country home built by the Jameses in Chocorua, New Hampshire.

Top right: In Keene Valley in the 1890s.
BY PERMISSION OF HOUGHTON LIBRARY, HARVARD UNIVERSITY

Bottom right: With philosopher Josiah Royce, of whom James said, "I feel as if I had made him, after a fashion," in Chocorua.
BY PERMISSION OF HOUGHTON LIBRARY, HARVARD UNIVERSITY

Left: Leonora Piper was the focus of James's psychical research for many years. This photograph is identified only by James's handwritten note: "Mrs. Piper in trance."
BY PERMISSION OF HOUGHTON LIBRARY, HARVARD UNIVERSITY

Below left: Pauline Goldmark, who made James feel "temporarily quite young again," at 22, in 1896.
BRYN MAWR ARCHIVES

Below right: At Château Carqueiranne, the home of French philosopher Charles Richet, in 1900.
BY PERMISSION OF HOUGHTON LIBRARY, HARVARD UNIVERSITY

Top: With his wife, Alice, at Lamb House in the 1890s.
BY PERMISSION OF HOUGHTON LIBRARY, HARVARD UNIVERSITY

Middle: William's younger brother, Robertson, shown here in the 1890s, caused the family continual distress.
BY PERMISSION OF HOUGHTON LIBRARY, HARVARD UNIVERSITY

Bottom: With Henry, William's most beloved sibling, whom he advised to "write a new book, with no twilight or mustiness in the plot, ... no psychological commentaries, and absolute straightness in the style." Henry responded that he would rather "descend to a dishonoured grave" than satisfy William's literary tastes.
THE GRANGER COLLECTION, NEW YORK

Early in July, he spent a few days at her home in Beverly, meeting a host of entertaining young people. Describing his stay to Alice, he anticipated her jealousy of Whitman, and assured her that she had no cause for concern. Sarah, he said, was "as remote from me *personally* as Sarah Bernhardt would be were she here. But *we* are both members of the same spiritual body of which she is another member, and the members ought to recognize each other."[52] Yet as much as James included Alice in this friendship, Whitman's attentions were focused on him.

Whitman responded with acclaim to what James considered "the most *continually* amusing" sections of the *Principles.* She begged for more, which James, eager to accommodate so flattering a reader, was delighted to send her. "Naturally I 'purr' like a cat at the handsome words you let fall about the 'Psychology.' Go on! But remember," he added slyly, "that you can do just as well without reading it: I shan't know the difference."[53] Mrs. Whitman, he confided to his sister, was "on the whole the best woman in Boston."[54]

Yet even Sarah Whitman's enthusiasm did not dispel the anxiety that James felt as he waited for his book to be published. For the first time, he would confront the marketplace that, so far, he had managed to avoid. Family history did not make him optimistic. His father had been a commercial failure; his own *Literary Remains of Henry James* had sold hardly any copies; and although his brother supported himself by his writing, he depended on serialization and a loyal literary audience to ensure his income. William took every opportunity to advise Henry that if he would only condense his tales, he might attract more readers. *The Tragic Muse,* for example, although it seemed to William "a most original, wonderful, delightful and admirable production," still was "too refined, too elaborate and minute, and requires to be read with too much leisure to appeal to any but the select few." There was no reason, he reminded Henry, "for not doing less elaborate things for wider audiences."[55]

Now, James had produced a manuscript so long that it had to be published in two volumes, with sections that he thought so tedious he wondered if even his friends would read them. Yet he was confident, as he wrote to his brother, that "[a]s 'Psychologies' go it is a good one."[56] The proofreading was finished in July; the index was done in August; and on September 26, 1890, just four months short of his forty-ninth birthday, James held in his hands his first original book.

Chapter 13

SURCHARGED WITH VITALITY

1890–1893

"WHO DOES NOT remember the sense of glowing delight with which we first read the pages of the big, cumbrous, ill-bound and rather ill-printed volumes?" recalled James Rowland Angell, who read *The Principles of Psychology* as a student at the University of Michigan. "It was like inhaling a rare, pungent mountain air, vital, bracing and almost intoxicating. . . . We read it as one reads the most fascinating tale of a master—spell-bound and transported and yet withal feeling ourselves acquiring new powers, and gaining command of pregnant thoughts."[1] Unlike other popularly assigned textbooks, James's was lively, vigorous, and, as another student put it, rooted in "the immediate reality of 'finite individual minds' with their 'thoughts and feelings.'"[2]

From all over the world, in private letters and journal reviews, James received accolades for his literary, lyrical, and, as William Dean Howells put it, "flavorous" book.[3] "Unrestricted and unqualified praise is after all the real thing which authors crave," James wrote to his friend Flournoy, whose review in the *Journal de Geneve* had just appeared, "and the adjectives need not fear to make themselves too superlative!"[4]

James's interest in theories that met the "urgent demand of common-sense," his willingness to debate the significance of current laboratory research, and his generosity in accepting personal introspection, philosophical speculation, and psychical research as valid bases of psychological theory earned the *Principles* an appreciative readership. But theoretical expansiveness was not its only appeal. The book, grounded in autobiography, was illuminated by the experiences of a vivid and heroic personality: William James himself. Where most textbook authors tried to hide behind a facade of rhetorical objectivity, James presented an abundance of personal anecdotes to sustain his celebration of intuition, to argue that knowledge is attainable through sensation, and to question the validity of psychological generalizations emerging so prolifically from college laboratories.

Although some philosophers already were familiar with James's ideas from the articles that he had published for more than a decade, his propositions were new to students and to the many nonacademic readers who made the book a financial success. The long and grateful attention that these readers gave to James's conception of a "stream of thought," to his ideas about attention and habit, and to his examination of multiple layers of personality reflected a cultural need for a psychology that allowed for personal evolution and sustained individual authority. Like James, many of his readers were dissatisfied with prevalent theories that put forth a view of personality as static and determined by forces—biological, social, metaphysical—that appeared immutable.

Among the questions that James addressed in his sprawling study, two emerged as especially significant: how do we maintain a consistent "personal consciousness" as we respond to novel experiences; and how do we communicate our identity to others? Arguing against John Locke and Alexander Bain, who posited consciousness as discrete "bits" of thought held together in a "chain" or "train," James expanded upon his metaphor of thought as a stream containing personal memories that inform a "community of self," or sense of perpetuating identity.

Although a "spiritual something" remains intact to inform our sense of identity, that identity is subject to change. James took issue with the widely held idea that certain stimuli necessarily produce certain responses in the same individual. His own responses, he knew, were contextual. At different ages, in different moods, in different "organic states" and with different motivations that shape our attention, we react differently.

He realized, of course, that every experience is not suffused with the "warmth and intimacy" of a lifetime of memories and searched for another metaphor to distinguish these moments from the enveloping stream; he found one in the flight of birds. We need only think of the "alternation of flights and perchings," he said, to understand the difference between "resting-places" of experience "usually occupied by sensorial imaginations of some sort" and "places of flight [that] are filled with thoughts of relations, static or dynamic" between the perchings.

For James, these places of flight are equally as significant as the "perching" that "arrests" experience and "makes a sort of crisis of it" by focusing our attention on it. The unarticulated "set of tactile, visual and other fancies" comprise what James called a "tendency of feeling" that also floats in the stream of one's personal consciousness. These tendencies can be discovered in the subtle, but crucial, relational terms that connect the more definitive nouns and verbs.

James was frustrated, as were many of the modernist writers who took up the notion of stream of thought as a literary strategy, by formal conventions of expression and by the emphasis on substantive parts of speech to convey meaning. Because nouns and verbs were inextricable from their historical connotations, they necessarily obscured the "delicate idiosyncrasy" of each person's individual response to experience. "And if we wish to *feel* that idiosyncrasy," James advised, "we must reproduce the thought as it was uttered, with every word fringed and the whole sentence bathed in that original halo of obscure relations, which, like an horizon, then spread about its meaning."[5] Perhaps no writer influenced by James came closest to creating this halo of obscure relations as well as his student Gertrude Stein.

The questions of identity central to James's study of thought emerged also in his chapter on habit, which he thought would be an inspiration to students. Here, James argues that the repetition of actions and thoughts shapes consciousness and, therefore, identity. Although he claims that habits ingrained by the time an individual is thirty are difficult to change, still he maintains that educating ourselves to new habits can "*make our nervous system our ally instead of our enemy.*" James offers two "great maxims," borrowed from his reading of Bain, to guide this reeducation: first, "we must take care to *launch ourselves with as strong and decided an initiative as possible.*" Second, "*Never suffer an exception to occur till the new habit is securely rooted in your life.*" To these he adds a third maxim of his own: "*Seize the very first possible opportunity to act on every resolution you make, and on every emotional prompting you may experience in the direction of the habits you aspire to gain.*" Never be distracted, even for a moment, from watching for an opportunity to change.

Throughout the chapter, James returns to the example of a musician learning to play the piano, but his advice on habit transcends learning skills. The habits he aimed to change, in his own life, were habits of attitude: pessimism, fear, anger, and indecision. "There is no more miserable human being," he wrote, "than one in whom nothing is habitual but indecision, and for whom the lighting of every cigar, the drinking of every cup, the time of rising and going to bed every day, and the beginning of every bit of work, are subjects of express volitional deliberation." Certainly James spoke from his own youthful experience. And only by practicing assiduously, by being "systemati-cally . . . heroic," did he manage to change.[6]

The possibility of change, however, brought up the question of consistent identity. Each individual, James wrote, was, in fact, a lay-ered personality, consisting of a public self—the self as actor, the em-pirical self—distinct from an underlying spiritual self, "the most enduring and intimate part of the self, that which we most verily seem to be." This was the self that contained "our moral sensibility and con-science" and "our indomitable will."[7] Self-hatred or emotional turmoil might result when this spiritual self conflicted with one's public self—certainly he had felt this turmoil himself; and frustration was certain when this inner, authentic self was not mirrored by those with whom one was intimate.

In portraying this frustration, James drew upon memories of his anguish during his courtship of Alice and his exultation when he fi-nally felt "recognized" by the woman he loved. "The most peculiar so-cial self which one is apt to have," James wrote, "is in the mind of the person one is in love with. The good or bad fortunes of this self cause the most intense elation and dejection. . . . To his own consciousness he *is* not, so long as this particular social self fails to get recognition, and when it is recognized his contentment passes all bounds."[8]

Some readers found such revelations in the text inappropriate. In a long and not flattering review, G. Stanley Hall noted that James dis-closed details "of his age, of his early school life, his daily habits, tastes, etc, and unintentionally compels the reader to imagine that he is the hero of many more of his stories and illustrations than is probably the case. His favorite theme, conscious states, also contributes to give the book in places a Rousseau like—we had almost said Bashkertsieff like—confessional flavor. Its personal frankness . . . is unequalled in the history of the subject."[9] To be compared with Rousseau was one thing, but to be compared with Marie Bashkertsieff was another. Her

Journal, published the year before, offered revelations so intimate that they seemed, to many readers, scandalous; this was not quite the tone James wanted to convey.

James's celebration of "the vague, the fugitive, the transitory, in consciousness" irritated others. Hugo Münsterberg, for one, while he admitted that James "disentangles the most complex states of mind and is able to describe the subtlest tints and shades of consciousness," still felt dissatisfied by James's conclusions; "such delightful intimacy and warmth," he remarked, "may sometimes antagonize the bloodless abstract theories towards which each science after all must tend."[10] James, though, was not aiming to create abstract theories; he would leave those to the experimental psychologists. If in 1878 he had begun the book enthusiastic over their work, by 1890 he had become disenchanted with the results of laboratory experimentation and believed his own contribution lay elsewhere: he wanted to explore varieties of knowing, thinking, and feeling; to suggest hidden, unexamined depths of personality; to create a philosophy of "mental science."

A Decided Success

RELIEVED AT THE immediate success of the *Principles,* happy, and hopeful about his own future—James reflected his uncommonly good spirits in his announcement to Henry of the birth of his fifth child on December 22, 1890. "This is to inform you that one of the most beautiful and touching spectacles which the Earth affords could have been witnessed in the accompanying house to day—a father sitting and ½ pas[t] 12 o'clock meditating on the features of his new born son, who lay embedded in blankets on the sofa in front of him!" The baby weighed a hefty eleven pounds, but Alice's labor was so easy, James said, "One doesn't see why it mightn't happen every week."[11] But it would not happen again; Alice, just a few months short of her forty-second birthday, had had her last child.

The Jameses were at a loss in choosing a name for this son. William suggested Francis Tweedy or perhaps Francis Temple. Henry approved of Francis, but liked neither middle name, suggesting that they invoke, instead, Mary James's maternal grandfather, Alexander Robertson, a name that at least "preserves the continuity one likes to preserve."[12] William declared that "Robertson . . . stands for *me* as a symbol of everything from which life demands emancipation," but Henry eventually prevailed.[13] Although the baby was called Tweedy throughout his infancy, he later took the name Alexander Robertson James and was called Aleck.

Perhaps because of his size, or perhaps responding to the unusual calm of the James household, Tweedy was a remarkably placid infant, sleeping through the night, hardly crying during the day. Alice recovered quickly from childbirth. William, joyful after completing his *Principles,* boasted that he had become

> more patriarchal than ever: . . . the idol of the group of relatives and dependents, dignified and serene, never worrying or "wishing," never depreciating present possessions, never protesting against the injustice of other's opinions, or contradicting or pinning them down, never discussing personal anecdotes from the point of view of abstract reasoning and absolute truth, never seeking a second metaphor, or a third, when the first or second were good enough, breathing in short an atmosphere of peace and rest wherever I go.[14]

At peace with himself and the rest of the world, James plunged energetically into writing a condensed version of the *Principles,* which Holt believed would prove more marketable for most college courses. Concerned with providing for his growing family, James lost no time in revising his long text. Working on it even during a respite at Putnam Camp, he borrowed a friend's copy, cut out paragraphs, and pasted them together to form new, shorter chapters. "By adding some twaddle about the senses, by leaving out all polemics and history, all bibliography and experimental details, all metaphysical subtleties and digressions, all quotations, all humor and pathos, all *interest* in short . . . ," he wrote to Holt, "I think I have produced a tome of pedagogic classic which will enrich both you and me, if not the student's mind."[15]

By the summer of 1891, James knew that the *Principles* would not repeat the failure of his edition of his father's works; the book was "a decided success—especially from the literary point of view," he boasted. "I begin to look down on Mark Twain!"[16] Unlike literary men, however, who built their reputations work by work, James believed that his ideas would gain more force and exert more influence if he were part of—if not the leader of—an intellectual movement. Now that he had established himself as a major figure in his field, it seemed to him possible to form "some kind of an intellectual school of psychology" based at Harvard that would compete favorably with "the raw philistinism of the Stanley Hall School" at Clark.[17] James knew that the success of such a school would depend on its laboratory research, and he set out to modernize the facilities where he had worked, with no great enthusiasm, since the mid-1870s. His laboratory had migrated all over the university for many years, sometimes taking over small basement rooms in the Museum of Comparative Zoology, sometimes using a room in Boylston Hall, until 1890, when the university allotted two laboratory rooms and lecture space in Dane Hall. It was up to James, however, to raise money for equipment; and after he succeeded in bringing in more than four thousand dollars, it was up to him to find someone to serve as director.

"In the laboratory," one of his students said, "it was plain that James had neither flair nor patience for experimental work, and that he didn't care who knew it."[18] Yet if Harvard were to gain eminent status in the new field, it needed a thriving laboratory, and James set out to lure to the university the best man for the job: his young friend Hugo Münsterberg.

"I am doing the disagreeable work of trying to beg 10,000 dollars for Münsterberg [sic] salary," James announced in the spring of 1892. "So far have collected 2000, and made the College assume 2000. It is terribly uphill and disagreeable work."[19] He succeeded, however, in raising $4,600, enough to attract Münsterberg to commit himself for a three-year trial period.

Münsterberg would relieve James of an onerous burden and allow him to spend more time on the research that really engaged him: collecting data on psychical experiences. When James learned from Harry Norman Gardiner, a professor of philosophy at Smith, that the well-respected, sixty-eight-year-old social reformer Caroline Wells Healey Dall had had a hallucination "or apparition of Theodore Parker, and also some telepathic experiences," James immediately wrote to Dall, begging for testimony.[20] He also continued to investigate Leonora Piper, sometimes taking his students with him to sittings. His lengthy report on Piper for the English SPR was received with such enthusiasm that Frederic Myers asked Henry to read it before the group at an October meeting. "You were very easy & interesting to read, & were altogether the 'feature' of the entertainment," Henry reported to William afterward.[21]

Alice's Will

"TO HIM WHO WAITS, all things come!" Alice exclaimed in her diary at the end of May 1891. Longing for some "palpable disease" to explain her many ailments, eager to foil the physicians who had patronized her by insisting that her symptoms were psychosomatic, Alice finally was diagnosed with breast cancer. True, she had suffered from "rheumatic gout" for some twenty years and "spinal neurosis" for seven, but the tumor had the decided advantage of being able to kill her, quickly. "To any one who has not been there," she reflected, "it will be hard to understand the enormous relief of Sir A. C.'s uncompromising verdict, lifting us out of the formless vague and setting us within the very heart of the sustaining concrete." At last, she was on her way to "the dark Valley of the Shadow of Death."[22]

Although Alice did not want to tell William about this new development, so as to avoid his "exaggerated sympathy for suffering," Harry thought better of it. William's response was a letter notable not for its exaggerated sympathy, but for its decided coolness. Her impending death was regrettable to be sure, he told Alice, but since she "never cared for life," since some mysterious "infernality in the body" suppressed the "really existing parts of the mind" and kept them "from participation in this world's experiences," death might allow her true personality—the repressed Alice—finally to emerge. "When that which is *you* passes out of the body," he told her, "I am sure that there will be an explosion of liberated force and life till then eclipsed and kept down. . . . Everyone will feel the shock, but you yourself will be more surprised than anyone else."

William predicted that someday, too late of course for Alice, there might be an explanation for the "doom of nervous weakness" that had so undermined her spirit and circumscribed her life. "These inhibitions, these split-up selves, all these new facts that are gradually coming to light about our organization, these enlargements of the self in trance etc., are bringing me to turn for light in the direction of all sorts of despised spiritualistic and unscientific ideas. Father would find in me to day a much more receptive listener—all that philosophy has got to be brought in."[23]

Katharine Loring apparently withheld William's letter from Alice, thinking, with good reason, that it might upset her. But when Alice finally read it, her response was not anger but a steadfast conviction of her own worth. "[Y]ou must believe," she informed him, "that you greatly exaggerate the tragic element in my commonplace little journey. . . . when I am gone, pray don't think of me simply as a creature who might have been something else had neurotic science been born; notwithstanding the poverty of my outside experience I have always had a significance for myself."[24] That significance eluded William, who, despite his rapacious interest in other people's lives, tended to judge their value by one standard: his own.

Reports from Harry kept him informed of Alice's decline; it was clear to William that she would not live until the spring when he planned to come to Europe with his family for his sabbatical year. In September, then, he sailed to England alone, to see his sister for the last time.

Although he expected that she would be changed physically, he found her much the same as when he saw her last, only weaker and uncomfortable, since she could lie in bed only in one position. She talked of almost nothing but her coming death; "it seems to fill her with positive glee," he said, a glee that only underscored for him what a "strange and wonderful little being" his sister was and, no doubt, inspired much exaggerated sympathy. During one of his three visits, she forced him to touch the tumor.

Alice did not record William's visits in her diary. While his presence may have offered her some solace, she knew that among her family, the only one whose sympathy she could depend on, the only one who would not patronize her, was her beloved Henry: "Henry the patient, I should call him," she said. Ever since she had arrived in England, she depended on his care, and he had shown her nothing but devotion. "He comes at my slightest sign," she wrote, "and hangs on to whatever organ may be in eruption and gives me calm and solace by assuring me that my nerves are his nerves and my stomach his stomach—this last a pitch of brotherly devotion never before approached by the race."[25] And surely not approached within the James family. It fell to Henry, aided by Katharine Loring and Alice's nurse, Emily Bradfield, to alleviate the pain of Alice's last months.

Katharine administered morphine, but its side effects were severe. William suggested the services of a physician expert in hypnosis, who managed to help Alice sleep. He taught the technique to Katharine; as Alice declined, the tireless Katharine was pressed into constant service, trying to hypnotize her every twenty minutes.

Her heart was weak, her resistance to infection so compromised that a cold she caught from her nurse resulted in a debilitating fever. She was emaciated, she was wracked by pain. "But don't be upset by all this," Henry added, incredibly, to William, "—the situation is after all simple."[26] On Saturday, March 5, Alice, barely able to speak, asked Henry to send a telegram to William and his family: "Tenderest love to all farewell Am going soon." That morning, Alice's pain seemed to abate, but by evening, after protesting that she could not live another day, she sank into a deep sleep. Her breathing, at first labored, gradually became more peaceful and, by Sunday afternoon, intermittent— one breath a minute, Henry said; and then, at four o'clock in the afternoon, the breathing stopped.

Henry telegraphed immediately: "Alice just passed away painless Wire Bob." Instead, William wired Henry: was he sure that Alice was dead, really dead, and not in a trance-state? "I telegraphed you this A.M.," he explained in a letter that followed, "to make sure the death was not merely apparent, because her neurotic temperament & chronically reduced vitality are just the field for trance-tricks to play themselves upon."[27]

"You wouldn't have thought your warning necessary if you had been with us, or were with us now," Henry assured him. William's "warning" reflected a pervasive suspicion about Alice's "neurotic temperament," her decades of mysterious illnesses, and, most of all, her "despotic" manipulation of her family. "What a relief!" he exclaimed to Henry, when he was sure Alice was, in fact, truly dead. "Poor little Alice! What a life! I can't believe that that imperious will and piercing judgment are snuffed out with the breath." If Alice had had some "mysterious debt" to the universe, William could not fathom what it was. To him, her "little life" seemed "shrunken and rounded. . . . What a blessed thing to be able to say '*that* task is over!'"

As much as Henry acknowledged the frustrations of Alice's life and "the consistency, as it were, of her character," he disagreed with William's insistence that she was "little" or "shrunken"; for Henry, she had been nothing less than a "rare & remarkable" woman. "The temper & nature of her spirit made the particular life & experience she had the only possible ones," he explained to William. "To this experience she lent herself with extraordinary courage & superiority—it is this last word, somehow, that expresses to me—vague as it is—most of what she was."[28]

He had loved her; he would miss her; and he felt great anxiety about his last duty to her: a funeral and, as she wished it, cremation. With Katharine Loring, Alice's faithful nurse, and the family's friend Annie Ashburner Richards, Henry accompanied Alice's body in a horse-drawn hearse to a chapel in Woking. The service was short, the "incineration," as Henry put it, took more than an hour. Carrying Alice's ashes, the four mourners returned to London. "It is the last, the last forever," Henry wrote to William.[29]

Alice's imperious spirit, however, still exerted itself. Shortly before her death, she had changed her will, removing William as executor and substituting Katharine Loring and Joseph Bangs Warner, the family's lawyer and friend. She divided her estate, worth some $80,000, according to her own sense of justice and merit. Her nephews received nothing; she left to her nieces—William's daughter Peggy, Bob's Mary, and Wilky's Alice—$2,500 each;[30] to her cousin Lilla Walsh and two women friends, one of whom was struggling to pursue a career in art, she left $1,000 each. Because Bob had married into a wealthy family and did not depend on her inheritance, she left him $10,000; the rest of the estate was to be divided among Henry, William, and Katharine Loring, all of whom, in Alice's estimation, had "no expectations" of wealth. The will seemed to Henry sensible and sensitive; William agreed, but he was apparently miffed at Alice's final note of condescension about his own lack of "expectations." "I do hope that you won't suffer one cent of Alice's *capital* to be invaded by you[r]self," he cautioned Henry. "You will need a good deal more than you are likely to have when your writing powers are cut short, as in the nature of things they must be some day if you live."[31] Henry, ever patient, chose to ignore the remark.

AS THEY GREW UP together, William saw Alice as a kindred spirit, suffering from the same unfortunate moral nature, plagued by the same demons as he. He applauded her demonstrations of will and attempts at independence although he saw that she was tethered, far more than he ever was, to her mother and aunt. Yet despite William's youthful sympathy for Alice, gender and age forced them into roles that precluded the kind of close camaraderie that William shared with Henry and, at times, with Bob.

Confronted again and again with Alice's nervous collapses, William advised her to "[k]eep a stiff upper lip & snap your fingers at fate."[32] When he saw that she was unable to snap her fingers to any effect, he predicted that she might "grow out" of whatever ailed her.[33] Alice did have some respites from her recurring breakdowns and depressions, caused at times by travel, by one or another therapeutic regimen, or by some productive activity. Since productivity had helped him weather his own crises, William assumed that Alice would benefit similarly. When he began to teach at Harvard, he thought he might find a job for her at the Museum of Comparative Zoology.

After 1878, however, when, by Alice's own admission, the dark waters of depression closed over her, never again to part, William was persuaded that she never would recover. Because he saw so much of himself in her, he tended to believe that her persistent nervous condition was a failure of will; if *he* had emerged from the dark waters, so could she; and if she did not, she cast her own vote for the universe in which she would live. If her recurrent depressions were not simply a failure of will, he, too—sharing her temperament—could become victimized by his hidden selves. He needed, then, to believe that Alice might have saved herself through her own efforts.

William's insensitivity toward his sister, his lack of sympathy for her trials, and his condescension reveal more about his perception of her personality and misunderstanding of her potential than his attitudes toward women in general. One of the first professors to support Elizabeth Agassiz's efforts to establish the Harvard Annex, James taught women students for most of his career and was notably generous with his serious help and encouragement.

At the time that Alice was dying, he was involved in a strenuous campaign to admit a brilliant young woman into Harvard's psychology department as a doctoral candidate. Mary Calkins had completed a bachelor's and master's degree at Smith College; was teaching Greek, philosophy, and psychology at Wellesley; and, at twenty-seven, wanted to begin studying for a Ph.D. in psychology at Harvard. James was delighted to take her on as a student, but Charles Eliot, speaking for the overseers, refused to allow him to do so. James suggested that she try

Hall's psychology department at Clark, at the same time assuring her that he would keep pressuring Eliot to give in.[34] "It is flagitious that you should be kept out," he wrote to her. "Enough to make dynamiters of you and all women. I hope and trust that your application will break the barrier."[35] She did not quite break the barrier: she could attend courses as a "guest," Eliot finally conceded, but not as a registered student.

Attending courses was at least a first step. Royce agreed to direct her independent reading, and James invited her to join his fall psychology seminar. "My students four in number seem of divergent tendencies," he told her, "and I don't know just what will come of the course. Having published my two rather fat tomes, I shan't lecture, but the thing will probably resolve itself into advice and possible some experimentation."[36] The seminar would meet in his own library at 7:15; he told her to come at 6:30 for tea. After a few weeks the other students, for whatever reasons, dropped out, creating for Calkins a private—and, she thought, privileged—tutorial.

According to James's high standards, Calkins was brilliant. He invited her to work in his laboratory; he invited her to lunch with him and Alice. He supervised her papers, which, one after another, were published. And in 1895, after she had completed all required graduate course work, Royce, who was then chairman of the department, gave her an unofficial examination for her doctorate. "[I]t was much the most brilliant examination for the Ph.D. that we have had at Harvard," James reported to an undergraduate at Smith. "It is a pity, in spite of this, that she still lacks the degree. Your downtrodden but unconquerable sex is fairly entitled to whatever glory and credit may accrue it from Miss Calkin's {sic} prowess."[37]

Calkins' prowess continued in the publication of many books and articles on psychology, about which she corresponded with James until his death. In 1905, she served as president of the American Psychological Association. But she never received a doctorate from Harvard; and in 1902, when Radcliffe offered to bestow upon her its own doctorate, she politely refused.

Like Calkins, James's students at Radcliffe felt respected and affirmed by his interest in them. Gertrude Stein, who took classes with James beginning in 1893, was among his most ardent admirers. "Is life worth living?" she wrote in an essay for an English composition course. "Yes, a thousand times yes when the world still holds such spirits as

Prof. James." Besides being "a scientist of force and originality" and "a metaphysician skilled in abstract thought," Stein was convinced that James was "too great to worship logic as his God, and narrow himself to a belief merely in the reason of man."[38]

The irreverence, openness, and intuitiveness that she cited help us to understand James's special impact on students who saw themselves as outsiders to the traditional college experience, and Stein saw herself as even more of an outsider: Jewish in a world of Unitarians, over-weight among her corseted classmates, and a lesbian who would never fulfill her culture's expectations to marry and have children. Strug-gling with a youthful crisis of identity as grievous as James's own, Stein descended into what she called the "Red Deeps" of depression. James's understanding managed to revive her spirits: He persuaded her to have faith in "a truer, more eternal world," in her own abilities, in her future accomplishments, and *to believe what is in the line of your needs,* for only by such belief is the need fulfilled."[39]

Stein made famous an anecdote, perhaps apocryphal, that under-scores her feeling of spiritual connection with James. At a final exami-nation, held on a beautiful spring day, Stein, tired from attending several nights at the opera, handed in her blank examination book with an apology: "I am so sorry," she wrote, "but really I do not feel like an examination paper in philosophy to-day." The next morning she received a postcard: James told her he understood perfectly and awarded her, she said, "the highest mark in his course."[40]

Appendage to a Nursery

AT THE END OF MAY, James began his fifteen-month sabbatical by boarding the *Friesland,* bound for Antwerp. Alice, who had not had a vacation from housekeeping since she returned from her honeymoon and who had never traveled abroad with her husband, finally, after four-teen years of marriage, was accompanying him. So were the children. Ranging in age from Tweedy's seventeen months to Harry's thirteen years, they were making their first transatlantic voyage. The trip marked another important first, too: the first time that James would be cloistered with his family, day and night, every day and every night. We can see how well Alice had sheltered him by his horrified reaction to his children's continual presence. "To combine novel anxieties of the most agonizing kind about your children's education, nocturnal and

diurnal contact of the most intimate sort with their shrieks, their quarrels, their questions, their rollings-about and tears, in short with all
their emotional, intellectual, and bodily functions, in what practically
in these close quarters amounts to one room—to combine these things
(I say) with a *holiday* for *oneself* is an idea worthy to emanate from a lunatic asylum," he complained. Why hadn't any of his friends warned
him of his folly? Why hadn't they stopped him before he herded his
family on board the ship?[41]

It was clear to him from the start that problems would outweigh
pleasures. First, the children simply were bored by the European experience. "When on the Rhine I try to interest Billy in castles," William
told Henry, "he counts the cars on the passing freight trains. When in
Cologne Cathedral I try to make Harry dilate with emotion, he says,
'Are we never going to get out of this?' etc etc." Moreover, all of the
children had caught colds, and Alice, who had hoped for some measure of holiday for *her*self, was exhausted.[42]

Most frustrating for James, the "education problem," he discovered, "was a hard nut to crack."[43] Harry's knowledge of Latin was not
good enough to put him in his proper class in a German school. Leaving the family in Germany—undoubtedly with great relief—James
went off to Switzerland to search for a school and for housing in
Lucerne. He was looking for a quiet, picturesque pension in the country, not too hot, not too cold, not too high in the mountains, not too
rustic, and definitely not too expensive. "You see how modest are my
requirements!" he confessed to Flournoy, who offered to help. It is not
surprising that he could not fulfill them. Inexpensive pensions were
too small, expensive places too charmless. He could not find families in
which Harry and Billy could get tutoring and board.

By mid-July he still had not found homes for his sons, and the
family had reconvened at a pension in Gryon. The claustrophobic atmosphere of their few small rooms was alleviated only by an iron balcony where, James disclosed, "all the innermost mysteries of the James
family are blazoned and bruited to the entire village. *Things* are dried
there, quarrels, screams and squeals rise incessantly to Heaven, dressing
and undressing are performed, punishments take place—recrimination,
arguments, execrations."[44] Besides the discomfort of tight quarters, the
Jameses also found Gryon so steep that Alice could not manage with
the baby. They moved to Lausanne.

Not until the end of July were Harry and Billy finally placed; and not until the end of August, fully three months into their trip, did William and Alice finally have two days apart from their children. Leaving Peggy and Tweedy with a governess in Lausanne, William and Alice checked into the Hotel de l'Ecu in Geneva, shopped, went to the theater, and listened to the silence.

As soon as they returned to Lausanne, however, their problems began again. Peggy, so quiet and easy as a baby, had turned into a moody child, "a second sister Alice," William once remarked.[45] At five, she was irritable and contrary: "the really bad element in our lives just now, poor little darling, and we the bad element in hers."[46] As Peggy recalled that period, she claimed that she suffered from "religious fears" generated by a French Catholic woman who told her that if she did not convert to Catholicism, she would go to hell. Afraid to tell her parents the reason for her fears, she took to screaming each night when she went to bed. Her distress continued long after the Jameses returned home.

Billy was not happy in the family with whom he boarded, and although Harry, docile Harry, was no problem at all, the Jameses decided to enroll both boys in the English school in Florence, where the family moved for the winter. Florence, they quickly discovered, posed new problems: heat, bugs, and inadequate housing. "Every day and all day long," Alice reported, "William and I climbed innumerable flights of stairs in the search after an apartment,"[47] trying to communicate their needs in broken Italian ("Aryan roots without terminations," as William described it). William's affection for the city lifted Alice's spirits for a while, but even he began to talk increasingly of their spacious, comfortable Cambridge house, and they wondered if sailing home was not their wisest option. Finally, however, they found an apartment, large, sunny, clean, but, according to Alice, "very ugly." "Why is one born poor and *so* fastidious!" William remarked.[48] Nevertheless, with two sitting rooms, William could have a separate study and retreat from the assaults of family life.

Finally, they were settled. William was able to write until eleven, then spent an hour and a half sightseeing with either Alice, Harry, or Billy. They had a wonderful cook, Raphaello, who managed to produce cheap and tasty meals even without an oven, and they had connected with several friends in the area, including William Wilberforce Baldwin, who, in fact, had found the clever cook.[49]

The close quarters, however, soon took their toll. When James left on a short trip to Padua in October to conduct an investigation for the SPR, his departure, as usual, incited discord. This time, however, the discord was intensified by months of frustration on both sides. Alice was incensed; and William, for once, was not moved to contrition. "It may seem mean," he wrote to her, "after being in such vile spirits when with you to write to you now when alone that I have rarely in my life passed a day of greater contentment, but you wish to know the truth and that is it."[50]

The truth did not help Alice's spirits, which continued to sink. What Alice needed, William decided, was a little diversion. "In the cars," he went on, "I had such a vision of your life history—when I first saw you you were a form of beauty, now you are a 'form of use.' I know darling Alice that when we begin to make excursions, this depressed feeling you have about yourself will melt like snow in the sun. I have all the variety, you all the monotony in this partnership."[51]

Perhaps he was right. After he returned from Padua, they involved themselves in what James called "a menace of 'sociability'" with new friends and old: Frank Duveneck, the widower of Lizzie Boott; art collector Charles Loeser, a former student of James; Mark Twain, who had come to Italy to write; Minister of Education Pasquale Villari and his wife; the Russian diplomat Count von der Osten-Sacken; assorted Americans passing through the city; relatives of Katharine Loring; and some of their own relatives: Bob's wife, Mary; Wilky's widow, Carrie; and Elizabeth Glendower Evans, who spent a few months at a nearby pension.

Evans, unfortunately, came to grate on James's nerves. She seemed to him one of those indefatigable reformers who lusted after some wrong to right. "Were some great work on hand, revolution, siege, or shipwreck," William wrote to Henry, "she'd take the lead as a duck takes to water, without an effort or an interfering thought." But spending much time in her company was wearing, since she seemed incapable of having a relaxed conversation, but instead responded to any offhand remark "in a way so curt that it dries one up."[52] Alice had more patience for her.

Evans, more intimately involved with the family than most other friends, noticed a decided friction between William and Alice over expenses. Although William knew that they were eroding his sister's legacy for the sabbatical, he did not want to practice the self-denial that came so naturally to his wife. Once, for example, Alice became visibly upset when William insisted on serving the dinner champagne when lunching at home with a friend. And though Alice was by then used to William's returning from excursions with small, but useless, souvenirs, she became irate when he came home one day with an oil painting under his arm. "Oh, William, how *could* you!" she exclaimed, inciting him to grab a pair of scissors and cut the painting into pieces. Alice was reduced to tears. Harry, who silently witnessed the argument, had never seen his parents so upset with one another. "It was the first agonizing revelation to me of the fact that two people who love each other can hurt each other so cruelly," he admitted later, "and it was long before I could understand it."[53]

Such a conflict, however, was rare, and the cruelty that Harry noticed so sadly inflicted only superficial wounds. When James took a second trip to Padua in December, this time to receive an honorary doctorate from the university, he did not leave Alice languishing unhappily. When he returned, she had decided, this time against *his* protests about unnecessary expenditures, to give a dinner party to reciprocate for the many invitations they had accepted during the fall. James tried valiantly to dissuade her, but she won, and on New Year's Day, 1893, they had such a successful evening that James begged her forgiveness. There was nothing to forgive, she said. William had been no more impossible than usual.[54]

What James described as "infernal . . . social interruptions," Alice saw as rewarding friendships. Her pleasure in Italy was increasing with the "dear people" she was coming to know: "The richest part of this rich year to me will be the feeling of goodness in the world," she told Elizabeth Evans, "goodness of such different forms, but flowering and making life fragrant in strange places."[55]

The Jameses had an intimate glimpse of life flowering when William's student Alfred Hodder and his wife, Jessie, arrived in Florence. Hodder was brilliant, James thought, with "a certain *insouciance* of character" his only flaw. That insouciance had created a precarious situation for him and Jessie; they were in Italy without a home and hardly a friend, and Jessie was about to give birth to their child. Alice took pity on the poor, wandering couple, especially Jessie. "I have known her but a short time," she wrote to Elizabeth Evans, "long enough to make me wish to aid her sweet helplessness. I think I am more nervous about her baby's advent than she is herself."[56] Since she and William were planning to leave Italy two months before their lease expired, Alice suggested that the Hodders take over the apartment for that time. At the end of April, Jessie gave birth to a daughter. William, not surprisingly, left the apartment in favor of traveling through Italy; and Alice, once she was sure that Jessie was recovering well from the delivery, soon joined him.

Hoping to have some time to travel together before they returned home at the end of the summer, the Jameses found a school for Harry and placed Billy, Peggy, and Tweedy with the dependable Cérésoles, where Harry had lived happily the summer before. The Cérésoles, James told Alice, were a fine couple: "He is a strong man, and his wife is a very sweet woman—reversing the rôles in our family."[57]

By the end of August, with home in sight, James wanted to be there immediately. From across the sea, Cambridge, he said, seemed "[s]urcharged with vitality."[58] He decided that he needed to return at least several weeks before classes began, and he begged Alice to leave Europe earlier than they had planned. For her part, she wanted to stay. The trip that had begun with tension and irritability had evolved into an exhilarating and inspiring respite. She had no need, and no desire, to return home early. James, seeing that his arguments were futile, enlisted the help of her mother. Couldn't she persuade Alice to return on the first of September instead of two weeks later? He knew, of course, that Alice did not want to return to the burdens of housekeeping. But for him, the *"minus* side" of the trip was "that fact that we are primarily and essentially a *nursery,* with *adults* attached, and I don't think that my truest vocation is to be an appendage to a nursery. The consciousness that I don't perform the duties required is as great a wear and tear as the duties themselves would be if I performed them at all."[59]

Perhaps Mrs. Gibbens put in a word on his behalf. The family sailed from England at the end of August, and by September 2, they were home.

Chapter 14

REAL FIGHTS

1894–1896

JAMES CAME HOME to an America that looked and felt far different from the country he had left in 1892. He perceived "a terrible grimness" in the land, which he blamed on his own "divided soul." "One should not be a cosmopolitan," he decided; "one's soul becomes 'disaggregated.' . . . Parts of it remain in different places, and the whole of it nowhere. One's native land seems foreign. It is not wholly a good thing, and I think I suffer from it."[1]

Europe, he said, invigorated him with its strength and prosperity; when he was in Switzerland or Germany or even England he felt manly and energetic. Of course, when he had been abroad, not engaged in the daily work that occupied him at home, he suffered no challenge to this stalwart sensibility; and he had forgotten, apparently, the many times he fled to Europe for resuscitation and returned home no stronger than he had left. Nevertheless, after fifteen months of a sabbatical, facing semester after semester of students, examinations, and faculty meetings from which he would have no respite for another seven years, he felt irresistibly drawn to what he saw as his European identity. The landscape of America—"the thin grass and ragged waysides, the poverty stricken land, and sad American sunlight over all"—served as a metaphor for his own discouragement.[2]

But the grimness that James noticed was not only in his imagination; it was real, the result of a devastating financial depression that had begun the previous June, causing farm prices to plummet, more than five hundred banks to close, and by the end of the year, sixteen thousand businesses to fail. Rising unemployment—even Harvard had to cut back on its teaching staff—caused a pervasive sense of panic. His brother Bob became frantic, accusing William of cheating him out of money he was owed from the family's Syracuse property.

Although James still was assured of his teaching salary, the depression had made "frightful ravages" in the family's savings, eating away two-thirds of Alice's legacy and forcing James to sell some stocks at a great loss. For years, he had hoped that he would be able to afford an early retirement so that he would have the time to write; but now, with this financial setback, liberation seemed increasingly remote. At fifty-two, as he thought about "the wild desert of old-age," he alerted younger men to "the paramount urgency of providing for the time when you'll be old fogies, by laying by from your very first year of service a fund on which you may be enabled to 'retire' before you're sixty and incapable of any cognitive operation that was n't ground into you twenty years before, or of any emotion save bewilderment and jealousy of the thinkers of the rising generation."[3]

James's obligation now was to provide for his family's current expenses. Like many other Americans, William and Alice were faced with the need to economize drastically. Alice, with her special talent for frugality, came up with a scheme whereby, she calculated, they could glean about three thousand dollars: they would rent the Cambridge house, she and the two younger children would move to Chocorua for the winter, Harry and Billy would live with Mrs. Gibbens, and James would rent a room. Much to James's relief, they could not find a tenant for the house. But he knew that their situation was difficult, and they were prepared, at the end of the year, to sell their Irving Street house and find more modest residence if their situation did not improve.

James admitted that the winter of 1893–94 was gloomy, but he had confidence that two controversial federal actions, the repeal of the Sherman Silver Purchase Act and the return to a gold standard, would bring about an economic revival. The crisis had not diminished his faith that the Democratic Party, to which he and his fellow mugwumps had defected in 1884, would save the country. After the elections in November, he rejoiced at "the Republican rout," deeming it "surely the greatest moral revolution we have had since Lincolns [sic] election in 1860 & on the whole a quite similar phenomenon."[4]

As for the continuing depression, it was "good and moralizing," James thought, "for people to 'lie low' as they are doing." In fact, James's standard of daily living had not been immediately affected by the depression. No doubt Alice chided him for any unnecessary expenditures, but the family still kept a cook and housekeeper, James still frequented the Friday Club, the Tavern Club, and the Saturday Club for an occasional dinner. And he could still afford mind-cure treatments which, he said, helped to lift him "from the really awful melancholy" of his first few months at home.

He came to reconcile his sense of ambiguous national identity by choosing, finally, to be an American: dauntless, spirited, even a bit rakish. America was a country that faced its problems intrepidly, convinced they could be solved; that celebrated consensus; that rejected the dusty scaffolding of social hierarchy. If sometimes the blare of American public life offended him, still the noise and turmoil energized him.

He knew that he, like his brother Henry, could slip too easily into the studied elegance of European intellectual life. If being an American meant that he must ration unsettling trips abroad, then he would stay at home. "It is no light matter to feel foreign in one's native land," he said.[5] "Like all ideal things, harmony of this kind [with one's country] must be worked for and bought by certain renunciations. We have many ideal things here, and the best thing an American can do is to stay at home as much as possible, and try to increase them."[6]

Increasing the nation's ideals meant contributing to a sense of optimism about America's future and a renewal of social spirit. The Chicago World's Columbian Exposition, for example, seemed to James just such an enterprise. Opening in the midst of the depression, the fair imparted to its twenty-seven million visitors an image of America as a triumphant nation that could overcome ephemeral problems and obliterate social blemishes. An homage to technology and inventiveness, dazzling exhibits defined the country's progress in terms of growing commercialism and industrialization.

"Everyone seems uplifted by it," James said, "and it appears actually to have been a purely ideal conception ideally carried out." William Dean Howells visited and found the fair inspiring; Münsterberg thought it offered a glimpse into a golden future. Charles Eliot

Norton, no easy convert to mass entertainment, returned from a visit transported by what he described as "a real communal spirit like that of ancient Athens where men feel as if they did not own themselves but held their life in fee for their city's service." The fair, James concluded, "acted like an unexpected revelation," its effect "quite religious in character."[7]

JAMES SUFFERED another challenge to his identity besides national "temperament": professional affiliation. He complained after returning from Europe that he had forgotten psychology, that "the subjects themselves have become so paltry and insignificant-seeming that each lecture has appeared a ghastly farce."[8] He accused experimental psychologists of devoting themselves to amassing minute and trivial data and claimed that he himself was "impatient (and incompetent) of details," preferring to "turn to broad abstractions. I wish to get relieved of psychology as soon as possible."[9]

Nevertheless, as one of the most prominent psychologists in America, he knew that he would be sacrificing himself, professionally and financially, if he did not promote his expertise. "The dreadful thing in life," he wrote to George Croom Robertson, "is the *trying* to do work to which one feels oneself incompetent, and when one *sincerely gives up,* in the old religious fashion, then one can *erst* look round one and take things in. The fever, the fret, the ambition, and the shame!—they are the worst of all. But willingly to *be* simply like the unnumbered herd, that must be peace."[10]

It was a peace that James would not know; beset by an ambitious and competitive temperament, he could do nothing else than catapult himself above the unnumbered herd. To that end, he attended a meeting of the American Psychological Association in New York in December 1893, and joined with his colleagues James McKeen Cattell, who taught at Columbia, and James Mark Baldwin, who taught at Princeton, in beginning a "broad and worthy" journal to rival Stanley Hall's "too narrow" *American Journal of Psychology.* His journal, James hoped, would allow more philosophically inclined psychologists to distinguish themselves from pure experimentalists and would help to create a cohesive and coherent American school of psychology.

American psychology, however, was not disposed to accept psychical research as part of the discipline. Although James continued investigating Leonora Piper, he discovered, much to his dismay, that some of his friends no longer shared his enthusiasm toward psychical research in general and Piper in particular. Ten years after the ASPR began, a lack of conclusive data discouraged many of its former supporters. Rivaled by prolific laboratory experimentation, psychical research seemed less and less likely to yield persuasive results. When James invited Hugo Münsterberg to participate in Piper's sittings, he absolutely refused. And even Royce, once so sympathetic, incited James's anger over his "cool and indifferent refusal to waste an hour over Mrs. P" at a sitting in James's house. "It is simply disgraceful to a man in his position," James complained, "the more so that (I fancy) he doesn't feel sure, as poor Münsterberg does, that Hodgson, Myers and I are dupes."[11] James convinced Nathaniel Shaler, Shaler's wife, and Charles Norton to attend sittings, but he worried that they would emerge deeming Piper "an ingenious fraud."[12]

Those sittings, however, validated James's own appraisal. Piper was able to give Mrs. Shaler many details related to her dead brother and to tell Norton facts that he believed no one else could know. But Piper herself seemed unusually irritated at the endless investigations and told Hodgson that she refused to sit for him again. A letter from James calmed her, although he had no sympathy for her claim of being exploited. "The poor innocent little woman," James remarked after Piper ended her strike, "—she has to stamp her foot and shake her head occasionally, to make believe she has any individuality left."[13]

Despite the coolness of some of his American colleagues, James's status among the English researchers was so exalted that they wished him to serve as president of the SPR, beginning in 1894. The request, from Myers, unfortunately came during the depths of James's melancholy, and he could see no way to accept yet another drain on his limited energy. He declined, using physical and emotional ill health as an excuse. Myers, however, would have none of it; and in a letter that Mary James could have written, he admonished James for his self-indulgence. "It seems to me," Myers wrote, "that your mental and physical disorganisation and decay is never by any chance perceptible to anyone but *yourself;* and, moreover, that when you are actually in the presence of friends you are able to make an effort (if such it be) which presents you to them as a source of wisdom and delight." If James had a bit more *"doggedness,"* Myers suggested, he might be more helpful to people; and besides, he assured James, all the SPR wanted was his name at the head of their roster of officers. It didn't much matter what, if anything, he actually did.[14] A few weeks later James, apparently chastened, telegraphed his acceptance.

Intimacies

BEGINNING IN THE fall of 1894, Rosina Emmet, the twenty-one-year-old daughter of James's cousin Ellen Temple Emmet, lived with the Jameses while she attended Radcliffe College. The pretty and spirited Rosina seemed to James "a regular trump. In fact," he wrote to Henry, "were I a youngster I should aim right at her 'hand.' "[15] James's enthusiasm for Rosina, and no doubt his playful flirting, irritated Alice, who began to complain of Rosina's inconsiderate behavior (she always arrived late to breakfast), her lack of affection for the Jameses, and her less-than-effusive gratitude for all that they offered her. By spring, James admitted that the fair Rosina had some definite shortcomings "in the line of selfishness and egotism," but still he enjoyed her liveliness and her "fine slap dash hit or miss perceptive intellect."[16] She reminded him of his beloved Minny Temple—"with more practical ability and less charm"—and stirred up some "dead and buried things" that made him feel a special affection for her.[17] Those feelings, he decided, were best kept secret from Alice. When Rosina was traveling in Europe after she left the Jameses, William sent one hundred dollars to Henry to give her for spending money. "*Don't acknowledge this specifically* when you write," he cautioned Henry, afraid of Alice's anger if she learned of his generosity.[18]

James's correspondence with Rosina suggests that she became a luminous figment of his imagination, colored by his memory of Minny, and intensified by Alice's scorn. "[Y]ou see the truth, irrespective of persons, as few people see it," he wrote to her, "and after all you care for that more than for anything else—and that means a rare and unusual destiny and ultimate salvation."[19]

James's affection for women whom Alice disparaged came to be a familiar pattern in his relationships. Early in his friendship with Sarah Wyman Whitman, at the time that Whitman was reading his *Principles* with such appreciation, he wrote to Alice defending his "flirtation": "you may say she's artificial, and an upstart, and what you like," he told Alice, "—but she has the real bottom thing in her, and in the long run I bet on her against the whole field, and I love her dearly—there!"[20]

While it is doubtful that his relationship with Whitman included physical intimacy (Alice would not have permitted his letters to her to survive if she had suspected anything of the kind), Whitman did serve as the object of his affections and, perhaps, of desire. Once, he reported a strange dream to her—one dream of many that centered around her—that suggests both her attraction to him and, perhaps, a yearning to be snared by her into a closer intimacy:

> The other night it was your three sisters whose acquaintance I made in a strange antique italian city. One of them was a singularly attractive person, though unlike you in every other respect. I asked which was the oldest of the family, as it was impossible to tell by their looks. "Oh!" she said, "of course *the Spider!*" by which surprising name I immediately understood *you* to be meant, believing it to refer to the gracility, so to speak, of your configuration, rather than to any moral analogy. Now how do you interpret *that* dream?[21]

By sharing his writing with Whitman, James spun his own web to draw her closer to him. And in the spring of 1894, he found another way to foster the intimacy that he desired.

Katharine Loring had made four copies of Alice's diary, and now, two years after Alice's death, she sent copies to William and Henry, asking their advice about whether to send a copy to the volatile Bob. Henry's immediate reaction was anxiety over "the sight of so many private names & allusions in print. I am still terrified by this—," he wrote to William, "—as I partly feel responsible as it were—being myself the source of so many of the things told, commented on &c."[22] The thought that it might be published, which Katharine said was Alice's intention, made him tremble with fear. The diary must be kept secret, he told William. Yes, Bob should be sent a copy—but only to avoid his recrimination when he found out about its existence; otherwise no one, no one, must find out.

William, on the other hand, thought the diary was a powerful literary work, deserving to be published. And as for keeping it secret, even before he instructed Katharine to send a copy to Bob, before anyone else except his wife knew of it, he decided to share the diary with

one special person, his "adored and adorable madam," Sarah Whitman.[23] "I think it best to leave poor sister Alice's diary with you to
day," he wrote to her. "Some parts of it will say nothing to you for lack
of a key to the persons etc.; some will bore you; but there are some
beautiful things well said, and beside the dramatic pathos as it nears
the end—she with her cancer—it seems to me a very vivid expression
of one of the most vivid and able characters I ever knew. . . . My real
reason for sending it to you," he confessed, "is that it brings you more
into the intimacy of the James family." Discovering Alice in the pages
of the diary, James knew, would give Whitman a new sense of intimacy
with him as well, with the context of his life and with the "hidden
self" that he felt he once had shared with his sister. He cautioned
Whitman to mention the diary to no one: "Not the Katharine Loring
should you meet her. My brother Bob is still ignorant of its existence,
and my wife hasn't yet communicated the fact to her mother and sister. So you see," he assured her, "how you are singled out!"[24]

Rosina Emmet and Sarah Whitman were not the only "adored and
adorable" women who would serve as James's confidantes and inspira-
tions. In the summer of 1895, in Keene Valley, James met Pauline
Goldmark. She was twenty-one, about to enter her senior year at Bryn
Mawr. He was fifty-three, and he was captivated.

Life Worth Living

"DARLING ALICE—I have been happy! *happy*! *happy*!—with the exquisite imperishable beauty of this place, the place I know so well,"
William wrote from Keene Valley, where he had returned at the end of
the summer, after a short lecture trip to Colorado.[25] Chocorua had its
appeal, but Putnam Camp remained a source of physical and spiritual
renewal, a place where he could rediscover the "real springs" of his life.
James often said that he retreated to Keene Valley to escape from the ir-
ritations of too much sociability, but he never was isolated in the
balsam-scented woods of Putnam Camp. The camp always was filled
with families—wives and children, cousins and friends—all of whom
he knew well: Bowditches, Putnams, various Lowells, Cabots, Lothrops,
Emersons, and Hoopers. "This is a strange world," he exclaimed once;
"here I am with a bevy of women and children and I *like* it!"

James was an enthusiastic participant in the rowdy, often silly, escapades that involved adults and children alike. Once, when Richard

Hodgson came to the camp, the children (and James) joined in a game of "capture," setting up a foot noose to trap the unsuspecting Hodgson after they pursued him around the grounds. There were customary evening theatricals and tableaux on the Stoop, complete with hand-made costumes; there was storytelling around a campfire at night; there were games of charades; there were impromptu celebrations of nothing in particular. When James Bryce, a friend of James's and an English ambassador, told the campers that he had never seen a torch-light parade, the group contrived one, complete with hastily crafted costumes, for that very evening. And there were silly songs, such as "Popsy Wopsy," which greeted the person unfortunate enough to ar-rive late to dinner; and equally silly poems, such as "The Great Cigar," commemorating James's smoking on the summit of the Gothics in the company of Jim Putnam, Richard Hodgson, and A. Lawrence Lowell:

> It was full eight inches long,
>   But not *pro rata* strong,
> And this was what the wily Willie thunk:
>   "I will nicotine my soul
>   And survey the godhead whole,
> And snatch celestial secrets by a drunk."
>
>   And first of all he bit it,
>   And next of all he lit it,
> Then sate him down to get the Giant view
>   With the first puff he did breathe, "Oh
>   My," he said, "Oh me, though,
> I fear I've bitten more than I can chew."

The poem continues for thirteen more stanzas, with references to James's experiments with other substances taken to expand his view: chloral, chloroform, hashish, opium, mescal; and to some of the psychological and philosophical theories that he was inclined to dis-cuss with his hiking companions.[26] James, Putnam, Hodgson, and Bowditch found enough time to talk about psychical research, a field to which Bowditch contributed with his famous "ghost pictures," overexposed photographs allegedly revealing the images of phantasms, developed in a darkroom that Bowditch had fitted at the Camp.

James had fond, even stirring memories of his honeymoon at Putnam Camp, where he and Alice "first truly made each other's acquaintance in the Putnam shanty all by ourselves." For others, as well, Putnam Camp was a place where romance blossomed and, as one camper recalled, "many a courtship was initiated or ripened. . . . The exhilaration of the mountains, the spirit of freedom which pervaded the place, made an ideal medium for the growth of romantic friendships."[27]

In that exhilarating landscape, James found himself suddenly overtaken by an unexpected feeling of romance. One of his former students, Dickinson Miller, took him to meet some friends of his, a family who had a summer home a half mile from Putnam Camp. The Goldmarks were an impressive group. Joseph Goldmark, a physician and chemist, had been a leading figure in Austria's revolution of 1848, forced to flee the country when he was convicted of high treason and complicity in the murder of the minister of war, and sentenced to death. Once in the United States, he married Regina Wehle, the daughter of a Prague businessman who had emigrated with his family because of the anti-Semitism and intractable economic problems throughout eastern Europe that had followed the incendiary revolutions of 1848. The couple raised their ten children in a large house in Brooklyn, New York, not far from Goldmark's percussion cap and cartridge factory. Describing himself as an ardent American patriot, Goldmark supplied the Union with munitions during the Civil War. Because of threats to his factory and family, a cadre of guards had surrounded his business and his home for several years.

The Goldmarks raised their children to be ardent Americans as well, outspoken, energetic, and responsive to social and political issues. The eldest daughter, Helen, married Felix Adler, founder of the Society for Ethical Culture and professor of political and social ethics at Columbia; another daughter, Alice, married jurist Louis Brandeis; the eldest son, Henry, became an engineer who was appointed to the Isthmian Canal Commission and spent eight years designing and supervising the building of the Panama Canal.

But the Goldmark most appealing to James was Pauline. "There is a perfect little serious rosebud of a Miss Goldmark whom Miller seems very sweet upon," he wrote to Alice. "She climbs cliffs like a monkey in his company—it would be jovial if they contracted an alliance."[28]

Whether Miller was attracted to her we do not know, but James was enchanted by her liveliness, her love of nature, her independence and self-possession. It was Pauline, after all, who inspired James's effusive letter to Alice declaring himself "happy! *happy*! *happy*!"; Pauline who made him recall his first intimacies with Alice at Putnam Camp during their honeymoon; Pauline who made him feel, he said, "temporarily quite young again."[29]

She was an exemplary young woman, and when his own daughter suffered from adolescent crises of identity, he wished Pauline were a central part of Peggy's life. "For Peggy's sake," he told Pauline, "I wish you could be 'around.' She is changed beyond all recognition, feels alone in the Universe, and needs some model of feminine character to show her in which direction to aspire, model,—or models! for she will certainly make her own choice. I wish she might choose to be like you."[30]

International Swagger

THE GOLDMARKS WERE among many of James's friends—including William Salter, Elizabeth Evans, and Thomas Davidson—who connected him to pressing social and political issues of his time and who urged him to make his views public. At first he preferred to express those opinions privately. But as his professional stature increased, he took a correspondingly active role in civic life, offering public declarations about the duties of citizenship, the nature of democracy, and the urgency of containing what he believed was an inherently bellicose human spirit. James's philosophical resistance to ideology, of course, informed his opinions about politics, as well.

In the summer of 1895, to James's consternation, President Cleveland decided to involve the United States in a dispute between Great Britain and Venezuela over the boundary line of British Guiana. America had offered to arbitrate in the dispute several years before, but by 1895 Cleveland felt so unpopular because of his failure to solve economic problems that he began searching for an issue that would inspire confidence in his leadership and that of the Democratic Party. Venezuela seemed to be that issue.

He directed Richard Olney, his secretary of state, to send an ultimatum to Great Britain, asserting that the United States was "practically sovereign" in the Americas. "Its infinite resources combined with its isolated position," Olney declared, "render it master of the situation and practically invulnerable as against any or all powers."[31] Hailing the Monroe Doctrine to justify his actions, Cleveland proposed nothing less than war if Great Britain did not concede. "Well," James wrote to

Frederic Myers in England, "our countries will soon be soaked in each other's gore. You will be disemboweling me, and Hodgson cleaving Lodge's skull. It will be a war of extermination when it comes, for neither side can tell when it is beaten, and the last man will bury the penultimate one, and then die himself. The French will then occupy England and the Spaniards America. Both will unite against the Germans, and no one can foretell the end."[32]

James made two public statements opposing the Cleveland-Olney proposition: one, a letter to Massachusetts congressman Samuel McCall; another, a published reply to a speech by Theodore Roosevelt, who asserted that anyone who questioned Cleveland's foreign policy was nothing less than a traitor.

But James discussed his feelings more elaborately in private letters, especially to his brother-in-law William Salter, who disagreed with his position. "Can any serious man pretend that the [Monroe] 'doctrine' has in the mind of one american out of a 1000 an ethical significance or that it would occur to any one to apply it between Chile & Peru?" he asked Salter. "Its only popular significance is that it claims as an ideal what Mr. Olney says is already a fact, the position of having our *fiat* recognized as law on this continent. We are pleased at challenging the big powers of Europe by this attitude, and apart from that exciting sensation there isn't one of us in 10,000 who has any use for such a doctrine."[33]

While Salter believed that the existence of such a doctrine required a nation to act consistently according to its provisions, James objected to the use of something so "abstract" to guide national policy. The government, he insisted, was hiding behind the doctrine to inflame Anglophobia and to justify actions that had nothing to do with a threat to American sovereignty, but more with the presence of gold in Venezuela, which would make some influential Americans rich. "A 'doctrine' that should oblige us in consistency to break with England for the sake of Venezuela carries its absurdity on its face," James argued. "Can any sane man believe in the 'menace to our institutions' etc. from European extension in S. A.? Absolutely the only institution menaced is the *Monroe Doctrine itself.*"[34]

Much to James's amazement, England, too distracted by problems with the Boers in South Africa to stand up to America's challenge, agreed to arbitration. Unfortunately, James believed, England's capitulation would convince many Americans that Cleveland's aggression had been justified; or perhaps, he suggested, "twisting the lion's tail . . . will be so safe hereafter as to lose all its zest and even pass into desuetude. . . . I do hope," he told Salter, "that as we get more and more drawn into the line of international swagger you won't applaud the fresh steps every time, as you have this one. . . . I know when I'm beaten," he added. "In matters political what succeeds is right and wise, so this is. Only our future history can tell whether permanently or temporarily wise. And to our future we now turn."[35]

James's reaction during the Venezuela crisis serves as a prelude to his more extensive involvement in political debate as America lunged further onto the international stage. What he opposed, he said, was adherence to any ideology, represented, for example, by the Monroe Doctrine; what he championed was "the good old rule of dealing with cases according to the expediencies and advisabilities of the moment."[36] What he opposed also were political leaders who appealed to what James called the base "fighting instinct" of the lowest classes of society. "The wise ruler and the wise country don't give the lower types their chance," he said. "The type that Cleveland has inflamed with the sense of its national authority is one of the lowest possible."[37]

For James, the "lower types," uneducated, unreflective, and unable to distinguish between responsible leaders and political opportunists, were the "internal enemy" that could undermine the country's moral life. These are the people who would give in to "mob hysteria" and who must be kept away from arms and the opportunity to use them. Unfortunately, he discovered that Rosina Emmet was among those enemies. Responding to Rosina's support of Cleveland's Venezuela policy, James said he regretted "that Radcliffe and its history courses didn't give you a somewhat broader view. The fighting temper into which the President's message has thrown a graceful and delicate girl like you is the best argument against it. . . . [I]t behooves rulers not to touch the fighting nerve till the cause is important and the moment unpostponeable. The European rulers know this: Ours, in their bottomless greenness and ignorance of the world know nothing."[38]

The susceptibility to war propaganda of even so thoughtful a young woman as Rosina made his own course clear. He needed to join "the party of civilization" that would "immediately, at any cost of discredit, . . . begin to agitate against any increase of either army, navy or coast defense. That is the one form of protection against the internal enemy on which we can most rely."[39] James saw two ways to agitate against this internal enemy: by participating in the growing peace movement and by campaigning for education of what he called the "moral faculties."

A Scale of Value

JAMES, BESET BY money worries, decided to augment the family's income by lecturing. In 1891–92, he had offered, under Harvard's auspices, a series of lectures to Cambridge teachers. As news of his "Talks to Teachers" spread, his audience increased at each session. Judging by this success, and the receptive audience of teachers that he addressed at the Concord Summer School, he decided to mine what seemed a lucrative field. If he charged fifty dollars per lecture, if he could sell a package of six to eight lectures in various cities throughout the country, he might bring in an extra thousand dollars each year, roughly equal to one-fourth of his Harvard salary.

Beginning in the fall of 1894, James delivered the lectures that he eventually published as *Talks to Teachers* in Boston; Cambridge; Norwich, Connecticut; Colorado Springs; Chicago; Buffalo; and Chautauqua. Basing his talks on the main points of the *Principles,* James offered to teachers more than a translation of the new psychology. He wanted to impart to them "a certain philosophic flexibility of mind, and easy look at life."[40] He wanted them to consider, or reconsider, the purpose of education. "The old notion that book learning can be a panacea for the vices of society lies pretty well shattered today," he said.[41] While he encouraged teachers to respect "the sacredness of individuality," he believed that education would necessarily produce a stratum of men and women who, because of their sense of pride, ambition, rivalry, or inner strength, would rise to become the nation's leaders.

Education, he told teachers, was nothing less than a battle for superiority. "We have of late been hearing much of the philosophy of tenderness in education," he told them; " 'interests' must be assiduously awakened in everything, difficulties must be smoothed away. *Soft* pedagogics have taken the place of the old steep and rocky path to learning. But from this lukewarm air the bracing oxygen of effort is left out."[42] Although he underscored his idea that a child's interests would focus his attention, he cautioned teachers against placing too much emphasis on responding to those interests. After all, he reminded

them, in adults, "interests are almost every one of them intensely artificial. . . . The objects of professional interest," he added, referring no
doubt to his own experiences, "are most of them, in their original nature, repulsive; but by their connections with such natively exciting
objects as one's own personal fortune, one's social responsibilities, and
especially by the force of inveterate habit, they grow to be the only
things for which in middle life a man profoundly cares."[43]

Instead of seeking out their students' interests, then, teachers must
appeal to an innate tendency to self-contempt and to an inherent "fighting impulse. . . . Make the pupil feel ashamed at being scared of fractions, of being 'downed' by the law of falling bodies; rouse his
pugnacity and pride, and he will rush at the difficult places with a sort
of inner wrath at himself that is one of his best moral faculties."[44] Education, though, was not limited to fractions and physics. Teachers must
have a clear sense of the moral values they wanted students to acquire.
"See to it now, I beg you," James urged, "that you make freemen of your
pupils by habituating them to act, whenever possible, under the notion
of a good."[45] It was one thing for educators to nurture intellectual independence; it was another, and more challenging task, to teach students
that their ideas must be tested against a rigorous "scale of value."[46]

This was the urgent message that James brought to the mostly
middle-aged women who, he confessed, seemed to him intellectually
limited. "I've been meeting minds so earnest and helpless," he told
Alice, "that it takes them ½ an hour to get from one idea to its immediately adjacent next-neighbor, and that with infinite creaking and
groaning. And when they've got to the next idea, they lie down on it
with their whole weight and can get no farther, like a cow on a door
mat, so that you can get neither in or out with them. Still glibness is
not all. Weight is something, even cow weight."[47]

"Talks to Teachers" kept him on the road throughout the mid-
1890s, despite James's weariness of the "woven wire mattresses" in
second-rate hotels and of the dullness of his listeners. His most vociferous complaints were inspired by his stay at the Chautauqua Institution in upstate New York, a larger and grander version of the Summer
School at Concord. Although James encouraged men and women to
take initiative in their own education, and although he insisted that the
academy had no corner on wisdom, still, he deemed few educational
enterprises as worthy as Harvard. Surely he saw nothing laudable in

Chautauqua: "that strange pool of philistinism . . . Good, but depressing from its mediocrity, in spite of a few fine human beings. Ten thousand people with no wilder excess to tempt them than 'ice cream
soda.'"[48] To these good, if timid, people he brought his message of intellectual pugnacity.

"Chautauqua," James said as he opened his first lecture, "resembles
a mouse trap. I am caught here and can't get away until I pay my ran-
som, and this is my only way of doing so."[49] Fortunately, his audience
thought he was joking, and they gave him a warm, admiring reception. One woman he met told him that she had his portrait in her bedroom with the words "I want to bring a balm to human lives" written
underneath. As if, he exclaimed to Alice, he would ever express such
soggy sentimentality.[50] After a few days he was sated with the "charmless goodness and seriousness of the place" and longed for "something
less blameless . . . The flash of a pistol, a dagger, or a devilish eye, anything to break the unlovely level of 10,000 good people, a crime, a
murder, rape, elopement, anything would do."[51]

Along with "Talks to Teachers," James came up with a new lecture
series, responding to his audience's interest in the more sensational aspects of psychological research. "Morbid psychology," James sensed,
would hold his audiences rapt. His writings on psychical research, his
own experiments with hypnotism, and his extensive reading on abnormal psychology became the basis for "Recent Researches into Exceptional Mental States," a series of six lectures that he gave at the
Brooklyn Institute of Arts and Sciences early in 1896, and eight well-
paid lectures that he delivered at the Lowell Institute in October and
November. The series included talks on trance states, multiple personality, hysteria, demoniacal possession, degeneration, mediumship, and
genius.

Besides filling his bank account and boosting his ego ("[T]he deepest principle of human nature," he said, "is the craving to be appreciated"),[52] these lectures gave James a chance to allay his listeners' fears
and misconceptions about alternative states of consciousness, mental
pathology, and the possibility of effective treatment. "The subject is in
the air," one newspaper report announced, "and haphazard faiths are so
common that such scientific deliverances as these have special attrac-
tiveness."[53] No doubt many in his audience also attended talks by promoters of many popular self-help movements such as the "Don't

Worry Movement" or "New Thought"; no doubt many had read such popular mental-health tracts as Annie Payson Call's *Power through Repose,* Horace Fletcher's *Happiness As Found in Forethought Minus Fearthought,* or Horatio Dresser's *Voices of Freedom.* But "Professor James of Harvard" spoke with an authority that none of these others possessed. He grounded his discussions of human behavior in scientific research. And besides, he was witty, charming, lively, and a huge success. "Boston may well be thankful for the privilege which she has enjoyed in listening to scholarly, carefully prepared addresses upon these intensely interesting subjects, by one whose authority is unquestioned," one newspaper reported.

Although the nine hundred people who filled Boston's Huntington Hall for the Lowell lectures hoped for scandalous revelations about "damnation in general," James persuaded them that what he was talking about was nothing less than the potential of the human mind: their mind. He maintained that his aim was not to titillate or to shock his listeners, but, he said, "to shape them towards optimistic and hygienic conclusions."[54]

Undergraduate women, he discovered, were eager to hear this message of optimism and mental hygiene, and James was eager to talk to them. "Will has lately taken to giving lectures, or speeches, at girls' colleges," Francis Child reported to a young woman friend, "and is fascinated with his hearers, whom he tells me that he addresses with unrestrained affectionate flattery. He will go anywhere to give a lecture to girls, he says. There are enough girls in the country to keep him tolerably busy if this gets out."[55] At Wellesley, Vassar, Bryn Mawr, and assorted normal schools, James offered three new lectures, "The Gospel of Relaxation," "What Makes a Life Significant," and, one of his favorites, "On a Certain Blindness in Human Beings." The message of these talks was self-trust, tolerance, and, above all, joy in living. Earnest young women, embracing unreflectively the religious and moral ideals of the past, responded to the ills of the world with feelings of sadness and despair. James urged them to look more closely at the reality of other people's lives, to understand that happiness may be enjoyed by poor as well as rich, and to recognize that ideals, changing as the world changes, needed to be tested against experience.

Many American women, James said, were so tense, so burdened by their feeling of moral responsibility, that they seemed like "bottled lightning." "The American over-tension and jerkiness and breathlessness and intensity and agony of expression," he told his listeners, were merely "*bad habits,* nothing more or less, bred of custom and example, born of the imitation of bad models and the cultivation of false personal ideals."[56] The world that his listeners might envision as ideal—the world represented, in effect, by the placid Chautauqua—would deny them, and others, a moral battlefield in which they could feel the satisfaction of a strenuous fight. "Sweat and effort," James said, "human nature strained to its uttermost and on the rack, yet getting through alive, and then turning its back on its success to pursue another more rare and arduous still" was, for James, the ideal life.[57]

"As I think over all the wise counsel I absorbed from James," wrote one Radcliffe undergraduate who studied with him in 1895, "perhaps his often repeated advice to live courageously is the most lasting. It was his belief that few people make use of their potential powers either of body, mind, or soul; that fields of accomplishment lie open before all individuals, ever widening if they will press bravely forward. He made his students feel that they had power that would grow with use and that they should live and work to the full, believing that new vistas would open, new possibilities be realized."[58]

Perhaps his most moving statement of these beliefs came in a talk he gave in Harvard's Holden Chapel, at the request of the Young Men's Christian Association, one April evening in 1895. The chapel was far too small for the eager students who crowded into it, and the evening was unusually warm. The crowd and the heat lent a special sense of urgency to the moment. At least, that is how one student remembered it: "As James stood there . . . reading with a sort of tumultuous rush from his nervous manuscript, perspiration streaming from his forehead, one felt almost palpably the tense absorption of the student group as he bared his own fighting faith in life's worthwhileness."[59] This was no academic topic for Harvard and Radcliffe students who may themselves have considered suicide as the only solution to their feelings of despair and rootlessness. There were some three thousand suicides each year in the country, James knew, and prevalence, especially among the young, of a "nightmare view of life."

James spoke as one familiar with that nightmare view, but also as one who had overcome it and taken another perspective on suffering. Personal hardship, he told his audience, only served to give life "a keener zest." In fact, if life were easy and comforting, it would be less interesting. "If this life be not a real fight," he wrote, "in which something is eternally gained for the universe by success, it is not better than a game of private theatricals from which one may withdraw at will. But it *feels* like a real fight—as if there were something really wild in the universe which we, with all our idealities and faithfulnesses, are needed to redeem; and first of all," he added, recalling his own nightmares, "to redeem our own hearts from atheisms and fears."[60]

Chapter 15

CIVIC GENIUS

1897–1898

"BRILLIANT, HIGH-STRUNG, dynamic, vivacious, resilient, unexpected, unconventional, picturesque."[1] That is how one Harvard student described James in the 1890s. Of all James's social selves, his most successful was that of teacher. Practiced since youth to offer brilliant public performances, James excelled in the classroom and lecture hall. Although he admitted to feeling anxiety and even stage fright as he walked across Harvard Yard to his classes, he fell into his role with unaccustomed ease. He dressed for the part in clothing that made him look more like a sportsman than a professor, cultivating an appearance that distinguished him, at a glance, from men he considered dull, cautious, and narrow.

Unlike other professors, he did not lecture to his students, but instead invited them to share in the stream of his thought as he worked through problems and responded to their questions. His task, as he saw it, was not to impart to his students a body of knowledge, but to teach them to philosophize, to understand philosophy not as a noun but as an active verb.

Philosophy for James, wrote George Santayana—his student and later a colleague—"was rather like a maze in which he happened to find himself wandering, and what he was looking for was the way out. In the presence of theories of any sort he was attentive, puzzled, suspicious, with a certain inner prompting to disregard them. He lived all his life among them, as a child lives among grown-up people; what a relief to turn from those stolid giants, with their prohibitions and exactions and tiresome talk, to another real child or a nice animal!"[2]

This attitude of puzzlement and especially suspicion appealed to his students' youthful philosophical rebellion. "As for philosophy, technically so called, or the reflection of man on his relations with the universe," James wrote early in his teaching career, "its educational essence lies in the quickening of the spirit to its *problems*." Students should "catch" from their teachers "the living, philosophic attitude of mind, the independent, personal look at all the data of life, and the eagerness to harmonize them."[3]

His notes for classes reflect his unusual teaching style. In planning his "Metaphysical Seminary—A Pluralistic Description of the World," for example, James listed among his objections to monism:

> Fatalistic. Violates free will. Makes notion of 'possible' illusory.
> Against this, only religious peace, & authority of mysticism.
>   'Central peace abiding at the heart of endless agitation.'
> Contrast between religion & morality.
> Pluralism the *moralistic* view
> Perfection necessary, vs.
>   "   " conditionally possible.
> Would you accept the latter world?
> Of course![4]

Questions, interjections, and emphatic outbursts marked his classroom performance. Sometimes, one student recalled, "James would rise with a peculiar suddenness and make bold and rapid strokes for a diagram on the black-board. I can remember his abstracted air as he wrestled with some idea, standing by his chair with one foot upon it, his elbow on his knee and his hand to his chin."[5] For some of his students, his apparent disorganization was troubling. "His work in the classroom was uneven," George Palmer had heard from some undergraduates, "his lectures—somewhat dependent on mood—often lacking continuity. If a student did not immediately 'catch on' he might go from one of them no richer than he came."[6]

James could be impatient with students who preferred to swallow knowledge whole, while at the same time he encouraged their more intrepid classmates to question and comment upon the course and upon assigned readings. When he first used his *Principles* as a text, James drew out his students' responses, and even their criticisms. Besides devoting class discussions to their questions, James asked for written submissions and always returned questions with a reply. He solicited suggestions on how to improve his courses, as well: "In a pretty full and varied experience of lecture-rooms at home and abroad," Dickinson Miller remarked, "I cannot recall another where the class was asked to criticize the methods of the lecturer."[7]

Believing that biography was a crucial subject for any undergraduate, James urged his students to study men's lives, preferably men of genius, rather than theories and systems, in order to learn about the possibilities of experience and the many perspectives from which individuals consider human problems. As he incorporated his own autobiography in his books, he hoped, no doubt, that his own genius would be applauded.

Despite his complaints each fall about the prospect of dull students and the burdens of preparing lectures and grading examinations, James was energized by his connection with students who thrived under his mentorship. Usually these were the "undisciplinables" who reminded him of his own youthful, vulnerable self. These young men and women believed that James was deeply interested in each of them as individuals, that he cared about their minds no less than their spirits. He paid special attention to them: inviting them to his home, to Chocorua, to Putnam Camp; visiting them in their rooms if they were ill or depressed; and most important, encouraging them to liberate themselves from self-defeating thoughts, keep an open mind, and act on their convictions.

When Walter Lippmann—an incipient social critic, even as an undergraduate—published an attack on Barrett Wendell's *The Privileged Classes,* in which Wendell asserted that the real privileged class in America was the working poor, James sought Lippmann out to congratulate him. The two met weekly thereafter for tea at James's home. After their first conversation, Lippmann reported to his mother that he had just experienced "the greatest thing that has happened to me in my college life."[8]

Lippmann's friend Hans von Kaltenborn shared his enthusiasm. Kaltenborn was twenty-seven and already had served in the Spanish-American War and traveled throughout Europe as a newspaper reporter by the time he entered Harvard as a special student. Of all his professors, Kaltenborn recalled, James stood out as "the most genuinely open-minded. . . . There was no aspect of human activity that did not interest him. . . . He was always responsive to something that might open a new door to knowledge. He appealed to me as a romantic adventurer in the realm of ideas, eagerly hospitable to new thoughts."⁹ When they talked privately, Kaltenborn found James to be "deeply spiritual and truly religious," and he believed that James helped him make sense of his own spiritual anxiety.¹⁰

James specialized in rescuing desperate students, perhaps none so despairing, nor so enduringly grateful, as Horace Kallen. As an undergraduate, Kallen felt stranded at Harvard, largely because of his orthodox Jewish upbringing—his father was a rabbi—which insisted on a religious unity. Because his own experiences contradicted that belief, Kallen decided that the only escape from his problem was to reject Judaism entirely.

But as a sophomore, Kallen took an English course in which he studied the Old Testament in historical and political context. Instead of feeling that his religious background was irrelevant to his identity as an intellectual, this perspective helped him see that Judaism could be consistent with a liberal worldview. Studying with James persuaded Kallen that religion, in any case, was not the only obstacle to his intellectual liberation. He needed to free himself from all superstitious beliefs, including "the superstition inherent in science . . . ; the superstition of logical staticism and physical necessitarianism, as well as the superstition of supernatural providence and cosmic purposes."¹¹

After Kallen returned to Harvard as a graduate student in 1905, James took a special interest in his career. When Kallen won a Sheldon Fellowship to study at Oxford, James supplemented the award with a hundred dollars of his own money, and wrote a letter of introduction for Kallen to his friend Canning Schiller. Kallen, James told Schiller, was "intense" and capable,

> with high potentialities of all round cultivation, an enthusiastic and aggressive "pragmatist," an active political worker, a *decidedly* original mind, neurotic disposition, but sails indefinitely long close to the wind without losing headway, a man with a positive future and possibly a great one and in good directions: *Revers de la médaille: sticky,* conceited, censorious of all institutions. Nevertheless faithful, candid, goodlooking and in favor of all good things.¹²

Neurotic pragmatists were perhaps James's favorite students.

James's dynamism, wit, and talent as a performer also endeared him to his audiences. He had a decided flair for making abstract philosophical

ideas accessible, for illuminating psychological theory with vivid anecdotes, and for generating in his listeners feelings of optimism and hope
about their own potential. Audiences adored him, and he basked in
their admiration.

From 1890, when his *Principles* earned him international fame in
the field of psychology, until 1899, when he began to work on the lectures that would become *The Varieties of Religious Experience,* James
shaped a new identity for himself within and outside of academia. Although he still taught—now with the more fitting title of professor of
philosophy—and reviewed books for professional journals, much of
his effort went into lecturing around the country, publishing articles in
such widely read magazines as *Scribner's* and the *Atlantic Monthly,* and
collecting his essays into two volumes addressed to the general public:
Talks to Teachers on Psychology: And to Students on Some of Life's Ideals and
The Will to Believe and Other Essays in Popular Philosophy.

In part, he was motivated by a need for public affirmation of his
worth, in part by an inherent intellectual restlessness that made him
bristle at being simply an academic philosopher, an identity as narrow
as anything his father had warned him against. He was not interested
in seeking refuge in a sanctuary of theory: if philosophy did not connect to the real world, if it did not change real lives, then for James it
had no value.

Not least among his motivations was money. Sure that his ideas
were a marketable commodity, he tried to negotiate the highest lecture
fees he could command and the most favorable book contracts. Dissatisfied with the terms he had received for the *Principles,* for example,
James risked severing his friendship with Holt when he tried to convince Scribner's to enter a bidding war for *The Will to Believe.* When
Scribner's declined, James, sorely disappointed, chose Longmans,
Green, who published the essay collection in the spring of 1897.

A Passionate Affirmation of Desire

THE TEN ESSAYS that James included in *The Will to Believe* contain
some of his most eloquent statements on the intellectual and emotional risks of religious belief; the philosopher's contribution to a society's moral life; the genesis and importance of genius; and the
accomplishments of psychical research. Although all of the essays had
been published before, some as early as 1879, and delivered as talks to

colleagues, students, and religious groups, together they sum up the issues that concerned James during the first twenty years of his professional career and stand as preface to the writings on pragmatism and pluralism that earned him enduring fame.

The most compelling piece in the collection is the title essay, James's response to Pascal's wager, and his defense of faith. At one point, he considered calling the essay "The Duty to Believe," but that title implied an obligation—perhaps to self, perhaps to society—that James did not intend. Then he thought he might call the essay "The Right to Believe," but that title could imply a right *bestowed*—and by whom? James meant something else: All human beings, he wrote, *want* to believe in a universe in which truth can be apprehended and, as Royce had persuaded him, in which goodness exists. Without the possibility of finding truth and achieving goodness, moral decisions would be futile exercises. Such a universe, however, cannot be defended by reason nor logic; it may exist for us only if we have faith, only if we show "a passionate affirmation of desire" for both truth and goodness, only if we will to believe that those qualities exist.

James knew that advocating faith made him an antagonist of those who hungered for scientific proof. As an empiricist himself he urged his readers to treat any so-called "facts" as hypotheses to be tested against their own experience. Yet he knew that empiricism would not suffice to guide his readers in making moral decisions. For James, the world consisted of "[r]eal possibilities, real indeterminations, real beginnings, real ends, real evil, real crises, catastrophes, and escape, a real God, and a real moral life."[13] And real people, who faced dilemmas, in their own lives and in the community, that required immediate action. Solutions to moral questions, he wrote, "cannot wait for sensible proof. A moral question is a question not of what sensibly exists, but of what is good, or would be good if it did exist."[14]

The "moral business" that so preoccupied him was inextricably connected to religious belief. Pascal's solution was, to James, not adequate. "Weigh what your gains and your losses would be if you should stake all you have on heads, or God's existence," James wrote, paraphrasing Pascal; "if you win in such a case, you gain eternal beatitude; if you lose, you lose nothing at all." But that proposal seemed to James unlikely to win converts to any religion. If faith requires willpower to shore itself up against science and logic, it also requires emotional and intellectual surrender to what James called "the instincts of the heart." The first step to faith is trust in one's own yearning to believe; the second, belief that the intellect is fallible.

James's passionate affirmation of faith was one among many popular books about spiritual issues published in the 1890s, convincing him that the public hungered for "religious philosophy that is both unconventional and untechnical"; his essay collection, he hoped, would find eager readers.[15] He had not miscalculated: by the fall, *The Will to Believe* had gone into its third printing of one thousand copies. Its popularity continued, with new printings almost yearly for the rest of James's life.

The demand on James to refine and expand his ideas about religion also continued. "Honours have been cast in my path with unusual frequency," James wrote to Henry early in 1897. Although Alice claimed that William showed "his usual incredible modesty" when honors were bestowed upon him, he had become well aware of his worth and his power to get what he wanted. One of the most prestigious honors strewn in his path was the coveted Gifford Lectureship on Natural Religion, offered alternately at the University of Aberdeen and the University of Edinburgh, Scotland. He was nominated for the Aberdeen series, to begin in 1899. As honored as he was by the nomination, he decided that Aberdeen was not the better choice: Edinburgh would be able to offer him the lecture series in 1901, giving him more time to prepare; equally important, Edinburgh paid more.

Alice, this time concerned more with glory than with gain, protested when William decided to gamble on being nominated for the Edinburgh lectureship, especially when he recommended Royce for the Aberdeen talks. "[T]hat," she told Henry, "will probably result in our missing the Gifford lectureship altogether. It is hardly probable that so rare a prize will be given to an American two years running."[16] But James won the gamble: the following year, he was nominated as the new Gifford lecturer at the University of Edinburgh. "The lectures are very highly paid," he admitted happily, "and the whole thing is a great honor."[17]

War Cant

JAMES RECEIVED SO many requests for lectures and addresses that he had to refuse most of them. "The public here grows increasingly eager to listen," Alice told Henry.[18] Two requests, however, were too important to turn down: the University of California, where his friend George Howison taught philosophy, offered him fifteen hundred dollars for a few lectures to students and teachers; in Boston, he was invited to be the main orator at the unveiling of Augustus Saint-Gaudens's long-awaited monument to Robert Gould Shaw on Decoration Day, 1897.

Charles Norton and Harvard's president Charles Eliot were among the candidates to deliver the oration, but Henry Lee Higginson, banker, philanthropist, and one of the event's planners, supported his old friend William James. Besides being the brother of Garth Wilkinson, who had been wounded in the battle that killed Shaw, James was a far more rousing speaker than either Norton or Eliot, or anyone else that Higginson knew. At the Tavern Club, the Friday Club, and the Saturday Club, where Higginson frequently dined with James, he had long admired James's wit and erudition: Higginson called James his mentor.

James reacted to the Shaw invitation with a mixture of pride and skepticism. Although he agreed with his brother Henry that the occasion would offer "a sort of beautiful, poetic justice" to Wilky's memory, he knew also that many of his contemporaries thought the commemoration sentimental and even hypocritical, an effort by politicians to turn the past into pageant and to glorify war.[19] John Chapman, a writer and editor with provocative political views, was one of the doubters. "I am just awfully glad you are going to speak at the Shaw Monument," Chapman wrote to James. "Down with the literary people. It might have been Norton or Eliot—very good—no offence in them—but Lord God, we have had literature done enough—hawked and styled to deadness. Let us express ourselves with brick-backs or pictures of ganglia. . . . Get up and say Shaw did well and sit down." Chapman warned James not to acquiesce to "the war reverence—the war cant—the eulogy business."[20]

The war cant, swelling since the Venezuela boundary dispute, had brought the nation close to another conflict, which James staunchly opposed. He did not want his commemoration of Shaw's sacrifice to serve as a defense of future aggression; instead, he wanted to urge his listeners that dissent was their right and duty. For James, the speech was a chance to revive the maverick political stand that the mugwumps, James among them, had taken thirteen years before, when they shunned the Republican Party, refusing to vote for the scandalous nominee James Blaine, and rallied around the Democratic candidate,

Grover Cleveland. Despite the mugwumps' identity as elite and academic, they proved themselves a formidable force in American politics.

The task he set for himself was not easy. After several drafts, he finally read the speech to Alice and his children, then, dissatisfied, set to work again. He brought it to Putnam Camp and read it to Thomas Davidson and some friends. Still unhappy, he revised, and revised again. "I tried to say *Truth,*" he wrote to Henry, "but every step I made in that direction proved a false one, and had to be retraced." At last, early in May, he had a speech that he thought would be "without praise and without blame."[21] He committed it to memory.

As James saw it, the bellicose spirit, which had served as a civilizing and socializing force in human evolution, no longer was necessary. "War," he told his listeners, "has been much praised and celebrated among us of late as a school of manly virtue," but it had outlasted its purpose of generating loyalty and a sense of common purpose toward achieving "wider tribal ends." Yet the "battle-instinct" still exerted its force, "and our pugnacity," James assured his audience, "is the virtue least in need of reinforcement by reflection, least in need of orator's or poet's help."[22]

The virtue that he hoped to inspire, he told them, was "civic courage," the courage to speak out against injustice, to resist "enthroned abuse," to recognize that the real threat to a nation's integrity was complacency and ignorance:

> The deadliest enemies of nations are not their foreign foes; they always dwell within their borders. And from these internal enemies civilization is always in need of being saved. The nation blest above all nations is she in whom the civic genius of the people does the saving day by day, by acts without external picturesqueness; by speaking, writing, voting reasonably; by smiting corruption swiftly; by good temper between parties; by the people knowing true men when they see them, and preferring them as leaders to rabid partisans or empty quacks. Such nations have no need of wars to save them.[23]

The present political climate, James believed, was no less divisive than it had been more than thirty years before and no less a test of America's independent spirit. The "American religion," he said, "baptized and reared" citizens to believe in their own self-reliance. "What

Shaw and his comrades stand for and show us," he said, "is that in such an emergency Americans of all complexions and conditions can go forth like brothers, and meet death cheerfully if need be, in order that this religion of our native land shall not become a failure on the earth."[24]

As much as James exhorted his listeners to protest against injustice and corruption, he believed that in a time of crisis—the time in which they lived—what the nation needed most was consensus. Yet his call for consensus always was tempered by a fear of the uneducated and unreflective populace. America's "true leaders" must come from his own class and kind, and those men must be allowed to take the reins of government. The survival of democracy, then, required citizens to cultivate two crucial habits: "trained and disciplined good temper towards the opposite party when it fairly wins its innings" and "fierce and merciless resentment towards every man or set of men who break the public peace."[25]

Although James regretted the "pathetic sentiment" pervading the air and felt that the day's pageantry made the memory of war "poetic and unreal," he realized that his impact on his audience was far greater than he had anticipated.[26] "You will read his address and feel its beauty," Alice wrote to Henry, "but you cannot measure the full power of it unless you had been one of that great audience in Music Hall, listening with rapt attention from the first word to the last."[27] For James, that power was unlike anything he had ever experienced; he had been recognized, at last, as a "true leader" among his peers.

The General Life of the World

ON THE NIGHT of February 15, 1898, 256 sailors were asleep on board the battleship *Maine,* anchored five hundred yards from the shore of Havana, when an explosion sent the men tumbling from their berths, shook the city, downed telegraph poles, and set the ship on fire. For nearly five hours, flames illuminated the harbor, as rescue boats picked up the wounded and the dead. Finally, at two the next morning, the wreck that had been the *Maine* sank into Cuban waters.

The United States reacted immediately, mobilizing ships and appropriating millions of dollars to investigate the explosion, for which Spain was blamed, and to protect against future attack. On April 11, President McKinley asked Congress to authorize military intervention on behalf of Cuban insurgents who, even as early as 1868, had been trying to oust Spain from the island; by April 25, America was at war.

"It is quite possible," James wrote to a French friend, "that, without the explosion of the Maine, we should still be at peace." But James knew that it was not probable. The spirit of war was in the air, and however intervention were rationalized, it was that spirit, James believed, not revenge for the *Maine,* not America's sympathy for oppressed Cubans, not the country's "sense of philanthropic duty," that served as the real impetus for war. "[O]nce the excitement of action gets loose, the taxes levied, the victories achieved, etc.," James said, "the old human instincts will get into play with all their old strength. . . . Human nature is everywhere the same; and at the least temptation all the old military passions rise, and sweep everything before them."[28]

Some of his contemporaries believed that the war had other causes, notably economic. American businessmen had fifty million dollars invested in Cuba, and some of those men believed their investment would be protected only if Spain relinquished its hold on the island. Besides, war would spur an economy that had been lagging since the depression of 1893. "After war," wrote William Dean Howells, who thought intervention "wickedly wrong," "will come the piling up of big fortunes again; the craze for wealth will fill all brains, and every good cause will be set back. We shall have an era of blood-bought prosperity, and the chains of capitalism will be welded on the nation more firmly than ever."[29]

For the public at large, however, especially those who read William Randolph Hearst's *New York Journal* and Joseph Pulitzer's *New York World,* Spain was the evil oppressor of a noble independence movement, a perpetrator of atrocities, and an arrogant insulter of the American government. American newspapermen were invested in Cuba, too, convinced that a war would sell more papers.

As soon as Congress authorized McKinley to take action against Spain, James saw a chance, at last, to offer a personal demonstration of "civic courage": that is, to speak out publicly against government policy and to try to change popular opinion. If war, as he saw it, was inevitable, if war were part of human nature, then his duty was to alert Americans to the power of their "old human instincts" and to urge them to consider whether their real motivation for supporting war was grounded in the actual situation before them. "I ought to say something about the war," he told Alice. "Events must now decide whether it shall turn out good for us or bad both for us and the world. . . . In any case it forces us out of our isolation and in so far forth becomes an educative influence."[30]

The war afforded many educative functions, according to James. First, it taught Americans that they were not exempt—as many thought they were—from the forces that shaped the history of European countries; America was not a "quaker nation," but as warlike as any other country. "It forces us immediately into the general life of the world," James said, "and into new and diversified responsibilities of a tremendous sort, in meeting which we shall *have* to put our very best qualities foremost." Unlike his friend Howells, James thought that the war would help generate reforms. "And we mugwumps will have a magnificent chance, on the new basis, in making the virtues of the country *live* in meeting the emergencies that are sure to arise."[31]

James's apparent optimism about the results of the war distinguished him from many other members of a growing anti-imperialist movement. These reformers, many of whom were James's friends and colleagues, did not see "a lot of good" in the war. Yet as much as James applauded the shattering of America's stubborn sense of moral superiority to Europe, he did join with other peace activists in decrying the public's call for revenge for the *Maine* "especially," he said, "as I can't help suspecting that the evidence for an external explosion is of the very slimmest."[32]

The brief war itself was not the only focus of James's protest. He was more concerned with foreign policy subsequent to the war: that is, with America's determination to take possession of the Philippines. The country's self-righteous mission of "impregnating the Philipinos with american ideals and educating them for freedom" seemed to him "sheer illusion, and can only mean rottenness and ruin to them," he told William Salter.[33]

Accusing Salter, who supported McKinley's decisions, of "jingoistic juvenility," James argued that as conflict intensified, diplomatic alternatives became increasingly remote. Most important to James, however, conflict abroad meant prolonged dissension at home, "indefinite postponement," he said, "of the hope that our already too barbarian and heterogeneous population may be at . . . last welded together into a people with well knit & consistent ideals."[34]

He was not necessarily a supporter of a community's consistent ideals, however, when they opposed his own views. When, for example, the Massachusetts Board of Health proposed a bill making it illegal to practice medicine without a license, James rose up in defense of such medical practitioners as mind curers, electricians, magnetic healers, Christian Scientists, and osteopathic physicians. He objected to the government's paternalism, the usurping of an individual's authority to make personal medical decisions, and most important, he argued that the progress of therapeutic medicine would be greatly hindered if unlicensed, experimental practitioners were deemed criminals. "I regard therapeutics as in too undeveloped a state for us to be able to afford to stamp out the contributions of all fanatics & one-sided geniuses," he wrote to the chairman of the Board of Health.[35]

He confessed to James Putnam, who agreed with his views, that speaking out for the mind healers was difficult, but unavoidable. "If you think I like this sort of thing you are mistaken," he told Putnam. "It cost me more effort than anything I have ever done in my life. But if Zola and Colonel Picquart can face the whole French army, cannot I face their disapproval? Far more easily than the reproach of my own conscience."[36]

Completest Union

"THAT SUMMER," James wrote to Pauline Goldmark, "when we walked over the 'Range' and I went to California to 'talk to teachers,' marked my completest union with my native land."[37] The spiritual consummation began in late June 1898, when James came to Keene Valley for a respite before his first trip across the country. One morning, he awakened at three, eager to set off for the day's hike, and eager, more, for a meeting later with Pauline Goldmark and some of her friends. He strapped on his eighteen-pound knapsack and started out alone to climb Mount Marcy, the highest peak in the Adirondacks. After a strenuous hike of five hours, he reached the top, rested until late afternoon, and then descended an hour to Panther Lodge Camp, where Pauline, her brother, and some of her Bryn Mawr friends had arrived to camp overnight.

Despite his early rising and the day's exertion, James found that he could not sleep. He blamed his wakefulness on the stimulation of the incomparable surroundings: the sky was unusually clear, the moon so luminous that only the brightest stars were visible, the temperature so perfect that he fell into "a state of spiritual alertness of the most vital description." Yet as he described the scene to Alice, he revealed other sources of his stirred feelings: "the wholesomeness of the people round me, especially the good Pauline, the thought of you and the children . . . all fermented within me till it became a regular Walpurgis Nacht." He wandered into the woods feeling bewitched, "as if the Gods of all the nature-mythologies were holding an indescribable meeting in my breast with the moral Gods of the inner life." He told Alice that the scene seemed to have an "intense significance" whose meaning eluded him, and yet enticed him.[38] Although James suggested that the moment was connected, somehow, to his thinking about his upcoming Gifford lectures on religion, his sensual description of his surroundings, his underscoring of the "wholesomeness" of his companions, his association of Pauline with Alice, and especially his sense of an inner war between pagan forces and moral inhibitions implies another cause for his aroused sensibilities: the attraction he felt for Pauline and his excitement at her closeness to him.[39]

After a sleepless night, James left the camp at six and again ascended to the peak of Mount Marcy, where the rest of the party soon joined him. The young people, who had slept soundly, felt fresh and eager for a day's hike: they descended Marcy, then scrambled up the scenic but difficult Basin Mountain, descended, and hiked up the challenging Gothics. "It was the steepest sort of work," James wrote to Alice, "and, as one looked from the summits, seemed sheer impossible, but the girls kept up splendidly, and were all fresher than I."[40] They were also more than thirty years younger than James, and after ten and a half hours of hiking, James was exhausted. He complained at first only of stiff thigh muscles, but as the summer wore on, he knew that the expedition had had more serious consequences. "My heart has been kicking about terribly of late, stopping, and hurrying and aching and so forth," he wrote to George Howison, who awaited him in California, "but I do not propose to give up to it too much."[41]

He did not, in any case, give up his trip across the country. As he traveled through Canada, he saw "grand and ferocious scenery," especially in the Canadian Pacific, but he noticed a landscape of desolation as soon as he descended into the United States. In Washington and Oregon, fires had destroyed huge tracts of forest; in Seattle, Portland,

and San Francisco, new buildings were notable for their "fantastic vile-
ness."[42] Yet despite the aesthetic poverty of the cities, James felt energized by his sense of a pervasive pioneering spirit.

His talks to California's teachers were a huge success: two lectures a
day, with from five hundred to eight hundred in the audience. Teachers
in the West, though, seemed no more intellectually astute than his Cambridge audiences. "Poor things," he told Henry, "they are so servile in
their natures as to furnish the most promising of all preys for systematic
mystification and pedantification on the part of the paedogogic author-
ities who write books for them, and when one talks plain common sense
with no technical terms, they regard it as a sort of revelation."[43]

A sort of revelation—heralded, perhaps, by the blare of trum-
pets—is what James had in mind for his address to the Philosophical
Union at Berkeley on August 26.[44] "Philosophical Conceptions and
Practical Results" marked an important moment in James's career as a
philosopher: the first time he defined as such the "principle of pragmatism" that had been evolving since the Metaphysical Club debates of
the 1870s. He began almost wistfully, hoping, he told his audience,
that he could offer "a message with a practical outcome and an emotional musical accompaniment, so to speak" that would elicit from his
listeners a grateful exclamation: "Why, that *is* the truth!—*that* is what
I have been believing, that is what I have really been living on all this
time, but I never could find the words for it before." Using a metaphor
drawn from his recent hiking vacation, he likened the philosopher's
task to that of the trailblazer, providing guideposts for spiritual wan-
derers, keeping them from becoming lost in the wilderness. "They give
you a direction," he said, "and a place to reach. . . . Though they create nothing, yet for this marking and fixing function of theirs we bless
their names and keep them on our lips."

In his talk, James revisited a trail that he had explored many times
and to which he would return often before his *Pragmatism* was published in 1907. Philosophy, he argued, could not be separated from an
individual's temperament: a person's needs and interests inspired attention to one philosophical issue over another and to one theory
rather than another. The choice of philosophical perspective shaped behavior, ethical decisions, and one's sense of authority to take action, or
not, in the face of moral dilemmas.

Although James had been thinking about the connection between philosophy and individual motivation since the beginning of his career, it was Charles Peirce, he said, who inspired him to focus on the connection between philosophy and practical consequences. Peirce, according to James, held that beliefs "are really rules for action; and the whole function of thinking is but one step in the production of habits of action." Beliefs need to make a difference, to have perceptible consequences, or they are not worth arguing over. The consequences of a belief, in fact, give meaning to the belief.

For his part, Peirce was not sure that he invented the term "pragmatism," for which James felt so indebted, but he did acknowledge their common goal. "You feel as I do," Peirce wrote to James, "that the importance of pragmatism is not confined to philosophy. The country is at this moment in imminent danger. . . . [O]ne simply can't form any conception that is other than pragmatistic."[45]

James, however, did not discuss political or social dangers in his Berkeley talk, but cited as the most compelling philosophical problem God's existence as "One in All and All in All" or as Many. What, James asked his listeners, was their personal stake in the resolution of that question? "In what ways does the oneness come home to your own personal life? By what difference does it express itself in your experience? How can you act differently towards a universe which is one?"

As he considered those questions in later works, James made much of the distinction between tough-minded and tender-minded thinkers, the tough-minded being empiricist and pluralistic on the one hand, but pessimistic and fatalistic on the other; and the tender-minded being rationalistic and idealistic, yet optimistic and "free-willist." James saw himself, like most other people, as "hankering for the good things on both sides of the line."[46] But in his Berkeley talk he made a more rigid distinction, one that he had held, he told his listeners, since boyhood, when he read the adventure stories of Captain Mayne Reid. "He was forever extolling the hunters and field-observers of living animals' habits, and keeping up a fire of invective against the 'closet-naturalists,' as he called them, the collectors and classifiers, and handlers of skeletons and skins. When I was a boy," he admitted, "I used to think that a closet-naturalist must be the vilest type of wretch under the sun." Similar to those closet-naturalists—but more vile still—were the "systematic theologians" who divorced themselves from concrete, visceral, tangled reality.

Trailblazer and field observer, James returned from California wreathed in accolades. The trip, he told Henry, "has done me a world of good, morally and intellectually, & made me see this world's affairs—I think also a bit the next world's—in a simpler broader light."[47]

Connected with Life

"JAMES DETESTED any system of the universe that professed to enclose everything," Santayana once remarked; "we must never set up boundaries that exclude romantic surprises. He retained the primitive feeling that death *might* open new worlds to us . . . ; also the primitive feeling that invisible spirits *might* be floating about among us, and might suddenly do something to hurt or to help us."[48]

This openness to the possibility of life after death informed James's Ingersoll Lecture on Human Immortality, delivered in the Fogg Museum at Harvard on November 10, 1897, and again, a month later, before the Society for Ethical Culture in Chicago. In his talk, he took up two objections to the possibility of an afterlife: the first posed by scientists, who maintained that thought was nothing more than a function of the brain's physical and chemical processes; the second, an objection by ordinary men and women who shuddered at the image of an overpopulated heaven, filled with immortal spirits of every individual who ever lived.

To the scientists, James responded by suggesting that rather than—or perhaps in addition to—producing thought, the brain might serve as a kind of conduit or sieve, able to filter thought already existing in a transcendental realm. "We need only suppose the continuity of our consciousness with a mother-sea," James wrote, "to allow for exceptional waves occasionally pouring over the dam" that the brain creates in each individual.[49]

This mother-sea would be infinite, able to contain "a literally endless accumulation of created lives," and therefore running no risk of overpopulation. Those who worried that heaven would become filled with the poor, uneducated, and unworthy were suffering, James said, from "a remnant of the old narrow-hearted aristocratic creed." Although James himself sometimes construed an image of heaven that seemed oddly like the rarefied community of Harvard Yard, heaven, as he presented it in his Ingersoll lecture, embraced diverse multitudes. To prepare themselves for this motley populace, James urged his listeners to develop a sense of empathy and to recognize "the inner joy" of each individual.

After James's lecture was published, he received hundreds of requests from readers asking where they could find the book. Besides those admirers, however, there were a few critics, who complained that James's idea of a "mother-sea" from which all individual spirits were generated precluded the integrity, in an afterlife, of each human soul. What was the use of surviving "beyond the veil" if one only merged into a vast swarm of psychical spirit?

James addressed this concern in a preface to the book's second edition, attempting, as he usually did when faced with criticism, to stretch his assertions to accommodate other views: many minds might exist in this mother-sea, he argued patiently, not just one. As long as one were imagining a spiritual realm, one might posit "as individualistic a form as one pleases." In fact, he said, it was possible to imagine, even more boldly, that each individual's brain altered the characteristics of the spiritual substance from which it had been derived, "just as . . . the stubs remain in a check-book whenever a check is used, to register the transaction, so these impressions on the transcendent self might constitute so many vouchers of the finite experiences of which the brain had been the mediator."[50]

The incompatibility of mother-sea and checkbook as metaphors suggests that James still had work to do in his thinking about the relationship between self and spirit. As he wrote his Gifford lectures, he pushed his ideas further: now, instead of conceiving of the brain as a filter, he argued that there existed within each individual a "subliminal self with a thin partition through which messages make irruption." Through this partition, he said, came the awareness "of a sphere of life larger and more powerful than our usual consciousness, with which the latter is nevertheless continuous."[51]

This idea of a hidden self receptive to a nonrational and nonprovable realm of existence made it possible for James to reconcile his "intellectual loyalty to . . . 'hard facts'" with his "craving of the heart to believe that behind nature there is a spirit whose expression nature is."[52] It was this yearning for "acquiescence and communion with the total soul of things" that made him envy his wife's unshakable belief in immortality, communicative spirits, and psychical experiences. But despite her convictions, she had not yet fulfilled the mission that James gave her after his father died, to help him "understand a little the value & meaning of religion in father's sense, in the mental life & destiny of man." James's faith, unlike his wife's and his father's, required the strenuous exertion of ferocious will.

His own yearning for spiritual communion was satisfied by Leonora Piper, whose integrity he continued to defend. He realized, however, that even his own reports on sittings with Piper conveyed little of the intense certainty of her authenticity that he felt when he was in her presence. "When you find your questions answered and your allusions understood; when allusions are made that you think you understand, and your thoughts are met by anticipation, denial, or corroboration; when you have approved, applauded, or exchanged banter, or thankfully listened to advice that you believe in; it is difficult," he said, "not to take away an impression of having encountered something sincere in the way of a social phenomenon." Yet while James recognized fully that the sitter's enthusiasm and will to believe shaped the "social phenomenon," he remained persuaded by Piper's psychical powers.

By the 1890s, Piper was living in the residential suburb of Arlington Heights, a half hour's train ride northwest of Boston, in a setting thoroughly middle-class and unpretentious. Her house was modest and welcoming, located on a hill that overlooked Boston, a lake, and many other small homes like her own. She had created an unlikely setting for psychical experiences, but those experiences occurred often. Richard Hodgson, still conducting a rigorous investigation of her powers, brought many sitters, including visitors from the London SPR; James, his family, and his Cambridge friends were frequent sitters. Piper's performance, on all occasions, was impeccable.

Sinking into her trance state as if anesthetized, her body relaxed, she began to breathe heavily and at times moaned softly. Her sittings lasted for about two hours, at which time she would slowly emerge, appearing frightened or disturbed, mumbling a few incoherent words that seemed to be the remnants of supernatural messages.

Besides transmitting messages aloud, she engaged in automatic writing, using her right hand both to write down spirit communications and, cupped, to serve as a mouthpiece into which sitters sent their own messages to the control. No matter how rarely she saw a sitter, Piper was able to recall minute details of their relationships, their problems, and their lives. She was voluble and forthcoming, very different from other mediums, who conveyed only terse and hesitant messages. Piper may have been a talented actress with a prodigious memory; James thought not. Acknowledging the "dramatic improbability" of finding a true psychic, still, he believed.[53]

Chapter 16

A GLEAM OF THE END

1899–1901

JAMES ENDED THE college year in the spring of 1899 feeling hopeful and energetic. He planned to spend his sabbatical in Europe, where he would write the Gifford lectures, deliver them in January 1900, and then set to work on a new book, his philosophical "message to the world."[1] At fifty-seven, James did not want to face the regret of "post-poned achievements." "I feel," he told his Berkeley audience in 1898, "that there is a center in truth's forest where I have never been: to track it out and get there is the secret spring of all my poor life's philosophical efforts; at moments I almost strike into the final valley, there is a gleam of the end, a sense of certainty, but always there comes still another ridge. . . . To-morrow it must be, or to-morrow, or to-morrow; and pretty surely death will overtake me ere the promise is fulfilled."[2] The Gifford lectures would be a step toward the fulfillment of his promise; but there were other books he wanted to write: a more sustained discussion of his ideas on pragmatism, for one; and a theoretical introduction to metaphysics, for another. His sabbatical year, he hoped, would give him precious time.

Looking forward to a summer and fall of intense work, James decided to take advantage of the weeks between the semester's end and his July 15 departure for a retreat to Keene Valley, where he could indulge in some mild hiking and, he thought, guaranteed refreshment. His plan, unfortunately, went awry; and his beloved Adirondacks, so often a source of sustenance, turned out to be his nemesis.

After climbing alone to the top of rugged Mount Marcy, he became hopelessly lost, confused after he took a recently blazed trail that he mistook for another, familiar, path. He had brought no food: twice he fainted. What should have been an easy three-hour descent turned into a long and strenuous ordeal.[3] At 10:15 that night, he staggered into Putnam Camp exhausted and frightened. His heart, strained the year before and never fully healed, pounded painfully.

When he returned to Cambridge, he realized that what he had described to friends as "a slight cardiac trouble" now was severely worsened. While Jim Putnam acknowledged some physical damage to the heart, he assured him that the tightness in his chest and his pounding heart were being exacerbated by anxiety and worry. Putnam seconded James's decision to seek treatment at Nauheim, the German spa famous for its attention to heart patients, which already was the first destination on James's itinerary. Calmed by Putnam's confidence in his recovery, James spent the few weeks until his departure working furiously: staying up late into the night reading, writing, taking notes, gathering material to bring with him. Overwork, coupled with increasing anxiety about the coming trip, drained him emotionally and physically: by the time he landed in Hamburg, his condition had declined. He could not walk more than a few feet without pain; he could not concentrate on his work; he was irritable and depressed. "I believe that Jim Putnam's diagnosis of William's breakdown is essentially right," Alice wrote to Fanny Morse, "that is, it's largely a nervous one. . . . Perhaps if he had gone to bed and rested instead of working for the two weeks before we sailed we might have escaped Nauheim and many subsequent woes, but the fact is that the William who landed at Hamburg was a much sicker one than the man Jim had seen."

Although Alice was well aware of the severity of her husband's heart condition, she—and James, as well—worried more about his emotional collapse. As she had observed many times, James's depressions could long outlast, and always aggravate, the physical ailments that precipitated them. She was upset when two eminent heart specialists consulted during the European trip, Theodor Schott at Nauheim and Bezly Thorne in London, failed to acknowledge what seemed too clear to her: that "a grave nervous disorder was complicating the heart symptoms." Overwhelmed by frustration, she consoled herself with "the Psalmist's prayer for 'enlightened understanding,'" but sometimes, Alice admitted, "I could cry out with the prophet in the wilderness, 'the journey is too great for me.'"[4]

This European journey was, indeed, a protracted affliction for Alice. What should have been a year's sabbatical stretched into two; instead of enjoying a well-deserved respite from the cares of home and family, Alice became William's protector, nurturer, and nurse. With little evidence that William ever would get well, Alice tried to maintain nothing less than steady calm and insistent hopefulness. Only briefly did her own good spirits fail her. William called her an angel, for good reason.

James's first months in Europe set a recurring pattern for the rest of the stay abroad. "My progress here is positive, but not vast in amount," James wrote to Henry early in September, when he hoped to leave Nauheim in a week.[5] In mid-September, he was still at the Villa Luise, and although Dr. Schott assured him that his chest pains would diminish after a few weeks, James felt frustrated by the slowness of both his physical improvement and his progress on the Gifford lectures. Although he knew that "[i]solation and freedom from all social entanglements of a[n] exhausting kind" were ideal for writing, the pressure of a deadline was sufficiently exhausting. He had boxes of books to read for the lectures, his drafts needed extensive revision, he had only four months in which to finish, and he was not as certain as his doctor about his imminent recovery.

At the end of September, the Jameses finally left Nauheim. Although their accommodations had been luxurious, William felt as if he had been under house arrest in a "morally deadening Serbonian bog"[6] among invalids who thought about, and talked about, nothing but their illnesses. Release, he said, felt glorious. After ten days of travel through Switzerland and a visit with Henry in Rye, William, Alice, and Peggy, their only child accompanying them on their travels, settled into Henry's London apartment. Initially, they exulted in Henry's sunny—relatively, for England—and spacious rooms.

But the Jameses' blithe spirits were short-lived: suddenly, Alice succumbed to severe headaches and depression. She and William apparently disagreed over Peggy's schooling, but that reason does not explain fully the tension that developed between them. She was overwhelmed by her duties to both William, still suffering chest pains, and Peggy, who at the moment was ill with tonsillitis; but she was more distressed by a sense of isolation from family and friends. "We are like two strange way-worn birds perching in a strange dark forest," she wrote to her son

Billy.[7] William tried as well as he could to comfort and console Alice; yet he realized that he, too, was sinking into a blackness darker than anything he had experienced for nearly thirty years.

One afternoon, when Alice was lying in her room with the shades drawn, trying to recover from a headache, he could no longer keep up the facade of cheerfulness that masked his own fears. "Alice," he exclaimed, "if I could have heard one word escape your lips during all this time in recognition of the facts that we *have* a home beyond the sea, *one* syllable of tenderness for Cambridge, *one* pleasant allusion to our house, to all the life we have left behind it would atone for everything—in that ideal vision we might forget the present. But no!"

Alice was indignant. She was more homesick than he, she insisted, and besides, she added, recalling their last trip abroad, she noticed his resentment whenever they were forced to be together during their travels. In Cambridge, he could come and go as he pleased, without thinking about her—or their children. William was shocked. He felt no resentment, he told her; his irritability, to which he readily admitted, had nothing to do with her and everything to do with the pains in his chest. "Of course all sorts of clouds were cleared away," he reported, "and in five minutes we were laughing most heartily."[8]

Oddly, the recipient of this account was Alice's mother; and the letter that contained it was written in Alice's hand, at William's dictation. Confessing his behavior to Mrs. Gibbens seems to have been part of his penance, written more to assure Alice, rather than her mother, of his devotion. However, as soon as Alice improved enough to care for him, William fell into another depression.

He became so weak that Thorne forbade any visits from friends and even so effortless an activity as sitting for the portrait that his cousin, Bay Emmet, had just begun. There was no question now of meeting the deadline for the Gifford lectures. James pleaded for, and received, an extension from both Edinburgh and Harvard: if possible, he would deliver the Gifford lectures in May instead of January; Charles Eliot was quick to reply that James could take another year's leave from the college. He need work on one project only: to recover his health.

At the end of the year, the Jameses left London for Malvern, a resort with a reputation for a curative climate; unfortunately, in William's case, it had the opposite effect. A "bad breakdown" sent the Jameses fleeing to Rye. As the English winter turned cold and damp, they searched for a more southerly location and accepted an invitation from James's friend Charles Richet to stay in his vacant château in Hyères, on the Mediterranean. The château was luxurious, with such amenities as a huge billiard room and an outbuilding as large as the Jameses' Irving Street home. The building usually contained a "flying machine" that Richet had constructed himself. "To my great relief," Alice wrote to her son Billy, "he has taken it away—otherwise Papa would surely have tried it."[9] James had a more pressing occupation: wrapped in blankets, he sat, day after day, in a rocking chair in front of the château, working on his lectures. "Things go well," William wrote to Henry, "and I seem to gain, though extremely slowly."[10]

By the end of April he was well enough to travel to Switzerland for a week with the Flournoys. In Geneva, a neurologist recommended that he return to Nauheim, more for its potential benefit to his nerves than to his heart, and this time put himself under the care of one Dr. Abbé. James doubted if his first stay at Nauheim had helped at all, but he decided to try again rather than do nothing. Alice, who intervened in every activity and every decision, apparently agreed. By early May, they were back at the Villa Luise.

By the end of May, against doctor's orders, they had fled.

"I wish I had never known the name of the accursed place," James said.[11] For the rest of the spring and summer, James took charge of his own health—"James M.D. is my only doctor," he announced—as he and Alice traveled through Europe in search of a restorative climate.[12] But he found none: in Switzerland James attributed his symptoms to the altitude; in Ostend he consented, at Alice's urging, to see a "magnetic healer" whose treatment, dismally for James, produced boils; in London, Thorne urgently recommended that he return to Nauheim "*now*!!! It may be all another expensive sham," James wrote to Henry, "but there is no alternative, except the anarchy of the past 3 months, and as far as the state of the circulatory organs goes, that has done no good. Any one adviser consistently obeyed is the safest thing, as a rule. So I obey."[13]

If James felt relatively sanguine about returning to Nauheim for the third time, Alice did not. She was homesick for her children, her mother, her sisters. Perhaps she would go home for a few months, she suggested. But the thought of being alone at Nauheim was unbearable for James. He did not want to "play the baby and stop her," he said, and yet he was certain that she "must *not* go."[14] Finally, after weeks of indecision on Alice's part and hopeful anticipation on William's, Alice decided, with some measure of regret, to stay at her husband's side.

Nauheim produced, as usual, "imperceptible results," but after a month, James felt able to travel; they went to Geneva and then, for the winter, to Rome. The first weeks in Italy were difficult: James suffered three gastrointestinal attacks that weakened him. But letters to Henry and to some friends hinted at a "therapeutic card to play" that James believed might effect a cure.[15] Henry was incredulous, wondering if the wild card were the mysterious "Albumen," a digestive aid that Mark Twain recently had recommended to him and, apparently, to William as well. But the miracle cure that James wanted to try was another substance entirely: injections with a mysterious solution called Roberts-Hawley Lymph Compound.

"[N]ot a glycerin or other solution . . . but the straight material sterilized by a process which is the inventor's secret," the compound included goats' lymph from the thoracic duct, and extracts from the lymphatic glands, brains, and testicles. The sites of extraction hint at the compound's alleged power: lymph from the thoracic duct, located near the heart and the main duct of the lymphatic system, should promote overall strength; lymph from the brain should hone mental acuity; and lymph from the testicles should cure the feeling of "pusillanimity," perhaps sexual impotence, of which James had often complained.

After a month of injections administered by Alice twice a day, James felt that he had improved markedly—at least physically. "Skin smoother, muscles *much* harder, face pinker, eyes brighter, temporal arteries never turgid, bronchial secretion entirely stopped, pulse regular and *much* softer, heart sounds (according to Baldwin) altered for the better, aortic murmur disappeared, aortic discomfort ditto, heart smaller. All these symptoms are positive and unquestionable, and are objective," James wrote to Frederic Myers, who himself suffered from heart disease. "The subjective symptoms haven't yet caught up. That is, I still get easily fatigued, and feel mentally dull & unexcited. I sleep much better, in fact well, but am below par in nervous strength."[16]

James began the new century with the same complaints that had plagued him throughout his life. He felt completely undermined, he said, by the "irritability and fits of despair, and invalid's egotism" that had long been symptoms of what he called his "neurasthenia."[17] "The fact is that my nervous system is utter trash, and always was so," he wrote to Henry. "It has been a hard burden to bear all these years, the more so as I have seemed to others perfectly well; and now it is on top and 'I' am under."[18] The "others" who were incredulous about his complaints even included those close to him: his mother, and now Alice. He sensed that behind her saintly forbearance there lay a suspicion that William had the power to get well, if only he willed it so. This time, though, he had no such power.

As he wrote the Gifford lectures, James, by his own admission, was obsessed with death: his own, certainly, and during the year, four men he knew and esteemed. In January, Frederic Myers succumbed with James at his bedside. In March, James learned from Hugo Münsterberg that Leon Mendez Solomons, a former student who had been teaching at the University of Nebraska, was dead at the age of twenty-seven, following an appendectomy.

In August, British psychical researcher Henry Sidgwick died of cancer; in September, his beloved friend Thomas Davidson. James thought he himself might be dead soon, too, before he realized his full potential. "I find myself in a cold, pinched, quaking state," he wrote in notes for his lectures,

> when I think of the probability of dying soon with all my music in me. My eyes are dry and hollow, my facial muscles won't contract, my throat quivers, my heart flutters, my breast and body feel as if stale and caked. . . . I have forgotten, really *forgotten,* that mass of this world's joyous facts which in my healthful days filled me with exultation about life. . . . The increasing pain & misery of more fully developed disease—the disgust, the final strangulation etc, begin to haunt me, I fear them; and the more I fear them, the more I think about them. I am turned into a pent-in egotist, beyond a doubt, having in my spiritual make-up no rescuing resources adapted to such a situation.[19]

Belief in God or any variety of religious experience would have provided those resources. But he was left, stranded, with nothing.

The Gifford lectures were his chance—perhaps, he thought, his final chance—to reconcile for himself the questions of faith that always had been central to his philosophy. As he mined autobiographies, confessions, popular self-help books, and serious studies of theology, he sought to understand how "a broken and contrite heart," such as his own, could achieve solace through some manner of faith, through some "transempirical" experience. A sense of yearning underlay James's writing: in nearly thirty years, he had not overcome the feeling he confessed to Minny Temple of being "separated from God." For thirty years, he had envied those who experienced religious epiphany, conversion, and consolation. When his Gifford lectures were published in 1902 as *The Varieties of Religious Experience,* he dedicated the book to E. P. G., his mother-in-law Eliza Putnam Gibbens, whose simplicity of faith, whose unquestioning belief in human immortality, psychical phenomena, and a vital world "behind the veil" he so desperately wished he could share.

Glorious Weather

AMONG THE DEATHS that contributed to James's "quaking state," Frederic Myers's proved the most shattering. Suffering from arteriosclerosis, Myers, desperately ill, had come to Rome in January to consult Dr. Baldwin, in hopes that some treatment might save his life. As James saw it, though, the case was more complicated than a mere heart condition.

The previous fall, Myers had been told by a medium that he would soon die, and ardent believer in psychical phenomena that he was, Myers proceeded to prove the medium correct. "I verily believe," James wrote to John Piddington, another member of the SPR, "that his subliminal is, to put it brutally, trying to kill him as well as it can." In an effort to save his friend, James asked Piddington to get "the 'other side' " to neutralize the prediction or counter it with another, in order to get Myers's hysteria to abate. If that were not possible, then James suggested that a "mendaciously concocted" prophecy be conveyed to Myers to counter the medium's devastating prediction.[20]

By the time he arrived in Rome, however, Myers was too ill for medical or psychical treatment. He had contracted double pneumonia, his breathing was labored, and on the afternoon of Thursday, January 17, James was summoned to Myers's bedside to administer morphine. When Axel Munthe, a Swedish physician called in as a consultant, pronounced death imminent, James kept a vigil just outside the door. He had promised Myers—author of the soon-to-be-published *Human Personality and Its Survival of Bodily Death*—that he would record any communication from "the other side" that Myers was able to make. James waited, a notebook resting on his knees, for a message. None came.

James took Myers's death "as a warning that one must not leave one's work to the morrow." When he had met Myers the year before at Carqueiranne, he had seemed to James so healthy "that when the medium Mrs. Thompson predicted his death within two years and my recovery, it looked more as if the names had been substituted for one another."[21] Now Myers had proven Mrs. Thompson correct, but James had yet to recover. "He is down again, nerves and sleep deplorable, aortic pain returned," Alice reported to Henry. Awaiting a new shipment of the lymph compound, James worried that a second series of injections would do as little for his nervous symptoms as the first had done.[22]

Fearful of dying with his music yet unsung, James suddenly rallied and focused on Myers's "heroic exit," as a source of inspiration, calling it "[t]he most elevating *moral* thing I've seen during these two years abroad."[23] He set to work with renewed energy, and by early March, when the Jameses left Rome, the Gifford lectures nearly were done. He and Alice spent the spring with Henry in Rye. In mid-May, they stopped in London so that William could order some clothing appropriate for the festivities in Edinburgh; there they were joined by Harry, who had come to attend his father's talks.

Edinburgh was glorious, the weather as "cold and bracing as the top of Mount Washington in early April," James said, and the people intellectually and spiritually "much like Boston, only stronger and with more temperament." James had sent word that his health was too delicate for much socializing, a caution that his considerate Scottish hosts, for the most part, heeded. Every afternoon, he and Alice took a carriage ride around the countryside. "The green is of the vividest, splendid trees and acres, and the air itself an *object,* holding watery vapor, tenuous smoke, and ancient sunshine in solution, so as to yield the most exquisite minglings and gradations of silvery brown and blue and pearly gray."[24]

But more than the climate, the people, and the countryside, James was delighted in his success. Whereas the Gifford lectures normally drew an audience of sixty, James delivered his first lecture to a packed house of two hundred fifty; and his audience grew. By the fifth lecture, he was speaking to more than three hundred.

Although his triumph in Edinburgh had strengthened him far more than any therapy had, James took one final cure at Nauheim before heading home at the end of August. As he improved—"it is evident," he declared, "that I am in a genuinely ameliorative phase of my existence"—Alice succumbed once again to a spate of severe headaches that lasted several days at a time. Both of them longed to be home, with their struggle behind them. "Happiness, I have lately discovered, is no positive feeling," James concluded in the final days of his European sojourn, "but a negative condition of freedom from a number of restrictive sensations of which our organism usually seems to be the seat. When they are wiped out, the clearness and cleanness of the contrast is happiness."[25]

Inheritance and Temperament

"ON THE WHOLE WE have been lucky with our brats," William told Fanny Morse, "—they are all at bottom reasonable—which, considering their half-cracked neurotic daddy, is nothing short of a special providence in Alice's behalf."[26] Still, James saw in Peggy's sensitivity and moodiness much of his own temperament. During the European trip, for example, Peggy was beset by anxieties: she was worried about her father's health; she was worried about making friends, especially about entering a school where she knew no one. Accustomed to being surrounded by siblings, friends, a doting grandmother, and her aunts, she felt isolated and lonely in Europe. Most of the time, she was separated from her parents, boarding with other families; in England, she stayed with their friends the Clarkes, whose children, Peggy complained, snubbed and harassed her. The Jameses thought that some of Peggy's complaints would stop once she began school, but finding a suitable school was more complicated than William and Alice had anticipated.

Not any school would do, they discovered, in a country where caste and class were so important. Henry recommended a certain Mademoiselle Souvestre who ran "a very highly esteemed school for girls at high, breezy Wimbledon, near London" attended by "the daughters of many of the very good English *advanced Liberal* political & professional connection."[27] When William suggested that Peggy might do well at a school in Scotland, Henry rushed to dissuade him: such a school would be "[f]earfully . . . 'middle class'—& you don't want that," he told them, "though you may think you do. The schooling of girls here is *mal vu*," he added, "& none will do but the very 'socially' best."[28]

Finally, the Jameses rescued Peggy from the Clarkes and enrolled her at Northlands, which seemed to them "unusually promising and charming"; Peggy, unfortunately, saw it as "a hopeless impossibility."[29] She felt alienated from the "socially best" because she was not a member of the Church of England, as were her classmates. When Alice realized that her distress would only get worse over time, she withdrew her and, despite Henry's concerns about her classmates' refinement, placed her in the more middle-class Hampstead High School, where she was decidedly happier.

Although James did not question the authenticity of his daughter's feelings, as his mother had done with him, still he had little patience for her complaints and preferred, just as his mother had, that children keep their feelings to themselves. "You will have to rely more on yourself," he told her, "and bottle up your feelings, and not expect pity or sympathy from parents, aunts, or grandmother."[30] He sent similar advice to Tweedy: "Keep motionless as much as you can," James wrote to his ten-year-old son. "Take in things without speaking—it'll make you a better man."[31] Tweedy tried to follow his father's advice, but Peggy rarely tried to bottle her feelings, instead taxing both her parents with noisy demonstrations of misery.

Fortunately for Peggy, her new environment proved beneficent; she made friends, joined in school activities, and enjoyed visiting her beloved uncle Henry. "Peggy has learnt this winter to play tennis well, to play basketball, rounders, to swim and to ride a little; also to be stretched on the rack of this tough world without too much complaining," James wrote to Francis Boott. "The way in which conventionalisms impress her imagination shows her to take more after her uncle Henry than after her father."[32]

If Harry and Peggy were impressed with conventionalisms, James could count on Billy to repudiate them. Billy, it seemed to James, was the child who most took after him. A freshman at Harvard, Billy had proved himself to be a champion rower. James, however, was afraid that the pressures of racing would cause a breakdown in his vulnerable son. Rowing, he cautioned Billy, was no sport "for a fellow of your inheritance and temperament. The strain on mere length of endurance and the dead pull of mental excitement make it quite a different sort of business from any of the other games, where the variety both to mind and muscles give so great a relief. I think that race-rowing can be done without risk by men of stolid make."[33]

Always concerned that Billy would be swayed by his peers, James cautioned his son to make friendships of a "rich and elevating" sort among the "best men" of his class.[34] And, he reminded his son, "Don't neglect prayers."[35] In James's view, Billy—like James at the same age—lacked the self-discipline and sense of direction that was so dominant a part of his brother Harry's personality. Of all the James children, Harry clearly was the most intellectual, Billy the most capricious. In 1899, when Billy and Harry took summer jobs with the U.S. Forestry Commission, James hoped that it might lead to a career for Billy as "a forester or landscape gardener. This will be a coup d'essai for him."[36]

Harry needed no such *coup d'essai*. He, according to William, was working in the Rocky Mountains merely "for the 'culture' involved." As an undergraduate at Harvard, Harry had not strained at sports, but instead became managing editor of the *Crimson*. After attending graduate school briefly, he decided, in 1901, to enter the Harvard Law School, where he was as impressive a student as he had been all through his academic career. "Harry has taken hold of law in a surprisingly rapid fashion," William reported proudly to Henry. As soon as he graduated and passed the bar, Harry took over William's role as overseer of the Syracuse property and served as the family's legal counselor for the rest of his life.

The young Francis Tweedy, who renamed himself Alexander Robertson—Aleck, to family and friends—eventually caused his father considerable consternation. Although James seemed to scoff at young Aleck's stupidity, he worried when the probability of Aleck's following his brothers at Harvard seemed increasingly remote. Nevertheless, James encouraged his ten-year-old son's interest in drawing; and Alice praised his writing. "Your Ma thinks you'll grow up into a filosopher like me and write books," William wrote to Aleck. "It is easy enuff, all but the writing. You just get it out of other books, and write it down."[37]

Relapse into Savagery

"I AM GLAD that William has been away during the election," Alice wrote to Elizabeth Glendower Evans in November 1900, "for he takes the country's errors so to heart."[38] Foremost among the country's errors, according to James, was the "deluge of militarism" that he believed characterized American foreign policy. "It seems like a regular relapse into savagery," he wrote to a former student. "In the Philippine Islands we are now simply pirates."[39]

As a result of the Spanish-American War, America had taken possession of the Philippines, much to the dismay of a growing anti-imperialist movement at home and a belligerent insurrectionist movement in the islands. Having defeated Spain, American soldiers now found themselves facing Filipino leader Emilio Aguinaldo, commander of guerrilla troops, who had declared war on the occupying forces. Reports of bloody American attacks against civilians and inhumane treatment of Filipino soldiers made their way into the press, fueling a debate between Republicans, who, with few exceptions, supported McKinley's policy of aggression, and Democrats, led by forty-year-old William Jennings Bryan.

Bryan had captured public attention in 1896, as leader of the silverites, Democrats who proposed that a silver standard for United States currency could solve the country's economic depression. His fiery "Cross of Gold" speech, delivered at the Democratic Convention, won him the presidential nomination. Although he lost the election, Bryan remained a noisy critic of Republican policies. In 1900, promising to campaign against expansionism and imperialism, Bryan again was chosen to lead the party against McKinley. Tall, slender, and younger than McKinley by seventeen years, Bryan seemed, to many Americans, representative of a new brand of independent and intrepid politician.

But his supporters did not, at first, include James. When Bryan emerged as the Democratic candidate in 1900, James had a cool response, wishing that the party could have found a stronger candidate. Articles in the press evaluating Bryan's chances for winning convinced him that a vote for Bryan was a vote wasted. Yet in the weeks before the election, as he read reports of the campaign and Bryan's earnest protests against American actions in the Philippines, he warmed to Bryan. "I have fallen in love with him so, for his character, that I am willing to forget his following," James wrote to Francis Boott. "The great thing is to get the republicans infernally *stopped;* and stopped quick!"[40]

"I pray for his victory," James wrote to Henry Higginson, a McKinley supporter. "There are worse things than financial troubles in a Nation's Career. To puke up its ancient soul, and the only things that gave it eminence among other nations, in five minutes without a wink of squeamishness, is worse; and that is what the Republicans would commit us to in the Philippines. Our conduct there has been one protracted infamy towards the Islanders, and one protracted lie towards ourselves." The Philippine problem, he told Higginson, "is one which is sure to determine the whole moral development of our policy in a good or a bad way for an indefinite future time."[41]

Although James saw the Philippine problem as a central concern in the election, at home the campaign often deflected focus on foreign policy. Expansionism had won many champions in both parties, perhaps none so enthusiastic as New York's outspoken governor, Theodore Roosevelt, who had been nominated as McKinley's running mate. Roosevelt exalted what he called "The Strenuous Life": bold risk taking, ruthless competitiveness, and aggressive militarism, all in the service of American "domination of the world" in the near future.[42] James called his former student "a combination of slime and grit, sand and soap" that could "scour anything away, even the moral sense of the country"; that moral sense, James thought, was compromised by the "abstract war-worship" that underlay the country's policy in the Philippines and shaped Roosevelt's ideas on foreign policy.[43]

Like many of his fellow anti-imperialists, James was concerned less with the rights of colonized peoples than with the motivations and rationalizations of the colonizers. It was too easy, he said, to cling to such abstractions as "responsibility for the islands" in defense of Philippine foreign policy. "Abstractness means empty simplicity," he wrote, "nonreference to features essential to the case." Stirred by the "organic excitement" of war, Americans, James feared, would fail to consider the concrete situation at hand: islands that yearned for self-government, a leader determined enough to fight for freedom, a populace eager to follow him. If America refused to respond to that situation, it was behaving no better than the bellicose European empires that stamped their way across the world.

"The white man's juggernaut car rolls over the poor yellow folk, who must find their 'consolation' in the certainty that History will write the truth," James wrote to his son Billy during the Boer War. "The English Jingoes have got into a mess with which I am heartily delighted. I hope it will rack the Empire to its very foundations and disgrace it, without destroying it." Destroying it, of course, might lead to anarchy, worse, in James's estimation, than imperialism. Still, imperialism was an evil that James hoped his sons would repudiate. "You boys," he told Billy, "have a tremendous duty hereafter now that our country has joined the beasts of prey for once and all, in working with the better element to keep the less ignoble aspects of the military vocation on top."[44]

"The better element," as James defined it, consisted of well-educated, articulate men and women who could discern worthy leaders from rabble-rousing politicians, who were not swayed by political rhetoric, and who were bold enough to speak out against injustice or foolishness. In America, it seemed to him, this intellectual elite had a chance of effecting change; not so in Europe. "We don't know what the word corruption means at home, with our improvised and shifting agencies of crude pecuniary bribery," he wrote to social activist Fanny Morse. Europe, on the other hand, was beset by "solidly intrenched and permanently organized corruptive geniuses of monarchy, nobility, church, army, that penetrate the very bosoms of the higher kind as well as the lower kind of people in all the european states (except Switzerland) and sophisticate all their motives away from the impulse to straightforward handling of any simple case."[45]

The case that James was watching with eagerness and horror was that of Alfred Dreyfus, which seemed to him a "still blacker nightmare" than anything happening in his own country. In 1894, Dreyfus, a French officer and Alsatian Jew, had been convicted of selling military secrets to Germany and sentenced to life imprisonment on Devil's Island. When evidence surfaced later that appeared to exonerate Dreyfus, his cause was embraced by French intellectuals—Anatole France; Joseph Reinach; and most famously, Émile Zola—who kept the case in the forefront of French politics until 1906, when Dreyfus finally was cleared and reinstated in the French army.

Like many of his countrymen, James followed the case with rapt attention. "As for Dreyfuss [sic]," James wrote to Frederic Myers in 1899, when a new trial was in progress, "we bkfst. dine & sup on his case, which daily developes more & more to the confusion of the opposition. . . . But I hardly dare to hope for an acquittal, such is caste-feeling and the prestige of so many generals."[46] Still, even though he anticipated the worst for Dreyfus, James appeared astounded when a new conviction was handed down. "The incredible has happened," he wrote to William Salter, "& Dreyfuss [sic] without one may say a single particle of *positive* evidence that he was guilty has been condemned again. The french republic . . . has slipped hell-ward. . . . But I don't believe the game is lost. 'Les intellectuels,' thanks to the republic, are now aggressively militant as they never were before, and will grow stronger and stronger."[47] As they would, he hoped, in America.

McKinley won in 1900, which James, after brief consideration, did not regret. A continued Republican administration gave anti-imperialist Republicans a chance to protest against the Philippine policy within their own party. And furthermore, the Republicans now had to face the consequences of their actions, and, James hoped, suffer public shame. "I am glad . . . that McKinley is elected," James remarked, "because four years more will surely bring divine punishment upon the Grand Old party, and it's much better that they should be in office to reap the whirlwind themselves."[48]

McKinley never reaped that whirlwind. On September 6, while attending the Buffalo Exposition, he was shot by a young anarchist who claimed he had been inspired by Emma Goldman. "[T]he old humbug now adds the martyr's crown to all the rest of his luck!" James wrote to Henry a few days later, when McKinley lay struggling for his life.[49] When he died, James surely was not among those who became "hysteric mad" over the event; nor was he among those who felt any particular loyalty toward the office of the presidency, which he saw as "irrational & idiotic," yet, he admitted, "a magnificent conservative force in a nation." Despite James's conviction that Roosevelt's war worship was intolerable, he decided that he admired the new president far more than he had admired McKinley. "Roosevelt has some splendid qualities & instincts, and may do well," he decided.[50]

Back Door to Heaven

JAMES WAS BACK in America by the time McKinley died and his successor installed. But his attention had shifted away from domestic politics. He was experiencing another "nervous smash-up" caused, he thought, by the enormous change in circumstances from the "ultra-protected and especially simplified life" he had been living in Europe. Although he was teaching only one lecture course at Harvard—The Psychological Elements of Religious Life—he found that he could not adjust to his old routines, despite the beneficial atmosphere—"intense and feminine and spiritual"—of America.[51] Those adjectives, surprisingly applied to American weather, seem more appropriate for Alice, who for two years had "ultra-protected" and nursed him so patiently. Now he complained that America seemed suddenly "strange & remote," which could well describe Alice during her first weeks at home, distracted as she was from his needs by reuniting with her mother, sisters, and sons; hiring new servants; and taking sole responsibility for repairs and renovations to their home.

As Alice's initial burdens were resolved, however, James improved. Within six weeks, he reported that he felt "on the rise," happy in his "comfortable house," which would soon be even more comfortable with the addition of a cook. He was seeing his friends more frequently, Alice could pay more attention to him, and his Harvard lectures served as "a useful stimulus" to his writing.[52] But being "on the rise" did not mean being completely well. Toward the end of October he was sufficiently concerned about his physical and emotional health to begin a new series of lymph injections, which he would continue for three months. His distress at that time may have been fueled, at least in part, by a controversy surrounding Leonora Piper that put into question his own commitment to psychical research.

On October 20, 1901, a shocking article appeared in the *New York Herald*: Leonora Piper, in an interview with a reporter, disclaimed her powers as a medium. She did not receive messages from the dead, she maintained, but instead was responding to mental telepathy on the part of her sitters. "I am inclined to accept the telepathic explanation of all of the so-called psychic phenomena," she said, "but beyond this I remain a student with the rest of the world." Thoroughly fed up by Richard Hodgson's condescending attitude toward her, she asserted that she had acted "simply as an automaton, going into what is called a trance condition to be studied for purposes of scientific investigation, and also for the comfort and help of many suffering souls who have accepted the spiritistic explanation of the words which I unconsciously spoke while in this dreamy state."[53]

She had allowed the investigation to continue, she said, because she herself wanted to determine if she were "possessed or obsessed," but sixteen years was enough: she felt that no further discoveries would be made by continuing the relentless examination. "I now desire to become a free agent," she said, "and devote myself and my time to other and more congenial pursuits."[54]

Despite the convictions of Hodgson, James, and other members of the SPR, Piper had been inspired to self-doubt by sittings with some other venerable men: Phillips Brooks, for example, who left a session saying, "It may be the back door to heaven, but I want to go in by the front door." And Charles Peirce, who did not believe that he was speaking to the departed spirits, although he admitted that "a real communication with the glorious dead would surely be the greatest conceivable satisfaction to one who could not be many years separated from the state in which they abide."[55]

The Piper interview generated a juicy scandal: Piper had, in effect, tweaked the noses of eminent intellectuals, James included, asserting her own authority to decide whether she was, or was not, truly a psychical phenomenon. But if she hoped to withdraw from public view, she did just the opposite. Newspaper reporters flocked to her Arlington Heights home to interview her; she refused to see them.

Hodgson, for his part, was irritated and embarrassed. Acknowledging his own strained relationship with Piper, he asked James to intervene. A letter from him apparently soothed her feelings, and within days of the *New York Herald* article, the *Boston Advertiser* reported that Piper had retracted her "confession": "I did not make any such statement as that published in the New York Herald to the effect that spirits of the departed do not control me," Piper announced. "My opinion is today as it was 18 years ago. Spirits of the departed may have controlled me and they may not. I confess that I do not know. . . . I fancy a feeling of envy prompted this statement."[56]

A few days later front-page headlines in the *Boston Morning Journal* read: "Hatchet Is Now Buried; Mrs. Piper and Dr. Hodgson Reach an Arrangement."[57] The hatchet, however, was still sharp. "I do not deny," Piper told the *Journal*'s reporter, "that I said something to the effect that I would never hold another sitting with Mr. Hodgson, and that I would die first, to a New York Herald reporter last summer, when I gave the original interview," and she still expressed doubts that her trance states were "spiritistic."[58]

The reaction of Hodgson, James, and other psychical researchers to Piper's protests suggests one reason for her decision to break with the

SPR. According to Hodgson, the agreement that the SPR made to investigate her trance states was not with Piper herself, but, incredibly, with Imperator, one of her controls. She had no right, therefore, to interfere. "In my own view," Hodgson wrote to the president of the New York Medico-Legal Society, which was debating spiritualism at several of its meetings, "Mrs. Piper's opinion, in any case, is of no value. She herself in past years has never had any opportunity of arriving independently at any definite conclusion by any investigation of her own, and she is, of course, not competent herself to deal with such a complicated problem. She herself has sometimes felt, owing to ignorance of her own work, and the reticence maintained by myself and other sitters, as if she would like to stop sitting altogether, and so put aside what to her has always seemed a mystery, which she herself had no hope of solving."[59]

The Piper scandal fueled continued skepticism about psychical phenomena among many of James's colleagues. James was sometimes hurt, sometimes angry, at their cavalier disdain. "No one thing so radically divided professional opinion of James as his support of the Psychical Research Movement," James Rowland Angell noted. But even in face of professional censure, James would not give up his steadfast conviction of the value of psychical research. "Why on evolutionary principles," he wrote to his friend Canning Schiller, "may not all these phenomena be residue of the chaos out of which our official universe extricated itself in such solidly organized shape? Parts imperfectly connected with the rest yet connected enough still to hang on and break in occasionally and not entirely disappear...?"[60] He would answer those questions, as well as he was able, in what he called his "very *objective* study," the huge, sprawling, and intensely subjective *Varieties of Religious Experience.*

Chapter 17

A TEMPER OF PEACE

1902–1905

IN JUNE 1902, James returned from his second series of Gifford lectures exhausted. Despite an effusive reception in Edinburgh—a hearty rendition of "He's a jolly good fellow" followed him from the hall at the conclusion of his last talk—he ended the trip in low spirits. The intellectual strain of writing, the emotional strain of self-analysis, and the physical strain of travel took a serious toll on his energies. "I was less well than I tho't I was when I started," he wrote to Pauline Goldmark, "having consumed my margin of improvement by writing that terrible book, so I rather went to pieces when I tried to plunge into social activities over there [in England]. . . . But a sexagenarian is no longer a boy, no longer an expansionist. . . ."[1]

But intellectual expansion was his goal: he was tired, he said, of the "squashy, popular-lecture style" of the books he had produced for the last ten years. Even his Gifford lectures, published soon after his return as *The Varieties of Religious Experience,* was not, in his estimation, a "serious, systematic, and syllogistic" contribution to the field of philosophy.[2] "I am convinced that the desire to formulate truths is a virulent disease," he told Sarah Whitman. "It has contracted an alliance lately in me with a feverish personal ambition, which I never had before, and which I recognize as an unholy thing in such a connection. I actually dread to die until I have settled the Universe's hash in one more book."[3] And, he hoped, a book that was nothing less than "epoch making."[4]

In the *Varieties,* James expanded upon the thesis of his *Will to Believe,* essentially for the same readers. As usual, he mined his own life and experiences for anecdotes and conclusions; supplementing this material, he drew upon a huge cache of data—"a barrelful and two large cartons"—amassed by one of his students, who, for a research project of his own, had circulated throughout the Harvard community a questionnaire about religious practices. The sheer weight of these sources made the book appear, James said, "objective" and even superficially "scientific."

His aim, however, was not to defend religion by scientific proof but to serve a volley in his long "battle of the Absolute" with such philosophical antagonists as Royce. In that battle, against naturalists, on the one hand, and philosophers whom James called "refined supernaturalists," on the other, James created for himself a special position. He was a "piecemeal supernaturalist," he said, one who "admits miracles and providential leadings, and finds no intellectual difficulty in mixing the ideal and the real worlds together."[5] As a piecemeal supernaturalist, he set himself the task of locating those places where the "ideal region" forced itself into "the real world's details" to cause experiences—prayer, epiphany, or visions, for example—that generated faith.

Because he was interested in an individual's response to these experiences, his subtitle, *A Study in Human Nature,* seems, in fact, an equally appropriate title for the book. What about human nature, he asked, caused a craving for spiritual communion and sustenance? What about human nature made it possible for some minds to be receptive to supernatural experiences and some minds to remain closed to them? The answer lay in the subliminal self.

James maintained that his only original contribution in the *Varieties* was "the suggestion (*very* brief) that our official self is continuous with more of us than appears (subliminal self) which accounts for the 'striking' experiences of religious persons." James's discussion of the subliminal, hardly brief, is central to the book. Mystical experiences, conversion, epiphany, elation, and a sense of spiritual connection to an invisible realm of physical energy all, in his view, resulted from a subliminal peculiarity in certain personalities. His wife, his mother-in-law, and Leonora Piper were among those closest to him who shared this openness. Hoping to achieve some measure of receptiveness for himself, he had experimented, rarely, with mind-altering drugs; he put more faith in the strategies of mind-cure therapy, which took a prominent place in his study.

Mind-cure movements, James explained, incorporated "traces of Christian mysticism, of transcendental idealism, of vedantism, and of the modern psychology of the subliminal self" to persuade adherents of their "inlet to the divine."[6] In both the "healthy-minded" and in what James called the congenitally pessimistic "sick soul," mind-cure practitioners drew upon religious rhetoric and practices to change their clients' perception of self, world, and possibility. The first step in transcending fear, pessimism, and worry was self-surrender: surrender, that is, to the idea that there exists a higher consciousness able to infiltrate and influence subliminal mental states, resulting in meliorism—the conviction that life would and must get better—and, consequently, in physical well-being. "The mind curers," James wrote, "have made a great discovery—viz. that health of soul and health of body hang together and that if you get *right,* you get right all over by the same stroke."[7]

The health of soul and the health of society also held together, James believed. Some mind curers agreed, claiming far-reaching implications of personal reform: when individuals "got right," the resulting society, they asserted, necessarily would be stable and strong. Notable among such mind-cure reformers was Horace Fletcher, whose work James championed in the *Varieties,* to his brother, among his friends, and to the Harvard community. In November 1905, the *Harvard Crimson* carried a letter by James urging students to attend a talk by Fletcher on an issue "of fundamental importance both to the individual and to the State. If his observations on diet, confirmed already on a limited scale, should prove true on a universal scale, it is impossible," James wrote, "to overestimate their revolutionary import."[8]

Like James, Fletcher had suffered from various physical ailments, including chronic indigestion and frequent fatigue, and a generally pessimistic outlook on life. He had experimented with popular cures, but his health and spirits did not improve. Depressed and hopeless, he retired from his work as a businessman and devoted himself to personal revival. In search of health, he traveled to Mexico, Central America, India, the Dutch East Indies, and finally to Japan, where he developed an admiration for the serenity of the samurai and Bushido warriors. The Orientalist Ernest Fenollosa, whom Fletcher befriended, convinced him that the only difference between Fletcher and the warriors he admired was self-control. Through willpower he, too, could eradicate anger and worry from his life and attain inner peace. Fletcher, skeptical, resolved to try.

At the same time, in the mid-1890s, Fletcher learned of a dietary innovation, popularized by British Prime Minister William Gladstone, that featured excessive chewing: each mouthful must be chewed thirty-two times. In addition, food choices must be simplified: instead of the large, fat-laden meals that were customary for lunch and dinner, one must eat mostly cereals and breads. The chew-chew movement, as it became known, seemed to Fletcher an easy exercise of the willpower that Fenollosa advocated. Within five months, the obese Fletcher lost sixty pounds, and felt exceedingly more energetic. More important, however, he found that he could, by willing it, feel optimistic, cheerful, and serene merely by acting that way: the emotion would follow the behavior. With this newly discovered strategy for health, he claimed a new vocation; he was a dietary expert, he said, and he spent the rest of his life publicizing his theories of self-control.

Although James tried fletcherizing himself, briefly, and recommended it to Henry (who made a longer commitment to it), he was not as interested in the chewing as in the implications for personal well-being and social reform. The healthy individual, Fletcher argued, necessarily would contribute to a healthy society. Once an individual conquered one enemy—food—he could conquer more insidious enemies, such as greed, pessimism, selfishness, violence. A person in control of his feeding would be moral, calm, and generous. These implications seemed to James reasonable and consistent with his own conclusions about the ways in which individual change affected the community.

Fletcher was only one among many other witnesses to the effectiveness of mind-cure treatments and the potential of faith and conversion as therapy. James's "pragmatic" approach to religion persuaded readers that they need not give up the benefits of religious belief ("[a]n assurance of safety and a temper of peace," James said) even if they chose not to adhere to any formal, established religious doctrine.[9] They were free to refuse theological intrusions into their own private experiences.

"No previous book of mine has got anything like the prompt and *thankful* recognition that has come to me in letters about this—many of them from strangers," he told Elizabeth Glendower Evans. "But I can't myself say on reflection that I do anything [except] leave the subject just where I find it, and everybody knows that the real life of religion springs from what may be called the mystical stratum of human nature."[10]

Powers of Darkness

THERE WAS NO doubt in James's mind about the necessity for deep social and political reform. America's policy of aggression and imperialism convinced James that the country had embraced a sad new identity. America, he said, "has deliberately pushed itself into the circle of international hatreds, and joined the common pack of wolves. . . . We are objects of fear to other lands. This makes of the old liberalism and the new liberalism of our country two discontinuous things. The older liberalism is in office, the new is in the opposition." As part of the opposition, he took his place among other intellectuals, in America and in Europe, who formed a "great international and cosmopolitan liberal party, the party of intelligence . . . carrying on the war against the powers of darkness here."[11]

The powers of darkness were "the deeper currents of human nature, or of the aboriginal capacity for murderous excitement which lies sleeping" within each individual. These "homicidal potentialities" not only incited war, but also infected the nation with what James called a "profound social disease": lynching. His former student W. E. B. Du Bois, teaching in Atlanta, had sent James newspaper clippings documenting recent lynchings, fueling James's conviction that an epidemic of violence was sweeping the country. Responding immediately in a letter to the liberal *Springfield Republican,* James called for swift and stringent legislation. "The fact seems recognized that local juries will not indict or condemn," he noted; "so that unless special legislation ad hoc is speedily enacted, and unless many 'leading citizens' are hung,— nothing short of this will check the epidemic in the slightest degree." The horror would not be limited to the South; soon, he predicted, blacks would be burned on the Cambridge Common, in Boston's Public Garden.[12]

While James was genuinely horrified by the violence generated by racial prejudice, some of his own remarks about blacks suggest that he was not immune to prevailing assumptions about the character and intellectual potential of non-Caucasian races. After the commemoration of the Robert Gould Shaw monument, for example, James praised "the darkey Washington's speech" and described the "respectable old darkey faces, the heavy animal look entirely absent" among the veteran soldiers.[13] Despite an occasional black student, such as W. E. B. Du Bois (who, James noted, was of mixed racial heritage), James had minimal experience with blacks or exposure to the southern culture that he saw as so oppressive. What he knew came from newspaper reports, articles in the *Nation,* and books such as the novel *Aliens,* by Mary Tappan Wright, which he recommended to Pauline Goldmark as offering a specially insightful portrait of "the 'Negro Problem' as it is today, in a small southern town. . . . I wondered in reading it," he added, "what kind of town she could mean, the civilization seemed so queer. . . . *Inferiority* is not a salubrious environment for any of us." He had glimpsed southern society only briefly during a visit to Charleston, which, he said "gave me the most curious impression of a second-rate & perfectly narrow-minded provincial respectability gone to utter decay" and to Savannah, which had "much more sympathetic elements."[14]

Aliens confirmed a view of the "Negro problem" and the differences between northern and southern culture that James shared with many of his friends. Its protagonist, Helen Thurston, is an educated northerner who comes to the fictional Tallawara after she marries a southern academic. She is shocked by the social constrictions on women's behavior and appalled by whites' attitudes toward the former slaves, now servants and menial laborers. When she dares to help a small band of northern "missionaries" by teaching in their school for black children, she is severely chastised even by the town's minister, the college's president, and her own husband. They are convinced that she, a northerner, cannot understand the consequences of reforms that affect relations between whites and blacks. "The question of the colored race," the minister tells her, "is one in which we will brook no interference. It is our own problem; we must be allowed to work it out at our own time and in our own way."[15] When Helen suggests that the "Negro problem" was shared by all Americans, she was roundly contradicted. It was a southern concern only, she was told, and one whose solution she could not possibly invent.

Helen, despite her liberal protestations and apparent sympathy for blacks, harbors the entrenched prejudices characteristic of many northern would-be reformers. Before grading her students' papers, she waves them over an open fire. "She is fumigating them," her husband explains, "as a preliminary to engaging in the elevation of mankind."[16]

Aliens was hardly the only novel that addressed what many perceived as a growing rift between north and south and, in more general terms, a crisis of unity for the country as a whole. In James's circle, those problems became the focus of many discussions at gatherings in Sarah Whitman's Beverly home, discussions that involved Oliver Wendell Holmes, a neighbor of Whitman's; the outspoken writer John Jay Chapman, whose magazine the *Political Nursery* James read regularly; and the novelist Owen Wister, a friend of both William and Henry.

Wister, born in Philadelphia in 1860, was educated in Europe; at the exclusive St. Paul's School; Harvard College—where he was a student of James's—and Harvard Law School. Resisting joining his father in business, Wister, like James in his youth, suffered a breakdown. In 1885, to regain his health, he lit out for the wide-open spaces of Wyoming. That trip, and fourteen subsequent forays to the West, informed his most famous novel, a portrait of the quintessential self-reliant American, the most famous cowboy of them all: *The Virginian.* When the book was published in 1902, Wister became one of the most celebrated writers in America.

Even before *The Virginian* appeared, however, Wister already had established himself as a writer of great promise. James thought his biography of Ulysses S. Grant "really colossal"; that work, and *Lady Baltimore,* a novel Wister published in 1906, reflect more directly the views that he shared with his friends at Sarah Whitman's about national problems and the possibility of social change. Like *Aliens, Lady Baltimore* addresses Americans who cherish their country's history and want to revive the spirit of patriotism, unity, and purpose that, they believe, informed the past.

The story is set in a small southern town, a town unchanged, in many ways, from what it was in the eighteenth century. Into quiet King's Port comes Augustus, the narrator, a northerner with an open mind and a fondness for gentility. While the novel is superficially about star-crossed lovers and the trials of romance, it is really about the conflict between the culture of the urban North, the seat of power in the country, and the dream of the American past.

In the North, the reader is told, "everybody is afraid of something: afraid of the legislature, afraid of the trusts, afraid of the strikes, afraid of what the papers will say, of what the neighbors will say, of what the cook will say; and most of all, and worst of all, afraid to be different from the general pattern."[17] In King's Port, on the other hand, idiosyncracy is accepted and understood. With its elegant, rambling houses; its charming gardens; its verandas and gazebos, the town maintains an air of individuality. And its people maintain their diversity while feeling that they are part of a huge extended American family, united by its past and its vision of the future.

Augustus thinks this sense of unity has been lost in the North. "There's nothing united about these States any more," he says, "except Standard Oil and discontent. We're no longer a small people living and dying for a great idea; we're a big people living and dying for money."[18] The revival of the great American idea seemed to Wister—and to his friends at Sarah Whitman's—essential for enduring social change. "We may say," Wister wrote, "that the Spanish War closed our first volume with a bang. And now in the second we bid good-by to the virgin wilderness, for it's explored; to the Indian, for he's conquered; to the pioneer, for he's dead; we've finished our wild, romantic adolescence and we find ourselves a recognized world-power of eighty million people, and of general commercial endlessness, and playtime over."[19]

For Wister, James, and their circle, the aggressive risk taking that characterized the country in its wild adolescence would not serve to guide a mature nation's decisions. What was required, they agreed, was a consensual code of ethics and a sustaining national philosophy. If that philosophy were based merely on the abstract ideals of the past, James believed, it would serve only to justify repeated warmongering, to foster divisiveness, and to generate unsettling moral consequences.

All One Tenderness

"IT WAS PERFECT this afternoon, dear friend," Sarah Whitman wrote to James, "full of that beauty which only human hearts can distil: and your words—skilled, reserved and passionate—more like the sunset of that day 91 years long."[20] The words James spoke at the Harvard Chapel on Sunday, May 8, 1904, honored Francis Boott, who, two months earlier, had died at the age of ninety-one. The oldest family friend of James's youth, Boott was a modest man of humanistic spirit and artistic sensibility. An 1831 graduate of Harvard, he dabbled at writing—mostly book reviews, letters to editors, and light verse—and devoted himself more seriously to composing music. If this enterprise gave him pleasure, it did not yield lasting fame. In his memorial address, James demurred from evaluating Boott's "musical genius."

Boott's great talent, it seemed, lay in friendship. Kind and loyal, Boott inspired devotion among many in the Cambridge community where he spent most of his life. Still, James sensed a loneliness borne of early losses: first of his young wife, and, in 1888, of his daughter, Lizzie, who as a young woman had seemed to Mary James a possible focus of William's affections. In the sixteen years since Lizzie's death, Boott's friends tried to offer him some measure of solace. Perhaps out of gratitude for their care, Boott remembered many of them in his will—including William and Henry James—with bequests that surprised them in their generosity. "Evidently Boott was rich enough to give reign to the pure instinct of friendliness in a large way," William wrote to Henry after learning that they each would receive five hundred dollars. "I didn't realize the amount of sentiment which the dear old boy possessed, and feel stricken at my own hardness of judgment towards him, not that I have anything to reproach myself in the way of hardness of conduct."

Death did serve as a reproach, however, reminding James of the disparity between his ebullient performance of friendship and his harsh private judgments. "To all people, even to ghosts," George Santayana once remarked, "William James was the soul of courtesy. . . . Nobody ever recognized more heartily the chance that others had of being right, and the right they had to be different."[21] But although James celebrated publicly each individual's right to behave, believe, and feel uniquely, he could be sharply intolerant of particular manifestations. Alice thought his intolerance was a peculiar family trait, inherited, no doubt, from his father. It might be overcome, James decided, only by an exertion of will. He resolved, he told Henry, to "abound and super-abound in every form of flattery and affectionate demonstration, blind to evil, seeing nothing but good, giving credit for ten times more than we see and laying aside that grudging, carping and critical attitude which Alice says is the moral keynote of the James family."[22]

Among James's friends, the adoring Sarah Whitman was exempt from his sharpest criticism. James believed that Whitman was genuinely entranced by him, that she connected, through some special intuition, with a hidden, genuine, part of his personality. Her interest excited him: once, after a visit to Whitman, James apologized for not writing immediately to thank her for her hospitality, "preferring," he said, "to wait till the tension should accumulate." His explanation suggests an emotional arousal that fueled his effusive letters.[23]

Santayana remembered one special dinner, held when Alice was out of town, where Whitman was the only woman at a party of James's students. With Santayana at her right and James across the table, Whitman presided as hostess for what Santayana described as "a semi-religious semi-festive mystery." Although it seemed odd to him at first that Whitman, and not Alice, was James's companion for the evening, he came to understand why James had invited her: he wanted to share with her this "chosen group of ambitious young men"; and he wanted to show off to them his elegant friend. Tall, graceful, and expensively dressed in green velvet and white silk, Whitman brought a radiance to the occasion that Alice, despite the genuine warmth of her hospitality, did not have. The meal, Santayana recalled, was suitably "lordly," with beer for the men, and a half bottle of champagne for Whitman.[24]

Like many of Whitman's closest friends, James sensed a sadness and dissatisfaction caused, he imagined, by an unhappy marriage. In the summer of 1901, when Whitman's husband died, Fanny Morse predicted that widowhood might liberate Sarah into a more fulfilling life. "Does it not seem as if her extraordinary gift of being friends with us all had been to her a sort of safety-valve for the expression of much that is usually taken up & absorbed into married life," Morse wrote to James, "and that now she may live her own life more."[25]

But her chance at happiness was cut short: by the spring of 1904, just after Boott's memorial service, Whitman herself lay dying of pneumonia. She was sixty-two, and, like James, she already had outlived many of her own friends. But James saw only her youthful enthusiasms and artistic passions; it was incomprehensible to him that her spirit could be extinguished. She reminded him, he told her, of a story he once read in which the heroine was a tightrope dancer who fell from her rope in " 'a helpless mass of youth and beauty.' It is as such, dear S. W., that I like to think of *you* lying at the old M. G. H. [Massachusetts General Hospital] of my childhood."[26]

A few days later, Sarah Whitman was dead, and James was shaken by the loss. Although he had shown Whitman extraordinary affection, even her death caused him to reproach himself for his lack of generosity: he admitted that sometimes he had felt resentment about "the way in which her individual friendships seemed mere elements in the great social 'business' which she kept going so extraordinarily." Her easy social graces—and his own insecurities—made him question just how much she really cherished him. Perhaps, he thought, he was just one among many of her distinguished friends and no more than that. But if James truly doubted her esteem, her bequests to him and Alice helped to allay those doubts: she left him a stained-glass window that she had designed; and, to both William and Alice, the munificent sum of five thousand dollars. "Mrs. Whitman's death," he wrote to Pauline Goldmark, "has made me and Alice both feel that the best thing life gives is friendship, and that we ought not to fail to make enough of the friends we have while we yet have them."[27]

He had not made enough of Whitman; he could not assuage her loneliness or unburden her of whatever secrets caused her sadness. Whitman, he exclaimed, had seemed so vulnerable, "[s]o lone, so naive, so friendly, so trustful, so interrupted!" And, James added, so mysterious. "Never did a 'behind the veil' suggest itself more forcibly. Even here she lived behind a veil."[28]

Now she was behind the veil forever—but where, he wondered. "And what does it all mean? I never had the pathos, or the mystery brought so sharply home, and one's thought of her now is all one tenderness."[29] Whitman's death, he said, made "a positive difference in the other side, now that she has gone over"; soon, another death made that difference ever more positive.[30]

On December 20, 1905, Richard Hodgson, in the middle of a strenuous game of handball at the Union Boat Club, collapsed from heart failure and died. "He was tremendously athletic," James wrote to Théodore Flournoy, "and said to a friend only a week before that he thought he could reasonably count on 25 years more of life." Hodgson had been an intimate of the James family, beloved especially by the children, and stood valiantly with James against those colleagues who would debunk psychical research. In fact, James deemed Hodgson a bit overzealous. "As a *man*," James said, "Hodgson was *splendid;* a real *man;* as an investigator, it is my private impression that he lately got into a sort of obsession about Mrs. Piper, cared too little for other clues, and continued working with her when all the sides of her mediumship were amply exhibited."[31] Convinced of Piper's authenticity, Hodgson often had claimed that if he died while Piper was alive, he would find a way to communicate with her from the other side and, he added, to "'control' her better than she had ever yet been controlled in her trances." James was ready: Hodgson, he said, "[m]ay he still be energizing somewhere—it's not a case of 'requiescat.'"[32]

James did not have to wait long. If controlling Piper eluded him in life, Hodgson's apparently impatient spirit took up the challenge just eight days after his death and continued to intrude for years every time she held a sitting. At first, he communicated through the domineering Rector, but soon he managed to speak for himself. His messages were so detailed and intimate that James, who chronicled the Hodgson-control, had to face squarely the question of their veracity. "I said that if I could get over there I would not make a botch of it," Hodgson declared through Piper. Now James had to decide if he truly had made contact from behind the veil.

Hodgson's long and close relationship with Piper left open the possibility that Piper merely was recalling details of his life from their conversations. But Hodgson was notably taciturn about personal anecdotes, James knew, and too professional to confide in the very woman he was investigating. The sittings, James admitted, gave him "the weirdest feelings," leading him to conclude that they reflected "a will of some kind, be it the will of R. H.'s spirit, of lower supernatural intelligences, or of Mrs. Piper's subliminal. . . . That a 'will to personate' is a factor in the Piper-phenomenon, I fully believe, and I believe with unshakeable firmness that this will is able to draw on supernormal sources of information." But what those sources of information were, James did not know: perhaps the sitter's memories, perhaps "some cosmic reservoir in which the memories of earth are stored," perhaps Hodgson's surviving spirit. Hodgson himself believed that sitters could act "psychometrically," that is, as a kind of receiving station for emanations of other lives, a possibility that James took seriously. Each individual's actions left certain "traces on the material universe. . . . During your life," he explained, "the traces are mainly in your brain; but after your death, since your brain is gone, they exist in the shape

of all the records of your actions which the outer world stores up."
Some people, such as mediums, apparently were sensitive to these
traces; some spirits, such as Hodgson's, capable of manipulating mediums to their own ends.[33]

Penetrating Minds

JAMES'S CIRCLE of friends was diminished by death, and the Irving
Street house became quieter as his children left to embark on their ca-
reers. By 1904, only Peggy and Aleck remained at home. James described his daughter as "rather a big souled and large minded pattern
of humanity."[34] One pattern was recurring depression which, as for her
father, worsened during winter. In the winter of 1904, however, she
approached her seventeenth birthday, in unusually good spirits, traveling with friends, attending dances, and, with her mother, planning
every detail of her "coming out." A young woman's social debut,
James learned, "was like the puberty-ordeals of savage tribes. . . . [O]f
all the rotten ideals I know," he said, "this that our young girls have,
of the momentous consequences of 'coming out' with 'success' is the
rottenest." Fortunately for him, the burden of Peggy's success lay on
Alice, and though Alice claimed to have collapsed afterward, she managed to steer Peggy happily through the experience.[35]

The emotional burden Alice felt, however, was evident in a series
of "curious dreams" that featured one recurring scene: "I seem to be
wandering in difficult places (last night it was over a trellis work built
above the water)," she wrote to William, "and always I am carrying in
my arms a baby, whose I know not, a weak ailing child whom I cannot
get rid of or lay to rest. I hope that this 'grief child' bodes no ill to you
or the dear family."[36]

Fourteen-year-old Aleck was less moody than his sister but sometimes inscrutable. Although James encouraged his youngest son's interests—in sports, bird-watching, and art, for example—he also
worried about his lack of interest in the intellectual pursuits that the
rest of the family valued. At the Browne and Nichols School in Cambridge, a preparatory school whose students were destined for Harvard
or Yale, Aleck was manager of the baseball team. It was not unusual,
one of Aleck's classmates recalled, to look up from the playing field to
see James sitting in the bleachers, huddled against a chill wind, root-
ing for his son's team. He always enjoyed hearing anecdotes about

games and practice sessions. But Aleck's performance in the classroom did not equal his success as a sportsman. Slower than his siblings, Aleck had unusual, inexplicable, trouble in school.[37]

In his senior year, when he failed to make progress at Browne and Nichols, the Jameses decided that he might improve with a total change of environment. To that end, they sent him to Oxford, to live with the family of Arthur Lionel Smith, who agreed to tutor him in preparation for Harvard's entrance examinations. "I hope he will learn the real manner of working wh. our schools don't seem able to impart," James wrote to Henry Bowditch. "Can school *impart* anything? It seems to me that they can only furnish oppti'ies, and the boy's own spontaneity has to do the work. At any rate when a boy gets 'stale' at one school, he ought to have a change, and I hope well of this one."[38]

Knowing that his parents expected him to succeed, Aleck was reluctant, or perhaps afraid, to admit that he was doing as badly with Smith as he had at home. When he visited with his uncle Henry, Aleck seemed "superficially serene" but did report that he had had no tutoring from Smith. Soon after, when Elizabeth Evans came to see him, bringing his mandolin from home, Aleck confided in her his unhappiness and frustration. His parents were wasting their tuition money, he told Evans; Smith was doing nothing to prepare him for college, and he was very lonely and unhappy. Henry, learning the facts from Evans, took it upon himself to advise his brother.

Perhaps recalling his own father's disappointment because he had never been as quick and aggressive as William, Henry wholeheartedly took Aleck's side. "What I do feel . . . is that he isn't a bit a shirker or a weakling," as William apparently felt, but rather a fine young man who deserved "*patience* & care & tenderness, & a certain intelligently *waiting* attitude. . . . He is *full value,* on his own lines, & growing, in his own way, now, quite remarkably fast."[39] Evidently, William decided to take Henry's advice; Aleck was brought home and tutored intensively for entrance to Harvard; he never managed to pass the exam.

Although there had been times when James worried as much about Billy as he did about Aleck, by the early 1900s, his second son appeared to be on a course for success. On Billy's twenty-first birthday, in June 1903, William told him that they both had passed a turning point: Billy no longer had to ask his father for advice, and James no longer had to support him. Neither, of course, occurred.

In Billy, James saw both an acting out, and a revision, of his own life story. Billy, he said, was "a 'private-spirited' cuss" who liked to work alone "rather than in some 'system' where he is remote from his object & gets at it through other men." Much to James's surprise, Billy decided to study medicine—first in Geneva, where Flournoy volunteered to serve as guide and mentor, and in 1903, at the Harvard Medical School. "It's a queer thing," James mused, "that you should be so identically repeating my experiences of 40 years ago, only with all the corresponding terms so much improved, for you are a much superior youth to what I was," he added generously, "and the town and the University are better."[40]

A year of medical school, however, convinced Billy that the profession was not for him, and once again he followed his father's footsteps: "Billy . . . has dropped the whole thing and gone in for *Art!*" James announced to Flournoy. "He smiles & makes jokes again and is more like unto his old & natural Self than we have seen him in two years. *I* never could apperceive him as a doctor."[41]

Yet even Billy, however much he seemed like James, and however much James wished it, was not a kindred spirit. For those, James found among his students many young men who reminded him of his youthful self; they shared his spiritual anguish and joined his philosophical quests. Prominent among them was Charles Augustus Strong.

Strong came to Harvard in 1885, already holding a bachelor's degree from the University of Rochester, prepared to follow in the footsteps of his father, Augustus Hopkins Strong, a Baptist minister. He left convinced that religion would never provide an adequate answer to the philosophical questions that had been sown in his studies with James and Royce, in his talks with Santayana, and even in his father's works.

Supported by a Walker Fellowship from Harvard, which he shared with Santayana, he traveled to the University of Berlin, where he studied under Friedrich Paulsen, an ethicist, philosopher, and acclaimed teacher who inspired his attraction to panpsychism, the subject of his first book, *Why the Mind Has a Body.* Panpsychism, which held that all matter was imbued by psychic force, enabled Strong to reconcile the mind-body duality that he, and many other philosophers of his time, found disturbing. For Strong, panpsychism transcended the prevalent theories of mind and brain that asserted either that mental states were the efforts of neurological events in the brain or that neurological events in the brain and mental states coexisted, but did not act upon one another.

Because panpsychism did not privilege the mind as the sole seat of consciousness, it allowed for the idea that mental states caused physical changes in the brain and, indeed, throughout the body. Drawing upon recent discoveries in physics and biology, Strong believed that mind-body unity—the ascribing of consciousness to all parts of the body—could be defended.

James, attracted to the idea of panpsychism, encouraged Strong to continue writing. Whenever they had a chance to meet, they spent long hours together, Strong taking notes, James spinning out ideas. "There is no one to whom I can talk so *straight* as to Strong or so profitably," he said.[42] "I never knew such an unremitting, untiring, monotonous addiction as that of his mind to truth," he wrote to Alice after a visit with Strong. "He goes by points, pinning each one definitely, and has, I think, the very clearest mind I ever knew. . . . I suspect that he will outgrow us all, for his rate accelerates, and he never stands still. He is an admirable philosophical figure, and I am glad to say that in most things he and I are fully in accord."[43]

Strong was handsome and personable—James once called him "polished"—but also could be shy and withdrawn. Teaching did not engage him as much as writing, and after his 1899 marriage to Bessie Rockefeller, daughter of the industrialist John D., he had no need to support himself from his teaching salary. In 1903 and 1904, when the Strongs were in residence in Lakewood, New Jersey, James took the opportunity to visit. There he first met the sixty-four-year-old Rockefeller, a man as notorious in the early 1900s as James's grandfather had been the century before. Although Rockefeller was reputed to be "the greatest business villain & pirate in the country," James saw something undeniably attractive about him: "simplicity and goodness are the attributes which his surface most immediately suggests," James reported to Billy. "A robust thickset animal, without a spear of hair upon his head or face (a recent affliction) flexible, dramatic, genial, anecdotal, a chiselled face (a regular *Pierrot* physiognomy) sharp, sly, a tremendously passionate nature which reveals itself underneath his studied habits of deliberate & deacon-like utterance—a most complex old scoundrel, who gives me a greater impression of *strength* than anyone I ever saw."[44] The old scoundrel was only three years older than James himself.

James boasted that Rockefeller confided in him with rare candor, divulging "his secretest sorrows, financial and moral." Hearing of the millionaire's financial straits, James generously offered "business advice—not in detail but from a broad and general point of view."[45]

James was fascinated by the complexity and contradictions of the man he called the "most powerful human organism I have ever seen." At the same time "cunning, flexible, a volcano of passion under absolute self-control," Rockefeller seemed entirely to lack reflection. He was, James soon learned, "a devout Christian of the narrowest sectarian type, not an interest except *business.*" Except for one interest, and one that affected James: Rockefeller had taken up—"as a fad or hobby"— the endowment of universities, notably the University of Chicago, where John Dewey and his colleagues had begun a school of philosophy that James envied. In James's estimation, Chicago was "a really magnificent institution." And Harvard, he feared, suffered by comparison.

Lonely Thinker

DURING THE LAST week of December 1905, the Departments of Philosophy and Psychology at Harvard moved into their permanent home with the formal opening of Emerson Hall, an event that coincided with meetings of the American Philosophical Association—of which James was elected president for 1906—and the American Psychological Association.

James thought the imposing red brick building an architectural horror and the festivities even more distressing: Hugo Münsterberg was in charge. On December 27, when Frank Duveneck's statue of a benignant Emerson was unveiled in the hall's entranceway, Münsterberg introduced the orators for the occasion, Charles Eliot and Edward Emerson. Within the hour, at a meeting of the American Philosophical Association, he again held forth by first introducing John Dewey, and then, when a discussion followed Dewey's address, by taking the floor as first speaker. "5 speeches in one hour," James complained to Charles Eliot, "and all this with no opportunity afforded to the visitors of the Emerson meeting to escape!" Moreover, Münsterberg and his wife held an evening reception at their home, a sign, if one was needed, that he "bossed the show."[46]

Although Münsterberg's prominent position in the event seemed to others entirely appropriate—he was chairman of the philosophy department and had been instrumental in funding and planning the new building—James saw Münsterberg as a dangerous rival, intent on changing the character of the department by elevating laboratory research at the expense of metaphysical inquiry.

Alice agreed with James's suspicions. When a professor from another college once asked James how Münsterberg was getting along at Harvard, James fell silent, with a pained expression on his face. Finally, Alice broke in, replying coldly, "Mr. Münsterberg has shown himself to be a very great organizer; he has almost organized us out of Harvard University."[47]

James's colleagues, however, did not share his disdain. In the spring of 1905, when Münsterberg was invited to fill the chair of philosophy at the University of Königsberg, once occupied by Kant, the Harvard philosophy department was horrified at the thought that they might lose their star. When Royce learned that Münsterberg had accepted, he spent long hours trying to convince him of the esteem Harvard felt for him and of the power he gained by associating himself with a major American university. Finally, to his great relief, Münsterberg changed his mind. Palmer, for one, was delighted: "I cannot believe you would have found any such opportunity for scholarly or public work in Königsberg as Cambridge affords," he exclaimed to his colleague. "We are pretty near the center of the earth. It isn't suitable to confine a man like you to some spot on its circumference."[48]

Both Royce and Palmer were convinced that Münsterberg was a philosopher in the Emersonian tradition, committed to questioning and transcending the mere accumulation of scientific data. During the dedication ceremonies, Münsterberg asserted that housing the new psychology department in Emerson Hall made clear Harvard's position on the affiliation of the two disciplines. "I have always insisted on the value of experiment, physics, and physiology in psychology," he said, "but that cannot lead me to identify psychology with the natural sciences." Questions of psychology, he believed, were, at heart, philosophical questions.[49]

James, however, lighted on Münsterberg's interest in laboratory experimentation as emblematic of wider changes in the university and, therefore, in the meaning of higher education. On the one hand, increasing specialization in all disciplines, especially in the fragmenting social sciences, made it difficult for a humanistic generalist, such as James, to find a place within the faculty. On the other hand, James did not want a university to retreat from the demands of the world, defending "a thing called 'higher' learning, or ideal education, or something the University is supposed to be faithful to *against* the vulgar demands of the world," he told John Chapman. "That whole notion spells to me nothing but *priggishness*—'oh! we are very *exclusive*.' I don't believe in any 'higher' learning, except as one item amid the very broad and miscellaneous demands of human beings for the instruction they want." Any college, he believed, "should minister to the general social life. . . . What in a broad way may be called a demand for 'engineering' knowledge is tremendously and justly urgent just now, and Harvard is becoming more and more extensively an engineering school in consequence. The new school of 'business' steps in the same direction. There is also a demand on the part of 'Society' that its children should be of Harvard as of a 'Club'—and this, kept within bounds, is also legitimate, and socially of use."[50]

Consistent with his critique of the aims of a university education, James regretted that the single most important criterion for hiring new faculty was their possession of a doctorate. Such self-taught men as he were no longer valued: "bare personality," James noticed, was "a mark of outcast estate." Yet, he asked, did a doctorate certify a talented teacher? Did a doctorate certify a creative mind? "Certain bare human beings," he insisted, "will always be better candidates for a given place than all the doctor-applicants on hand."[51] At the time he criticized what he called "The Ph.D. Octopus," James himself, with no earned doctorate, was feeling a bit bare: in the present market, he never would have been invited to join the Harvard faculty.

But James not only lacked a doctorate, he lacked a Harvard degree. This feeling of being an outsider to the clublike atmosphere that prevailed on campus and among alumni was aggravated each year at commencement, when James, along with other non-Harvard men, did not have a class with whom to walk in the graduation procession. In June 1903, the university finally tried to remedy that situation by conferring upon him an honorary doctorate, a gesture "of personal good will" from his friends among the overseers and the faculty. Although James had received other honorary doctorates from European universities, he took Harvard's gesture as a special honor. The event, not surprisingly, flooded him with anxiety. A week before graduation, he divulged the news of the impending ceremony to his son Billy, confessing that he was "in a bad funk" over the speech he was scheduled to deliver at Commencement Dinner in Memorial Hall. "But the gospel of relaxation is the right thing for such cases," he added, "and I am practising it as well as I can."[52]

He was worried, too, that in presenting the degree, Eliot would describe him as " 'talker to teachers,' 'religious experiencer,' or 'willer to believe,' " all epithets that referred to James as a popularizer of philosophy, rather than a serious theorist.[53] His own speech, delivered from memory, insisted on his identity as a "truth-seeking and independent and often very solitary" thinker, an innovator who had managed to flourish at Harvard, but who might not continue to be welcomed if Harvard reshaped its identity. On that June evening, he took his stand against that redefinition.

"I want to use my present privilege," he said, "to say a word for these outsiders with whom I belong." These outsiders, he said, may come from remote parts of the country and from poor families. They may not have attended the best preparatory schools of the East, nor, during their residence at Harvard, join the Hasty Pudding Club and the Porcellian, but, he said, "they nevertheless are intoxicated and exultant with the nourishment they find here; and their loyalty is deeper and subtle and more a matter of the inmost soul than the gregarious loyalty of the club-house pattern often is." These were the men who sought him out after class, who sat with him in his library; these were the men, filled with doubts and dreams, who took inspiration in his teaching. Harvard's most precious function, James told his listeners, was to draw such men of "exceptionality and excentricity"—such men as he—and to serve as "a nursery for independent and lonely thinkers. . . . Our undisciplinables," he told the commencement class of 1903, "are our proudest product."[54]

Celebrating his identity as lone thinker, James, at the same time, wished that he could surround himself with disciples and establish the kind of philosophical community he envied at the University of Chicago. "Chicago has a school of thought!" James announced, "a school of thought which, it is safe to predict, will figure in literature as the School of Chicago for twenty-five years to come." John Dewey, "long-necked &

abstracted dreamer" as he seemed to James, led a contingent of at least ten scholars in shaping a perspective "so simple, massive, and positive that," James said, "it deserves the title of a new system of philosophy."[55]

This new system was defined in a collection of essays, *Studies in Logical Theory,* in which the members of Chicago's philosophy department acknowledged their debt to James for "the forging of the tools with which the writers have worked."[56] As much as they were indebted to him, however, they did not embrace James within their fold, nor did James seek to join them. Instead, he looked for a way to improve upon their work.

As James understood them, the Chicago philosophers were empiricists who did not distinguish between fact and theory—both being intellectual constructions—and who believed that truth was "in process of formation like all other things . . . [and] not in conformity or correspondence with an externally fixed archetype or model." James saw the Chicago School as mediating between empiricism and transcendentalism, which he applauded, but noticed two gaps in its philosophy: "no positive account of the order of physical fact, as contrasted with mental fact, and no account of the fact . . . that different subjects share a common object-world."[57] These gaps would be addressed in his own work, he promised, but he regretted that there were no colleagues at Harvard who would rally around him to bolster the impact of his ideas. "Here we have thought, but no school," he remarked. "At Yale a school, but no thought. Chicago has both."[58]

But James's sense of rivalry, his abiding need to be recognized as a singular genius, made the formation of a cohesive Harvard School of Philosophy impossible, even if there had been a more like-minded department. James, said Ralph Barton Perry, "was incapable of that patient brooding upon the academic nest that is necessary for the hatching of disciples." His strength, as Perry saw it, and as scores of his students gratefully remarked, was in his ability to inspire and encourage other solitary geniuses. "The number of those who borrowed his ideas is small and insignificant," Perry said, "beside the number of those that through him were brought to have ideas of their own. His greatness as teacher lay in his implanting and fostering of intellectual independence."[59] His favorite students were, like him, the undisciplinables.

Part of his difficulty in creating a philosophical school lay in the confusion generated by his ideas. As James tried out his "program" on various groups of philosophers and students, he found the same puzzled response. In August 1903, he had expounded his "gospel," as he put it, at Glenmore, the summer school of philosophy established by his late friend Thomas Davidson. He gave five lectures "just to hear how the stuff would sound when packed in to that bulk," but he discovered that it sounded "*queer*," and, he added, "I must make it sound less so to the common mind."[60] The very terms he used— "pragmatism," "pluralism," and "radical empiricism"—seemed fraught with difficulties.

Although his Glenmore audience thought James personally "genial" and "charming," some deemed his philosophy so "simple-minded" as to be laughable. "The whole philosophy to me," one student reported to William Torrey Harris, "is one of common sense with the emphasis on the word common." James, he said, did not adequately refute the idea that diversity could be consistent with an underlying unity; he could not fully explain what he meant by stream of consciousness, nor, if individuals created their own streams, how those streams came to a consensus about the reality of the world. In explaining the relation between mind and body, he fell upon Strong's panpsychism: there were higher streams of consciousness, James asserted, that filtered through each individual consciousness. Just so there might be a God: not an omniscient, omnipotent God, but some higher form of consciousness that could justify religion and faith.[61]

James decided that his Glenmore listeners simply misunderstood him. But his progress in articulating his ideas during the winter and spring of 1904 was slowed by an onslaught of illness: two attacks of influenza, three of gout, and one of the skin inflammation erysipelas. Planning to produce four hundred pages by summer, he had been able to write only thirty-two. But by June, he had recovered, ready to devote his energies to an explication of a philosophy that "represents order as being gradually won and always in the making." This emphasis on process and chance, he insisted, did not preclude the existence of God. His philosophy, he told his friend and ally François Pillon, "is theistic but not *essentially* so. It rejects all doctrines of the Absolute. It is finitist; but it does not attribute to the question of the Infinite the great methodological importance which you and Renouvier attribute to it. I fear that you may find my system too *bottomless* and romantic." Yet James was convinced that whether it were "in the end judged true or false, it is essential to the evolution of clearness in philosophic thought that *someone* should defend a pluralistic empiricism radically."[62]

As James worked, the possibility of being misunderstood and censured even by philosophers who admired him inspired a feeling of generalized vulnerability. In the fall of 1904, when he was in New Hampshire with Henry, who had begun a six-month tour of his native land, James related to Alice a strange dream:

> I dreamed the night before last that I had grown so intolerable that you suddenly "left" me. The news was broken to me by a sort of compound of Mary, your Aunt Susan, and your mother. I took it very naturally, saying I knew that you had been on the point of it for ever so long, and went about my lonely business. It seemed intensely real—rather cold & austere.

In the dream, he did not try to find her, but two weeks later, he came home certain that she had returned. Even then, however, he did not look through the house for her, but simply went into a downstairs bedroom and fell asleep. At dawn, "remembering to look for you," he went upstairs and found "a large mass with the bedclothes over it, which I identified with such a thrill of joy as to wake me immediately up," but not before he learned that Alice had spent her absence with another man, "and I happy that it had been so good a man. A very real and impressive dream!" he added.[63]

Certainly Alice may have complained recently about her onerous wifely duties. According to James, she had spent the winter playing "sick nurse" both to him and to Billy, besides having "a h-ll of a time with painters & plumbers & carpenters in Cambridge in May & June, ditto at Chocorua in August, etc. etc."[64] Alice's irritability may have been one cause for the dream. But rejection and abandonment were James's constant fears as he worked to overcome "the difficulty of making one's self understood in these matters even to one's closest cronies."[65]

James received a welcome boost during a three-month trip to Europe in the spring of 1905. At the end of April, in Rome for the Fifth International Congress of Psychology, he went to the conference hall to register, "and when I gave my name," he told Alice, "the lady who was taking them almost fainted, saying that all Italy loved me, or words to that effect." His effusive admirer called in one of the officers of the congress, who, just as impressed, implored James to give a talk at one of the general meetings. "So I'm in for it again," James admitted with delight, "having no power to resist flattery."[66]

For his talk, he condensed—and speedily translated into French—his recently published "Does 'Consciousness' Exist?"[67] Responding to the prevalent notions of mind-body dualism that he had questioned in the *Principles,* James argued that consciousness "as it is commonly represented, either as an entity, or as pure activity, but in any case as being fluid, unextended, diaphanous, devoid of content of its own, but directly self-knowing—spiritual, in short" was nothing more than "pure fancy." What did exist, according to James, were "pure experiences" of objects, events, or people, that "succeed one another; they enter into infinitely varied relations; and these relations are themselves essential parts of the web of experiences." That consciousness of experience is shaped by each individual's "biography": that is, past experiences, interests, memories, needs. Distinguishing between "subject" and "object," "thing" and "thought," therefore, was not philosophically useful. The knower and the known were inseparable components of any experience.[68] "In my view," James said, "self-transcendency is everywhere denied. Instead of it, and performing the same function, we have the continuity of adjacents. It is clear that too much attention cannot be brought to bear upon this notion."[69]

Although James discovered that his international audience, like many of his American colleagues, "had wholly failed to catch the point of view," he quickly was swept off by a "Florentine band" of philosophers who hailed James as their mentor. Led by twenty-four-year-old Giovanni Papini—"the most enthusiastic pragmatist of them all," James said—the group published a monthly journal, *Leonardo,* with writing so refreshingly "cutting and untechnical" that James wished American philosophers could use it as a model.

Papini's literary skill, especially his talent with adjectives and metaphors, seemed to James just what was needed to communicate his own ideas. He thought especially fruitful Papini's definition of pragmatism as "a collection of attitudes and methods" that took a position of "armed neutrality in the midst of doctrines. It is like a corridor in a hotel, from which a hundred doors open into a hundred chambers. In one you may see a man on his knees praying to regain his faith; in another a desk at which sits some one eager to destroy all metaphysics; in a third a laboratory with an investigator looking for new footholds by which to advance upon the future. But the corridor belongs to all, and all must pass there. Pragmatism, in short, is a great *corridor-theory.*"[70]

In Papini, James recognized an iconoclast who believed, as he did, that philosophy should liberate the imagination. "It is your *temper of carelessness,*" James wrote to Papini later, "quite as much as your particular formulas, that has had such an emancipating effect on my intelligence."[71] Papini was extravagant, emotional—and very likely he seemed to James unstable. James thought better of an initial impulse to include Papini in the dedication to his *Pragmatism;* and in 1909, he perpetuated a rumor (false, as it turned out) that Papini had died of insanity.

Nevertheless, Papini and his compatriots had succeeded in countering James's despondency about his potential contribution to philosophy. James spent the rest of his European holiday in Greece, Switzerland, England, and France, where meetings with Schiller, Flournoy, and Henri Bergson proved to be "realities of the best sort."[72] Although he felt physically exhausted and worried about a recurrence of his "old heart sensibilities," he returned home inspired.

James's resolve to write, however, soon was interrupted. By January 1, 1906, he was closeted in the stuffy compartment of a Santa Fe Railway train, making his way to the Pacific Coast where he would spend the spring semester as visiting professor in Stanford University's philosophy department. After James's first trip to California in 1898, Stanford's president David Starr Jordan began campaigning to lure James to the campus, but his repeated invitations were met with one or another excuse: poor health, fatigue, and competing obligations, James told him, stood as obstacles to another trip west.

Jordan persisted; and finally, in the summer of 1904, James acquiesced, but only if his terms were met. He would teach no more than three hours a week, only for one semester, must have the hour from two to three o'clock free for his daily nap, and would not come for less than three thousand dollars. Compared with faculty salaries nationwide, the fee was high, but James knew his market value, and, in the end, Jordan was able to offer five thousand dollars to get him to the campus and serve as adviser in shaping the university's philosophy department.[73]

On his way to California, James stopped at the Grand Canyon, arriving just after sunset on a blustery evening. Although he was nearly blinded by gusts of snow, he found "the abyss," as he called it, "equal to the brag." The next morning, he planned to join a tour descending into the canyon, but the cold weather—it was three above zero—canceled the excursion. James, who hated heights, was relieved. "As Chas. Lamb says," he wrote to Pauline Goldmark, "there is nothing so nice as doing good by stealth and being found out by accident, so I now say it is even nicer to make heroic decisions and to be prevented by 'circumstances beyond your control' from even trying to execute them."[74]

"All very beautiful and promising," James wrote in his diary when he finally arrived in Palo Alto. Then, in the only other entry for the day, he added, "Feel lonely and scared."[75] Alice was remaining in Cambridge for several weeks to steer Peggy through her social debut, and he missed her. Besides, he felt homesick for the bracing New England winter, his library, and his friends. California was vast and sunny, but vacuous. "Multiply the Irving Street circle by 100 or 1000," he wrote to Alice, "throw in the crudest business block, composed mainly of telegraf poles, and you have all California. As for any *past,* you can listen and actually hear the historic silence. It is startling."[76]

In the weeks before Alice arrived, James's irritability was exacerbated by a case of gout brought on, he insisted, by tension over a talk that he delivered to the Pacific Coast Unitarian Club. Although "Reason and Faith" appears to be nothing more than a distillation of some portions of *The Will to Believe,* still James was as worried about the occasion as if he were trying out new propositions, confessing to George Howison, another of the evening's speakers, that he felt "fear and trembling" at the prospect of the Unitarian gathering.[77] Afterward, James decided that Howison's speech had been received more warmly than his own, yet he was pleased enough with one of his ideas—the image of a "faith-ladder"—to repeat it in later works.

The "faith-ladder" represented a progression of thought that ended in belief in a truth:

> It *might* be true somewhere, you say, for it is not self-contradictory.
> It *may* be true, you continue, even here and now.
> If it is *fit* to be true, it would be *well if it were true,* it *ought* to be true, you presently feel.
> It *must* be true, something persuasive in you whispers next; and then—as a final result—
> It shall be *held for true,* you decide; it *shall be* as if true, for *you.*

The faith-ladder was not logical, James said, "yet it is the way in which monists and pluralists alike espouse and hold fast to their visions. It is life exceeding logic."[78]

"Reason and Faith" was only one of several speaking engagements that James accepted in addition to his teaching duties. He also joined a special convocation, a teach-in as it were, on international arbitration, held at Stanford on Washington's Birthday. A resolution passed by the Lake Mohonk Conference on International Arbitration called for colleges throughout the country to devote the day to meetings focusing on peace. James called his talk "The Psychology of the War Spirit." Not for the first time nor the last, he asserted that the "bellicose constitution of human nature" was so deeply inbred that humans could not help but love war. " 'Peace' in military mouths to day," he said, "is a synonym for 'war expected.' " Yet he believed it was possible that educated and responsible leaders—such as the British diplomats who had avoided military conflict over the Venezuela boundary dispute— could both prevent war and invent ways to divert aggression into peaceable enterprises.[79] The spirit of "pugnacity," as he put it, need not result in murder and destruction. Competitiveness, valor, risk taking, inventiveness, vigor, and discipline—all these qualities could be directed to the benefit of humankind.

"The Psychology of the War Spirit" reprised some of the ideas James had presented at the Thirteenth Universal Peace Congress in Boston in October 1904[80] and informed his most famous statement on the subject, "The Moral Equivalent of War," published, finally, in 1910.

James's first weeks at Stanford were pressured and disorienting. In addition to the stresses of public speaking, the discomfort of gout, and loneliness for Alice, James complained of frustration at not working on his new, groundbreaking philosophical work. But frustration does not fully explain a particularly unsettling experience that occurred just before Alice arrived.

Chapter 18

MENTAL PIROUETTES

1906–1907

ON THE MORNING of February 12, James was awakening, conscious of having been dreaming peacefully, when suddenly he recalled another dream, "very elaborate, of lions, and tragic," that merged itself into the first. This "mingling of two dreams" was something he had never experienced, and he found it disturbing—disturbing enough, it seems, to influence his sleep on the following night.

This time he awoke from a deep sleep, suddenly overwhelmed by three dreams merging together. "Whence comes *these dreams?*" he asked himself. "They were close to *me,* and fresh, as if I had just dreamed them; and yet they were far away *from the first dream.*" The dreams were unrelated in any way, he said, one set in London, the other two in America: "One involved the trying on of a coat . . . the other was a sort of nightmare and had to do with soldiers." Yet it was not the disparate content that disturbed him, but the feeling that the dreams had not occurred in succession, and that he could no longer tell which one he had been dreaming when he awakened. He had the uncanny sensation that he belonged "to three different dream-systems at once, no one of which would connect itself either with the others or with my waking life. I began to feel curiously confused and *scared.* . . . Presently a cold shiver of dread ran over me: *am I getting into other people's dreams?* Is this a 'telepathic' experience? Or an invasion of double (or treble) personality? Or is it a thrombus in a cortical artery? and the beginning of a general mental 'confusion' and disorientation which is going on to develop who knows how far?"

His sense of control over his hidden selves—a control that at various times in his life felt alarmingly fragile—suddenly became threatened, leaving him stranded, terrified by the idea that he was losing his coherent "self" either through "invasion" by other mind states or by his own submerged personalities. He became convinced that he was being overtaken by psychic or physical forces, that these two nights of increasingly complicated dream states were the beginning of a long descent into mental deterioration.

Besides being rooted in his abiding fear of harboring a morbid secondary self, James's panic about the possible disintegration of his personality, far out of proportion to the dream experiences, can be located, in part, in a book he received just before leaving for California: Morton Prince's groundbreaking study, *The Dissociation of a Personality*. This case history of a multiple personality already was familiar to James from Prince's earlier articles in the *Proceedings of the Society for Psychical Research*, articles that James found fertile and provocative in their implications for understanding identity, for defining the "normal" self, and for gaining access to subliminal mental states. Those questions always had more than academic interest to James; they took on a new urgency after his shattering dreams.

Prince's patient, whom he called Christine Beauchamp, was a refined, well-bred, and well-educated woman who suddenly, at the age of twenty-three, developed severe symptoms of neurasthenia. She sought the help of Prince, a physician and psychologist who happened to be a former student of James's, and she remained his patient for seven years. During treatment, Prince hypnotized Beauchamp and discovered a "family" of three other personalities besides the conventional "social self" that Beauchamp presented to the world. These personalities were distinct, each with its own set of memories.

As Prince presented the case, the disintegration afflicting Beauchamp was not a bizarre anomaly, but something that could happen to anyone; her various personalities were really manifestations—or at most, exaggerations—of character traits that any individual might embody: saintliness, devilishness, aggression, inhibition. "Miss Beauchamp is simply ourselves 'writ larger,'" one reviewer noted; "ourselves passed on to a stage of chronic mental disease."[1] Furthermore, Prince's study implied, one might become afflicted and never reveal it: hardly anyone in her circle knew of Beauchamp's problems, not even when she spent the morning taking four baths, so that each identity was satisfied about her cleanliness. Social life was complicated, but it went on.

James admired Beauchamp's heroic ability to maintain a facade of coherence, her ability to hide her affliction from others and to proceed with a life that appeared, to everyone except Dr. Prince, perfectly conventional. When Prince's detractors suggested that the personalities were "organized & solidified by the operators suggestion," James insisted that Prince's intervention was not the issue. "The point that is psychologically interesting," he said, "is not how they arose, but the fact that a human being can continue to exist in that strangely divided shape."[2]

The most dangerous of Beauchamp's selves called herself Sally. Outspoken, sexually aggressive, and sardonic, she hated the reticent and conventional Christine, and she managed, for a while, to gain control over the other personalities. It was clear to Prince, as he searched for the "real" Miss Beauchamp among the four personalities, that Sally could never be that identity and therefore, through hypnotic suggestion, must be eliminated. This "drastic treatment" sparked lurid headlines in the popular press; Prince, according to an article in the *Boston Sunday Globe,* was nothing less than the "annihilator of a woman's soul."[3]

The prospect of annihilation may have contributed to James's anxiety. By early 1906, after all, James was feeling attacked for the intellectual divisions that he presented as a philosopher and psychologist. His irreverence toward entrenched philosophical ideas made him a kind of "Sally" to the academic community where he wanted affirmation and where he feared rejection. He was increasingly pressed by his colleagues and readers to present a coherent intellectual self in his writings and lectures, to resolve the contradictions that many readers noticed between his insistent belief in psychic phenomena and panpsychism and at the same time his championing of a philosophy that tested itself against concrete experience. As he anticipated presenting his ideas—the very ideas that he planned to expound upon in his much-anticipated new work—to his classes, he worried about being misunderstood and derided. Burdened by questions of identity and authenticity, James reacted violently to the strange dream experiences.

When he recalled the experiences later, he claimed that he resolved his immediate feeling of dread by rationalizing that two of the dreams actually were memories of previous dreams, an explanation that seemed to him reasonable and allayed his fears of mental disintegration. More likely, he recovered quickly because Alice, finally, arrived to care for him.

Anyone who feared disintegration of the self needed a "principle of steadiness to hold on to," he wrote. "We ought to assure them and reassure them that we will stand by them, and recognize the true self in them to the end."[4] Alice always had served that purpose for her husband. She treated his moods, depressions, anger, and self-deprecation not as evidence of hidden selves, but as transitory states of mind. She was certain, if sometimes he was not, of the integrity of his personality.

Uplift

ALTHOUGH SUFFERING from anxieties in the solitude of his rooms, James presented to his colleagues a familiar air of self-assurance. He had come to serve as adviser, after all, and nothing, not even an incipient breakdown, would prevent him from offering his counsel. Despite his initial sense of the intellectual vacuousness in Palo Alto, James soon decided that Stanford's setting, architecture, and climate gave the university extraordinary potential. "There couldn't be imagined a better environment for an intellectual man to teach and work in," he told Flournoy, if not for some underlying problems—the most pressing of which was the demoralized faculty.[5]

"The day after he arrived," faculty member Frank Angell remembered, "I took him for a walk in the fields and his first remark was, 'Anyone seeing us out walking together might suppose we were discussing philosophy or psychology. But the matter that really interests a professor is salaries. Now how are the men paid here?' "[6] Not well, as it turned out. But the meager salaries were not the only reason Stanford failed to attract faculty. Among the conventions of academic life, an annual trip to Europe was a cherished ritual. That trip became more difficult when it first required a transcontinental train journey.

To change the character of the university would require money, but as James saw it, both Jordan and his board of trustees suffered from a lack of imagination and fiscal generosity. Still, James tried to help, recommending several candidates, Ralph Barton Perry among them, to serve as philosophy department chair. Perry, however, saw a brighter future at Harvard, especially with James's retirement imminent; other candidates also declined Jordan's offers; and James soon grew discouraged

about exerting an energizing influence at Stanford. As he wrote to
Charles Eliot, "Things here won't admit of reform *yet,* and a volcanic
explosion of some sort will probably have to occur first."[7] A violent upheaval did occur: on Wednesday morning, April 18.

At 5:13 A.M., James already was awake when suddenly his room
began to sway. He gripped the edge of his bed, but the swaying became fiercer, throwing him to the floor. As his bureau crashed beside
him, he heard the immense din of furniture falling in other rooms and
buildings crumbling outside. It was an earthquake, he realized, and it
seemed to him, he later wrote to Henry, "absolutely as a permanent
Entity that had been holding back its activity all these months, and on
this exquisite early morning saying 'nun geht's los!' Now *give* it to
them!"[8] James was exhilarated. *"Go* it," he nearly cried, "and go it
stronger!"[9]

At nine on the seismographic scale, the quake was strong indeed.
In forty-eight seconds, much of Stanford was demolished. The church
tower, the Memorial Arch, and the powerhouse smokestack were now
piles of rubble. A statue of Louis Agassiz was upended, its head buried
in a cement sidewalk: "from the abstract into the concrete," someone
quipped.[10] Only two of Stanford's fifteen tile-roofed, sandstone buildings were left standing, although wooden houses were hardly dam-
aged; losses were estimated at between three and four million dollars.

The Jameses suffered no injuries and only the minor loss of some
pottery. In fact, for James, who so rarely faced physical hardship or
danger, whose participation in the "strenuous life" consisted of hiking
in the Adirondacks, the earthquake became a "supremely thrilling excitement," a welcome relief from "Habit's tediousness. . . . The dams
of routine burst, and boundless prospects open."[11] To expand those
prospects, he decided to take the single train that was running into San
Francisco, accompanying his colleague Lillien Martin, who feared for
the welfare of her sister.

San Francisco, James discovered, was nothing like Stanford, where
one student and one fireman had been killed on the campus. In San
Francisco, hundreds lay buried beneath rubble, and hundreds more
were missing. The largest water main was disrupted, having been lain,
unfortunately, along the seismic rift. When gas from broken mains ignited, the blaze, uncontained, began to consume one street after another. As the heat rose to the hilltops, bits of burned wallpaper and

shingles wafted up in the morning breeze. Dragging boxes, trunks, and suitcases, people poured out of their homes, pursued by fire. In an effort to control the flames, soldiers stationed at the Presidio were ordered to dynamite the ruptured gas mains. Explosions and aftershocks kept the earth trembling and San Franciscans shivering in fear. Some managed to reach the Oakland ferry and escaped. Most were forced to remain: James saw stunned families gathered in Golden Gate Park, guarding the furniture that they managed to rescue from the rubble that once had been their homes.

In the East—and in England, where Henry and Billy anxiously awaited word from the Jameses—the news was shocking. "Even at this distance the tidings are hideous," Elizabeth Agassiz noted in her journal three days after the earthquake, "—what can it be on the spot?"[12] James's friends were horrified: "You have lived through the great Civil War," William Dean Howells wrote to Charles Norton, "but has your experience of life anything in it like this awful San Francisco earthquake? While it shrinks in fact, it rather grows in the imagination and centres all the appallingness of historical disaster in our point of time. Is it true that William James was at Stanford University when it happened?"[13] Henry feared the worst—that William and Alice "were thrown bedless & roofless upon the world, semi-clad & semi-starving" among the thronging rabble.[14] But he need not have worried. "In general," William assured him, "you may be sure that when any disaster befalls our country it will be *you* only who are wringing of hands, and we who are smiling with 'interest,' or laughing with gleeful excitement." During several visits to San Francisco, William claimed, he did not hear "one pathetic word" spoken.[15]

James's reports to Henry reflect his desire to show bravery, if not bravura, in the face of his brother's characteristic acute anxiety. But James was excited for another reason, as well: if he looked at the earthquake as an analogy to war, it seemed a stimulating test of courage rather than a terrifying disaster. Convinced that such an event must lead to moral uplift, he paid attention more to evidence of triumph than to misery and suffering. He decided, for example, that the earthquake could not have occurred in a better place because in San Francisco "everyone knew about camping, and was familiar with the creation of civilization out of the bare ground." Rested after a good night's sleep, how could they fail to take on this challenge with gusto? "Everyone at

San Francisco seemed in a good hearty frame of mind," he noted; "there was work for every moment of the day and a . . . sense of a 'common lot' that took away the sense of loneliness that (I imagine) gives the sharpest edge to the more usual kind of misfortune that may befall a man."[16]

Although James himself responded to misfortunes with feelings of desolation, this physical upheaval seemed to him qualitatively different; he simply could not bring himself to empathize with the sufferers in San Francisco, but insisted that work and a sense of community were prescriptions for overcoming the disaster. "[I]n battle, sieges, and other great calamities," he assured Henry, "the pathos and agony is in general solely felt by those at a distance, and although physical pain is suffered most by its immediate victims, those at the *scene of the action* have no *sentimental* suffering whatever."[17] Unscathed, he and Alice managed to start for home the next week, and by the beginning of May he was well-settled in his Irving Street home.

Heroes

FOR MONTHS AFTERWARD the Jameses found themselves talking about little but their California experience and becoming "thoroly accustomed to the 'pose' of heroes."[18] Alice was even invited by her "mother's group" to give a talk about the earthquake. Feeling uncomfortable about giving a public presentation, she used as a text her husband's "On Some Mental Effects of the Earthquake," which he wrote for *Youth's Companion* within weeks of his return to Cambridge.

That essay was one of several distractions during the summer of 1906 that kept James from renewing his work on the major theoretical expositions that he hoped would earn him acclaim. He also delivered five lectures on "Religious Philosophy and Individualism" at the Harvard Summer School of Theology, and he consented to research and write a report on Hodgson's control of Leonora Piper for the Psychical Research Society, a commitment that required his presence at many more sittings than he might ordinarily have attended.

He had not lost touch with Piper, however, even before he agreed to investigate the Hodgson-control. Just before Alice left for California, she had gone to a sitting at which she believed she heard, through the control of Rector, a message from Mary James to Henry. "He must be anxious no more for the end shall be as he desires," Rector said. Although Billy thought that Henry would not understand what the message meant, Alice felt obligated to relay it to her brother-in-law and, furthermore, to ask him if there was any message for Mary that she could bring to the next sitting. "I think it was your thought of your mother," Alice told Henry, "—I meant the intensified consciousness of her which made this communication possible. If the spirits of the departed are to reach us, 'tis we somehow who must keep the path open." Rector advised Alice to "*pray,* much and often, that we may help. . . . I believe we must pray," she concurred, "and I am trying to do it—to keep the way open to the dear and beneficent powers who are more than ready to help us."[19]

For William, messages from both his mother and Hodgson only deepened the conundrum. As he worked on his report for the SPR, he wavered between finding the evidence "*Not* convincing, to me: but baffling exceedingly," and feeling so sure of Hodgson's spiritual presence that he felt chills down his spine. One message from Hodgson, referring to a private conversation the two men once had, seemed especially persuasive.[20] At another sitting, which Alice also attended, James told Peggy that "Rector spoke of you & spoke to *her* with extraordinary discernment."[21] Although he admitted that some "residual doubt" always would trouble him, he wanted to believe that Hodgson truly had found a way to communicate to the living. "It will be sad indeed," he told Flournoy, "if this undecided verdict will be all that I can reach after so many years."[22] Collecting data and writing the Hodgson report would compete with James's other work until the spring of 1909.

Whether as a result of intense intellectual work or frustration in actually getting to that work, James suffered a bout of insomnia and restlessness so severe that in July he turned to a mind-cure practitioner for help. This time, he told his daughter, he had an unusually successful experience.[23] Freed from debilitating fatigue, he did not immediately return to his writing table, but instead took off to Keene Valley for two weeks in late August and early September, visiting one afternoon with the Goldmarks, including Pauline and the Goldmarks' sons-in-law Felix Adler and Louis Brandeis, to whom he expounded—"probably at too much length," he admitted—about Mrs. Piper.[24] James also became involved, if only peripherally, in a sexual scandal.

Maxim Gorky, Russian writer and political activist, had arrived in New York in April to the great excitement of American intellectuals and social reformers. Hailed as a hero of the Russian uprising of 1905, Gorky was portrayed as a darkly Byronic figure, young, impetuous, and passionate. A large circle of influential men and women—William Dean Howells, Mark Twain, and Jane Addams among them—arranged speaking engagements and dinners to help him raise money for the cause of freedom in Russia.

In his first days in the country, Gorky was lionized; but on April 14, the *New York World* published on its front page two shocking photographs—one, of Gorky's wife and child in Russia; the other, of Gorky and Russian actress Maria Andreyeva, the woman he had introduced to Americans as his wife. Within hours, Gorky and Andreyeva were evicted from their Manhattan hotel rooms and refused lodging anywhere else. Finally, they were invited to take refuge at the Staten Island home of John Martin, a professor, socialist, and reformer.

Some of Gorky's more worldly friends were not so much shocked as disappointed. Gorky was not playing the right role in the drama that Americans hoped to witness. They needed him to be upright, morally impeccable. Instead, he had shown himself to be naive at best, arrogant at worst. "[T]here is no considerable body of people in this country who will follow as a leader or respect as a teacher one whose teaching or whose example indicates a disregard for the sacredness of the family," proclaimed one magazine editorial.[25]

It hardly mattered that Gorky's wife had rushed a statement to America testifying that she had not been abandoned, that the two had long been separated but, according to Russian law, could not be divorced. Still, speeches, dinners, and receptions were canceled. It is no wonder that when John Martin offered Gorky and Andreyeva the use of his cabin in the Adirondacks, they were glad to accept. Away from the scandalized population of New York City, Gorky might at least have a chance to write.

When James discovered that Gorky was staying not far from Putnam Camp, he suggested to Alice that he might go to meet him, although he worried about trying to have a conversation with someone who spoke no English and little French, and someone who was harboring bitter feelings toward Americans in general. Furthermore, local gossip had it that Gorky wanted only to write and spent fourteen hours a day sequestered in his room. "I *may* get round there to morrow A.M.," William wrote to his wife, "and *possibly,* for your sake offer them our spare room. For my sake too, if I find them simpatici."[26] Apparently, James did make a call, but the interaction sparked no feeling of camaraderie. "James is a nice old chap," Gorky remarked, "but, he, too, is an American."[27]

Coincidentally with James's visit to Gorky, Alice decided to take an active role in a less public, though no less shocking, scandal. Her friend Jessie Hodder decided to sue Alfred Hodder for bigamy. Jessie needed evidence, and Alice was intent on finding some. Day after day, she sat in the stifling attic of her Irving Street home, rummaging through letters, "trying," James said, "to discover among [them] something that may serve to incriminate all the more deeply that arch-villain Hodder." James knew that Alice had been suspicious of Hodder from the beginning. "Her prophetic soul," he admitted, "got onto him much more quickly & infallibly than mine did."[28]

After the birth of a daughter in the Jameses' Florence apartment, Jessie had another child with Hodder. In 1898, Hodder sent Jessie and their two children to Switzerland, while he continued to teach at Bryn Mawr. There, he began an affair with another instructor, whom he married. Hodder's colleagues at Bryn Mawr, including the president, M. Carey Thomas, believed that Hodder and Jessie had divorced before Jessie went to live abroad, but in fact, the two had never married. Still, Jessie considered herself Hodder's common-law wife—as did Alice; and in 1906, after the death of her daughter, Jessie returned to Boston and, taking Alice's advice, initiated a suit.

Perhaps because of his wife's passion for the case, James accompanied Jessie's lawyer to see M. Carey Thomas, hoping to persuade her to testify that Jessie had been accepted as Hodder's wife among the members of the Bryn Mawr community. Although Thomas first refused to testify, eventually she came to censure Hodder for his behavior; her testimony never was needed, however: Hodder died on March 3, 1907, before the suit came to trial.

The Jameses continued to help Jessie Hodder: through them she met Elizabeth Glendower Evans, who found a job for Hodder as housemother at the Industrial School for Girls in Lancaster, Massachusetts. Through Evans, Hodder met Richard C. Cabot, the founder of medical social work, for whom she worked as a counselor to unwed mothers and other needy patients at the Massachusetts General Hospital. By 1910, Hodder was superintendent of the Massachusetts Prison and Reformatory for Women in Framingham.

The Essence of Humanism

WHEN JAMES RETURNED to Cambridge at the end of September, he set to work, finally, on a series of Lowell lectures scheduled for early November, to be repeated at Columbia University in January. Although he complained, as usual, that the lectures demanded nothing more than a popularized version of his ideas, he found himself newly inspired by this effort to write a coherent exposition about pragmatism.[29] "I didn't know, until I came to prepare them," he told Flournoy, "how full of power to found a 'school' and to become a 'cause,' the pragmatistic idea was. But now I am all aflame with it, as displacing all rationalistic systems . . . and I mean to turn the lectures into a solid little cube of a book . . . which will, I am confident, make the pragmatic method appear, to you also, as the philosophy of the future."[30]

"Pragmatism," he said, was nothing more than a new name for old ways of thinking, ways of thinking that preceded the separation of science from its origins in philosophy. This attempt to ensure the status of philosophy by drawing it closer to its scientific origins was, as Charles Peirce observed, trendy scholarship, and not unique to James. "Today," Peirce remarked, "the animating endeavor of the younger philosophers is to bring their queen within the circle of the genuine sciences."[31] Certainly James, even at the age of sixty-four, saw himself among those "younger" philosophers (he was "eternally young," Royce said enviously)[32] who argued that philosophy and science essentially rely on the same methods: "observing, comparing, classifying, tracing analogies, making hypotheses." But philosophy, for at least three hundred years, had been focused on developing "closed systems" that increasingly divorced it from the "vicious, tangled, painful" exigencies of real life. "Philosophy," James insisted, "*should* become as empirical as any science."

For James, pragmatism tempered empiricism with humanism; the observer, the thinker, the seeker after truth, was necessarily implicated in the process of inquiry and experimentation. Pragmatism, then, invested each individual with the authority to determine truths; privileged what James called "percepts" over abstract concepts; and linked philosophical decisions to moral actions.

Even as he worked on his Lowell lectures, James knew that among his colleagues in America and abroad, considerable doubt had surfaced about pragmatism as a theory of truth and as a justification of religious belief. One cause of objection was the term "pragmatism" itself, too easily confused with practicality or mere *expediency*. But when his fellow pragmatist Canning Schiller suggested the more widely accepted "humanism," James balked. That term, he believed, was too historically embedded in theological discussions and did not imply, as much as James wanted to, a focus on concrete consequences.

Still, as much as they debated about the impact of "pragmatism" versus "humanism," James and Schiller believed themselves allies in a war against intellectualism. In the last decades of James's life, Ferdinand Canning Schiller served as his most reliable and zealous supporter.

Schiller, twenty-two years younger than James, had been educated at Oxford and came to the United States in 1893 to continue studying at Cornell, where he also taught. During the Christmas holidays of 1896, he visited with James, who found him "a most peculiarly delightful fellow" whose philosophy was congruent with James's. When Schiller decided to leave Cornell in 1897, James wished that Harvard could recruit him; but no positions were vacant, and Schiller returned to Oxford, where he remained affiliated for the rest of his career.

Besides formulating a philosophy that echoed James's pragmatism, besides praising James's books and essays, Schiller was just the kind of open-minded intellectual who attracted James. "He is boyish in temperament," James wrote to Schiller's Oxford colleague Francis Herbert Bradley, who most decidedly was not, "and far too fond of puns and practical jokes (which have hurt *him* as a philosopher in the reading eye more than they have ever hurt anyone else) . . . but he is, I think, not conceited in any reprehensible sense, and his writings have been absolutely objective."[33] As James worked to clarify his own ideas on pragmatism, pluralism, and radical empiricism, Schiller served as sympathetic respondent, urging James to push forward despite criticism from his colleagues.

Schiller understood that critics were upset that their own authority as philosophers, the elite status that they conferred upon themselves, was threatened by James. By insisting that any individual, and every individual, had the authority to recognize reality and identify truth, James undermined the very profession of philosophy. "James," Schiller explained, "had carried respect for personality to the pitch of profess-ing willingness to consider whether it was not as good a clue to reality as the method of abstractions." Giving personality "metaphysical sta-tus and value," Schiller saw, "was not only a revolutionary suggestion, but one bound to gall traditional philosophy in a very sore point."[34]

Schiller also realized that besides protecting their authority as in-tellectuals, many philosophers were "*weary* of their personality, and re-sentful of its omnipresence. They long to escape from themselves, and make appeal to scientific methods to give them extraneous support and to relieve them of the burden of their being."[35] James, of course, had been raised by one such philosopher and, especially in his early de-velopment of pragmatism, influenced by another.

Santiago

SELF-DEPRECATING and at the same time egotistical, angry enough to explode in fearsome rages, Charles Peirce may have reminded James of his own father and of what he himself might have become if he had not experienced a series of personal liberations: reading Renouvier, for ex-ample, or being hired to teach at Harvard or marrying Alice.

Although Peirce had few friends, he knew he could count on James's unwavering loyalty. "All the rivalship which is likely to exist between us two, I don't think will ever touch our friendship," Peirce once wrote to James.[36] As soon as James found himself in a position to help Peirce, he did, proposing Peirce for one or another teaching posi-tion at Johns Hopkins, Harvard, Chicago. But Peirce's indiscretions, his too-public marital problems, and his arrogance led to repeated dis-missals. As Peirce's fortunes plummeted—making a "rivalship" im-possible—James tried aggressively to help. For many months, he mounted a campaign to convince the Carnegie Commission to fund Peirce's proposed *Logic,* a twelve-volume opus that Peirce considered the culmination of his life's work. When a Carnegie representative ex-pressed concern that Peirce actually would produce the text, James suggested that payments be made according to a strict contract: funds released for chapters completed. The Carnegie fund, in the end, re-jected the proposal.

Although Peirce was genuinely grateful to James—even adding Santiago (St. James) to his own name as a gesture of homage—Peirce could be an acerbic critic of James's work. He published a particularly cavilling review of the *Principles* in the *Nation;* a few years later, he circulated among philosophers in Cambridge a manuscript that called James a "slap-dash" thinker who "has but the vaguest notion of how he has come by his principles."[37] The paper seemed so scandalous to some of James's friends that Peirce took it upon himself to apologize to Alice, claiming that his "exaggerated terms" were a result only of his "hermit life" and not of his disrespect for James.[38]

As much as James acknowledged Peirce's influence on his work— he dedicated *The Will to Believe* to the friend "whose philosophical comradeship in old times and . . . whose writings in more recent years I owe more incitement and help than I can express or repay"—Peirce, in his letters to James, tried mightily to disassociate himself from James's version of pragmatism, in which scientific experimentation was linked to personality. He repeatedly contended that James and Schiller were making assertions about pragmatism with which he disagreed.[39] He chided James for being unclear and unsystematic. "I have just one lingering wish," he wrote after reading *Pragmatism.* "It is that you, if you are not too old, would try to learn to think with more exactitude."[40]

Yet even Peirce acknowledged some affinities: certainly they agreed, as Peirce put it, that "the true idealism, the pragmatistic idealism, is that reality consists in the *future*";[41] they shared a belief that pragmatism was essential for making moral political decisions. "The country is at this moment in imminent danger on which I need not expatiate," Peirce wrote to James in 1902. "In philosophy those who think themselves pragmatists, like Mr. Schiller, miss the very point of it, that one simply can't form any conception that is other than pragmatistic."[42] They agreed, too, that pragmatism was intended to wrest philosophy from an intellectual elite that both men disdained. "Pragmatism," Peirce contended, "makes or ought to make no pretension to throwing positive light on any problem. It is merely a logical maxim for laying the dust of pseudoproblems, and thus enabling us to discern what pertinent facts the phenomena may present."[43]

But James had long been more interested than Peirce in formulating both a philosophy of psychology and a psychology of philosophy. Identity influenced attention, James had insisted in the *Principles* and elsewhere, and attention generated questions; questions shaped the kind of experimentation that Peirce thought would lead to the discovery of truths. "Different minds may set out with the most antagonistic views," Peirce wrote in his seminal essay "How to Make Our Ideas Clear," "but the progress of investigation carries them by a force outside of themselves to one and the same conclusion. . . . No modification of the point of view taken, no selection of other facts for study, no natural bent of mind even, can enable a man to escape the predestinate opinion." This consensual "opinion," according to Peirce, "is what we mean by the truth, and the object represented in this opinion is the real. That is the way I would explain reality."[44]

For James, however, every experiment was complicated by the needs, desires, perceptions, past experiences, and beliefs of the experimenter. Pragmatism, as a method and "logical maxim" surely could yield truths, but not the kind of certainty that Peirce anticipated. "A thing is not truth till it is so strongly believed in that the believer is convinced that its existence does not depend on him," James wrote. "This cuts off the pragmatist from knowing what truth is."[45] As a philosophical method, pragmatism reflected and shaped the temperament of the individual investigating the qualities and dimensions of reality, and making decisions, small and momentous, in the course of daily life. When an individual asks, "Shall I commit this crime? choose that profession? accept that office, or marry this fortune?" James wrote in the *Principles,* "—his choice really lies between one of several equally possible future Characters. What he shall *become* is fixed by the conduct of this moment. . . . The problem with the man is less what act he shall now choose to do, than what being he shall now resolve to become."[46]

Peirce argued with James about his interpretation of pragmatism, and in 1903, James persuaded Charles Eliot to hire Peirce for a series of lectures in which he could present his own ideas. James had cautioned Peirce earlier, however, that unless he wanted his audience to dwindle to a handful of students, he needed to "be a good boy" and adopt a popular style.[47] Being a good boy, however, was not among Peirce's talents; "practical eccentricity and irresponsibility," James said, were his chief personality traits.[48]

Early in 1907, Peirce seemed at the nadir of his misfortunes. He was living in a Cambridge rooming house, nearly starving, depressed and suicidal. James, who apparently knew nothing of Peirce's destitute state, was shocked when he learned of the situation and rushed to rescue him. It was clear that Peirce needed money, and he set out to raise enough funds for a yearly pension of five hundred dollars. The pension would not be given directly to Peirce, James assured those he was soliciting, because "Charles is unfit to handle money, having no notion of the difference between a dollar and a hundred."[49] In the end, James managed to raise ample funds from contributors who included Alexander Graham Bell; Charles Strong, whose work Peirce had praised; and, of course, James himself.[50]

Intellectual Larking

ON TUESDAY, JANUARY 22, 1907, James taught his last class at Harvard, a section of Philosophy D (General Problems of Philosophy). His lecture room in Emerson Hall swelled with students, many of whom had enrolled in the course because they knew it was their last chance to study with him. Among those students, a few took it upon themselves to plan a celebration of their professor, and just moments before James was to end his class—and his teaching career—the "committee" marched to the front of the lecture hall bearing a silver-mounted inkwell, a gift from his graduate students and teaching assistants, and a silver loving cup from his undergraduates, past and present. Alice, who had slipped in quietly, watched from the back of the room.

For James, the "manifestation" as he put it, caught him by surprise. Harvard, he said, was "a place so little given to gush, so little given to the expression of the softer emotions," that sometimes he wondered what his students thought of him. Now, he was persuaded, at least for the moment, of "how warm-hearted the world around one is."[51]

"A professor has two functions," James wrote shortly before he retired: "1) to be learned and distribute bibliographical information 2) to communicate truth. The 1st function is the essential one, officially considered. The 2nd is the only one I care for. Hitherto I have always felt like a humbug as a professor, for I am so weak in the 1st requirement."[52]

A week after he officially retired, James resumed his second professorial function when he repeated his Lowell lectures at Columbia University. The Boston series had been a huge success: at the final talk on December 8, his audience of five hundred—"the intellectual elite of Boston," he said—gave him a thunderous ovation.[53] And at Columbia in January, he was lionized as never before. As James described his visit, New York's robust vitality seemed to reflect and heighten his new, intoxicating sense of power.

Although at first he felt overwhelmed by the city's "clangor, disorder, and permanent earthquake conditions," soon, he told Henry, he "caught the pulse of the machine, took up the rhythm, and vibrated *mit*, & found it simply magnificent." Each day he took the "space-devouring Subway," in itself a heady experience, from his rooms at the Harvard Club in midtown Manhattan to Columbia. "It is an *entirely* new N.Y., in soul as well as in body, from the old one, which looks like a village in retrospect. The courage, the heaven scaling audacity of it all, and the *lightness* withal . . . & the great pulses and bounds of progress . . . give a kind of *drumming background* of life that I never felt before."[54]

He never had felt before, either, the celebration that this visit accorded him. This time, instead of meeting only with academics and a few sad, aging relatives, he dined with luminaries from the worlds of journalism, politics, and literature, including magazine editor Norman Hapgood, his partner Robert Collier, satirist Finley Peter Dunne, and Mark Twain ("a dear little genius," James said). He hardly had a meal alone, including four dinners at the Columbia University faculty club, where he was pressed to talk about pragmatism by colleagues and former students.

Although on previous trips he often complained about feeling besieged by social demands, this time he welcomed any proof of his fame. He was so flattered, for example, when the photographer Alice Boughton, who had taken some impressive publicity portraits of Henry, asked William to sit for her, that he simply appeared at her studio one morning, impeccably dressed, top hat in hand, prepared to spend several hours.[55] When Boughton asked James if she had permission to publish the photographs or sell them to his friends, he agreed without hesitation—and only one exception: "You won't let the yellow press have it, will you?" he asked.

If the yellow press was not clamoring for his likeness, he knew that many others in New York were eager to hear and to meet him. His audience, as usual, increased from lecture to lecture, forcing moves to larger and larger halls. At the end, he was speaking to a thousand, but still, James managed to create an atmosphere at once informal and intimate. Dickinson Miller, a Columbia faculty member at the time, remembered that after one lecture, James came to the front of the platform, sat down with his feet dangling over the edge, and patiently, attentively, answered each questioner. If the trip proved anything, it was that adoration was more curative than lymph compound. "It was certainly the high tide of my existence," he told Henry, "so far as *energizing* and being 'recognized' were concerned."[56]

James's New York experience only fueled his conviction that *Pragmatism* would be his most notable contribution. "It is exceedingly untechnical," he wrote to Flournoy in March, as he corrected proofs, "and I can't help suspecting that it will make a real impression." Even Münsterberg, who had been "pooh-poohing" James's arguments, offered what James saw as a positive response. After reading a chapter on truth, Münsterberg declared that James seemed "ignorant that Kant ever wrote, Kant having already said all that I say. I regard this as a very good symptom. The third stage of opinion about a new idea, already arrived:—1st: absurd! 2nd, trivial!, 3rd WE discovered it!"[57]

After he sent off the proofs in April, while awaiting the finished copies, he explained to Henry that although the book was "a very unconventional utterance, not particularly original at any one point," he believed that, compared with other such works, it had "just that amount of squeak and shrillness in the voice that enables one book to *tell,* when others don't, to supersede its brethren, and be treated later as 'representative.' I shouldn't be surprised if 10 years hence it should be rated as 'epoch-making,' . . . I believe it to be something quite like the protestant reformation."[58] But within a few months, as readers communicated their disdain, James found himself shocked, disappointed, and frustrated.

Years before, Henry and Alice noticed that some reviewers of *The Principles of Psychology* criticized James for his "mental pirouettes and . . . his daring to go lightly amid the solemnities." As Henry put it, "they can't understand intellectual larking."[59] That intellectual larking irritated readers of *Pragmatism,* as well. The book was attacked, gently by some of James's friends, viciously by some of his adversaries.

Its apparent endorsement of relativism was one source of discomfort. Truth simply could not be whatever anyone determined that it was. James Rowland Angell, while he agreed with James that truth depended on interpretation, still argued that "what you *can* make and still have it true, is subject to limitations set by something which we may loosely call 'events.' It is this fact," he told James, "that I feel you slur. We are in other words not wholly foot-free in the interpretations which we make."[60]

James Putnam, while agreeing that pragmatism could have important value practically, believed that it unfortunately might encourage
"a too narrow conservatism of a materialistic stamp" among some
people.[61] Royce, more kindly, advised James that the fault of his book
lay more in style than substance. "Consider your own manner &
method in the 'Dilemma of Determinism' as well as in the *Varieties of
Rel. Exp.* & the rest," he told James. "It *does* seem to me that then there
was no danger of having the people regard the discussion just as some
of them now do regard the *Pragmatism*,—viz., as in large part a splendid joke,—a brilliant *reductio ad absurdum* of all attempts at serious
grappling with any philosophical issue." Surely Royce knew that the
book revealed James at his most serious, but "the externals,—the mere
setting & style of the *Pragmatism*, tend to produce on the man in the
street this impression,—an impression that those earlier papers would
not make, and that you in no sense mean these to make."[62]

James was ready to believe that if he had avoided a "free and easy
style" he would not have generated so much outrage.[63] Or perhaps if he
had simply chosen another term to name his philosophy, there would
not have been such misunderstanding. "I think the word pragmatism
has been very unlucky," he wrote to Charles Strong. "Everyone takes it
as *exclusive* of purely intellectual interests, or purely mental adaptations
of reality, making us signify that all our agreements with reality must
be of an externally and immediately utilitarian sort. You don't do this,
so I bless you."[64] But in the end, James had to admit that objections to
the book were deeper and more damning than mere reproach of inappropriate style. He could not ignore, for example, such influential critics as Arthur Lovejoy.

Lovejoy, who had been a graduate student at Harvard at the same
time as Ralph Barton Perry, never surrendered to James's spell. From
the beginning, he found James idiosyncratic, confusing, and, most
damning to Lovejoy, illogical. As Lovejoy understood the tenets of
pragmatism, James was arguing that "judgments are not known to be
true until they become true, and until they become true they have no
use . . . for their reference is to the dead past. Our intellect is condemned, according to this doctrine, to subsist wholly by a system of deferred payments; it gets no cash down; and . . . when the payments are
finally made, they are always made in outlawed currency." As a theory
of knowledge, then, pragmatism left the knower with no basis for judg-

ing "what predictions are to be accepted as sound *while they are still pre-dictions.*"[65] If James were concerned that the past—ancient ideas, as he put it—shaped and limited our judgment of present experiences, Love-joy saw no less risk in making judgments according to effects.

James complained about Lovejoy's criticisms to his friends Schiller ("I'm getting tired of being treated as ½ idiot, ½ scoundrel")[66] and Kallen (Lovejoy was "fearfully off the track in parts").[67] But Lovejoy persisted in believing James to be anti-intellectual; illogical; distracted by the concrete; "prone, in his enthusiasm for the point which he was at the moment expounding, to forget the qualifying considerations which he elsewhere plainly enough acknowledged"; and, Lovejoy added, "likely sometimes to overstate the truth immediately before his mind, especially if it seemed to him a truth that had been shabbily treated, a deserving philosophical waif that had been arrogantly turned away from the doors of all the respectable and established doctrines."[68]

James did not want to be known as the champion of philosophical waifs; nor did he want only the praise of such eccentric philosophers as Benjamin Paul Blood, who called *Pragmatism* "the fastest, the *brainiest* head-on collision with experience that I have been into."[69]

And so, as soon as he realized that *Pragmatism* would not fulfill his ambitions, he set himself to work again. "I want to write and publish, if I can do it," he wrote to Henry, "another immortal work, less popu-lar but more original than 'pragmatism' which latter no one seems rightly to understand, representing it as a philosophy got up for the use of engineers, electricians and doctors, whereas it really grew up from a more subtle and delicate theoretic analysis of the function of knowing, than previous philosophers had been willing to make. I know," he added hopefully, "that it will end by winning its way & triumphing!"[70]

Chapter 19

THE PITCH OF LIFE

1908–1909

AS MUCH AS JAMES insisted that he wanted to do nothing else but write something "ultra dry in form, impersonal and exact," he succumbed to yet another distraction by agreeing to deliver the Hibbert lectures at Manchester College, Oxford, in the spring of 1908. The invitation, he said, was too important to turn down, especially since it meant that he would add another honorary degree to his collection. Although he knew that his audience would be largely academics, he complained that these talks, like the Lowell lectures, forced him "to relapse into the 'popular lecture' form just as I thought I had done with it forever." Once again, he would have to revert to a "free and easy & personal way of writing . . . [that] has made me an object of loathing to many respectable academic minds, and," he confessed, "I am rather tired of awakening that feeling."[1]

Nevertheless, he plunged into writing the lectures with his customary zeal, generating his customary anxiety: an "infernal nervous condition," accompanied by insomnia, resulted by late March. This time, however, instead of visiting a mind-cure practitioner, James put himself into the hands of one Dr. James Taylor, a homeopathic physician who successfully had treated both his sister-in-law Mary and the family's dentist. On the strength of their testimony, James committed himself to daily visits and followed Taylor's orders to limit his social engagements.[2]

Taylor faced an enormous challenge in treating his new patient: James suffered not only from nervous exhaustion, but had been weakened by illness during the course of the winter: colds, dyspepsia, and a long bout with influenza left him feeling "seedy" and prone to attacks of vertigo. Nevertheless, by mid-April, James managed to complete six of his eight lectures (he attributed his progress to Taylor's treatments), admitted that "they've panned out good, so far," and deemed himself "in good fighting trim" to take on the "wretched clerical defenders" of the Absolute who would comprise his Oxford audience.[3] On April 21, he and Alice sailed for England on the *Ivernia*.

James knew that pragmatism was being discussed vigorously at Oxford, but he also recognized among Oxford empiricists a "steep and brittle attitude" of "monastic dogmatism" that he deplored; he had little hope that his listeners would be sympathetic to radical empiricism. "If Oxford men could be ignorant of anything," he told them, "it might almost seem that they had remained ignorant of the great empirical movement towards a pluralistic panpsychic view of the universe, into which our own generation has been drawn."[4] He took it upon himself to persuade them of this new development.

As he would continue to do for the rest of his life, James made a passionate case against intellectualism and rationalism. "Reality, life, experience, concreteness, immediacy, use what word you will," he told his listeners, "exceeds our logic, overflows and surrounds it. . . . I prefer bluntly to call reality if not irrational then at least non-rational in its constitution,—and by reality here I mean where things *happen*."[5] Forcing nonrational reality into an intellectual frame corrupts the essence of experience; defining experience according to concepts precludes one's sense of intimacy with the world. "[T]o understand life by concepts," James said, "is to arrest its movement, cutting it up into bits as if with scissors, and immobilizing these in our logical herbarium where, comparing them as dried specimens, we can ascertain which of them statically includes or excludes which other."[6]

Surprised at the "sweepingly impressionist glance" of James's perspective, Oxonians nevertheless overflowed the library in which he delivered his first lecture: three hundred seats filled immediately, with about a hundred more listeners perched on bookcases and pressed against the walls. Many were turned away at the door, disappointed. So many people complained of the crowds, the heat, and, not least, the odor, that Manchester College decided to move the talks to a larger, airier hall. An even larger audience came to James's next presentations.

Despite the audience's apparent interest, however, James found Oxford philosophers curiously reticent to debate his ideas. Part of their reluctance seems to have come from their awe of the famous American pragmatist. John Jay Chapman, who attended one of James's talks, noticed "the reverence which that very un-revering class of men—the University dons—evinced towards James, largely on account of his appearance and personality."[7] While James was gratified by rumors of admiration overheard by Alice, he felt disappointed by the lack of direct response. "Philosophical work seems to me to go on in silence and in print exclusively," he complained to Flournoy.[8]

Like all of James's previous trips to England, this one was filled with social engagements, including reunions with Americans abroad. After spending a few days with the Putnams in early May, James was surprised to meet Richard and Ella Cabot, "he one of the most original minds & characters in Boston," he told Henry, "and very *good,* altho' he hates my philosophy. He is putting a new moral tone into the whole medical professional life of Boston."[9] For many years part of James's circle, Cabot was a physician influential in curriculum changes at Harvard Medical School—he introduced the case system for medical students at Massachusetts General Hospital—and was the founder of medical social work. He may not have hated James's philosophy, but surely he deemed religion "the one place in the world where a man can be certain" and challenged James to disprove religious doctrines. James, however, would not take up the challenge. "So far from its being my duty to prove that religious doctrines can be doubted," he wrote to Cabot, "it seems to me it is your duty to show that any one of them may not."[10]

After the lectures were over, the Jameses spent the rest of the spring in England. The same man who had spent the winter and spring lamenting his poor health and savoring every moment of productivity now set on a course of vigorous travel and social engagements. His only respites were at Rye, with Henry; but these interludes were few, as James, Alice, and one or another of their children cavorted across England and the Continent. There was too much to do, and, James feared, too little time.

While Alice visited friends in Harrow, James stopped to see Sir Oliver Lodge, a British physicist and member of the SPR, with whom he stayed up until midnight discussing pragmatism. Early in June, he and Alice spent a few days at Newington, the grand country house of Ethel Sands, an American painter whose reputation derived more from her parties than her contributions to art. Besides the Jameses, Sands's guests included Roger Fry; Ottoline Morrell and her husband, the MP Philip Morrell; and James's old friend Logan Pearsall Smith. Smith brought him to visit Bernard Berenson and his wife. Mary Berenson engaged James in a conversation about his philosophy, but came away feeling unsatisfied. "I could not find that he had any real foundation for his beliefs," she said, "and he certainly had no God to offer me that I could depend on."[11]

The long weekend at Newington, James wrote, was "the climax of our visit, and the family relation, so to speak, with so many good people . . . have meant a real enlargement of our moral horizon."[12] Although James was used to socializing with literary luminaries and Boston Brahmins, British aristocracy—"high bred and well bred," as he put it—inspired a new level of adulation.[13] He and Alice were especially admiring of Lady Ottoline Morrell. "She looks like a Flemish saint of ages ago," Alice wrote to Billy, "and she and Loving Dad are sworn friends."[14] At the end of June, when James learned that Henry might be a guest at Newington House, he urged his brother to go, suggesting that "it would be a very educative thing" if he could bring Peggy along.[15]

From Newington, some eight miles north of London, they went on to the Cotswold town of Bibury and toured York Cathedral before stopping for a few days in Durham, where James was awarded another honorary degree. Their next destination was the Lake District, where the Jameses spent only a few days together before Alice went back to London to meet the newly arrived Peggy.

The Lake District put James in a sentimental and nostalgic mood, in part because the landscape reminded him of his beloved Keene Valley: "Mountains and valleys compressed together as in the Adirondacks, great reaches of pink and green hillsides and lovely lakes, the higher parts quite fully Alpine in character but for the fact that no snow mountains form the distant background."[16] But James's sudden longing for the past, for youth, for a sense of vigor that he knew was lost to him forever was inspired also by letters he was receiving from Pauline Goldmark, herself traveling through Europe, just then on her way from Greece to Italy. "How I wish I might have been with you there for 24 hours!" he exclaimed; but he was tired, he confessed, "tired as I have seldom been. . . . I've grown fearfully old in the past year," he told her, "except 'philosophically,' where I still keep young, but I can't keep pace with your strong young life at all any more, and you do well to drop me out of your calculations." But Pauline never thought of ignoring him. When he arrived at the Ullswater Hotel in Patterdale, he found her letter waiting for him.

For a few days in early July, with Alice still away, James wrote to Pauline every morning, offering her reflections about Britons, reminiscences of his own travels in Italy, advice about places she should not fail to see, and luminous descriptions of the countryside—Keswick, Grasmere, Ambleside—through which he had been motoring with a couple he and Alice had met in Durham. He wished Pauline could be in England to share the experiences with him. Writing to her, he said, "makes me feel temporarily quite young again,—not more than 34 years old, or 34 and a half." And it made him realize how much he missed her. "Ah Pauline, Pauline," he sighed as he ended one letter. "God bless you! Your W. J."[17]

Being older—and being famous—had its compensations: James was lionized by those he admired. One afternoon, H. G. Wells arrived at Henry's home in Rye to take James and Peggy to his own home, Sandgate, where, James said, they had "delicious talks." After reading *The Future in America, In the Days of the Comet,* and Wells's frequent contributions to American magazines, James called the young writer "one of the few most original literary forces of our time," and nothing less than a real pragmatist.[18] "With you and Chesterton and Bernard Shaw," James told Wells, "no one can now accuse this age of lack of genius."

James had a chance to meet the second genius on his list when he and Wells happened to bump into G. K. Chesterton. Happily for James, Chesterton invited him to tea; and a few days later, after Alice and Peggy had left for Geneva, he returned to spend an evening with Chesterton and Hilaire Belloc, drinking port until midnight, and discussing, among other topics, military history.[19] Fortunately, the conversation did not turn to philosophy. Chesterton was an admirer of James, but not of pragmatism. "It was his glory that he popularised philosophy," Chesterton said of James. "It was his destruction that he popularised his own philosophy." As Chesterton understood it, pragmatism "substantially means that the sun being useful is the same thing as the sun being there," a notion that Chesterton dismissed as "bosh."[20] But James, unaware of Chesterton's disdain, was pleased to think they shared an intellectual kinship.

Before leaving England to join Alice and Peggy in Brussels, James spent an afternoon, finally, with Pauline Goldmark, just arrived in London, who lunched with him and accompanied him to an art exhibition. The next day, he boarded a boat for Ostend, the first stop in the bustling itinerary that the family had planned for the next weeks. Antwerp, Rotterdam, Delft, The Hague, Ghent, Amsterdam, Bruges: in each city, the Jameses visited churches, museums, historic sites, galleries—besides doing the obligatory shopping. In September, after a few days in Paris so that Alice and Peggy could buy hats, they were back in England, Alice and Peggy to Rye; William to London, where he met Aleck, who was about to begin his tutorial in Oxford, and then to Rye, but not for long.

He returned to Oxford for more talks with Schiller, visited splendid Newington House once again, and just before he left for home, had a warm and fruitful meeting with Henri Bergson, with whom he felt a great intellectual sympathy. James thought Bergson "a marvel . . . and a very easy talker . . . but very shy and timid I think, with bad nerves and habitual fear of their playing him tricks. Like *me,* du reste!"[21] Finally, on October 6, the Jameses boarded the *Saxonia* for home. They arrived on October 16; next morning, with only one night's sleep to refresh him, James took the train to Silver Lake, New Hampshire, to partake of the "sweetness" of the New England fall.

Talking Cures

THE PROGRESS TOWARD health that James had made in the spring eroded during his frenetic European stay. By the time he returned in the fall, he was exhausted, suffering from chest pains and dizziness. He decided, once again, to seek help from Taylor, who, James believed, was worth the high fee of three dollars a visit. "It requires frightful patience, trust, and moneybags," he remarked. This time, however, improvement was so slow that his patience wore out.[22] After ten weeks of daily treatment, he told Taylor that his symptoms had not abated, and he gave the doctor an ultimatum: four more weeks, and if there was no change, James would leave.

Taylor, unintimidated, offered reassurance: there soon would be discernible improvement, he said, if James continued to follow his many prescriptions for health. "His treatment," James reported, "consists in 8 minutes of 'vibration' along the spine, in 6 minutes of 'high frequency' electricity, in 12 daily inhalations of a certain vapor, and in homoeopathic pellets 6 times a day." Although James was a dutiful patient, he was also dubious: "I have no reason whatever to think that these things exert any effect beyond that of making me feel that something is being done and I'm in for it."

It is clear from James's testimony that Taylor's power over him derived more from the strength of his personality than from pellets and vapors. "He's a poor talker," James told Henry, "and a relatively uneducated man, but he has extraordinarily shrewd perceptions, and a marvellous insight into the dynamics of the human machine." Dr. Taylor's real talent, it seemed, lay in a kind of commonsensical psychotherapy. Despite his seeming to be a "poor talker," he managed to convince James that he needed to reform his behavior radically: "What tells in the long run, he says, is the 'pitch' at which a man lives. . . ." It came as no surprise to James that his own "pitch" was "unnecessarily high." He summarized what he had learned about himself for his brother's edification:

> Suffice it to say that I have been racing too much, kept in a state of inner tension, anticipated the environment, braced myself to meet and resist it ere it was due . . . left the present act inattentively done because I am preoccupied with the next act, failed to listen, etc, because I was too eager to speak, kept *up,* when I ought to have kept *down,* been jerky, angular, rapid, precipitate, let my mind run ahead of my body, etc, etc., and impaired my efficiency, as well as flushed my head, and made my tissues fibrous, in consequence.

Taylor's diagnosis seemed absolutely sensible, and James knew that he would have to relax considerably if he wanted to succeed in any "remodelling" of his clogged arteries and weak heart. But he claimed that he was willing to try. Taylor, he said, "has at last got his suggestive hook into my gills, and aroused my confidence, and it will be interesting to see what comes."[23]

James's faith in unconventional mind-cure strategies did not extend to the special talking cure associated with Sigmund Freud. Among James's circle, many, including James, believed that Freud inappropriately emphasized the relationship between sexuality and mental pathology. James Jackson Putnam, on the other hand, saw in

Freud's ideas significant therapeutic potential. Where early in his career Putnam had subscribed largely to electrotherapeutics—that is, the administering of low doses of electricity as a massage of stimulation to parts of the body—by the 1890s he was trying hypnosis and his own version of the talking cure with considerable success.

Yet even Putnam, as interested as he was in Freud, preferred to use "the Freud method," as he called it, not to dredge up repressed feelings, but to substitute new ideas and new associations for the obsessive or "morbid" ideas that patients found so debilitating. While he admitted that insight into a patient's behavior depended on knowledge of a patient's history, he believed that specific past experiences need not be specifically exorcised.

Putnam—and James—feared that Freud's method of psychoanalysis would lead to the patient's dependency on the authoritative physician, a dependency that surely would impede the autonomy that any individual needed for a healthy mental life. Far better in the long run, they thought, were strategies that taught self-control and raised a patient's self-esteem.

In September 1909, James had a chance finally to meet Freud at a special convocation to celebrate the twentieth anniversary of Clark University. Freud was one among many important social scientists attending, including anthropologist Franz Boas, Swiss-born psychiatrist Adolf Meyer ("A splendid character!" James exclaimed) and Carl Jung.[24] James was favorably impressed with Jung, but less admiring of the fifty-three-year-old Freud, who lectured on dreams, a talk that James found troubling because of its sexual references. Freud, he said, seemed to him "a man obsessed by fixed ideas. I make nothing in my own case with his dream theories, and obviously 'symbolism' is a most dangerous method." Moreover, James was offended that Freud dismissed "American religious therapy"—that is, mind-cure therapy—as " 'dangerous' because so 'unscientific.' " James invited Freud's continuing contribution to the dialogue about mental pathology in the interest of clarity as much as for revolutionary insight. "I hope that Freud and his pupils will push their ideas to their utmost limits," he remarked to Flournoy, "so that we may learn what they are."[25]

James's second, and more direct, encounter occurred when Freud accompanied him to the Worcester train depot on the evening that James left the convocation. Throughout the summer James had suffered, he said, from "violent pre-cardial pain whenever I exert myself strongly or rapidly, or whenever I get into any mental hesitation, trepidation, or flurry."[26] Nevertheless, he decided to walk the mile and a half, carrying his overnight case. The exertion, perhaps coupled with his anxiety at talking with Freud, resulted in an attack of angina so severe that he had to stop, most likely to take a dose of nitroglycerin. He asked Freud to hold his suitcase and to walk on ahead, saying that he would catch up when the pain abated. Trying to hide his symptoms—symptoms that hardly would have alarmed another physician—is, of course, consistent with James's determination to present a hale and hearty public self. Freud interpreted James's behavior as reflecting courage, rather than fear, shame, or regret.[27]

Endowing Insanity

JAMES'S RETICENCE to embrace Freud's ideas contrasted with his exuberant support of many others working in the field of mental health. In 1905, thirty-year-old Clifford Beers, who had spent several years in mental hospitals suffering from manic depression, began a chronicle detailing his illness and the often inadequate and inhumane treatment he received. For Beers, the book was no mere confessional: he aimed not only to bear witness to the plight of the mentally ill, but to mount an aggressive campaign for the reform of mental institutions. At a time when popular magazines trumpeted "the literature of exposure" written by outspoken muckrakers, Beers knew that a document such as his had the potential to effect enormous change if it were taken up by influential readers.

Family and friends thought that Beers's illness was best kept private, but Beers was undeterred. Early in June 1906, he sent part of his manuscript to James, who decided immediately that it was worth publishing. "It is the best written out 'case' that I have seen," he replied to Beers, encouraging him to complete the manuscript. "[Y]ou have no doubt put your finger on the weak spots of our treatment of the insane, and suggested the right line of remedy. I have long thought that if I were a millionaire, with money to leave for public purposes, I should endow 'Insanity' exclusively."[28]

James looked forward to a time when mental illness would be more widely and publicly understood, and, he hoped, prevented. Throughout his career, he found visiting mental institutions a shattering experience. The portals of the mental hospital at Ward's Island, he said after visiting there in the 1890s, should have inscribed above them Dante's warning at the entrance to Purgatory, "Forsake all hope, ye who enter here." And Ward's Island was one among many. "Nowhere," he told Beers, "is there massed together as much suffering as in the asylums. Nowhere is there so much sodden routine, and fatalistic insensibility in those who have to treat it."[29]

James's interest in mental-health reform went beyond professional concerns. Certainly there were times in his life when he feared that he himself might end up, cowering and forgotten, in a mental asylum. In his searches to find a suitable place for his brother Bob, he visited local facilities that, with few exceptions, were shockingly degrading. Reform, he told Beers, was crucial.

From 1906, therefore, when he first read Beers's draft, James worked in whatever way he could to publicize and strengthen his new friend's efforts. His endorsement of the book helped to get it published, and Beers took his advice in negotiating his first book contract. A Mind That Found Itself appeared from Longmans, Green in 1908, prefaced by a laudatory letter from James to Beers. James accepted a post as honorary trustee for Beers's pioneering Connecticut Society for Mental Hygiene, and he contributed the magnanimous sum of one thousand dollars to Beers's organization. In addition, James actively solicited friends and colleagues (Francis Peabody and Charles Eliot, for example) for Beers's board of advisers and lent his name to Beers's solicitations, even agreeing to "attack" John D. Rockefeller for a contribution.[30]

While James usually offered unqualified encouragement, leaving the details of the project to Beers, on one issue he stood firmly against him: the naming of the first state reform organization. Beers voted for the term "mental hygiene," as part of the name, but James objected. "It doesn't *bite*," he complained. "It suggests diffuseness, 'new thought,' etc." He preferred the simple "insanity." " 'Insanity' arrests attention; and it's what we're after. If we do abolish insanity (!!) we can change our title, but much water will flow before then."[31] Beers, however, saw the advantage to the less stinging "mental hygiene" and overrode James's objections.

As Beers tirelessly pursued his work, generating publicity and excitement throughout the reform communities of the Northeast, James was writing the books he believed would be his last. The contrast between what Beers was achieving and what James was not elicited a sad reflection: "I inhabit such a realm of abstractions," he wrote to Beers, "that I only get credit for what I do in that spectral empire; but you are not only a moral idealist and philanthropic enthusiast, (and good fellow!) but a *tip-top man of business* in addition. . . . Your name will loom big hereafter, for your movement must prosper, but mine will not survive unless some other effort of mine saves it."[32] While Beers was effecting a "momentous practical matter," James wrote, it seemed possible that his own reputation would pale in comparison, that he himself would be remembered only as "a mere metaphysician and sponsor of cranks."[33]

Dramatic Probabilities

JAMES'S FEAR OF being denounced as a crank, however, failed to divert his engagement in psychical research. In early December 1908, James attended several séances at which a table, encircled by a brass rail, exhibited some strange movements. It seems that the brass rail slid around from no physical cause, first when the sitters' hands or wrists were in place upon it, and then by itself. One sitter went so far as to put a piece of chewing gum on the rail to follow its movements. James concluded that "no room for fakery seemed possible" and hoped that "this is the crack in the levee of scientific routing through wh. the whole Mississippi of supernaturalism may pour in."[34]

The levee seemed ready to shatter at the end of September 1909. Shortly after returning from the Clark convocation, James learned that the notorious Eusapia Palladino, a fifty-five-year-old Italian medium, was being brought to America to be investigated by Hereward Carrington for the Society for Psychical Research. Palladino long had been the subject of controversy among psychical researchers. The Sidgwicks, Myers, and Hodgson deemed her a fraud, but Flournoy, who attended her séances in Paris, came away believing that she could create phenomena "inexplicable by any known laws of physics or physiology."[35]

By the time she arrived in America, Palladino's reputation had preceded her. Where Leonora Piper earned credibility because she was a quiet, conventional housewife, Eusapia Palladino was portrayed as a Neapolitan peasant, an opportunist, and, by some, a hysteric. Because she was a physical medium, moving tables and causing guitar strings to vibrate, investigators monitored her movements by holding her hands and ankles, or sitting with her feet on theirs. Investigating Palladino became a salacious attraction, and reports of her trance states read like pages from lurid fiction. One investigator noted her "truly feminine languor" and the "strange and feeling passion" in her trembling voice when calling for a spirit to appear. Carrington himself described her flushed face, "demoniacal look" and "brilliant and languid" eyes as manifestations "of the erotic ecstasy."

> She says "*mio caro*" ("my dear"), leans her head upon the shoulder of her neighbor, and courts caresses when she believes that he is sympathetic. It is at this point that phenomena are produced, the success of which causes her agreeable and even voluptuous thrills. During this time her legs and her arms are in a state of marked tension, almost rigid, or even undergo convulsive contractions. Sometimes a tremor goes through her entire body.[36]

Not surprisingly, Palladino became a sought-after subject for investigation. Despite her doubtful reputation, James was not alone in hoping that Palladino might yield verifiable psychical phenomena. Her situation, he said, reminded him of the torrid controversy that ensued after the publication of Darwin's *Origin of Species,* and he recalled the advice of his teacher, Jeffries Wyman. When a theory "gets propounded over and over again," Wyman told him, "coming up afresh after each time orthodox criticism has buried it, and each time seeming solider and harder to abolish, you may be sure that there is truth in it."[37] Palladino, after each alleged exposure, nevertheless continued to be hailed by some as a genuine psychic.

Eager to gather witnesses to Palladino's talents, James dared Hugo Münsterberg to attend some of her séances by publicly denouncing his rejection of psychical research as "shallow dogmatism." "My natural instinct, of course, would be not to touch that whole affair," Münsterberg wrote, responding to an invitation from Carrington, but James's attack provoked him.

As was customary for physical mediums, Palladino performed in a cabinet, darkened by heavy black curtains, containing a lightweight table around which the sitters assembled. For the purposes of the inquiry, electric burglar alarms had been placed at all windows, and the sitters on either side of Palladino held her hands and knees. Her feet were placed on the foot of each of her two neighbors. At each sitting, Palladino called for the spirit "John" to materialize and make contact with the sitters, at which time the table would levitate. This event occurred at the first séance without incident; at the second séance, however, just as "John" appeared, Palladino let out a chilling scream: one of the investigators, stretched out on the floor beneath the table, had grabbed Palladino's left foot, apparently as she was trying to lift the table with it. Only the shoe, Münsterberg reported, remained on top of his own foot.

Palladino's footwork created the scandal for which Münsterberg had hoped; James, predictably, was irritated and disappointed. Her occasional cheating, he thought, was no reason to reject the possibility of her authenticity. After all, he himself, assisting once in a scientific demonstration, "cheated" to make sure the demonstration succeeded in presenting a phenomenon that he knew to be true. Still, James realized at last that associating with the slippery Palladino would make him appear foolish, and he advised Carrington to withdraw as well. "Her methods are too detestable for nomenclature!" he told Carrington, suggesting that he "pass to more deserving subjects," such as a new Polish medium about whom he had recently heard interesting testimony.

For his own part, James produced several articles testifying to his career in psychical research, including a long and detailed report about Hodgson's control of Piper and his autobiographical essay, "The Confidences of a 'Psychical Researcher.'"

He was frustrated, he admitted, that after twenty years as a psychical researcher, he had not yet succeeded in adequately verifying spiritual phenomena. "[A]t times," he said, "I have been tempted to believe that the creator has eternally intended this department of nature to remain *baffling*." Except for those rare moments of doubt, however, he felt certain of the "dramatic probabilities of nature"; certain that there existed a vast, hidden, and unsettling layer of human experience that would, and must, yield its secrets to persistent researchers. "There is a hazy penumbra in us all," he wrote, "where lying and delusion meet, where passion rules beliefs as well as conduct, and where the term 'scoundrel' does not clear up everything to the depths as it did for our forefathers." He had made a contribution at the very beginnings of psychical research; now, his goals must be pursued by investigators as daring as he. After all, he asked, "when was not the science of the future stirred to its conquering activities by the little rebellious exceptions to the science of the present?"[38]

Heart's Desires

NONE OF JAMES'S children emulated his professional work, none followed him into science, philosophy, or any other corner of academia. But two sons picked up the trajectory of his career at a critical turning point: the point at which he gave up art and settled into science. Both sons made the opposite decision—Billy giving up medicine, Aleck giving up a traditional undergraduate education—to become painters. James encouraged, even applauded, their choice.

"If Aleck would only develope the passion for painting that animates Bill, it would be too good to be true, almost," William commented to Alice after Aleck was settled into the home of his Oxford tutor.[39] By the next spring, his wish seemed likely to be fulfilled. Aleck, discouraged with his progress, decided that he wanted to give up college entirely to follow "his heart's desire" and study painting. William's response was far different from his own father's when, at the same age as Aleck, he declared art to be his vocation. Immediately, he cabled Aleck to return home.

After Aleck arrived in Cambridge, however, he wavered, not quite sure about dropping his college plans. While James investigated special student status at Harvard, Aleck began a tutorial—at a cost of five hundred dollars for two months—to prepare for his entrance examinations. "I'm sick of the whole business of 'literary' education," William complained, tired especially of the exorbitant cost of tuition. "How little *we* had of it, yet how well we've done!"[40]

As it turned out, all the literary education that James could buy did not help Aleck. By early July, it was clear that he would fail most of the entrance examinations and could not join the Harvard class of 1913. Instead, he went to Dublin, New Hampshire, to visit Albert Thayer, an artist friend and returned, William said happily, firmly "desirous of being a painter."[41]

James's support of Billy's and Aleck's decision to become artists appears motivated more from his feeling of identification with these two sons than from an objective assessment of their artistic talents. Much later, Harry commented that Aleck "temperamentally . . . was more like Dad than any of us"; certainly he was more like his father than Harry, whose law career James spoke about with a tone of distant admiration, but little sense of connection.[42] Billy and Aleck, on the other hand, allowed James to experience vicariously the artistic career that he had rejected—a decision that he sometimes appeared to regret.

Similarly, Alice hoped that Peggy would achieve her own unfulfilled goals. When her daughter was thirteen, Alice recalled her excitement at hearing George Herbert Palmer lecture at the Harvard Annex shortly after her marriage. "I have never forgotten it," Alice told Elizabeth Evans. "How I longed to join that very class, and how I wish now that I had had the course! We generally rue the day when courage gives out. It seemed to me then that I had no right to take the time for anything so delightful. But Peggy shall do all the good things—and better than I."[43] But by 1909, Peggy's future seemed precarious. Although she had completed two years at Bryn Mawr, periodic nervous collapses—"Peggy has a crisis," James once noted in his diary—worried her parents enough to persuade her to withdraw.[44] "Her nervous delicacy is such that she has to live very *voluntarily,* wh. is expensive," James said, "but she *succeeds,* and will, I trust, grow solider as the years advance."[45] According to James, Peggy had to practice healthful living: going to bed by nine, resting for an hour a day, and avoiding strenuous sports.[46] Otherwise, he cautioned, she might become a nervous invalid, like the aunt she never met, but whose fate Peggy knew. Of course, there was also her father.

Pot Boiler

BY THE SPRING of 1909, James's cardiac symptoms had returned, and he became "[t]ormented by desire to go to Nauheim."[47] The usually reliable Hawley Lymph Compound provided no improvement, and by fall he had descended to "a state of nervous prostration like that which I fell into after Nauheim 10 years ago."[48] One physician prescribed laxatives, but they only made the symptoms worse.

It is no surprise that James's collapse coincided with the publication of his Hibbert lectures and the hostile reaction the book received. James tried to convince himself that the criticism really indicated the significance of his work. "It is already evident from the letters I am getting about the 'Pluralistic Universe,'" he informed Flournoy, "that the book will 1), be *read;* 2), be *rejected* almost unanimously at first, and for very diverse reasons; but 3), will continue to be bought and referred to, and will end by strongly influencing english philosophy."[49]

Henry understood immediately that his brother needed praise and more praise. "It may sustain & inspire you a little to know that I'm *with* you, all along the line—& can conceive of no sense in any philosophy that is not yours!" he told William. "As an artist & a 'creator' I can catch on, hold on, to pragmatism, & can work in the light of it & apply it."[50]

Not for the first time, Henry confessed his affinity for his brother's philosophical writings, but William, no doubt, was continually surprised that his philosophy inspired prose that he once described as "interminable elaboration of suggestive reference." Throughout Henry's career, William proved an intractable reader, always urging his brother toward clarity and directness, while Henry protested against William's taste in literature and bristled at his advice. After reading The *Golden Bowl,* William urged Henry "just to please Brother, [to] sit down and write a new book, with no twilight or mustiness in the plot, with great vigor and decisiveness in the action, no fencing in the dialogue, no psychological commentaries, and absolute straightness in the style."[51] But Henry retorted that he would rather "descend to a dishonoured grave" than to write anything that William found stylistically admirable.

"I hear of your reading anything of mine, & always hope you won't," he wrote to William, after receiving the criticism of *The Golden Bowl,* "— you seem to me so constitutionally unable to 'enjoy' it, & so condemned to look at it from a point of view remotely alien to mine in writing it." He begged William to read his works with more generosity, if he would read them at all. "I can read *you* with rapture," Henry insisted, and asked William to send him whatever he published.[52]

As much as they differed in their literary tastes, William still had more in common with Henry, intellectually, than he had with his brother Bob, who followed William's career with a cold eye, and who saw himself in fierce competition with William over their ability to understand their father's ideas. "I picture to myself dear Old father & mother & Alice and Wilkie. I know all the truth you and Harry and I had in boyhood came swift from God through the generous sweet and trusting love of these departed ones," Bob wrote to William. "That *truth,* always has been & always will be. Nothing that culture or reason can give will ever make it better or worse. Burn your false books," he advised.

Like his father, Bob claimed that Truth, Knowledge, and Goodness emanated directly from God through the seeker; philosophizing
never would offer William an epiphany. If William would only recall
his childhood in Boulogne or London or Geneva, he would be able to
recapture "the truth of Trust" that illuminated the glowing memory.
"For Gods sake stop your research for Truth (pragmatic or otherwise),"
Bob wrote to William, "and try and enjoy life." Bob, by this time, had
come to an unusually peaceful stage in his own life. He had become a
painter, spending his afternoons with his oils and easel in the woods
around Walden Pond. "Please," he added in a postscript, "don't think
it necessary to answer this. I am too busy painting pictures . . . to notice you."[53]

His brothers, of course, were not the readers to whom James addressed his writing, and if he appreciated Henry's moral support, still
he wanted praise from other quarters. That praise, however, did not
come after the publication of *A Pluralistic Universe.* Nor did it come the
following September, when James published a sequel to his maligned
Pragmatism. He hoped that *The Meaning of Truth* would "keep the pot
of public interest in the subject boiling."[54]

Perhaps the pot was boiling, but James felt scorched by some critics, notably his former student Dickinson Miller; the young American
philosopher Boyd Henry Bode, who aired his objections to James in
the *Journal of Philosophy;* and the brilliant, thirty-six-year-old British
philosopher Bertrand Russell, who had met James during a visit to
America in 1896, and whose *Principles of Mathematics,* when it appeared
in 1902, established him as a logician of formidable stature.

Because James thought that he and Russell shared philosophical
interests—Russell claimed to be a pluralist, opposed to the Absolute—
he was especially frustrated that Russell so adamantly misunderstood
his ideas. Russell was disturbed, for example, that pragmatism encouraged religious belief by allowing for the existence of an Absolute
merely because "useful consequences" derive from that belief. "With
regard to religion," Russell told James, "I notice one purely temperamental difference: that the first demand you make of your God is that
you should be able to love him, whereas my first demand is that I
should be able to worship him. I do not desire familiarity lest it should
breed contempt."[55]

Russell's most extensive criticisms, however, were focused on James's definition of truth. Like many other critics, Russell took James to assert that whatever was useful was true, leaving James to insist, repeatedly, that utility was not crucial to knowing truth. To Russell's conclusion that "pragmatists are almost wholly directed to proving that utility is a *criterion*" and therefore "that utility is the *meaning* of truth," James asked simply: "who? Surely not W. J.!"[56]

Russell, he said, was misreading him. "In my own treatment of the God problem, I simply illustrated the fact that men do (and always will) use moral satisfactoriness as an ingredient in the truth of a belief."[57] But Russell, and other readers, understood "moral satisfactoriness" to mean personal predilection: anything useful to justify one's thoughts or actions, therefore, might as well be true. Not so, James argued: "'the true' means not 'the useful' but 'the useful in the [w]ay of [l]eading to [a] reality.' Many beliefs are useful in *that* sense, only when the realities are useful also."[58] Russell, he added, was not seeing the essential duality "between *fact* (or *reality*) and our beliefs about it. . . . The reality has a 'sphere of influence,' and so has the belief. If the two spheres don't touch, I ask 'what then is the belief's truth *made* of?' If they do touch, a verification-process becomes possible. . . . A fish that avoids the hook has a 'truer' sense of it than one who makes straight at it & swallows it. *The mere existence* of the hook does n't unambiguously and adequately determine what shall count as true about it."[59] Still, as much as he wanted to dismiss Russell's objections to his work, he believed that Russell, along with his other critics, might help him to clarify the ideas that he never, to his own satisfaction, managed to convey adequately. "Russell's def'n. of truth may not only be an enormous *summarizer*," he noted. "May it be a specific sort of inspirer?"[60]

Chapter 20

ECLIPSE

1910

"BIG PREPARATIONS for banquet," James noted in his diary on January 18, a week after his sixty-eighth birthday. In their Irving Street home, the family was preparing to host a dinner celebrating the presentation of Bay Emmet's portrait of James to the university. Peggy decorated and set the tables, Alice supervised the cook, and Billy roasted a goose he had shot in New Brunswick, which supplemented an ovenful of chickens. Predictably, the excitement caused James to have an attack of angina.

More than any other occasion, this dinner, attended by twenty-two of James's eminent colleagues and close friends, marked the end of his Harvard career. If it was a moment of celebration, it moved James to question, not for the first time, how he would be remembered by the academic community, by his philosophical heirs, by his friends, by us. He himself had delivered enough eulogies to know that the memory left by any man, however intellectually robust he may have been, undergoes an inevitable "diminution and abridgment."[1] That diminution, he thought, already had occurred in the very portrait that his friends had gathered to extol.

Illuminated by the glow of candlelight, sitting around his own table, his guests—Charles William Eliot, A. Lawrence Lowell, Henry Higginson, George Dorr, the Reverend George Gordon, and the senior members of the philosophy department, among them—praised Bay Emmet's rendering of a professorial James, standing before a wall of books: kindly, wise, and benign. The portrait, James thought, was not quite good enough: "surely good in all that it gets of you," Josiah

Royce remarked, "—especially the eyes, brow, pose, and pleasing impression." But Royce, like James, had hoped for more. "I see in you more Titanic features, *beside* those that the portrait gets."[2]

But if he were to be remembered as a philosophical titan, James knew, it would not be from affectionate portraits. In whatever time he had left, he needed to write, to explicate, to shape his legacy.

"FOR THIRTY-FIVE years," James wrote to Schiller after he retired, "I have been suffering from the exigencies of being [a professor], the pretension and the duty, namely, of meeting the mental needs and difficulties of other persons, needs that I could n't possibly imagine and difficulties that I could n't possibly understand; and now that I have shuffled off the professional coil, the sense of freedom that comes to me is as surprising as it is exquisite."[3] Yet despite his exaltation of intellectual freedom, James decided that his last book, his message to the world, his essential statement of a coherent philosophy, would be an introductory textbook for undergraduates.

It seems an odd choice, in light of James's frustration at not being taken seriously by academic philosophers. Yet in deciding to write a textbook, he was motivated by the same forces that had shaped the whole of his career. He disdained philosophers who gave in to "the rules of the professorial game—they think and write from each other and for each other and at each other exclusively." Within that cloistered intellectual environment, he thought, "all true perspective gets lost, extremes and oddities count as much as sanities," and anyone who writes in a popular, accessible, and concrete style is considered a shallow thinker.[4]

Writing an introductory textbook that explained pragmatism, pluralism, and radical empiricism was consistent, certainly, with James's role as liberator of students. He wanted to give them confidence in their own feelings, decisions, and intuitions; to free them from subjugation by an intellectual hierarchy, where they held tremulously to the bottom rung. He had not forgotten the intellectual oppression he had felt as his father's son: "The mind of man," he had written in his diary when he was seventeen, "naturally yields to necessity and our wishes soon subside when we see the impossibility of their being gratified."[5]

In the spring of 1896, when he delivered "The Will to Believe" at Yale and Brown, James wrote to a friend explaining his goal: "There is a sort of bullying of the human soul by scientific agnosticism that goes on a great scale now-a-days and that takes advantage of a very noble feeling in people—'love of truth' 'intellectual honesty' etc. I confess that I like to do what I can to set myself and others free from the paralysis it often brings about."[6]

Sympathy for students, however, was not James's only motivation for writing a textbook. A readership of undergraduates freed him from the intellectual demands of his colleagues—demands that he thought were irrelevant to formulating a persuasive and significant argument. Defending his book's lack of complexity to Schiller, he explained that "for College use . . . (I want it to *sell*) the 'eternal' view of concepts can do no particular harm."[7]

A desire to sell, and sell many copies, affected his decision as well. His *Introduction,* he admitted, was planned "partly as a market venture" and "partly to popularize the pragmatic method."[8] When he first conceived of the book, perhaps as early as 1903, he saw it as another opportunity to publish a work—like the *Principles* and its briefer version that became the standard psychology textbook at Harvard—that would provide royalties for many years to come. By the time he actually set to work, however, early in 1910, he was not certain that he would live to complete it.

Late in 1909, James had collapsed, mentally and physically, suffering from depression and severe angina. He bought the services of one L. G. Strang, a Christian Science practitioner in Boston, but after twenty-one treatments, his physical symptoms had not been alleviated. James saw Strang's failure as his own: throughout his life, mind-cure therapies from one or another practitioner had never effected lasting changes. "I think," he said, "there is a certain impediment in the minds of people brought up as I have been, which keeps the bolt from flying back, and letting the door of the more absolutely grounded life open. They can't back out of their system of finite prudences and intellectual scruples, even though in *words* they may admit that there are other ways of living, and more successful ones."[9]

James's diary is a sad chronicle of worsening chest pains, complicated by rheumatism, toothaches, colds, and depression. He was ill and weak and frustrated by the apparent intractability of his readers. "The problem of mutual misunderstanding in philosophy seems infinite, and grows discouraging," he said.[10] His *Introduction,* he knew, might be his last word; and there is a sense of desperation in the first paragraphs of the book, which serve not only as a defense of philosophy, but as a declaration of his own genius.

> The progress of society is due to the fact that individuals vary from the human average in all sorts of directions, and that the originality which they show is often so attractive or useful, that they are recognized by their tribe as leaders, and become setters of new ideals and objects of envy or imitation.
>
> Among the variations, every generation of men produces some individuals exceptionally preoccupied with theory. Such men find matter for puzzle and astonishment where no one else does. Their imagination invents explanations and combines them. They store up the learning of their time, utter prophecies and warnings, and are regarded as sages. Philosophy, etymologically meaning the love of wisdom, is the work of this class of minds, regarded with an indulgent relish, if not with admiration, even by those who do not understand them or believe much in the truth which they proclaim.

Having classed himself as exceptional and admirable, James set out to define his philosophy, borrowing substantially from *Pragmatism, The Meaning of Truth,* and from many essays—"Does 'Consciousness' Exist?" and "How Two Minds Can Know One Thing," for example— that he had published long before.

James devoted more than half of his manuscript to distinguishing between concept and percept, and to restating his objections to intellectualism. Concepts, terms generalized from experience, were necessarily abstractions. "We *harness* perceptual reality in concepts," James wrote, "in order to drive it better to our ends."[11] This harnessing, however, limited one's perception of new situations and experiences. Concepts affirm the history of experience; they cannot "divine the new" except "in ready-made and ancient terms. . . . Properly speaking," he wrote, "concepts are post-mortem preparations, sufficient only for retrospective understanding."[12]

His philosophy of pure experience, he insisted, would prepare students for "the superabounding, growing, ever-varying and novelty producing" world of the new century; for understanding the potential of more, and more complicated, technology; for the discoveries made by the rich new disciplines of sociology, anthropology, and psychology.[13]

His book, he said, "will immediately prove a centre of crystallization and a new rallying point of opinion in philosophy. The times are fairly crying aloud for it."[14] Perhaps they were, but he would never hear cries of gratitude for these illuminating ideas. The book that James wanted to be called "A beginning of an introduction to philosophy," was published as *Some Problems of Philosophy* nine months after his death.

One Long Fortitude

AS JAMES SUFFERED from his own physical problems and the depression that they caused, he received distressing news from his brother in England. Just after Christmas, Henry suffered a breakdown—"trepidation, agitation, general dreadfulness," is how he described it—complicated by digestive troubles, for which he blamed "too-prolonged & too-consistent Fletcherism."[15] Although he experienced "flares & flickers up" from depression, he repeatedly sank into a "deep & disheartening" emotional abyss.[16] He was lonely, frightened, and desperate for the company of William and Alice.

Alice wanted to rush to his side, but William, concerned as he was, thought it better to wait. Alice had just begun a series of vibratory massage treatments with Dr. Taylor; William wanted to arrange appointments for himself with Dr. Alexandre Moutier, a Parisian heart specialist; and, once again, he planned a stay at Nauheim. Meanwhile, they sent Harry as the family's ambassador while they booked passage on the *Megantic,* sailing on March 29.

If William proclaimed to friends that he would return "resurgent like a phoenix" from Nauheim, in small gestures he revealed his doubts about returning at all. Sometime shortly before he and Alice departed, James sat at his desk, opened his copy of the Harvard catalog, and looked through the list of faculty members, men who had been his colleagues, men who had been his friends, for the past several decades. "A thousand regrets cover every beloved name," he wrote above the roster. There was no time to say good-bye.

"I don't think *death* ought to have any terrors for one who has a positive life-record behind him," James had written a few months before to Henry Bowditch; "and when one's mind has once given up the *claim* on life (which is kept up mainly by one's vanity, I think) the prospect of death is gentle. . . . The great thing is to live *in* the passing day, and not look farther!"[17] But James had not relinquished his claim on life, had not completed his "life-record," and never had learned to live in the passing day. If death held no terror for him, its prospect filled him with regret.

When the Jameses arrived in Rye early in April, they found Henry so grateful to see them that he appeared better than they expected. With Alice to minister to his needs, he decided that he no longer needed the nurse whose domineering presence irritated him. All he needed, Henry said, was his precious family: his companions, his supporters. He could not bear to be alone.

Together, the two invalids and Alice took long drives in a car that Edith Wharton had sent, along with her chauffeur, from Paris. But after a few days, the drives proved too strenuous for Henry. He wanted nothing more than to sit by the hearth in Lamb House, reminiscing about his childhood, with his sister-in-law and brother beside him. But William was restless. His angina and dyspnea had become frighteningly painful; he had great hopes in Moutier's diagnosis and treatment, and each day in Rye seemed a day wasted. Finally, early in May, Henry seemed stable enough for William to leave. Alice watched him depart with a feeling of trepidation; she wanted to be with him, but at the moment Henry seemed to need her more.

Moutier's experimental treatment apparently lowered blood pressure, but hypertension was not James's problem. Instead, Moutier diagnosed a dilation of the aorta, and although he administered his treatment of high-frequency "d'Arsonval currents," he had little confidence that it would relieve James's pain. James, he advised, could do nothing better than to continue taking nitroglycerin for his angina attacks and to pursue a course of treatment at Nauheim. Despite his disappointment that Moutier could not help him, James was pleased—as his sister Alice had been when she finally received a diagnosis of breast cancer—that his symptoms had "a respectable organic basis, and are not, as so many of my friends tell me, due to pure 'nervousness.' "[18] He would not be an accomplice to his own death.

Debilitated and depressed, James nevertheless kept up an intense social life during his ten days in Paris. He saw Edith Wharton, stayed for a few days with Charles Strong, and visited with Émile Boutroux, a French philosopher who recently had been a guest of the Jameses' in Cambridge. He talked with the always inspiring Bergson, and he had a bemusing encounter with his thirty-seven-year-old nephew Edward,

Bob's son, whose eccentric political ideas seemed to James "the most harmless lunacy of reform I have yet met."[19] He even attended a séance at the Institut de France.

To all of these friends, he presented as vigorous an appearance as he could. Only one, Henry Adams, was not taken in by James's determined heartiness. When Adams last saw James, he said, he seemed "a delightful sparkling boy." Now he was shockingly changed. "William James came up yesterday, and looked like a schoolmaster of retired senescence," Adams wrote to a friend in sad surprise.[20]

From Paris, James went directly to Nauheim, while Alice accompanied Henry to a friend's house in Epping Forest. For a few weeks, William and Henry competed for her attentions. "I can tread on the wine-press alone, and live on Alice's letters!" William wrote to Henry. "It is honorable to both you and her that you don't yet get tired of each other." But as much as he appeared to encourage her travels with Henry, he repeatedly tried to entice them both to Nauheim by describing the "sweet and pure" air and by finding "3 excellent rooms— perhaps the best in the place" which they must reserve immediately.[21] Henry, however, was not inclined to rush. "Alice is a perfect angel of mercy & tower of strength," Henry wrote to William. Of course, William knew that and wanted her at his own side.[22] Finally, on June 8, she arrived in Nauheim with Henry.

Nauheim had changed since the Jameses' last visit, but it was not the elegant art nouveau buildings or the expanded gardens that impressed them. James had come for the baths, the physicians, and the medical technology. A radiogram and X rays confirmed Moutier's diagnosis of aortic enlargement and "insufficiency" of the mitral valve regulating blood flow from left auricle to ventricle. The baths, William believed, "won't cure, but will help to adapt the heart. There's life in the old dog yet!" he proclaimed.[23]

The cure, though, was enervating in itself, and he was uncertain about its effects. As usual during one of his protracted illnesses, Alice took the brunt of his irritability and frustration. On some days, every remark she made seemed wrong.[24] Henry, whose gradual improvement was punctuated with days of darkest depression, still was far easier to care for.

At the end of June, when the three Jameses left Nauheim, William attributed his general weakness to the first effects of the baths. Hoping for the kind of marked recovery he had felt in the past, he decided that they all would go to Switzerland before sailing home in mid-August. He would engage in some pleasant walks, he thought; and he would have a private talk with his friend Flournoy. But the trip from Germany to Geneva was more tiring than he anticipated. He sent a postcard to Flournoy telling him that he would take a taxi to see him, to consult "about certain things apart from my brother," but the meeting never occurred. First, James complained that he was too tired from the trip, then too strained by a visit from Dickinson Miller, to make even a short visit.[25] "My dyspnoea gets worse at an accelerated rate," he wrote to Flournoy, "and all I care for now is to get home—doing *nothing* on the way. It is partly a spasmodic phenomenon I am sure, for the aeration of my tissues, judging by the colour of my lips, seems to be sufficient."[26]

The spasmodic phenomenon, however, persisted. At the end of July, back at Lamb House, William was too ill and too weak even to write to his friends. "His nights are dreadful and the hours one long fortitude," Alice wrote to Schiller. "The Nauheim experiment has been all a disaster and every move seems to diminish his slight strength." James Mackenzie, a London physician who attended him, insisted that "acute neurasthenia" played a decisive role in exacerbating James's symptoms. For William, the diagnosis was a reproach, a moral condemnation. Alice, though, wanted to believe Mackenzie: if William's suffering was caused mostly by his intractable "pitch of life," then he would not die, not now. "I 'keep a good hope to the future' for him," Alice told Schiller, "for he never was more *vital* in spirit, or wiser in thought than now."[27]

At that moment, William felt little hope in the future. He never would write again, he knew, and although he professed not to care— "in the least pathetically or tragically, at any rate"—he did care about two unfinished projects: "I have other business in life," he had written to Alice from Nauheim, "—'my Father's' business namely,—to say nothing of the embalming and perfuming of my own invincibly squalid little corpus!"[28]

He attended to his father's business—reconciling, as well as he could, pragmatism and pluralism with mysticism and monism—in his last article, an homage to his longtime admirer Benjamin Paul Blood, who saw in James "the presence of that transcendent which we call genius," a quality he first had noticed in Henry Sr.[29] Surely James was susceptible to Blood's continued and unabashed flattery of him and his works; but there was more: a reminder, in Blood's mysticism, his crankiness, and most decidedly in his failure to attract any readership for his writings, of the personality and career of Henry Sr. But Blood succeeded, where Henry defiantly would not, in rejecting monism for pluralism, and therefore in aligning himself with James's philosophy. "I feel now," James wrote, "as if my own pluralism were not without the kind of support which mystical corroboration may confer. Monism can no longer claim to be the only beneficiary of whatever right mysticism may possess to lend *prestige.*"[30]

In "A Pluralistic Mystic," James extracted from Blood's works passages that defended *Pragmatism, A Pluralistic Universe,* and *The Meaning of Truth,* and more important, argued against intellectualism. "The 'inexplicable,' the 'mystery,'" James wrote, must be "met and dealt with by faculties more akin to our activities and heroisms and willingnesses, than to our logical powers." He allowed Blood the last words of the article—the last words that James would publish in his own lifetime: "There is no conclusion. What has concluded, that we might conclude in regard to it? There are no fortunes to be told, and there is no advice to be given.—Farewell."[31]

James's longer farewell was his "squalid little corpus"—the *Introduction* that Peggy, in Cambridge, had just finished typing. When he received it at the end of May, he immediately began to make corrections, supplementing the editing he already had done on his own typescript. One morning, a few weeks before they set sail for home, James asked Alice for his copy of the manuscript, kept it briefly, and then gave it to her to pack. "I have made a note of the help I want from Kallen when you publish my unfinished book," he told her.[32] It was a task that Alice could not bear to consider.

Horace Kallen, with his newly earned doctorate in philosophy, was a safe choice to be editor of James's final work. At the beginning of his career, lacking power or influence within the philosophical community, Kallen was unlikely to exert his own authority over James's manuscript. Deeply indebted to William and Alice for financial help and emotional support, he would feel compelled to obey James's wishes. The other possible candidate for role of editor was Ralph Barton Perry, but Perry already had served as chairman of Harvard's philosophy department, had published two books, and had a reputation for self-interest that made him less trustworthy for this special, delicate task. James intended *Some Problems of Philosophy* to enhance his own reputation, not his editor's.

William's note instructed Alice to pay Kallen $250 to edit the manuscript, being sure that he compared the corrections on the two typescripts, but adding nothing of his own except perhaps clarifications of "obvious obscurities or carelessnesses" and only necessary annotations. But besides these few mundane instructions, there was a more emotional message: "Say it is fragmentary and unrevised," he pleaded. "Call it: 'A beginning of an introduction to Philosophy.' Say that I hoped by it to round my system, which now is too much like an arch built only on one side."[33]

Fragmentary and unrevised though it was, *Some Problems of Philosophy* at least had a shape and form that would allow it to be published. With his manuscript in Alice's safekeeping, he was ready for a strenuous trip. He wanted desperately to return to America. "I am still in pretty miserable shape with *athemnoth* & weakness," he wrote to Flournoy en route to Liverpool, "but near home now, & not afraid of the voyage."[34]

WHILE WILLIAM and Henry were struggling to recover their health in Europe, Bob, sixty-three, suffered a serious decline at home.[35] During the winter of 1909, he again began drinking heavily. His wife, furious, decided that the situation was intolerable and left him for several months of European travel. Bob was alone and lonely when he received word about William and Henry. "The James brothers are beginning to crumble fast," he wrote to his daughter, "and are a good deal more than half way on a return to the paradise in which they grew up."[36] Within weeks, Bob had a heart attack in his sleep and died, apparently with a smile on his face. His body was not discovered for two days.

The Jameses received a report of Bob's death from a shocked and worried Peggy. "I am constantly thinking of you and Dad and Uncle Henry," she wrote to her mother. Although not notified in time to attend Bob's funeral, Peggy and Harry went to visit their cousin Mary, who had come to Concord to pack up her father's possessions. "'I would have done more for Father, if he had let me,'" Mary told Peggy, "'but he never would and now it is too late.' Those fatal words 'too late,'" Peggy told her parents, "they grip one by the throat and make one fairly suffocate under the load of chances lost. We must draw the circle closer while we are here together, and do all we can for one another while it is still time."[37] Peggy knew, as they all knew, that there was little time. When William was told of Bob's death, he remarked that he would like to die as peacefully.

A FEW DAYS BEFORE sailing home on the *Empress of Britain,* Alice wrote to Harry, informing him of their scheduled arrival in Quebec on August 19. "I want you to pass round the good tidings that Papa is really better," she told him, as if a consensus of belief in William's good health would insure his recovery. "He is very weak and the breathing still troubles him," she admitted, "but he has had two good nights, and Skinner [Henry's physician] says his heart is *much* better. So we have a right to expect improvement now all along the line."[38]

Yet in a letter to her mother, Alice revealed an unmistakable sense of foreboding: "It is a strangely haunted and haunting morning," she wrote. "The sun comes and withdraws. The bees buzz about the great bush of blossoming lavender beside the door, the wind sounds a menacing note, as of rain to come, and I am thinking of all the anxious hours I have lived through."[39] And, no doubt, envisioning all the anxious hours still to come.

William was so weak that he had to be carried on board. Although the voyage was unusually calm, the sea air and seclusion did nothing to improve his symptoms. Every breath was so painful, Henry reported, that he "suffered piteously & dreadfully." By the time they disembarked in Quebec he still could not walk unaided. But as dire as his condition seemed at the moment, Alice apparently convinced herself that this time, as in times before, he would recover. She did not interfere, then, when Harry, who met them at the boat with his brother, left immediately for a few days' vacation with a friend, hunting and fishing in Canada. Billy drove them to Chocorua, where Peggy and Mrs. Gibbens were waiting to greet them. The long voyage finally ended, James was overcome with relief, collapsing into a chair and sobbing, "Oh, it's so good to be home!"

He was put to bed immediately and the household mobilized to serve him. In the first days after their return, Alice wrote to many friends in Boston, assuring them that William was improving. Soon, however, it became clear that he was not, and her hopes changed to fear: William was sinking. The local physician, Dr. George Shedd, arranged for his son, also a physician, to move into the James house. But Alice wanted William to be seen by a specialist, and on August 25, Dr. Smith, responding to Alice's phone call, drove up from Boston. "It is wonderful here now what the ubiquitous telephone & the extra-ordinarily multiplied motor together achieve," Henry remarked. Smith examined James, declared that he had "a fighting chance," but dispelled none of Alice's anxiety.

As much as she and Henry wanted to believe him, they knew that William was dying: "he suffered so & only wanted, wanted more & more, to go," Henry said. The next day, he was worse. He told Alice he longed to die and asked her to rejoice for him. Early in the afternoon of August 26, Alice came into William's bedroom with some milk, the only sustenance he had been able to take since he came home. At first she thought he was asleep, but suddenly she realized that something had changed: he was unconscious. She cradled his head in her arms, listening to his quiet breathing. Just before 2:30, still lying in Alice's arms, he died.

Billy photographed his father's body as it lay in rumpled white sheets on the iron bed; he made a death mask, and then the body was removed for the autopsy that Alice had requested. "Acute enlargement of the heart," she recorded in her diary. "He had worn himself out."[40] He had not simply willed himself to die.

"I BELIEVE IN immortality," Alice wrote to Horace Kallen, "—really believe that he is safe and living, loving and working, never to be wholly gone from us."[41] If Alice's spiritual convictions could sustain her now, Henry had no such consolation. "My own fears are of the blackest," he wrote to his friend Grace Norton; "[F]rom as far back as in dimmest childhood, I have so yearningly always counted on him, I feel nothing but the abject weakness of grief and even terror."[42] He had hoped his sister's death would be "the last, the last forever" that he would suffer; but he had been wrong. This was the last, and the worst. "His extinction changes the face of life for me," Henry wrote to Tom Perry, one of the Jameses' oldest friends, "—besides the mere missing of his inexhaustible company and personality, originality, the whole unspeakably vivid and beautiful presence of him."[43]

Many of James's friends and colleagues learned of his death from newspaper announcements and obituaries, based on information sent by Alice and Henry from Chocorua. Most were shocked: they had not realized that he had been so ill; his public enactment of strength and vigor had deceived them. Even Alice, who had witnessed most intimately her husband's long decline, described his death as sudden, and stunning. "But he wanted to go," she explained, "and departed swiftly as he always has when he made up his mind to move on."[44]

Scores of notices in the *Boston Herald, Globe,* and *Transcript,* in the major London dailies, and in Italy, France, and Switzerland announced that the world had lost "the most distinguished and influential American philosopher of our day."[45] But to James's friends, the loss had little to do with the books he published or the lectures he gave. "Much as William achieved," Alice wrote to one of her husband's admirers, "he was more than anything he did."[46]

His friends felt orphaned, bereft of a spiritual strength and warmth that they could compare only to the power of light. He was a rare and luminous spirit: a member, one of Aleck's friends commented, of the "great society of encouragers." It seemed incomprehensible that he *could* be dead, that so robust, so vigorous a spirit simply ceased to be. Again and again, his friends describe their immediate reaction to the news as an overwhelming sense of darkness: darkness and abandonment.

Elizabeth Glendower Evans saw an obituary in a Wisconsin newspaper. "I felt as if it eclipsed the light of the sky," she recalled. "It seemed impossible—impossible that such a vital creature should be lying still and cold, to be covered in the silence of the grave from the eyes that delighted in him."[47] When John Elof Boodin saw the "brutal headlines" in a newspaper, he broke down and wept as he had not wept since his father's death. "A light and a love had gone out of my life which could not be replaced. We feel like orphans in our bereavement," he said. "Who like him will follow our feeble efforts? Who like him will cheer us on to do our best? Who like him will have the generosity to praise the little service we have done?"[48]

"None of us will ever see a man like William James again: there is no doubt about that," John Jay Chapman wrote. "And yet it is hard to state what it was in him that gave him either his charm or his power, what it was that penetrated and influenced us, what it is that we lack and feel the need of, now that he has so unexpectedly and incredibly died. I always thought that William James would continue forever; and I relied upon his sanctity as if it were sunlight."[49]

"He did surely shed light to man, and *gave,* of his own great spirit and beautiful genius, with splendid generosity," Henry wrote to H. G. Wells. "Of my personal loss—the extinction of so shining a presence in my own life, and from so far back (really from dimmest childhood) I won't pretend to speak. He had an inexhaustible authority for me, and I feel abandoned and afraid, even as a lost child."[50]

"WHEN YOU BURY ME," William had written to Alice sixteen years earlier, after the funeral of a friend, "do it in a cathedral with a ritual. Dignity befits the business better than sincerity."[51] But Alice never questioned her own religious sincerity, nor her husband's. "He said to me once, many years ago," she wrote to one of William's friends, " 'I am *really* a religious man'—and so he was."[52]

Wanting both dignity and sincerity, she called upon the services of George Angier Gordon, minister of the prestigious Old South Church in Boston, and one of James's former students. "I want you to officiate at his funeral as one of William's friends and also as a man of faith," Alice wrote to Gordon. "That's what he was; I want no hesitation or diluted utterance at William's funeral."[53]

There were no diluted utterances in Harvard's Appleton Chapel on the afternoon of August 30. Chauvet's "Funeral Prelude" began the service. Baritone William Walker sang "O Rest in the Lord" from Mendelssohn's *Elijah.* Gordon eulogized James as a profoundly religious man "by nature and by conviction."

The friends and colleagues who, ten months before, had celebrated James's career, now stood as honorary pallbearers: Harvard's president Lowell, MIT's former president James Crafts, George Herbert Palmer, James's old and dear friends James Jackson Putnam and Henry L. Higginson, and his beloved allies George Dorr and Charles Strong. The casket, covered with a purple pall on which lay two palm branches and a spray of asparagus, was carried from the chapel by six pallbearers. The body was cremated.

For the next several months, Henry stayed on with Alice and the children, partly because he still needed, as he put it, to cling to her, partly because she hoped, and he encouraged her in the hope, that William would succeed in communicating with them from the spiritual realm in which she knew he was now, profoundly, alive. Just as she had after the death of her young child, she sought out likely mediums and held several séances in her home. There was no message, and yet Alice, who wore black for the rest of her life, never felt quite alone.

THERE ARE TWO large graveyards in Cambridge. One, the luxurious and manicured Mount Auburn Cemetery has been a tourist attraction since it opened in 1831. With its rare and exotic plantings, elegant statuary and monuments, chapels and crypts, with ten miles of carefully tended paths, it offers a serene respite for the world-weary visitor. More than seventy-five thousand have been buried there, including some of New England's most famous luminaries: James's teacher Louis Agassiz; his dear friend Josiah Royce; his colleagues Charles Eliot Norton and Phillips Brooks; Mary Baker Eddy, whose Christian Science movement James defended; Charles William Eliot, who first hired James to teach at Harvard. One can hardly walk down any path and not find a headstone for someone whose life touched James's.

James, however, is not among them.

The James family plot is at the rim of the vast, undistinguished Cambridge Cemetery, a cluster of five small headstones facing away from the rest of the dead and toward the life of the city. There Henry James Sr. was buried beside his wife, Mary. There James and his wife had stood, overcome with grief, as their eighteen-month-old son was laid into the earth. There, the ashes of James's sister, Alice, were interred. And there a simple, polished stone, unexpectedly small, marks the grave of William James.

ACKNOWLEDGMENTS

ANY ACKNOWLEDGMENT PAGE seems inadequate to thank all the friends and colleagues whose enthusiasm for this project has sustained me through years of research and writing. Still: my thanks, first to John Mc-Dermott, in whose classes I first encountered William James; to Ignas Skrupskelis and Elizabeth Berkeley, upon whose scholarship all James researchers depend.

And many thanks, as well, to those who kindly read portions of the manuscript: John De Cuevas, Erika Dreifus, Emily Gottreich, Alfred Habegger, Emily Haddad, Lilian Handlin, Alex Johnson, Sue Lonoff, Barbara Petzen, Kathy Richman, and Kathryn Slanski. Thanks to Betty Smith, for sharing her research on Sarah Wyman Whitman; Cornelia Wheeler, for conversations about Chocorua; Benjamin Apt, for conducting research in Germany; Suzi Naiburg, for conversations about the Jameses; Luise Erdmann, for judicious suggestions; Ruth Tiffany Barnhouse, for memories of McLean's; Ruth Rischin, for insights on James's international impact; Terry Bragg and the Institutional Review Board for allowing me to conduct historical research at the McLean Hospital; Janice Hamel, who allowed me to tour James's home in Chocorua; Lyford Merrow II, for helpful details about the Chocorua home and property; John and Kathleen Case, for allowing me to examine the logs and photograph albums at Putnam Camp; Michael James, for his kind words about *William James Remembered;* Bay James, for her generous responses to many queries and for permission to quote from unpublished material by William James and reproduce photographs from the James archives.

Many librarians responded helpfully to my requests for material from their archives. I especially thank Jim Meehan, Curatorial Assistant, and Jerold Pepper, Librarian at the Adirondack Museum; and Melanie Wisner,

Susan Halpert, Jennie Rathbun, Emily Walhout, Denison Beach, Jozef Zajac, Tom Ford, and Virginia L. Smyers of Harvard University's Houghton Library.

Thanks in abundance to my editor, Walt Bode, for his superb reading of the manuscript, his gentle prodding, unfailing patience, and inspiring encouragement; to his assistant, Theo Lieber, who greeted my anxieties with uncommon serenity; to Rachel Myers for scrupulous copyediting; and to my literary agent, Elaine Markson, for her abiding and generous enthusiasm.

Finally, gratitude unbounded to my husband, Thilo Ullmann, and my son, Aaron Simon: liberating and loving spirits.

PERMISSIONS

UNIVERSITY PRESS of Virginia, for permission to quote from previously published material in the *Correspondence of William James,* volumes 1 through 5. Portions of Chapters 9 and 10 appeared in different form as the Introduction to Volume 5. Houghton Library, Harvard University, for permission to quote from unpublished material in the James Family Papers and to publish photographs from the William James collection. Beinecke Library, Yale University, for permission to quote from William James's letter to E. Stettheimer.

NOTES

KEY TO ABBREVIATIONS IN THE NOTES

Archival Sources

Houghton   Houghton Library, Harvard University houses the major collection of James family papers.

Schlesinger   Radcliffe College, Schlesinger Library for Women's History.

Beinecke   Beinecke Library, Rare Book and Manuscript Collection, Yale University.

Colby   Miller Library, Colby College.

Selected Works by the James Family

The works and published correspondence of William James, the autobiographical works of his brother Henry, and selected biographical works are listed below. When these works are referred to in the notes by a short form, the abbreviation is indicated to the right of the entry below. All references to William James's works, unless otherwise indicated, are to the Harvard University Press editions, edited by Frederick H. Burkhardt, Fredson Bowers, and Ignas Skrupskelis.

> James, Alice. *The Diary of Alice James*. Edited with an introduction by Leon Edel. New York: Dodd, Mead, 1964.
>
> ———. *The Death and Letters of Alice James*. Edited by Ruth Bernard Yeazell. Berkeley: University of California Press, 1981.
>
> James, Henry, Sr. *The Literary Remains of the Late Henry James*. Edited with an introduction by William James. Boston: Osgood, 1884.

James, Henry. *Henry James Letters.* Edited by Leon Edel. 4 vols. Cambridge: Harvard University Press, 1974, 1975.

————. *The Notebooks of Henry James.* Edited by F. O. Matthiessen and Kenneth B. Murdock. New York: Oxford University Press, 1947.

————. *Henry James Autobiography.* Edited with an introduction
SBO by F. W. Dupee. New York: Criterion, 1956. Contains *A Small*
NSB *Boy and Others* and *Notes of a Son and Brother.*
CER James, William. *Collected Essays and Reviews.* New York: Longmans, Green, 1920.
ECR ————. *Essays, Comments, and Reviews.* Introduction by Ignas Skrupskelis, 1987.
EPhil ————. *Essays in Philosophy.* Introduction by John J. McDermott, 1978.
EPR ————. *Essays in Psychical Research.* Introduction by Robert A. McDermott, 1986.
EPsych ————. *Essays in Psychology.* Introduction by William R. Woodward, 1983.
ERE ————. *Essays in Radical Empiricism.* Introduction by John J. McDermott, 1976.
ERM ————. *Essays in Religion and Morality.* Introduction by John J. McDermott, 1982.
MEN ————. *Manuscript Essays and Notes.* Introduction by Ignas Skrupskelis, 1988.
ML ————. *Manuscript Lectures.* Introduction by Ignas Skrupskelis, 1988.
MT ————. *The Meaning of Truth.* Introduction by H. S. Thayer, 1975.

————. *Memories and Studies.* New York: Longmans, Green, 1911.

————. *A Pluralistic Universe.* Introduction by Richard J. Bernstein, 1977.

————. *Pragmatism.* Introduction by H. S. Thayer, 1975.

————. *The Principles of Psychology.* 3 vols. Introductions by Gerald E. Myers and Rand B. Evans, 1983. Because the pages are numbered consecutively throughout the three volumes, volume numbers are not included in the notes.

————. *Psychology: Briefer Course.* Introduction by Michael M. Sokal, 1984.

————. *Some Problems of Philosophy.* Introduction by Peter H. Hare, 1979.

———. *Talks to Teachers on Psychology: And to Students on Some of Life's Ideals.* Introduction by Gerald E. Myers, 1983.

———. *The Varieties of Religious Experience.* Introduction by John E. Smith, 1985.

WB   ———. *The Will to Believe.* Introduction by Edward H. Madden, 1979.

William James Published Correspondence

Letters   James, Henry, III, ed. *Letters of William James.* 2 vols. Boston: Atlantic Monthly Press, 1926.

Le Clair   Le Clair, Robert, ed. *The Letters of William James and Théodore Flournoy.* Madison: University of Wisconsin Press, 1966.

Scott   Scott, Frederick J. D., ed. *Selected Unpublished Correspondence, 1885–1910.* Columbus: Ohio State University Press, 1986.

Correspondence   Skrupskelis, Ignas, and Elizabeth M. Berkeley, *The Correspondence of William James,* 5 vols. Charlottesville: University Press of Virginia, 1992–1997. This ongoing project will comprise thirteen volumes.

Biographical Sources

Allen   Allen, Gay Wilson. *William James.* New York: Viking, 1967.

Myers   Myers, Gerald. *William James: His Life and Thought.* New Haven: Yale University Press, 1986.

Perry   Perry, Ralph Barton. *The Thought and Character of William James,* 2 vols. Boston: Little, Brown, 1935.

WJR   Simon, Linda, ed. *William James Remembered.* Lincoln: University of Nebraska Press, 1996.

Additional sources follow the Notes.

NOTES TO THE TEXT

Introduction

1. WJ, "Emerson," in *ERM,* 109.
2. WJ to AHJ, 22 April 1897, Houghton; WJ to HJ, 4 April 1897, *Correspondence,* 3:6.
3. WJ to Charles Renouvier, 29 July 1876, *Letters,* 1: 188.
4. WJ to Thomas Ward, 30 December 1876, *Correspondence,* 4:552.
5. WJ to HJ, 7 February 1897, *Correspondence,* 3:1.

6. WJ, *Principles of Psychology*, 280.
7. John Jay Chapman, "William James," in *WJR*, 54.
8. Walter Lippmann, "William James: An Open Mind," in *WJR*, 257.
9. HJ to WJ, 25 February 1897, *Correspondence*, 3:5.
10. WJ to HJ, 5 June 1897; AHJ to HJ, 31 May 1897, *ERM*, 221, 220.
11. WJ to E. Stettheimer, 16 May 1909, Beinecke Library, Yale.
12. See Deborah J. Coon, "One Moment in the World's Salvation: Anarchism and the Radicalization of William James," *Journal of American History* 83 (June 1996). Other recent scholars who consider James's political views include George Cotkin, James Kloppenberg, Frank Lentricchia, and Cornel West. References to their works appear in the bibliography.
13. WJ to H. G. Wells, 11 September 1906, *Letters*, 2:260.
14. *Ibid.*
15. WJ, "Confidences of a 'Psychical Researcher,'" *EPR*, 374.
16. WJ, *WB*, ix.
17. Théodore Flournoy, "Artistic Temperament," in *WJR*, 85.
18. Gertrude Stein, *Picasso*. Boston: Beacon Press, 1959 (1938), 49.
19. John Elof Boodin, "William James as I Knew Him," in *WJR*, 209.
20. WJ to George Croom Robertson, 22 August 1888, Houghton.

Chapter 1: Mortification

1. HJSr., *The Literary Remains of the Late Henry James*, ed. WJ, 189.
2. *Ibid.*, 173.
3. *Ibid.*, 163.
4. *Ibid.*, 154.
5. *Ibid.*, 172–73.
6. Henry's age at the time of this accident is in dispute. Henry James III, when editing the letters of William James, commented that Henry Sr. was thirteen at the time, setting the year for the accident in 1824. Austin Warren, in *The Elder Henry James* (New York: Macmillan, 1934), repeats this information, but adds that the tutor was Joseph Henry. But Joseph Henry apparently did not join the staff at the Academy until 1926. Jean Strouse, in *Alice James* (Boston: Houghton Mifflin, 1980), writes that the accident occurred in 1828, when Henry was seventeen, basing her conclusion on a May 6, 1828, letter from Augustus James to Reverend William James, announcing that Henry's leg had been amputated. Since Augustus does not imply that this was a second amputation, Strouse assumes that the accident recently occurred. But Henry's sister Jannet had written to Marcia James (wife of the Reverend William) on November 16, 1827, that

"Henry's leg is not as well at present as it was in the Spring, instead of progressing it goes back and there is a greater space to heal now than there was before." This letter indicates that the wound occurred at the latest in the spring of 1827, and probably earlier, even in the fall or winter of 1826, which would make it possible that Joseph Henry was involved.

7. Quoted in Strouse, *Alice James,* 8.
8. *Boston Medical and Surgical Journal* (22 July 1828), 367. Details about the procedure for amputation were taken from a hospital report of an amputation below the knee, 365–67.
9. HJSr., *Literary Remains,* 185–86.
10. McIntyre to HJSr., 12 November 1829, Houghton. Quoted in Warren, *The Elder Henry James,* 17.
11. HJSr. to Isaac Jackson, 12 January 1830, Houghton. Quotations that follow regarding James's stay in Boston are from this letter.
12. William James to McIntyre, 2 December 1829, Houghton.
13. William James to McIntyre, n.d., Houghton.
14. William James to McIntyre, n.d., Houghton.
15. HJSr. to Reverend William James, 14 November 1827, Houghton.
16. HJSr. to Julia Kellogg, 8 September n.y., Houghton.
17. HJSr. to Reverend William James, 3 November 1827, Colby College.
18. HJSr., *Literary Remains,* 124.
19. HJSr. to Joseph Henry, 9 July 1843, Houghton.
20. HJSr. to Ralph Waldo Emerson, 9 March (1865? 1868?), Houghton.
21. HJSr., "Is Marriage Holy?" *The Atlantic Monthly,* March 1870, 364.

Chapter 2: Gestation

1. HJSr. to Reverend William James, 21 December (n.d.), Colby College.
2. HJSr. to R. W. Emerson, March 1842, Houghton. Also published in Perry, 1:40.
3. HJSr. to Joseph Henry, 9 July 1943, quoted in Perry, 1:16.
4. *Emerson in His Journals.* Edited by Joel Porte, Cambridge: Harvard University Press, 1850, 142.
5. *Emerson in His Journals,* 279.
6. HJ, *SBO,* 7.
7. H. D. Thoreau to Emerson, 8 June 1843, in F. B. Sanborn, ed. *Familiar Letters of Henry David Thoreau.* Boston: Houghton Mifflin, 1894, 95.
8. HJSr. to Emerson, 11 May 1843, Perry, 1:48.

9. HJSr. to Emerson, 11 May 1843, Perry, 1:46.

10. Mary James to Mary Holton James, n.d., in Jane Maher, *Biography of Broken Fortunes*. Hamden, Conn.: Archon Books, 1986, 122; Mary James to Mrs. J. J. Garth Wilkinson, quoted in Maher, 2; Robertson James, quoted in Maher, 3.

11. HJSr. to Emerson, (1842? or 1843?), Houghton. Quoted in Perry, 1:43.

12. Thoreau to Emerson, 7 August 1843, *Familiar Letters of Henry David Thoreau*, 133.

13. HJSr. to Emerson, 3 October 1843. Quoted in Perry, 1:50.

14. HJSr., *Society the Redeemed Form of Man*. Boston: Houghton, Osgood, 1879, 43–44.

15. HJSr. to Emerson, 11 May 1843, Houghton.

16. Margaret Fuller, *Memoirs of Margaret Fuller Ossoli*, vol. 2. Boston: Phillips, Sampson & Company, 1852, 186.

17. Carlyle to Emerson, n.d., quoted in Warren, *The Elder Henry James*, 50.

18. Quoted in Warren, *The Elder Henry James*, 53.

19. HJSr. to Catharine Barber James, 1 May 1844, Houghton. Quoted in Perry, 1:178.

20. HJSr. to Catharine Barber James, 1 May 1844, Houghton. Quoted in Perry, 1:179.

21. HJSr. to Catharine Barber James, 1 May 1844, Houghton. Quoted in Perry, 1:179.

22. HJSr., *Society the Redeemed Form of Man*, 43ff.

23. "The essential feature of a Panic Attack is a discrete period of intense fear or discomfort that is accompanied by at least 4 of 13 somatic or cognitive symptoms. The attack has a sudden onset and builds to a peak rapidly (usually in 10 minutes or less) and is often accompanied by a sense of imminent danger or impending doom and an urge to escape. The 13 somatic or cognitive symptoms are palpitations, sweating, trembling or shaking, sensations of shortness of breath or smothering, feeling of choking, chest pain or discomfort, nausea or abdominal distress, dizziness or lightheadedness, derealization or depersonalization, fear of losing control of 'going crazy,' fear of dying, paresthesias, and chills or hot flushes." *Diagnostic and Statistical Manual of Mental Disorders*, 4th edition (American Psychiatric Association, 1994), 394.

24. HJSr. to WJ, 27 September 1867, Houghton.

25. HJSr., "Spiritual Rappings," in *Lectures and Miscellanies*. New York: Redfield, 1852, 411.

26. HJSr. to Sarah Sturgis Shaw, 10 May 1859, Houghton.

27. HJSr. to Sarah Sturgis Shaw, 1 June (1859), Houghton.

28. WJ, *The Principles of Psychology*, 296–97.

29. HJSr., *Society the Redeemed Form of Man*, 46–47.

30. *Ibid.*, 48–49.

31. Emerson, *Journals, 1841–44*, 185.

32. HJSr., *Society*, 75–76.

33. HJSr., "Spiritual Rappings," *Lectures and Miscellanies*, 411.

34. *Ibid.*, 412–13.

35. Mary James to Mrs. Garth Wilkinson, Albany, 29 November 1846, Houghton.

Chapter 3: Appetites and Affections

1. Clarence L. F. Gohdes, *The Periodicals of American Transcendentalism.* Durham: Duke University Press, 1931, 103.

2. HJSr. to Edmund Tweedy, 5 September 1852, Houghton.

3. HJSr., "Morality and the Perfect Life," in *Moralism and Christianity.* New York: Redfield, 1850, 114–15.

4. HJSr., "Socialism and Civilization in Relation to the Development of the Individual Life," in *Moralism and Christianity*, 60.

5. *Ibid.*, 61.

6. HJSr., "Morality and the Perfect Life," in *Moralism and Christianity*, 150.

7. Stephen Pearl Andrews, *Love, Marriage and Divorce*, quoted in Warren, *The Elder Henry James*, 124.

8. "horror of pen and ink": HJSr. to JJG Wilkinson, 6 September 1852, quoted in Perry, 1:23; "literary men": HJSr. to Emerson, 31 August 1849, quoted in Perry, 1:57.

9. HJSr. to Emerson, 31 August 1849, quoted in Perry, 1:59.

10. Bronson Alcott, *The Journals of Bronson Alcott.* Edited by Odell Shepard. Boston: Little, Brown, 1938, 245–57.

11. HJSr., *Literary Remains*, 16.

12. HJ, *SBO*, 109.

13. Alcott (2 March 1851), *Journals*, 241–42.

14. HJ, *SBO*, 29–30.

15. WJ to AJ, 31 August (1865), *Correspondence*, 4:116. A paper cutter is a slab of seasoned hardwood, fitted with a sliding gauge and metal blade, from six to fourteen inches long; or WJ may have meant the paper knife HJSr. used to slit uncut book pages.

16. HJ, *SBO*, 123.

17. HJSr., "A Scientific Statement of the Christian Doctrine of the Lord, or Divine Man," in *Moralism and Christianity*, 25.
18. HJSr., "The Principle of Universality in Art," in *Lecture and Miscellanies*, 126.
19. HJSr. to Catharine James, 24 July 1854, Houghton.
20. HJSr. to Edmund Tweedy, 19 September (1853), Houghton.
21. AJ to WJ, 22 March 1889, Ruth Bernard Yeazell, ed. *The Death and Letters of Alice James*. Berkeley: University of California Press, 1981, 162.
22. WJ to AJ, 14 November 1866, *Letters*, 1:80; *Correspondence*, 4:145.
23. Obituary of Charles Marshall, quoted in Jean Strouse, *Alice James*. Boston: Houghton Mifflin, 1980, 34–35. Marshall died in 1865.
24. HJ to WJ, 27 (December) 1869, *Correspondence*, 1:139.
25. HJ, *SBO*, 119.
26. *Ibid.*, 146.
27. *Ibid.*, 60.
28. *Ibid.*, 146.
29. WJ to Edgar Van Winkle, 1 March 1858, *Correspondence*, 4:11.
30. HJSr., "Democracy and Its Issues," in *Lectures and Miscellanies*, 4–5.

Chapter 4: Other People's Rules

1. HJ, *SBO*, 158.
2. *Ibid.*, 165.
3. *Ibid.*, 164.
4. HJ to Catharine Barber James, 13 August (1855), quoted in Robert Le Clair, *Young Henry James*. New York: Bookman, 1955, 156–57.
5. HJSr., *New York Daily Tribune*, 3 September 1855, quoted in Le Clair, *Young Henry James*, 162.
6. HJSr. to Catharine Barber James, 25 September 1855, quoted in Le Clair, *Young Henry James*, 171–72.
7. HJSr.'s advertisement quoted in Alfred Habegger, *The Father*, 372.
8. Thomson later established his own school in Edinburgh, which Robert Louis Stevenson attended from 1864–67.
9. HJ, *SBO*, 170.
10. HJSr. to Emerson, 1856, Houghton.
11. HJSr. to Edmund Tweedy, 14 September 1856, Houghton.
12. WJ to Edgar Van Winkle, 1 July 1856, *Correspondence*, 4:1.
13. WJ to Edgar Van Winkle, 25 July 1856, *Correspondence*, 4:2–3.
14. WJ to Edgar Van Winkle, 2 August 1856, *Correspondence*, 4:3.

15. WJ to AHJ, 23 February 1883, *Correspondence,* 5:427.

16. WJ to Edgar Van Winkle, 4 January 1858, *Correspondence,* 4:10.

17. WJ to Edgar Van Winkle, 4 January 1858, *Correspondence,* 4:9.

18. WJ to Edgar Van Winkle, 4 September 1857, *Correspondence,* 4:6.

19. WJ to Edgar Van Winkle, 4 January 1858, *Correspondence,* 4:9.

20. WJ to Edgar Van Winkle, 1 March 1858, *Correspondence,* 4:11–15.

21. WJ to Edgar Van Winkle, 1 March 1858, *Correspondence,* 4:14.

22. WJ to Edgar Van Winkle, 26 May 1858, *Correspondence,* 4:16.

23. WJ to Edgar Van Winkle, 26 May 1858, *Correspondence,* 4:16–17.

24. WJ to Edgar Van Winkle, 26 May 1858, *Correspondence,* 4:18.

25. WJ to Edgar Van Winkle, 12 August 1858, *Correspondence,* 4:19.

26. HJ, *SBO,* 303, 304.

27. WJ to Edgar Van Winkle, 18 September 1858, *Correspondence,* 4:21.

28. Thomas Wentworth Higginson, "Life in Cambridge Town," in *The Cambridge of Eighteen Hundred and Ninety-Six.* Cambridge, Mass.: Riverside Press, 1896, 39.

29. HJSr. to Samuel Gray Ward, 7 September 1858, Houghton.

30. WJ to Edgar Van Winkle, 12 November 1858, *Correspondence,* 4:22.

31. Percy MacKaye, *Epoch: The Life of Steele MacKaye,* vol. 1. New York: Boni & Liveright, 1927, 76n.

32. WJ to Edgar Van Winkle, 12 November 1858, *Correspondence,* 4:24.

33. WJ to Edgar Van Winkle, 12 November 1858, *Correspondence,* 4:23.

34. HJSr., "Man," in *Lectures and Miscellanies,* 346–56.

35. HJSr., "Morality," in *Lectures and Miscellanies,* 362–74.

36. Henry Adams, "The Contradictions of William Morris Hunt," in *William Morris Hunt: A Memorial Exhibition,* by M. Hoppin and H. Adams. Boston: Museum of Fine Arts, 1979, 25–26.

37. Helen Knowlton, ed., *William Morris Hunt's Talks on Art.* Boston: Houghton, Osgood, 1880, 6.

38. Edward Waldo Emerson, *The Early Years of the Saturday Club.* Boston: Houghton Mifflin, 1918, 472.

39. William Morris Hunt, quoted in Adams, *op. cit.,* 22.

40. M. De Wolfe Howe, *Memories of a Hostess.* Boston: Atlantic Monthly Press, 1922.

41. HJ, *NSB,* 285.

42. Knowlton, ed., *Talks on Art,* 57.

43. HJSr. to Edmund Tweedy, 24–30 July (1860), Houghton.

44. F. B. Sanborn, *Memoir of Bronson Alcott,* vol. 1. New York: Biblo and Tannen, 1965, 277 n.1.

45. HJSr. to Catharine James, 24 July 1854, Houghton.

46. HJSr. to Edmund Tweedy, 24–30 July (1860), Houghton.

47. AJ, *The Diary of Alice James,* ed. Leon Edel. New York: Dodd, Mead, 1964, 72.

48. WJ to Edgar Van Winkle, 18 September 1859, *Correspondence,* 4:21.

49. WJ to Edgar Van Winkle, 18 December 1859, *Correspondence,* 4:25.

50. HJ to Thomas Sergeant Perry, 8 October (1859), *Henry James Letters,* vol. 1, ed. Leon Edel (Cambridge: Harvard University Press, 1974), 6.

51. WJ to Edgar Van Winkle, 18 December 1859, *Correspondence,* 4:25–26.

52. HJ to Thomas S. Perry, 13 May 1860, *HJ Letters,* ed. Edel, 1:20.

53. HJ to Thomas S. Perry, 18 July 1860. *HJ Letters,* ed. Edel, 1:24.

54. HJSr. to Edmund Tweedy, 18 July (1860), Perry, 1:191.

55. HJ to Thomas S. Perry, 18 July 1860, *HJ Letters,* ed. Edel, 1:22.

56. HJSr. to Edmund Tweedy, 24 July (1860), Perry, 1:193.

Chapter 5: Spiritual Dangers

1. WJ to AJ, 30 July (1872), Houghton. Harry, visiting Newport in 1868, wrote, "The place struck me with a chill and horror." HJ to Thomas Perry, 27 March 1868, *HJ Letters,* ed. Edel, 1:83–84.

2. WJ to HJSr. (19 August 1860), *Correspondence,* 4:36–38.

3. WJ to HJSr. (24 August 1860), *Correspondence,* 4:40.

4. WJ to HJSr. (24 August 1860), *Correspondence,* 4:40.

5. HJ to Thomas S. Perry, 5 August 1860, *HJ Letters,* ed. Edel, 1:32.

6. HJ, *NSB,* 277.

7. MacKaye, *Epoch,* 76.

8. HJ, *NSB,* 287.

9. *Ibid.,* 288.

10. *Ibid.,* 287.

11. HJSr., *Literary Remains,* 345.

12. *Ibid.,* 343.

13. HJSr. to Edmund Tweedy, 1 October 1860, Houghton.

14. HJ, *SBO,* 124.

15. HJSr. to WJ, 18 March 1868, Houghton.

16. Ellen Tucker Emerson, *Letters,* ed. Edith Gregg. Kent, Ohio: Kent State University Press, 1982, 291.

17. Virginia Harlow, *Thomas Sergeant Perry: A Biography.* Durham: Duke University Press, 1950, 18.

18. Quoted in Strouse, *Alice James,* 44.

19. AJ to HJSr., 11 March 1860, *Death and Letters,* 49.

20. WJ to HJSr. (19 August 1860), *Correspondence,* 4:38.

21. AJ to WJ, 28 May 1867, *Correspondence*, 4:167.

22. HJ to Thomas S. Perry, 25 March (1864), *HJ Letters*, ed. Edel, 1:50.

23. AJ to Annie Ashburner, 12 April 1876. *Death and Letters*, 73, 74.

24. Julian Hawthorne, in Maher, *Biography of Broken Fortunes*, 19–20.

25. WJ, "'Person and Personality': From *Johnson's Universal Cyclopaedia*," in *EPsych*, 315.

26. HJ, *NSB*, 308.

27. WJ to HJ, 22 March 1869, *Correspondence*, 1:61.

28. In "Henry James and the Civil War," *New England Quarterly* 62 (December 1989): 529–52, Charles and Tess Hoffmann also come to this conclusion (537). The Hoffmanns, however, agree with Leon Edel that William decided to give up painting because of the Civil War (535–36).

29. WJ to his family, 16 September 1861, *Letters*, 1:35; *Correspondence*, 4:43.

30. WJ to HJ (7 September 1861), *Correspondence*, 1:1–3.

31. WJ to Mary James, 10 September (1861), Perry, 1:210; *Correspondence*, 4:41.

32. Frank Higginson to Henry Lee Higginson, *The Letters of Henry Lee Higginson*. Edited by Bliss Perry. Boston: Atlantic Monthly Press, 1921, 133.

33. WJ to his family, 16 September 1861, *Letters*, 1:35; *Correspondence*, 4:43. Eliot's remarks: *Letters*, 1:31–32.

34. WJ to his family, 25 December (1861), Perry, 1:211; *Correspondence*, 4:63.

35. WJ to Katharine James Prince, 12 September 1863, *Letters*, 1:43–44; *Correspondence*, 4:81.

36. WJ to Mary James (2 November 1863), *Correspondence*, 4:86.

37. WJ to Jeannette Barber Gourlay, 21 February 1864, Perry, 1:216; *Correspondence*, 4:90.

38. In the end, it seems to have cost several times more. See WJ to HJSr., 3 June 1865, *Letters*, 1:61.

39. WJ to his family, 3 June 1865, *Letters*, 1:62; *Correspondence*, 4:107.

40. WJ to his parents, 21 April 1865, *Letters*, 1:58; *Correspondence*, 4:101.

41. WJ to HJ, 3 May 1865, *Correspondence*, 1:8.

42. WJ to his family, 3 June 1865, *Letters*, 1:61–63; *Correspondence*, 4:107.

43. WJ to his family, 7 June 1865, in Carleton Sprague Smith, "William James in Brazil," in *Four Papers Presented in the Institute for Brazilian Studies*. Nashville: Vanderbilt University Press, 1951, 104.

44. Louis Agassiz to Nathaniel Thayer, 25 November 1865, Museum of Comparative Zoology, Harvard.
45. WJ to Mary James, 23 August (1865), *Correspondence,* 4:110–13.
46. *Ibid.,* 111.
47. *Letters,* 1:56.
48. WJ to AJ, 1 September 1865, *Correspondence,* 4:120.
49. WJ to Joao, early December 1865, Smith, "William James in Brazil," 136.
50. Quoted in Smith, "William James in Brazil," 125–26.
51. Smith, "William James in Brazil," 132.
52. WJ to Mary James, 9 December 1865, Perry, 1:225; *Correspondence,* 4:132.

Chapter 6: Descent

1. HJSr. to Edmund Tweedy, 18 July (1860), Houghton.
2. HJSr. to Robertson James, 28 April 1865, quoted in Maher, *Biography of Broken Fortunes,* 74.
3. HJSr., "Is Marriage Holy?" *The Atlantic Monthly,* March 1870, 364.
4. WJ to his parents, 12 August (1860), Perry, 1:195; *Correspondence,* 4:35.
5. AJ to HJSr., 11 March 1860, *Death and Letters,* 49.
6. WJ, Review of *Women's Suffrage* by Horace Bushnell and *The Subjection of Women* by John Stuart Mill, in *ECR,* 253. Originally published in *North American Review* 109 (October 1869).
7. AJ, *Diary,* 155.
8. WJ to Garth Wilkinson James, 21 March (1866), Perry, 1:228; *Correspondence,* 4:135.
9. Mrs. Holmes to Oliver Wendell Holmes Jr., 3 July 1866, quoted in Liva Baker, *The Justice from Beacon Hill.* New York: HarperCollins, 1991, 181.
10. WJ to Tom Ward, 8 June 1866, *Letters,* 1:78; *Correspondence,* 4:140.
11. WJ to Tom Ward, (7) January 1868, *Correspondence,* 4:248.
12. WJ to AJ, 12 December (1866), *Correspondence,* 4:148.
13. WJ to AJ, 14 November 1866, *Letters,* 1:80–81; *Correspondence,* 4:145.
14. Mary James to AJ, April 1867, Houghton.
15. WJ to Oliver Wendell Holmes Jr., (10 April 1867), Harvard Law School Archives.
16. WJ to AJ, 19 November 1867, *Correspondence,* 4:228. WJ used this phrase in reference to his friendship with Fräulein Bornemann, a young woman he met through the Grimms.
17. WJ to Tom Ward, 14 March 1870, *Correspondence,* 4:403.

18. Charles Eliot Norton to G. W. Curtis, *Letters of Charles Eliot Norton,* vol. 1, ed. Sara Norton and M. A. De Wolfe Howe. Boston: Houghton Mifflin, 1913, 410–11.

19. WJ to Henry Pickering Bowditch, 12 December 1867, *Correspondence,* 4:233.

20. WJ to Mary James, 12 June 1867, *Letters,* 1:93; *Correspondence,* 4:176.

21. WJ to his parents, 27 May 1867, *Letters,* 1:87; *Correspondence,* 4:160.

22. WJ to his family, 24 July 1867, Perry, 1:241; *Correspondence,* 4:184.

23. WJ to HJSr., 26 September 1867, *Correspondence,* 4:203.

24. WJ to Tom Ward, 7 January 1868, *Correspondence,* 4:249.

25. HJSr., "The Ontology of Swedenborg," *North American Review* 105 (1867): 89–123. HJSr. reviewed a biography of Swedenborg and two new translations of Swedenborg's work.

26. HJSr. to WJ, 27 September 1867, *Correspondence,* 4:204.

27. WJ to HJSr., 28 October 1867, *Correspondence,* 4:221.

28. WJ to Tom Ward, 7 January 1868, *Correspondence,* 4:249–50.

29. WJ to HJSr., 5 September 1867, *Correspondence,* 4:194.

30. WJ to Henry Bowditch, 12 December 1867, *Correspondence,* 4:234–35.

31. HJ to WJ, 22 November (1867), *Correspondence,* 1:25–26.

32. Mary James to WJ, 21 November 1867, *Correspondence,* 4:230.

33. WJ to Oliver Wendell Holmes, 15 May 1868, *Correspondence,* 4:300.

34. WJ to Oliver Wendell Holmes, 18 May 1868, *Correspondence,* 4:301.

35. WJ to Henry Bowditch, 5 May 1868, *Correspondence,* 4:292. This letter was misdated 5 April 1868.

36. WJ to Oliver Wendell Holmes, 18 May 1868, *Correspondence,* 4:302.

37. WJ to Tom Ward, (7) January 1868, *Correspondence,* 4:250.

38. WJ, Review of *Rapport sur les progrès et la marche de la physiologie générale en France,* in *ECR,* 222–28. Originally published in *North American Review* 107 (July 1868): 322–28.

39. WJ to HJ, 12 February 1868, *Correspondence,* 1:31–32.

40. WJ, diary, 22 May 1868, Houghton.

41. WJ, diary, 27 May 1868, Houghton.

42. WJ to Tom Ward, 24 May 1868, *Correspondence,* 4:305.

43. WJ to Catherine Havens, 29 August 1868, *Correspondence,* 4:334.

44. HJSr. to WJ, 27 September 1867, *Correspondence,* 4:208.

45. WJ to Tom Ward, 29 October (1868), Perry, 1:288.

46. AJ, *Diary,* 149.

47. WJ to HJ, 22 March 1869, *Correspondence,* 1:61.

48. WJ to Tom Ward, 16 December 1868, *Correspondence,* 4:353.

49. WJ to Henry Bowditch, 12 August 1869, *Correspondence,* 4:383.

50. Mary James to HJ, 24 July 1869, Houghton.
51. Mary James to HJ, 24 July 1869, Houghton.
52. Mary James to HJ, 25 July 1869, Houghton.
53. WJ to Oliver Wendell Holmes, n.d., Harvard Law Library Archives.
54. WJ to HJ, 1 June 1869, *Correspondence,* 1:80.
55. Wilhelm von Humboldt, *Letters of William von Humboldt to a Female Friend,* 2 vols, trans. Catharine M. A. Couper. London: J. Chapman, 1849, xiii.
56. *Ibid.,* 10.
57. WJ to HJ, 5 December 1869, *Correspondence,* 1:129.
58. See Mary James to HJ, 1 July 1873, Houghton. WJ compares his nervous condition to Alice's.
59. J. G. Spurzheim, *Observations on the Deranged Manifestations of the Mind or Insanity.* London: Baldwin, Cradock & Joy, 1817, 243.
60. Edward Charles Spitzka, *Insanity: Its Classification, Diagnosis, and Treatment.* New York: E. B. Treat, 1887, 190.
61. WJ, "The Powers of Men," *ERM,* 156.
62. WJ to Tom Ward, (7) January 1868, *Correspondence,* 4:248–49.
63. Mary Temple to John Gray, 7 January 1869, Houghton.
64. Mary Temple to John Gray, 27 January 1869, Houghton.
65. Mary Temple to John Gray, 25 January 1870, quoted in Alfred Habegger, "New Light on William James and Minny Temple," *New England Quarterly* (March 1987), 50.
66. Mary Temple to WJ, 10 February 1870, Houghton. Copy in the hand of Alice Gibbens James.
67. Mary Temple to John Gray, 21 January 1870, Houghton.
68. WJ, journal entry, 21 December 1869, Houghton.
69. WJ, diary, 1 February 1870, Houghton.

Chapter 7: Absolute Beginnings

1. WJ, "Frederic Myers' Services to Psychology," in *Memories and Studies.* New York: Longmans, Green, 1911, 148–49.
2. HJ to WJ, 24 July 1872, *Correspondence,* 1:161.
3. WJ, *Varieties of Religious Experience,* 136–37.
4. *Ibid.,* 134–35.
5. WJ to HJ, 7 May 1870, *Correspondence,* 1:159.
6. WJ to Tom Ward, (7) January 1868, *Correspondence,* 4:249.
7. WJ, diary, 30 April 1870, Houghton.
8. WJ, "Renouvier's Contribution to *La critique philosophique,*" in *ECR,* 266.

9. WJ, diary, 30 April 1870, Houghton.

10. WJ to Tom Ward, (7) January 1868, *Correspondence*, 4:248.

11. Robert Browning, "Bishop Bloughram's Apology," *Poetical Works*. London: Oxford University Press, 1967, 444.

12. John Jay Chapman, *Memories and Milestones*. Freeport, N.Y.: Books for Libraries Press, 1971 (1915), 167, 171–72.

13. WJ to Henry Bowditch, 22 May 1869, *Correspondence*, 4:379.

14. WJ to Henry Bowditch, 12 August 1869, *Correspondence*, 4:385.

15. Charles William Eliot, "Inaugural Address as President of Harvard College, 19 October 1869," quoted in W. Bruce Fye, "Why a Physiologist? The Case of Henry P. Bowditch," *Bulletin of the History of Medicine* 56 (1982): 26.

16. WJ to HJ, 24 August 1872, *Correspondence*, 1:167.

17. WJ to HJ, (10) October 1872, *Correspondence*, 1:173.

18. WJ to HJ, 13 February 1873, *Correspondence*, 1:191.

19. Mary James to HJ, 1 March 1873, Houghton.

20. Mary James to HJ, 15 December 1872, Houghton.

21. HJSr. to HJ, 18 March 1873, Perry, 1:339–40.

22. WJ, diary, 10 February 1873, quoted in Perry, 1:335.

23. WJ, "Two Reviews of *Principles of Mental Physiology* by William B. Carpenter," in *ECR*, 274, 273. Originally published in *North American Review* (July 1874).

24. WJ to HJ, 11 May 1873, *Correspondence*, 1:203.

25. WJ to HJ, 6 April 1873, *Correspondence*, 1:194.

26. WJ to HJ, 25 May 1873, *Correspondence*, 1:208–9.

27. WJ to HJ, 14 July (1873), *Correspondence*, 1:214–15.

28. Mary James to HJ, 12 September 1873, Houghton.

29. WJ to HJ, 2 September 1873, *Correspondence*, 1:219.

30. WJ to the James family, 25 October 1873, *Correspondence*, 4:449.

31. WJ to Mary James, 6 November (1873), *Correspondence*, 4:452.

32. Mary James to HJ, 8 December 1873, Houghton.

33. HJ to Charles Eliot Norton, 16 January 1871, *HJ Letters*, ed. Edel, 253.

34. WJ to AJ, 17 December 1873; WJ to Mary James, 26 January 1874; WJ to HJSr., 4 January 1874, *Correspondence*, 4:472, 480, 475; HJ to his parents, 5 February (1874), *HJ Letters*, ed. Edel, 430.

35. WJ to AJ, 23 November 1873, *Correspondence*, 4:458.

36. HJ to his parents, 3 December (1873), *HJ Letters*, ed. Edel, 413.

37. Mary James to HJ, 6 July 1874, Houghton.

38. WJ, 10 March 1869, in *EPR*, 1–4.

39. WJ to Catherine Havens, 14 June 1874, *Correspondence*, 4:496.

40. Benjamin Paul Blood to WJ, 20 June (1895), Perry, 2:229.
41. WJ, "*The Anaesthetic Revelation,* by Benjamin Paul Blood," in *ECR,* 285–88. Originally published in *Atlantic Monthly,* November 1874.
42. WJ to HJ, 14 November 1875, *Correspondence,* 1:243.

Chapter 8: Engaged

1. WJ to HJ, 14 November 1875, *Correspondence,* 1:243.
2. WJ to HJ, 12 December 1875, *Correspondence,* 1:247.
3. WJ to Catherine Havens, 26 December 1874, *Correspondence,* 4:506.
4. WJ to HJ, 1 January 1876, *Correspondence,* 1:249.
5. WJ, *ECR,* 296–97, 301. Originally published in *North American Review,* July 1875.
6. WJ to Carl Stumpf, 6 February 1887, *Letters,* 1:263.
7. WJ, "*The Emotions and the Will,* by Alexander Bain and *Essais de critique générale* by Charles Renouvier," in *ECR,* 325, 326. Originally published in *Nation,* 8 June 1876.
8. WJ to HJ, 14 November 1875, *Correspondence,* 1:243.
9. HJ to Charles Norton, quoted in Max Fisch, "Was There a Metaphysical Club in Cambridge?" in *Studies in the Philosophy of C. S. Peirce,* ed. Edward C. Moore and Richard S. Robin. Amherst: University of Massachusetts Press, 1964, 4.
10. Chauncey Wright to Grace Norton, 18 July 1875, Perry, 1:530.
11. "Notes by Chauncey Wright," in Perry, 2:718.
12. WJ to his family, 16 September (18)61, *Correspondence,* 4:43.
13. C. S. Peirce to WJ, 21 November 1875, *Correspondence,* 4:523.
14. WJ to HJ, 12 December (18)75, *Correspondence,* 1:246.
15. M. E. F. Sargent, *Sketches and Reminiscences of the Radical Club of Chestnut Street.* Edited by Mrs. John T. Sargent. Boston: Osgood, 1880, 383.
16. Julia Ward Howe, *Reminiscences, 1819–1899.* Boston: Houghton Mifflin, 1899, 282.
17. Daniel Gibbens to AHG, 28 July 1859, Houghton.
18. Daniel Gibbens to AHG, 10 June 1865, Houghton.
19. AHJ to John Chapman, 30 March 1919, Houghton.
20. Daniel Gibbens to AHG, 22 May 1865, Houghton.
21. Daniel Gibbens to AHG, 9 June 1865, Houghton.
22. Daniel Gibbens to AHG, 28 November 1862, Houghton.
23. Daniel Gibbens to AHG, 4 July 1865, Houghton.
24. Daniel Gibbens to AHG, 9 June 1865, Houghton.
25. Daniel Gibbens to AHG, 10 October 1865, Houghton.

26. *Mobile Daily Times,* 31 October 1865.
27. Daniel Gibbens to AHG, 25 May 1865, Houghton.
28. Daniel Gibbens to AHG, 17 July 1865, Houghton.
29. Vida Scudder, *On Journey.* New York: Dutton, 1937, 33.
30. WJ to AHJ, 13 May 1888, Houghton.
31. WJ to AHJ, 10 August 1898, Houghton.
32. WJ to HJ, 3 June 1876, *Correspondence,* 1:261.
33. WJ to Robertson James, 11 June (1876); WJ to Catherine Havens, 13 July 1876, *Correspondence,* 4:537, 540.
34. WJ, "Vacations," *ECR,* 4.
35. James Jackson Putnam, "William James," *WJR,* 15–16.
36. WJ to AHG, 6 October 1876, *Correspondence,* 4:547.
37. WJ to AHG, (Fall) 1876, Houghton.
38. WJ, *Principles of Psychology,* 1053–55.
39. *Ibid.,* 238.
40. WJ to AHG (September 1876), *Correspondence,* 4:544.
41. WJ to AHG (9 October 1876), 12 November 1876, *Correspondence,* 4:547, 549.
42. WJ to AHG (6 October 1876), *Correspondence,* 4:547.
43. WJ to AHG, 30 April (1877), *Correspondence,* 4:561.
44. WJ to AHG, 15 April 1877, *Correspondence,* 4:557.
45. WJ to AHG, 7 June 1877, *Correspondence,* 4:571.

Chapter 9: Gifts

1. Mary Tweedy to WJ, 14 May 1878, *Correspondence,* 5:10.
2. Garth Wilkinson James to WJ, 16 May 1878, *Correspondence,* 5:10.
3. WJ to Frances Rollins Morse, 26 May (1878), *Correspondence,* 5:13.
4. WJ to AHG, 24 February 1878, *Correspondence,* 5:3.
5. WJ, diary, 30 April 1870, Houghton.
6. WJ, *Varieties of Religious Experience,* 126–27.
7. AHG to John Greenleaf Whittier, n.d., Essex Institute.
8. WJ to Fanny Morse, 26 May 1878, *Correspondence,* 5:13.
9. HJ to WJ, 23 July (1878), *Correspondence,* 1:305.
10. AJ, *Diary,* 230.
11. HJ to Robertson James, 17 September (1878), quoted in Strouse, *Alice James,* 186.
12. WJ to Harris, 6 December 1877, *Correspondence,* 4:587.
13. WJ to Thomas Ward, 30 December 1876, *Correspondence,* 4:552.
14. WJ, "Remarks on Spencer's Definition of Mind as Correspondence," *EPhil,* 12–13.

15. *Ibid.*, 11n.
16. George Santayana, *Persons and Places*, vol. 1. London: Constable, 1944, 253.
17. WJ to G. S. Hall, 3 September 1879, *Correspondence*, 5:61.
18. WJ to Royce, 3 February 1880, *Correspondence*, 5:84.
19. George Croom Robertson, "Prefatory Words," *Mind* (January 1876): 3.
20. WJ to Arthur Sedgwick, 20 September 1878, *Correspondence*, 5:22.
21. WJ to AHJ, 24 May 1890, Houghton.
22. WJ to Daniel Coit Gilman, 18 January 1879, *Correspondence*, 5:35.
23. WJ to Arthur Gilman, 18 February 1879, *Correspondence*, 5:41.
24. George Angier Gordon, "A Profoundly Religious Man," in *WJR*, 46–47.
25. WJ to Robertson James, 26 May 1879, *Correspondence*, 5:52.
26. George Angier Gordon, "A Profoundly Religious Man," in *WJR*, 46.
27. WJ to Robertson James, 28 April 1880, *Correspondence*, 5:91.
28. WJ, *EPhil*, 32.
29. WJ, *Ibid.*, 37.
30. WJ, *Ibid.*, 38.
31. WJ, "Rationality, Activity and Faith," in *WB*, 74.
32. WJ to AHJ, 27 June 1880, *Correspondence*, 5:108.
33. WJ to AHJ, 28 June 1880, *Correspondence*, 5:111.
34. WJ to AHJ, 10 July 1880, *Correspondence*, 5:118.
35. WJ to AHJ, 27 June 1880, *Correspondence*, 5:109.
36. WJ, "Great Men, Great Thoughts and The Environment," in *WB*, 164.
37. HJSr., "Some Personal Recollections of Carlyle," *Atlantic Monthly*, May 1881, 603.
38. WJ to Daniel Coit Gilman, 3 April 1881, *Correspondence*, 5:157.
39. WJ to AHJ, 8 April 1881, *Correspondence*, 5:160.
40. WJ to Daniel Coit Gilman, 18 April 1881, *Correspondence*, 5:162.
41. WJ to Thomas Davidson, 16 April 1882, *Correspondence*, 5:204.
42. WJ to Emma Wilkinson Pertz, 6 January 1884, *Correspondence*, 5:478.
43. Royce to George Coale, 24 January 1883, *Letters of Josiah Royce*, ed. John Clendenning, 123.
44. WJ to AHJ, 22 September 1882, *Correspondence*, 5:257.

Chapter 10: An Entirely New Segment of Life

1. WJ to AHJ, 24 September 1882, *Correspondence*, 5:254.
2. WJ to Henry James III, 1 October 1882, *Correspondence*, 5:261.
3. HJSr. to WJ, 7 November 1882, *Correspondence*, 5:293.

4. AHJ to WJ, 30 November (1882), *Correspondence,* 5:313.

5. AJ, *Diary,* 125.

6. Quoted in Habegger, *The Father,* 499.

7. WJ to AHJ, 11 December (1882), *Correspondence,* 5:321–22.

8. AHJ to WJ, 30 November 1882, *Correspondence,* 5:313.

9. WJ to Henry James III, 1 October 1882, *Correspondence,* 5:261.

10. WJ to AHJ, 11 October 1882, *Correspondence,* 5:269.

11. WJ to AHJ, 15 December 1882, *Correspondence,* 5:330.

12. WJ to AHJ, 15 December 1882, *Correspondence,* 5:330.

13. WJ to HJSr., 14 December 1882, *Correspondence,* 5:327–28.

14. AHJ to WJ, 21 December 1882, *Correspondence,* 5:344.

15. HJ to WJ, 28 December (1882), *Correspondence,* 1:340–41.

16. HJ to WJ, 26 December (1882), *Correspondence,* 1:340.

17. WJ to HJ, 20 December 1882, *Correspondence,* 1:337.

18. WJ to AJ, 20 December 1882, *Correspondence,* 5:340.

19. WJ to AHJ, 22 December 1882, *Correspondence,* 5:346.

20. WJ to AJ, 20 December 1882, *Correspondence,* 5:340.

21. AHJ to WJ, 27 January 1883, *Correspondence,* 5:407.

22. AHJ to WJ, 1 January 1883, *Correspondence,* 5:371.

23. WJ to AJ, 20 December 1882, *Correspondence,* 5:341.

24. AHJ to WJ, 21 December 1882, *Correspondence,* 5:344.

25. WJ to AHJ, 9 April 1888, Houghton.

26. WJ to AHJ, 6 January 1883, *Correspondence,* 5:378.

27. HJ to WJ, 11 January (1883), *Correspondence,* 1:348–52.

28. WJ to HJ, 23 January (1883), *Correspondence,* 1:354–55.

29. WJ to AHJ, 23 February 1883, *Correspondence,* 5:428.

30. WJ to AHJ, 23 February 1883, *Correspondence,* 5:427.

31. Single admission to the lectures cost fifty cents, and lecturers were paid fifteen dollars for each talk.

32. James delivered his lectures on July 18, 20, and 23.

33. WJ, *EPsych,* 146.

34. WJ to Frederick George Bromberg, 30 June 1884, *Correspondence,* 5:505.

35. WJ, *EPsych,* 170.

36. *Ibid.,* 178.

37. WJ, "The Dilemma of Determinism," in *Unitarian Review,* September 1884; *WB,* 114–40.

38. WJ, *WB,* 119.

39. *Ibid.,* 123.

40. WJ to Mary James, 4 October 1884, *Correspondence,* 5:527.

41. WJ to HJ, 6 January 1884, *Correspondence*, 5:478–79.
42. WJ to AHJ, 13 September 1884, *Correspondence*, 5:571.
43. HJ to WJ, 26 March (1884), *Correspondence*, 1:377–78.
44. WJ to AHJ, 7 August 1884, *Correspondence*, 5:513.
45. HJSr., *Literary Remains*, 9.
46. *Ibid.*, 10.
47. *Ibid.*, 48n.
48. *Ibid.*, 15.
49. *Ibid.*, 116–17.
50. *Ibid.*, 118.
51. WJ to HJ, 17 September 1885, *Correspondence*, 2:29.
52. WJ, "Frederic Myers's Service to Psychology," in *EPR*, 193–94.
53. WJ to Carl Stumpf, 1 January 1886, *Letters*, 1:248.
54. WJ to Thomas Davidson, 30 March 1884, *Correspondence*, 5:499.
55. WJ to AHJ, 29 August 1884, *Correspondence*, 5:521.
56. AHJ to WJ, 1 January 1883, *Correspondence*, 5:370.
57. WJ to Katharine James Prince, 24 December 1884, *Correspondence*, 5:542.
58. Edward Gurney to WJ, 23 September 1883, *Correspondence*, 5:462.
59. William Barrett, Report on "The Prospects of Psychical Research in America," *Journal of Society for Psychical Research* (November 1884): 174.
60. William Barrett, quoted in WJ, *EPR*, 7.
61. WJ to Thomas Davidson, 1 February 1885, *Letters*, 1:250.

Chapter 11: The Lost Child

1. WJ to Charles Marseilles, 23 April 1885, Scott: 29.
2. Quoted in Liva Baker, *The Justice from Beacon Hill*, 245.
3. Elizabeth Glendower Evans, "William James and His Wife," in *WJR*, 62.
4. WJ to AJ, 20 March 1885, Houghton.
5. WJ to Catharine Walsh, 28 June 1885, Houghton.
6. WJ to Catharine Walsh, 28 June 1885, Houghton.
7. WJ to AHJ, 27 June 1885, Houghton.
8. WJ to Catharine Walsh, 11 July 1885, Houghton.
9. WJ to HJ, 11 July 1885, *Correspondence*, 2:21.
10. WJ to AHJ, 25 September 1882, *Correspondence*, 5:255–56.
11. WJ, *Principles of Psychology*, 1055–56.
12. WJ to AHJ, n.d. (three weeks after Herman's death), Houghton.
13. HJ to WJ (24 July 1885), *Correspondence*, 2:23.

14. Elizabeth Glendower Evans, "William James and His Wife," in *WJR*, 62.

15. AHJ to Elizabeth Glendower Evans, "William James and His Wife," in *WJR*, 62–63.

16. WJ to Katharine James Prince, 12 July 1885, Houghton.

17. There is some debate about how, in fact, the Jameses heard of Piper. See WJ, *EPR*, 393–400. Since the Jameses were in Jaffrey, New Hampshire, from mid-July through August, it seems likely that they discovered Piper after their return in late summer.

18. WJ to Katharine James Prince, 1 June 1885, Houghton.

19. George Herbert Palmer, "William James," in *WJR*, 32. See also "Letter on Mrs. Ross, the Medium" in WJ, *EPR*, 29–32, for James's severe castigation of one Mrs. H. V. Ross.

20. WJ, *Human Immortality*. Boston: Houghton Mifflin, 1900, 15.

21. When James recounted this first visit to Piper in "Certain Phenomena of Trance," he said that Herman had died "the previous year." However, since a letter of 25 September 1885 already refers to sittings with Piper, their first encounter must have occurred in summer or early fall, 1885, a few months after Herman's death. See WJ, *EPR*, 79–88.

22. AHJ to Elizabeth Glendower Evans, 5 December (1885?), Schlesinger.

23. WJ, *EPR*, 88.

24. WJ, *Pragmatism*, 140.

25. WJ to AHJ, 6 January 1883, *Correspondence*, 5:379.

26. Santayana, *Persons and Places*, 252.

27. Royce, *The Religious Aspect of Philosophy*. Boston: Houghton Mifflin, 1885, vi.

28. WJ to Carl Stumpf, 6 February 1887, *Letters*, 1:265.

29. WJ, Review of *Lectures and Essays* and *Seeing and Thinking* by William K. Clifford (1879), *ECR*, 359.

30. WJ to Hodgson, 12 September 1886, *Letters*, 1:256–57.

31. Royce, *Religious Aspect*, 6–7.

32. *Ibid.*, 6.

33. WJ to Thomas Davidson, 8 January 1882, *Correspondence*, 5:195.

34. WJ, "Philosophical Conceptions and Practical Results," in *Pragmatism*, 267.

35. Royce, *Religious Aspect*, 112.

36. Royce, *Religious Aspect*, 116, 117. For James's comment on the romantic, see WJ to Shadworth Hodgson, 12 September 1886, *Letters*, 1:256–57.

37. WJ to Henry Bowditch, 8 April 1871, *Correspondence,* 4:417.
38. WJ to HJ, 9 May 1886, *Correspondence,* 2:40.
39. WJ to William Mackintyre Salter, 24 March (1886), Houghton.
40. WJ to HJ, 9 May 1886, *Correspondence,* 2:40.
41. WJ to Salter, 7 November 1887, Houghton.
42. WJ to HJ, 17 September (1886), *Correspondence,* 2:51.
43. WJ to HJ, 14 October 1888, *Correspondence,* 2:91.
44. WJ to AHJ, 19 October 1887, Houghton.
45. WJ to AHJ, 24 May (n.y.), Houghton.
46. WJ to AHJ, 26 May (n.y.), Houghton.
47. WJ to George Croom Robertson, 29 August 1886, Perry, 1:602.
48. Hodgson to J. T. Hackett, 23 December 1888, quoted in Arthur S. Berger, *Lives and Letters in American Parapsychology.* Jefferson, N.C.: McFarland, 1988, 22.
49. WJ to George Croom Robertson, 13 August 1885, Houghton.
50. WJ to AJ, 5 February 1887, *Letters,* 1:261.
51. WJ to Katharine Prince, 3 February 1887, Houghton.
52. WJ to HJ, 10 March 1887, *Correspondence,* 2:59.
53. WJ to AHJ, 6 October 1887, Houghton.
54. WJ to AHJ, 4 March 1888, Houghton.
55. WJ to HJ, 12 April 1887, *Correspondence,* 2:62–63.
56. WJ to Henry Bowditch, 26 March 1887, *Letters,* 1:267.
57. WJ to HJ, 28 September 1890, *Correspondence,* 2:149.
58. WJ to HJ, 6 February 1888, *Correspondence,* 2:79–80.
59. John J. Chapman, "William James," *WJR,* 55.

Chapter 12: Family Romance

1. WJ to AHJ, 17 January 1888, Houghton.
2. AHJ to WJ, 3 January (1883), *Correspondence,* 5:375.
3. WJ to Eliza Gibbens, 10 December 1900, Houghton.
4. WJ to AHJ, 15 February 1888, Houghton.
5. WJ, *Principles of Psychology,* 1055.
6. WJ to AHJ, 22 March 1888, Houghton.
7. WJ to AHJ, 21 March 1888, Houghton.
8. WJ to Baldwin, 7 March 1891, Houghton.
9. WJ to HJ, 11 July 1888, *Correspondence,* 2:89–90.
10. WJ to AHJ, 5 or 6 April 1888, Houghton.
11. WJ to AHJ, 30 June 1889, Houghton.
12. WJ to HJ, 12 April 1887, *Correspondence,* 2:63.
13. WJ to HJ, 6 February 1888, *Correspondence,* 2:80.

14. G. Stanley Hall to WJ, 26 October 1879, *Correspondence,* 5:66.
15. WJ to G. Stanley Hall, 16 January 1880, *Correspondence,* 5:82.
16. WJ to Hall, 5 November 1887, Scott, 47; 10 November 1887, Scott, 50.
17. WJ to George Croom Robertson, 9 November 1887, Houghton. James was more generous toward Hall after he suffered a great personal tragedy—the asphyxiation of his wife and daughter in the spring of 1890. See WJ to Hall, 16 May 1890, Scott, 64.
18. WJ, *Talks to Teachers,* in *Psychology,* 50.
19. WJ to HJ, 19 April 1888, Houghton.
20. WJ to AHJ, 19 April 1888, Houghton.
21. WJ to AHJ, 24 April 1888, Houghton.
22. HJ to WJ, 8 March (1889), *Correspondence,* 2:106.
23. AJ to WJ, 7 April (1889), *Death and Letters,* 167.
24. WJ to HJ, 12 May 1889, *Correspondence,* 2:108–9.
25. WJ to AHJ, 19 July 1889, Houghton.
26. AJ, *Diary,* 51–52.
27. AJ, *Diary,* 25.
28. WJ to AHJ, 19 July 1889, *Letters,* 1:288.
29. WJ to HJ, 11 July 1888, *Letters,* 1:280.
30. WJ to AHJ, 25 July 1889, Houghton.
31. WJ to AHJ, 29 July 1889, Houghton.
32. Théodore Flournoy, *Spiritism and Psychology,* trans. Hereward Carrington. New York: Harper, 1911, vii.
33. *Ibid.,* vii.
34. James, *Principles of Psychology,* 3:1556n.
35. WJ to HJ, 11 April 1892, *Correspondence,* 2:217.
36. Rollo Walter Brown, *Harvard Yard in the Golden Age.* New York: Current Books, 1948, 49.
37. WJ to Royce, 22 June 1892, in Perry, 2:141.
38. WJ to HJ, 30 August 1889, *Correspondence,* 2:121.
39. We do know, however, that James was delighted to have more children, as he wrote to her on 16 October 1887. "For though simplification has its charms *for a change,* life has its charms also; and God knows, darling girl, that I have use enough of you when you come—even if we do have another child, I'm willing! The three are so nice; and you such a good mother, that my old feeling is gone, I know not where. Only I should like to have you, for one day, alone.—I trust you are not offended by the perhaps somewhat transparent sense of these remarks." (Houghton)

40. WJ to HJ, 15 December 1889, *Correspondence,* 2:129.
41. AJ, *Diary,* 68.
42. WJ to HJ, 15 December 1889, *Correspondence,* 2:129.
43. WJ to HJ, 19 September 1887, *Correspondence,* 2:68.
44. WJ to HJ, 22 August 1890, *Correspondence,* 2:146.
45. WJ to Howells, 20 August 1890, *Letters,* 1:298.
46. WJ to AHJ, 17 May 1890, Houghton.
47. WJ to Christine Ladd-Franklin, 19 May (1890), Scott, 65.
48. WJ to AHJ, 24 May 1890, Houghton.
49. WJ to HJ, 22 August 1890, *Correspondence,* 2:146.
50. Chapman, *Memories,* 105.
51. WJ to HJ, 22 August 1890, *Correspondence,* 2:147.
52. WJ to AHJ, 7 July 1890, Houghton.
53. WJ to Sarah Whitman, 15 October 1890, *Letters,* 1:303–4.
54. WJ to AJ, 23 July 1890, Houghton.
55. WJ to HJ, 26 June (1890), *Correspondence,* 2:142–43.
56. WJ to HJ, 4 June 1890, *Correspondence,* 2:138.

Chapter 13: Surcharged with Vitality

1. James Rowland Angell, "William James," *WJR,* 134–35.
2. Mary Whiton Calkins, in *History of Psychology in Autobiography,* 31.
3. Howells, quoted in Perry, 2:109.
4. WJ to Flournoy, 31 May 1891, Robert Le Clair, ed., *The Letters of William James and Théodore Flournoy.* Madison: University of Wisconsin Press, 1966, 7.
5. WJ, *Principles of Psychology,* 266.
6. *Ibid.,* 126–30.
7. *Ibid.,* 283.
8. *Ibid.,* 282.
9. G. Stanley Hall, Review of *The Principles of Psychology, American Journal of Psychology,* 3, no. 4: 585.
10. Hugo Münsterberg, "Professor James as a Psychologist," in *WJR,* 110.
11. WJ to HJ, 22 December (1890), *Correspondence,* 2:162.
12. HJ to WJ, 12 February (1891), *Correspondence,* 2:171–73.
13. WJ to HJ, 1 June 1891, *Correspondence,* 2:177.
14. *Ibid.*
15. WJ to Holt, 24 July 1891, *Letters,* 1:314.
16. *Ibid.*
17. WJ to James Mark Baldwin, 11 January 1891, Houghton.
18. Roswell Parker Angier, "Another Student's Impressions of James at the Turn of the Century," in *WJR,* 234.

19. WJ to HJ, 16 April 1892, *Correspondence,* 2:219.

20. WJ to Caroline Healey Dall, 14 October 1890, Massachusetts Historical Society.

21. HJ to WJ, 7 November 1890, *Correspondence,* 2:154–55.

22. AJ, *Diary,* 206–7. Sir A. C. was Sir Andrew Clark, a well-regarded physician and surgeon.

23. WJ to AJ, 6 July 1891, *Letters,* 1:309–11.

24. AJ to WJ, 30 July (1891), *Death and Letters,* 185.

25. AJ, *Diary,* 104.

26. HJ to WJ, 2 March 1892, *Correspondence,* 2:203.

27. *Correspondence,* 2:204, n.1; HJ to WJ, (6 March 1892), and WJ to HJ, 7 March 1892, *Correspondence,* 2:205.

28. HJ to WJ, 19 March 1892, *Correspondence,* 2:211–12.

29. HJ to WJ, 9 March (1892), *Correspondence,* 2:211.

30. When Peggy was born, Alice wrote to her sister-in-law: "You have my warmest sympathy & congratulations. That 'he is a girl' delights me, it will be so good for the boys, elevate the tone of the house and be some one for *me* to associate with in the future!" Alice never lived to meet her niece. (AJ to AHJ, 3 April 1887, *Death and Letters,* 123.)

31. WJ to HJ, 22 March (18)92, *Correspondence,* 2:213.

32. WJ to AJ, 4 June (18)68, *Correspondence,* 4:315.

33. WJ to HJSr., 7 August (18)68, *Correspondence,* 4:331.

34. WJ to Mary Whiton Calkins, 29 May 1890, Wellesley College Archives.

35. WJ to Calkins, 30 July 1890, quoted in Elizabeth Scarborough and Laurel Furumoto, *Untold Lives: The First Generation of American Women Psychologists.* New York: Columbia University Press, 1987, 33.

36. WJ to Calkins, 3 October 1890, quoted in Scarborough and Furumoto, 35.

37. WJ to Smith College student, 29 June 1895, Scarborough and Furumoto, 46.

38. Quoted in Rosalind Miller, *Gertrude Stein: Form and Intelligibility.* New York: Exposition Press, 1949, 146.

39. WJ, "Is Life Worth Living?" in *The Will to Believe,* 54.

40. Gertrude Stein, *The Autobiography of Alice B. Toklas,* in *The Selected Writings of Gertrude Stein.* New York: Vintage, 1972, 74–75.

41. WJ to Grace Ashburner, 13 July 1892, *Letters,* 1:321.

42. WJ to HJ, 23 June 1892, *Correspondence,* 2:222.

43. WJ to HJ, 10 July 1892, *Correspondence,* 2:222.

44. WJ to Grace Ashburner, 13 July 1892, *Letters,* 1:321-22.

45. WJ to HJ, 15 December 1889, *Correspondence,* 2:129-30.

46. WJ to AHJ, 19 July 1892, Houghton.

47. AHJ to HJ, 11 October (1892), *Correspondence,* 2:235.

48. WJ to AHJ, 17 November 1892, Houghton.

49. AHJ to HJ, 11 October (1892), *Correspondence,* 2:235.

50. WJ to AHJ, 2 November 1892, Houghton.

51. WJ to AHJ (9 November 1892), Houghton.

52. WJ to HJ, 3 June (1893), *Correspondence,* 2:268–69.

53. Henry James III to Elizabeth Glendower Evans, 25 May 1931, Schlesinger.

54. WJ to Margaret Gibbens, 3 January 1893, *Letters,* 1:340.

55. AHJ to Elizabeth Glendower Evans, quoted in Evans, "William James and His Wife," in *WJR,* 73.

56. AHJ to Elizabeth Glendower Evans, 6 April 1893, Schlesinger.

57. WJ to AHJ, 19 April 1893, Houghton.

58. WJ to Josiah Royce, 18 December 1892, *Letters,* 1:335.

59. WJ to Eliza Gibbens, 9 May 1893, Houghton.

Chapter 14: Real Fights

1. WJ to Carl Stumpf, 24 January 1894, Perry, 2:189.

2. WJ to HJ, 22 September 1893, *Correspondence,* 2:280.

3. WJ to Dickinson Miller, 19 November 1893, *Letters,* 2:17.

4. WJ to Eliza Gibbens, 12 November 1893, Houghton.

5. WJ to Carl Stumpf, 18 December 1895, Perry, 2:189.

6. WJ to Carl Stumpf, 24–28 November 1896, Perry, 2:191.

7. WJ to HJ, 29 October 1893, *Correspondence,* 2:287.

8. WJ to Dickinson Miller, 19 November 1893, *Letters,* 2:17.

9. WJ to Carl Stumpf, 18 December 1895, Perry, 2:189–90.

10. WJ to George Croom Robertson, 11 July 1892, Houghton.

11. WJ to AHJ, 19 May 1894, Houghton.

12. WJ to AHJ, 24 May 1894, Houghton.

13. WJ to AHJ, 28 May 1894, Houghton.

14. Myers to WJ, 16 November 1893, Perry, 2:157–58.

15. WJ to HJ, 12 December 1894, *Correspondence,* 2:331.

16. WJ to HJ, 17 March 1895, *Correspondence,* 2:352.

17. WJ to HJ, 8 April 1895, *Correspondence,* 2:355–56.

18. WJ to HJ, 9 December 1896, *Correspondence,* 2:417.

19. WJ to Rosina Emmet, 9 September 1898, Houghton.

20. WJ, on back of letter from Sarah Whitman, 3 August 1890, Houghton.

21. WJ to Sarah Wyman Whitman, 9 September 1890, Houghton.

22. HJ to WJ, 25 May (1894), *Correspondence,* 2:307–8.

23. WJ to Sarah Wyman Whitman, 18 July 1895, Houghton.

24. WJ to Sarah Wyman Whitman, 27 May (1894), Houghton.

25. WJ to AHJ, 5 September 1895, Houghton.

26. "The Great Cigar," Putnam Camp log, 11 September 1896.

27. Elizabeth Putnam McIver, "Early Days at Putnam Camp," Keene Valley Historical Society, 1941: 12.

28. WJ to AHJ, 5 September 1895, Houghton.

29. WJ to Pauline Goldmark, 5 July 1908, Houghton.

30. WJ to Pauline Goldmark, 1 August 1902, Houghton.

31. Quoted in Vincent P. DeSantis, *The Shaping of Modern America.* Arlington Heights, Ill: Forum Press, 1989, 72.

32. WJ to Myers, 1 January 1896, *Letters,* 2:30–31.

33. WJ to William Mackintyre Salter, 10 February 1896, Houghton.

34. WJ to Salter, 13 February 1896, Houghton.

35. WJ to Salter, 13 February 1896, Houghton.

36. WJ to Salter, 22 February 1896, Houghton.

37. WJ to Salter, 10 February 1896, Houghton.

38. WJ to Rosina Emmet, 5 January 1896, Houghton.

39. WJ, quoted in Evans, "William James and His Wife," in *WJR,* 67.

40. WJ to George Howison, 27 October 1897, Perry, 2:131.

41. WJ, "The True Harvard," in *ECR,* 75.

42. WJ, *Talks to Teachers,* 41–42.

43. *Ibid.,* 65.

44. *Ibid.,* 41–42.

45. *Ibid.,* 113.

46. WJ, "The True Harvard," in *ECR,* 76–77.

47. WJ to AHJ, 24 July 1896, Houghton.

48. WJ to HJ, 15 August 1896, *Correspondence,* 2:406.

49. *Chautauqua Assembly Herald,* 25 July 1896.

50. WJ to AHJ, 26 July 1896, Houghton.

51. WJ to AHJ, 29 July 1896, Houghton.

52. Mary Raymond, "Memories of William James," *New England Quarterly* (September 1937), 423.

53. *Boston Evening Transcript,* 31 October 1896, *ML,* 521.

54. WJ to George Howison, 5 April 1897, Perry, 2:129.

55. Francis Child, 23 December 1895, *A Scholar's Letters to a Young Lady.* Boston: Atlantic Monthly Press, 1920, 147.

56. WJ, *Talks to Teachers,* 123–24.

57. *Ibid.,* 153.

58. Mary Raymond, "Memories of William James," 429.
59. Roswell Angier, "Another Student's Impression of James at the Turn of the Century," in *WJR*, 235.
60. WJ, "Is Life Worth Living?" in *WB*, 40–41, 45, 55.

Chapter 15: Civic Genius

1. Roswell Angier, "Another Student's Impression of James at the Turn of the Century," in *WJR*, 236.
2. George Santayana, "William James," *WJR*, 103.
3. WJ, "The Teaching of Philosophy in Our Colleges," in *EPhil*, 5.
4. WJ, *ML*, 273.
5. Dickinson Miller, "A Memory of William James," in *WJR*, 129.
6. George Herbert Palmer, "William James," in *WJR*, 32. Also see Dickinson Miller, *WJR*, 126, for a similar conclusion.
7. Dickinson Miller, "A Memory of William James," in *WJR*, 126.
8. Quoted in Ronald Steel, *Walter Lippmann and the American Century*. Boston: Little, Brown, 1980, 17.
9. *Ibid.*, 47–48.
10. *Ibid.*, 48.
11. Horace Kallen, "Remembering William James," in *In Commemoration of William James, 1842–1942*. New York: Columbia University Press, 1942, 12.
12. WJ to Schiller, 15 July 1907, Scott, 443.
13. WJ, *WB*, 5–6.
14. *Ibid.*
15. WJ to Helen Merriman, 22 December 1898, Scott, 177.
16. AHJ to HJ, 23 April 1898, in WJ, *Varieties of Religious Experience*, 521–22.
17. WJ to François Pillon, 31 January 1898, in *Varieties of Religious Experience*, 522.
18. AHJ to HJ, 4 February 1898, Houghton.
19. HJ to WJ, 25 February 1897, *Correspondence*, 3:5.
20. John Chapman to WJ, 17 March 1897, 164.
21. WJ to HJ, 9 May 1897, *Correspondence*, 3:8.
22. WJ, "Robert Gould Shaw," in *ERM*, 72.
23 *Ibid.*, 72–73.
24. *Ibid.*, 66–67.
25. *Ibid.*, 74.
26. WJ to HJ, 5 June 1897, *Correspondence*, 3:9.
27. AHJ to HJ, 31 May 1897, in WJ, *ERM*, 220.
28. WJ to François Pillon, 15 June 1898, *Letters*, 2:73–74.

29. William Dean Howells to Aurelia Howells, 3 April 1898, *Life and Letters of William Dean Howells,* vol. 2. Edited by Mildred Howells, New York: Russell & Russell, 1968 (1928), 90.

30. WJ to AHJ, 21 April 1898, Houghton.

31. WJ to William Mackintyre Salter, 8 April 1898, Houghton.

32. WJ to Salter, 21 April 1898, Houghton.

33. WJ to Salter, 5 January 1898, Houghton.

34. WJ to Salter, 18 November 1898, Houghton.

35. WJ to Henry Walcott, 1 April 1894, in WJ, *ECR,* 684.

36. Quoted in Putnam, "William James," in *WJR,* 11–12.

37. WJ to Pauline Goldmark, quoted in Goldmark, "An Adirondack Friendship," in *WJR,* 185.

38. WJ to AHJ, 9 July 1898, *Letters,* 2:75–77.

39. See Saul Rosenzweig, *Freud, Jung, and Hall the King-Maker.* Seattle, Wash.: Hogrefe & Huber, 1992, 182–186, for a discussion of this episode.

40. WJ to AHJ, 9 July 1898, *Letters,* 2:77.

41. WJ to George Howison, *Letters,* 2:78.

42. WJ to AHJ, 10 August 1898, Houghton. WJ to HJ, 11 August 1898, *Correspondence,* 3:38.

43. WJ to HJ, 22 September 1898, *Correspondence,* 3:40–41.

44. WJ, "Philosophical Conceptions and Practical Results," in *Pragmatism,* 257–70. All quotations cited in the discussion of this address come from this source.

45. Charles Sanders Peirce to WJ, 25 November 1902, *Collected Papers of Charles Sanders Peirce,* vol. 7, ed. Arthur W. Burks. Cambridge: Harvard University Press, 1958, 188.

46. WJ, *Pragmatism,* 14.

47. WJ to HJ, 22 September 1898, *Correspondence,* 3:40.

48. George Santayana, *Persons and Places* (London: Constable, 1944), 249.

49. WJ, *ERM,* 94.

50. *Ibid.,* 76.

51. WJ to Henry William Rankin, 16 June 1901, in *Varieties of Religious Experience,* 434.

52. WJ, *WB,* 40–41.

53. WJ, "Report on Mrs. Piper's Hodgson-Control," in *EPR,* 281–85.

Chapter 16: A Gleam of the End

1. WJ to Mary Raymond, 2 March 1899, "Memories of William James," *New England Quarterly,* September 1937, 426.

2. WJ, "Philosophical Conceptions and Practical Results," *Pragmatism*, 258.

3. James told Pauline Goldmark about his "seven hours' scramble" after which he arrived in Keene Valley at 10:15 P.M. (12 August 1899, *Letters*, 2:95). To Henry, he wrote that the "scramble" took thirteen hours "without food and with anxiety" (8 August 1899, *Correspondence*, 3:77).

4. AHJ to Frances Morse, 4 January (1901), Houghton.

5. WJ to HJ, 3 September 1899, *Correspondence*, 3:84.

6. WJ to HJ, 23 September 1899, *Correspondence*, 3:88.

7. AHJ to William James Jr., 24 October 1899, quoted in Allen, 403.

8. WJ to Eliza Gibbens, 29 October 1899, Houghton.

9. AHJ to William James Jr., quoted in Allen, *William James*, 411.

10. WJ to HJ, 30 January 1900, *Correspondence*, 3:99.

11. WJ to Ralph Barton Perry, 17 June 1900, Scott, 231.

12. WJ to James Mark Baldwin, 19 June (1900), Scott, 232.

13. WJ to HJ (14 August 1900), *Correspondence*, 3:131.

14. WJ to HJ, 23 September (1900), *Correspondence*, 3:135.

15. Among the correspondence in which James alluded to this secret cure is his letter to Josiah Royce, 26 September 1900, *Letters*, 2:138.

16. WJ to Frederic Myers, 12 December 1900, Houghton.

17. WJ to Eliza Gibbens, 6 May 1900, Houghton.

18. WJ to HJ, 1 January 1901, *Correspondence*, 3:153–54.

19. WJ, appendix 4, in *Varieties of Religious Experience*, 498–99. This passage was extracted from notes that contain emendations made by the volume's editor.

20. WJ to John Piddington, 5 January 1901, Houghton.

21. WJ to HJ, 17 January 1901, *Correspondence*, 3:157.

22. WJ to HJ (partly written in Alice's hand), 25 January 1901, *Correspondence*, 3:160.

23. WJ to E. L. Godkin, 29 August 1901, *Letters*, 2:161.

24. WJ to Frances Morse, 17 May and 30 May 1901, *Letters*, 2:146, 147.

25. WJ to Frances Morse, 10 July 1901, *Letters*, 2:158.

26. WJ to Frances Morse, 30 April 1901, Houghton.

27. HJ to WJ, 9 August (1899), *Correspondence*, 3:77.

28. HJ to WJ (14 August 1899), *Correspondence*, 3:82.

29. WJ to Eliza Gibbens, 29 October 1899, Houghton.

30. WJ to Margaret Mary James, 2 August 1899, Houghton.

31. WJ to Alexander Robertson James (3 May 1900), *Letters*, 2:129.

32. WJ to Francis Boott, 8 September 1900, Houghton.

33. WJ to William James Jr., 21 September 1900, Houghton.

34. WJ to William James Jr., 8 January 1900, Houghton.

35. WJ to William James Jr., 8 November 1900, Houghton.

36. WJ to HJ, 19 March 1899, *Correspondence,* 3:55.

37. WJ to Alexander Robertson James, (3 May 1900), *Letters,* 2:129. James's spelling in this letter reflects his support of the spelling reform movement, which counted among its members some of the most influential literary figures of the time. Simplified spelling would lead to increased literacy, equality, and democracy, according to its promoters.

38. AHJ to Elizabeth Glendower Evans, quoted in Evans, "William James and His Wife," in *WJR,* 76.

39. WJ to Mary Raymond, 2 March 1899, "Memories of William James," *New England Quarterly,* September 1937, 426.

40. WJ to Francis Boott, 15 September 1900, Houghton.

41. WJ to Henry Higginson, 18 September 1900, in Bliss Perry, ed., *Letters of Henry Lee Higginson.* Boston: Atlantic Monthly Press, 1921, 429.

42. Theodore Roosevelt, "The Strenuous Life," in *The Strenuous Life: Essays and Addresses.* New York: Century, 1900, 21.

43. WJ to Henry Bowditch, 25 May 1900, Houghton. "Governor Roosevelt's Oration," *ECR,* 163.

44. WJ to William James Jr. (Billy), 8 January 1900, Houghton.

45. WJ to Frances Morse, 17 September 1899, Houghton.

46. WJ to Frederic Myers, 13 August 1899, Houghton.

47. WJ to William Mackintyre Salter, 11 September 1899, Houghton.

48. WJ to Francis Boott, 14 November 1900, Houghton.

49. WJ to HJ, 10 September 1901, *Correspondence,* 3:178.

50. WJ to HJ, 21 September 1901, *Correspondence,* 3:180–81.

51. WJ to HJ (14 October 1901), *Correspondence,* 3:181–82.

52. WJ to HJ, 27 October 1901, 14 November (1901), *Correspondence,* 3:182, 187.

53. Clark Bell, *Spiritism, Hypnotism and Telepathy: as involved in the Case of Mrs. Leonora Piper and the Society for Psychical Research.* New York: Medico-Legal Journal, 1904.

54. *Ibid.,* 161.

55. *Ibid.,* 163.

56. *Boston Advertiser,* 25 October 1901, quoted in Bell, *Spiritism,* 126.

57. *Boston Morning Journal,* 29 October 1901, quoted in Bell, *Spiritism.*

58. Leonora Piper in *Boston Morning Journal,* 29 October 1901, quoted in Bell, *Spiritism,* 125.

59. Bell, *Spiritism,* 123.
60. WJ to F. C. S. Schiller, 15 March 1900, Scott, 222–23.

Chapter 17: A Temper of Peace

1. WJ to Pauline Goldmark, 1 August 1902, Houghton.
2. WJ to Elizabeth Glendower Evans, quoted in Evans, "William James and His Wife," in *WJR,* 66.
3. WJ to Sarah Wyman Whitman, 22 August 1903, Schlesinger.
4. WJ to Mary Raymond, 14 September 1904, "Memories of William James," 428.
5. WJ, *Varieties of Religious Experience,* 410.
6. *Ibid.,* 88, 93.
7. WJ to Rosina Emmet, 26 August 1902, Houghton.
8. WJ, *ECR,* 184.
9. WJ, *Varieties of Religious Experience,* 383.
10. WJ to Elizabeth Glendower Evans, quoted in Evans, "William James and His Wife," in *WJR,* 66.
11. Obituary, *New York City Post,* 27 August 1910, Harvard Archives.
12. "A Strong Note of Warning Regarding the Lynching Epidemic," *ECR,* 170–73.
13. WJ to HJ, 5 June 1897, *Correspondence,* 3:9.
14. WJ to Pauline Goldmark, 24 February 1904, Houghton.
15. Mary Tappan Wright, *Aliens.* New York: Scribner's, 1902, 362.
16. *Ibid.,* 360.
17. Owen Wister, *Lady Baltimore.* New York: Macmillan, 1906, 24.
18. *Ibid.,* 65.
19. *Ibid.,* 112.
20. Sarah Wyman Whitman to WJ, 8 May 1904, Schlesinger.
21. George Santayana, *Character and Opinion in the United States.* New York: Doubleday Anchor, n.d., 93.
22. WJ to HJ, 14 March (1904), *Correspondence,* 3:263–64.
23. WJ to Sarah Whitman, 22 August 1903, Houghton.
24. George Santayana, *The Middle Span,* 127–28.
25. Frances Morse to WJ, 28 July 1901, Houghton.
26. WJ to Sarah Whitman, 20 June 1904, Houghton.
27. WJ to Pauline Goldmark, 30 June 1904, Houghton.
28. WJ to Frances Parkman, 28 June 1904, Houghton.
29. WJ to Frances Morse, 30 June 1904, Houghton.
30. WJ to John Jay Chapman, 26 September 1904, Houghton.
31. WJ to Théodore Flournoy, 9 February 1906, Le Clair, ed., *Letters,* 174.
32. WJ to F. C. S. Schiller, 16 January 1906, Scott, 395.

33. WJ, "Report on Mrs. Piper's Hodgson-Control," in *EPR,* 269, 355, 358.
34. WJ to HJ, 1 January 1904, *Correspondence,* 3:254–55.
35. WJ to HJ, 1 February 1906, *Correspondence,* 3:307.
36. AHJ to WJ, 28 May 1905, Houghton.
37. R. W. B. Lewis claims that Aleck suffered from undiagnosed dyslexia. See *The Jameses.* New York: Farrar, Straus & Giroux, 1991, 626.
38. WJ to Henry Bowditch, 13 September 1908, Houghton.
39. HJ to WJ, 12 January 1909, *Correspondence,* 4:374.
40. WJ to William James Jr., 22 November 1902, Houghton.
41. WJ to Flournoy, 11 October 1904, Le Clair, ed., *Letters,* 162.
42. WJ to AHJ, n.d., Houghton.
43. WJ to AHJ, 13 May 1905, *Letters,* 2:229–30.
44. WJ to William James Jr., 26 January 1903, Houghton.
45. WJ to AHJ, 11 April 1904, Houghton.
46. WJ to Charles William Eliot, 28 December 1905, Scott, 388.
47. Frank Angell to Henry James III, 25 February 1937, Houghton.
48. Margaret Münsterberg, *Hugo Münsterberg: His Life and Work.* New York: Appleton, 1922, 126.
49. *The Philosophical Review* 15, no. 2: 173.
50. WJ to John Jay Chapman, 7 October 1909, Houghton.
51. WJ, "The Ph.D. Octopus," in *ECR,* 69–71.
52. WJ to William James Jr., 18 June 1903, quoted in *ECR,* 661.
53. WJ to William James Jr., 4 July 1903, Houghton.
54. WJ, "The True Harvard," in *ECR,* 76–77.
55. WJ, "The Chicago School," in *EPhil,* 102; WJ to Pauline Goldmark, 23 February 1904, Houghton.
56. Quoted in Perry, 2:523.
57. WJ, "The Chicago School," in *EPhil,* 105.
58. WJ to Sarah Wyman Whitman, 29 October 1903, *Letters,* 2:201–2.
59. Ralph Barton Perry, *Present Philosophical Tendencies.* New York: Longmans, Green, 1912, 378.
60. WJ to F. C. S. Schiller, 4 September 1903, Scott, 319–20.
61. Lewis S. Feuer, "The East Side Philosophers: William James and Thomas Davidson," *American Jewish History* 76 (March 1987), 288.
62. WJ to François Pillon, 12 June 1904, *Letters,* 2:203–4.
63. WJ to AHJ, 25 September 1904, Houghton.
64. WJ to Katherine and Henrietta Rodgers, 20 September 1904, Scott, 351.
65. WJ to F. C. S. Schiller, 9 October 1904, Scott, 353.
66. WJ to AHJ, 25 April 1905, Houghton.

67. WJ, "Does 'Consciousness' Exist?" in *Journal of Philosophy, Psychology, and Scientific Methods,* 1 September 1904, 477–91.

68. "La notion de conscience," WJ, in *ERE,* 261–71.

69. WJ, *ML,* 320.

70. WJ, "G. Papini and the Pragmatist Movement in Italy," in *EPhil,* 146.

71. WJ to G. Papini, 27 April 1906, Perry, 2:572.

72. WJ to AHJ, 28 May 1905, Houghton.

73. WJ to David Starr Jordan, 14 January 1905, Stanford University Archives.

74. WJ to Pauline Goldmark, quoted in Goldmark, "An Adirondack Friendship," in *WJR,* 195.

75. WJ, diary, 1906, Houghton.

76. WJ to AHJ, 11 January 1906, Houghton.

77. WJ to George Howison, 23 January 1906, in *ERM,* 243.

78. WJ, *A Pluralistic Universe,* 148. See also "Reason and Faith," in *ERM,* 125.

79. WJ, "The Psychology of the War Spirit," in *ERM,* 251, 164.

80. Other speakers at that conference included Booker T. Washington and the noted anti-war activist Baroness Bertha von Suttner, who won the Nobel Peace Prize in 1905. James gave the closing remarks at the daylong conference.

Chapter 18: Mental Pirouettes

1. *Boston Herald,* 9 April 1906, quoted in Otto Marx, "Morton Prince and the Dissociation of a Personality," *Journal of the History of the Behaviorial Sciences* 6 (1970): 124.

2. WJ to Flournoy, 18 November 1908, Le Clair, ed., *Letters,* 207.

3. Quoted in Otto Marx, "Morton Prince and the Dissociation of a Personality," *Journal of the History of the Behaviorial Sciences* 6 (1970): 121.

4. WJ, "A Suggestion about Mysticism," in *EPhil,* 157–65. Erik H. Erikson offers a cursory interpretation of this dream, which he misdated, in *Identity, Youth, and Crisis* (New York: Norton, 1968), 204–7. Saul Rosenzweig asserts a connection between James's dream and his relationship with Pauline Goldmark in *Freud, Jung, and Hall the King-Maker,* 189–195.

5. WJ to Théodore Flournoy, 9 February 1906, in Le Clair, ed., *Letters,* 174–75.

6. Frank Angell to Henry James III, 23 March 1937, Houghton.

7. WJ to Charles William Eliot, 18 March (1906), Scott, 408–9.

8. WJ to HJ, 22 April 1906, *Correspondence,* 3:311.

9. WJ, "On Some Mental Effects of the Earthquake," in *Memories and Studies.* New York: Longmans, Green, 1917, 211. This essay first appeared in *Youth's Companion,* 7 June 1906.

10. Edith Mirrieless, *Stanford: The Story of a University.* New York: Putnam's, 1959, 135.

11. WJ, "Remarks at the Peace Banquet," in *ERM,* 122.

12. Elizabeth Agassiz, journal, 21 April 1906, Schlesinger.

13. William Dean Howells to Charles Eliot Norton, 22 April 1906, *Life and Letters of William Dean Howells,* vol 2. Edited by Mildred Howells. New York: Russell & Russell, 1968 (1928), 175.

14. HJ to WJ, 4 May 1906, *Correspondence,* 3:314.

15. WJ to HJ, 9 May 1906, *Correspondence,* 3:316.

16. *Ibid.*

17. *Ibid.*

18. WJ to Frank Angell, 13 May 1906, Scott, 412.

19. AHJ to HJ, 6 April 1906, *Correspondence,* 3:309.

20. WJ to F. C. S. Schiller, 24 August 1906, Scott, 415; WJ to HJ, 9 May 1906, *Correspondence,* 3:316–17. In February 1906, James Hyslop, who had taken over Hodgson's role as investigator of Piper, had asked James about an allusion made by the Hodgson-control about a conversation between James and Hodgson. Although James could not recall the conversation at the time, in early May he suddenly remembered it. It was this conversation that made him feel suddenly close to Hodgson's departed spirit.

21. WJ to Margaret Mary James, 9 October 1906, Houghton.

22. WJ to Théodore Flournoy, 1 July 1906, Le Clair, ed., *Letters,* 179.

23. WJ to Margaret Mary James, 5 July 1906, Houghton.

24. WJ to Margaret Mary James, 1 September 1906, Houghton.

25. *The Outlook,* 21 April 1906, 878.

26. WJ to AHJ, 25 August 1906, Houghton.

27. Maxim Gorky, *The City of the Yellow Devil: Pamphlets, Articles and Letters about America.* Moscow: Progress Publishers, 1972, 133.

28. WJ to William James Jr., 22 August 1906, Houghton.

29. James had written about pragmatism in many articles published between the *Varieties of Religious Experience* in 1902 and *Pragmatism* in 1907, including:

"Pragmatic and Pragmatism," (1902), in *EPhil,* 94; Review of Schiller's *Humanism,* (1904), in *ECR,* 550; "Humanism and Truth," (1904), in *MT,* 37–60; "The Pragmatic Method,"

(1904), in *EPhil,* 123–39; "The Experience of Activity," (1905), in *ERE,* 79–96; "The Essence of Humanism," (1905), in *ERE,* 97–104; "Humanism and Truth Once More," (1905), in *ERE,* 127–36; "G. Papini and the Pragmatist Movement in Italy," (1906), in *EPhil,* 144–48.

30. WJ to Théodore Flournoy, 2 January 1907, Le Clair, ed., *Letters,* 181.
31. Peirce, Review of Charles Strong's *Why the Mind Has a Body* (1903) in *Collected Papers of Charles Sanders Peirce,* vol. 8. Cambridge: Harvard University Press, 1958, 141.
32. Josiah Royce to Alfred Deakin, 18 April 1908, Clendenning, ed., *Letters of Josiah Royce,* 522.
33. WJ to F. H. Bradley, 16 July 1904, quoted in J. C. Kenna, "Ten Unpublished Letters from James to Bradley," *Mind,* July 1966, 318.
34. Schiller, *Must Philosophers Disagree?* London: Macmillan, 1934, 82.
35. *Ibid.,* 83.
36. Peirce to WJ, 1 May 1877, *Correspondence,* 4:561.
37. Quoted in Perry, 2:422.
38. Peirce to AHJ, 12 April (1902), quoted in Perry, 2:423.
39. Peirce, *Collected Papers,* 8:190.
40. Peirce to WJ, 13 June 1907, Perry, 2:437.
41. Peirce, *Collected Papers,* 8:199.
42. Charles Peirce to WJ (25 November 1903), *Collected Papers,* 8:188.
43. Peirce, Review of Strong's *Why the Mind Has a Body,* in *Collected Papers,* 8:142.
44. Charles Peirce, "How to Make Our Ideas Clear" (1878), in *Pragmatism,* edited by Russell Goodman. New York: Routledge, 1995, 47.
45. WJ to John Jay Chapman, 12 October 1909, Houghton.
46. WJ, *Principles of Psychology,* 276–77.
47. WJ to Peirce, 22 December (1897), Perry, 2:418.
48. WJ to John Shaw Billings, 20 June (1902), Scott, 287.
49. WJ to Henry Bowditch, 26 January 1907, quoted in Joseph Brent, *Charles Sanders Peirce.* Bloomington: Indiana University Press, 1993, 306.
50. In gratitude, Peirce named Henry James III as his beneficiary if Peirce's wife died before him.
51. Hans von Kaltenborn, "William James at Harvard," *The Harvard Illustrated Magazine,* February 1907.
52. WJ to Flournoy, 26 March 1907, Le Clair, ed., *Letters,* 188.
53. WJ to HJ, 9 December 1906, *Correspondence,* 3:330.
54. WJ to HJ, 14 February 1907, *Correspondence,* 3:332–33.

55. Boughton's recollection of the sitting appeared in *Photographing the Famous,* and was reprinted in Matthiessen, *The James Family* (New York: Knopf, 1947), xv.

56. WJ to HJ, 14 February 1907, *Correspondence,* 3:332–33.

57. WJ to Flournoy, 26 March 1907, Le Clair, ed., *Letters,* 187–88.

58. WJ to HJ, 4 May, (19)07, *Correspondence,* 3:339.

59. AJ, *Diary,* 217.

60. James Angell to WJ, 16 January 1908, Houghton.

61. James Jackson Putnam, "William James," in *WJR,* 24.

62. Royce to WJ (1907), Clendenning, ed., *Letters of Josiah Royce,* 511.

63. WJ to F. C. S. Schiller, 4 January 1908, Scott, 459.

64. WJ to Charles Augustus Strong, 21 August 1907, Houghton.

65. Arthur Lovejoy, "The Thirteen Pragmatisms," in *The Thirteen Pragmatisms and Other Essays.* Baltimore: Johns Hopkins, 1963, 11–12.

66. WJ to F. C. S. Schiller, 17 January 1908, Scott, 465.

67. WJ to Horace Meyer Kallen, 12 February 1908, Scott, 473.

68. Lovejoy, "William James as Philosopher," in *The Thirteen Pragmatisms,* 92.

69. Benjamin Paul Blood to WJ, 29 September 1907, Houghton.

70. WJ to HJ, 8 September 1907, *Correspondence,* 3:344.

Chapter 19: The Pitch of Life

1. WJ to Flournoy, 3 January 1908, Le Clair, ed., *Letters,* 195.

2. James's first record of a visit to Dr. Taylor appears in his diary of 28 March. On 20 April, just before sailing to Europe, he had his last treatment: there were 44 in all, at a cost of $152. (Houghton)

3. WJ to HJ, 15 April (19)08, 29 April (19)08, *Correspondence,* 3:358, 360.

4. WJ, *A Pluralistic Universe,* 141–42.

5. *Ibid.,* 96–97.

6. *Ibid.*

7. John Jay Chapman, "William James," in *WJR,* 56.

8. WJ to Flournoy, 9 August 1908, Le Clair, ed., *Letters,* 198.

9. WJ to HJ, 3 June (1908), *Correspondence,* 3:361.

10. WJ to Richard Cabot, 22 March (1899), Harvard Archives.

11. *Mary Berenson, a Self-Portrait from Her Letters and Diaries.* Edited by Barbara Strachey and Jayne Samuels. New York: Norton, 1983, 198–99.

12. WJ to Ottoline Morrell, 13 June 1908, Scott, 478.

13. WJ to F. C. S. Schiller, 15 June 1908, Scott, 481.

14. AHJ to William James Jr., 12 June 1908, quoted in Allen, *William James,* 462.

15. WJ to HJ, 29 June (19)08, *Correspondence,* 3:362.
16. WJ to Pauline Goldmark, 2 July 1908, in "An Adirondack Friendship," in *WJR,* 187–88.
17. WJ to Pauline Goldmark, 31 May, 2 July, 3 July, 5 July (19)08, in "An Adirondack Friendship," in *WJR,* 186–90.
18. WJ to Theodora Sedgwick, 26 July 1908, Houghton.
19. WJ to AHJ, 3 August 1908, Houghton.
20. G. K. Chesterton, "The Philosophy of William James," in *WJR,* 264–65.
21. WJ to F. C. S. Schiller (5 October 1908), Scott, 489–90.
22. WJ, diary 1909, 12 January. James wrote that he had a "candid talk with Taylor," suggesting that this was the date he delivered his ultimatum. (Houghton)
23. WJ to HJ, 6 March (19)09, *Correspondence,* 3:385–86.
24. WJ to Clifford Beers, 22 September 1909, Houghton.
25. WJ to Flournoy, 28 September 1909, Le Clair, ed., *Letters,* 224.
26. WJ to Flournoy, 18 June 1909, Le Clair, ed., *Letters,* 216–17.
27. See Saul Rosenzweig, *Freud, Jung, and Hall the King-Maker,* for a detailed discussion of James's encounters with Freud. Rosenzweig offers another interpretation of James's dream experience, discussed here in chapter 18.
28. WJ to Clifford Beers, 1 July 1906, in *ECR,* 188.
29. WJ to Clifford Beers, 21 April 1907, *Letters,* 2:274.
30. WJ to John D. Rockefeller, 1 June 1909, Menninger Archives.
31. WJ to Clifford Beers, 24 February 1909, Houghton.
32. WJ to Clifford Beers, 17 January 1910, Houghton.
33. WJ to Clifford Beers, 3 March 1910, Houghton.
34. WJ to AHJ, 4 December 1908, in *EPR,* 424.
35. Théodore Flournoy, *Spiritism and Psychology,* trans. Hereward Carrington. New York: Harper, 1911, 245.
36. Hereward Carrington, *Eusapia Palladino and Her Phenomena.* New York: Dodge, 1909, 332, 333.
37. WJ, "Confidences of a 'Psychical Researcher,'" in *EPR,* 362–63.
38. *Ibid.,* 372, 375.
39. WJ to AHJ, 21 July 1908, Houghton.
40. WJ to HJ, 31 May (19)09, *Correspondence,* 3:388.
41. WJ, diary, 1909: 15 January, 5 March, 29 April, 1 July, 6 November, Houghton.
42. Quoted in Lewis, *The Jameses,* 630.
43. Elizabeth Glendower Evans, "William James and His Wife," in *WJR,* 76.

44. WJ, diary, 1909: 2 May, Houghton.
45. WJ to HJ, 6 October (19)09, *Correspondence,* 3:399.
46. WJ to Margaret Mary James, 4 March 1907, Houghton.
47. WJ, diary, 28 April 1909, Houghton.
48. WJ to Henry Bowditch, 30 October 1909, Houghton.
49. WJ to Flournoy, 18 June 1909, Le Clair, ed., *Letters,* 218.
50. HJ to WJ, 18 July (1909), *Correspondence,* 3:393.
51. WJ to HJ, 22 October 1905, *Correspondence,* 3:301.
52. HJ to WJ, 23 November 1905, *Correspondence,* 3:305.
53. Robertson James to WJ (18 November 1909), Houghton.
54. WJ to James Pratt, 9 March (19)09, in *MT,* 312.
55. Bertrand Russell to WJ, 22 July 1909, in *MT,* 303.
56. WJ, comments on Bertrand Russell's "Transatlantic Truth," in *MT,* 307.
57. *Ibid.,* 309.
58. *Ibid.,* 307.
59. *Ibid.,* 310.
60. WJ, *MEN,* 237.

Chapter 20: Eclipse

1. WJ, "Emerson," in *ERM,* 109.
2. Josiah Royce to WJ (January 1910), Clendenning, ed., *Letters of Josiah Royce,* 539.
3. WJ to F. C. S. Schiller, 18 May 1907, Perry, 2:506.
4. WJ, *A Pluralistic Universe,* 13.
5. WJ, notebook, Geneva 1859, Houghton.
6. WJ to Amy Lothrop, 26 April 1896, Massachusetts Historical Society.
7. WJ to Schiller, 27 April 1910, *Some Problems of Philosophy,* 206.
8. WJ to J. E. Boodin, 26 September 1906, John Elof Boodin, "William James as I Knew Him," in *WJR,* 224.
9. WJ to Alice Runnells, 15 December 1909, Houghton.
10. WJ to Shadworth Hodgson, 3 October 1908, *Letters,* 2:312.
11. WJ, *Some Problems of Philosophy,* 39.
12. *Ibid.,* 54–55.
13. WJ, "A French Philosopher at Harvard," in *EPhil,* 169.
14. WJ to F. C. S. Schiller, 8 April 1903, in *Some Problems of Philosophy,* 199.
15. HJ to Jocelyn Persse, 28 April 1910, *HJ Letters,* ed. Edel, 4:551; HJ to WJ, 8 February 1910, *Correspondence,* 3:409.
16. HJ to WJ, 4 March 1910, *Correspondence,* 3:413.
17. WJ to Henry Bowditch, 6 November 1909, Houghton.

18. WJ to Henry Bowditch, 4 June 1910, *Letters,* 2:341.
19. WJ to Margaret Mary James, 18 May 1910; WJ to AHJ, 14 May 1910, Houghton.
20. Henry Adams to Elizabeth Cameron, 12 May 1910, *Letters of Henry Adams,* vol. 2. Edited by Worthington Chauncey Ford. Boston: Houghton Mifflin, 1938, 539.
21. WJ to HJ, 30 May 1910 and 26 May 1910, *Correspondence,* 3:422, 420.
22. HJ to WJ, 5 June (1910), *Correspondence,* 3:425.
23. WJ to Ralph Barton Perry, 28 May 1910, Scott, 553.
24. AHJ diary, cited in Allen, *William James,* 484.
25. WJ to Flournoy, 4 July 1910, 7 July 1910, Le Clair, ed., *Letters,* 237.
26. WJ to Flournoy (9 July 1910), Le Clair, ed., *Letters,* 239.
27. AHJ to F. C. S. Schiller, 25 July 1910, Scott, 556–57.
28. WJ to Flournoy (9 July 1910), Le Clair, ed., *Letters,* 239; WJ to AHJ, 20 May 1910, Houghton.
29. Benjamin Paul Blood to WJ, 20 June (1895), Perry, 2:229.
30. WJ, "A Pluralistic Mystic," *EPhil,* 173.
31. *Ibid.,* 190.
32. AHJ to Horace Kallen, 3 September 1910, American Jewish Archives, Hebrew Union College.
33. The note is dated 26 July 1910.
34. WJ to Flournoy, 12 August 1910, Le Clair, ed., *Letters,* 241.
35. When William and Alice had visited Bob on 15 November 1908, they found out that he had taken up fletcherizing following a bout of indigestion; Mary told them that Bob had had occasional drinking sprees, but lasting only one day at a time. Bob seemed to the Jameses "very grave and not very genial." See WJ to HJ, 15 November (19)08, *Correspondence,* 3:370.
36. Robertson James to Mary James Vaux, 7 June 1910, quoted in Maher, *Biography of Broken Fortunes,* 191.
37. Margaret James to AHJ, 9 July 1910, quoted in Maher, *Biography of Broken Fortunes,* 192.
38. AHJ to Henry James III. Quoted in Allen, *William James,* 488.
39. AHJ to Eliza Gibbens, 7 August 1910, Houghton.
40. Quoted in Allen, *William James,* 491–92.
41. AHJ to Horace Kallen, 3 September 1910, American Jewish Archives, Hebrew Union College.
42. HJ to Grace Norton, 26 August 1910, *HJ Letters,* ed. Edel, 4:559–60.
43. HJ to Thomas Perry, 2 September 1910, *HJ Letters,* ed. Edel, 4:561.

44. AHJ to Pauline Goldmark, 14 September 1910, Houghton.

45. *Springfield Daily Republican,* 27 August 1910.

46. AHJ to H. V. Knox, 7 November 1910, quoted in Marjorie R. Kaufman, "William James's Letters to a Young Pragmatist," *Journal of the History of Ideas,* July 1963, 421.

47. Elizabeth Glendower Evans, "William James and His Wife," in *WJR,* 81.

48. John Elof Boodin, "William James as I Knew Him," in *WJR,* 231.

49. John Jay Chapman, "William James," in *WJR,* 53.

50. HJ to H. G. Wells, 11 September 1910, *HJ Letters,* ed. Edel, 4:561–62.

51. WJ to AHJ, 16 September 1894, Houghton.

52. AHJ to James B. Pratt, 23 October 1911, Williams College Archives.

53. AHJ to George Gordon, in George Angier Gordon, "A Profoundly Religious Man," in *WJR,* 48.

BIBLIOGRAPHY

SELECTED SOURCES

Ackerknecht, Erwin H. *Medicine at the Paris Hospital, 1794–1848*. Baltimore: Johns Hopkins University Press, 1967.

Addams, Jane. *Newer Ideals of Peace*. New York: Macmillan, 1915 (1907).

———. *Twenty Years at Hull House*. New York: Macmillan, 1910.

Agassiz, Louis, and Elizabeth Agassiz. *A Journey in Brazil*. Boston: Fields, Osgood, 1869.

Alcott, Amos Bronson. *The Journals of Bronson Alcott*. Edited by Odell Shepard. Boston: Little, Brown, 1938.

———. *Letters of A. Bronson Alcott*. Edited by Richard L. Herrnstadt. Ames: Iowa State University Press, 1969.

Alexander, Gray. "The Hypothesized God of C. S. Peirce and William James." *Journal of Religion*. July 1987, 67:3 (304).

Allen, Gay Wilson. *William James*. New York: Viking, 1967.

Allport, Gordon. "The Productive Paradoxes of William James." *Psychological Review* 50 (1943): 95–120.

Anderson, James William. "An Interview with Leon Edel on the James Family." *Psychohistory Review* 8, no. 1-2 (1979): 15–22.

———. "In Search of Mary James." *Psychohistory Review* 8, no. 1–2 (1979): 63–70.

Angell, James R. "James R. Angell," in *History of Psychology in Autobiography*. Edited by C. Murchison. Vol. 3. Worcester: Clark University Press, 1936. 1–38.

Baida, Peter. "The admirable three millions." *American Heritage*. July–August, 1988. 39:5–16.

Bain, Alexander. *The Emotions and the Will*. London: Parker, 1859.

Baird, Alexander. *Richard Hodgson*. London: Psychic Press, 1949.

Baker, Liva. *The Justice from Beacon Hill: The Life and Times of Oliver Wendell Holmes*. New York: HarperCollins, 1991.

Barnes, William Abner. *Personal Influence (Practical Psychology): An Aid to Health, Success, and Happiness*. Boston: Foreign Language Press Co., 1906.

Barrett, William F. *On the Threshold of the Unseen: An Examination of the Phenomena of Spiritualism and of the Evidence for Survival after Death*. New York: E. P. Dutton & Co., 1917.

Barzun, Jacques. *A Stroll with William James*. New York: Harper & Row, 1983.

Basu, Sankari Prasad, and S. B. Ghosh, eds. *Vivekananda in Indian Newspapers, 1893–1902*. Calcutta: Basu Bhattacharyyal, 1969.

Baum, Maurice. "The Development of James's Pragmatism Prior to 1879." *Journal of Philosophy* 30 (January 1933): 43–51.

Bayley, James E. "A Jamesian Theory of Self." *Transactions of the Peirce Society* 12 (Spring 1976): 148–65.

Beard, George Miller. *American Nervousness: Its Causes and Consequences*. New York: Putnam, 1881.

———. *Eating and Drinking: A Popular Manual of Food and Diet in Health and Disease*. New York: Putnam, 1871.

Beisner, Robert L. *Twelve against Empire: The Anti-Imperialists, 1898–1900*. New York: McGraw-Hill, 1968.

Benjamin, Ludy T., et al. "Wundt's American Doctoral Students." *American Psychologist* 47, no. 2 (February 1992): 123–31.

Berger, Arthur S. "The Early History of the ASPR: Origins to 1907." *The Journal of the American Society for Psychical Research* 79 (January 1985): 39–57.

Bixler, Julius. "The Existentialists and William James." *The American Scholar* 28, no. 1 (Winter 1958–59): 80–90.

Bjork, Daniel. *The Compromised Scientist: William James in the Development of American Psychology*. New York: Columbia University Press, 1983.

———. *William James: The Center of His Vision*. New York: Columbia University Press, 1988.

Bjorkman, F. M. "Fletcher and Fletcherism." *Independent* 64 (March 19, 1908): 623–26.

Blecher, Henry K., and Mark D. Altschule. *Medicine at Harvard: The First Three Hundred Years*. Hanover, N.H: University Press of New England, 1977.

Boutroux, Émile. *William James*. Translated by Archibald and Barbara Henderson. New York: Longmans, Green, 1912.

Brand, Dana. "William James's Reformulation of Emerson and Whitman." *ESQ: A Journal of the American Renaissance* 31, no. 1 (1985): 38–48.

Brent, Joseph. *Charles Sanders Peirce: A Life*. Bloomington: Indiana University Press, 1993.

Brown, Rollo Walter. *Harvard Yard in the Golden Age*. New York: Current Books, 1948.

Browning, Don S. *Pluralism and Personality: William James and Some Contemporary Cultures of Psychology*. Lewisburg, Pa.: Bucknell University Press, 1980.

———. "William James's Philosophy of the Person: The Concept of the Strenuous Life." *Zygon* 10 (June 1975): 162–74.

Brugger, Robert. *Our Selves/Our Past: Psychological Approaches to American History*. Baltimore: Johns Hopkins University Press, 1981.

Buckham, John Wright. "George Herbert Palmer, 1842–1942." *The Personalist* 23, no. 3 (Summer 1942): 229–38.

Burr, Anna Robeson. *Alice James, Her Brothers—Her Journal*. New York: Dodd, Mead & Co., 1934.

———. *Weir Mitchell: His Life and Letters*. 2nd ed. New York: Duffield, 1930.

Cabot, Ella Lyman. *Everyday Ethics*. New York: Holt, 1906.

Cabot, Richard C. *Adventures on the Borderlands of Ethics*. New York: Harper, 1926.

———. *The Meaning of Right and Wrong*. New York: Macmillan, 1933.

———. *What Men Live By: Work, Play, Love, Worship*. Boston: Houghton Mifflin, 1914.

Cacioppo, John T., and Louis G. Tassinay. "Centenary of William James's 'Principles of Psychology': From the Chaos of Mental Life to the Science of Psychology." *Personality and Social Psychology Bulletin* 16, no. 4 (Dec. 1990): 601.

Calkins, Mary Whiton. *The Good Man and the Good*. New York: Macmillan, 1918.

Campbell, James. "William James and the Ethics of Fulfillment." *Proceedings of the Charles S. Peirce Society* 17, no. 3 (Spring 1981): 224–40.

Carpenter, Frederic I. "William James and Emerson." *American Literature* 11 (1939): 39–57.

Cattell, James McKeen. "Psychology in America." *Proceedings and Papers: Ninth International Congress of Psychology* (1929): 12–32.

Chapman, John Jay. *Memories and Milestones*. Freeport, N.Y.: Books for Libraries Press, 1971 (1915).

——. *Practical Agitation.* New York: Scribner's, 1900.

——. *John Jay Chapman and His Letters.* Edited by M. A. De Wolfe Howe. Boston: Houghton Mifflin, 1937.

——. *Selected Writings.* Edited by Jacques Barzun. New York: Farrar, Straus & Cudahy, 1957.

Chesterton, G. K. *Autobiography.* Introduction by Anthony Burgess. London: Hutchinson, 1969.

——. *The Ball and the Cross.* Philadelphia: Dufour, 1963 (1910).

——. *The Collected Works of G. K. Chesterton.* Vol. 28. Edited by Lawrence J. Clipper. San Francisco: Ignatius Press, 1987.

——. *The Common Man.* New York: Sheed & Ward, 1950.

——. *Heretics.* New York: John Lane, 1905.

Clarke, Edwin, and L. S. Jacyna. *Nineteenth-Century Origins of Neuroscientific Concepts.* Berkeley: University of California Press, 1987.

Clendenning, John. *The Life and Thought of Josiah Royce.* Madison: University of Wisconsin Press, 1985.

Cohen, Morris Raphael. *A Dreamer's Journey.* Glencoe, Ill.: Free Press, 1949.

Coon, Deborah J. "One Moment in the World's Salvation: Anarchism and the Radicalization of William James." *The Journal of American History* 83, no. 1 (June 1996): 70–99.

Cope, Jackson I. "William James's Correspondence with Daniel Coit Gilman, 1877–1881." *Journal of the History of Ideas* 12 (October 1951): 609–27.

Cortissoz, Royal. *John La Farge: A Memoir and a Study.* Boston: Houghton Mifflin, 1911.

Cotkin, George. "Fathers and Sons, Texts and Contexts: Henry James, Sr., and William James." *American Quarterly* 36 (Winter 1984): 719–24.

——. "William James and Emerson as Public Philosophers." *Historian* 49 (November 1986): 49–63.

——. "William James and the 'Weightless' Nature of Modern Existence." *San Jose Studies* 12 (Spring 1986): 7–19.

——. *William James: Public Philosopher.* Baltimore: Johns Hopkins University Press, 1990.

Coughlan, Neil. *Young John Dewey: An Essay in American Intellectual History.* Chicago: University of Chicago Press, 1975.

Cromer, Ward, and Paula Anderson. "Freud's Visit to America: Newspaper Coverage." *Journal of the History of the Behaviorial Sciences* 6 (October 1970): 349–53.

Danziger, Kurt. "On the Threshold of the New Psychology: Situating Wundt and James." In *Wundt Studies: A Centennial Collection,* edited by

Wolfgang G. Bringmann and Ryan D. Tweney, 363–79. Toronto: Hogrefe, 1980.

Deck, Raymond H., Jr. "Notes on the Theology of Henry James, Sr." *Psychohistory Review* (1979): 60–62.

Diggins, John Patrick. *The Promise of Pragmatism: Modernism and the Crisis of Knowledge and Authority*. Chicago: University of Chicago Press, 1994.

Donley, John E. "On Neurasthenia as a Disintegration of Personality." *Journal of Abnormal Psychology* (June 1906): 55–68.

Drinka, George Frederick. *The Birth of Neurosis: Myth, Malady, and the Victorians*. New York: Simon & Schuster, 1984.

Edel, Leon. *Henry James*. 5 vols. Philadelphia: Lippincott, 1953–1972.

———, and Gordon N. Ray, eds. *Henry James and H. G. Wells: A Record of Their Friendship, Their Debate on the Art of Fiction, and Their Quarrel*. Urbana: University of Illinois Press, 1958.

Emerson, Edward Waldo. *The Early Years of the Saturday Club, 1855–1870*. Boston: Houghton Mifflin, 1918.

Emerson, Ralph Waldo. *Emerson in his Journals*. Edited by Joel Porte. Cambridge: Harvard University Press, 1982.

———. *Journals 1841–44*. Vol. 6. Cambridge: Riverside Press, 1911.

Erikson, Erik H. "William James's Terminal Dream." In *Identity, Youth, & Crisis*, 204–7. New York: Norton, 1968.

Feinstein, Howard. *Becoming William James*. Ithaca, N.Y.: Cornell University Press, 1984.

———. "The Use and Abuse of Illness in the James Family Circle: A View of Neurasthenia as a Social Phenomenon." *Psychohistory Review* (Summer/Fall 1979): 6–14.

Feuer, Lewis S. "The East Side Philosophers: William James and Thomas Davidson." *American Jewish History* 76 (March 1987): 287–310.

Fisch, Max. "Philosophical Clubs in Cambridge and Boston." Parts 1–3. *Coranto* 2 (Fall 1964): 12-23; 2 (Spring 1965): 12–25; 3 (Fall 1965): 16–29.

———. "Was There a Metaphysical Club in Cambridge?" In *Studies in the Philosophy of Charles Sanders Peirce*, edited by Edward C. Moore and Richard S. Robin, 2–32. Amherst: University of Massachusetts Press, 1964.

Flournoy, Théodore. *The Philosophy of William James*. Translated by Edwin B. Holt and William James, Jr. New York: Holt, 1917.

Flower, Elizabeth, and Murray G. Murphey. *A History of Philosophy in America*. Vol. 2. New York: Putnam, 1977.

Fontinell, Eugene. *Self, God, and Immortality: A Jamesian Investigation*. Philadelphia: Temple University Press, 1986.

Ford, Marcus. "William James: Panpsychist and Metaphysical Realist." *Transactions of the Peirce Society* 17 (Spring 1981): 158–70.

———. *William James's Philosophy: A New Perspective.* Amherst: University of Massachusetts Press, 1982.

Gifford, George Edmund, ed. *Psychoanalysis, Psychotherapy, and the New England Medical Scene, 1894–1944.* New York: Science History Publications, 1978.

Gordon, George Angier. *My Education and Religion.* Boston: Houghton Mifflin, 1953 (1925).

Gosling, Francis G. *Before Freud: Neurasthenia and the American Medical Community, 1870–1910.* Urbana: University of Illinois Press, 1987.

Greenspan, Henry Miller. "William James's Eyes: The Thought Behind the Man." *Psychohistory Review* (1979): 26–46.

Grohskopf, Bernice. "'I'll Be a Farmer': Boyhood Letters of William James." *Virginia Quarterly Review* 66 (Fall 1990): 585–600.

Habegger, Alfred. *The Father, A Life of Henry James, Sr.* New York: Farrar, Straus & Giroux, 1994.

———. "New Light on William James and Minny Temple." *New England Quarterly* (March 1987): 28.

Hale, Nathan. *Freud and the Americans.* New York: Oxford University Press, 1971.

———, ed. *James Jackson Putnam and Psychoanalysis.* Cambridge: Harvard University Press, 1971.

Hall, G. Stanley. "Philosophy in the United States." *Mind* (1879): 89–105.

Hare, Peter. "William James, Dickinson Miller, & C. J. Ducasse on the Ethics of Belief." *Transactions of the Peirce Society* 4 (1968): 115–29.

Harlow, Virginia. *Thomas Sergeant Perry: A Biography.* Durham: Duke University Press, 1950.

Harper, Robert S. "The Laboratory of William James." *Harvard Alumni Bulletin* 52 (5 November 1948).

Harrington, Fred H. "The Anti-Imperialist Movement in the United States." *Mississippi Valley Historical Review* 22 (1935): 211–30.

Hastings, Katherine. "William James of Albany, New York (1771–1832) and His Descendants." *New York Genealogical and Biographical Records* 55 (1924).

Hawkins, Hugh. *Between Harvard and America: The Educational Leadership of Charles W. Eliot.* New York: Oxford University Press, 1972.

Hawthorne, Julian. *The Memoirs of Julian Hawthorne.* Edited by Edith G. Hawthorne. New York: Macmillan, 1938.

Haynes, Renee. *The Society for Psychical Research, 1882–1982: A History.* London: Macdonald & Co., 1982.

Higgins, Hubert. *Humaniculture.* New York: F. A. Stokes, 1906.

Higginson, Henry Lee. *The Letters of Henry Lee Higginson.* Edited by Bliss Perry. Boston: Atlantic Monthly Press, 1921.

Hine, Robert V. *Josiah Royce: From Grass Valley to Harvard.* Norman: University of Oklahoma Press, 1992.

Hodysh, Henry W. "Social Ideals and the Educational Purpose of History in the Philosophy of William James." *Educational Theory* 39 (Winter 1989): 63–69.

Hoffman, Charles, and Tess Hoffman. "Henry James and the Civil War." *New England Quarterly* 62 (Dec. 1989): 529–52.

Hollinger, David. *In the American Province: Studies in the History and Historiography of Ideas.* Bloomington: Indiana University Press, 1985.

Holmes, Oliver Wendell. *The Holmes-Einstein Letters.* Edited by James Bishop Peabody. London: Macmillan, 1964.

———. *The Holmes-Laski Letters,* Vols. 1 and 2. Edited by M. A. De Wolfe Howe. Cambridge: Harvard University Press, 1953.

———. *The Holmes-Pollack Letters.* 2 vols. Edited by M. A. De Wolfe Howe. Cambridge: Harvard University Press, 1941.

Hoppin, Martha, and Henry Adams. *William Morris Hunt: A Memorial Exhibition.* Boston: Museum of Fine Arts, 1979.

Howe, Julia Ward. *Reminiscences, 1819–1899.* Boston: Houghton Mifflin, 1899.

Howe, M. A. De Wolfe. *Later Years of the Saturday Club, 1870–1920.* Boston: Houghton Mifflin, 1927.

———. *A Memoir of Richard Hodgson.* Boston: Tavern Club, 1906.

———. *A Partial (And Not Impartial) Semi-Centennial History of the Tavern Club, 1884–1934.* Boston: Tavern Club, 1934.

Howells, Dorothy Elia. *A Century to Celebrate: Radcliffe College, 1879–1979.* Cambridge: Radcliffe College, 1978.

Howells, William Dean. *Life in Letters of William Dean Howells.* 2 vols. Edited by Mildred Howells. New York: Russell & Russell, 1968 (1928).

Humboldt, Wilhelm von. *Letters of William von Humboldt to a Female Friend.* 2 vols. Translated by Catharine M. A. Couper. London: J. Chapman, 1849.

Janet, Pierre. *The Major Symptoms of Hysteria.* New York: Macmillan, 1907.

Jones, Robert E. "Moral Treatment: The Basis of Private Mental Hospital Care." *The Psychiatric Hospital* 14, no. 1: 5–9.

Jordan, David Starr. *The Days of a Man: Being Memories of a Naturalist, Teacher, and Minor Prophet of Democracy.* 2 vols. Yonkers-on-Hudson, N.Y.: World Book Co., 1922.

Kallen, Horace. "Mussolini, William James, and the Rationalists." *Social Frontier* 4 (May 1938): 253–56.

———. "Remembering William James." In *In Commemoration of William James, 1842–1942*, 11–23. New York: Columbia University Press, 1942.

———. *What I Believe and Why—Maybe: Essays for the Modern World.* Edited by Alfred J. Marrow. New York: Horizon, 1971.

Kaltenborn, Hans von. *Fifty Fabulous Years.* New York: Putnam, 1950.

———. "William James at Harvard." *The Harvard Illustrated Magazine* 8 (February 1907).

Kaufman, Marjorie R. "William James's Letters to a Young Pragmatist." *Journal of the History of Ideas* (July 1963): 413–21.

Kazin, Alfred. "William James: To Be Born Again." *Princeton University Library Chronicle* 54 (Winter–Spring 1993): 244–58.

Keller, Phyllis. *States of Belonging: German-American Intellectuals and the First World War.* Cambridge: Harvard University Press, 1979.

Kellogg, Julia A. *The Philosophy of Henry James.* New York: J. W. Lovell Company, 1883.

King, John Owen. *The Iron of Melancholy: Structures of Spiritual Conversion in America from the Puritan Conscience to Victorian Neurosis.* Middletown: Wesleyan University Press, 1983.

Kingsbury, Forrest A. "The History of the Department of Psychology at the University of Chicago." *Psychological Bulletin* 43 (1946): 259–71.

Kloppenberg, James T. "Pragmatism: An Old Name for Some New Ways of Thinking?" *Journal of American History* 83, no. 1 (June 1996): 100–38.

———. *Uncertain Victory: Social Democracy and Progressivism in European and American Thought, 1870–1920.* New York: Oxford University Press, 1986.

Knowlton, Helen M., ed. *William Morris Hunt's Talks on Art.* Boston: Houghton, Osgood, 1880.

Konvitz, Milton R., ed. *The Legacy of Horace M. Kallen.* Rutherford, N.J.: Fairleigh Dickinson University Press, 1987.

Kuklick, Bruce. *The Rise of American Philosophy: Cambridge, Massachusetts, 1860–1930.* New Haven: Yale University Press, 1977.

Ladd, George Trumbull. *Elements of Physiological Psychology: A Treatise of the Activities and Nature of the Mind from the Physical and Experimental Point of View.* New York: Scribner's, 1887.

Landy, Frank J. "Hugo Münsterberg: Victim or Visionary?" *Journal of Applied Psychology* 77, no. 6 (1992): 787–802.

Larrabee, Harold. "The Flight of Henry James the First." *New England Quarterly* (December 1937): 774–75.

————. "Henry James, Sr. '30 at Union.'" *Union Alumni Monthly* 15 (1926): 236–47.

Lasch, Christopher. "The Anti-Imperialists, the Philippines, and the Inequality of Man." *Journal of Southern History* 24 (1958): 319–31.

Lears, T. J. Jackson. *No Place of Grace: Antimodernism and the Transformation of American Culture, 1880–1920.* New York: Pantheon Books, 1981.

Leary, David E. "Telling Likely Stories: The Rhetoric of the New Psychology, 1880–1920." *Journal of the History of the Behavioral Sciences* 23 (October 1987): 316–31.

Le Clair, Robert. "Henry James and Minny Temple." *American Literature* (1949): 35–48.

————. *Young Henry James, 1843–1870.* New York: Bookman, 1955.

Leidecker, Kurt F. *Yankee Teacher: The Life of William Torrey Harris.* New York: Philosophical Library, 1946.

Lentricchia, Frank. "Philosophers of Modernism at Harvard, circa 1900." *South Atlantic Quarterly* 89, no. 4 (Fall 1990): 787–834.

————. "On the Ideologies of Poetic Modernism, 1890–1913: The Example of William James." In *Reconstructing American Literary History*, edited by Sacvan Bercovitch, 220–49. Cambridge: Harvard University Press, 1986.

————. "The Return of William James." *Cultural Critique* (Fall 1986): 5–31.

Lesch, John E. *Science and Medicine in France: The Emergence of Experimental Physiology, 1790–1855.* Cambridge: Harvard University Press, 1984.

Leveretter, W. E. "Simple Living and the Patrician Academic: The Case of William James." *Journal of American Culture* 6 (Winter 1983): 36–43.

Levinson, Henry Samuel. *The Religious Investigations of William James.* Chapel Hill: University of North Carolina Press, 1981.

Lewis, R. W. B. *The Jameses: A Family Narrative.* New York: Farrar, Straus & Giroux, 1991.

Linderman, Gerald F. *The Mirror of War: American Society and the Spanish-American War.* Ann Arbor: University of Michigan Press, 1974.

Lippmann, Walter. *Early Writings.* New York: Liveright, 1970.

Lovejoy, Arthur O. *The Great Chain of Being: A Study of the History of an Idea.* Cambridge: Harvard University Press, 1966 (1936, 1964).

————. *The Thirteen Pragmatisms and Other Essays.* Baltimore: Johns Hopkins University Press, 1963.

Lovett, Sidney. "A Boy's Recollections of William James." *Yale Review* 76, no. 2 (Winter 1987): 247–55.

Lurie, Edward. *Louis Agassiz: A Life in Science.* Chicago: University of Chicago Press, 1960.

McCaughey, Robert. "The Transformation of American Academic Life: Harvard University, 1821–1892." *Perspectives in American History* 8 (1974): 239–332.

McConnell, Francis John. *Borden Parker Bowne: His Life and His Philosophy.* New York: Abingdon Press, 1929.

McDermott, John. *Streams of Experience: Reflections on the History and Philosophy of American Culture.* Amherst: University of Massachusetts Press, 1986.

McFarland, Gerald W., ed. *The Mupwumps, 1884–1900: Moralists or Pragmatists?* New York: Simon & Schuster, 1975.

MacKaye, Percy. *Epoch: The Life of Steele MacKaye, Genius of the Theater.* 2 vols. New York: Boni & Liveright, 1927.

Madden, Edward H. *Chauncey Wright and the Foundations of Pragmatism.* Seattle: University of Washington Press, 1963.

————, and George Giacaman. "Miller and James on Analysis and Determinism." *Journal of the History of Philosophy,* 16 (1978): 209–18.

————, and Robert Giuffrada. "James on Meaning and Significance." *Transactions of the Peirce Society* 11 (1975): 18–36.

Madsen, Truman. "William James: Philosopher-Educator." *Brigham Young University Studies* 4 (Autumn 1961): 81–105.

Maher, Jane. *Biography of Broken Fortunes: Wilkie and Bob, Brothers of William, Henry, and Alice James.* Hamden, Conn.: Archon Books, 1986.

Marchand, C. Roland. *The American Peace Movement and Social Reform, 1898–1918.* Princeton: Princeton University Press, 1972.

Martin, Jane Roland. "Martial Virtues or Capital Vices? William James's 'Moral Equivalent of War' Revisited." *Journal of Thought* 22 (Fall 1987): 32–44.

Marx, Otto. "American Philosophy Without William James." *Bulletin of the History of Medicine* 42 (1968): 52–61.

————. "Morton Prince and the Dissociation of a Personality." *Journal of the History of the Behavioral Sciences* (1970): 120–30.

Mason, Daniel Gregory. "At Harvard in the Nineties." *New England Quarterly* (March 1936): 43–70.

Massaro, Dominic W. "A Century Later: Reflections on 'The Principles of Psychology' by William James and on the review by G. Stanley Hall." *American Journal of Psychology* 103, no. 4 (Winter 1990): 539.

Matthiessen, F. O. *The James Family.* New York: Knopf, 1947.

Mauskopf, Seymour. "The History of the American Society for Psychical Research: An Interpretation." *Journal of the American Society for Psychical Research* 83 (January 1989): 7–19.

————, and Michael R. McVaugh. *The Elusive Science: Origins of Experimental Psychical Research.* Baltimore: Johns Hopkins University Press, 1980.

May, Henry. *The End of American Innocence: A Study of the First Years of Our Own Time, 1912–1917.* New York: Oxford University Press, 1979 (1959).

"A Member of the Class of 1878." *Harvard Graduates Magazine* 39 (1920): 324.

Meyers, Robert G. "Natural Realism and Illusion in James's Radical Empiricism." *Transactions of the Peirce Society* 5, no. 4 (Fall 1969): 211–23.

Miller, Dickinson S. "Beloved Psychologist." In *Great Teachers: Portrayed by Those Who Studied Under Them,* edited by Houston Peterson, 223–28. New York: Random House, 1946.

———. "Mr. Santayana and William James." *Harvard Graduates Magazine* (March 1921): 348–64.

———. *Philosophical Analysis and Human Welfare: Selected Essays and Chapters from Six Decades.* Edited by Loyd Easton. Dordrecht, Holland: D. Reidel, 1975.

———. "Some of the Tendencies of Professor James's Work." *Journal of Philosophy* 7 (24 November 1910): 645–64.

Moore, G. E. "Prof. James' 'Pragmatism.'" *Proceedings of the Aristotelian Society for the Study of Philosophy* 8 (1907–08): 33–77.

Moore, Merrill. "Morton Prince, M.D., 1854–1929." *Journal of Nervous and Mental Disease* 87 (1938): 701–10.

Moraitis, George, and George H. Pollock, eds. *Psychoanalytic Studies of Biography.* Madison, Conn.: International Universities Press, 1987.

Morse, John T., Jr. *Thomas Sergeant Perry: A Memoir.* Boston: Houghton Mifflin, 1929.

Moyer, Albert E. *A Scientist's Voice in American Culture: Simon Newcomb and the Rhetoric of Scientific Method.* Berkeley: University of California Press, 1992.

Munsell, Joel. *Collections on the History of Albany from Its Discovery to the Present Time.* Vol. 2, 444–46. Albany, N.Y.: J. Munsell, 1867.

Münsterberg, Margaret. *Hugo Münsterberg: His Life and Work.* New York: D. Appleton, 1922.

Munthe, Axel. *The Story of San Michele.* New York: E. P. Dutton, 1929.

Myerson, Joel. *The New England Transcendentalists and the "Dial": A History of the Magazine and Its Contributors.* Rutherford: Fairleigh Dickinson University Press, 1980.

Neilson, William Allan. "William James as Lecturer and Writer." *The Harvard Illustrated Magazine* 8 (February 1907).

Nethery, Wallace, ed. "Pragmatist to Publisher, Letters of William James to W. T. Harris." *The Personalist* 49 (Autumn 1968): 489–508.

Newcomb, Simon. *The Reminiscences of an Astronomer.* Boston: Houghton Mifflin, 1903.

Norton, Charles Eliot. *Letters of Charles Eliot Norton.* 2 vols. Edited by Sara Norton and M. A. De Wolfe Howe. Boston: Houghton Mifflin, 1913.

Novick, Sheldon. *Honorable Justice: The Life of Oliver Wendell Holmes.* Boston: Little, Brown, 1989.

O'Brien, Laurie. "'A Bold Plunge into the Sea of Values.' The Career of Dr. Richard Cabot." *New England Quarterly* (December 1985): 533–53.

"Official Report of the Thirteenth Universal Peace Congress." Boston: Peace Congress Committee, 1904.

Olin, Doris, ed. *William James, Pragmatism in Focus.* London: Routledge, 1992.

Olivier, Sydney. *Sydney Olivier: Letters and Selected Writings.* Edited by Margaret Olivier. London: Allen & Unwin, 1948.

Orcutt, William Dana. *From My Library Walls: A Kaleidoscope of Memories.* New York: Longmans, Green, 1945.

———. *In Quest of the Perfect Book: Reminiscences and Reflections of a Bookman.* Boston: Little, Brown, 1926.

Otto, Max C. "On a Certain Blindness in William James." *Ethics* 53 (April 1943): 184–91.

Palmer, George Herbert. *The Autobiography of a Philosopher.* Boston: Houghton Mifflin, 1930.

———. *The Life of Alice Freeman Palmer.* Boston: Houghton Mifflin, 1908.

Parker, Gail T. *The History of the Mind Cure in New England.* Hanover: University Press of New England, 1975.

Patterson, David S. *Toward a Warless World: The Travail of the American Peace Movement, 1887–1914.* Bloomington: Indiana University Press, 1976.

Peabody, Francis G. *The Christian Life in the Modern World.* New York: Macmillan, 1914.

Perry, Ralph Barton. "First Personal." *Atlantic Monthly* (October 1946): 106–8.

———. *Present Philosophical Tendencies: A Critical Survey of Naturalism, Idealism, Pragmatism, and Realism, Together with a Synopsis of the Philosophy of William James.* New York: Longmans, Green, 1912.

———. "The Religious Experience." *The Monist* 14 (October 1904): 752–66.

Piper, Alta. *The Life and Work of Mrs. Piper.* London: Kegan Paul, 1929.

Pochman, Henry A. *New England Transcendentalism and St. Louis Hegelianism: Phases in the History of American Idealism.* Philadelphia: Carl Schurz Memorial Foundation, 1948.

Posnock, Ross. *The Trial of Curiosity: Henry James, William James, and the Challenge of Modernity.* New York: Oxford University Press, 1991.

Potts, David. "Social Ethics at Harvard, 1881–1931." In *The Social Sciences at Harvard, 1860–1920: From Inculcation to Open Mind,* edited by Paul Buck, 113–14. Cambridge: Harvard University Press, 1965.

Prince, Morton. *The Dissociation of a Personality: A Biographical Study in Abnormal Psychology.* New York: Longmans, Green, 1908 (December 1905).

Randall, John Herman. *The Culture of Personality.* New York: Dodge, 1912.

Raymond, Mary E. "Memories of William James." *New England Quarterly* (September 1937): 419–29.

Richards, Robert J. "The Personal Equation in Science: William James's Psychological and Moral Uses of Darwinian Theory." *Harvard Library Bulletin* 30 (1982): 387–425.

Robbins, Anna Manning. *Both Sides of the Veil: A Personal Experience.* Boston: Sherman, French, 1909.

Rose, Anne C. *Transcendentalism as a Social Movement, 1830–1850.* New Haven: Yale University Press, 1981.

———. *Voices of the Marketplace: American Thought and Culture, 1830–1860.* New York: Twayne, 1995.

Rosenberg, Charles. *The Cholera Years: The United States in 1832, 1849, and 1866.* Chicago: University of Chicago Press, 1987.

Rosenfield, Leonora Cohen. *Portrait of a Philosopher: Morris R. Cohen in Life and Letters.* New York: Harcourt, Brace & World, 1962.

Rosenzweig, Saul. "Erik Erikson on William James's Dream." *Journal of the History of the Behavioral Sciences* 6 (July 1970): 258–60.

———. *Freud, Jung, and Hall the King-Maker: The Historic Expedition to America (1909).* Seattle: Hogrefe & Huber, 1992.

Rosovsky, Nitza. *The Jewish Experience at Harvard and Radcliffe.* Cambridge: Harvard Semitic Museum, 1986.

Ross, Dorothy. *The Origins of American Social Science.* New York: Cambridge University Press, 1991.

Roth, John K. *Freedom and the Moral Life: The Ethics of William James.* Philadelphia: Westminster Press, 1969.

Royce, Josiah. *The Letters of Josiah Royce.* Edited by John Clendenning. Chicago: University of Chicago Press, 1970.

———. *The Religious Aspect of Philosophy: A Critique of the Bases of Conduct and of Faith.* Boston: Houghton Mifflin, 1885.

————. *William James and Other Essays on the Philosophy of Life.* New York: Macmillan, 1911.

Ryan, Judith. *The Vanishing Subject: Early Psychology and Literary Modernism.* Chicago: University of Chicago Press, 1991.

Saint-Gaudens, Augustus. *The Reminiscences of Augustus Saint-Gaudens.* Edited by Homer Saint-Gaudens. Vol. 2. New York: Century, 1913.

Salter, William Mackintyre. *First Steps in Philosophy.* Chicago: C. H. Kerr, 1892.

Sanborn, F. B. *Recollections of Seventy Years.* 2 vols. Boston: Gorham Press, 1909.

Santayana, George. *Character and Opinion in the United States: With Reminiscences of William James and Josiah Royce and Academic Life in America.* New York, Scribner's, 1920.

————. *The Letters of George Santayana,* ed. by Daniel Cory. New York: Scribner's, 1955.

————. *Persons and Places: The Background of My Life.* London: Constable, 1944.

————. *Persons and Places: The Middle Span.* New York: Scribner's, 1945.

Sargent, Mary Elizabeth. *Sketches and Reminiscences of the Radical Club of Chestnut Street.* Edited by Mrs. John T. Sargent. Boston: Osgood, 1880.

Scarborough, Elizabeth, and Laurel Furumoto. *Untold Lives: The First Generation of American Women Psychologists.* New York: Columbia University Press, 1987.

Schaub, Edward L., ed. *William Torrey Harris, 1835–1935: A Collection of Essays.* Chicago: Open Court, 1936.

Schiller, F. C. S. *Must Philosophers Disagree?* London: Macmillan, 1934.

Schilpp, Paul Arthur, ed. *The Philosophy of George Santayana.* 2nd ed. New York: Tudor, 1951 (1940).

Scott, Frederick J. Down. "William James and Stanford University: 1906." *San Jose Studies* (May 1975): 28–43.

Seigfried, Charlene Haddock. *Chaos and Context: A Study in William James.* Athens: Ohio University Press, 1978.

————. *William James's Radical Reconstruction of Philosophy.* Albany: SUNY Press, 1990.

Shafer, Roy. "The Pursuit of Failure and the Idealization of Unhappiness." *American Psychologist* (April 1984): 398–405.

Shaler, Nathaniel. *The Autobiography of Nathaniel Southgate Shaler.* Boston: Houghton Mifflin, 1900.

Sharpless, Stephen P. "Some Reminiscences of the Lawrence Scientific School." *Harvard Graduate Magazine* 26 (1918): 532–40.

Smith, Carleton Sprague. "William James in Brazil." In *Four Papers Presented in the Institute for Brazilian Studies*. Nashville: Vanderbilt University Press, 1951.

Snider, Denton Jaques. *The St. Louis Movement in Philosophy, Literature, Education, Psychology, with Chapters of Autobiography*. St. Louis: Sigma Publishing Company, 1920.

Sokal, Michael M. "Origins and Early Years of the American Psychological Association, 1890–1906." *American Psychologist* 47 (February 1992): 111–22.

Sotheran, Charles. *Horace Greeley and Other Pioneers of American Socialism*. New York: Mitchell Kennerley, 1915.

The Spanish-American War by Eye Witnesses. Chicago: Herbert S. Stone & Co., 1899.

Spitzka, Edward C. *Insanity: Its Classification, Diagnosis, and Treatment*. New York: E. B. Treat, 1887.

Stafford, William T. "Emerson and the James Family." *American Literature* 24 (1954): 433–61.

Starbuck, Edwin Diller. *The Psychology of Religion: An Empirical Study of the Growth of Religious Consciousness*. Preface by William James. New York: Scribner's, 1911 (1899).

Steel, Ronald. *Walter Lippmann and the American Century*. Boston: Little, Brown, 1980.

Steinmeyer, Henry G. *Staten Island, 1524–1898*. Richmondtown, N.Y.: Staten Island Historical Society, 1987.

Stoddard, Henry L. *Horace Greeley: Printer, Editor, Crusader*. New York: Putnam's, 1946.

Strouse, Jean. *Alice James*. Boston: Houghton Mifflin, 1980.

———. "Katharine James Prince: A Partial Portrait." In *Essaying Biography*. Edited by Gloria Fromm. Honolulu: University of Hawaii Press, 1986.

Strout, Cushing. "William James and the Twice-Born Sick Soul." *Daedalus* 97 (Summer 1968): 1062–82.

Suckiel, Ellen Kappy. *The Pragmatic Philosophy of William James*. University of Notre Dame Press, 1982.

Taylor, Eugene. *William James on Consciousness beyond the Margin*. Princeton: Princeton University Press, 1997.

———. *William James on Exceptional Mental States: The 1896 Lowell Lectures*. New York: Scribner's, 1983.

Taylor, W. S. *Morton Prince and Abnormal Psychology*. New York: Appleton, 1928.

Thielman, Samuel B. "Madness and Medicine: Trends in American Medical Therapeutics for Insanity, 1820–1860." *Bulletin of the History of Medicine* 61 (1987): 25–46.

Thomas, Joseph M. "Figures of Habit in William James." *New England Quarterly* 66 (March 1993): 3–26.

Thoreau, Henry David. *Familiar Letters of Henry David Thoreau.* Edited by F. B. Sanborn. Boston: Houghton Mifflin, 1894.

Thorndike, E. L. "James's Influence on the Psychology of Perception and Thought." *Psychological Review* 50 (1943): 87–94.

Turner, James. *Without God, Without Creed: The Origins of Unbelief in America.* Baltimore: Johns Hopkins University Press, 1985.

Warren, Austin. *The Elder Henry James.* New York: Macmillan, 1934.

Weber, Hermann, and F. Parkes Weber. *The Spas and Mineral Waters of Europe: with Notes on Baines-Therapeutic Management in Various Diseases and Morbid Conditions.* London: Smith, Elder, 1896.

Webster, Sally. *William Morris Hunt, 1824–1879.* Cambridge: Cambridge University Press, 1991.

Weissbourd, Katherine. *Growing Up in the James Family: Henry James, Sr., as Son and Father.* Ann Arbor: UMI Research Press, 1985.

Wiener, Philip P. *Evolution and the Founders of Pragmatism.* Cambridge: Harvard University Press, 1949.

Welch, Richard E., Jr. *Response to Imperialism, The United States and the Philippine-American War, 1899–1902.* Chapel Hill: University of North Carolina Press, 1979.

Wells, H. G. *Experiment in Autobiography: Discoveries and Conclusions of a Very Ordinary Brain.* New York: Macmillan, 1934.

Wendell, Barrett. *Barrett Wendell and His Letters.* Edited by M. A. De Wolfe Howe. Boston: Atlantic Monthly Press, 1924.

West, Cornel. *The American Evasion of Philosophy.* Madison: University of Wisconsin Press, 1989.

Whittier, John Greenleaf. *Letters of John Greenleaf Whittier.* Vol. 3, 1861–1892. Edited by John B. Pickard. Cambridge: Belknap Press of Harvard University Press, 1975.

Wilkerson, Marcus M. *Public Opinion and the Spanish-American War: A Study in War Propaganda.* New York: Russell & Russell, 1967 (1932).

"William James." *Journal of Philosophy, Psychology, and Scientific Methods* 7 (15 September 1910).

Wilshire, Bruce. "Protophenomenology in the Psychology of William James." *Transactions of the Peirce Society* 5 (Winter 1969): 25–43.

Wilson, Daniel J. *Arthur O. Lovejoy and the Quest for Intelligibility*. Chapel Hill: University of North Carolina Press, 1980.

————. *Science, Community, and the Transformation of American Philosophy, 1860–1930*. Chicago: University of Chicago, 1990.

Wood, Henry. *The New Thought Simplified: How to Gain Harmony and Health*. Boston: Lee & Shepard, 1903.

Wright, Chauncey. *Letters of Chauncey Wright: With Some Account of His Life*. Edited by James Bradley Thayer. Cambridge: John Wilson, 1878.

Wundt, Wilhelm. *Outlines of Psychology*. Translated by Charles H. Judd. Leipzig: W. Engelmann, 1902.

Zeldin, David. *The Educational Ideas of Charles Fourier (1772–1837)*. London: Cass, 1969.

INDEX